HOSKER HAYNES

SELLING YOUR COINS & BANKNOTES?

Warwick and Warwick have an expanding requirement for coin and banknote collections, British and worldwide and for coins and notes of individual value. Our customer base is increasing dramatically and we need an ever larger supply of quality material to keep pace with demand. The market has never been stronger and if you are considering the sale of your collection, now is the time to act.

FREE VALUATIONS

We will provide a free, professional and without obligation valuation of your collection. Either we will make you a fair, binding private treaty offer, or we will recommend inclusion of your property in our next specialist public auction.

FREE TRANSPORTATION

We can arrange insured transportation of your collection to our Warwick offices completely free of charge. If you decline our offer, we ask you to cover the return carriage costs only.

FREE VISITS

Visits by our valuers are possible anywhere in the country or abroad, usually within 48 hours, in order to value larger collections. Please telephone for details.

ADVISORY DAYS

We are staging a series of advisory days and will be visiting all areas of England, Scotland, Wales and Ireland during the coming months. Please visit our website or telephone for further details.

EXCELLENT PRICES

Because of the strength of our customer base we are in a position to offer prices that we feel sure will exceed your expectations.

ACT NOW

Telephone or email Richard Beale today with details of your property.

Get to know and understand your

Financial Instruments

Collecting the financial instruments of the past – gold, silver or copper coins – is a pursuit many of us turn to as an escape from the tribulations of everyday life in our hectic world.

But acquisition is only part of the picture. To really know and understand the coins of a particular period or ruler, take the opportunity to look at some of the masterly works of scholarship that have appeared in the pages of the *British Numismatic Journal* since before the First World War. Scholarship that is now available to you, online, at **www.britnumsoc.org**.

We're not just about coins, though. Among our 600-plus membership are collectors and students of tokens, medals and paper money of the British Isles, the Commonwealth and other territories that have been subject to British rule. Our monthly meetings in London feature talks on all aspects of numismatics, from the Iron Age and Roman periods right up to the present, so there's something for everyone, and we also have an annual meeting in New York in January.

There has never been a better time to join the Society as we are currently running a special reduced rate of £15 per annum for the first two years of membership (normally £32). Under 25 or in full-time study? Then enjoy a further reduction to only £10 per annum. To apply, visit **www.britnumsoc.org/membership** today.

The British Numismatic Society

Promoting the study of British numismatics since 1903

For Quality British Coins
RODERICK RICHARDSON LTD
Numismatist
Specialist in English Hammered - Early Milled Coins

WANTED

...IONS AND CHOICE INDIVIDUAL PIECES

For appointments in London or my latest circular, please contact me at
Old Granary Antiques Centre, Kings Staithe Lane,
King's Lynn, Norfolk, England PE30 1LZ

Tel: +44 (0)1553 670833   Mob: +44 (0)7786 372444
...uk
...n

000003192912

R. INGRAM COINS

2 Avonborne Way, Eastleigh, SO53 1TF
023 80275079 & 07730 782810

info@ringramcoins.com www.ringramcoins.com

We stock the largest selection of British and foreign coins in the UK. We sell:

English Gold, Silver, Copper and Bronze coins, Maundy sets and odds, Roman and Hammered coins, Silver proofs, Proof and uncirculated sets, Irish, Scottish, US and Foreign Gold and Silver. We also stock a big selection of lots and a large number of banknotes.

We issue 6 catalogues a year. Each one has 92 pages and includes 16,000 coins. It is free. For your copy, send us your contact details. You can telephone, e-mail, write or message us on Facebook. Most of our buyers have been with us a long time, some for decades; join them. Get the UK's most extensive list.

Twitter: @ringramcoins
Facebook: R. Ingram Coins

www.ringramcoins.com

From beginner to numismatist

The new collector can best advance to becoming an experienced numismatist by examining as many coins as possible, noting their distinctive features and by learning to use the many books of reference that are available. It will be an advantage to join a local numismatic society, as this will provide an opportunity for meeting other enthusiasts and obtaining advice from more experienced collectors. Most societies have a varied programme of lectures, exhibitions and occasional auctions of members' duplicates.

Those who become members of one or both of the national societies, the Royal Numismatic Society and the British Numismatic Society, receive an annual journal containing authoritative papers and have access to the societies' library and programme of lectures.

Many museums have coin collections available for study, although they may not always be displayed, and a number of museum curators are qualified numismatists. Many collectors enjoy deepening their knowledge of the coins they collect by referring to books and articles which provide detailed study of specific coins and coinages. These provide more detail on varieties than can be included here in the Standard Catalogue. References to relevant studies and books are given within this catalogue to allow for more detailed study. Appendix 1 gives details of a selection of key works useful to the specialist collector.

SOME NUMISMATIC TERMS EXPLAINED

Obverse	That side of the coin which normally shows the monarch's head or name.
Reverse	The side opposite to the obverse, the 'Tails'.
Blank	The coin as a blank piece of metal, i.e. before it is struck.
Flan	The whole piece of metal after striking.
Type	The main, central design.
Legend	The inscription. Coins lacking a legend are called 'mute' or anepigraphic.
Field	That flat part of the coin between the main design and the inscription or edge.
Exergue	That part of the coin below the main design, usually separated by a horizontal line, and normally occupied by the date.
Die	The block of metal, with design cut into it, which actually impresses the coin blank with the design.
Die variety	Coin showing slight variation of design.
Mule	A coin with the current type on one side and the previous (and usually obsolete) type on the other side, or a piece struck from two dies that are not normally used together.
Graining or reeding	The crenellations around the edge of the coin, commonly known as 'milling'.
Proof	Carefully struck coin from special dies with a mirror-like or matt surface. (In this country 'Proof' is not a term used to describe the state of preservation, but the method of striking.)
Hammered	Refers to the old craft method of striking a coin between dies hammered by hand.
Milled	Coins struck by dies worked in a coining press. The presses were hand powered from 1560-1800, powered by steam from 1790 and by electricity from 1895.

CELTIC COINAGE EXPLAINED

The Celtic or Ancient British issues are amongst the most interesting and varied of all British coins. They are our earliest coins and are the product of a society that left no historical sources of its own. It is therefore often difficult to be specific about for whom, when or where they were produced. Despite only being used for approximately a hundred and fifty years they do provide a rich variety of designs and types in gold, silver and bronze. Collectors looking for a theme to concentrate on may find the coins of one tribe, an individual ruler or a particular phase in the coinage interesting.

Grading Celtic Coins
The majority of Celtic coins were struck by hand, sometimes resulting in a loss of definition through weak striking. In addition, the design on the dies was often bigger than the blank flan employed, resulting in the loss of some of the design. Coins with full legends are generally more valuable than examples with incomplete legends. Bronze coins in good condition (VF or better) and especially toned examples attract a premium. Factors that detract from a coin's value are chips, scratches and verdigris on bronze coins. It is important to take into account these factors as well as the amount of wear on a coin when assessing its grade.

Cunobelin Bronze Unit   Epaticcus Silver Unit   Cunobelin Gold Stater

Fine

Very Fine

Plated Coins
Plated gold staters, quarter staters and silver units are recorded for many known types. They vary considerably in the quality of their production and are usually priced at around a quarter of the substantive type's value. Their exact purpose or relation to the type they copy is not fully understood.

References and Select Bibliography.
ABC   Rudd, C. (2010), Ancient British Coinage.
V   Van Arsdell, R.D. (1989), Celtic Coinage of Britain.
BMC   Hobbs, R. (1996), British Iron Age Coins in the British Museum.

de Jersey, P. (1996), Celtic Coinage in Britain. *A good general introduction to the series.*
Nash, D. (1987), Coinage in the Celtic World. *Sets the coinage in its social context.*

The layout of the following list is derived from the standard works by Van Arsdell and the British Museum Catalogue by Richard Hobbs. References are made to these works where possible, in the case of the last work it should be noted that the British Museum collection is not exhaustive, and therefore should not be used to assess the rarity of a coin with, for example Rudd ABC listing many more varieties than can be listed here.

IMPORTED COINAGE

The earliest coinage in the British isles originated as continental imports around the middle of the 2nd Century BC, and primarily from the various tribes inhabiting northern Gaul (modern-day France and Belgium). It is not clear how the coins first came to be used, but surviving historical records suggest a period in which British and Gallic tribes shared close socio-economic and political ties. The development of Royal hierarchies within these tribal communities, as well as the hiring and sharing of mercenaries during times of conflict, further aided circulation, as in the case of Caesar's 'Gallic Wars' at the end of this period.

These gold staters are principally subdivided into the 'Gallo-Belgic' series A-F. The earliest (A), is attributed to the Ambiani tribe (sited around the Somme Valley and Amiens), and is most notable for its supreme artistry and close imitation of Philip II of Macedon's prototype (359-336 BC) which would serve as a canon for this entire series. As the coinage developed, the quality of *Ambiani* workmanship rapidly deteriorated to the extent that the once-recognisable laureate head of Apollo and the depiction of a charioteer became merely an assortment of disarticulated crescents, pellets or other abstract motifs (C and E). Recent studies have suggested the 'defaced' issues (B) could relate to the *Nervii* (Brussels and Hainault) or the *Caletes* (NE Normandy), whilst the triple-tailed horse issues of series F can be confidently associated with the *Suessiones* (Soissons). Quarter-Staters can be subdivided along similar lines, the only exception being found in series D, where the distinctive 'Boat-Tree' design is attributed to the sea-faring *Morini* tribe (Pas-de-Calais).

GALLO-BELGIC ISSUES

	2	5	7	9		
					F	VF
					£	£

From 150 B.C.

		F	VF
1	**Gold Stater**. *Large flan*. Series A, head r., R. horse and charioteer l., rosette below. *VA 10; ABC 1*	2250	8500
2	— — —, head l., R. horse r. *VA 12; ABC 4 ['Bellovaci']*	1250	5250
3	— *Small flan*. B, defaced obverse die, R. as last *VA 30; ABC 7*	750	3250
4	— — —, similar, R. horse and rider l., lyre motif below *VA 33; ABC 10*	900	4000
5	— — C, devolved head r., R. horse r. *VA 44; ABC 13*	375	1200
6	**Gold Quarter Stater**. *Large flan*. Series A, as S.1. *VA 15; ABC 28*	300	1000
7	— — —, as S.2. *VA 20; ABC 31 ['Bellovaci']*	275	950
8	— *Small flan*. B, as S.3 *VA 35; ABC 34*	350	675
9	— — —, as S.4. *VA 37; ABC 37*	225	675
10	— — D, various abstract symbols or uniface, R. tree-motif surrounded by geometric lines, rings or pellets, cf. S.46 *VA 67-69; ABC 40-49*	125	275

c.60-50 B.C. (Gallic War issues)

	11	11 (Var.)	14		
				F	VF
				£	£

		F	VF
11	**Gold Stater**. Series E, uniface or with detail to periphery [rare], R̶. dis-jointed horse r., various patterns around and in exergue. *VA 50-56; ABC 16*	225	575
12	— F, devolved head r., R̶. triple-tailed horse r. *VA 85; ABC 22*	575	2250
13	— Xc, digamma monogram in blank field, R̶. sinuous horse r., normal or reversed 'S' below *VA 87; ABC 19*	275	900

Armorica (Channel Islands and North-west Gaul): c.75-50 B.C.

		F	VF
14	**Billon Stater**. Type I, head r. with corded hair, R̶. stylised horse r., with rider and Victory, lash ends in loop, boar below	50	250
15	— II, similar, R̶. Victory only, lash ends in small cross of pellets	40	200
16	— III, similar, anchor-shaped nose, R̶. similar to S.14	45	225
17	— IV, similar, rev. horse and rider with reins, lash ends in three prongs, lyre-motif below..	50	250
18	— V, similar, R̶. lash ends in long cross of pellets	60	300
19	— VI, similar, R̶. lash ends in 'ladder' motif	60	300
20	**Billon Quarter Stater**, various types, as above.......................................	75	350

CELTIC COINS STRUCK IN BRITAIN

Coin production in Britain began at the very end of the second century B.C. with the cast potin coinage of Kent (Nos 62-64). Inspired by Gaulish issues and ultimately derived from the potin coins of Massalia (Marseilles) in southern Gaul, the precise function and period of use of this coinage is not fully understood. The domestic production of gold coins started around 70 B.C., these issues are traditionally known as British A-P and are derived from imported Gallo-Belgic issues. Broadly contemporary with these issues are quarter staters, silver units, and bronze units. Work by John Sills has further enhanced our understanding of this crucial early period with the identification of two new British staters (Insular Belgic C or Kentish A and the Ingoldisthorpe type) and their related quarters and a Westerham quarter stater. The Insular Belgic C or Kentish A type derived from Gallo-Belgic C now becomes the first British stater.

EARLY UNINSCRIBED COINAGE FROM c.65 B.C.

20A 20B

		F	*VF*
		£	£
20A	**Gold Stater**. Kentish A [Insular-Belgic C], as S.5, Ʀ. horse r., rosette behind or before. *Sills 457-459; ABC 515*	575	2250
20B	— '*Ingoldisthorpe*', similar, Ʀ. crescents or zig-zag in exergue. *Sills -; ABC 2421-24*	525	2000

21 22 23 24 25

21	— British A, '*Westerham*', devolved head r., Ʀ. abstract horse formed of pellets, crescents and lines. *BMC 1-32; VA 200-202; ABC 482, 2430*	275	825
22	— B, '*Chute*', similar, Ʀ. 'crab' motif below. *BMC 35-76; VA 1205; ABC 746*	250	750
23	— C, '*Yarmouth*', similar, three-pronged 'eye', rev. linear horse right, 'bird-headed' star before. *BMC 78-85; VA 1220; ABC 518*	1250	3750
24	— D, '*Cheriton*', as B, with large crescent face. *BMC 86-128; VA 1215; ABC 755*	275	800
25	— E, '*Waldingfield*', similar to A, Ʀ. annulets below *VA 1462; ABC 2335*	525	2000

27 28

		F £	VF £

26 — F, '*Clacton*', type I, similar to A, ℞. rosette below. *BMC 137-144; VA 1458; ABC 2332 ['Late']* 575 2250

27 — G, — type II, as last, ℞. sinuous horse r., pellet and lines below. *BMC 145-179; VA 30, 1455; ABC 2326-29 ['Early']* 350 1250

28 — H, North-East Coast, type I, similar to F and G, ℞. horse r., rosette below. *BMC 181-191; VA 800; ABC 1716-19* 275 850

29 30 31

29 — I, —, type II, as last, ℞. horse l., pellet, rosette or star below. *BMC 193-211; VA 804-807; ABC 1722, 1728-1734, 1740* 225 700

30 — J, Norfolk Wolf, type I, as S.5 and 20A, ℞. wolf r., pellets above. *BMC 212-216; VA 610; ABC 1393* 675 2500

31 — — —, type II [base gold issue], as last, ℞. wolf l. *BMC 217-278; VA 610; ABC 1396-99* 375 1350

32 (Middle) 32 (Early)

32 — L, '*Whaddon Chase*', Early-Middle types, as F and G, ℞. horse r., rosette below. *BMC 279-343; VA 1470, 1485; ABC 2240; 2347; 2433-45* 300 950

33 33A

33 — —, Late types, uniface, ℞. similar to last, annulet below. *BMC 344-346; VA 1498-1505; ABC 2338-44* 325 1000

33A — '*Climping*', similar to S.32, ℞. horse l., bird motif above, pellets-in-annulets around. *BMC —; VA —; ABC —* 625 2000

34   35

		F £	VF £
34	— Lx, North-Thames, blank except reversed 'SS' motif, ℞. as S.33. *BMC 350; VA 1509; ABC 2237*	675	2250
35	— Lz, Weald, uniface, ℞. horse r., 'thumbs-up' motif above, large wheel below. *BMC 347-349; VA 1507; ABC 186*	900	3250

36

| 36 | — Ma, *'Wonersh'*, crossed wreath, crescents back-to-back at centre, ℞. horse r., rosette below. *BMC 351-356; VA 1520; ABC 527* .... | 725 | 2500 |

37   38

| 37 | — Mb, *'Savernake Forest'*, uniface, ℞. as last. *BMC 361-364; VA 1526; ABC 2091* .... | 200 | 700 |
| 38 | — Qa, British 'Remic' types, devolved head right, ℞. triple-tailed horse r., wheel below. *BMC 445-458; VA 210-214; ABC 485, 494-497* .... | 325 | 1000 |

39   39B

39	— Qb, —, uniface, ℞. similar. *BMC 461-476; VA 216; ABC 488*	250	800
39A	**Gold Quarter Stater**. Kentish A [Insular-Belgic C], similar to S.10, but rosette in obverse field. *Sills 431; ABC 530*	375	1250
39B	— *'Ingoldisthorpe'*, similar to last, spermatozoids in fields. *ABC 2448* ..	400	1350
39C	— British A, *'Westerham'*, similar to last, L-shapes in fields. (*ABC 2448*)	325	1050
40	— D, *'Cheriton'*, as S.24, ℞. cross motif with pellets. *BMC 129-136; cf. VA 143; cf. ABC 770*	400	1350

41   43

		F £	VF £
41	— F/G, '*Clacton*', blank or with faint patterns, R. ornamental cross with pellets. *BMC 180; VA 1460; ABC 2356*	150	475
42	— H, -, de Jersey type, blank or with faint patterns, R. ornamental cross with pellets. *BMC 192; ABC 2350*	150	475
43	— Lx, North Thames, stylised wreath on corded line, 'faces' in two angles, R. horse r., various motifs. *BMC 365-367; VA 234; ABC 2463-66*	200	625

44   45

		F £	VF £
44	— Ly, North Kent, uniface, R. horse r., U-shaped motif above. *BMC 371-374; VA 158; ABC 201*	150	475
45	— Lz, Weald, straight wreath with crescents or annulets in fields, R. horse r., floral sun above or below. *BMC 375, 548-50; VA 250; ABC 623-626*	200	575
45A	— — —, similar to last, R. triple-tailed horse l., floral sun above, cog-wheel below. *BMC 552; ABC 629 [48]*	325	1050
45B	— Mc, '*Wonersh*', as S.36, R. horse l. or r., floral sun or wheel below. *VA 1688; ABC 617-620*	375	1250

46   47

		F £	VF £
46	— O, Geometric types, unintelligible patterns, some blank on obv. *BMC 410-432; VA 143, 1225-29; ABC 533-536, 767*	110	325
47	— P, Trophy types, blank on obv., R. 'trophy' surrounded by various motifs. *BMC 437-444; VA 145, 147; ABC 192-195, 2243*	125	375
47A	— — —, Eastern variants, four-petalled flower or reversed S, R. similar to last. *BMC 436; VA 146; ABC 2246-49*	175	525

48

		F £	VF £
48	— Qc, British 'Remic' types, devolved head r., R. [usually] triple-tailed horse l. or r., various motifs surround. *BMC 478-538; VA 220-232; ABC 500-512, 554-584, 2093-99, 2225-2234, 2359-62, 2368-71*	200	625
48A	— — —, Ornamental variants, R. triple-tailed horse l., various motifs around. *BMC 539-544; VA 236, 256; ABC 779-791*	375	1000
48B	— — —, Wreath variants, ringed annulet or flower at centre, R. horse l. or r., various motifs surround. *(BMC 545-546; VA 242-244; ABC 602-605, 611-614, 2365-71, 2469*	275	900

49

		F £	VF £

49 — Xd, diademed head of good style l., reversed S before, Ɽ. sinuous horse l., wheel below. *BMC 571-575; VA 78; ABC 551* 475 1500

50   50 (Var.)

50 **Silver Unit**. head left or right, Ɽ. horse l. or r. *BMC 376-382; VA 80, 1546, 1549, 1555; ABC 1507, 2472-75, 2481-84 [53]*....................................... 125 425

51   53

51 — head l., Ɽ. stag or goat with horns r. *BMC 383; VA 1552; ABC 2487 [54]* 135 450
52 **Silver Half Unit**. Zoomorphic types, annulate horses and beasts. *BMC 391-400; VA 474, 1626, 1643; ABC 719, 935-941, 2283-2309, 2401, 2496-2502, 2535 [55]* 125 425
53 **Silver Unit**. British Lz, Danebury group, head r., with corded hair, Ɽ. annulate horse l, flower above. *BMC 580-582; VA 262; ABC 1013* 150 525

54   54A

54 — helmeted head r., Ɽ. annulate horse r., wheel below. *BMC 583-592; VA 264; ABC 662 [58]*.. 135 475
54A **Silver Half Unit**. Cruciform pattern with ornaments in angles, Ɽ. horse l., motifs surround. *ABC 2505* 200 650
55 **Silver Minim**. helmeted head r., Ɽ. horse r., pellet mane. *BMC 642-643; VA 268-270; ABC 728 [59]*.. 65 225

56

56 **Silver Unit**. horned head r., Ɽ. as S.54. *BMC 595-601; VA 280; ABC 866* 100 350
57 — head l., pellet-in-ring before, Ɽ. as S.54. *BMC 610-612; VA 284; ABC 857* 75 250

58

		F £	*VF* £
58	—, serpentine dragon l., head back-turned, R. similar to S.54. *BMC 631-633; VA 286; ABC 896*	150	525

59   61

59	**Silver Minim**. Concave square, R. two-tailed annulate horse l., wheel above. *BMC 654-656; VA 482; ABC 1046*	50	175
60	**Bronze Unit.** Lx. Winged horse l. R. Winged horse l. *ABC 273; V. 1629; BMC 401*	70	250
61	Chichester Cock type. Head r. R. Head r. surmounted by cock. *ABC 737; V. — BMC 657-59*	80	275

POTIN, c.120-100 B.C.
(Cast copper/tin alloy, mainly Kent)

62

		F £	VF £
62	**Unit.** Thurrock type.Head l. ℞. Bull butting l. or r. *ABC 120, 123, 126, 129, 132; V. 1402-42; BMC 660-666.*	35	100

63   64

63	Class I type. Crude head. ℞. Lines representing bull *(Allen types A-L.) ABC 147, 150, 153, 156, 162, 165, 168, 171; V. 104, 106, 108, 112, 114, 115, 117, 119, 120, 122, 123, 125, 127, 129, 131, 133; BMC 667-714.*	40	125
64	Class II type. Smaller flan, large central pellet. *(Allen types M-P.)* 30ABC 174; *V. 135-39; BMC 715-23.*	35	100

CELTIC DYNASTIC AND LATER UNINSCRIBED COINAGE

From Julius Caesar's expeditions to Britain in 55/54 B.C. and his conquest of Gaul in 52 B.C. to the Claudian invasion in A.D. 43, southern Britain was increasingly drawn into the orbit of the Roman world. This process is reflected not only in the coins but also in what we know about their issuers and the tribes they ruled. Latin legends begin to appear for the first time and increasingly accompany objects and designs drawn from the classical world. A lot of what we know about the Celtic tribes and their rulers, beyond just their names on coins, is drawn from contemporary and slightly later Roman historical sources. A great deal however is still uncertain and almost all attributions to either tribes or historically attested individuals have to be seen as tentative.

The coin-producing tribes of Britain can be divided into two groups, those of the core and those of the periphery. The tribes of the core, the Atrebates/Regni, Trinovantes/Catuvellauni and Cantii, by virtue of their geographical location controlled contact with the Roman world. Unlike the tribes of the periphery they widely employed Latin legends, classical designs and used bronze coinage in addition to gold and silver.

Following the Roman invasion of A.D. 43 it is likely that some coinage continued to be produced for a short time. However in A.D. 61 with the death of King Prasutagus and the suppression of the Boudiccan revolt that followed, it is likely that Celtic coinage came to an end.

TRIBAL MAP

ATREBATES AND REGNI

The joint tribal area of these two groups corresponds roughly with Berkshire and Sussex and parts of northern and eastern Hampshire. The Atrebatic portion being in the north of this region with its main centre at Calleva (Silchester). The Regni occupying the southern part of the region centred around Chichester.

COMMIUS
(Mid to Late 1st Century B.C.)

The first inscribed staters to appear in Britain, closely resemble British Q staters (no.38) and are inscribed 'COMMIOS'. Staters and silver units with an inscribed 'E' are also thought to be related. Traditionally this Commius was thought to be the Gaulish chieftain who Caesar refers to in De Bello Gallico, as firstly serving him in his expeditions to Britain and finally fleeing to Britain c. 50 B.C. This attribution does however present chronological problems, and the appearance of a few early staters reading 'COM COMMIOS' suggests that the Commius who issued coins is more likely to have been the son of Caesar's Commius.

65

		F £	VF £
65	**Gold Stater**. Devolved head r, ℞. triple-tailed horse r., COM-MIOS below. *BMC 724-729; VA 350; ABC 1022*	375	1100

66   67

66	—, similar to last, ℞. E above horse. *BMC 730; VA 352; ABC 1025*	425	1250
67	**Gold Quarter Stater**. Blank except for digamma, ℞. annulate horse l., E above, annulet and corded line below. *BMC 724-729; VA 353-1; ABC 1028*......	200	575
68	—, similar to last, ℞. cogwheel above horse. *VA 353-5; ABC 1031 [67]*.	175	475

69

| 69 | **Silver Unit**. Head l., concentric rings before, ℞. horse l., wheel or E above. *BMC 731-758; VA 355; ABC 1034-40*......... | 75 | 275 |

70

| 70 | **Silver Minim**. Similar to last. *BMC 759-760; VA 358; ABC 1043* .... | 50 | 175 |

TINCOMARUS or TINCOMMIUS
(Late 1st Century B.C. – Early 1st Century A.D.)

Successor to Commius and on his coins styled as 'COM.F' (son of Commius). Early coins of the reign like his predecessors are very obviously Celtic in their style. However later coins exhibit an increasing tendency towards Roman designs. Indeed Tincommius is recorded as a suppliant king of the Roman emperor Augustus (Res Gestae, xxxii), finally fleeing to Rome in the early 1st century A.D. The discovery of the Alton Hoard in 1996 brought to light gold staters with the new legend TINCOMARVS.

72   73

		F £	VF £
71	**Gold Stater.** *Celtic style*. Devolved Apollo head r. ℞. TINC COMM. F. around horse. *ABC* —; *V. 362; BMC* —.	1100	3500
72	Similar but legend reads TINCOMARVS. *ABC 1049; V. 363; BMC 761-765.*	575	1750
73	**Gold Quarter Stater.** Spiral with pellet centre. ℞. Horse r. T above. *ABC 1094; V. 366; BMC 781-797.*	150	525

74   75

| 74 | TINCOM, zig-zag ornament below. ℞. Horse l. *ABC 1073; V. 365; BMC 798-810.* | 225 | 750 |
| 75 | **Gold Stater.** *Classical style*. TINC(O) on a sunk tablet. ℞. Horseman with javelin r. often with CF in field. *ABC 1055, 1058, 1061; V. 375-76; BMC 765-769.* | 475 | 1500 |

76   77

76	COM.(F). on a sunk tablet. ℞. Horseman with javelin r. TIN in field *ABC 1067; V. 385; BMC 770-774.*	425	1350
77	**Gold Quarter Stater.** TINC on a tablet, C above, A or B below. ℞. Winged head (Medusa?) facing. *ABC 1076; V. 378; BMC 811-826.*	575	1750
78	TIN on tablet. ℞. Boar l. *ABC 1079; V. 379; BMC 827-837.*	150	450

		F	VF
		£	£
79	COMF on tablet. R. Horse r. TIN around. *ABC 1082; V. 387; BMC 838-841.*	165	525
80	— R. Horse l. TIC around. *ABC 1088; V. 388; BMC 842-851.*	165	525
81	COM on tablet. R. Horse l. T above. *ABC 1091; V. 389; BMC 852-3.*	200	625
82	COMF on tablet. R. Horse r. TINC around. *ABC 1085; V. 390; BMC 854-879.*	165	525
83	**Silver Unit.** Laureate head r. TINCOM in front, V behind. R. Eagle stg. on snake. *ABC 1106; V. 397; BMC 880-905.*	80	325
84	Laureate head l. R. Bull l. TINC around. *ABC 1112; V. 396; BMC 906-910.*	80	325
85	Laureate head r. R. Bull r. TIN(C) around. *ABC 1115, 1118; V. 381; BMC 911-925.*	80	325

86	Facing head. R. Bull l. TINC around. *ABC 1109; V. 370; BMC 926-29*	110	450
87	TINC in angles of cross, R. Lion l. *ABC 1124; V. 372; BMC 930-45.*	80	325
88	Star. R. Boy riding dolphin r. TINC in field. *ABC 1127; V. 371; BMC 946-977.*	65	250
89	TINC around pellet. R. Lion l. *ABC 1121; V. 382; BMC 978-80.*	90	350
90	Head l. TINCOMMIVS in front. R. Horse l. lyre above. *ABC 1100; V. 473; BMC —-. (Formerly attributed to Verica)*	80	325
91	**Silver Minim.** CF within two interlinked squares. R. Boar? r. TINC. *ABC 1136; V. 383-1; BMC 981-82.*	40	150
92	As above but CO. R. Bull r. TI. *ABC 1139; V. 383-5; BMC —-*...............	50	175
93	C inside box, box above and below. R. Bull r. TIN. *ABC 1274; V. 383-7; BMC 983*	50	175

| 94 | Cross, T? in angles. R. uncertain object. *ABC 1142; V. 483; BMC 984-85. (Formerly attributed to Verica)* .... | 45 | 160 |

EPPILLUS
(Later 1st Century B.C. – Early 1st Century A.D.)

His reign is likely to have coincided with that of Tincommius's. Eppillus also claimed to be a son of Commius. Two coinages appear in his name, one for Kent and one minted at Calleva (Silchester, Hants.) in the northern part of the territory of the Atrebates and Regni. The coins of Calleva conform to the southern denominational structure of gold and silver with fractions of each, whilst the Kentish series is distinctly tri-metallic, replacing the silver minim with bronze. A joint coinage was issued by Eppillus and Verica. It is not understood if Eppillus held both territories simultaneously.

COINAGE STRUCK AT CALLEVA

	F £	VF £
95	95	96

		F £	VF £
95	**Gold Stater.** Devolved Apollo head r. ℞. EPPI COMMI F around horse. *ABC 1145; V. 405; BMC —*	2500	9500
96	**Gold Quarter Stater.** CALLEV, star above and below. ℞. Hound r. EPPI. *ABC 1148, 1151; V. 407-08; BMC 986-1005.*	175	525

	97	98

		F £	VF £
97	COMM F EPPILV, around crescent. ℞. Horse r. *ABC 1157; V. 409; BMC 1006-1009.*	225	750
98	EPPI COMF in two lines. ℞. Winged horse r. *ABC 1154; V. 435; BMC 1010-15.*	185	575

	99	100	103

		F	VF
99	**Silver Unit.** Crescent REX CALLE above and below. ℞. Eagle r. EPP. *ABC 1160; V .415. BMC 1016-1060.*	85	350
100	Bearded hd. r. in wreath. ℞. Boar r. EPPI(L) F CO(M). *ABC 1163; V. 416; BMC 1061-87.*	90	375
101	Bearded hd. in pellet border. ℞. Lion r. EPP COMF. *ABC 1166; V. 417; BMC 1088-1115.*	90	375
102	**Silver Minim.** Floral cross. ℞. Eagle r. EPPI. *ABC 1169; V. 420; BMC 1116-17*	65	225
103	Spiral and pellets. ℞. Ram r. EPP. *ABC 1172; V. 421; BMC 1118-20.*	65	225
104	Bulls head facing. ℞. Ram r. EPP. *ABC 1175; V. 422; BMC 1121-24.*	75	250
105	Wreath pattern. ℞. Boar r. EPP. *ABC 1280; V. 423; BMC —-*	90	325
106	Crescent cross. ℞. Hand holding trident. *ABC 1298; V. 487; BMC —.* ...	75	250

KENTISH TYPES

107

		F £	VF £
107	**Gold Stater.** COMF within wreath. Ŗ. Horseman l. EPPILLVS above. *ABC 384; V. 430; BMC 1125-26.*	3000	12500
108	Victory holding wreath l., within wreath. Ŗ. Horseman r. holding carnyx, F EPPI COM below. *ABC 387; V. 431; BMC 1127-28.*	3750	15000
109	**Gold Quarter Stater.** Crossed wreaths, EPPI in angles. Ŗ. Horse l. *ABC 390; V. 436; BMC 1129.*	575	1750
110	COMF in pellet border. Ŗ. Horse r. EPPI. *ABC 393; V. 437; BMC 1130-31.*	525	1600
111	**Silver Unit.** Head l. EPPIL in field. Ŗ. Horseman holding carnyx, EPPILL. *ABC 399; V. 441; BMC 1132.*	375	1350
112	**Bronze Unit.** Bow cross, EPPI COMF around. Ŗ. Eagle facing. *ABC 408; V. 450; BMC 1137-38.*	60	275
113	Bull r., EPPI COF around. Ŗ. eagle facing. *ABC 411; V. 451; BMC 1139-41.*	60	275
114	Head l., EPPI in front. Ŗ. Victory l. holding wreath and standard. *ABC 414; V. 452; BMC 1142.*	70	300
115	Bearded hd. r., EPPI CF. Ŗ. Biga r. CF. *ABC 417; V. 453; BMC −*	90	375

JOINT TYPES OF EPPILUS AND VERICA

116 117

116	**Silver Unit.** Diademed head l., TOVTO before. Ŗ. Victory walking r., E-P in field. *BMC 1133-34; VA 442; ABC 432*	675	2500
117	Head r. VIR CO in front. Ŗ. Capricorn l. EPPI COMF. *ABC 435; V. 443; BMC 1135-36.*	200	750

VERICA
(c. 10.-c. A.D. 40)

The exact details of Verica's succession and relationship to Eppillus and Tincommius are not fully understood. However by c. A.D. 10 it seems likely that Verica was the sole ruler of the southern region. His close contact with Rome, both political and economic, seen in the increasing use of classical designs on his coins, culminated in his flight to Rome in c. A.D. 42 to seek assistance from Claudius.

		F £	VF £
118	**Gold Stater.** COM:F on tablet. R̟. Horseman r. holding spear, VIR below. *ABC 1187; V. 460; BMC 1143-44.*	525	1750
119	COM.F. on tablet, pellet in ring ornament above and below. R̟. Similar to last. *ABC 1184; 461; BMC 1146-53.*	525	1750

120   121

120	COM.F on tablet. R̟. Horseman r. holding spear, VIR above, REX below. *ABC 1190; V. 500; BMC 1155-58.*	450	1500
121	Vine-leaf dividing VI RI. R̟. Horseman r. with shield and spear. COF in field. *ABC 1193; V. 520-1; BMC 1159-73.*	450	1500
122	Similar, reads VE RI. *ABC 1193; V. 520-5/7; BMC 1174-76.*	525	1750

123   124

123	**Gold Quarter Stater.** COMF on tablet. R̟. Horse l. VIR. *ABC 1196; V. 465; BMC 1177-78.*	175	575
124	COMF on tablet, pellet in ring ornament above and below R̟. Horse r. VI. *ABC 1199; V. 466; BMC 1179-1206.*	160	500
125	COMF on tablet, pellet border. R̟. Horse r. VI above. *ABC 1202; V. 467; BMC 1207-16.*	200	675

126   127   128

126	COM FILI. in two lines, scroll in between. R̟. Horse r. VIR(I) above. *ABC 1205; V. 468; BMC 1217-22.*	225	750
127	VERI COMF, crescent above, star below. R̟. Horse r. REX below. *ABC 1208; V. 501; BMC 1223-36.*	225	750
128	VERI beneath vine-leaf. R̟. Horseman r. with sword and shield, FRX in field. *ABC 1211; V. 525; BMC 1237-38.*	475	1500
129	COM, horseman r. R̟. Seated figure, VERICA around. *ABC 1214; V. 526; BMC 1239.*	750	2500
130	Similar to last. R̟. Laureate bust r., VIRI in front. *ABC 1217; V. 527; BMC 1240.*	750	2500

131 132 133 134

	F £	VF £
131 **Silver Unit.** COMF, crescent and or pellet in ring above and below. ℞. Boar r. VI(RI) below. *ABC 1220, 1223; V. 470/72; BMC 1241-1331.*	75	325
132 VERICA COMMI F around pellet in ring. ℞. Lion r. REX below. *ABC 1229; V. 505; BMC 1332-1359.*	80	350
133 COMMI F, horseman with shield r. ℞. VERI CA, mounted warrior with spear r. *ABC 1238; V. 530; BMC 1360-92.*	80	350

135 136 137 138

	F £	VF £
134 Two cornucopiae, COMMI F. ℞. Figure seated r. VERICA. *ABC 1241; V. 531; BMC 1393-1419.*	65	275
135 Bust r. VIRI. ℞. Figure seated l. *ABC 1244; V. 532; BMC 1420.*	225	900
136 Naked figure l. ℞. Laureate bust r., COMMI F. *ABC 1250; V. 533; BMC 1421-49.*	65	275

141 143 146 148 149

	F £	VF £
137 VERICA REX, bull r. ℞. Figure stg. l., COMMI F. *ABC 1235; V. 506; BMC 1450-84.*	65	275
138 COMF, in tablet and scroll. ℞. Eagle facing, VI RI. *ABC 1226; V. 471; BMC 1485-1505.*	65	275
139 VIRIC across field, ornaments above and below. ℞. Pegasus r., star design below. *ABC 1256; V. —; BMC —.*	135	500
140 Head r. Verica. ℞. COMMI F., eagle l. *ABC 1253; V. 534; BMC —.*	150	575
141 **Silver Minim.** COF in tablet, ℞. Facing head (Medusa?), VE below. *ABC 1271; V. 384; BMC 1506.. (Formerly attributed to Tincommius)*	60	220
142 Head r. ℞. Horse r., VIRICO. *ABC 1289; V. 480; BMC —.*	75	275
143 Pellet and ring pattern. ℞. Lion r. VIR. *ABC 1292; V. 484; BMC 1514-17.*	50	185
144 VIRIC reversed. ℞. Boar r. *ABC 1283; V. 485; BMC 1518*	50	185
145 Cross. ℞. Trident. *ABC 1295; V. 486-1; BMC —-*	75	275
146 Uncertain. ℞. Boar r. *ABC 1280; V. 510-1; BMC —.*	45	175
147 Crescent cross. ℞. Boar r. *ABC 1301; V. 510-5; BMC 1521-23.*	50	185
148 VIR VAR in tablets. ℞. Winged horse r. CO. *ABC 1262; V. 511; BMC 1507-12.*	55	200
149 Vine-leaf, CFO. ℞. Horse r. VERI CA. *ABC 1307; V. 550; BMC 1524-25*	55	200

150 152

	F £	VF £
150 CF in torc. ℞. Head r. VERIC. *ABC 1310; V. 551; BMC 1526-33.*	45	180
151 Altar, CF, ℞. Bull's head facing, VERICA. *ABC 1313; V. 552; BMC 1534-37.*	100	350
152 Temple, CF. ℞. Bull r, VER REX. *ABC 1316; V. 553; BMC 1538-41*	45	180

153 157 162

		F	VF
		£	£
153	Cornucopia, VER COM. R. Lion r. *ABC 1319; V. 554; BMC 1542*........	60	220
154	Two cornucopiae. R. Eagle l. *ABC 1322; V. 555; BMC 1543-58*............	45	175
155	Floral pattern, CF. R. Lion r. *ABC 1325; V. 556; BMC 1559-63.*	50	185
156	Sphinx r., CF, R. dog curled up, VERI. *ABC 1328; V. 557; BMC 1564-68.*	45	180
157	VERI. R. Urn, COMMI F. *ABC 1286; V. 559; BMC —-*.........................	60	225
158	A in star. R. Bird r. *ABC 1133; V. 561; BMC 1569-71*	125	450
159	Urn, Rex. R. Eagle r., VERRICA COMMI F. *ABC 1331; V. 563; BMC 1572-78.*	50	200
160	VIR inside tablet. R. Boars head r. *ABC 1268; V. 564; BMC 1579-81.* ..	45	180
161	Cross. R. bull l. *ABC 1334; V. —; BMC 1582*	60	225
162	Boars head r., CF, R. Eagle, VE. *ABC 1337; V. —; BMC 1583-86*	45	175
163	Head r, COMM IF., R. Sphinx, R VE. *ABC 1340; V. —; BMC 1587-89* .	50	200
164	A in tablet. R. Boar r. VI CO. *ABC 1277; V. —; BMC 1590*	100	350
	The two following coins are possibly issues of Epatticus.		
165	Bull r. R. Eagle with snake l. *ABC 1358; V. 512; BMC 2366-70*	60	225
166	Bust r. R. dog r. *ABC 1361; V. 558; BMC 2371-74*	60	225

CANTII

The Cantii, who gave their name to Kent, occupied a similar area to that of the modern county.Caesar considered this the most civilised part of Britain and the early production of potin units in Kent can be seen as indicative of this. A number of Kentish rulers for whom we have coins, appear to be dynasts from the two neighbouring kingdoms, who were involved in struggles to acquire territory. Eppillus (see Atrebates and Regni) produced coins specifically for circulation in Kent and like those of Cunobelin they circulated widely.

EARLY UNINSCRIBED

167	**Gold Stater.** Ly. Blank. R. Horse l. numerous ring ornaments in field. *ABC 183; V. 142; BMC 2472.*	1100	3750
168	Blank. R. Horse r. numerous ornaments in field. *ABC 294; V. 157; BMC—*	1250	4000

169 170 171

169	Lz. Blank. R. Horse l., box with cross hatching below. *ABC 177, 180; V. 150, 144; BMC 2466-68.*	1350	4250
170	**Gold Quarter Stater.** Ly. Blank. R. Horse r., pentagram below. *ABC 309; V. 163; BMC 2473-74.*	200	625
171	Blank. R. Horse r., 'V' shape above. *ABC 312; V. 170; BMC 2475-77.* .	185	575
172	Lz. Blank. R. Horse l., 'V' shape above. *ABC 198; V. 151; BMC 2469-70.*	175	525

173 175 176

173	**Silver Unit.** Curved star. R. Horse r. Pentagram below. *ABC 2258; V. 164; BMC—.*	325	1100

	F £	VF £
174 Serpent torc. R. Horse r., box with cross hatching below. *cf Mossop 8; ABC 243; BMC 2478*	475	1500
175 **Silver Half Unit.** Spiral of three arms. R. Horse l. *ABC 2261; V. —; BMC 2479*	175	650
176 **Bronze Unit.** Various animal types, R. Various animal types. *ABC 258, 267, 270, 285, 288, 291; V. 154/167; BMC 2480-91. (80/141-44)*	75	325

INSCRIBED

DUBNOVELLAUNUS
(Late 1st Century B.C.)

Likely to be the same Dubnovellaunus recorded on coins in Essex (see Trinovantes / Catuvellauni). The two coinages share the same denominational structure and have some stylistic similarities. It has been suggested that Dubnovellaunus is the British king of that name mentioned along with Tincommius as a client king in the Res Gestae of the Roman emperor Augustus.

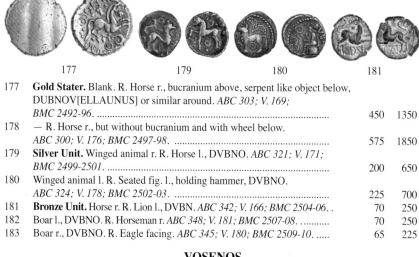

177　　　　　179　　　　　180　　　　181

	F £	VF £
177 **Gold Stater.** Blank. R. Horse r., bucranium above, serpent like object below, DUBNOV[ELLAUNUS] or similar around. *ABC 303; V. 169; BMC 2492-96.*	450	1350
178 — R. Horse r., but without bucranium and with wheel below. *ABC 300; V. 176; BMC 2497-98.*	575	1850
179 **Silver Unit.** Winged animal r. R. Horse l., DVBNO. *ABC 321; V. 171; BMC 2499-2501.*	200	650
180 Winged animal l. R. Seated fig. l., holding hammer, DVBNO. *ABC 324; V. 178; BMC 2502-03.*	225	700
181 **Bronze Unit.** Horse r. R. Lion l., DVBN. *ABC 342; V. 166; BMC 2504-06.*	70	250
182 Boar l., DVBNO. R. Horseman r. *ABC 348; V. 181; BMC 2507-08.*	70	250
183 Boar r., DVBNO. R. Eagle facing. *ABC 345; V. 180; BMC 2509-10.*	65	225

VOSENOS
(Late 1st Century B.C./ Early 1st Century A.D.)

Little is known of this ruler who issued coins in a characteristically Kentish style similar to those of Dubnovellaunus.

184　　　　　　　　185

	F £	VF £
184 **Gold Stater.** Blank. R. Horse l., bucranium above, serpent like object below., [VOSE]NOS. *ABC 357; V. 184; BMC 2511-12.*	3000	11000
185 **Gold Quarter Stater.** Blank. R. Horse r., VOSI below. *ABC 360; V. 185; BMC 2514-15.*	625	2000
186 **Silver Unit.** Horse and griffin. R. Horse r., retrograde legend. *ABC 363; V. 186; BMC —.*	300	1000

"SA" or "SAM"

(Late 1st Century B.C./ Early 1st Century A.D.)

An historically unattested individual whose coins are stylistically associated with those of Dubnovellaunus and Vosenos. His coins have been predominantly found in north Kent

187

187B

		F £	VF £
187	**Silver Unit.** Head l., R. Horse l., SA below. *ABC 369; V. —; BMC —*	300	1000
187A	**Bronze Unit.** Boar l., R. Horse l., SA below. *ABC 375; V. 187; BMC 2516-19.*	80	275
187B	Horse l., SAM below. R. Horse l., SAM below. *ABC 281; V. —; BMC —*	85	300

AMMINUS

(Early 1st Century A.D.)

Issued a coinage stylistically distinct from other Kentish types and with strong affinities to those of Cunobelin. Indeed it has been suggested that he is the Adminius recorded by Suetonius, as a son of Cunobelin. The enigmatic legend DVN or DVNO may be an unknown mint site.

189

188	**Silver Unit.** Plant, AMMINUS around. R. Winged horse r., DVN. *ABC 456; V. 192; BMC 2522-23.*	135	475
189	(Last year 190). A in wreath. R. Capricorn r., S AM (I). *ABC 468; V. 194; BMC 2520-21.*	135	475
190	**Bronze Unit.** (Last year 189). AM in wreath. R. Horse r., DVNO. *ABC 462; V. 193; BMC — —*	70	250
191	Head r. R. Hippocamp r., AM. *ABC 471; V. 195; BMC 2524.*	80	300

BELGAE
ESUNERTOS
(c. 50-30 BC)

Esunertos is an unexpected addition to an extremely limited corpus of early inscribed native British coinage, and is only known from only three coins found in the vicinity of Danebury hill fort since the early 1980s. Esunertos translates as "Mighty as the God Esos" and has been documented on a few Romano-Gallic inscriptions dating to the 1st Century AD. Etymologically, his name is indicative of a Belgic elder.

193

	F £	VF £
193 **Gold Quarter-Stater**. IISVNIIRTOS around debased laureate head r., wheel at centre, R. Annulate horse l., wheel above, E-motif before	2000	7500
194 **Silver Unit**. Similar to above	950	2500

TRINOVANTES AND CATUVELLAUNI

Occupying the broad area of Essex, southern Suffolk, Bedfordshire, Buckinghamshire, Hertfordshire, parts of Oxfordshire, Cambridgeshire and Northamptonshire, they are likely to have been two separate tribes for most of their history. The Trinovantes were originally located in the eastern half of this area, with their main centre at Camulodunum (Colchester). The original Catuvellauni heartland was further west, with their main centre at Verulamium (St.Albans). The whole area eventually came under the control of Cunobelin at the end of the period.

TRINOVANTES

ADDEDOMAROS
(Late 1st Century B.C.)

Unknown to history, he appears to have been a contemporary of Tasciovanus. The design of his staters is based on the Whaddon Chase type (No.32) which circulated widely in this region.

200	201	202

		F	VF
200	**Gold Stater**. Crossed wreath. R. Horse r., wheel below, AθθIIDOM above. *ABC 2514; V. 1605; BMC 2390-94.*	475	1500
201	Six armed spiral. R. Horse r., cornucopia below, AθθIIDOM above. *ABC 2517; V. 1620; BMC 2396-2404.*	400	1250
202	Two opposed crescents. R. Horse r., branch below, spiral or wheel above, AθθDIIDOM. *ABC 2511; V. 1635; BMC 2405-2415.*	600	1850

203   204

		F £	VF £
203	**Gold Quarter Stater.** Circular flower pattern. ℞. Horse r. *ABC 2526; V. 1608; BMC 2416.*	225	675
204	Cross shaped flower pattern. ℞. Horse r. *ABC 2529; V. 1623; BMC 2417-21.*	175	575
205	Two opposed crescents. ℞. Horse r., AθθDIIDOM around. *ABC 2520, 2541; V. 1638; BMC 2422-24.*	225	675
206	**Bronze Unit.** Head l. ℞. Horse l. *ABC 2544; V. 1615/46 BMC 2450-60.*	40	125

DUBNOVELLAUNUS
(Late 1st Century B.C./ Early 1st Century A.D.)

Dubnovellaunus is likely to have been the successor to Addedomaros, with whom his coins are stylistically related. It is not clear if he was the same Dubnovellaunus who also issued coins in Kent (see Cantii) or if he is the same Dumnobeallaunos mentioned in the Res Gestae of the emperor Augustus c. A.D. 14.

207   208   210

		F £	VF £
207	**Gold Stater.** Two crescents on wreath. ℞. Horse l., leaf below, pellet in ring, DVBNOVAIIAVNOS above. *ABC 2392; V. 1650; BMC 2425-40.*	550	1750
208	**Gold Quarter Stater.** Similar. *ABC 2395; V. 1660; BMC 2442.*	175	525
209	**Silver Unit.** Head l., DVBNO. ℞. Winged horse r., lattice box below. *ABC 315; V. 165; BMC 2443-44.*	150	525
210	Head l., legend ?, ℞. Horse l. DVB[NOV]. *ABC 2404; V. 1667; BMC 2445.*	125	450
211	**Bronze Unit.** Head l., ℞. Horse l., DVBNO above. *ABC 2407; V. 1669; BMC 2446-48.*	50	175
212	Head r., ℞. Horse l. *ABC 2410; V. 1665; BMC 2461-65.*	50	175

DIRAS
(Late 1st Century B.C./ Early 1st Century A.D.)
An historically unattested ruler, responsible for a gold stater related stylistically to Dubnovellaunus's.

	F £	VF £
213 **Gold Stater.** Blank. R. Horse r., DIRAS? above, yoke like object above. *ABC 297; V. 162; BMC 2449.*	3000	11000

CATUVELLAUNI

TASCIOVANUS
(Late 1st Century B.C./ Early 1st Century A.D.)
The early gold coins of Tasciovanus, like those of his contemporary Addedomaros, are based on the Whaddon Chase stater. Verulamium (St. Albans) appears to have been his principal mint, appearing as VER or VERL on the coinage. Staters and quarter staters inscribed CAM (Camulodunum/ Colchester) are known and perhaps suggest brief or weak control of the territory to the east. The later coins of Tasciovanus use increasingly Romanised designs. The adoption of the title RICON, perhaps a Celtic equivalent to the Latin REX (King), can be seen as a parallel move to that of his contemporary Tincommius to the south.

	214	217	219
214	**Gold Stater.** Crescents in wreath. R. TASCIAV and bucranium over horse r. *ABC 2553; V. 1680; BMC 1591-1603.*	600	2000
215	— R. Similar reads TAXCIAV. *ABC 2550; V. 1682; BMC 1604-05.*	650	2250
216	— R. Similar reads TASCIOVAN above, CAM below. *ABC 2559; V. 1684; BMC 1606-07.*	1350	4500
217	— R. Horseman r. helmeted and with carnyx, TASC in field. *ABC 2562, 2565; V. 1730-32; BMC 1608-1613.*	525	1750
218	Crescents in wreath, with V or VER in design. R. Similar to last. *ABC 2568, 2571; V. 1734-35; BMC 1623-24.*	625	2100

	221	224	226
219	TASCIO(V) RICON in panel. R. Horseman l., wearing armour and holding sword and shield. *ABC 2577, 2580; V. 1780; BMC 1628-36.*	675	2250
220	**Gold Quarter Stater.** Floral design. R. Horse r. *ABC 2583; V. —; BMC 1638-39*	275	900
221	Crossed Wreath. R. Horse l. *ABC 2586; V. 1688; BMC 1651-53.*	185	600
222	— R. Horse r., CAM. *ABC 2589; V. 1694; BMC 1640.*	275	900
223	Similar, TASCI in wreath. R. Horse r., TASC. *ABC 2595; V. 1692; BMC 1641.*	200	675
224	Similar, VERO in wreath. R. Horse l., TAS. *ABC 2598; V. 1690; BMC 1642-43.*	185	600
225	TASCIO on tablet. R. Horse l. *ABC 444; V. 1848; BMC 1646.*	450	1350
226	TASC on tablet. R. Horse l. *ABC 2601; V. 1786; BMC 1647-50.*	200	675

		F	VF
		£	£
227	**Silver Unit.** Head l. ℞. Horse r. *ABC 2604; V. 1698; BMC 1654*	95	325
228	Cross and box. ℞. Horse r., VER in front. *ABC 2631; V. −; BMC 1655*.	95	325
229	Cross and crescent. ℞. Horse l., TASCI. *ABC 2607; V. −; BMC 1665-57*	95	325
230	Bearded head l. ℞. Horseman r., TASCIO. *ABC 2610; V. 1745; BMC 1667-68.*	125	500
231	Winged horse l., TAS. ℞. Griffin r., within circle of pellets. *ABC 2649; V. 1790; BMC 1660.*	110	425
232	Eagle stg. l., TASCIA. ℞. Griffin r. *ABC 2646; V. 1792; BMC 1658-59.*	110	400
233	VER in beaded circle. ℞. Horse r., TASCIA. *ABC 2622; V. 1699; BMC 1670-73.*	100	375
234	− ℞. Naked horseman. *ABC 2625; V. 1747; BMC 1674-76.*	110	400

235   238

235	Laureate hd. r., TASCIA. ℞. Bull l. *ABC 2643; V. 1794; BMC 1681-82.*	110	400
236	Cross and box, VERL. ℞. Boar r. TAS. *ABC 2628; V. 1796; BMC 1661-62.*	100	375
237	TASC in panel. ℞. Winged horse l. *ABC 2637; V. 1798; BMC 1664-65.*	95	350
238	− ℞. Horseman l., carrying long shield. *ABC 2640; V. 1800; BMC 1677-79.*	110	400
239	Two crescents. ℞. Winged griffin, VIR. *ABC 2619; V. −; BMC 1666*	120	450
240	Head r., TAS?. ℞. Horseman r. *ABC −; V. −; BMC 1669*	150	525

241

241	**Bronze Double Unit.** Head r., TASCIA, VA. ℞. Horseman r. *ABC 2652; V. 1818; BMC 1685-87.*	95	275

242

242	**Bronze Unit.** Two heads in profile, one bearded. ℞. Ram l., TASC. *ABC 2655; V. 1705; BMC 1711-13.*	40	185
243	Bearded head r. VER(L). ℞. Horse l., VIIR or VER. *ABC 2658; V. 1707; BMC 1714-21.*	35	170
244	Bearded head r. ℞. Horse l., TAS. *ABC 2661; V. 1709; BMC 1722-23.* ..	40	185
245	Head r., TASC. ℞. Winged horse l., VER. *ABC 2664; V. 1711; BMC 1688-89.*	35	170
246	− ℞. Horseman r., holding carnyx, VIR. *ABC 2676; V. 1750; BMC 1724-27.*	35	170

247

		F	VF
		£	£
247	VERLAMIO between rays of star. Ŗ. Bull l. *ABC 2679; V. 1808;*		
	BMC 1745-51.	30	160
248	Similar without legend. Ŗ. Bull r. *ABC 2685; V. 1810; BMC 1752-55.* ..	40	185
249	Similar. Ŗ. Horse l., TASCI. *ABC 2688; V. 1812; BMC 1709-10.*	40	185
250	Head r., TASCIO. Ŗ. Lion r., TA SCI. *ABC 2691; V. 1814; BMC 1736-38.*	35	170
251	Head r. Ŗ. Figure std. l., VER below. *ABC 2751; V. 1816; BMC 1739-44.*	45	200
252	Cross and Crescents. Ŗ. Boar r., VER. *ABC 2667; V. 1713;*		
	BMC 1702-05.	35	170
253	Laureate head r. Ŗ. Horse l., VIR. *ABC 2694; V. 1820; BMC 1706-08.* ..	35	170
254	Raised band across centre, VER or VERL below. Ŗ. Horse grazing r.		
	ABC 2673; V. 1717; BMC −.	45	200
255	**Bronze Fractional Unit.** Animal r. Ŗ. Sphinx l. *ABC 2700; V. 1824;*		
	BMC 1760-61.	35	160
256	Head l., VER. Ŗ. Goat r. *ABC 2709; V. 1715; BMC 1765-68.*	30	150
257	Head r. Ŗ. Boar r. *ABC 2712; V. 1826; BMC 1762-64.*	30	160
258	Head l. Ŗ. Animal with curved tail. *ABC 2697; V. 1822; BMC 1759.*	35	160

ASSOCIATES OF TASCIOVANUS

(Early 1st Century A.D.)

Towards the end of his reign, a number of joint issues bearing his name and the name of either Sego or Dias appear. In addition coins similar in style to those of Tasciovanus appear with either the name Andoco or Rues. It has been suggested that these issues belong to a period of struggle following the death of Tasciovanus and are all rival contestants for the throne. Another theory is that they are associates or sub-kings of Tasciovanus responsible for areas within the wider territory.

SEGO

259

259	**Gold Stater.** TASCIO in tablet, annulets above. Ŗ. Horseman with carnyx r.,		
	SEGO. *ABC 441; V. 1845; BMC 1625-27.*	2750	9000

9 out of 10 Celtic coins sold by Chris Rudd have been found by metal detectorists

260

		F £	VF £

260 **Silver Unit.** SEGO on panel. ℞. Horseman r. *ABC 447; V. 1851; BMC 1684.* 450 1500

261 **Bronze Unit.** Star shaped pattern. ℞. Winged sphinx l., SEGO. *ABC 453; V. 1855; BMC 1690.* 135 450

ANDOCO

262

262 **Gold Stater.** Crescents in wreath. ℞. Bucranium over horse r., AND below. *ABC 2715; V. 1860; BMC 2011-14.* 900 3000

263 **Gold Quarter Stater.** Crossed wreaths, ANDO in angles. ℞. Horse l. *ABC 2718; V. 1863; BMC 2015-17.* 250 900

264

264 **Silver Unit.** Bearded head l. ℞. Winged horse l., ANDOC. *ABC 2721; V. 1868; BMC 2018.* 150 525

265

265 **Bronze Unit.** Head r., ANDOCO. ℞. Horse r., ANDOCO. *ABC 2727; V. 1871; BMC 2019-20.* 45 225

266 Head r., TAS ANDO. ℞. Horse r. *ABC 2730; V. 1873; BMC —.* 60 275

DIAS

267   268

267 **Silver Unit.** Saltire over cross within square. ℞. Boar r., TASC DIAS. *ABC 2742; V. —; BMC 1663.* 110 375

268 DIAS CO, in star. ℞. Horse l., VIR. *ABC 2739; V. 1877; BMC 1683.* 110 375

269

| | | F | VF |
| | | £ | £ |

269   **Bronze Unit.** Bearded head r., DIAS TASC. R̂. Centaur r., playing pan pipes.
ABC 2748; V. 1882; BMC 1728-35.   45   250

RUES

270   **Bronze Unit.** Lion r., RVII. R̂. Eagle. *ABC 2760; V. 1890; BMC 1691.* .   40   200
271   — R̂. Similar reads RVE. *ABC 2760; V. 1890-3; BMC 1692.*   35   185

272   273

272   Bearded head r., RVIIS. R̂. Horseman r., VIR. *ABC 2754; V. 1892;*
BMC 1698-1701.   35   185
273   RVIIS on tablet. R̂. Winged sphinx l. *ABC 2757; V. 1895;*
BMC 1693-97.   35   185
274   **Bronze Fractional Unit.** Annulet within square with curved sides. R̂.
Eagle l.,RVII. *ABC 2763; V. 1903; BMC 1756-58.*   40   200

CUNOBELIN
(Early 1st Century A.D. to *c*. A.D. 40)

Styled as son of Tasciovanus on some of his coins, Cunobelin appears to have ruled over the unified territories of the Trinovantes and Catuvellauni, with additional territory in Kent. His aggressive policy of expansion that involved members of his family eventually led to Roman concern over the extent of his power. Following his death just prior to A.D. 43, the emperor Claudius took the decision to invade Britain.

During his long reign an extensive issue of gold, silver and bronze coins used ever increasingly Romanised designs. It has been estimated from a study of known dies that around one million of his gold corn ear staters were produced. His main centre and mint was at Camulodunum (Colchester) appearing as the mint signature CAMV. The names SOLIDV and AGR appear on a few coins associated with Cunobelin and are likely to represent personal names.

280   281

280   **Gold Stater.** Biga type. CAMVL on panel. R̂. Two horses l., wheel below,
CVNOBELIN. *ABC 2771; V. 1910; BMC 1769-71.*   750   2500
281   Linear type. Corn ear dividing CA MV. R̂. Horse r., branch above., CVN.
ABC 2774; V. 1925; BMC 1772-76.   400   1100

	F £	VF £

282 — Similar, privy mark 'x' above a letter in *obv.* legend. *ABC 2774; VA 1925-3/5; BMC 1777-81.* 450 1350

283 285

283 Wild type. Corn ear dividing CA MV. R. Horse r., branch above., CVN(O). *ABC 2783; V. 1931/33; BMC 1784-92/1804-08.* 350 1000

284 — Similar, heart shaped object between horses forelegs. *ABC 2780; V. 1931-3; BMC 1793.* 525 1750

285 — Similar, privy mark pellet or pellet triangle above a letter(s) in *obv.* legend. *ABC 2777; V. 1931-5/7/9; BMC 1797-1803.* 425 1250

286 288

286 Plastic type. Corn ear dividing CA MV. R. Horse r., branch above., CVNO. *ABC 2786, 2792; V. 2010-1/3/5; BMC 1809-11/15-23.* 400 1100

287 — Similar, 'B' in front of horse. *ABC 2789; V. 2010-7; BMC 1813.* 625 2000

289 290

288 Classic type. Corn ear dividing CA MV. R. Horse r., branch above., CVNO. *ABC 2795, 2798; V. 2025/27; BMC 1827-31/33.* 500 1500

289 — Similar, horse l., lis like object above. *ABC 2804; V. 2029; BMC 1834-35.* 675 2250

290 **Gold Quarter Stater.** Biga type. Similar to 280. *ABC 2807; V. 1913; BMC 1836/A.* 400 1100

292 296

292 Linear type. Similar to 281. *ABC 2810; V. 1927; BMC 1837-42.* 200 550

293 Wild type. Similar to 283. *ABC 2813; V. 1935; BMC 1843-44.* 200 550

294 Plastic type. Similar to 286. *ABC 2816; V. 2015; BMC 1846-48.* 175 475

295 — Similar but corn ear dividing CAM CVN. *ABC 2819; V. 2017; BMC 1845.* 225 600

296 Classic type. Similar to 288. *ABC 2822; V. 2038; BMC —.* 250 750

299

		F £	VF £
299	**Silver Unit.** Two bull headed serpents, inter twined. ℞. Horse l., CVNO. *ABC 2831; V. 1947; BMC 1856.*	185	650
300	Curled serpent inside wheel. ℞. Winged horse l., CVN. *ABC 2834; V. —; BMC 1857*	185	650
301	CVN on panel ℞. Dog l., (C)M. *ABC 2846; V. 1949; BMC 1858-59.*	120	475
302	CVNO BELI on two panels. ℞. CVN below horseman r. *ABC 2858, 2861; V. 1951/53; BMC 1862.*	110	425
303	Head l., CAMVL. ℞. CVNO beneath Victory std. r. *ABC 2855; V. 2045; BMV 1863-65.*	110	425

304   305

304	Two leaves dividing CVN. ℞. Horseman r., CAM. *ABC 2888; V. 2047; BMC 1866-67.*	100	400
305	Flower dividing CAMV. ℞. CVNO below horse r. *ABC 2885; V. 2049; BMC1867A.*	135	525
306	CVNO on panel. ℞. CAMV on panel below griffin. *ABC 2897; V. 2051; BMC 1868-69.*	185	650
307	CAMVL on panel. ℞. CVNO below centaur l. carrying palm. *ABC 2828; V. 1918; BMC —.*	135	525
308	CAMVL on panel. ℞. Figure seated l. holding wine amphora, CVNOBE. *ABC 2849; V. —; BMC —.*	120	450
309	Plant, CVNOBELINVS. ℞. Figure stg. r. holding club and thunderbolt dividing CA MV. *ABC 2906; V .—; BMC 1897.*	185	650
310	Laur. hd. r., CVNOBELINVS. ℞. Winged horse springing l., CAMV below. *ABC 2909; V. —; BMC —.*	185	650
311	CVNO on panel, wreath around. ℞. Winged horse r., TASC F. *ABC 2876; V. 2053; BMC 1870.*	120	475

312   313

312	Head r., CVNOBELINI. ℞. Horse r., TASCIO. *M. ABC 2873; V. 2055; BMC 1871-73.*	100	400
313	Winged bust r., CVNO. ℞. Sphinx std. l., TASCIO. *ABC 2870; V. 2057; BMC 1874-78.*	85	350

314   316   318

	F £	VF £
314 Draped female fig. r., TASCIIOVAN. ℞. Figure std. r. playing lyre, tree behind. *ABC 2867; V. 2059; BMC 1879-82.*	100	400
315 Figure stg. l., holding club and lionskin., CVNO. ℞. Female rider r., TASCIOVA. *ABC 2864; V. 2061; BMC 1884-85.*	90	375
316 Female head r., CVNOBELINVS. ℞. Victory r., TASCIO(VAN). *ABC 2882; V. −; BMC 1883.*	90	375
317 Fig. r. carrying dead animal, CVNOBELINVS. ℞. Fig. stg. holding bow, dog at side, TASCIIOVANI. *ABC 2879; V. 2063; BMC 1886-88.*	100	400
318 CVNO on panel, horn above, dolphin below. ℞. Fig. stg. r. altar behind. *ABC 2900; V. 2065; BMC 1889-90.*	125	525
319 CVN on panel. ℞. Fig. holding club walking r., CVN. *ABC 2840; V. 2067; BMC 1891-92.*	150	575
320 CVN in wreath. ℞. CAM, dog? trampling on serpent r. *ABC 2891; V. 2069; BMC 1893.*	200	750
321 Winged horse l., CVN. ℞. Std. fig. r. *ABC 2903; V. 2071; BMC 1896.*	175	650
322 CVNO in angles of cross. ℞. Capricorn r., CVNO. *ABC 2843; V. −; BMC 1898*	125	500
323 **Bronze Unit.** Head l., CVNO. ℞. Boar l., branch above. *ABC 2993; V. 1969; BMC−.*	50	200
324 CVNOB ELINI in two panels. ℞. Victory std. l., TASC. *ABC 2918; V. 1971; BMC 1921-27.*	40	175
325 Winged horse l., CAM. ℞. Winged Victory stg l., CVN. *ABC 2921; V. 1973; BMC 1938-43.*	50	200

326

326 Bearded head facing ℞. Boar l., CVN. *ABC 2912; V.1963; BMC 1904-05.*	50	200
327 Ram-headed animal coiled up in double ornamental circle. ℞. Animal l., CAM. *ABC 2915; V. 1965; BMC −.*	50	200
328 Griffin r., CAMV. ℞. Horse r., CVN. *ABC 2945; V. 2081; BMC 1909-12.*	50	200
329 Bearded head l., CAMV. ℞. CVN or CVNO below horse l. *ABC 2951; V. 2085/2131; BMC 1900-01.*	60	250
330 Laureate head r., CVNO. ℞. CVN below bull butting l. *ABC 2948; V. 2083; BMC 1902-03.*	60	250
331 Crude head r., CVN. ℞. Figure stg. l., CVN. *ABC −; V. 2135; BMC −.*	60	250

332

		F £	VF £
332	CAMVL / ODVNO in two panels. ℞. CVNO beneath sphinx crouching l. *ABC 2924; V. 1977; BMC 1928-30.*	45	175
333	Winged horse l., CAMV. ℞. Victory stg. r. divides CV NO. *ABC 2927; V. 1979; BMC 1931-34.*	50	200
334	Victory walking r. ℞. CVN below, horseman r. *ABC 2930; V. 1981; BMC 1935.*	60	250
335	Head l., CAM. ℞. CVNO below eagle. *ABC 2954; V. 2087; BMC −.*	60	250

336 337

336	Head l., CVNOBELINI. ℞. Centaur r., TASCIOVANI.F. *ABC 2957; V. 2089; BMC 1968-71.*	40	175
337	Helmeted bust r. ℞. TASCIIOVANII above, sow stg. r., F below. *ABC 2960; V. 2091; BMC 1956-60.*	40	175
338	Horseman galloping r. holding dart and shield, CVNOB. ℞. Warrior stg. l., TASCIIOVANTIS. *ABC 2963; V. 2093; BMC 1961-67.*	40	175

339 340

339	Helmeted bust l., CVOBELINVS REX. ℞. TASC FIL below boar l., std. on haunches. *ABC 2933; V. 1983; BMC 1952-55.*	50	200
340	Bare head r., CVNOBELINVS REX. ℞. TASC below bull butting r. *ABC 2966; V. 2095; BMC 1944-51.*	40	175
341	Bare head l., CVNO. ℞. TASC below bull stg. r. *ABC 2996; V. 1985; BMC −.*	50	200

342 343

342	Head l., CVNOBELIN. ℞. Metal worker std. r. holding hammer, working on a vase, TASCIO. *ABC 2969; V. 2097; BMC 1972-83.*	45	185
343	Winged horse r., CVNO. ℞. Victory r. sacrificing bull, TASCI. *ABC 2972; V. 2099; BMC 1913-19.*	35	150
344	CVNO on panel within wreath. ℞. CAMV below horse, prancing r. *ABC 2975; V. 2101; BMC 1987-90.*	50	200

345   346

		F £	VF £
345	Bearded head of Jupiter Ammon l., CVNOBELIN. R. CAM below horseman galloping r. *ABC 2978; V. 2103; BMC 1984-86.*	50	200
346	Janus head, CVNO below. R. CAMV on panel below, sow std. r. beneath a tree. *ABC 2981; V. 2105; BMC 1998-2003.*	50	200

347

347	Bearded head of Jupiter Ammon r., CVNOB. R. CAM on panel below lion crouched r. *ABC 2984; V. 2107; BMC 1991-97.*	45	185
348	Sphinx r., CVNO. R. Fig stg. l. divides CA M. *ABC 2987; V. 2109; BMC 2004-09.*	45	185
349	Horse r. R. CVN below horseman r. *ABC 2936; V. 1987; BMC 1936-47.* ...	60	250
350	Animal l. looking back. R. CVN below horse l. *ABC 2990; V. 1967; BMC−*	50	200
350A	Ship, CVN below. R. Fig. r. dividing S E. *ABC 2939; V. 1989; BMC 2010.*	225	900

"SOLIDV"

351

351	**Silver Unit.** SOLIDV in centre of looped circle. R, Stg. fig. l., CVNO. *ABC 474; V. 2073; BMC 1894-95.*	325	1050

"AGR"

352   353

352	**Gold Quarter Stater**. Corn ear dividing CAM CVN. R. Horse r., branch above., AGR below. *ABC 3002; V. −; BMC 1854*	375	1100
353	— R. Horse r., branch above., cross and A below. *ABC 2999; V. −; BMC 1855*	400	1250

354

	F £	VF £
354 **Silver Unit.** AGR inside wreath. Ŗ. Female dog r., AGR below. *ABC 3005; V. —;* *BMC 1899*	300	900

EPATICCUS
(1st Half 1st Century A.D.)

Epaticcus, styled as a son of Tasciovanus on his coins, was most probably a brother of Cunobelin. The corn ear employed on his staters is similar to those his brother produced at Colchester. His coins appear in northern Atrebatic territory and conform to the area's denominational structure. It seems likely that Epaticcus's coinage reflects an incursion into Atrebatic territory by the Trinovantian/ Catuvellaunian dynasty.

355

355 **Gold Stater.** Corn ear dividing TAS CIF. Ŗ. Horseman r., with spear and shield. EPATI. *ABC 1343; V. 575; BMC 2021-23.*	1250	4500

356   357   358

356 **Silver Unit.** Head of Hercules r., EPAT(I). Ŗ. Eagle stg. on snake. *ABC 1346; V. 580; BMC 2024-2268/2270-76.*	65	200
357 Victory seated r. TASCIOV. Ŗ. Boar r., EPAT. *ABC 1349; V. 581; BMC 2294-2328.*	75	250
358 Bearded head l., TASCIO. Ŗ. EPATI below lion r. *ABC 1352; V. 582; BMC 2329*	175	650
359 EPATI inside panel. Ŗ. Lion r. *ABC 1355; V. 583; BMC 2330.*	200	750

360 (x1.5)   361 (x1.5)

360 **Silver Minim.** EPATI. Ŗ. Boars head r., TA. *ABC 1370; V. 585; BMC 2331-46.*	40	160
361 TA inside star. Ŗ. Winged horse r., EPA below. *ABC 1367; V. 560; BMC 2351-57.*	40	165
362 Helmeted head r. Ŗ. Horse r., E below. *ABC 1364; V. —; BMC 2358-63*	40	165
363 EPATI. Ŗ. Winged horse r., cross below. *ABC 1373; V .—; BMC 2365...*	65	225

CARATACUS
(1st Half 1st Century A.D.)

Coins inscribed CARA have been traditionally associated with the historically attested son of Cunobelin, Caratacus the leader of British resistance against Rome. His coins appear in the same area as those of Epaticcus and he may have been his successor.

364   364A (x1.5)

		F	VF
		£	£
363A	**Gold Stater.** Corn ear dividing CV NO. Ṛ. Horseman r. with spear and shield. CARAT. *Rudd 173, lot 14*...*Extremely rare*		
364	**Silver Unit.** Head of Hercules r., CARA. Ṛ. Eagle stg. on snake. *ABC 1376; V. 593; BMC 2376-84.*	275	850
364A	**Silver Minim.** CARA around pellet in ring. Ṛ. Winged horse r. *ABC 1379; V. 595; BMC 2385-89.*	135	450

DUROTRIGES
(Mid 1st Century B.C. to Mid 1st Century A.D.)

The Durotriges inhabited West Hampshire, Dorset and adjoining parts of Somerset and Wiltshire. Their coinage is one of the most distinctive in Britain due to its rapid debasement. The disappearance of precious metals from the coinage should perhaps be linked to the declining trade between the south-west and western Gaul, following the Roman conquest of the Gaul. Hengistbury Head is the probable mint site of the cast bronzes. Coins inscribed CRAB have been traditionally associated with the tribe.

UNINSCRIBED

| 365 | **Silver Stater.** White Gold type. Derived from Westerham stater (no. 21). *ABC 2157; V. 1235, 52, 54, 55; BMC 2525-2731.* .... | 150 | 525 |

366   368

366	Silver type. Similar. *ABC 2169; V. 1235, 52, 54, 55; BMC 2525-2731.* .	80	250
367	Billon type. Similar. *ABC 2166; V. 1235, 52, 54, 55; BMC 2525-2731.* .	40	135
368	**Silver Quarter Stater.** Geometric type. Crescent design. Ṛ. Zig-zag pattern. *ABC 2205, 2208, 2211, 2214, 2217; V. 1242/29; BMC 2734-79.* . *Quality of metal varies, obv.almost blank on later issues*	40	135

369

371

		F £	VF £
369	Starfish type. Spiral. Ŗ. Zig-zag pattern. *ABC 2220; V. 1270; BMC 2780-81*	135	450
370	Hampshire Thin Flan type. Crude head of lines and pellets. Ŗ. Stylised horse l. *ABC 911; V. 1280; BMC 2782-87.*	150	525
371	**Bronze Stater.** Struck Bronze type. Similar to No.365-67. *ABC 2175; V. 1290; BMC 2790-2859.*	35	100

372

		F	VF
372	Cast Bronze type. Many varities, as illustration. *ABC 2178, 2181, 2184, 2187, 2190, 2193, 2196, 2199; V. 1322-70; BMC 2860-2936.*	40	135

INSCRIBED

"CRAB"

373

		F	VF
373	**Silver Unit.** CRAB in angles of cross. Ŗ. Eagle. *ABC 1385; V. 1285; BMC 2788.*	275	950
373A	**Silver Minim.** CRAB on tablet. Ŗ. Star shape. *ABC 1388; V. 1286; BMC 2789.*	175	525

DOBUNNI
(Mid 1st Century B.C. to Mid 1st Century A.D.)

Dobunnic territory stretched over Gloucestershire, Hereford and Worcester and into parts of Somerset, Wiltshire and Gwent. The earliest Dobunnic coins are developed from the British Q stater, and have the distinctive tree-like motif of the tribe on the obverse. The inscribed coinage is difficult to arrange chronologically and it may be that some of the rulers named held different parts of the territory simultaneously.

UNINSCRIBED

374

374 (variant)

375

		F £	VF £
374	**Gold Stater.** Plain except for tree-like object. ℞. Triple tailed horse r., wheel below. *ABC 2003; V. 1005; BMC 2937-40.*	750	2750
375	**Gold Quarter Stater.** Plain with traces of wreath pattern. ℞. Horse r. *ABC 2009; V. 1010-3; BMC 2942-46.*	225	850
376	Wreath pattern. ℞. Horse l., pellet in ring motifs in field. *ABC 2105; V. 1015; BMC 2949.*	250	800

377   378

| 377 | **Silver Unit.** Allen types A-F/I-J. Regular series. Head r. ℞. Triple tailed horse l. or r. *ABC 2012, 2015, 2018, 2021, 2024, 2027, 2036; V. 1020/45/49/74/78/95/ 1135/1137; BMC 2950-3011. (63-64). Style becomes progressively more abstract, from-* | 70 | 225 |
| 378 | Allen types L-O. Irregular series. Similar to last. *ABC 2030, 2122, 2125, 2137, 2140; V. 1170-85; BMC 3012-22. (63-64)* | 85 | 300 |

INSCRIBED
The following types are not arranged chronologically.

ANTED

379

| 379 | **Gold Stater.** Dobunnic emblem. ℞. ANTED or ANTEDRIG over triple tailed horse r., wheel below. *ABC 2066, 2069; V. 1062-69; BMC 3023-3031.* | 600 | 2000 |

	F £	VF £

380 **Silver Unit.** Crude head r. R. ANTED over horse. *ABC 2072; V. 1082; BMC 3032-38.* 85 325

EISV

381 382

381 **Gold Stater.** Dobunnic emblem. R. EISV or EISVRIG over triple tailed horse r., wheel below. *ABC 2078; V. 1105; BMC 3039-42.* 600 2000

382 **Silver Unit.** Crude head r. R. Horse l., EISV. *ABC 2081, 2084; V. 1110; BMC 3043-55.* 65 225

INAM or INARA

383 **Gold Stater.** Dobunnic emblem. R. INAM or INARA over triple tailed horse r., wheel below. *ABC 2060; V. 1140; BMC 3056.* 1750 5750

CATTI

384

384 **Gold Stater.** Dobunnic emblem. R. CATTI over triple tailed horse r., wheel below. *ABC 2057; V. 1130; BMC 3057-60.* 525 1750

COMUX

385

385 **Gold Stater.** Dobunnic emblem. R. COMVX retrograde, over triple tailed horse r., wheel below. *ABC 2054; V. 1092; BMC 3061-63.* 1350 5000

CORIO

386   387

		F £	VF £

386   **Gold Stater.** Dobunnic emblem. R. CORIO over triple tailed horse r., wheel
below. *ABC 2048; V. 1035; BMC 3064-3133.* 475   1650
387   **Gold Quarter Stater.** COR in centre. R. Horse r., without legend. *ABC 2051;
V. 1039; BMC 3134.* 375   1250

BODVOC

388   389

388   **Gold Stater.** BODVOC across field. R. Horse r., without legend. *ABC 2039;
V. 1052; BMC 3135-42.* 1000   3500
389   **Silver Unit.** Head l., BODVOC. R. Horse r., without legend. *ABC 2042; V. 1057;
BMC 3143-45.* 135   450

CORIELTAUVI

The Corieltauvi, formerly known as the Coritani, occupied Lincolnshire and adjoining parts of
Yorkshire, Northamptonshire, Leicestershire and Nottinghamshire. The earliest staters, the South
Ferriby type, are developed from Gallo-Belgic C staters, and are associated with the silver Boar/
Horse types. The distinctive dish shaped scyphate coinages have no parallels in Britain and stand
apart from the main series. The later inscribed issues present a complex system of inscriptions. It
has been suggested that some of the later inscriptions refer to pairs of names, possibly joint rulers or
moneyers and rulers.

EARLY UNINSCRIBED
(Mid to Late 1st Century B.C.)

390

390   **Gold Stater.** South Ferriby type. Crude laureate head. R. Disjointed horse l.,
rosette or star below, anchor shape and pellets above. *ABC 1737, 1743,
1746, 1752; V. 809-815/19; BMC 3146-3179.* 225   675

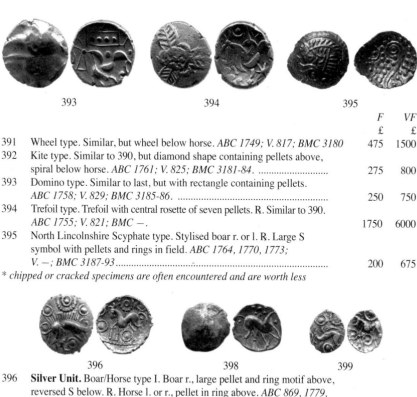

393 394 395

		F £	VF £

391 Wheel type. Similar, but wheel below horse. *ABC 1749; V. 817; BMC 3180* — 475 — 1500

392 Kite type. Similar to 390, but diamond shape containing pellets above, spiral below horse. *ABC 1761; V. 825; BMC 3181-84.* .... 275 — 800

393 Domino type. Similar to last, but with rectangle containing pellets. *ABC 1758; V. 829; BMC 3185-86.* .... 250 — 750

394 Trefoil type. Trefoil with central rosette of seven pellets. Ṛ. Similar to 390. *ABC 1755; V. 821; BMC —.* 1750 — 6000

395 North Lincolnshire Scyphate type. Stylised boar r. or l. Ṛ. Large S symbol with pellets and rings in field. *ABC 1764, 1770, 1773; V. —; BMC 3187-93* .... 200 — 675

* chipped or cracked specimens are often encountered and are worth less

396 398 399

396 **Silver Unit.** Boar/Horse type I. Boar r., large pellet and ring motif above, reversed S below. Ṛ. Horse l. or r., pellet in ring above. *ABC 869, 1779, 1782, 1785, 1791, 1797; V. 855-60, 864, 867; BMC 3194-3214.* .... 100 — 375

397 Boar Horse type II. Vestiges of boar on obv. Ṛ. Horse l. or r. *ABC 1800; V. 875-877; BMC 3214-27.* .... 65 — 200

398 Boar Horse type III. Blank. Ṛ. Horse l.or r. *ABC 1803, 1806, 1812, 1815; BMC 3228-35.* .... 40 — 120

399 **Silver Fractional Unit.** Similar to 396-97. *ABC 1827, 1836; V. 862/66; BMC 3236-3250.* .... 35 — 110

400 Similar to 398. *ABC 1833; V. 877-81; BMC 3251-55. (70/71)* .... 35 — 100

401 Pattern/Horse. Flower pattern. Ṛ. Horse l. *ABC 1606; V. —; BMC 3256-57.* 85 — 325

INSCRIBED
(Early to Mid 1st Century A.D.)
The following types are not arranged chronologically.

AVN COST

402   403

		F £	VF £
402	**Gold Stater.** Crude wreath design. R. Disjointed horse l., AVN COST. *ABC 1929; V. 910; BMC 3258.*	400	1350
403	**Silver Unit.** Remains of wreath or blank. R. AVN COST, horse l. *ABC 1935, 1938; V. 914; BMC 3261-66.*	50	185
403A	**Silver Unit.** Inscription between three lines. R. Horse l. AVN. *ABC −; V-; BMC −.*	85	300
404	**Silver Fractional Unit.** Similar. *ABC 1953; 1 V. 918; BMC 3267-68.* ...	35	110

ESVP RASV

405

		F £	VF £
405	**Gold Stater.** Crude wreath design. R. Disjointed horse l., IISVP RASV. *ABC 1917; V. 920; BMC 3269.*	325	1100
406	**Silver Unit.** Similar. *ABC 1920; V. 924; BMC 3272-73.*	60	225

VEP

407

		F £	VF £
407	**Gold Stater.** Blank or with traces of wreath. R. Disjointed horse l., VEP. *ABC 1851; V. 905; BMC 3274-75.*	450	1500
408	**Silver Unit.** Blank or with traces of wreath. R. VEP, horse r. *ABC 1866; V. 963; BMC 3277-82.*	45	175
409	**Silver Half Unit.** Similar. *ABC 1887; V. 967; BMC 3283-3295.*	40	135

VEP CORF

410 412

		F £	VF £
410	**Gold Stater.** Crude wreath design. R. Disjointed horse l., VEP CORF. *ABC 1854, 1857, 1860, 1863; V. 930/40/60; BMC 3296-3304.*	300	950
411	**Silver Unit.** Similar. *ABC 1869, 1878, 1881; V. 934/50; BMC 3305-14.*	60	225
412	Similar but VEPOC (M)ES, pellet in ring below horse. *ABC 1869; V. 955; BMC –.*	60	225
413	**Silver Half Unit.** Similar. *ABC 1890, 1893, 1896, 1899, 1902, 1908; V. 938/58; BMC 3316-24. (293/95)*	40	135

DVMNO TIGIR SENO

414 415

414	**Gold Stater.** DVMN(OC) across wreath. R. Horse l., TIGIR SENO. *ABC 1971; V. 972; BMC 3325-27.*	575	2000
415	**Silver Unit.** DVMNOC in two lines. R. Horse r., TIGIR SENO. *ABC 1974; V. 974; BMC 3328-29.*	150	575

VOLISIOS DVMNOCOVEROS

416

416	**Gold Stater.** VOLISIOS between three lines in wreath. R. Horse r. or l., DVMNOCOVEROS. *ABC 1980; V. 978-80; BMC 3330-3336.*	375	1250
417	**Silver Unit.** Similar. R. Horse r., DVMNOCO. *ABC 1983; V. 980; BMC 3339.*	150	575
418	**Silver Half Unit.** Similar. *ABC 1986; V. 984; BMC 3340-41.*	70	250

VOLISIOS DVMNOVELLAUNOS

419

		F	VF
		£	£
419	**Gold Stater.** VOLISIOS between three lines in wreath. R. Horse r. or l., DVMNOVELAVNOS. *ABC 1995; V .988; BMC 3342-43.*	400	1350
420	**Silver Half Unit.** As last but DVMNOVE. *ABC 1998; V. 992; BMC 3344-46.*	120	475

VOLISIOS CARTIVEL

| 420A | **Gold Stater.** VOLISIOS between three lines in wreath. R. Horse l. CARTILLAVNOS. *ABC —; VA 933; BMC —.* .... | 1250 | 4500 |
| 421 | **Silver Half Unit.** VOLISIOS between three lines in wreath. R. Horse r., CARTILEV. *ABC 1992; V. 994; BMC 3347-48.* .... | 250 | 900 |

IAT ISO E

| 422 | **Silver Unit.** IAT ISO (retrograde) on tablet, rosettes above and below. R. Horse r., E above. *ABC 1959; V. 998; BMC 3349-51.* .... | 135 | 500 |

CAT

| 422A | **Silver Unit.** Boar r., pellet ring above, CAT above. R. Horse r. *ABC 1845; V. —; BMC 3352* .... | 250 | 950 |

LAT ISON

423

| 423 | **Gold Stater.** LAT ISO(N) in two lines retrograde. R. Horse r., ISO in box above, N below. *ABC 1956; V. —; BMC —. Only recorded as an AE/AV plated core, as illustrated.* .... | *Extremely rare* |

ICENI

The Iceni, centred on Norfolk but also occupying neighbouring parts of Suffolk and Cambridgeshire, are well attested in the post conquest period as the tribe who under Boudicca revolted against Roman rule. Their earliest coins are likely to have been the British J staters, Norfolk Wolf type (no.30/31), replaced around the mid first century B.C. by the Snettisham, Freckenham and Irstead type gold staters and quarter staters. Contemporary with these are silver Boar/Horse and Face/Horse units and fractions. The introduction of legends around the beginning of the millennia led to the adoption of a new obverse design of back to back crescents. The continuation of the coinage after the Roman invasion is attested by the coins of King Prasutagus. Some of the Face/Horse units (no.434) have been attributed to Queen Boudicca but this attribution is uncertain.

EARLY UNINSCRIBED
(Mid to Late 1st Century B.C.)

424

		F £	VF £
424	**Gold Stater.** Snettisham type. Blank or with traces of pellet cross. R. Horse r., serpent like pellet in ring motif above. *ABC 1402, 1405; V .—; BMC 3353-59*	850	3000
425	Similar. Blank or with three short curved lines. R. Horse r., symbol above more degraded. *ABC 1408, 1411; V. —; BMC 3360-83*	625	2250

426   427

426	Freckenham type. Two opposed crescents with stars or pellets in field. R. Horse r., various symbols in field. *ABC 1441, 1444, 1447, 1450; V. 620; BMC 3384-89.*	475	1750
427	Similar. Blank or with traces of pellet cross. R. Horse r., wheel or arch containing pellets above. *ABC 1414, 1417, 1420; V.624; BMC 3390-95.* ...	850	3000

. 428

428	Similar. Trefoil on cross design. R. Similar. *ABC 1423, 1426, 1432, 1435; V. 626; BMC 3396-3419.*	475	1750

		F	VF
		£	£
429	**Gold Quarter Stater.** Snettisham type. Wreath cross. ℞. Horse r. *ABC 1462; V. —; BMC 3420-35*	225	750
430	Irstead type. Hatched box, wreaths at sides. ℞. Horse r. *ABC 1474, 1480; V. 628; BMC 3436-39.*	185	600
431	**Silver Unit.** Boar / Horse type. Boar r. ℞. Horse r. *ABC 1576, 1579, 1582; V. 655-59; BMC 3440-3512.*	65	200
432	Bury type. Head l. or r. ℞. Horse l. or r. *ABC 1495, 1498, 1501; V. —; BMC 3524-35*	110	400
433	Early Face / Horse type. Celticised head l. or r. ℞. Horse l. or r. *ABC 1522, 1525, 1531, 1537, 1540, 1546, 1549, 1552, 1555, 1558; BMC 3536-3555.*	135	525
434	Face / Horse Regular type. Head r. ℞. Horse r. *ABC 1564, 1567; V. 790-94; BMC 3556-3759. Attributed to Queen Boudicca by R.D. van Arsdell*	75	250
435	Early Pattern / Horse type. Cross of two opposed crescents. ℞. Horse l. or r. *ABC 1588, 1591; V. 675-79; BMC 3763-74.*	50	175
436	ECEN symbol type. Two opposed crescents. ℞. Horse r. *ABC 1678, 1681; V. 752; BMC 4297-4325*	35	130

	F £	VF £

437   **Silver Half Unit.** Boar / Horse type. Similar to 431. *ABC 1621, 1624; V. 661;*
BMC 3513-20. 60   200

438   **Silver Fractional Unit.** Early Pattern / Horse type. Similar to 435.
ABC 1612, 1693; V. 681-83; BMC 3775-89. (76/A) 60   200

INSCRIBED
(Early to Mid 1st Century A.D.)
The following types are not arranged chronologically.

CAN DVRO

439

439   **Silver Unit.** Boar. R. Horse r., CAN(S) above, DVRO below. *ABC 1630;*
V. 663; BMC 3521-23. 110   425

ANTED

440

440   **Gold Stater.** Triple crescent design. R. Horse r., ANTED monogram below.
ABC 1639; V. 705; BMC 3790. 900   3500

441

441   **Silver Unit.** Two opposed crescents. R. Horse r., ANTED. *ABC 1642, 1645;*
V. 710-11/15; BMC 3791-4025. 35   135

442   **Silver Fractional Unit.** Similar to last. *ABC 1648; V. 720; BMC 4028-31.*   50   175

ECEN

443

		F £	VF £
443	**Gold Stater.** Triple crescent design. R. Horse r., ECEN below. *ABC 1651; V. 725; BMC 4032*	1000	3750
443A	**Silver Unit.** Two opposed crescents. R, Horse r., ECEN. *ABC 1657; V. 730; BMC 4033-4215.*	45	165
443B	**Silver Half Unit.** Similar to last. *ABC 1684; V. 736; BMC 4216-17.*	40	150

EDN

| 444 | **Silver Unit.** Two opposed crescents. R, Horse r., ED, E, EI or EDN. *ABC 1672, 1675; V. 734/40; BMC 4219-81.* .... | 50 | 175 |

ECE

| 444A | **Gold Stater** Triple crescent design R. Horse r., ECE. *ABC — ; V. — ;* .. | 1250 | 4250 |

445

| 445 | **Silver Unit.** Two opposed crescents. R, Horse r., ECE. *ABC 1660, 1663, 1666, 1669; V. 761-66; BMC 4348-4538. (278-80)* .... | 40 | 150 |

SAENU

| 446 | **Silver Unit.** Two opposed crescents. R. Horse r., SAENV. *ABC 1699; V. 770; BMC 4540-57.* .... | 55 | 185 |

AESU

447

| 447 | **Silver Unit.** Two opposed crescents. R. Horse r., AESV. *ABC 1702; V. 775; BMC 4558-72.* .... | 60 | 200 |

ALE SCA

| 448 | **Silver Unit.** Boar r., ALE. R. Horse r., SCA. *ABC 1708; V. 996; BMC 4576* | 225 | 850 |

AEDIC SIA

	F £	VF £
449 **Silver Unit.** AEDIC in two lines. R. Horse r., SIA? below. *ABC 1633; V.—; BMC 4581*	450	1500

PRASUTAGUS

450

450 **Silver Unit.** Romanised head l., SUB RII PRASTO. R. Rearing horse r., ESICO FECIT. *ABC 1711; V. 780; BMC 4577-80.* 900 3500

This legend translates as "Under King Prasto, Esico made me", giving the name of both King and moneyer.

The systematic conquest of Britain by the Romans began in A.D. 43 when the Emperor Claudius (41-54), anxious to enhance his military reputation, authorised an invasion in which he personally participated, albeit in a purely symbolic role. The initial military contact between the two cultures had taken place almost a century before when Julius Caesar, during the course of his conquest of Celtic Gaul, led expeditions to the island in 55 and 54 B.C. Although no actual Roman occupation of Britain resulted from Caesar's reconnoitring campaigns, commercial intercourse was certainly accelerated, as evidenced by the 'Romanisation' of the British Celtic coinage in the final decades of its production.

The Claudian conquest, commencing in A.D. 43, brought about a complete change in the nature of the currency circulating in Britain and ushered in a period lasting more than three and a half centuries during which Roman coinage was the only official medium of exchange. Local copies of the money brought with them by the four legions of the invading army began to appear at a very early stage, the most popular type for imitation being the well-known Claudian copper as with reverse type fighting Minerva. Some of these copies are well-executed and of a style not much inferior to the prototype, suggesting that their local minting may have been officially sanctioned by the Roman government in order to make good a shortage of currency in the newly-conquered territory. Other examples are of much poorer style and execution and are frequently well below the normal weight of a Claudian as (usually between 10 and 11 grams). These copies must have been issued unofficially and provide evidence of the huge demand for this type of currency in a population which had never before experienced the benefits of having base metal coins available for small everyday transactions.

In the decades that followed, the boundaries of the Roman province of Britannia were continually pushed further north and west until, under the celebrated Flavian governor Gnaeus Julius Agricola, the Roman army even penetrated to northern Scotland (A.D. 83/4). A few years later, under Trajan, the northern frontier was established along the Tyne-Solway line, a barrier made permanent by the construction of Hadrian's Wall following the emperor's visit to the province in 122. For a brief period in the mid-2nd century the frontier was temporarily advanced to the Forth-Clyde line with the building of the Antonine Wall, though this seems to have been abandoned early in the reign of Marcus Aurelius (ca. 163) when the Hadrianic barrier was re-commissioned and became the permanent frontier. The security thus provided to the now-peaceful province in the south facilitated urban expansion and the development of commerce. The new prosperity brought a flood of Roman coinage into the island-province and it was no longer necessary for shortages to be made good by large scale local imitation.

Until the mid-3rd century the production of Roman coinage remained the prerogative of the mint in the capital, with only occasional issues from provincial centres to serve short-term local needs. But with the deepening political and economic crisis in the third quarter of the century there was a dramatic decentralisation of minting operations, with permanent establishments being set up in many important cities in the western as well as the eastern provinces. Britain, however, still remained without an official mint at this time and in the dark days of the 270s, when the separatist Gallic Empire to which Britain belonged was close to collapse, large scale production of imitative antoniniani (commonly called 'barbarous radiates') occurred in the province. The integrity and prestige of the Empire was, to some extent, restored by a rapid succession of Illyrian 'soldier emperors', until the situation was finally stabilised by Diocletian (A.D. 284-305) who established the tetrarchy system under which governmental responsibility was shared by four rulers. By the end of the 3rd century Britain had been reorganised into a civil diocese of four provinces: it had already been subdivided into Britannia Superior and Britannia Inferior almost a hundred years before, under Septimius Severus or Caracalla.

It was left to the colourful and enigmatic usurper Carausius (A.D. 287-293) to establish mints in Britain. It was, of course, vital for him to do so as his dominion was mostly confined to the island-province. Londinium (London) was his principal mint, with a secondary establishment at a place usually signing itself 'C' (probably Camulodunum, modern Colchester). After the downfall of Carausius' murderer and successor Allectus (293-296) Britain was restored to the central government, an event commemorated by the celebrated gold medallion of Constantius I showing the Caesar riding alongside the Thames approaching the gateway of the city of Londinium. At this point the mysterious 'C' mint disappears from the picture. Londinium, on the other hand, retained its status as an official mint under Diocletian's tetrarchy and its successors down to A.D. 325, when it was closed by Constantine the Great who regarded it as superfluous to his needs. In nearly four decades of existence as a Roman mint Londinium had produced a varied and extensive coinage in the names of almost all the emperors, empresses and Caesars of the period. It was destined never again to be active during Roman times, unless the extremely rare gold and silver issues of the late 4th century usurper Magnus Maximus, signed AVG, AVGOB and AVGPS, are correctly attributed to Londinium under its late Roman name of Augusta.

The termination of Roman rule in the British provinces is traditionally dated to A.D. 410 when the emperor Honorius, in response to an appeal for aid from his British subjects, told them to arrange for their own defence as best they might ('Rescript of Honorius'). In reality, the end probably came quite gradually. As the machinery of government ground to a halt and the soldiers stopped receiving their pay there would have been a steady drift of population away from the semi-ruinous cities and military installations to the countryside, where they could better provide for themselves through farming. Under these conditions the need for coinage would have been drastically reduced, as a primitive economy based on barter would largely have replaced the complex monetary economy of the late Roman period. In any case the supply of coinage from the Continent would now have dried up. The few monetary transactions which still took place were made with worn-out coins from earlier periods augmented by local imitations, production of which in Britain had resumed in the mid-4th century. Such was the pitiful end of the long tradition of Roman coinage in the remote island-province of Britannia. More than two centuries of 'Dark Ages' were to elapse before England's new rulers, the Anglo-Saxons, commenced the issue of gold thrymsas, the designs of many of which were based on late Roman types.

As Rome's Imperial coinage provided the currency needs of this country over a period of almost four centuries no representative collection of British coins is complete without some examples of these important issues. The following listing is divided into four categories: 1. Regular Roman issues, all of which would have been legal tender in Britain after A.D. 43; 2. Issues with types referring specifically to the province of Britannia, usually in commemoration of military campaigns in the north; 3. Official Roman coinage struck in Britain; 4. Imitations of Roman coins produced in Britain, all but possibly some of the earliest being of unofficial origin. The reference 'R.R.C.' is to the listing of the type in Michael Crawford's *Roman Republican Coinage* (Cambridge, 1974); and 'R.I.C.' to *Roman Imperial Coinage* (Spink, London, 1923-2019, in ten volumes).

For more detailed collectors' information on Roman coinage, including a more comprehensive listing of types, the reader is referred to *Roman Coins and their Values Volumes I to V* by David R. Sear. A complete catalogue of silver issues may be found in the 5 volumes of *Roman Silver Coins* (H.A. Seaby and C.E. King) which provides a quick and convenient reference and is especially aimed at the collector. Gilbert Askew's *The Coinage of Roman Britain* (2nd edition) concentrates on those issues which are particularly associated with the Roman province of Britannia, but does not provide valuations. Other works on this subject include R. Reece's *Coinage in Roman Britain* and *The Coinage of Roman Britain*, and also David R. Sear's *The History and Coinage of the Roman Imperators, 49−27 BC* which is devoted to the vital two decades of transition from Republic to Empire. Some of these titles are now out of print, but many can be bought via Spink Books, www.spinkbooks.com, or by emailing books@spink.com.

The standard works on the coinages of the Roman Republic and the Roman Empire have already been mentioned *(Roman Republican Coinage and Roman Imperial Coinage)*. These monumental publications are essential to the advanced collector and student and their importance cannot be overstated. The British Museum Catalogues are also vital. They contain superb interpretive material in their introductions and are very fully illustrated. A similar work is Anne S. Robertson's *Roman Imperial Coins in the Hunter Coin Cabinet*, in 5 volumes (volume 4 is especially important for the later 3rd century coinage). For more general reading we may recommend J.P.C. Kent and M. & A. Hirmer's *Roman Coins*, undoubtedly the most lavishly illustrated book on the subject; C.H.V. Sutherland's *Roman Coins;* and R.A.G. Carson's *Coins of the Roman Empire*. Finally, for a most useful single-volume work on interpretation and background information, we would suggest *A Dictionary of Ancient Roman Coins* by John Melville Jones.

1. REGULAR ROMAN ISSUES

A token selection of the types of Roman coins which might be found on Romano-British archaeological sites. Many of the rarer emperors and empresses have been omitted and the types listed often represent only one of hundreds of variant forms which might be encountered.

		F £	VF £
451	**THE REPUBLIC: P. Aelius Paetus** (moneyer), 138 B.C. Æ *denarius.* Helmeted hd. of Roma r. Rev. The Dioscuri galloping r. R.R.C. 233/1 ...	50	140

Although dating from long before the Roman conquest many Republican coins circulated well into the Imperial period and found their way to Britain where they are often represented in early hoards.

| 452 | **L. Thorius Balbus** (moneyer), 105 B.C. Æ denarius. Hd. of Juno Sospita r., clad in goat's skin. Rev. Bull charging r. *R.R.C. 316/1.* .... | 55 | 150 |
| 453 | **Q. Antonius Balbus** (moneyer), 83-82 B.C. Æ *denarius.* Laur. hd. of Jupiter r. Rev. Victory in quadriga r. *R.R.C. 364/1.* .... | 55 | 150 |

454   455B

454	**C. Calpurnius Piso** (moneyer), 67 B.C. Æ *denarius.* Laur. hd. of Apollo r. Rev. Horseman galloping r., holding palm-branch. *R.R.C. 408/1a.*	55	150
455	**Mn. Acilius Glabrio** (moneyer), 49 B.C. Æ *denarius.* Laur. hd. of Salus r. Rev. Valetudo stg. l., holding snake and resting on column. *R.R.C. 442/1.*	50	140
455A	**Pompey the Great** (imperator) 49-48 BC. Æ *denarius.* Diademed head of Numa r. Rev. MAGN PRO COS. Prow of galley r. *R.R.C. 446/1.*	260	650
455B	**Scipio** (imperator) 47-46 BC, Æ *denarius.* Laureate head of Jupiter r. Rev. SCIPIO IMP. Elephant r. *R.R.C. 459/1.*	150	375
455C	**Pompey Junior** (imperator) 46-45 BC. Æ *denarius.* Helmeted head of Roma r. Rev. CN MAGNVS IMP. Hispania stg r presenting palm branch to Pompeian soldier. *RRC 469/1a.*	200	400
455D	**Sextus Pompey** (imperator) 45-36 B.C. Æ *denarius.* Bare head of Pompey. Rev. Neptune stg l between brothers Anapias and Amphinomus. *R.R.C. 511/3a.*	400	1050
455E	**Julius Caesar** (dictator), visited Britain 55 and 54 B.C., died 44 B.C. Ν *aureus.* Veiled head of Vesta r. Rev. A. HIRTIVS PR. Jug between lituus and axe. *R.R.C. 466/1.*	1800	4200

456   456B

456	Æ *denarius.* CAESAR. Elephant r. Rev. Priestly emblems. *R.R.C. 443/1.*	275	700
456A	— Wreathed hd. of Caesar r. Rev. P. SEPVLLIVS MACER. Venus stg. l., holding Victory and sceptre. *R.R.C. 480/9.*	800	2200
456B	Head of Venus. Rev CAESAR. Aeneas l bearing his father Anchises on shoulder. *R.R.C. 458/1.*	200	460

456F

		F	VF
		£	£
456C	Head of Venus r. Rev. CAESAR. Trophy of Gallic arms between seated captives. *R.R.C. 468/1*	220	500
456D	**Brutus** (imperator) 42 BC. Æ *denarius*. Head of Apollo r. Rev. BRVTVS IMP. Trophy. *R.R.C. 506/2.*	300	700
456E	**Cassius** (imperator) 42 BC. Æ *denarius*. Head of Libertas. Rev. LENTVLVS SPINT. Jug and lituus. *R.R.C. 500/3*	210	500
456F	**Ahenobarbus** (imperator) 41-40 BC. Æ *denarius*. Bare head r. Rev. CN DOMITIVS IMP. Prow of galley r, surmounted by trophy. *R.R.C. 519/2*.	400	1000
457	**Mark Antony** (triumvir), died 30 B.C. Æ *denarius*. Galley r. Rev. LEG. II. Legionary eagle between two standards. *R.R.C. 544/14.*	175	420
457A	Head of Antony r. Rev. CAESAR DIC. Head of Caesar r. *R.R.C. 488/2.*	400	1020
457B	Bare head of Antony. Rev. CAESAR IMP PONT III VIR RPC. Bare head of Octavian. *R.R.C. 517/2*	300	725
457C	**Cleopatra VII** 34 BC Æ *denarius*. Bust of Cleopatra r. Rev. ANTONI ARMENIA DEVICTA. Head of Antony r. *R.R.C. 543/1.*	3200	7500

458 459

458	**Octavian** (triumvir), named Augustus 27 B.C. Æ *denarius*. Bare hd. of Octavian r. Rev. IMP. CAESAR. Trophy set on prow. *R.I.C. 265a*	220	525
458A	**THE EMPIRE: Augustus,** 27 B.C.-A.D. 14. *N aureus*. Rev. IMP XII ACT. Apollo stg r, holding lyre. *R.I.C. 192a*.	2400	5750
459	Æ *denarius*. Rev. C. L. CAESARES AVGVSTI F COS DESIG PRINC IVVENT. The emperor's grandsons, Gaius and Lucius, stg. facing, with spears and shields. *R.I.C. 207*	175	420
	Almost all the coins in the Roman Imperial series have a head or bust of the emperor, empress or prince as their obverse type. Therefore, in most instances only the reverses will be described in the following listings.		
459A	— Rev IMP X. Bull butting r. *R.I.C. 167a.*	200	500
460	Æ *as*. ROM. ET AVG. The altar of Lugdunum. *R.I.C. 230.*	90	240
460A	Æ *quadrans*. Obv. Anvil. Rev. Moneyers' inscription around large S. C. *R.I.C. 443*	35	90
461	**Augustus and Agrippa,** general and designated heir of Augustus, died 12 B.C. Æ *dupondius*. Obv. Their hds. back to back. Rev. COL. NEM. Crocodile r., chained to palm-branch. *R.I.C. 159.*	140	325
	See also no. 468.		
461A	**Gaius Caesar**, 17 BC, grandson of Augustus. Æ *denarius*. Rev. AVGVST. Candelabrum within floral wreath. *R.I.C. 539*	460	1300

464

		F	VF
		£	£
462	**Divus Augustus,** deified A.D. 14. Æ as. PROVIDENT S. C. Large altar. *R.I.C. 81*............................	90	240
463	**Tiberius,** A.D. 14-37. *N aureus.* PONTIF MAXIM. Livia (?) seated r., holding sceptre and branch. *R.I.C. 29*........................	1600	3750
464	*R denarius.* Similar. *R.I.C. 30.*	190	480
	This type is commonly referred to as the 'Tribute Penny' of the Bible (Matthew 22, 17-21).		
464A	Æ *sestertius.* Tiberius seated l. Rev Inscription around large S. C. *R.I.C. 48.*	330	950
464B	Æ *as.* Inscription around large S. C. *R.I.C. 44*........................	85	230
465	**Livia,** wife of Augustus, mother of Tiberius. Æ *dupondius.* Obv. Veiled bust of Livia as Pietas r. Rev. Inscription of Drusus Caesar around large S. C. *R.I.C. 43.*	190	490
466	**Drusus,** son of Tiberius. Æ *as.* Inscription around large S. C. *R.I.C. 45.*	90	240
466A	**Caligula,** A.D. 37-41. *N aureus.* Rev. SPQR/PP/OBCS in three lines within oak wreath. R.I.C. 27....................	4500	11000
466B	*R denarius,* SPQR/PP/OBCS in three lines within oak wreath, *R.I.C. 28.*	840	2500
466C	Æ *sestertius.* Rev. ADLOCVT COH. Caligula stg l on platform, haranguing soldiers. *R.I.C. 40.*	480	1600

467

467	Æ *as.* VESTA S. C. Vesta seated l. *R.I.C. 38*...........................	120	400

468

468	**Agrippa,** grandfather of Caligula, died 12 B.C. Æ *as.* S. C. Neptune stg. l., holding dolphin and trident. *R.I.C. 58.*	100	280
	See also no. 461 and under Category 4.		

	F	VF
	£	£

469 **Germanicus,** father of Caligula, brother of Claudius, died A.D. 19. Æ *as*.
Inscription of Caligula around large S. C. *R.I.C. 35*. 95 250

470 **Agrippina Senior,** mother of Caligula, died A.D. 33. Æ *sestertius*. S.P.Q.R.
MEMORIAE AGRIPPINAE. Carpentum drawn l. by two mules. *R.I.C. 55*. 575 2000

470A **Claudius,** A.D. 41-54, initiated the conquest of Britain by his invasion in
A.D. 43. *N aureus* Rev. EX SC/OBCIVES/SERVATOS in three lines within
oak wreath. *R.I.C. 15*. 2400 6000

470B *R denarius*. PACI AVGVSTAE, winged Nemesis advancing r, snake at feet.
R.I.C. 52. .... 550 1600

470C Æ *sestertius*. Rev. SPES AVGVSTA SC. Spes walking l, holding flower.
R.I.C. 115. (see also no 744) 300 850

471   474

471 Æ *as*. LIBERTAS AVGVSTA S. C. Libertas stg. r., holding pileus.
R.I.C. 113. .... 85 240

471A Æ *quadrans*. Obv. Hand holding scales. Rev. Inscription around large
S. C. *R.I.C. 85*. 35 80
See also under Categories 2 and 4.

472 **Nero Claudius Drusus,** father of Claudius, died 9 B.C. Æ *sestertius*.
TI. CLAVDIVS CAESAR AVG. P. M. TR .P. IMP. P. P. S. C. Claudius seated
l. on curule chair amidst arms. *R.I.C. 109*. 340 1250
See also under Category 4.

473 **Antonia,** mother of Claudius, died A.D. 37. Æ *dupondius*. TI. CLAVDIVS
CAESAR AVG P.M. TR. P. IMP. S. C. Claudius stg. l., holding simpulum.
R.I.C. 92 .... 150 425
See also under Category 4.

474 **Nero,** 54-68, emperor at the time of Queen Boudicca's rebellion in Britain.
N aureus. SALVS. Salus seated l. *R.I.C. 66*. 1500 3800

475 *R denarius*. IVPPITER CVSTOS. Jupiter seated l. *R.I.C. 53*. 180 520

476 Æ *sestertius*. ROMA S. C. Roma seated l., holding Victory and parazonium.
R.I.C. 274 .... 360 1400

476A Æ *as*. S. C. Victory hovering l., holding shield inscribed S. P. Q. R. *R.I.C. 312*. 100 290

476B **Civil Wars** (Gaul). *R denarius*. Clasped hands. Rev. FIDES PRAETOR
IANORUM. Clasped r hands. R.I.C. 121. .... 350 975

476C **Galba,** 68-69. *N aureus*. Rev. SPQR/OB CS in two lines within oak
wreath. *R.I.C. 164* 3200 7800

477 *R denarius*. S.P.Q.R. / OB / C.S. within oak-wreath. *R.I.C. 167*. 230 640

477A **Otho,** 69. *N aureus*. Rev. SECVRITAS PR. Securitas stg l, holding wreath
and sceptre. *R.I.C. 7*. 4900 13000

478 *R denarius*. SECVRITAS P. R. Securitas stg. l. *R.I.C. 10* 425 1200

478A **Vitellius,** 69. *N aureus*. Rev. CONCORDIA PR. Concordia seated l, holding
patera and cornucopiae. *R.I.C. 72* 3400 8500

		F	VF
		£	£
479	Æ denarius. CONCORDIA P. R. Concordia seated l. *R.I.C. 90*...............	230	575
480	**Vespasian,** 69-79, commanded Legio II in the Claudian invasion of Britain (43) and appointed Agricola to governorship of the province in 77/8. Æ *aureus.* ANNONA AVG. Annona seated l. *R.I.C. 131a.*	1300	3400

481

		F	VF
481	Æ *denarius.* VICTORIA AVGVSTI. Victory advancing r., crowning standard. *R.I.C. 52.*...	65	150
481A	Æ *sestertius.* Rev. JVDAEA CAPTA SC. Palm tree with standing Jewish captive r and female captive seated r. *R.I.C. 424*....................................	600	1750
481B	Æ *dupondius.* FELICITAS PVBLICA S. C. Felicitas stg. l. *R.I.C. 554*...	65	200
481C	**Titus,** 79-81 (Caesar 69-79). Æ *aureus.* Rev. TRP VIIII IMP XIIII COS VII PP. Venus stg r resting on column. *R.I.C. 9.*	1850	4500
482	Æ *denarius.* TR. P. IX. IMP. XV. COS. VIII. P. P. Thunderbolt on throne. *R.I.C. 23a*...	120	340
482A	**Julia Titi,** daughter of Titus and mistress of Domitian. Æ *denarius.* Rev. VENVS AVGVST. Venus stg r resting on column. *R.I.C. 56*...................	380	1050
482B	**Domitian,** 81-96 (Caesar 69-81), recalled Agricola in 83/4 and abandoned the conquest of northern Scotland (ca. 87). Æ *aureus.* Rev. GERMANICVS COS XV. Minerva stg l holding spear. *R.I.C. 163*...	1700	4000

483   485

		F	VF
483	Æ *denarius.* IMP. XIX. COS. XIIII. CENS. P. P. P. Minerva stg. l., resting on spear. *R.I.C. 140*...	· 70	200
483A	Æ *sestertius.* Rev. IOVI VICTORI SC. Jupiter seated l, holding Victory and sceptre. *R.I.C. 358*...	200	525
484	Æ *dupondius.* VIRTVTI AVGVSTI S. C. Virtus stg. r. *R.I.C. 393*...........	60	175
484A	Æ *as.* MONETA AVGVSTI S. C. Moneta stg. l. *R.I.C. 354b.*	60	175
484B	**Domitia,** wife of Domitian. Æ *denarius.* Rev CONCORDIA AVGVST. Peacock stg r. *R.I.C. 212*..	625	1750
484C	**Nerva,** 96-98. Æ *aureus.* Rev. CONCORDIA EXERCITVVM. Clasped r hands. *R.I.C. 14*..	2700	6000
485	Æ denarius. AEQVITAS AVGVST. Aequitas stg. l. *R.I.C. 13*.................	110	300
485A	Æ *as.* LIBERTAS PVBLICA S. C. Libertas stg. l. *R.I.C. 86*....................	90	275
486	**Trajan,** 98-117, established the northern frontier in Britain along the Tyne-Solway line (ca. 100). Æ *aureus.* P. M. TR. P. COS. VI. P. P. S. P. Q. R. Genius stg. l., holding patera and corn-ears. *R.I.C. 347.*...........................	1650	3900

487   489

		F	VF
		£	£

487   Æ *denarius*. COS. V. P. P. S. P. Q. R. OPTIMO PRINC. Military trophy.
       R.I.C. 147. 60   150

488   Æ *sestertius*. S. P. Q. R. OPTIMO PRINCIPI S. C. Spes walking l.,
       holding flower. *R.I.C. 519.* 110   450

488A Æ *dupondius*. SENATVS POPVLVSQVE ROMANVS S. C. Emperor
       advancing between two trophies. *R.I.C. 676.* 75   180

489   **Hadrian,** 117-138, visited Britain in 122 and initiated the construction of
       a fortified frontier line (Hadrian's Wall). Æ *aureus*. HISPANIA. Hispania
       reclining l. *R.I.C. 305* 1750   4300

490   Æ *denarius*. P. M. TR. P. COS. III. Roma stg. l., holding Victory and spear.
       R.I.C. 76. 70   200

491   Æ *sestertius*. COS. III. S. C. Neptune stg. r., holding dolphin and trident,
       foot on prow. *R.I.C. 632.* 130   475

491A Æ *as*. FELICITATI AVG COS. III. P. P. S. C. Galley travelling l. over waves.
       R.I.C. 719. 75   200
       See also under Category 2.

492   **Sabina,** wife of Hadrian. Æ *denarius*. IVNONI REGINAE. Juno stg. l.
       R.I.C. 395a. 85   220

493   **Aelius Caesar,** heir of Hadrian, 136-138. Æ *denarius*. CONCORD. TR.
       POT. COS. II. Concordia seated l. *R.I.C. 436.* 150   375

493A Æ *as*. TR. POT. COS. II. S. C. Spes walking l., holding flower. *R.I.C. 1067.*   95   250

494   **Antoninus Pius,** 138-161, ordered the expansion of the Roman province to
       include southern Scotland and constructed the Antonine Wall on the Forth-Clyde
       line (beginning ca. 143). An uprising in northern Britain in the 150s resulting in a
       permanent withdrawal to the Hadrianic frontier early in the next reign.
       Æ *aureus*. COS. IIII. Togate emperor stg. l., holding globe. *R.I.C. 233b.*   1500   3750

495   Æ *denarius*. PIETATI AVG. COS. IIII. Pietas stg. l. between two children,
       holding two more in her arms. *R.I.C. 313c* 50   120

496

496   Æ *sestertius*. SALVS AVG. S. C. Salus stg. l. at altar, feeding snake.
       R.I.C. 635 100   375

496A Æ *dupondius*. TR. POT. XX. COS. IIII. S. C. Providentia stg. l., pointing
       at globe at her feet and holding sceptre. *R.I.C. 2025* 55   130
       See also under Categories 2 and 3.

		F £	VF £
497	**Antoninus Pius and Marcus Aurelius Caesar**. *R denarius*. Obv. Laur. hd. of Antoninus Pius r. Rev. AVRELIVS CAESAR AVG PII F. COS. Bare hd. of young Marcus Aurelius r. *R.I.C. 417a*.	150	360

498

501

		F £	VF £
498	**Divus Antoninus Pius,** deified 161. *R denarius*. CONSECRATIO. Four-storeyed crematorium of Antoninus Pius. *R.I.C. 436*.	55	130
499	**Diva Faustina Senior,** wife of Antoninus Pius, deified 141. *R denarius*. AETERNITAS. Aeternitas stg. l., holding globe and billowing veil. *R.I.C. 351*.	50	120
499A	Æ *sestertius*. AVGVSTA S. C. Ceres stg. l., holding two torches. *R.I.C. 1120*.	80	230
500	**Marcus Aurelius,** 161-180 (Caesar 139-161), re-established Hadrian's Wall as the permanent northern frontier of the province, ca. 163. *N aureus*. PROV. DEOR. TR. P. XV. COS. III. Providentia stg. l., holding globe and cornucopiae. *R.I.C. 19*.	1700	4000
501	*R denarius*. PIETAS AVG. Priestly emblems. *R.I.C. 424a*.	60	150
501A	— SALVTI AVG. COS. III. Salus stg. l. at altar, feeding snake. *R.I.C. 222*.	60	150
502	Æ *sestertius*. CONCORD. AVGVSTOR. TR. P. XVI. COS. III. S. C. Marcus Aurelius and Lucius Verus stg. face to face, clasping hands. *R.I.C. 826*.	120	475
502A	Æ *as*. HONOS TR. POT. II. COS. II. S. C. Honos stg. r. *R.I.C. 1271a*.	55	170
503	**Divus Marcus Aurelius,** deified 180. *R denarius*. CONSECRATIO. Eagle stg. r. on altar. *R.I.C. 272*.	55	140

504

506A

		F £	VF £
504	**Faustina Junior,** daughter of Antoninus Pius, wife of Marcus Aurelius. *R denarius*. FECVNDITAS. Fecunditas stg. r., holding sceptre and child. *R.I.C. 677*.	50	120
504A	Æ *sestertius*. HILARITAS S. C. Hilaritas stg. l. *R.I.C. 1642*.	80	270
505	**Diva Faustina Junior,** deified 175. Æ *as*. S. C. Crescent and seven stars. *R.I.C. 1714*.	55	170
506	**Lucius Verus,** 161-169. *R denarius*. PAX TR. P. VI. IMP. IIII. COS. II. Pax stg. l. *R.I.C. 561*.	80	230
506A	Æ *dupondius*. TR. P. IIII. IMP. II. COS. II. S. C. Mars stg. r., resting on spear and shield. *R.I.C. 1387*.	70	220
507	**Lucilla,** daughter of Marcus Aurelius, wife of Lucius Verus. *R denarius*. IVNONI LVCINAE. Juno stg. l., holding child in swaddling clothes. *R.I.C. 771*.	60	150
507A	Æ *sestertius*. PIETAS S. C. Pietas stg. l., altar at feet. *R.I.C. 1756*.	90	320

	F	VF
	£	£

508 **Commodus,** 177-192 (Caesar 175-177), major warfare on the British
frontier early in the reign; situation restored by Ulpius Marcellus in 184/5,
followed by unrest in the British legions. Æ *denarius.* LIB. AVG. IIII. TR.
P. VI. IMP. IIII. COS. III. P. P. Liberalitas stg. l. *R.I.C. 22*....................... 65 160

509   511

509 Æ *sestertius.* IOVI VICTORI IMP. III. COS. II. P. P. S. C. Jupiter seated l.
R.I.C. 1612.... 100 400
509A Æ *as.* ANN. AVG. TR. P. VII. IMP. IIII. COS. III. P. P. S. C. Annona stg. l.,
modius at feet. *R.I.C. 339 (See also under Category 2.)*......................... 50 130
510 **Crispina,** wife of Commodus. Æ *denarius.* CONCORDIA. Clasped hands.
R.I.C. 279.... 65 160
511 **Pertinax,** January-March 193, formerly governor of Britain, ca. 185-7. Æ
denarius. PROVID. DEOR. COS. II. Providentia stg l., reaching up to star.
R.I.C. 11a.... 400 1050

512   513   514A

512 **Didius Julianus,** March-June 193. Æ *denarius.* CONCORD MILIT.
Concordia Militum stg. l., holding standards. *R.I.C. 1.*............................. 760 1800
513 **Clodius Albinus,** 195-197 (Caesar 193-195), governor of Britain (from
191/2) at the time of his imperial proclamation by his troops. Æ *denarius.*
MINER. PACIF. COS. II. Minerva stg. l. *R.I.C. 7.*.................................. 110 275
513A — FIDES LEGION. COS. II. Clasped hands holding legionary eagle. *R.I.C. 20b.* 130 300
514 **Septimius Severus,** 193-211, restored the frontier forts in northern Britain
following the downfall of Clodius Albinus; later repaired Hadrian's Wall, and
spent the years 208-11 in Britain campaigning in Scotland; divided Britannia into
two provinces, Superior and Inferior; died at York, February 211. Æ *denarius.*
VIRT AVGG. Roma stg. l., holding Victory, spear and shield. *R.I.C. 171a.* 35 80
514A — P.M. TR. P. XVIII. COS. III. P. P. Jupiter stg. l. between two children.
R.I.C. 240 (See also under Category 2.) 35 80
515 **Julia Domna,** wife of Septimius Severus, mother of Caracalla and Geta,
accompanied her husband and sons on the British expedition, 208-211, and
probably resided in London during the northern campaigns. Æ *denarius.*
VENERI VICTR. Venus stg. r., resting on column. *R.I.C. 536.*............... 35 75
515A — VESTA. Vesta stg. l., holding palladium and sceptre. *R.I.C. 390.*........ 35 75

516   519

		F	VF
		£	£

516 **Caracalla,** 198-217 (Caesar 196-198), accompanied his father and brother
on the British expedition, 208-211, and led the final campaign in Scotland
in 210 during Severus' illness; made frontier dispositions before returning
to Rome and finalized his father's arrangements for the division of Britain
into two provinces. Æ *antoninianus (double denarius,* introduced in 215).
VENVS VICTRIX. Venus stg. l., holding Victory and resting on shield.
R.I.C. 311c. 85 220

517 Æ *denarius.* PART. MAX. PONT. TR. P. IIII. Trophy with two captives at
base. *R.I.C. 54b.*.. 40 90

517A — P. M. TR. P. XV. COS. III. P. P. Hercules stg. l., holding olive-branch
and club. *R.I.C. 192.* 40 90
See also under Category 2.

518 **Plautilla,** wife of Caracalla. Æ *denarius.* PROPAGO IMPERI. Caracalla
and Plautilla clasping hands. *R.I.C. 362.* 50 120

519 **Geta,** 209-212 (Caesar 198-209), accompanied his father and brother on
the British expedition, 208-211, and took charge of the civil administration
in London during the northern campaigns. Æ *denarius.* PRINC. IVVENTVTIS.
Prince stg. l. beside trophy, holding branch and spear. *R.I.C. 18.* 55 130

519A — FORT RED TR. P. III. COS. II. Fortuna seated l. *R.I.C. 75.* 50 120
See also under Category 2.

520 **Macrinus,** 217-218. Æ *denarius.* PROVIDENTIA DEORVM. Providentia
stg. l., globe at feet. *R.I.C. 80.* 75 190

521 **Diadumenian,** 218 (Caesar 217-218). Æ *denarius.* PRINC. IVVENTVTIS.
Prince stg. l., two standards behind. *R.I.C. 109.*...................... 170 420

522

522 **Elagabalus,** 218-222. Æ *antoninianus.* MARS VICTOR. Mars advancing r.
R.I.C. 122.... 85 220

522A Æ *denarius.* P. M. TR. P. III. COS. III. P. P. Jupiter seated l., eagle at feet
R.I.C. 27.... 45 100

523 **Julia Paula,** first wife of Elagabalus. Æ *denarius.* CONCORDIA.
Concordia seated l. *R.I.C. 211.* 70 160

524 **Aquilia Severa,** second wife of Elagabalus. Æ *denarius.* CONCORDIA.
Concordia stg. l., altar at feet. *R.I.C. 226.* 80 200

525 **Julia Soaemias,** mother of Elagabalus. Æ *denarius.* VENVS CAELESTIS.
Venus seated l., child at feet. *R.I.C. 243.* 55 120

	F £	VF £
526 **Julia Maesa,** grandmother of Elagabalus and Severus Alexander. Æ *denarius*. SAECVLI FELICITAS. Felicitas stg. l., altar at feet. *R.I.C. 271.*	45	110
527 **Severus Alexander,** 222-235 (Caesar 221-222). Æ *denarius*. PAX AETERNA AVG. Pax stg. l. *R.I.C. 165.*	45	95
527A — P. M. TR. P. XIII. COS. III. P. P. Sol advancing l., holding whip. *R.I.C. 123.*	45	95

528

528 Æ *sestertius*. MARS VLTOR S. C. Mars advancing r., with spear and shield. *R.I.C. 635.*	60	170
529 **Orbiana,** wife of Severus Alexander. Æ *denarius*. CONCORDIA AVGG. Concordia seated l. *R.I.C. 319.*	120	280

530 531A

530 **Julia Mamaea,** mother of Severus Alexander. Æ *denarius*. VESTA. Vesta stg. l. *R.I.C. 362.*	40	85
530A Æ *sestertius*. FELICITAS PVBLICA S. C. Felicitas stg. facing, hd. l., resting on column. *R.I.C. 676.*	55	140
531 **Maximinus I,** 235-238. Æ *denarius*. PAX AVGVSTI. Pax stg. l. *R.I.C. 12.*	45	100
531A Æ *sestertius*. SALVS AVGVSTI S. C. Salus seated l., feeding snake arising from altar. *R.I.C. 85.*	60	170
532 **Maximus Caesar,** son of Maximinus I. Æ *denarius*. PRINC IVVENTVTIS. Prince stg. l., two standards behind. *R.I.C. 3.*	85	240
533 **Gordian I Africanus,** March-April 238, governor of Britannia Inferior late in the reign of Caracalla. Æ *denarius*. P. M. TR. P. COS. P. P. Togate emperor stg. l. *R.I.C. 1.*	600	1550
534 **Gordian II Africanus,** March-April 238. Æ *denarius*. VIRTVS AVGG. Virtus stg. l., with shield and spear. *R.I.C. 3.*	600	1550
535 **Balbinus,** April-July 238. Æ *antoninianus*. FIDES MVTVA AVGG. Clasped hands. *R.I.C. 11.*	140	325
535A Æ *denarius*. PROVIDENTIA DEORVM. Providentia stg. l., globe at feet. *R.I.C. 7.*	120	290
536 **Pupienus,** April-July 238. Æ *antoninianus*. AMOR MVTVVS AVGG. Clasped hands. *R.I.C. 9a.*	140	325
536A Æ *denarius*. PAX PVBLICA. Pax seated l. *R.I.C. 4.*	110	270

537   539

		F	VF
		£	£
537	**Gordian III,** 238-244 (Caesar 238). Æ *antoninianus*. LAETITIA AVG. N. Laetitia stg. l. *R.I.C. 86*.	25	50
538	Æ *denarius*. DIANA LVCIFERA. Diana stg. r., holding torch. *R.I.C. 127*.	25	50
538A	Æ *sestertius*. AETERNITATI AVG. S.C. Sol stg. l., holding globe. *R.I.C. 297a*.	50	120
539	**Philip I,** 244-249. Æ *antoninianus*. ROMAE AETERNAE. Roma seated l. *R.I.C. 65*.	30	60
539A	Æ *sestertius*. SECVRIT. ORBIS S. C. Securitas seated l. *R.I.C. 190*.	55	140
540	**Otacilia Severa,** wife of Philip I. Æ *antoninianus*. PIETAS AVGVSTAE. Pietas stg. l. *R.I.C. 125c*.	35	70
540A	Æ *sestertius*. CONCORDIA AVGG. S. C. Concordia seated l. *R.I.C. 203a*.	55	140
541	**Philip II,** 247-249 (Caesar 244-247). Æ *antoninianus*. PRINCIPI IVVENT. Prince stg. l., holding globe and spear. *R.I.C. 218d*.	35	80
541A	Æ *sestertius*. PAX AETERNA S. C. Pax stg. l. *R.I.C. 268c*.	55	140

542   543

		F	VF
542	**Trajan Decius,** 249-251. Æ *antoninianus*. DACIA. Dacia stg. l., holding staff with ass's hd. *R.I.C. 12b*.	35	85
542A	Æ *sestertius*. PANNONIAE S. C. The two Pannoniae stg., each holding standard. *R.I.C. 124a*.	65	170
543	**Herennia Etruscilla,** wife of Trajan Decius. Æ *antoninianus*. PVDICITIA AVG. Pudicitia stg. l. *R.I.C. 58b*.	40	85
544	**Herennius Etruscus,** 251 (Caesar 250-251). Æ *antoninianus*. PIETAS AVGG. Mercury stg. l., holding purse and caduceus. *R.I.C. 142b*.	45	110
545	**Hostilian,** 251 (Caesar 251). Æ *antoninianus*. PRINCIPI IVVENTVTIS. Apollo seated l., holding branch. *R.I.C. 180*.	65	160
546	**Trebonianus Gallus,** 251-253. Æ *antoninianus*. FELICITAS PVBLICA. Felicitas stg. l., resting on column. *R.I.C. 34A*.	35	75
546A	Æ *sestertius*. SALVS AVGG S. C. Salus stg. r., feeding snake held in her arms. *R.I.C. 121a*.	70	180
547	**Volusian,** 251-253 (Caesar 251). Æ *antoninianus*. VIRTVS AVGG. Virtus stg. l. *R.I.C. 186*.	35	80
548	**Aemilian,** 253. Æ *antoninianus*. PACI AVG. Pax stg. l., resting on column. *R.I.C. 8*.	120	280
549	**Valerian,** 253-260. Billon antoninianus. FIDES MILITVM. Fides stg. r., holding two standards. *R.I.C. 241*.	35	75

		F £	*VF* £

550 **Diva Mariniana,** wife of Valerian, deified 253. Billon *antoninianus*.
CONSECRATIO. Empress seated on peacock flying r. *R.I.C. 6*. 77 190

551 **Gallienus,** 253-268, during whose reign Rome temporarily lost control
over Britain when Postumus rebelled and established the independent
Gallic Empire in 260. Billon *antoninianus*. VIRT GALLIENI AVG.
Emperor advancing r., captive at feet. *R.I.C. 54*. 15 35

552

552 — DIANAE CONS. AVG. Doe l. *R.I.C. 176*. 15 35
552A — SOLI INVICTO. Sol stg. l., holding globe. *R.I.C. 658*. 15 30
553 **Salonina,** wife of Gallienus. Billon *antoninianus*. VENVS FELIX. Venus
seated l., child at feet. *R.I.C. 7*. 15 35
553A — IVNONI CONS. AVG. Doe l. *R.I.C. 16*. 15 35
554 **Valerian Junior,** son of Gallienus, Caesar 256-258. Billon *antoninianus*.
IOVI CRESCENTI. Infant Jupiter seated on goat r. *R.I.C. 13*. 35 75
555 **Divus Valerian Junior,** deified 258. Billon *antoninianus*. CONSECRATIO.
Large altar. *R.I.C. 24*. 35 75
556 **Saloninus,** 260 (Caesar 258-260). Billon *antoninianus*. PIETAS AVG.
Priestly emblems. *R.I.C. 9*. 35 75
557 **Macrianus,** usurper in the East, 260-261. Billon *antoninianus*. SOL.
INVICTO. Sol stg. l., holding globe. *R.I.C. 12*. 70 160
558 **Quietus,** usurper in the East, 260-261. Billon *antoninianus*.
INDVLGENTIAE AVG. Indulgentia seated l. *R.I.C. 5*. 70 160

559

559 **Postumus,** usurper in the West, 260-268, founder of the 'Gallic Empire'
which temporarily detached Britain from the rule of the central government,
a state of affairs which continued until Aurelian's defeat of Tetricus in
273. Billon *antoninianus*. HERC. DEVSONIENSI. Hercules stg. r. *R.I.C. 64*. 20 45
560 — MONETA AVG. Moneta stg. l. *R.I.C. 75*. 15 40
560A Æ *sestertius*. FIDES MILITVM. Fides stg. l., holding two standards.
R.I.C. 128. .... 85 240
561 **Laelianus,** usurper in the West, 268. Billon *antoninianus*. VICTORIA AVG.
Victory advancing r. *R.I.C. 9*. 360 875
562 **Marius,** usurper in the West, 268. Billon *antoninianus*. CONCORDIA
MILITVM. Clasped hands. *R.I.C. 7*. 110 275

	F	VF
	£	£

563   **Victorinus**, usurper in the West, 268-270. Billon *antoninianus*. INVICTVS.
Sol advancing l. *R.I.C. 114.*   15   30

564   **Tetricus**, usurper in the West, 270-273, defeated by Aurelian, thus ending
the 'Gallic Empire' and the isolation of Britain from the authority of Rome.
Billon *antoninianus*. LAETITIA AVGG. Laetitia stg. l. *R.I.C. 87.*   15   30
See also under Category 4.

565   **Tetricus Junior,** son of Tetricus, Caesar 270-273. Billon *antoninianus*.
SPES PVBLICA. Spes walking l., holding flower *R.I.C. 272.*   15   30
See also under Category 4.

566   **Claudius II Gothicus,** 268-270. Billon *antoninianus*. IOVI STATORI.
Jupiter stg. r. *R.I.C. 52.*   15   30

567   **Divus Claudius II,** deified 270. Billon *antoninianus*. CONSECRATIO.
Large altar. *R.I.C. 261*   15   30
See also under Category 4.

568   **Quintillus,** 270. Billon *antoninianus*. DIANA LVCIF. Diana stg. r.,
holding torch. *R.I.C. 49.*   35   100

569   **Aurelian,** 270-275, restored Britain to the rule of the central government
through his defeat of Tetricus in 273; possibly began construction of the
chain of 'Saxon Shore' forts on the eastern and southern coastlines. Billon
antoninianus. ORIENS AVG. Sol stg. l. between two captives. *R.I.C. 63.*   25   60

569A — RESTITVT. ORBIS. Female stg. r., presenting wreath to emperor stg. l.
R.I.C. 399.   25   60

570   **Aurelian and Vabalathus,** ruler of Palmyra 267-272 and usurper in the
East from 271. Billon *antoninianus*. Obv. Laur. bust of Vabalathus r. Rev.
Rad. bust of Aurelian r. *R.I.C. 381*   55   140

571   574A

571   **Severina,** wife of Aurelian. Billon *antoninianus*. PROVIDEN. DEOR.
Concordia (or Fides) Militum stg. r., facing Sol stg. l. *R.I.C. 9.*   30   75

572   **Tacitus,** 275-276. Billon *antoninianus*. SECVRIT. PERP. Securitas stg. l.,
leaning on column. *R.I.C. 163.*   30   75

573   **Florian,** 276. Billon *antoninianus*. LAETITIA FVND. Laetitia stg. l.
R.I.C. 34.   55   140

574   **Probus,** 276-282, suppressed governor's revolt in Britain and lifted
restrictions on viticulture in Britain and Gaul. Billon *antoninianus*.
ADVENTVS PROBI AVG. Emperor on horseback l., captive seated
before. *R.I.C. 160.*   20   45

574A — VICTORIA GERM. Trophy between two captives. *R.I.C. 222.*   25   55

574B **Proculus** (usurper 280-281) Billon *antoninianus*. VICTORIA AUG. Female
figure stg l.   14000   40000

575   **Carus,** 282-283. Billon *antoninianus*. PAX EXERCITI. Pax stg. l., holding
olive-branch and standard. *R.I.C. 75.*   35   85

		F	*VF*
		£	£

576   **Divus Carus,** deified 283. Billon *antoninianus*. CONSECRATIO. Eagle
       facing, hd. l. *R.I.C. 28*..   35   85

577   **Carinus,** 283-285 (Caesar 282-283). Billon *antoninianus*. SAECVLI
       FELICITAS. Emperor stg. r. *R.I.C. 214*.   30   75

578   **Magnia Urbica,** wife of Carinus. Billon *antoninianus*. VENVS VICTRIX.
       Venus stg. l., holding helmet, shield at feet. *R.I.C. 343*............................   75   190

579   **Numerian,** 283-284 (Caesar 282-283). Billon *antoninianus*. CLEMENTIA
       TEMP. Emperor stg. r., receiving globe from Jupiter stg. l. *R.I.C. 463*....   35   85

580   **Diocletian,** 284-305. Æ *argenteus*. VIRTVS MILITVM. The four tetrarchs
       sacrificing before gateway of military camp. *R.I.C. 27a (Rome)*.............   170   380

581   Billon *antoninianus*. IOVI CONSERVAT AVGG. Jupiter stg. l. *R.I.C. 162.*   20   45

582   Æ *follis*. GENIO POPVLI ROMANI. Genius stg. l. R.I.C. 14a *(Alexandria)*.   20   45

582A — (post-abdication coinage, after 305). PROVIDENTIA DEORVM QVIES
       AVGG. Quies and Providentia stg. facing each other. *R.I.C. 676a (Treveri)*.   35   90
       See also under Category 3.

583   **Maximian,** 286-305 and 306-308, failed in his attempts to suppress the
       usurpation of Carausius in Britain. Æ *argenteus*. VICTORIA SARMAT. The
       four tetrarchs sacrificing before gateway of military camp. *R.I.C. 37b (Rome)*.   160   340

584

584   Billon *antoninianus*. SALVS AVGG. Salus stg. r., feeding snake held in
       her arms. *R.I.C. 417*..   20   40

585   Æ *follis*. SAC. MON. VRB. AVGG. ET CAESS. NN. Moneta stg. l.
       R.I.C. 105b (Rome).   20   45

585A — (second reign). CONSERVATORES VRB SVAE. Roma seated in
       hexastyle temple. *R.I.C. 84b (Ticinum)*.   20   45
       See also under Category 3.

       *[For coins of the usurpers **Carausius** and **Allectus** see under Category 3]*

586   **Constantius I,** 305-306 (Caesar 293-305), invaded Britain 296 and defeated
       the usurper Allectus, thus restoring the island to the rule of the central government;
       Britain now divided into four provinces and the northern frontier defences
       reconstructed; died at York, July 306. Æ *argenteus*. PROVIDENTIA AVGG.
       The four tetrarchs sacrificing before gateway of military camp. *R.I.C. 11a (Rome)*.   180   400

587

587   Æ *follis*. GENIO POPVLI ROMANI. Genius stg. l. *R.I.C. 26a (Aquileia)*.   20   45

| | | F | VF |
| | | £ | £ |

587A — SALVIS AVGG. ET CAESS. FEL. KART. Carthage stg. l., holding
fruits. *R.I.C. 30a (Carthage).* 20   45
See also under Category 3.

588   593

No.	Description	F	VF
588	**Galerius,** 305-311 (Caesar 293-305). Æ argenteus. VIRTVS MILITVM. The four tetrarchs sacrificing before gateway of military camp. *R.I.C. 15b (Ticinum).*	170	380
588A	— XC / VI in wreath. *R.I.C. 16b (Carthage).*	220	550
589	Æ *follis.* GENIO AVGG ET CAESARVM NN. Genius stg. l. *R.I.C. 11b (Cyzicus).*	20	45
589A	— GENIO IMPERATORIS. Genius stg. l. *R.I.C. 101a (Alexandria)*...... *See also under Category 3.*	20	40
590	**Galeria Valeria,** wife of Galerius. Æ *follis.* VENERI VICTRICI. Venus stg. l. *R.I.C. 110 (Alexandria).*	45	110
591	**Severus II,** 306-307 (Caesar 305-306). Æ *follis.* FIDES MILITVM. Fides seated l. *R.I.C. 73 (Ticinum).* .... *See also under Category 3.*	45	110
592	**Maximinus II,** 310-313 (Caesar 305-310). Æ *follis.* GENIO CAESARIS. Genius stg. l. *R.I.C. 64 (Alexandria).*	20	40
592A	— GENIO POP. ROM. Genius stg. l. *R.I.C. 845a (Treveri).* .... *See also under Category 3.*	15	35
593	**Maxentius,** 306-312 (Caesar 306). Æ *follis.* CONSERV. VRB. SVAE. Roma seated in hexastyle temple. *R.I.C. 210 (Rome).*	20	40
594	**Romulus,** son of Maxentius, deified 309. Æ *quarter follis.* AETERNAE MEMORIAE. Temple with domed roof. *R.I.C. 58 (Ostia).*	90	220
595	**Licinius,** 308-324. Æ *follis.* GENIO AVGVSTI. Genius stg. l. *R.I.C. 198b (Siscia).*	20	35
595A	Æ 3. IOVI CONSERVATORI AVGG. Jupiter stg. l. *R.I.C. 24 (Nicomedia).* *See also under Category 3.*	20	35
596	**Licinius Junior,** son of Licinius, Caesar 317-324. Æ 3. CAESARVM NOSTRORVM around wreath containing VOT. / V. *R.I.C. 92 (Thessalonica).*	20	35
597	**Constantine I, the Great,** 307-337 (Caesar 306-307), campaigned with his father Constantius I against the Picts in northern Britain, summer 306, and proclaimed emperor by the legions at York on Constantius' death in July; closed the London mint early in 325 ending almost four decades of operation. Æ *follis.* GENIO POP ROM. Genius stg. l. *R.I.C. 719b (Treveri).*	20	45
598	— SOLI INVICTO COMITI. Sol stg. l. *R.I.C. 307 (Lugdunum).*	20	35
598A	Æ 3. PROVIDENTIAE AVGG. Gateway of military camp. *R.I.C. 153 (Thessalonica)*..	15	30

599　　　　　　　599B　　　　　　　600

		F	VF
		£	£

599 — VIRTVS EXERCIT. Trophy between two captives. *R.I.C. 280 (Treveri).* 20 40

599A Æ 3/4. GLORIA EXERCITVS. Two soldiers stg. either side of two standards.
R.I.C. 518 (Treveri).. 10 20
See also under Category 3.

599B Silver third siliqua, after 330. Obv Female bust r. Rev. K within border of
pellets. *(Constantinopolis)*.. 120 300

600 **'Urbs Roma'**, after 330. Æ 3/4. Obv. Helmeted bust of Roma l. Rev.
She-wolf l., suckling twins. *R.I.C. 195 (Nicomedia)*................................. 10 25

601　　　　　　　　604

601 **'Constantinopolis'**, after 330. Æ 3/4. Obv. Helmeted bust of
Constantinopolis l. Rev. Victory stg. l., foot on prow. *R.I.C. 339 (Rome).* 10 25

602 **Fausta,** wife of Constantine I. Æ 3. SALVS REIPVBLICAE. Empress
stg. l., holding two children. *R.I.C. 459 (Treveri)*..................................... 20 50
See also under Category 3.

603 **Helena,** mother of Constantine I. Æ 3. SECVRITAS REIPVBLICAE.
Empress stg. l., holding branch. *R.I.C. 38 (Alexandria)*............................ 20 50

603A Æ 4 (posthumous issue, 337-340). PAX PVBLICA. Pax stg. l. *R.I.C. 78*
(Treveri). 15 30
See also under Category 3.

604 **Theodora,** second wife of Constantius I. Æ 4 (posthumous issue, 337-340).
PIETAS ROMANA. Pietas stg. r., holding child. R.I.C. 43 *(Treveri)*...... 15 35

605 **Crispus,** eldest son of Constantine I, Caesar 317-326. Æ 3. CAESARVM
NOSTRORVM around wreath containing VOT. / V. *R.I.C. 68 (Aquileia).* 15 35
See also under Category 3.

606 **Delmatius,** nephew of Constantine I, Caesar 335-337. Æ 3/4. GLORIA
EXERCITVS. Two soldiers stg. either side of two standards. *R.I.C. 90*
(Antioch). 35 90

607 **Hanniballianus,** nephew of Constantine I, Rex 335-337. Æ 4. SECVRITAS
PVBLICA. River-god Euphrates reclining r. *R.I.C. 147 (Constantinople).* 175 380

608 **Constantine II,** 337-340 (Caesar 317-337). Æ 3. BEATA
TRANQVILLITAS. Altar inscribed VOT / IS / XX. *R.I.C. 312 (Treveri).* 15 35

608A Æ 3/4. GLORIA EXERCITVS. Two soldiers stg. either side of standard.
R.I.C. 392 (Rome) (See also under Category 3.)..................................... 10 25

609 **Constans,** 337-350 (Caesar 333-337), visited Britain in 343, the last
reigning emperor to do so. Æ 2. FEL. TEMP. REPARATIO. Soldier r.,
dragging barbarian from hut beneath tree. *R.I.C. 103 (Aquileia).*............ 30 60

609A   611B

	F £	VF £

609A — FEL. TEMP. REPARATIO. Emperor stg. l. on galley steered by Victory.
R.I.C. 219 (Treveri)... 25 50

609B Æ 4. VICTORIAE DD. AVGG. Q. NN. Two Victories stg. face to face.
R.I.C. 195 (Treveri)... 10 25

610 **Constantius II,** 337-361 (Caesar 324-337). Æ 3/4. GLORIA EXERCITVS.
Two soldiers stg. either side of two standards. *R.I.C. 85 (Cyzicus)*.......... 10 25

611 Æ *siliqua*. VOTIS / XXX. / MVLTIS / XXXX. in wreath. *R.I.C. 207 (Arelate)*. 75 200

611A Æ 2. FEL. TEMP. REPARATIO. Emperor stg. l. on galley. *R.I.C. 218
(Treveri)*. 30 60

611B Æ 3. FEL. TEMP. REPARATIO. Soldier advancing l., spearing fallen
horseman. *R.I.C. 189 (Lugdunum)*... 10 25
See also under Categories 3 and 4.

612   616

612 **Magnentius,** usurper in the West, 350-353, temporarily detached Britain
from the rule of the legitimate Constantinian dynasty. Æ 1. SALVS DD.
NN. AVG. ET CAES. *Chi-Rho* Christian monogram between Alpha
and Omega. *R.I.C. 34 (Ambianum)*... 150 350

612A Æ 2. FELICITAS REIPVBLICAE. Emperor stg. l., holding Victory and
labarum. *R.I.C. 264 (Treveri)*.. 35 75
See also under Category 4.

613 **Decentius,** brother of Magnentius, Caesar 351-353. Æ 2. VICTORIAE DD.
NN. AVG. ET CAE. Two Victories supporting between them shield
inscribed VOT. / V. / MVLT. / X. *R.I.C. 146 (Lugdunum)*. 45 100
See also under Category 4.

614 **Vetranio,** 'usurper' in the Balkans, 350. Æ 2. CONCORDIA MILITVM.
Emperor stg. l., holding two labara. *R.I.C. 281 (Siscia)*........................... 55 130

615 **Constantius Gallus,** Caesar under Constantius II, 351-354. Æ 2. FEL.
TEMP. REPARATIO. Soldier advancing l., spearing fallen horseman.
R.I.C. 94 (Cyzicus)... 30 60

615A **Julian II,** 360-363 (Caesar 355-360). Æ *miliarense*. Rev. VIRTVS
EXERCITVM. Soldier stg l, holding spear and resting on shield. *R.I.C. 290.
(Arelate)* 550 1300

616 Æ *siliqua*. VOT. / X. / MVLT. / XX. in wreath. *R.I.C. 309 (Arelate)*. 75 200

	F	VF
	£	£

617   Æ 1. SECVRITAS REIPVB. Bull stg. r. *R.I.C. 411 (Siscia)*. .... | 60 | 180

Beware of recent forgeries.

617A Æ 3. VOT. / X. / MVLT. / XX. in wreath. *R.I.C. 108 (Sirmium)*.............. | 15 | 35

618   **Jovian,** 363-364. Æ 3. VOT. / V. / MVLT. / X. in wreath. *R.I.C. 426 (Siscia)*. | 30 | 60

619   620

619   **Valentinian I,** 364-375 (in the West), during whose reign the Roman
province of Britannia was devastated by the simultaneous attack of hordes
of invaders on several fronts (the 'Barbarian Conspiracy'); order eventually
restored by Count Theodosius, father of the future emperor . *N solidus.*
RESTITVTOR REIPVBLICAE. Emperor stg. r., holding standard and
Victory. *R.I.C. 2b (Antioch)*. .... | 400 | 900

619A Æ *miliarense*. Rev. VICTORIA AVGVSTORVM. Victory
stg r, inscribing shield. *R.I.C. 24a. (Trier)*... | 450 | 1200

619B Æ *siliqua*. Rev. VRBS ROMA. Roma seated l. *R.I.C. 27a (Trier)*.......... | 80 | 220

619C Æ 3. GLORIA ROMANORVM. Emperor advancing r., dragging
barbarian and holding labarum. *R.I.C. 14a (Siscia)*. .... | 15 | 30

619D — SECVRITAS REIPVBLICAE. Victory advancing l. *R.I.C. 32a (Treveri)*. | 15 | 30

619E **Valens,** 364-378 (in the East). *N solidus*. Rev. RESTITVTOR REIPVBLICAE.
Valens stg , holding labarum and Victory. *R.I.C. 2d (Antioch)* .... | 400 | 900

619F Æ *miliarense*. Rev. VIRTVS EXERCITVS. Valens stg, holding standard.
R.I.C. 26c (Trier) .... | 425 | 1100

620   Æ *siliqua*. VRBS ROMA. Roma seated l. *R.I.C. 27e (Treveri)*. .... | 80 | 220

620A Æ 3. SECVRITAS REIPVBLICAE. Victory advancing l. *R.I.C. 42b
(Constantinople)*. .... | 15 | 30

621   **Procopius,** usurper in the East, 365-366. Æ 3. REPARATIO FEL. TEMP.
Emperor stg. r., holding standard and shield. *R.I.C. 17a (Constantinople)*. | 55 | 140

621A **Gratian,** 367-383 (in the West), overthrown by Magnus Maximus who had
been proclaimed emperor by the army in Britain. *N solidus*. Rev. VICTORIA
AVGG. Two Emperors enthroned holding globe, Victory behind. *R.I.C. 17g
(Trier)* .... | 425 | 1000

621B Æ *miliarense*. Rev. VIRTVS EXERCITVS. Gratian stg, holding standard.
R.I.C. 40 .(Lugdunum) .... | 450 | 1000

622   Æ *siliqua*. VRBS ROMA. Roma seated l. *R.I.C. 27f (Treveri)*.............. | 80 | 220

622A **Valentinian II,** 375-392 (in the West). *N solidus*. Rev. VICTORIA AVGG.
Two Emperors enthroned holding globe, Victory behind. *R.I.C. 34b
(Thessalonica)* .... | 450 | 1100

622B Æ *miliarense*. Rev. GLORIA ROMANORVM. Valentinian stg , holding
standard. *R.I.C. 40 (lugdunum)* .... | 450 | 1200

622C Æ *siliqua*. Rev. VIRTVS ROMANORVM. Roma seated l. *R.I.C. 43a.
(Lugdunum)*... | 85 | 220

623   Æ 2. REPARATIO REIPVB. Emperor stg. l., raising kneeling female figure.
R.I.C. 20c (Arelate).. | 25 | 50

623A Æ 4. SALVS REIPVBLICAE. Victory advancing l., dragging barbarian.
R.I.C. 20a (Alexandria). .... | 15 | 30

	F	VF
	£	£

623B **Theodosius I,** the Great, 379-395 (in the East), son of the Count Theodosius who
had cleared Britain of barbarian invaders in the reign of Valentinian I; the Emperor
Theodosiua twice restored Britain to the rule of the central government, by his
defeat of the usurpers Magnus Maximus (in 388) and Eugenius (in 394).
N solidus. Rev. CONCORDIA AUGGG. Constantinopolis seated, holding
sceptre and shield. *R.I.C. 71a (Constantinople)* 425   1050

623C *R miliarense.* Rev. VIRTUS EXERCITUS. Theodosius stg , holding standard.
R.I.C. 53c (Trier) 450   1200

624 *R siliqua.* CONCORDIA AVGGG. Constantinopolis enthroned facing, foot
on prow. *R.I.C. 55a (Treveri)* 80   220

624A

624A — VIRTVS ROMANORVM. Roma enthroned facing. *R.I.C (Aquileia) 28d.*   80   220

624B Æ 2. VIRTVS EXERCIT. Emperor stg. r., foot on captive, holding
labarum and globe. *R.I.C. 24b (Heraclea)*   30   60

625 **Aelia Flaccilla,** wife of Theodosius I. Æ 2. SALVS REIPVBLICAE. Victory
seated r., inscribing Christian monogram on shield set on cippus.
R.I.C. 81 (Constantinople)   30   80

625A **Magnus Maximus,** usurper in the West, 383-388, proclaimed emperor by the
army in Britain, invaded Gaul, and overthrew the legitimate western emperor
Gratian; possibly reopened the London mint for a brief issue of precious metal
coinage (Rudyard Kipling presented a rather fanciful version of his career in
"Puck of Pook's Hill"). *N solidus.* Rev. RESTITVTOR REPVBLICAE.
Maximus stg, holding labarum and Victory. *R.I.C. 76 (Trier)* 1600   3750

625B *R miliarense.* Rev. VIRTVS EXERCITVS. Maximus stg, holding labarum.
R.I.C. 82 (Trier) 850   2100

626   627

626 *R siliqua.* VIRTVS ROMANORVM. Roma enthroned facing. *R.I.C. 84b (Treveri)*
(See also under Category 3.)   95   260

626A **Flavius Victor,** son of Magnus Maximus, co-emperor 387-388. *R siliqua.*
VIRTVS ROMANORVM. Roma seated facing on throne. *R.I.C. 84d (Treveri)*   380   900

627 Æ 4. SPES ROMANORVM. Gateway of military camp. *RIC 55b (Aquileia).*   60   150

627A **Eugenius,** usurper in the West, 392-394, recognized in Britain until his defeat
by Theodosius the Great. *N solidus.* VICTORIA AUGG. Two emperors
enthroned facing holding globe. *R.I.C. 28 (Treveri)* 3500   9250

627B *R miliarense.* Rev. VIRTVS EXERCITVS. Eugenius stg, holding standard.
R.I.C. 105 (Trier) 1900   4600

628   629

		F	VF
		£	£
628	Æ *siliqua*. VIRTVS ROMANORVM. Roma seated l. on cuirass. *R.I.C. 32c (Milan)*.	380	900
629	**Arcadius,** 395-408 (in the East, co-emperor with his father Theodosius I from 383). *N solidus*. VICTORIA AVGGG. Emperor stg. r., foot on captive, holding standard and Victory. *R.I.C. 1205 (Milan)*.	425	1050
629A	Æ *miliarense*. Rev. GLORIA ROMANORVM. Arcadius stg, raising r hand and holding globe in l. *R.I.C. 25b (Milan)*	475	1200
629B	Æ *siliqua*. Rev. VOT V MVLT X in wreath. *R.I.C. 13 (Milan)*	85	220
629C	Æ 2. GLORIA ROMANORVM. Emperor stg. l., holding standard and shield, captive at feet. *R.I.C. 41 (Antioch)*.	30	70
630	**Honorius,** 395-423 (in the West, co-emperor with his father Theodosius I and brother Arcadius from 393), this reign saw the end of Roman rule in Britain following a succession of usurpations in the province, culminating in that of Constantine III against whom the Britons rebelled in 409; Honorius' celebrated ' Rescript' of the following year instructed the provincials to look to their own defence as he was no longer able to assist them. *N solidus*. VICTORIA AVGGG. Emperor stg. r., foot on captive, holding standard and Victory. *R.I.C. 1287 (Ravenna)*.	400	900
630A	Æ *miliarense*. Rev. VIRTVS EXERCITVS *(Rome)*	480	1175
630B	Æ *siliqua*. VIRTVS ROMANORVM. Roma seated l. on cuirass. *R.I.C. 1228 (Milan)*	80	200

631

631	**Constantine III,** usurper in the West, 407-411, proclaimed emperor by the army in Britain, but his authority rejected by the Romano-Britons two years later, thus effectively ending 366 years of Roman rule in Britain. Æ *siliqua*. VICTORIA AVGGG. Roma enthroned l. *R.I.C. 1532 (Treveri)*	240	550
632	**Valentinian III,** 425-455 (in the West), during whose reign the Saxon conquest of the former Roman province commenced, following the final unsuccessful appeal of the Romano-Britons for help addressed to the general Aetius in 446. *N solidus*. VICTORIA AVGGG. Emperor stg. facing, foot on human-headed serpent. *R.I.C. 2010 (Ravenna)*.	425	1000
632A	Æ 4. VOT. PVB. Gateway of military camp. *R.I.C. 2123 (Rome)*.	35	100

2. ISSUES WITH TYPES REFERRING SPECIFICALLY
TO THE PROVINCE OF BRITANNIA

Struck in Rome, unless otherwise indicated. These usually commemorate military operations in the northern frontier region of the province or beyond.

633   635

		F £	VF £
633	**Claudius,** A.D. 41-54. AV aureus, celebrating the early stages of the Roman conquest of Britain which commenced in A.D. 43. DE BRITANN on architrave of triumphal arch. *R.I.C. 33.*	3200	7000
634	Æ *denarius. Similar. R.I.C. 34.*	800	2000
634A	Æ *didrachm* of Caesarea in Cappadocia. DE BRITANNIS. Emperor in triumphal quadriga r. *R.I.C. 122.*	700	1800
635	**Hadrian,** 117-138. Æ as, commemorating the restoration of order in the province following a serious uprising (or invasion) in the north, probably early in the governorship of Q. Pompeius Falco (118-122). BRITANNIA PONT. MAX. TR. POT. COS. III. S. C. Britannia seated facing on rock. *R.I.C. 577a.*	380	950
636	Æ *sestertius,* commemorating Hadrian's visit to the province in 122, when he planned and initiated the construction of the northern frontier system which bears his name. ADVENTVI AVG. BRITANNIAE S.C. Emperor and Britannia stg. either side of altar. *R.I.C. 882*	6500	21200

638A

637	— BRITANNIA S. C. Britannia seated facing, foot resting on rock. *R.I.C. 845.*	6800	22400
637A	Æ *dupondius* or as. *Similar. R.I.C. 846*	700	1900
638	Æ *sestertius,* commemorating Hadrian's attention to the legionary garrison strength of the province, principally his transfer of *VI Victrix* from Germany in 122. EXERC. BRITANNICVS S. C. Emperor on horseback r., addressing gathering of troops. *R.I.C. 912.*	6500	21200
638A	— EXERC. BRITANNICVS S.C. Emperor stg. r. on tribunal, addressing gathering of troops. *R.I.C. 913.*	6500	21200

	F	VF
	£	£

639 **Antoninus Pius,** 138-161. *N aureus,* commemorating the conquests in Scotland by the governor Q. Lollius Urbicus (138/9-142/3) at which time construction of the Antonine Wall was begun. BRITAN. IMPERATOR II. Victory stg. l. on globe. *R.I.C. 113* 2600 6000

640

640	Æ *sestertius.* BRITANNIA S. C. Britannia seated l. on rock, holding standard. *R.I.C. 742.*	925	2350
641	— BRITAN. IMPERATOR II. S. C. Helmeted Britannia seated l., foot on rock. *R.I.C. 743*	925	2350
642	— BRITAN. IMPERATOR II. S. C. Britannia seated l. on globe above waves, holding standard. *R.I.C. 744.*	1000	2750
643	— BRITAN. IMPERATOR II. S. C. Victory stg. l. on globe. *R.I.C. 719.*	360	875
643A	— BRITANNIA IMPERATOR II. S. C. Britannia seated l. on rock, holding standard. *R.I.C. 745.*	925	2350
644	Æ *as.* IMPERATOR II. S. C. Victory hovering l., holding shield inscribed BRI / TAN. *R.I.C. 732.*	185	425
645	Æ *dupondius,* commemorating the quelling of a serious uprising in the north, ca. 154/5, necessitating the evacuation of the recently constructed Antonine Wall in Scotland. BRITANNIA COS. IIII. S. C. Britannia seated l. on rock, shield and vexillum in background. *R.I.C. 930.*	360	850
646	Æ *as.* Similar. *R.I.C. 934.*	160	425

Many specimens of this type are carelessly struck on inadequate flans. Moreover, they have been found in significant quantities on Romano-British sites, notably in Coventina's Well at Carrawburgh fort on Hadrian's Wall, raising the interesting possibility that they may have been issued from a temporary mint in Britain. The style of the engraving is quite regular, indicating that even if locally produced these coins would have been struck from normal Roman dies brought to Britain especially for this purpose. See under Category 3.

647 **Commodus,** 177-192. Æ *sestertius,* commemorating the victories in Scotland of the governor Ulpius Marcellus in 184/5. These were in retribution for a major barbarian invasion several years earlier resulting in serious damage to Hadrian's Wall, which had been temporarily overrun, and the defeat and death of an unknown governor. BRITT. P. M. TR. P. VIIII. IMP. VII. COS. IIII. P. P. S. C. Britannia stg. l., holding curved sword and helmet. *R.I.C. 437.* 5800 18750

648

	F	VF
	£	£

648   — VICT. BRIT. P. M. TR. P. VIIII. (or X.) IMP. VII. COS. IIII. P. P. S. C.
Victory seated r., about to inscribe shield. *R.I.C. 440, 452*...................... 260   750

649

649   **Septimius Severus,** 193-211. *N aureus,* commemorating the success of
the punitive Roman campaigns in Scotland during 209 and 210 culminating
in the illness and death of Severus at York in Feb. 211. VICTORIAE BRIT.
Victory advancing l. *R.I.C. 334.* 3200   8000

650   — VICTORIAE BRIT. Victory advancing r., leading child by hand.
R.I.C. 302.. 3400   8250

651   *R denarius.* VICTORIAE BRIT. Victory advancing r. *R.I.C. 332.* 80   170

651A   — VICTORIAE BRIT. Victory stg. facing beside palm-tree with shield
attached. *R.I.C. 336*.. 85   180

651B   — VICTORIAE BRIT. Victory stg. l. *R.I.C. 333.*.................................... 85   180

651C   — VICTORIAE BRIT. Victory seated l., holding shield. *R.I.C. 335.*....... 85   180

652

652   Æ *sestertius.* VICTORIAE BRITTANNICAE S. C. Two Victories placing
shield on palm-tree with captives at base. *R.I.C. 818*............................... 525   1600

653   — P. M. TR. P. XVIII. COS. III. P. P. S. C. Similar. *R.I.C. 796.* 325   760

654   Æ *dupondius.* VICT. BRIT. P. M. TR. P. XIX. COS. III. P. P. S. C. Victory
stg. r. between two captives, holding vexillum. *R.I.C. 809.* 190   500

655   Æ *as.* VICTORIAE BRITTANNICAE S. C. Similar. *R.I.C. 837a*........... 220   550

		F £	VF £

656   Billon *tetradrachm* of Alexandria in Egypt. NEIKH KATA BRET. Nike
flying l. *Milne 2726.*   950   2300

657   **Caracalla,** 198-217. *N aureus,* commemorating the victories achieved
by the Romans in Scotland during the campaigns led jointly by Severus
and Caracalla in 209, and by Caracalla alone the following year during
his father's illness. VICTORIAE BRIT. Victory seated l., holding shield.
R.I.C. 174.   3400   8000

658   659A

658   *R denarius.* VICTORIAE BRIT. Victory advancing l. *R.I.C. 231.*   85   180
658A   — VICTORIAE BRIT. Victory advancing r., holding trophy. *R.I.C. 231A.*   85   180
659   Æ *sestertius.* VICTORIAE BRITTANNICAE S. C. Victory stg. r., erecting
trophy to r. of which Britannia stands facing, captive at feet. *R.I.C. 464.*   450   1200
659A   — VICT. BRIT. TR. P. XIIII. COS. III. S.C. Similar. *Cf. R.I.C. 483c.*   375   1000
660   Æ *dupondius.* VICTORIAE BRITTANNICAE S. C. Victory stg. r.,
inscribing shield set on palm-tree. *R.I.C. 467*   190   475
661   Æ *as.* VICT. BRIT. TR. P. XIIII. COS. III. S. C. Similar. *R.I.C. 490*   170   425
662   **Geta,** 209-212. *R denarius,* commemorating the victories achieved by
his father and brother in Scotland in 209-10 while he and his mother were
resident in London. VICTORIAE BRIT. Victory stg. l. *R.I.C. 92*   90   190
662A   — VICTORIAE BRIT. Victory advancing r. *R.I.C. 91.*   90   190

663

663   Æ *sestertius.* VICTORIAE BRITTANNICAE S. C. Victory seated r.,
inscribing shield set on knee. *R.I.C. 166.*   525   1550
663A   — VICT. BRIT. TR. P. III. COS. II. S. C. Similar. *R.I.C. 172b.*   450   1150
664   Æ *as.* VICTORIAE BRITTANNICAE S. C. Victory seated l., balancing
shield on knee. *R.I.C. 191a*   190   525
665   Billon *tetradrachm* of Alexandria in Egypt. NEIKH KATA BRETAN.
Nike advancing l. *B.M.C. (Alexandria) 1481.*   1000   2500

3. OFFICIAL ROMAN COINAGE STRUCK IN BRITAIN

The London mint, and the associated 'C' mint (new research indicates that this was a secondary mint that operated initially in North London and subsequently moved around the country with Carausius), were created by the usurper Carausius soon after his seizure of Britain in 287. Prior to this, in the mid-2nd century, there may have been minting of 'Britannia' asses of Antoninus Pius in the province using dies brought from Rome, though this has not been firmly established. After the downfall of the rebel British regime in 296 the minting establishment in London (though not the subsidiary mint) was retained by the tetrarchal government and the succeeding Constantinian administration. Early in 325, however, Constantine the Great closed the London mint after almost four decades of operation. A possible brief revival under the usurper Magnus Maximus has been postulated for gold and silver coins marked 'AVG', 'AVGOB' and 'AVGPS', though the attribution has not received universal acceptance.

For more on the bronze coinage struck at London Mint c.296-97 to c.325 see Cloke, H.J. and Toone, L., *The London Mint of Constantius and Constantine* (Spink 2015).

		F	VF
		£	£
666	**Antoninus Pius,** 138-161. Æ *as,* struck in northern Britain (?) in 155. BRITANNIA COS. IIII. S. C. Britannia seated l. on rock, shield and vexillum in background. *R.I.C. 930.*	200	550

Many poorly struck examples of this type have been found on Romano-British sites, notably at Brocolitia (Carrawburgh) fort on Hadrian's Wall in Northumberland, where no fewer than 327 specimens were discovered in the great votive deposit in the well which formed part of the shrine of the water-nymph Coventina. There appears to be a very real possibility that many of these 'Britannia' asses had been issued from a temporary mint in Britain, most likely situated in the north. The dies, however, are quite regular, and would thus have been brought from Rome to the island province for the express purpose of supplementing the money supply at a time of crisis.

667	**Carausius,** usurper in Britain and northwestern Gaul, A.D. 286-293. *N aureus,* London. CONSERVAT. AVG. Jupiter stg. l., eagle at feet, ML in ex. *R.I.C. 1.*	38000	105000
667A	*R denarius* ADVENTVS AUG. Emperor riding l, captive before horse. *R.I.C. 1068*	1800	4200
667B	— CONCORDIA AVG. Clasped hands. RSR. *R.I.C. 545*	1400	3300
668	— EXPECTATE VENI. Britannia stg. r. and emperor l., clasping hands, RSR in ex. *R.I.C. 555.*	1750	3900

669   672A

669	— RENOVAT. ROMANO. She-wolf r., suckling twins, RSR in ex. *R.I.C. 571.*	1550	3500
669A	— Rev. VIRTVS AVG. Lion walking l. RSR in exergue. *R.I.C. 591*	2000	4500
669B	— Rev. VOTO PVBLICO, MVLTIS XX IMP in altar. RSR below. *R.I.C. 595.*	1600	3700
670	Billon *antoninianus,* London. COMES AVG. Victory stg. l., S—P in field, ML in ex. *R.I.C. 14.*	130	360
670A	— HILARITAS AVG. Hilaritas stg. l., B—E in field, MLXXI in ex. *R.I.C. 41.*	100	250

		F	VF
		£	£
671	— LAETITIA AVG. Laetitia stg. l., F—O in field, ML in ex. *R.I.C. 50.*.	80	200
671A	— LEG. II. AVG. Capricorn l., ML in ex. *R.I.C. 58.*................................	180	450
	Legio II Augusta was stationed at Isca (Caerleon in South Wales).		
672	— LEG. XX. V. V. Boar stg. r. *R.I.C. 82.*.....................................	200	500
	Legio XX Valeria Victrix was stationed at Deva (Chester in the northwest		
	Midlands).		
672A	— PAX AVG. Pax stg. l., F—O in field, ML in ex. *R.I.C. 101.*	65	175
673	— Similar, but without mint mark. *R.I.C. 880.*	60	160
673A	— PROVIDENT. AVG. Providentia stg. l., B—E in field, MLXXI in ex.		
	R.I.C. 149...	80	200
674	— SALVS AVGGG. Salus stg. r., feeding snake held in her arms, S—P		
	in field, ML in ex. *R.I.C. 164.*...	110	275
	The reverse legends with triple-ending (AVGGG.) presumably are subsequent		
	to Carausius' recognition by Diocletian and Maximian in 289 following the		
	failure of the latter's attempt to dislodge the usurper from his island stronghold.		
674A	— TEMPORVM FELICITAS. Felicitas stg. l., B—E in field, ML in ex.		
	R.I.C. 172...	80	200
675	— VIRTVS AVGGG. Mars (or Virtus) stg. r., holding spear and shield,		
	S—P in field, MLXXI in ex. *R.I.C. 183.*	110	275
676	Billon *antoninianus,* Colchester (?). CONCORDIA MILIT. Emperor stg.		
	r. and Concordia l., clasping hands, C in ex. *R.I.C. 205.*	160	425
676A	— EXPECTATE VENI. Britannia stg. r. and emperor l., clasping hands,		
	MSC in ex. *R.I.C. 216.*...	230	640
677	— FELICITAS AVG. Galley with mast and rowers, CXXI in ex. *R.I.C. 221.*	220	600
677A	— FORTVNA RAEDVX. Fortuna seated l., SPC in ex. *R.I.C. 237.*	130	325
678	— LAETITIA AVG. Laetitia stg. l., globe at feet, S—P in field, C in ex.		
	R.I.C. 255...	80	200
678A	—-MONETA AVG. Moneta stg. l., CXXI in ex. *R.I.C. 287.*	100	240
679	— ORIENS AVG. Sol stg. l., C in ex. *R.I.C. 293.*.................................	110	275
679A	— PAX AVGGG. Pax stg. l., S—P in field, MC in ex. *R.I.C. 335.*...........	70	160

680

680	— PROVID. AVG. Providentia stg. l., S—P in field, C in ex. *R.I.C. 353.*	80	200
680A	— SALVS AVG. Salus stg. l. at altar, feeding snake, S—C in field,		
	C in ex. *R.I.C. 396.*	100	250
681	— SPES PVBLICA. Spes walking l., holding flower, S—P in field,		
	C in ex. *R.I.C. 413.*	110	275
681A	— VICTORIA AVG. Victory advancing l., captive at feet, MC in ex. *R.I.C. 429.*	120	325
682	**Carausius, Diocletian and Maximian,** after 289. Billon *antoninianus,*		
	Colchester (?). Obv. CARAVSIVS ET FRATRES SVI. Conjoined busts		
	of the three emperors l. Rev. PAX AVGGG. Pax stg. l., S—P in field,		
	C in ex. *R.I.C. 1.*	2100	5500

682A 683

	F	VF
	£	£

682A — MONETA AVGGG. Moneta stg. l., S—P in field, C in ex. *R.I.C.* —.. 2300 5750
See also nos. 693-4 and 698-700 as well as regular Carausian types with the triple-ending 'AVGGG.' on reverse.

683 **Allectus,** usurper in Britain, 293-296. *N aureus,* London. ORIENS AVG. Sol stg. l. between two captives, ML in ex. *R.I.C. 4*.................................. 42000 125000

684 *Æ antoninianus,* London. LAETITIA AVG. Laetitia stg. l., S—A in field, 35000MSL in ex. *R.I.C. 22.*.. 100 240

684A

684A — PAX AVG. Pax stg. l., S—A in field, ML in ex. *R.I.C. 28.* 80 200

685 — PROVID. AVG. Providentia stg. l., holding globe and cornucopiae, S—P in field, ML in ex. *R.I.C. 36.* 100 240

685A — SALVS AVG. Salus stg. r., feeding snake held in her arms, S—A in field, MSL in ex. *R.I.C. 42*.. 110 280

686 — TEMPOR. FELICITAS. Felicitas stg. l., S—A in field, ML in ex. *R.I.C. 47.* 100 240

686A — VICTORIA AVG. Victory advancing l., S—P in field, ML in ex. *R.I.C. 48.* 130 325

687 *Æ antoninianus,* Colchester (?). AEQVITAS AVG. Aequitas stg. l., S—P in field, C in ex. *R.I.C. 63*.. 100 240

687A — FIDES MILITVM. Fides stg. l., holding two standards, S—P in field, C in ex. *R.I.C. 69.* 130 325

688A

688 — LAETITIA AVG. Laetitia stg. l., S—P in field, CL in ex. *R.I.C. 79.* ... 100 250
This form of mint mark has given rise to the alternative identification of this mint as Clausentum (Bitterne, Hants.)

688A — MONETA AVG. Moneta stg. l., S—P in field, C in ex. *R.I.C. 82.* 100 240

	F	VF
	£	£

689 — PAX AVG. Pax stg. l., S—P in field, C in ex. *R.I.C. 86.* 80 200

689A — PROVIDENTIA AVG. Providentia stg. l., globe at feet, S—P in field,
C in ex. *R.I.C. 111.*.. 90 220

690 — TEMPORVM FELIC. Felicitas stg. l., S—P in field, CL in ex. *R.I.C. 117.* 100 240

690A — VIRTVS AVG. Mars stg. r., holding spear and shield, S—P in field,
C in ex. *R.I.C. 121.*.. 110 280

691 Æ *'quinarius'*, London. VIRTVS AVG. Galley l., QL in ex. *R.I.C. 55.*... 85 220
*An experimental denomination issued only during this reign, the types of
the so-called 'quinarius' would seem to indicate that it was in some way
associated with the operations of the fleet upon which the survival of the
rebel regime in Britain was totally dependent.*

692 693

692 Æ *'quinarius'*, Colchester (?). LAETITIA AVG. Galley r., QC in ex.
R.I.C. 124.... 85 220

692A — VIRTVS AVG. Galley l., QC in ex. *R.I.C. 128.*.................................... 85 220

693 **Diocletian,** 284-305. Billon *antoninianus* of London, struck by Carausius
between 289 and 293. PAX AVGGG. Pax stg. l., S—P in field, MLXXI
in ex. *R.I.C. 9.*... 80 210

694 Billon *antoninianus* of Colchester (?), same date. PROVID AVGGG.
Providentia stg. l., globe at feet, S—P in field, C in ex. *R.I.C. 22*............ 85 230

695

695 Æ *follis*, London. GENIO POPVLI ROMANI. Genius stg. l., LON in ex.
R.I.C. 1a... 220 550
*By the time the central government had recovered control of Britain in 296
the antoninianus had been replaced by the larger follis under Diocletian's
sweeping currency reform. London was retained as an official imperial
mint, but the secondary British establishment (at Colchester?) was now
abandoned. Except for its initial issue in 297 (marked 'LON') the London
mint under the tetrarchic government produced only unsigned folles
throughout its first decade of operation. Perhaps Constantius did not
wish to draw attention to his employment of a mint which had been the
creation of a rebel regime.*

696 — Similar, but without mint mark. *R.I.C. 6a.* 30 65

		F	VF
		£	£

697 — (post-abdication coinage, after 305). PROVIDENTIA DEORVM
QVIES AVGG. Quies and Providentia stg. facing each other (no mint mark).
R.I.C. 77a..   50   110

697A   704

697A — QVIES AVGG. Quies stg. l., holding branch and sceptre, PLN in ex.
R.I.C. 98..   50   110

698 **Maximian,** 286-305 and 306-308. *N aureus* of London, struck by
Carausius between 289 and 293. SALVS AVGGG. Salus stg. r., feeding
snake held in her arms, ML in ex. *R.I.C. 32.* 30000 82000

699 Billon *antoninianus* of London, same date. PROVIDENTIA AVGGG.
Providentia stg. l., S—P in field, MLXXI in ex. *R.I.C. 37.*.....................   70   180

700 Billon *antoninianus* of Colchester (?), same date. PAX AVGGG. Pax stg.
l., S—P in field, C in ex. *R.I.C. 42.*   70   180

701 Æ *follis,* London. GENIO POPVLI ROMANI. Genius stg. l., LON in ex.
R.I.C. 2...   190   450

702 — Similar, but without mint mark. *R.I.C. 23b.*   30   70

703 — (post-abdication coinage, after 305). PROVIDENTIA DEORVM
QVIES AVGG. Quies and Providentia stg. facing each other (no mint mark).
R.I.C. 77b..   45   100

706

704 — (second reign). GENIO POP. ROM. Genius stg. l., PLN in ex. *R.I.C. 90.*   35   80

704A — HERCVLI CONSERVATORI. Hercules stg. l., resting on club,
PLN in ex. *R.I.C. 91.*   45   110

705 **Constantius I,** 305-306 (Caesar 293-305). Æ *follis,* London (as Caesar).
GENIO POPVLI ROMANI. Genius stg. l., LON in ex. *R.I.C. 4a.*..........   220   550

706 — Similar, but without mint mark. *R.I.C. 30.*   25   55

707 — (as Augustus). Similar. *R.I.C. 52a.*   30   65

708 **Divus Constantius I,** deified 306. Æ *follis,* London. MEMORIA FELIX.
Altar flanked by eagles, PLN in ex. *R.I.C. 110*..   35   90

709 **Galerius,** 305-311 (Caesar 293-305). Æ *follis,* London (as Caesar).
GENIO POPVLI ROMANI. Genius stg. l., LON in ex. *R.I.C. 4b.*   190   450

		F £	VF £
710	— Similar, but without mint mark. *R.I.C. 15.*	25	50
711	— (as Augustus). Similar. *R.I.C. 42.*	25	50
711A	— GENIO POP. ROM. Genius stg. l., PLN in ex. *R.I.C. 86.*	30	65
712	**Severus II,** 306-307 (Caesar 305-306). Æ *follis,* London (as Caesar). GENIO POPVLI ROMANI. Genius stg. l. (no mint mark). *R.I.C. 58a*	50	120
713	— (as Augustus). Similar. *R.I.C. 52c*	50	120
714	**Maximinus II,** 310-313 (Caesar 305-310). Æ *follis,* London (as Caesar). GENIO POPVLI ROMANI. Genius stg. l. (no mint mark). *R.I.C. 57.*	25	55
715	—-GENIO POP. ROM. Genius stg. l., PLN in ex. *R.I.C. 89a*	25	60
716	— (as Augustus). Similar, but with star in r. field. *R.I.C. 209b.*	25	55
717	**Licinius,** 308-324. Æ *follis,* London. GENIO POP. ROM. Genius stg. l., star in r. field, PLN in ex. *R.I.C. 209c.*	25	55
717A	— Similar, but with S—F in field. *R.I.C. 3.*	25	50
718	— SOLI INVICTO COMITI. Sol stg. l., holding globe, S—P in field, MSL in ex. *R.I.C. 79.*	25	50
719	**Constantine I, the Great,** 307-337 (Caesar 306-307). Æ *follis,* London (as Caesar). GENIO POPVLI ROMANI. Genius stg. l. (no mint mark). *R.I.C. 72.*	35	80
719A	— GENIO POP. ROM. Genius stg. l., PLN in ex. *R.I.C. 88b*	25	55
720	— PRINCIPI IVVENTVTIS. Prince stg. l., holding standards, PLN in ex. *R.I.C. 97.*	35	85
721	— (as Augustus). ADVENTVS AVG. Emperor on horseback l., captive on ground before, star in r. field, PLN in ex. *R.I.C. 133*	40	90
722	— COMITI AVGG. NN. Sol stg. l., holding globe and whip, same mint mark. *R.I.C. 155*	30	65
723	— CONCORD. MILIT. Concordia stg. l., holding standards, same mint mark. *R.I.C. 195*	25	60
724	— MARTI CONSERVATORI. Mars. stg. r., holding spear and shield, star in l. field, PLN in ex. *R.I.C. 254.*	25	60
724A	— SOLI INVICTO COMITI. Sol stg. l., holding globe, S—F in field, MLL in ex. *R.I.C. 27*	20	45
725	Æ 3, London. VICTORIAE LAETAE PRINC. PERP. Two Victories supporting shield, inscribed VOT. / P. R., over altar, PLN in ex. *R.I.C. 159.*	20	40

726

		F £	VF £
726	— VIRTVS EXERCIT. Vexillum, inscribed VOT. / XX., between two captives, PLN in ex. R.I.C. 191.	20	45
727	— BEAT. TRANQLITAS. Altar, inscribed VOT / IS / XX., surmounted by globe and three stars, PLON in ex. *R.I.C. 267*	20	45
727A	— SARMATIA DEVICTA. Victory advancing r., trampling captive, PLON and crescent in ex. *R.I.C. 289.*	30	60
728	— PROVIDENTIAE AVGG. Gateway of military camp, PLON in ex. *R.I.C. 293.*	20	45

	F	VF
	£	£

729 **Fausta,** wife of Constantine I. Æ 3, London. SALVS REIPVBLICAE.
Empress stg. l., holding two children, PLON in ex. *R.I.C. 300*.............. 140 400

730 **Helena,** mother of Constantine I. Æ 3, London. SECVRITAS REIPVBLICE.
Empress stg. l., holding branch, PLON in ex. *R.I.C. 299.*........................ 140 400

731 **Crispus,** eldest son of Constantine I, Caesar 317-326. Æ 3, London.
SOLI INVICTO COMITI. Sol stg. l., holding globe, crescent in l. field,
PLN in ex. *R.I.C. 144.* 25 50

731A — VIRTVS EXERCIT. Vexillum, inscribed VOT. / XX., between two
captives, PLN in ex. *R.I.C. 194.* 25 55

732 — BEATA TRANQVILLITAS. Altar, inscribed VOT / IS / XX.,
surmounted by globe and three stars, P—A in field, PLON in ex. *R.I.C. 211.* 20 45

733 — CAESARVM NOSTRORVM around wreath containing VOT. / X.,
PLON and crescent in ex. *R.I.C. 291*.. 20 45

734

734 — PROVIDENTIAE CAESS. Gateway of military camp, PLON in ex.
R.I.C. 295... 20 45

735 **Constantine II,** 337-340 (Caesar 317-337). Æ 3, London (as Caesar).
CLARITAS REIPVBLICAE. Sol stg. l., holding globe, crescent in l. field,
PLN in ex. *R.I.C. 131.* 20 45

736 — VICTORIAE LAETAE PRINC. PERP. Two Victories supporting shield,
inscribed VOT. / P. R., over altar ornamented with wreath, PLN in ex.
R.I.C. 182.... 20 45

737 — VIRTVS EXERCIT. Vexillum, inscribed VOT. / XX., between two
captives, PLON in ex. *R.I.C. 190.* 20 45

737A

737A — BEATA TRANQVILLITAS. Altar, inscribed VOT / IS / XX.,
surmounted by globe and three stars, PLON in ex. *R.I.C. 236*................. 20 45

738 — CAESARVM NOSTRORVM around wreath containing VOT. / X.,
PLON and crescent in ex. *R.I.C. 292*.. 20 45

738A — PROVIDENTIAE CAESS. Gateway of military camp, PLON in ex.
R.I.C. 296... 20 45

739 **Constantius II,** 337-361 (Caesar 324-337). Æ 3, London (as Caesar).
PROVIDENTIAE CAESS. Gateway of military camp, PLON in ex.
R.I.C. 298... 35 85

	F	VF
	£	£

740 **Magnus Maximus,** usurper in the West, 383-388. *N solidus*, London (?).
RESTITVTOR REIPVBLICAE. Emperor stg. r., holding labarum and
Victory, AVG in ex. *R.I.C. 1*. ....   *Unique*
The attribution to London of this rare series has not been firmly established,
though Maximus was certainly proclaimed emperor in Britain and it is
well attested that the principal city of the British provinces bore the name
'Augusta' in the late Roman period (Ammianus Marcellinus XXVII, 8, 7;
XXVIII, 3, 7).

741

741   — VICTORIA AVGG. Two emperors enthroned facing, Victory hovering
in background between them, AVGOB in ex. *R.I.C. 2b*.   7500   25000
Maximus appears to have struck a similar type in the name of the eastern
emperor Theodosius I (cf. R.I.C. 2a), though it is presently known only
from a silver-gilt specimen preserved in the British Museum.
742   *R siliqua*, London (?). VOT. / V. / MVLT. / X. within wreath, AVG below.
R.I.C. 4.   1200   3400
742A — VICTORIA AVGG. Victory advancing l., AVGPS in ex. *R.I.C. 3*.......   1100   2800

4. IMITATIONS OF ROMAN COINS PRODUCED IN BRITAIN

At certain periods during the three and a half centuries of its occupation Roman Britain seems to
have been the source of much local imitation of the official imported coinage. This began soon
after the Claudian invasion in A.D. 43 when significant quantities of sestertii, dupondii and asses
(especially the last) were produced in the newly conquered territory, as evidenced by the frequency
of their occurrence in archaeological finds. The technical excellence of many of these 'copies',
together with the surprising extent of their minting, would seem to indicate that some, at least, of
these coins were produced with official sanction in order to make good an unexpected deficiency in
the currency supply. Others are much poorer and well below weight, representing the 'unofficial'
branch of this operation, some of it probably emanating from territory as yet unconquered. As
conditions in the new province settled down rapid Romanisation and urbanisation of British society
brought a general increase in wealth, and with it a much greater volume of currency flowing into
the country. Local imitation now virtually ceased, except for the occasional activities of criminal
counterfeiters, and this state of affairs lasted down to the great political crisis and financial collapse
of the second half of the 3rd century. At this point large scale minting of imitations of the debased
antoniniani of the late 260s and early 270s began in Britain and in the other northwestern provinces,
all of which had been serioulsy affected by the political dislocation of this turbulent era. This
class of imitations is usually referred to as 'barbarous radiates', the emperor's spiky crown being
a constant and conspicuous feature of the obverses. Most frequently copied were the antoniniani
of the Gallic rulers Tetricus Senior and Tetricus Junior (ca. 270-273) and the posthumous issues
of Claudius Gothicus (died 270). The quality of the 'barbarous radiates' is variable in the extreme,
some exhibiting what appears to be a revival of Celtic art forms, others so tiny that it is virtually

impossible to see anything of the design. Their production appears to have ended abruptly with Aurelian's reconquest of the western provinces in 273. A similar phenomenon, though on a lesser scale, occurred in the middle decades of the following century when normal life in Britain was again disrupted, not only by usurpation but additionally by foreign invasion. With supplies of currency from the Continent temporarily disrupted, local imitation, particularly of the 'Æ 2' and 'Æ 3' issues of Constantius II and the usurper Magnentius, began in earnest. How long this continued is difficult to determine as life in the island province was now subject to increasingly frequent episodes of dislocation. By now urban life in Britain was in serious decline and when Roman rule ended early in the 5th century, bringing a total cessation of currency supplies, the catastrophic decline in monetary commerce in the former provinces rendered it no longer necessary for the deficiency to be made good.

	F	VF
	£	£
743 **Agrippa,** died 12 B.C. Æ as, of irregular British mintage, imitating the Roman issue made under Agrippa's grandson Caligula, A.D. 37-41. S. C. Neptune stg. l., holding dolphin and trident.	65	175

743 **Agrippa,** died 12 B.C. Æ as, of irregular British mintage, imitating the Roman issue made under Agrippa's grandson Caligula, A.D. 37-41. S. C. Neptune stg. l., holding dolphin and trident. 65 175
The large official issue of Agrippa asses was made shortly before the Claudian invasion of Britain in A.D. 43 and would thus have comprised a significant proportion of the 'aes' in circulation at this time. In consequence, it would soon have become familiar to the new provincials providing an ideal prototype for imitation.

744 **Claudius,** 41-54. Æ *sestertius,* of irregular British mintage. SPES AVGVSTA S. C. Spes walking l., holding flower. 140 475

745 Æ *dupondius,* of irregular British mintage. CERES AVGVSTA S. C. Ceres enthroned l., holding corn- ears and torch..................................... 55 150

746

746 Æ *as,* of irregular British mintage. S. C. Minerva advancing r., brandishing spear and holding shield. 50 130
This is by far the commonest of the Claudian imitations and the prototypes must have represented the bulk of the aes coinage carried by the legions at the time of the invasion. The martial type may well have been specially selected as a suitable theme for the initial import of coinage into the newly conquered territory.

747 **Nero Claudius Drusus,** father of Claudius, died 9 B.C. Æ *sestertius,* of irregular British mintage. TI. CLAVDIVS CAESAR AVG. P. M. TR .P. IMP. S. C. Claudius seated l. on curule chair amidst arms 175 480
This type was issued by Claudius half a century after his father's death and would thus have been prominently represented in the initial wave of coinage imported into the new province.

748 **Antonia,** mother of Claudius, died A.D. 37. Æ *dupondius,* of irregular British mintage. TI. CLAVDIVS CAESAR AVG P.M. TR. P. IMP. P. P. S. C. Claudius stg. l., holding simpulum. 100 325
Another Claudian issue for a deceased parent, this represents one of only two dupondius types struck during this reign and would have entered Britain in significant quantities at the time of the invasion in A.D. 43.

749A   749B   749C

| | F | VF |
| | £ | £ |

749   **'Barbarous radiates',** ca. 270-273. British and Continental imitations of billon *antoniniani,* principally of Divus Claudius II (A), Tetricus Senior (B) and Tetricus Junior (C). The inscriptions are usually blundered and the types sometimes unrecognizable. British mintage can only be established by provenance.   10   20

750   **Barbarous 4th century,** mostly of the second half of the century, and principally imitated from 'Æ 2' and 'Æ 3' issues of the later Constantinian period, notably those of Constantius II ('soldier spearing fallen horseman' type), and the usurpers Magnentius and Decentius ('two Victories' type). The copies, especially those of Magnentius and Decentius, are often of excellent style and execution, though the legends frequently contain small errors. Those of Constantius II are sometimes very barbarous and poorly struck, occasionally over regular issues of the earlier Constantinian period. Again, the likelihood of British mintage can only be established by provenance.   15-20   20-25

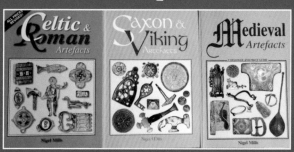

Grading of Hammered Coins

As the name suggests, hammered coins were struck by hand with a hammer. This can lead to the coin being struck off-centre, double struck, areas of the design not being struck up as well as cracks or other defects in the flan. It is important to take these factors into account along with surface wear, quality of the metal and patina when assessing the grade of this series. Value is considerably reduced if the coin is holed, pierced, plugged or mounted. Coins with proven provenance from important old collections will carry a price premium. For further detail on condition see pages ix to x.

Extremely Fine	**Very Fine**	**Fine**

William I PAXS type penny

Henry VIII 1st coinage gold Angel

Edward VI silver shilling

EARLY & MIDDLE ANGLO-SAXON KINGDOMS & MINTS (c.650-973)

EARLY ANGLO-SAXON PERIOD, *c.* 600-*c.* 775

The withdrawal of Roman forces from Britain early in the 5th century A.D. and the gradual decline of central administration resulted in a rapid deterioration of the money supply. The arrival of Germanic raiders and settlers, even in relatively small numbers, disrupted life and it was probably not until late in the 6th century that renewed political, cultural and commercial links with the kingdom of the Merovingian Franks led to the appearance of small quantities of Merovingian gold *tremisses* (one-third solidus) in England. A purse containing 37 such pieces (plus 3 gold blanks and 2 ingots) was found in the Sutton Hoo ship-burial; a further hoard of at least 60 Continental tremisses came to light in Norfolk in 2014. Native Anglo-Saxon gold shillings (*thrymsas*) were minted from the c.620s, initially in the style of their continental prototypes or copied from obsolete Roman coinage with others in pure Anglo-Saxon style. The mixed Crondall hoard of 101 gold coins (1 Byzantine, 24 Merovingian or Frankish, 69 Anglo-Saxon, 7 others) gives structure to the arrangement of thrymsas with types found in this hoard differentiated from those, some of the same date, that were not. By the middle of the 7th century the gold coinage was being increasingly debased with silver, and according to recent scientific analysis of grave goods gold had been superseded entirely by the 660s.

The silver coins, contemporary with the *deniers or denarii* of the Merovingian Franks, are the first English pennies, typically referred to as *sceats* or *sceattas* (pronounced 'skeets' or 'shatters' possibly meaning 'treasure' or 'wealth'); the singular is *sceat*. The term early-penny is now favoured. They provide important material for the student of Anglo-Saxon art. Indeed, it could be said that, until recently, the largely anonymous, anepigraphic, nature of the sceatta coinage detracted from its numismatic character, however, Anna Gannon's work on the subtle iconography of this period has elevated its status significantly.

The silver coins of the early ('primary') phase, c.680-710, are a transition from the gold coinage and are conservative in style. Those of the 'secondary' period, c.710-60, are far more diverse in design. Trading types were issued in substantial numbers (probably tens of millions) especially by the Frisians of the Low Countries ('Continental'), evidencing the significant volume of North Sea trade, and their central role in the economic resurgence. Early coins are of good silver content, though the quality deteriorates early in the 8th century, with weights then averaging around 1.00 g. The secondary types exist in numerous varieties, though the survival rate, for the non-trading types is low and for some types, extremely low. The designs on many of these mix Christian with pagan symbolism though the iconography is often, and probably intentionally, ambiguous. In this the coinage reflects the changes taking place during the period when Christianity was being adopted with the designs looking appealing to differing cultural strands in Anglo-Saxon England at the time. As well as the official issues there are mules and other varieties, which may be contemporary imitations; there is no clear line of demarcation. The 'eclectic' types are those which do not sit comfortably in the alphabetic Serial classification. However, Abramson's listing of varieties recognised here attempts to bring the eclectic issues into the general classification.

Many of the sceats were issued at the time of Aethelbald, King of Mercia, (A.D. 716-757) who was overlord of the southern English, but as few bear inscriptions it is only in recent years that research has enabled their correct dating and the attribution of certain types to specific areas. The Northumbrian issues are more literate and facilitate attribution to issuers. The Aston Rowant (Oxon.) hoard of 324 sceats, deposited *c*. 710, separates the primary and secondary phases. The sceatta 'penny' coinage came to an end c.780 when it was replaced by the broad flan penny initially in Kent before its wider adoption in Mercia. The Northumbrian kingdom continued to use the small flan sceatta which after 810 was increasingly a copper coinage, known as stycas, this ending with Danish conquest of York in 867.

Through recent detector finds and continued research, a definitive classification is evolving but remains fluid. The arrangement given below is informed by Michael Metcalf's work on the series, developing Rigold's alphabetical classification. In this listing, the primary sceats are followed by the Continental then the secondary and, finally, the eclectic. This is not chronologically precise as there is some overlap but has been adopted for ease of reference and identification. This list is more extensive than previously published in *Coins of England* but is not exhaustive. The reference Abr. refers to the type listing by Abramson; 'B.M.C.' to the type given in *British Museum Catalogue: Anglo-Saxon Coins*. The reference *M* is to an illustration, and *M. p.* to a page, in Metcalf (below).

Useful reference works include:

Abramson, T., *Sceatta List: An Illustrated and Priced Catalogue of Sceats for Collectors* (2017).

Abramson, T., *The Abramson Collection: Coins of Early Anglo-Saxon England and the North Sea Area*, SCBI, 69 (2018).

Gannon, A., *The Iconography of Early Anglo-Saxon Coinage* (2003).

Gannon, A., British Museum, Anglo Saxon Coins I, *SCBI* 63 (2013).

Lyon, S., 'The Lyon Collection of Anglo-Saxon Coins', *SCBI* 68, (2016).

Metcalf, D. M., *Thrymsas and Sceattas in the Ashmolean Museum,* Vols I-III.

Op den Velde, W., & Klaassen, C.J.F., *Sceattas and Merovingian Deniers from Domburg and Westenschovwen* (2004)

Rigold, S. E., 'The two primary series of sceattas', *B.N.J.*, XXX (1960).

Sutherland, C. H. V., *Anglo-Saxon Gold Coinage in the light of the Crondall Hoard* (1948).

ᚠᚪᚦᚻᚱᚴ·ᚷᛈᚾ�∔ᛁ ᚢᛄᚳᚣᚾᛏᛒᛗᚻᚱᚷᚻᚩᚠᚪᛏᚪ

f u th o r k z w h n i j jh p x s t b e m l ng d oe a Æ ea y

Early Anglo-Saxon Runes (Futhark)

GOLD

752

	F	VF
	£	£

A.   EARLY PIECES, OF UNCERTAIN MONETARY STATUS

751   Thrymsa. Name and portrait of Bishop Liudhard (chaplain to Queen Bertha
of Kent). ℞. Cross. ....   *Extremely rare*

752   Solidus. Imitating solidi of Roman rulers. Blundered legends, some with runes.   *Extremely rare*

753   754   758

B.   CRONDALL TYPES, *c.* 620 – *c.* 645

Twelve different types, which are almost certainly English, were found in the Crondall hoard of 1828. All are thrysmas, containing 40-70% gold.

		F	VF
753	'Witmen' type. Bust r. with trident. ℞. Cross. Legend normally blundered. *M. 1-21*	1100	3750
754	London-derived type. Head r. with pseudo-legend. ℞. Cross. Pseudo-legend. *M. 22-32*	3750	15000
755	'Licinius' type. Elegant imitation of Roman triens. Bust l. ℞. VOT XX. *M. 33-41*	3250	13500
756	'LEMC' type. Head l. ℞. Maltese cross with letters L, E, M, C in angles, or cross on steps. *M. 42-9*	2500	10000
757	'LONDINIV' type. Facing bust, crosslets l. and r. ℞. Tall cross, LONDVNIV and pseudo-legend around. *M. 51-7*	3750	15000
758	Eadbald of Kent (616-40) London. Bust r. AVDVARLD REGES. ℞. Cross on globule, LONDENVS. Usually garbled. *M. 50*	5750	22500
758A	— Canterbury. As 758 but DOROVERNVS M. *M-*..............................	6500	25000
759	Other crude types, usually with head or bust, ℞. Cross. *M. 58-72*	900	3250

C.   ULTRA-CRONDALL TYPES, *c*. 620 – *c*. 655

Thrymsas not represented in the Crondall hoard, but probably of the same date range.

760   761

		F £	VF £
760	'Benutigo' type. Bust r., blundered legend. R. Cross on steps, runic legend (Benutigoii?)	2500	10000
761	'Wuneetton' type. Bust r., cross before. R. Cross. Blundered legend (WVNEETON or similar). *M*. 77	1500	5250
762	'York' group, inscribed type, stylised face cross each side, lattice pattern below, R. uncertain blundered legend. *M*. 76	3000	12500

762   762B

		F £	VF £
762A	— uninscribed, similar, R., four 'faces' around central square or similar	3750	15000
762B	— uninscribed, standing facing figure facing hold long cross each side, R., cross within inner circle, symbols around	4000	16000
763	— Bishop Paulinus of York (c.625-633), as 762, rev. :PAOLIENVS EP legend some letters inverted	4500	17500

D.   POST-CRONDALL TYPES, *c*. 655 – *c*. 675

Pale gold types, visibly debased and sometimes almost silvery, containing 10-35% gold. The description "standard" is a reference to the Roman legionary ensign bearing the legend e.g. VOTIS X MVLTIS XX also carried in Anglo-Saxon episcopal processions. The legend is reduced to TOTII on the coinage and may be described as the "votive standard".

764   764B   766   767

		F £	VF £
764	'Crispus' type. Helmeted bust, r. CRISPVS NOB CAES. R. Cross and XX in wreath, runic legend DESAIONA. *N*.7	2500	9500
764A	'Daisy and annulet-cross' type. Flower pattern. R. annulet Latin cross in pseudo wreath.	2500	9500
764B	'Head and annulet cross' type, bare head within coiled snake, R. similar to last.	4500	17500
765	'Concordia' type. Radiate bust r. R. Clasped hands. *N*.5	3000	12500
766	'Oath-taking' type. Bust r. or l. with hand placed against cross. R. Lyre-shaped object, or eight-rayed symbol. *N*.6	2000	8000
767	'Two emperors' type. Helmeted bust r. R. Bust of angel with wings above two facing heads. *M*. 79-80	950	3500

768A   769   771

		F	VF
		£	£
768	'Pada', Type Ia. Helmeted bust r. ℞. Runic PADA on panel. *M.p.73.*	1100	4000
768A	— Type Ib. Similar. ℞. Standard TTXX, PADA in runes in legend. *M. 81*	850	2750
769	— Type IIa. bust r. ℞. PADA in runes in field, blundered legend around,		
	M.p.73.	525	1650
769A	— Type IIb. Similar. ℞. Cross on steps in double beaded border............	900	3000
770	— Type III. bust r. ℞. Cross with annulets in angles, legend		
	includes runic PADA and other lettering *M.p.73.*	750	2250
771	'Vanimundus', Type A. bust r. holding sceptre. ℞. Cross, with		
	CA in lower angles. VANIMVNDVS MONE. *M.p.82*	1250	4500
772	— Type B. Similar. ℞. Small cross in double circle of dots. *M. 84*..........	750	2500

SILVER

773

SCEATTA COINAGE, *c*. 675 – *c*. 760
A.   EARLY TRANSITIONAL TYPES BY THRYMSA MONEYERS, c.675 – c.685

773	'Pada', Type III. As 770, but silver. *Abr. 1, M. 82, M. p. 73-9*	300	950
774	'Vanimundus', Type B. As 772, but silver. *Abr. 2, M. 85-7. M. p. 80-4* ..	325	1000

B.   PRIMARY PHASE, *c*. 680 – *c*. 710
Minted in various regions of south-eastern and eastern England.

775

775	**Series A 2a**. Radiate bust r., TIC. ℞. Standard, TOTII. Several varieties. *Abr. 3* 90	325

776   777

776	**Series BX**. Diademed bust r., VANTAVMA or similar. ℞. Bird r. above cross on		
	steps, annulets and pellets in field vary. *Abr. 15, B.M.C. 26. M. 97-9, M. p. 99*	110	375
777	**Series BI**. Diademed head r. within serpent circle. ℞. Bird r. on cross. Some with		
	symbols by bird. *Abr. 16, B.M.C. 27a. M. 100-106, M. 113-16*	50	175

777A: varieties   778

	F £	VF £

777A Series BIIIA, Type 27a. Diademed head r. with either protruding jaw or pointed nose, symbols before, serpent circle. R. Full bodied or linear bird on cross within serpent circle, annulets either side, pellets below. *Abr. 16.70-80, M. p. 158-65 `*. **75   275**

778 Series BZ. Abstract facing head. R. Simplified bird on cross in linear style, blundered legend. *Abr. 17, BMC 29a, M. 138-9. M. p. 136-7* **175   650**

779 C1   779 C2

779 Series C. Radiate bust r., similar to 775 but runic ᚠᛗᚳᚠ replaces TIC. R. Variety C1, standard, TOTII; variety C2, four crosses around standard, variety C2, cross abuts standard. *Abr. 4, B.M.C. 2b. M. 117-125, 132-2. M. P. 106-13* **50   175**

780   781

780 Attributed to King Aethelred of Mercia (674-704). Degenerate head. R. 'Æthiliræd' in runes in two lines. *Abr. 92, M. 134-5, M. p. 120-4* **250   800**

781 Series F. Bust r., with pelleted helmet, blundered legend. R. Small cross on steps, arrangement of surrounding annulets and letters "T" and "I" varies, as do styles. *Abr. 106, M. 136-7, M. p. 125-32* **70   250**

782: various styles

782 Series Z. Broad facing portrait (Christ?) with forked or straight beard. R. Hound running r., legs straight or crossed, tail curled beneath or above, erect ears sometimes with chevrons above, various styles known. Some coarse. *Abr. 102.10-60, BMC 66, M. 140-2, M. p. 137-8* **375   1250**

782A   783

782A Series Z-related. Skeletal hound r., perhaps copy of 782. R. Saltire standard or cross-crosslet design, various styles known. *Abr. 102.70-80, M. 143-4, M. p. 138-9*.. **200   750**

783 'Vernus' group, Types 2b, 3b and 91. Degenerate head r., VER before, execution deteriorates in later issues. R. Standard, various styles known. *Abr. 6, M. 146-8, M. p. 140-6* **75   275**

784   785   786

		F	VF
		£	£

784   **'Saroaldo'**, Type 11. Bust r. becoming increasingly stylized R. Pseudo-legend
        SAROALDO(?) around standard. Some with FIT/RV inscribed (rare) or with saltire and
        pellets, various styles. *Abr. 7, M. 151-3, M. p. 147-51*   135   575
785   **'Stepped cross'**, Type 53. Degenerate 'porcupine' head. R. Stepped cross,
        annulet at centre. *Abr. 91, M. 258-62, M. p. 140, M. p. 243-5*   65   225
786   **'SEDE'**. Type 89. Quilled serpent, pellet in mouth, coiled around cross.
        R. Small central saltire, S E D E in angles with saltires between.
        Abr. 93, M. 263, M. p. 682   350   1350

787: various styles

787   **Series W**. Half- to full-length figure, head r., holding long cross pommée or
        annulet cross either side. R. Cross crosslet on saltire. *Abr. 108, BMC 54,*
        M. 155, M. p. 152-7   325   1200

788: Series W related

788   **Series W related**. Monogram (Marseilles?) or monster l. looking back R.
        Cross crosslet on saltire. *Abr. 53*   150   525

C.   CONTINENTAL ISSUES, *c*. 695 – *c*. 740

Most Continental sceattas emanate from the former Rhine mouth area, Frisia, particularly
the emporia of Domburg and Dorestad. The obverse motif of Series E, commonly
referred to as the "porcupine", is now recognized as a degenerate diademed bust. Series
D bust takes English Series C as its prototype retaining the runic inscription ÆPA.

790   790A *VICO*

790   **Series E**. Degenerate head enclosing three bars. R Votive standard
        with TOTII design, various styles. *Abr. 94*   35   110
790A   —, **'Vico' type**. Degenerate head enclosing bars. R. 'Standard' with letters possibly
        reading VIC (*wic*, emporium) around central annulet. *Abr. 88, M. p. 211-16*   40   120

790B   790C   791

		F	VF
		£	£

790B —, variety D. Degenerate head, various symbols in field. R. 'Standard' with four
pellets around central annulet. *Dorestad. Abr. 90, M. 209-11.* 35 110

790C —, variety E. Degenerate head. R. 'Standard' with four lines and central annulet.
Abr. 89, M. p. 216-19 .... 35 100

790D Later issues. Degenerate head. Innumerable varieties. R. 'Standard'.
Abr. 94-97, M. 214-53, M. p. 222-42. .... 35 100

791 —, plumed bird, usually r. R. Standard with a variety of symmetrical geometric
symbols. *Abr. 87, M. 190-3, M. p.206-11* 50 175

792   792 var.

792 **Series D**, Type 2c. Bust r. (types with bust l. are possibly English
and imitative), runic ÆPA before bust. R. Plain cross with pellets in angles,
pseudo-letters around. *Abr. 8, M. 158-80, M. p. 184-90.* 45 150

793   794

		F	VF
		£	£

793   — Type 8. Crude standard with angular symbols. R. central cross pommée,
pellets in angles. *Abr. 10, M. 183-6, M. p. 191-5* .... | 40 | 125
A variety has a wheel device in standard, R. Bifurcated cross, chevrons above.

794   Type 10. Degenerate bust r., runic AEPA or APA. R. Profile 'moon' face,
blundered legend. *Abr. 9, M. p.248* .... | 150 | 575

795   796

795   **Interlace Cross Type** (formerly 'Maastricht' Type). Crude head l. or r. R.
Quatrefoil interlaced cross. Some coins possibly English. *Abr. 60, M. 265-6,
M. p. 258-60* .... | 125 | 450

796   **'Hexagon' Type** (formerly 'Herstal' Type and possibly a Denier).
Hexagram enclosing central cross. R. Unbalanced radial arrangement, cross
near centre and sometimes above. *Abr. 109, M. 325-8,* M. p. 256-8 .... | 120 | 450

797   797 (cruder style)

797   **Series X**. Facing 'Wodan' head, of various styles. R. Crested monster r. or l.,
tail raised to mouth, claws below, prominent member, die mark below jaw.
Ribe, Jutland, M. 275-81, M. p. 275-86, same cruder style possibly English.
Abr. 103-4, M. 282, M. p. 286-3 .... | 175 | 650

D.   SECONDARY PHASE, *c.* 710 – *c.* 760

Die duplication is the exception in this coinage, with a substantial variation of execution and
fabric within each type. It is assumed that quality deteriorates over time and late issues may
be of more interest monetarily than aesthetically. This coinage was issued in all the main
regions of southern and eastern England. Some boundaries between Series remain indistinct
e.g. K and L, C and R.

800 varieties

800   **Series G**, Type 3a. Diademed bust r., heavenward gaze, cross before. R. Standard
with 3 or 4 saltires. *Abr. 21, M. 267-70, M. p. 266-72* .... | 75 | 250

		F £	VF £
801	**Series H ('Hamwic')**, Type 39. Pecking bird. ℞. Celtic cross. *Abr. 46, M. 283-4, M. p. 324-5*	135	475
801A	— Type 49. 'Wodan' head, 5-11 bosses around. ℞. Pecking bird in various styles. *Abr. 48, M. 285-8, M. p. 325-32.*	175	650
801B	— Type 48. Whorl of 3 wolf heads. ℞. Celtic cross. *Abr. 47, M. 289-92, M. p. 333-40*	125	450

802	**Series J ('York')**, Type 85. Large diademed head r. ℞. Outline bird on cross. *Abr. 18.20, M. 293-5, M. p. 345-50*	65	225
802A	— Type 37. Two diademed heads face-to-face. ℞. Four birds clockwise around cross. *Abr. 19.30, M. 296-300, M. p. 351-3*	85	325
802B	— Type 60. Diademed head r. ℞. Two serpents coiled clockwise with beaded bodies, heads central. *Abr. 18.10, M. p. 354-5*	250	850

| 802C | — Type 72. Two diademed heads face-to-face. ℞. Bird r., looking back at serpent. *Abr. 19.10-20, M. 303, M. p. 355-6.* One variety has bird looking forward | 120 | 400 |
| 802D | — Type 36. Diademed bust r., cross before. ℞. Two birds. *Abr. 20.10-30, M. 301-2, M. p. 361-4* .... | 100 | 325 |

803	**Series K ('Kent')**, Type 33. Diademed bust r., cross before. ℞. Wolf's head with long tongue, l. or r. *Abr. 38, M. 306, M. p. 388-91*	140	525
803A	— Type 42. Diademed bust r. with bird, cross or flower. ℞. Hound l. looking back, plant behind, various styles. *Abr. 41, M. 311-3, M. p. 391-5*	135	500
803B	— Type 75. Roulette wheel of 11 compartments . ℞. Hound l. looking back, plant behind. *Abr. 41.50*	275	1000

803C

	F	*VF*
	£	£

803C — Type 32a. Bust r. with cross before, cupped in hand. ℞. Wolf curled
head to tail or wolf headed serpent. *Abr. 39, M. 309, 310, M. p. 395-402*   140   525

803D

803D — — Similar. ℞. Wolf-headed serpent r. or l. *Abr. 40, M. 310, M. p. 400*   150   550

803E: Series K, Type 20   obv var.

803E — Type 20. Bust r. cross or chalice before. ℞. Standing figure in crescent boat
holding cross and hawk. *Abr. 33, M. 314-18, M. p. 402-5*.......................... 100   375

803F

803F — Type 16. Bust r. floral scroll before. ℞. Standing figure in crescent boat
holding cross and hawk. *Abr. 33.80, M. 314-18, M. p. 402-5*................... 135   525

804   804C   804D

804   **Series L ('London'),** Type 12. Bust r., LVNDONIA. ℞. Standing figure in
crescent boat holding two crosses. *Abr. 23, M. 319-22 M. p. 409-11* 200   750

804A — Type 13. Similar. ℞. Seated figure holding hawk and cross. *Abr. 23.20,
M. p. 409* 375   1500

804B — Type 14. Similar, but bust l. ℞. Celtic cross. (as S.822). *Abr. 27.10, M. p. 427* 325   1250

804C — Type 15. Diademed bust r. with cross, no legend. ℞. Standing figure
holding two crosses. *Abr. 35.20, M. 323-6* 125   450

804D — Type 16. Bust r. with floral scroll before. ℞. Standing figure holding
two crosses. *Abr. 35.40, M. 329-30*... 125   450

804E — Type 17. Bust l. with long cross before. ℞. Standing figure holding two
crosses. *Abr. 36* 135   525

804F　804G　804H

	F £	VF £
804F — Type 18. Diademed bust l. or r. with chalice and sometimes cross above. R. Standing figure in crescent boat holding cross and bird. *Abr. 33.10-30, M. 331-3*	110	400
804G — Type 19. Diademed bust l. or r., long cross before. R. Standing figure in crescent boat holding cross and bird. *Abr. 33.40-80, 100-110, M. 335 ....*	135	525
804H — Type 23e. Standing figure holding two long crosses. R. Whorl of 3 wolf heads. *Abr. 43, M. 359-62 M. p. 451-2*	125	450

805

805	**Series M**, Type 45. Sinuous animal r. R. Spiral vine. *Abr. 61, M. 363-6, M. p. 453-8*	150	575

806: type 41a　type 41b

806	**Series N**, Type 41. Two standing figures, one or both looking across or facing. R. Crested monster r. or l., looking back, claws beneath, tail raised, pellet outline. *Abr. 52, M. 368-72, M. p. 459-69.*	90	325

807

807	**Series O**, Type 38. Bust r. blundered legend or cable border. R. Bird r. in torc. *Abr. 58, M. 373-5, M. p. 470-2*	135	525
807A	— Type 21. Similar, but peg-nosed bust l. R. Standing figure with two crosses. *Abr. 59, M. 376, M. p. 472-4*	200	750

807B

807C   807D various

	F £	VF £

807B — Type 40. Standing figure holding two long crosses. R. Monster l. looking
back, curled tail and foreleg raised, claw beneath, "feathered" coat below.
Abr. 55, M. 379-81, M. p. 477-81, 490. 110   450

807C — Type 57. Peg-nosed bust r. in cable border. R. Monster looking back r.
or l. curled tail and foreleg raised, claw beneath, "feathered" coat below.
Abr. 54, M. 377, M. p. 474-5.. 150   575

807D — Type 40 variety. Monster r., looking back, tail and crest raised, foreleg
raised behind head. R. Elaborate beaded standard in beaded circle, outer linear
border with annulets or standard, votive or beaded. *Abr. 57, M. p. 490* ... 175   650

808

808   **Series Q**, variety IA-D. Two Standing figures with long crosses. R. Monster r. or l.,
looking back, crest raised or lowered, tail raised, claws below, several varieties.
Abr. 63.10-40, M. p. 488, 489, 491. 200   750

808A   808B

808A —, variety IE, Type 67. Diademed bust r., cross before. R. Walking bird l.,
pellets in field. *Abr. 63.50-70, M. 383, M. p. 490-1* 175   650

808B —, variety IF, Type 71. Standing facing figure with two crosses. R. Walking bird l.,
pellets in field. *Abr. 63.80, M. 384.* 275   1000

808C   808D

808C —, variety IG, Type 95. Facing head. R. Long-legged quadruped looking
back, crest intertwines legs, tail raised. *Abr. 63.100-110, M. p. 492.* 300   1100

808D —, variety IH. Half-length profile figure holding cross r. R. Long-legged
quadruped looking back, crest raised, tail intertwines legs. *Abr. 63.90,
M. 385, M. p. 492*.. 275   1000

809

		F	VF
		£	£

809   —, variety II. Quadruped l. or r., tail intertwines legs. R. Bird l. wings spread,
cross by wing. *Abr. 64, M. p. 494*   200   750

810

810   —, variety III. Quadruped l or r. with tail ending with triquetra. R. Bird l. or r.
often with triquetra. *Abr.65, M. p. 496*..   200   750

811

811   — variety IV. Bird or lion r. or l. R. Bird or lion r. or l. *Abr. 66, M. p. 499, 501*   175   650

812 mules of Series R and Q   812 Q/R mule

812   **Series R and Q** MULES, Type 73. Crude radiate bust r. or l. blundered runes.
R. Quadruped or bird r. *M. 388, M.p.496-8 & 518*, vars. R/Q and Q/R mules.
Abr. 12, 67,..   110   400

813 (R1)   813 (R3)   813 (R4)

813   **Series R**. Varieties R1-R6, bust r. on pyramidal neck. Epa in runes, sometimes
retrograde. R. Standard, various angular symbols in and around. *Abr. 11,
M. 391-428, M. p. 507-14*   60   200

813A: Series R7, Spi   813A: Series R10, Wigræd   813A: Series R11, Tilbeorht

813A   —, varieties R7-R12, Head r. or l. with no neck. Spi, Wigræd or Tilbeorht in
runes r. or l. R. Standard with angular symbols. *Abr. 11, M. 391-428,
M. p. 514-23*   65   225

814   815

	F £	VF £
814 **Series S**, Type 47. Female centaur 1. Palm fronds either side, tail beaded or linear, with or without finial. R. Whorl of 4 wolf heads, beaded tongues meet in centre. *Abr. 68, M. 438-41, M. p. 537-44*	175	600
815 **Series T**, Type 9. Diademed bust r., +LEL or + TΛNVM. R. Degenerate 'porcupine' head l or r. *Abr. 25, M. 442-4, M. p. 545-51*	200	750

816 varieties

816 **Series U**, Type 23. Standing figure facing or profile in crescent boat holding two crosses. R. Pecking bird in vine. *Abr. 45, M. 445-52, M. p. 552-569.*......	185	675

817

817 **Series V**, Type 7. Wolf and twins. R. Bird in stalks of wheat. *Abr. 62, M. 453, M. p. 570-5.*..	250	950

E.   **ECLECTIC SCEATTAS, *c*. 710 – *c*. 760**

Included here are groups of types, related often by a common reverse motif (Triquetras, Celtic cross, interlace, saltire, annulet cross groups and Type 70) that do not easily fit into the main alphabetical classification, even though there may be some features in common with or derived from the types therein. There are numerous 'mules' in this coinage, typically imitative combinations of known obverse and reverse types. Only a few of these are included.

820: C ARIP group, some varieties

820 **'Carip' group**. Bust r., CARIP, often blundered. R. include pecking bird, wolf-serpent, or standing figure. *Abr. 26, M. 336-40, M. p. 416-21*	150	575

821: Triquetras group

	F	*VF*
	£	£

821   **'Triquetras' group**. Man and crosses, winged figure, facing bust, or pecking
bird. R. Interlaced cross with triquetra terminals, rosettes or pellets between.
Abr. 110, M. p. 422-5.   225   850

822: Celtic cross group, some obverse varieties

822: Celtic cross group, some reverse varieties

822   **'Celtic Cross' group**. Bust r. or l. with or without legend, cross or sprig
(34a(828A)) before; one or two standing figure(s) with long crosses, cross in
torc, wolf-worm or pecking bird. R. Celtic cross, void or with superimposed
pellet cross or cross pattée, rosettes in angles. *Abr. 27-31, M. p. 426-32.*   200   750

823: Rosette type, various styles

823   **'Rosette'**, Type 68, Series L-related. Bust r., one or two rosettes in field. R.
Standing figure usually with two crosses. *Abr. 32.30-50, M. 347, M. p. 433-4*   175   650

823A

823A   — Type 32b. Bust l. rosettes in field. R. Wolf-serpent within torc. *Abr. 32.10-20,*
M. 307-8, M. p. 433-4   225   850

824:Monita Scorum type   824A

824   **'(Monita) Scorum' type**. Bust r., MONITA SCORVM. R. Degenerate 'porcupine'
head l., figure with two crosses, or triquetra cross. *Abr. 24, M. p. 435-6.*   400   1500

824A   — . Bust r., DE LVNDONIA. R. porcupine l., SCORVM. *Abr. 24.50, 25.50,*
M. p. 436   375   1350

826: Hen type

	F	VF
	£	£

825   **'Archer' group**. Kneeling archer r. R. Large bird (swan?) on branch r. or l.,
looking back. *Abr. 50*, *M. 349*, *M. p. 437-9*   675   2500

826   **'Hen' type**. Hen r. or l. R. Large bird (swan?) on branch r. or l. looking back
and biting berries. *Abr. 51*   450   1750

827: Victory group

827   **'Victory'** Type 22. Victory standing with wreath. R. Standing figure
holding two crosses, winged figure in crescent boat, or diademed bust.
Abr. 111, *M. 350-1*, *M. p. 440-3*   300   1250

828: K/N group

828   **K/N related group**. Standing figure with two long crosses. R. Monster of Type
41 r. or l. looking back. *Abr. 37*, *M. p. 445*.   150   575

829: Animal mask group

829   **'Animal mask' group**. Facing animal (feline?) with erect ears. R. Standing
figure with bird and cross, bird with cross before, segmented circle or monster.
Abr. 112, *M. 354-6* , *M. p. 446-8*   400   1500

830: K/R mule

830   **K/R mule**. Wolf worm curled r. or l. R. Standard with annulet cross or
central Annulet. *Abr. 42*, *M. p. 449*   125   450

831: Type 43

831   — Type 43. Monster of Type 40, l. looking back. R. Interlace cross.
(See also S.795.) *Abr. 54-58*, *M. p. 482*   250   900

832: Fledgling type   833: Saltire standard group, varieties

	F	VF
	£	£

832   **'Fledgling' type**. Type 33 wolf head r. R. Running fledgling with fish in mouth. Style degenerates to linear style. *Abr. 44*   600   2250

833   **'Saltire Standard' types**. Two standing figures or bust l. or r.. R. Saltire and pellets in square. *Abr. 13.80-90, M. 432-5, M. p. 530-2*   110   400

833A: Saltire standard group, geometric reverses   833B: Saltire standard group, Type 70

833A   'Saltire Standard' geometric types. Double croix ancrée or annulet cross. R. Saltire and pellets in square. *Abr. 13.150, 14.110-120, M. 432-5, M. p. 530-2*   100   350

833B   **Saltire-standard and geometric symbols**, Type 70. Many varieties, typically base. R. Standard. *Abr. 13.160-170, M. 436-7, M. p. 532-4*   60   225

834: Annulets group: some varieties

834   **'Annulet cross' types**. Bust r. or l. with runic legend, 'Wodan' face, coiled serpent or saltire cross. R. Annulet cross. *Abr. 14, M. p. 534-6*   175   600

835: 'Wodan' head varieties

835   **'Wodan' Head**, Type 30. Facing 'Wodan' head various styles some coarse. R. Two standing figures, standard or Series N, type 41 monster r. *Abr. 105, M. 429-31, M. p. 527-30*...   250   800

836: Flying monster type

836   **'Flying Monster'**. Monster in flight r. or l., looking back, tail erect. R. Swan-like bird r. or l., looking back, alternate with groups of pellets on limbs of central cross fourchée. *Abr. 107*   225   800

KINGS OF NORTHUMBRIA AND ARCHBISHOPS OF YORK

The issues associated with pre-Viking Northumbria comprise the York group of gold Shillings c. 630-80 (S.762-763), followed by silver sceattas which became increasingly debased after c. 810, becoming a copper alloy coin referred to as a Styca. There are two special presentation issues, Eanred's broad Penny and Wigmund's gold *Solidus,* for neither of which is there yet evidence of monetary use within the kingdom.

The stycas developed in two phases, becoming a robust currency of small-denomination coins, which seem to have been of great practical use. Production may have ceased early in Osberht's reign, although the old money may have continued in circulation until the Viking capture of York in 867. The official styca coinage, however, does appear to have been overwhelmed by irregular issues, which may reflect a period of civil war during the years c. 843 to c. 855.

James Booth's classification of the silver Sceatta coinage of the eighth century is used here, with newly discovered types and variants added ('Sceattas in Northumbria' in Hill and Metcalf, *Sceattas in England and on the Continent, BAR* 128 (1984), pp.71-111, and 'Coinage and Northumbrian History: c. 790-c. 810, in D.M. Metcalf, *Coinage in ninth-century Northumbria, BAR* 180 (1987), pp.57-90).

For the styca coinage of the *ninth-century* Elizabeth Pirie provides an indispensable illustrated corpus of the known material in her *Coins of the Kingdom of Northumbria c. 700-867,* 1996. Her classification is however over-complex for practical use, and several aspects of it, including her division of the coins of Aethelred II between his two reigns, have not been accepted by other scholars. The division here is that which is customarily adopted in volumes in the SCBI series. Moneyers' names are shown as they appear on the coinage.

Further reading: See SCBI 68, Lyon, C.S.S., *The Lyon Collection of Anglo-Saxon Coins* (2016). The introduction to this, sections 2 and 3, provides a useful up to date assessment of the Northumbrian Sceatta and Styca coinage along with illustrations of coins in the Lyon collection; Bude, R., *The joint coinage of Ecgberht and Eadberht of Northumbria,* in BNJ 86, 2016.

SILVER SCEATTA COINAGE - A: REGAL ISSUES

846: Aldfrith

846   **Aldfrith** (685-705). ALðFRIDVS in semi-uncial lettering around central boss. Ꞃ. Lion(?) l. triple tail above. *Abr. 69*   375   1250

847 vars classes

847   **Eadberht** (737-758). Classes A-F. Small cross (mainly). Ꞃ. Stylized stag, to l. or r., various ornaments. *Abr. 70*   110   400

848

	F £	VF £

848   **Aethelwald Moll** (759-765) ΛD+ELΛΑΓDRE (A and R inverted) around
      central boss. R. His son ΛEDILRED+R (second R reversed), around central
      cross. *Abr. 77*   4250   13500

849   850   851

849   **Alchred** (765-774). Small cross. R. Stylized stag to l. or r., cross below. *Abr. 71.*   275   900
850   **Aethelred I** (first reign, 774-779/80). R. Stylized stag to l. or r., triquetra
      below. *Abr. 72*.   400   1500
851   **Aelfwald I** (779/80-788). R. Stylized stag to l. or r., various ornaments,
      Abr. 73   425   1600

SILVER SCEATTA COINAGE - B: JOINT ISSUES BY KINGS OF NORTHUMBRIA AND ARCHBISHOPS OF YORK

852   854   855

852   **Eadberht** with **Abp. Ecgberht** (737-758). Small cross. R. Mitred figure
      holding two crosses. *Abr.74*   175   650
853   **Aethelwald Moll** with **Abp. Ecgberht** (759-765). Cross each side. *Abr.76*   2000   7500
854   **Alchred** with **Abp. Ecgberht** (765-766). Cross each side. *Abr. 74*   275   900
855   **Aethelred I,** with **Abp. Eanbald I** (*c.* 779-780). Various motifs. *Abr. 78*   275   900

SILVER SCEATTA COINAGE - C: REGAL ISSUES WITH NAMED MONEYERS

856

856   **Aethelred I** (second reign, 789-796). R. CEOLBALD, CVDHEARD, HNIFVLA,
      TIDVVLF, central motifs vary. *Abr.80, 82-84*   110   375

857 858

		F	VF
		£	£
857	– Base metal. R. 'Shrine', "CVDCLS" (the moneyer Cuthgils)	375	1350
858	**Eardwulf** (first reign, 796-806). R. Small cross, CVDHEARD	1500	6000

SPECIAL ISSUES

863A

861A	**Eanred,** *c*. 830. Æ *penny*. Bust right. R. Cross, part moline part crosslet	7500	32500
863A	**Abp. Wigmund** (837-849/50). Aʹ *solidus*. Facing bust. R. Cross in wreath	45000	200000

STYCA COINAGE - A: BASE SILVER REGAL ISSUES, *c*. 810 – *c*. 830

859

859	**Aelfwald II** (806-808). R. Small cross, CVDhEARD	450	1750

860

860	**Eanred** (810-841 (total reign)). R. CVDhEARD, CYNVVLF, DAEGBERCT, EADVINI,EDILECH, HERREÐ, [HEARDVVLF, correctly VVLFHEARD], HVAETRED, TIDVINI, VILHEAH, VVLFHEARD, various central motifs	45	175

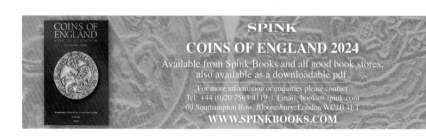

STYCA COINAGE - B: BASE SILVER ARCHIEPISCOPAL ISSUES, *c.* 830 – *c.* 867

861

		F £	VF £
861	**Abp. Eanbald II** (796-835 (total tenure)). R. EODWVLF or EDILWEARD	60	225

STYCA COINAGE - C: COPPER ALLOY REGAL ISSUES, *c.* 810 – *c.* 830

862

| 862 | **Eanred.** R. ALDATES, BADIGILS, BROD(E)R, FORDRED, FVLCNOD, MONNE, ODILO, W(D)IHTRED, VVLFRED, various central motifs | 40 | 125 |

865

| 865 | **Aethelred II** (first reign, 841-843/4), R. ALGHERE, BRODER, COENRED, CVNEMVND, EANRED, FORDRED, HVNLAF, LEOFDEGN, MONNE, ODILO, VENDELBERHT, W(D)IHTRED, VVLFRED, VVLFSIG , various central motifs .... | 40 | 125 |

866: varieties

| 866 | – Leofdegn's 'Special' motifs, R. Hound 1., LEOFDEGN .... | 525 | 1850 |

866A

| 866A | –various elaborate cruciform central devices, LEOFDEGN .... | 85 | 275 |

867   868   869

867	**Redwulf** (843/4). R. ALGHERE, BROTHER, COENRED, CVDBEREhT, EANRED, FORDRED, HVAETNOD, MONNE	90	300
868	**Aethelred II** (second reign 843/4-849/50), R. EANVVLF, EARDVVLF, FORDRED, MONNE, ODILO, VVLFRED	40	125
869	**Osberht** (849/50-867). R. EANVVLF, EDELHELM, MONNE, VINIBERHT, VVLFSIXT, VVLFRED	60	225

STYCA COINAGE - D: COPPER ALLOY ARCHIEPISCOPAL ISSUES, *c.* 830 – *c.* 867

870   871

		F £	VF £
870	**Abp. Wigmund** (837-849/50). R. COENRED, EDELHELM, EDILVEARD, HVNLAF	40	135
871	**Abp. Wulfhere** (849/50-900). R. VVLFRED	110	400

STYCA COINAGE - E: IRREGULAR ISSUES IN COPPER ALLOY, *c.* 843/4 – *c.* 855

872	**Irregular Issues** (*c*.843/4-*c*.855). Various types; legends blundered.....	30	120

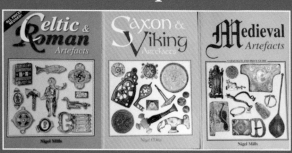

In the kingdom of the Franks a reformed coinage of good quality *deniers* struck on broad flans had been introduced by Pepin in 755 and continued by his son Charlemagne and his descendants. A new coinage of *pennies* of similar size and weighing about 20 grains (1.3 gms) was introduced into England, probably by Offa (757-96), the powerful king of Mercia, c.780, though early pennies also exist of two little known kings of Kent, Heaberht and Ecgberht, of about the same period.

The silver penny (*Lat.* 'denarius', hence the *d.* of our *£ s. d.*) remained virtually the sole denomination of English coinage for almost five centuries, with the rare exception of occasional gold coins and the somewhat less rare silver halfpence. The penny reached a weight of 24 grains (c.1.55g), i.e., a 'pennyweight' during the reign of Alfred the Great. Silver pennies of this period normally bear the ruler's name, though not always his portrait, and the name of the moneyer responsible for their manufacture.

Pennies were issued by various rulers of the Heptarchy for the kingdoms of Kent, Mercia, East Anglia, Wessex and by the Danish settlers in the Danelaw and the Hiberno-Norse kings of York, and also by the Archbishops of Canterbury and a Bishop of London. Under Eadgar, who became the sole ruler of England, a uniform coinage was instituted throughout the country, and it was he who set the pattern for the 'reformed' coinage of the later Anglo-Saxon and Norman period.

Halfpence were issued by most rulers from the time of Alfred until the reform of Eadgar, c.871-973 for southern England, and although all are rare today, it is probable that reasonable quantities were made.

Nos. 873-1378 are all silver pennies except where stated.

NB. Many pennies of the early part of this period have chipped flans and prices should be reduced accordingly.

Further Reading: R. Naismith, *The Coinage of Southern England 796-865*, 2011; C.E. Blunt, B.H.I.H. Stewart & C.S.S. Lyon, *Coinage in Tenth-century England: From Edward the Elder to Edgar's Reform*, 1989.

KINGS OF KENT

874   875

876   877

		F	VF
		£	£
873	**Heaberht** (*c.* 765). Monogram for REX. R̃. Five annulets, each containing a pellet, joined to form a cross	12500	40000
874	**Ecgberht** (*c.* 780). Similar. R̃. Varied	2000	6750
875	**Eadberht Praen.** Type 1. (796-798). As illustration. R̃. Varied	1850	6500
875A	— Type 2. (*c.* 798). His name around, Ϻ in centre, R̃. Moneyer's name in angles of a tribrach	2000	7000
876	**Cuthred** (798-807). *Canterbury.* Various types without portrait	950	3500
877	— — Portrait. R̃. Cross and wedges or A	1350	4750

878

880 881

		F	*VF*
		£	£
878	**Anonymous** (*c*. 822-823). *Canterbury*. As illustration or 'Baldred' style head	1350	5000
879	**Baldred** (*c*. 823-825). *Canterbury*. diademed head r. ℞. DRVR CITS within		
	inner circle	1850	6500
880	— Cross each side	1100	3750
881	*Rochester*. Bust r. ℞. Cross moline or wheel design	1750	6000

ARCHBISHOPS OF CANTERBURY

882

881A	**Jaenberht** (765-792). New type (early). Under Ecgberht II of Kent (?). (before *c*. 780 ?) His name around small cross of pellets in centre. ℞. PONTIFEX in three lines	2000	6500
882	Under Offa of Mercia (*c*. 780-792) His name around central ornament or cross and wedges. ℞. OFFA REX in two lines	1250	4500
883	— His name in three lines. ℞. OFFA or OFFA REX between the limbs of Celtic cross	1350	4750
884	**Aethelheard** (el. 792, cons. 793, d. 805). With Offa as overlord. First issue (792-?), with title *Pontifex*...	1100	4250

885 886

885	— Second issue (?-796), with title *Archiepiscopus*	900	3500
885A	— Third issue (*c*. 796-798), with title *Archiepiscopus*. His name and AR around EP in centre. ℞. Moneyer's name, EADGAR or CIOLHARD.....	1100	4250
886	— With Coenwulf as overlord. (798-800 ?) Fourth Issue. As last. ℞. King's name in the angles of a tribrach	950	3750

886A   887   888 (rev.)

		F	VF
		£	£
886A	— Fifth issue (*c.* 798-805?). As last R. Coenwulf's name around Ⓜ in centre	825	3250
887	**Wulfred** (805-832). group I (805-*c.* 810). As illustration. R. Crosslet, alpha-omega........................	1250	4500
888	— Group II (*c.* 810). As last. R. DOROVERNIA C monogram	1100	4000
889	— Group III (pre- 823). Bust extends to edge of coin. R. As last	950	3750
890	— Groups IV and V (*c.* 822-823). Anonymous under Ecgberht. Moneyer's name in place of the Archbishop's. R. DOROBERNIA CIVITAS in three or five lines	1350	5000
891	— Group VI (*c.* 823-825). Baldred type. Crude portrait. R. DRVR CITS in two lines........................	1500	5500
892	— Group VII (*c.* 832). Second monogram (Ecgberht) type. Crude portrait r., PLFRED. R. DORIB C. Monogram as 1035	1500	5500

893   894

893	**Ceolnoth** (833-870). Group I with name CIALNOD. Tonsured bust facing. R. Varied	900	3250
894	— Group II. Similar but CEOLNOD. R. inscribed cross	1000	3750
894A	— —. O. as last, R. as 1054, cross fleury over floreate cross	1500	6000

895   896

895	— Group III. Diad. bust r. R. Moneyer's name in and between lunettes .	1350	5250
896	**Aethelred** (870-889). Bust r. R. As illustration or with long cross with lozenge panel	2750	10500
897	— Cross pattée. R. ELF / STAN.................................	1500	6000

898 900

		F	VF
		£	£
898	**Plegmund** (890-914). DORO in circle. R. As illustration above, various moneyers	1100	4000
899	— Similar, but title EPISC, and XDF in centre	1250	4500
900	— Small cross pattée. R. moneyers name in two lines	950	3500
901	— Crosses moline and pommée on *obv.*	1250	4500
901A	— Halfpenny. As 900	1500	6000

KINGS OF MERCIA

Until 825 Canterbury was the principal mint of the Kings of Mercia and some moneyers also struck coins for the Kings of Kent and Archbishops of Canterbury.

GOLD

902 903

902	**Offa** (757-796). Gold *dinar*. Copy of Arabic dinar of Caliph Al Mansur, dated 157 A.H. (A.D. 774), with OFFA REX added on *rev.*	175000	750000
903	Gold *penny*. Bust r., moneyer's name. R. Standing figure, moneyer's name	45000	200000

A copy of a solidus with a diademed bust appears to read CIOLHEARD and is probably Mercian of this or the following reign.
For further information see: *The Coinage of Offa and his Contemporaries* by Derek Chick, 2010.

SILVER

904 905

904	**Offa** (757-796). Light Coinage. (*c.* 780?-792) *London and Canterbury.* Various types without portraits. Small flans	575	1750
905	— (*c.* 780?-792) *London and Canterbury.* Various types with portraits. Small flans.	1100	3750

906   908

		F	VF
		£	£
906	— East Anglia. Various types with portraits. R. Some with runic letters, small flans	1250	4250
907	— — Various types without portraits. R. often with runic letters, small flans	675	2250
908	Heavy Coinage (*c.* 792-796) *London, Canterbury and East Anglia.* Various types without portraits, large flans.	650	2000

909   911

909	**Cynethryth** (wife of Offa). Coins as light coinage of Offa. With bust as illustration	2750	9500
910	— O. without bust, as rev. of last, R, moneyers name on cross of lobes, usually EOBA	2000	7000
911	**Eadberht** (Bishop of London, died 787/789). EADBERHT EP in three lines or ADBERHT in two lines within a beaded rectangle, EP below. R. various with name of Offa	1100	4500

912   912A

912	**Coenwulf, King of Mercia** (796-821). Gold *penny* or *Mancus* of 30 pence. London, diademed bust of Coenwulf right, finely drawn with four horizontal lines on the shoulders	65000	250000
912A	Penny Group I (796-805). *London.* Without portrait, three line inscription. R. Varied	675	2250
913	— *Canterbury.* Name around ᛗ as illus. below. R. Moneyer's name in two lines	800	2500

914   915

914	— *Both mints.* Tribrach type	525	1500
915	— Group II (*c.* 805-810). *Canterbury.* With portrait. Small flans. R. Varied but usually cross and wedges	750	2500

916

919

		F	VF
		£	£
916	— Groups III and IV (*c*. 810-820). *Canterbury*. Similar but larger flans. ℞. Varied	800	2750
917	— *Rochester*. Large diad. bust of coarse style. ℞. Varied. (Moneyers: Dun, Ealhstan)	850	3000
918	— *London*. With portrait generally of Roman style. ℞. Crosslet	950	3500
919	— *E. Anglia*. Crude diad. bust r. ℞. Moneyer's name LVL on leaves in arms of cross	750	2500
920	— — *O*. as last. ℞. Various types	725	2400

921

927

921	**Ceolwulf I** (821-823). *Canterbury*. Group I. Bust r. ℞. Varied. (Moneyers: Oba, Sigestef)	1750	6500
922	— — Group II. *London*. Crosslet. ℞. Varied	1100	4500
923	— — Group III. Tall cross with MERCIORV̄. ℞. Crosslet. SIGESTEF DOROBERNIA	1250	4750
924	— *Rochester*. Group I. Bust r. ℞. Varied	1350	5250
925	— — Group IIA. As last but head r.	1350	5250
926	— — Group IIB. Ecclesiastical issue by Bp. of Rochester. With mint name, DOROBREBIA, but no moneyer	1650	6000
927	— *East Anglia*. Crude style and lettering with coarse portrait. ℞. Varied	1100	4500

928

929

928	**Beornwulf** (823-825). Group I. *East Anglia*. Bust r. ℞. Moneyer's name in three lines	1750	6500
929	— Group II. *East Anglia* or *London*. ℞. Cross crosslet in centre	1500	6000
929A	— — *London*. Alpha-Omega monogram. ℞. As 929	1850	7000
930	Group III. *East Anglia*. Similar to 928 but moneyer's name in two lines with crosses between	1750	6500
931	**Ludica** (825-827). *East Anglia*. Bust r. ℞. Moneyer's name in three lines as 928	7500	30000

932   932A

		F	VF
		£	£
932	— Similar. *East Anglia*. R̃. Moneyer's name around cross crosslet in centre, as 929	8000	32500
932A	*London*. Diademed bust r. R. LUNDONIA CIVIT in three lines.	8500	35000

933

| 933 | **Wiglaf,** first reign (827-829). *London*. Crude head r. R̃. Crosslet | 5000 | 17500 |

934   935

934	Second reign (830-840). *London*. Cross and pellets, or ⚡ R̃. Moneyer's name in three lines or between lunettes of pellets	2250	8500
935	**Berhtwulf** (840-852). Various types with bust	1750	7000
936	— without bust	1350	5500
937	As before. R̃. IAETHELWLF REX. cross pommée over cross pattée (crude die copying on obverse of Aethelwulf of Wessex)	1250	5000

938 (rev. A)   939A   939B

938	**Burgred (852-874)** Ia, 852-c.855, bust r, looks up, almond eye, r. A (MacKay P1)	800	3000
939A	Ib, c.855-c.858-60, bust r, coarse style, annulet or almond eye, two panel or triangular tunic, r. A, C, D, (MacKay P2, P4)	500	1500
939B	— — bust r, pellet in almond eye, low shoulders, high neck r. A, C (MacKay P3)	575	1750

		940C
940A (rev. D)	940B (rev. C)	

	F	VF
	£	£

940A IIa, c.858/60-c.866, bust r, almond eye, neat bust, lips sometimes omitted,
r. A, C, D (MacKay H1, H2) 400 1100
940B — —, bust r, as Aethelberht of Wessex Floreate type (S.1054), often six pellets
below neck, some coarse r. C (MacKay H3-H4: coarse,H5) 750 2250
940C — —, bust r, coarse style, large annulet eye, outward wedge lips,
r. A, C, D (MacKay V1) 500 1500

941A	941B	942A

941A IIb, c.866-868/70, bust r, various styles incl. with large annulet eye, ill-
proportioned bust, realistic pointed nose narrow tunic, r. A, C, D (MacKay H6-8) 350 950
941B — —, bust r, outward or upward wedge lips, steeply angled diadem, various
styles, incl. with wide tunic, double inner-circle, narrow diameter i.c, r. D
(MacKay V2-4) 375 1000
942A III, c.868/70-874, bust r, pellet eye, diadem cuts across eye, r. A, D (MacKay H10) 350 950

942B	942C	942D (rev. B)

942B — —, bust r, crescent below pellet eye, r. A, D (MacKay H11).............. 350 950
942C — —, bust r, pellet eye, small crescent above and below, r. A, often with six
pellets in one angle (MacKay H12) 325 900
942D — —, bust r, rather crude, steeply pitched diadem, outward or upward wedge
lips, r. A (MacKay V5) 300 850

Reverse types most commonly found are listed above; type A, closed lunettes (commonly found); B, open at base and top (very rare); C, open at sides (rare); D, 'crooks' without lunettes semi-circles (scarce); E, as D with large M symbol added above and below dividing legend (very rare).
Prices for Lunettes types can vary with rare types worth more than commoner types.

Lunette A ....*from*	300	850
Lunette B ....*from*	750	2250
Lunette C ....*from*	400	1100
Lunette D..*from*	350	950
Lunette E ....*from*	1350	4500

For further reading see; *MacKay, The Coinage of Burgred 852-874,* BNJ 85, 2015, pp 101-237.

			F	VF
			£	£
943	**Ceolwulf II** (874-*c*. 880). Bust r. ℞. Two emperors seated. Victory above		6750	27500

944

944	— ℞. Moneyer's name in angles of long cross with lozenge centre	1750	7500
944A	— Halfpenny, similar to 944	3500	12500

KINGS OF EAST ANGLIA

945   947

945	**Beonna,** King of East Anglia, *c*. 758. Æ sceat. Pellet in centre, Runic inscription. ℞. EFE in Roman characters around saltire cross. *Abr.113.10*	1000	3500
945A	— Similar. ℞. WILRED or WERFERTH in runic around pellet or cross. *Abr. 113.20-30*..................	1100	3750
945B	— Similar. ℞. Interlace pattern (large flans). *Abr.113.40*	2250	8500
945C	**Alberht** (749-?). Pellet in centre, AETHELBERT (runic) around ℞. Rosette in circle, TIAELRED (runic) around. *Abr. 114*............................	5750	22500
946	**Aethelberht** (d. 794). bust r. ℞. wolf and twins	11000	40000
946A	— King's name EDILBERHT around cross and pellets. ℞. Lozenge intersecting large cross fourchée, LVL in angles.............................	7250	27500
947	**Eadwald** (*c*. 798). King's name in three lines. ℞. Moneyer's name in quatrefoil, around cross or tribrach...	1350	5250
947A	— King's name around cross or Ϣ in centre. ℞. Moneyer's name in quartrefoil	1500	6000

949   950 (obv,)   951

948	**Aethelstan I** (*c*. 825-840). Bust r. or l. ℞. Crosslet or star	1750	6750
949	Bust r. ℞. Moneyer's name in three or four lines.....................................	1750	6750
950	Alpha or A. ℞. Varied..	675	2500
951	*O*. and *rev*. Cross with or without wedges or pellets in angles	675	2500
952	— Similar, with king's name both sides	800	3000
952A	Name around ship in centre. ℞. Moneyer Eadgar, around cross of pellets or in two lines (Possibly the earliest of his coins.)	6750	27500

953 954

	F £	VF £
953 **Aethelweard** (*c.* 840-*c.* 855), A, Omega or cross and crescents. ℞. Cross with pellets or wedges	1100	4500
954 **Edmund** (855-870). Alpha or A. ℞. Cross with pellets or wedges	525	1500
955 — *O*. Varied. ℞. Similar...	525	1500

For the St. Edmund coins and the Danish issues struck in East Anglia bearing the name of Aethelred I, see Danish East Anglia.

ANGLO-VIKING COINAGES *c.* 885-954

DANISH EAST ANGLIA, *c.* 885-915

Following the treaty of Wedmore in 880 the Viking invaders were ceded control of Eastern Mercia including all territory east of Watling street. Coinage issued in this area after 880 initially imitated Wessex types of Alfred. Independent coinages were struck from early 880s in East Anglia, the east midlands and Northumbria.

956 **Aethelstan II** Guthrum (878-890), Cross pattée. ℞. Moneyer's name in two lines..	2250	8500
957 **Oswald** (unknown except from his coins). Alpha or A. ℞. Cross pattée..	2750	12500
958 — Copy of Carolingian 'temple' type. ℞ Cross and pellets	2750	12500
959 **Aethelred** (*c.*870). As last, with name Aethelred. ℞. As last, or cross-crosslet	2250	8500
959A — As 954	1850	7500

Oswald and Aethelred, both unattested historically, are thought to be East Anglian kings in the period after the death of Eadmund in 870 before Guthrum took control of the East Anglia c.880.

960 962

960 **St. Edmund,** memorial coinage, Æ *penny,* type as illus. above, various legends of good style	225	575
961 — Similar, but barbarous or semi-barbarous legends...............................	200	550
962 *Halfpenny*. Similar	950	3750
963 **St. Martin of Lincoln.** Sword dividing legend. ℞. Cross in voided cross. LINCOI A CIVIT.	4250	15000

SOUTHERN DANELAW *c.* **880-910**

965   970

		F £	VF £
964	**Alfred.** Imitation of London Monogram types- see 1061, 1062, some very barbarous, bust usually right, R. *Londonia* monogram (wt. c.1.2-1.4g) ..	2250	8500
964A	— Similar, crude bust, blundered legends, R. *Lincolla* or *Roiseng* monogram (possibly an official issue, Chester?)	4250	15000
965	— Similar to 1062, with moneyer's name (Aelfstan, Heawulf, Herewulf, Heremod, Winurdal)	3500	12500
966	— Imitation of two line types (1066, 1069), small cross, R. some read REX DORO	650	1750
967	— Similar. R. 'St. Edmund type' A in centre..	950	3500
968	— Imitation of Two Emperors type, as 943 and 964	4500	15000
969	*Halfpenny.* Imitation of London Monogram types - see 1063..................	1350	5250
970	— Imitation of two line types	950	3500

971   975

971	— Imitation of Oxford type, as 1071A, ELFRED between ORSNA and FORDA, R. Moneyer's name in two lines (sometimes divided by horizontal long cross)	800	2750
972	— *Halfpenny.* Similar, of very crude appearance	950	3500
973	**Alfred/Archbishop Plegmund.** *Obv.* ELFRED REX PLEGN	2000	7500
974	**Archbishop Plegmund.** Imitative of two line type, as 900	850	2750
975	**Earl Sihtric.** Type as 971. SCELDFOR between GVNDI BERTVS. R SITRIC COMES in two lines	6750	25000

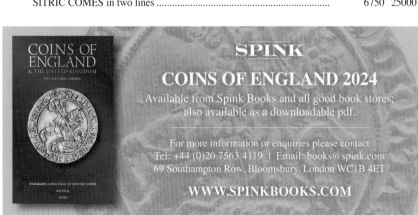

COINAGES OF THE VIKING KINGDOM OF YORK, *c.* 895-920

References are to 'The Classification of Northumbrian Viking Coins in the Cuerdale hoard', by
C. S. S. Lyon and B. H. I. H. Stewart, in Numismatic Chronicle, 1964, p. 281 ff.

		F	VF
		£	£
975A	**Guthfrith.** GV DE F. RE Small cross. ℞. Moneyer's name in two lines.	5000	17500
976	**Siefred.** C. SIEFRE DIIS REX in two lines. ℞. EBRAICE CIVITAS (or		
	contractions), small cross. *L. & S. Ia, Ie, Ii*	675	2500
977	— Cross on steps between. ℞. As last. *L. & S. If, Ij*	1000	3500
978	— Long cross. ℞. As last. *L. & S. Ik*	750	2750

979

980

984

979	SIEFREDVS REX, cross crosslet within legend. ℞. As last. *L. & S. Ih...*	575	2000
980	SIEVERT REX, cross crosslet to edge of coin. ℞. As last. *L. & S. Ic, Ig, Im*	525	1850
981	— Cross on steps between. ℞. As last. *L. & S. Il*	850	3000
982	— Patriarchal cross. ℞. DNS DS REX, small cross. *L. & S. Va*	525	1850
983	— — ℞. MIRABILIA FECIT, small cross. *L. & S. VIb*	750	2750
984	REX, at ends of cross crosslet. ℞. SIEFREDVS, small cross. *L. & S. IIIa, b*	575	2000
985	— Long cross. ℞. As last. *L. & S. IIIc*	525	1850
986	*Halfpenny.* Types as 977, *L. & S. Ib;* 980, *Ic;* and 983, *VIb*	1100	3750
987	**Cnut.** CNVT REX, cross crosslet to edge of coin. ℞. EBRAICE CIVITAS,		
	small cross. *L. & S. Io, Iq*	500	1750
988	— — ℞. CVNNETTI, small cross. *L. & S. IIc*	475	1500

989

993

989	— Long cross. ℞. EBRAICE CIVITAS, small cross. *L. & S. Id, In, Ir....*	325	1100
990	— — ℞. CVNNETTI, small cross. *L. & S. IIa, IId*	250	750
991	— Patriarchal cross. ℞. EBRAICE CIVITAS, small cross. *L. & S. Ip, Is*	240	700
992	— — ℞.— *Karolus* monogram in centre. *L. & S . It*	1000	3500
993	— — ℞. CVNNETTI, small cross. *L. & S. IIb, IIe*	225	675

995   998

		F	VF
		£	£
994	*Halfpenny.* Types as 987, *L. & S. Iq; 989, Id; 991, Is; 992, Iu; 993, IIb and e*	900	2750
995	*Halfpenny.* As 992, but CVNNETTI around *Karolus* monogram. *L. & S. IIf*	1000	3500
996	**Cnut and/or Siefred.** CNVT REX, patriarchal cross. ℞. SIEFREDVS, small cross. *L. & S. IIId*	575	2000
997	— — ℞. DNS DS REX, small cross. *L. & S. Vc.*	525	1850

1000   1002

998	— — ℞. MIRABILIA FECIT. *L. & S. VId*	425	1350
999	EBRAICE C, patriarchal cross. ℞. DNS DS REX, small cross. *L. & S. Vb*	575	2000
1000	— — ℞. MIRABILIA FECIT. *L. & S. VIc*	425	1350
1001	DNS DS REX in two lines. ℞. ALVALDVS, small cross. *L. & S. IVa*	1750	6500
1002	DNS DS O REX, similar. ℞. MIRABILIA FECIT. *L. & S. VIa*	575	2000
1003	*Halfpenny.* As last. *L. & S. VIa*	950	3000

1004   1006

1004	**'Cnut'.** Name blundered around cross pattée with extended limbs. ℞. QVENTOVICI around small cross. *L. & S. VII*	1250	4000
1005	*Halfpenny.* Similar. *L. & S. VII*	1100	3500
1006	**St. Peter coinage,** *c.* 905-915. Swordless type. Early issues. SCI PETRI MO in two lines. ℞. Cross pattée	475	1500
1007	— similar. ℞. 'Karolus' monogram	1250	4000
1008	*Halfpenny.* Similar. ℞. Cross pattée	1100	3500

1009

		F £	VF £

1009 **Regnald** (blundered types). RAIENALT, head to l. or r. Ŗ. EARICE CT,
'Karolus' monogram 5750 20000

1010

1010	— Open hand. Ŗ. Similar	2500	9000
1011	— Hammer. Ŗ. Bow and arrow	2750	10500
1012	Anonymous Ŗ. Sword..	1750	6000

ENGLISH COINS OF THE HIBERNO-NORSE VIKINGS OF YORK *c.* 919-954

1015

1016

EARLY PERIOD, *c.* 919-925

1013	**Sihtric** (921-927). SITRIC REX, sword. Ŗ. cross, hammer, mallet or T (Lincoln)	3750	12500
1014	**St. Peter coinage.** Sword type. Late issues SCI PETRI MO, sword and hammer. Ŗ. EBORACEI, cross and pellets	1350	4500
1015	— Similar. Ŗ. Voided hammer..	1500	5500
1016	— Similar. Ŗ. Solid hammer..	1650	6000

St. Peter coins with blundered legends are rather cheaper.

LATER PERIOD, 939-954 (after the battle of Brunanburh, 937). Mostly struck at York.

1017	**Anlaf Guthfrithsson,** 939-941. Flower type. Small cross, ANLAF REX TO D. Ŗ. Flower above moneyer's name	5250	18500
1018	— Circumscription type, with small cross each side, ANLAF CVNVNC, M in field on reverse *(Derby)*	3500	13500
1018A	— Two line type. ONLAF REX. Large letter both sides *(Lincoln?)*........	2750	12500

1019   1020

	F	VF
	£	£
1019 — Raven type. As illustration, ANLAF CVNVNC	2250	9000
1020 **Anlaf Sihtricsson,** first reign, 941-944. Triquetra type, ANLAF CVNVNC. R. Danish standard	2250	8500

1021   1022

1021 — Circumscription type (a). Small cross each side, ANLAF CVNVNC, R. MONETR	2500	9500
1022 — Cross moline type, ANLAF CVNVN C. R. Small cross	2250	8500

1024

1023 — Two line type. Small cross. R. ONLAF REX. R. Name in two lines	2500	9500
1024 **Regnald Guthfrithsson,** 943-944. Triquetra type. As 1020. REGNALD CVNVNC	4750	17500
1025 — Cross moline type. As 1022, but REGNALD CVNVNC	4500	16500
1026 **Sihtric Sihtricsson,** c. 942. Triquetra type. As 1020, SITRIC CVNVNC	2750	12500
1027 — Circumscription type. Small cross each side	2750	12500

1027A

1027A **Anonymous?** Two line type. Small cross ELTANGERHT. R. RERNART in two lines	1100	4000
1028 **Eric Blood-Axe,** first reign, 948. Two line type. Small cross, ERICVC REX A; ERIC REX AL; or ERIC REX EFOR. R. Name in two lines	8500	32500

	F £	VF £
1029 **Anlaf Sihtricsson,** second reign, 948-952. Circumscription type (b). Small cross each side, ONLAF REX, R. MONE.............	2250	8500
1029A — Flower type. small cross ANLAF REX R. Flower above moneyer's name..........	3500	13500
1029B — Two line type. Small cross, ONLAF REX. R. Moneyer's name in two lines..........	2500	9500

1030

1030 **Eric Blood-Axe,** second reign, 952-954. Sword type. ERIC REX in two lines, sword between. R. Small cross	13500	47500

For more on the Anglo-Viking Coinages - see Blackburn M.A.S., *Viking Coinage in the British Isles (Spink 2011)*

KINGS OF WESSEX, 786-924

BEORHTRIC, 786-802
Beorhtric was dependent on Offa of Mercia and married a daughter of Offa.

1031

	F	VF
1031 As illustration..........	10000	40000
1032 Alpha and omega in centre. R. Omega in centre	9500	37500

ECGBERHT, 802-839
King of Wessex only, 802-825; then also of Kent, Sussex, Surrey, Essex and East Anglia, 825-839, and of Mercia also, 829-830.

1035

1033 *Canterbury.* Group I. Diad. hd. r. within inner circle. R. Various.............	2000	7000
1034 — II. Non-portrait types. R. Various	1500	5750
1035 — III. Bust r. breaking inner circle. R. DORIB C	1750	6500
1036 *London.* Cross potent. R. LVN / DONIA / CIVIT	2750	10000
1037 — — R. REDMVND MONE around TA..........	1750	6500
1037A — — R. REDMVND in three lines..........	2500	9000

1041

		F	VF
		£	£
1038	*Rochester,* royal mint. Non-portrait types with king's name ECGBEO RHT	1500	5750
1039	— — Portrait types, ECGBEORHT	1750	6500
1040	*Rochester,* bishop's mint. Bust r. ℞. SCS ANDREAS (APOSTOLVS)....	2250	8000
1041	*Winchester.* SAXON monogram or SAXONIORVM in three lines. ℞. Cross	1850	6250

AETHELWULF, 839-858

Son of Ecgberht; sub-King of Essex, Kent, Surrey and Sussex, 825-839; King of all southern England, 839-855; King of Essex, Kent and Sussex only, 855-858. No coins are known of his son Aethelbald who ruled over Wessex proper, 855-860.

1043   1045

1047

1042	*Canterbury.* Phase I (839-c. 843). Head within inner circle. ℞. Various. *Br. 3*	1100	4000
1043	— — Larger bust breaking inner circle. ℞. A. *Br. 1 and 2*	1200	4250
1044	— — Cross and wedges. ℞. SAXONIORVM in three lines in centre. *Br. 10*	750	2750
1045	— — Similar, but OCCIDENTALIVM in place of moneyer. *Br. 11*	850	3000
1046	— Phase II (*c.* 843-848?). Cross and wedges. ℞. Various, but chiefly a form of cross or a large A. *Br. 4*	725	2500
1047	— — New portrait, somewhat as 1043. ℞. As last. *Br. 7*	1100	4000
1048	— — Smaller portrait. ℞. As last, with *Chi/Rho* monogram. *Br. 7*	1200	4250

1049   1051

	F	VF
	£	£
1049 — Phase III (*c.* 848/851-*c.* 855). DORIB in centre. ℞. CANT mon. *Br. 5*	700	2500
1050 — — CANT mon. ℞. CAN M in angles of cross. *Br. 6*	900	3250
1051 — Phase IV (*c.* 855-859). Mostly Canterbury rarely Rochester. New neat style bust ℞. Large voided long cross. *Br. 8*	975	3500
1052 *Winchester.* SAXON mon. ℞. Cross and wedges. *Br. 9*	1050	3750

AETHELBERHT, 858-865

Son of Aethelwulf; sub-King of Kent, Essex and Sussex, 858-860; King of all southern England, 860-865/6.

1053   1053A (rev.)

1053 Bust r., ℞ large voided long cross. Mostly Canterbury, also known for Rochester	975	3500
1053A *O.* As 1053, ℞ large cross pattée	1500	6000

1054

1054 *O.* Diad. bust r., ℞. Cross fleury over floreate cross	1350	5250

Son of Aethelwulf; succeeded his brother Aethelberht.

1055

		F	*VF*
		£	£
1055	As illustration, Wessex Lunettes, Canterbury, usually with bonnet ...	1000	3500
1055A	— —, London obv. dies in style as Burgred	1100	4000
1056	Similar, but moneyer's name in four lines, Canterbury or Winchester	1350	5500

For another coin with the name Aethelred see 959 under Viking coinages.
For further reading see: *Lyons & MacKay,* BNJ 2007

ALFRED THE GREAT, 871-899

Brother and successor to Aethelred, Alfred had to contend with invading Danish armies for much of his reign. In 878 he and Guthrum the Dane divided the country, with Alfred holding all England south and west of Watling Street. Alfred asserted over-lordship of Mercia and London from c.880.

Types with portraits

1057   1058   1061

1057	As illustration, Wessex Lunettes, Canterbury, bust with bonnet. r. ℞. As Aethelred I. *Br. 1 (name often AELBRED)*	1350	4250
1057A	— —, London obv. dies in style as Burgred	1500	4500
1058	— ℞. Long cross with lozenge centre, as 944, *Br. 5*	2250	9500
1059	— ℞. Two seated figures, as 943. *Br. 2*	8500	30000
1060	— ℞. As Archbp. Aethered; cross within large quatrefoil. *Br. 3*	6250	22500

1062   1063

1061	*London.* Various busts. ℞. LONDONIA monogram, moneyer not named	3500	12500
	For contemporary Viking copies see 964.		
1062	— ℞. Similar, but with moneyer's name (Tilewine) added	4000	13500
1063	— *Halfpenny.* Bust r. or rarely l. ℞. LONDONIA monogram as 1061	1750	6500
1064	*Gloucester.* ℞. Æ GLEAPA in angles of three limbed cross....................	9500	35000

	F	VF
	£	£

Types without portraits

1065 King's name on limbs of cross, trefoils in angles. R. Moneyer's name in quatrefoil. *Br. 4.* 4750 17500

1066   1067

1066 Various styles, Cross pattée, legend in four parts. R. Moneyer's name in two lines. *Br. 6* 750 2000

1067 — As last, legend in three parts. R as Edward the Elder, 1087 .... 800 2250

1068 — *Halfpenny.* As 1066.. 1100 4000

1069

1069 *Canterbury.* As last but DORO added on *obv. Br. 6a* 900 2500

1070 *Exeter?* King name in four lines. R. EXA vertical 6500 22500

1071 *Winchester?* Similar to last, but PIN... 6500 22500

1071A *Oxford.* Elfred between OHSNA and FORDA. R. Moneyer's name in two lines (much commoner as a Viking Imitation - see 971) 1250 4000

1072 'Offering penny'. Very large and heavy. AELFRED REX SAXORVM in four lines. R. ELIMO in two lines i.e. (*Elimosina*, alms)........................ 13500 52500

For other pieces bearing the name of Alfred see under the Viking coinages.

For further reading see: *Lyons & MacKay, The Lunettes Coinage of Alfred the Great* BNJ 2008.

EDWARD THE ELDER, 899-924

Edward, the son of Alfred, aided by his sister Aethelflaed 'Lady of the Mericians', annexed all England south of the Humber and built many new fortified boroughs to protect the kingdom.

Rare types

1074

1073 *Br. 1. Bath?* R. BA... 3500 12500

1074 — *2. Canterbury.* Cross moline on cross pommée. R. Moneyer's name . 2000 6500

	F	VF
	£	£
1075 — 3. *Chester?* Small cross. ℞. Minster	5000	17500
1076 — 4. — Small cross. ℞. Moneyer's name in single line..........................	1500	5000
1077 — 5. — ℞. Two stars	2500	9500

1078   1079

| 1078 — 6. — ℞. Flower above central line, name below .... | 3750 | 12500 |

1081   1083

1079 — 7. — ℞. Floral design with name across field....................................	4000	13500
1080 — 8. — ℞. Bird holding twig	6000	22500
1081 — 9. — ℞. Hand of Providence, several varieties...................................	5000	17500
1082 — 10. — ℞. City gate of Roman style..	2750	10000
1083 — 11. — ℞. Anglo-Saxon burg...	2500	9500

Ordinary types

1084   1087

1084 *Br. 12.* Bust l. var. styles ℞. Moneyer's name in two lines	1100	4250
1086 — 12a. Similar, but bust r. of crude style	1350	5250
1087 — 13. Small cross. ℞. Moneyers name in two lines.................................	325	950
1087A — — As last, but in *gold*	35000	150000
1088 **Halfpenny.** Similar to 1087	1350	5000
1088A — — ℞. Hand of Providence...	1850	6750

Imitations of the types of Edward the Elder were also struck in the Danelaw territories. They are usually of lighter weight and coarser execution than the official Wessex issues of Edward the Elder.

AETHELSTAN, 924-939

Aethelstan, the eldest son of Edward, completed the re-conquest of territories controlled by the Danes with the capture of York in 927. He decreed that money should be coined only in a borough, that every borough should have one moneyer and that some of the more important boroughs should have more than one moneyer.

1089   1093

		F	VF
		£	£
1089	**Main issues.** Small cross. ℞. Moneyer's name in two lines..........	475	1350
1090	Diad. bust r. ℞. As last	1350	5000
1091	— ℞. Small cross	1250	4500
1092	Small cross both sides...	525	1750
1093	— Similar, but mint name added	625	2000
1094	Crowned bust r. As illustration. ℞. Small cross	1000	3750

1095   1100

1095	— Similar, but mint name added	1250	4250
1096	**Local Issues.** *N. Mercian mints.* Star between two pellets. ℞. As 1089...	1250	4250
1097	— Small cross. ℞. Floral ornaments above and below moneyer's name .	1500	5500
1098	— Rosette of pellets each side...................................	550	1850
1099	— Small cross one side, rosette on the other side	650	2000
1100	*N.E. mints.* Small cross. ℞. Tower over moneyer's name............	1750	6500

1102

1101	Similar, but mint name added	1850	7000
1102	— Bust in high relief r. or l. ℞. Small cross.......................	1350	4750
1103	— Bust r. in high relief. ℞. Cross-crosslet	1350	4750
1104	'Helmeted' bust or head r. ℞. As last or small cross	1000	3500
1104A	**Halfpenny.** Small cross or floral lozenge. ℞. Moneyer's name in two lines .	1250	4500

Eadmund was a half brother of Aethelstan. At the start of his reign he lost the kingdom of York and faced renewed Viking incursions into North East England; however, by the end of his reign he had regained control of those territories.

1105   1106

1107   1111

1112

		F £	VF £
1105	Small cross, rosette or annulet. ℞. Moneyer's name in two lines with crosses or rosettes between	400	1200
1106	Crowned bust r. ℞. Small cross	1250	4500
1107	Similar, but with mint name	1350	4750
1108	Small cross either side, or rosette on one side	675	2250
1109	Cross of five pellets. ℞. Moneyer's name in two lines	575	1850
1110	Small cross. ℞. Flower above name	1750	6500
1111	'Helmeted' bust r. ℞. Cross-crosslet	1250	4500
1112	**Halfpenny**. small cross, ℞. Moneyer's name in two lines or one line between rosettes	1200	4250
1112A	— Flower. ℞. As 1105	1350	5000

Eadred was another of the sons of Edward. He faced renewed Viking attempts to recover York whose last king, Eric Bloodaxe, he drove out in 954 to finally secure Northumbria for the English.

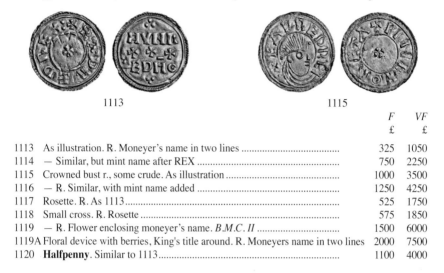

1113   1115

		F £	VF £
1113	As illustration. R. Moneyer's name in two lines	325	1050
1114	— Similar, but mint name after REX	750	2250
1115	Crowned bust r., some crude. As illustration	1000	3500
1116	— R. Similar, with mint name added	1250	4250
1117	Rosette. R. As 1113	525	1750
1118	Small cross. R. Rosette	575	1850
1119	— R. Flower enclosing moneyer's name. *B.M.C. II*	1500	6000
1119A	Floral device with berries, King's title around. R. Moneyers name in two lines	2000	7500
1120	**Halfpenny**. Similar to 1113	1100	4000

HOWEL DDA, d. 949/950

Grandson of Rhodri Mawr, Howel succeeded to the kingdom of Dyfed *c.* 904, to Seisyllog *c.* 920 and became King of Gwynedd and all Wales, 942.

1121

1121	HOᵽÆL REX, small cross or rosette. R. Moneyer's name in two lines ..	17500	60000

EADWIG, 955-959

Elder son of Eadmund, Eadwig lost Mercia and Northumbria to his brother Eadgar in 957.

1122   1123

1122	*Br. 1*. Type as illustration	1000	3000
1123	— — Similar, but mint name in place of crosses	1250	3750

		F	VF
		£	£
1124	— 2. As 1122, but moneyer's name in one line	1500	4500
1125	— 3. Similar. R. Floral design	2000	7500
1126	— 4. Similar. R. Rosette or small cross	1000	3250
1127	— 5. Bust r. R. Small cross	12500	40000

1128

1128	**Halfpenny**. Small cross. R. Flower above moneyer's name	1500	5000
1128A	— Similar. R. PIN (Winchester) across field	1750	5250
1128B	— Star. R. Moneyer's name in two lines	1250	4500

EADGAR, 959-975

King in Mercia and Northumbria from 957; King of all England 959-975. He was crowned King of England at Bath in 973 in the first coronation of an English King. His reign was largely free from Viking invasions, leading him to be given the sobriquet of 'The Peaceful'.

PRE-REFORM COINAGE BEFORE 973
It is now possible on the basis of the lettering to divide up the majority of Eadgar's coins into issues from the following regions: N.E. England, N.W. England, York, East Anglia, Midlands, S.E. England, Southern England, and S.W. England. (See 'Anglo-Saxon Coins', ed. R. H. M. Dolley.)

1129

1129	*Br I*. Small cross. R. Moneyer's name in two lines, crosses between, trefoils top and bottom	275	900
1130	— — R. Similar, but rosettes top and bottom (a N.W. variety)	325	1100
1131	— — R. Similar, but annulets between	325	1100
1132	— — R. Similar, but mint name between (a late N.W. type)	625	1850
1133	— 2. — R. Floral design	1600	5500
1133A	Voided cross, lys in angles, R. cross pattée dividing alpha and omega	1750	5750
1134	— 4. Small cross either side	300	950

1135

		F £	VF £
1135	— — Similar, with mint name...	625	1850

1136   1138

		F	VF
1136	— — Rosette either side...	450	1350
1137	— — Similar, with mint name..	675	2000
1138	— 5. Large bust to r. R. Small cross	1100	3750
1139	— — Similar, with mint name..	1500	5500
1140	**Halfpenny**. (8.5 grains / c.0.6 g)) *Br. 3*. Small cross. R. Flower above name	1100	4000

1140A   1140B

		F	VF
1140A	— — R. Mint name around cross (Chichester, Wilton)	1350	4750
1140B	— Bust r. R. 'Londonia' monogram	1500	5500

For Eadgar 'reform' issues see next page.

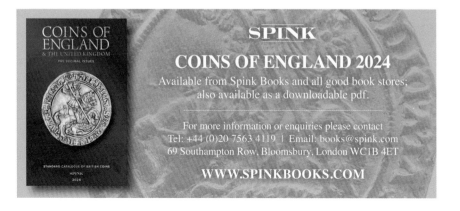

KINGS OF ENGLAND, 973-1066

In 973 Eadgar introduced a new coinage. A royal portrait now became a regular feature and the reverses normally have a cruciform pattern with the name of the mint in addition to that of the moneyer. Most fortified towns of burghal status were allowed a mint, the number of moneyers varying according to their size and importance: some royal manors also had a mint and some moneyers were allowed certain ecclesiastical authorities. In all some seventy locations are recorded with striking coins in this period (see list of mints pp.144-46).

The control of the currency was retained firmly in the hands of the central government, unlike the situation in France and the Empire where feudal barons and bishops controlled their own coinage. Coinage types were changed at intervals to enable the Exchequer to raise revenue from new dies and periodic demonetisation of old coin types helped to maintain the currency in a good state. No halfpence were minted during this period. During the latter part of this era, full pennies were sheared into 'halfpennies' and 'farthings'. They are far rarer than later 'cut' coins.

Further Reading: On the initial reform of the coinage under Eadgar see K. Jonsson, *The NewEra: The Reformation of the Late Anglo-Saxon Coinage* (London: 1987). The nature and purpose of frequent periodic recoinages is explored by I. Stewart, 'Coinage and recoinage after Edgar's reform', in *Studies in Late Anglo-Saxon Coinage*, ed. K. Jonsson (Stockholm: 1990), 455-85. References to individual types for mints and moneyers for much of the first half of the period may be found in K. Jonsson, *Viking Age Hoards and Late Anglo-Saxon Coins* (Stockholm: 1986).

EADGAR, 959-975 *(continued)*

REFORM COINAGE, 973-975

1141

	F	VF
	£	£
1141 **Penny**. Reform Small Cross type. Small diademed bust left. King's name 'Eadgar'. R. Small cross, name of moneyer and mint.............................	1250	4250

EDWARD THE MARTYR, 975-978

The son of Eadgar by his first wife, Æthelflaed, Edward was murdered at Corfe in Dorset.

1142

| 1142 Sole type. As 1141, but reading 'Eadward'... | 1750 | 5750 |

LATE ANGLO-SAXON MINTS (973-1066)

1. Gothabyrig*	16. Cadbury	31. Cricklade	46. Canterbury	61. Ipswich	76. Tamworth
2. Launceston	17. Bruton	32. Oxford	47. Rochester	62. Norwich	77. Derby
3. Lydford	18. Dorchester	33. Wallingford	48. Horndon	63. Thetford	78. Leicester
4. Barnstaple	19. Wareham	34. Reading	49. Southwark	64. Huntingdon	79. Nottingham
5. Totnes	20. Shaftesbury	35. Guildford	50. London	65. Northampton	80. Melton Mowbray
6. Exeter	21. Warminster	36. Chichester	51. Hertford	66. Warwick	81. Stamford
7. Watchet	22. Bath	37. Cissbury	52. Aylesbury	67. Worcester	82. Newark
8. Taunton	23. Bristol	38. Steyning	53. Buckingham	68. Pershore	83. Torksey
9. Langport	24. Berkeley	39. Lewes	54. Newport Pagnell	69. Winchcombe	84. Lincoln
10. Petherton	25. Malmesbury	40. Hastings	55. Bedford	70. Gloucester	85. Horncastle
11. Crewkerne	26. Wilton	41. Romney	56. Cambridge	71. Hereford	86. Caistor
12. Bridport	27. Salisbury	42. Lympne	57. Bury St Edmunds	72. Grantham*	87. York
13. Axbridge	28. Southampton	43. Hythe	58. Sudbury	73. Shrewsbury	88. Wilton. Norfolk*
14. Ilchester	29. Winchester	44. Dover	59. Maldon	74. Chester	89. Frome
15. Miborne Port	30. Bedwyn	45. Sandwich	60. Colchester	75. Stafford	90. Droitwich

*Possible location of uncertain mint

Son of Eadgar by his second wife Ælfthryth, Æthelred ascended the throne on the murder of his half-brother. He is known to posterity as 'The Unready' from 'Unrede', meaning 'without counsel', an epithet gained from the weakness of his royal government. During this reign England was subjected to Viking raids of increasing frequency and strength, and a large amount of tribute was paid in order to secure peace. Large hoards have been found in Scandinavia and the Baltic region and coins are often found peck-marked. There is a high degree of regional variation in the style of dies, particularly in Last Small Cross type, for which readers are advised to consult the following paper: C.S.S. Lyon, *'Die cutting styles in the Last Small Cross issue of c.1009-1017...'*, *BNJ* 68 (1998), 21-41.

1143

1144

	F	VF
	£	£
1143 First Small Cross type. Diademed bust left, usually with three pellets before in field. No line to indicate shoulder. *B.M.C I*	900	3250
1144 First Hand type. Diademed bust right, without sceptre. R. Hand of providence between alpha and omega, issuing from cloud composed of parallel curved or angular lines. *B.M.C IIa*	225	600
1145 — —, similar but bust left. *B.M.C IIb*	750	2750

1146

1147

1146 Second Hand type. Diademed bust right, with sceptre. R. Hand of providence between alpha and omega, issuing from clouds with edges that billow outward. *B.M.C IId*	210	550
1147 Benediction Hand type. *O.* as last. R. Hand gives Latin benediction, fields without alpha and omega. *B.M.C IIf*	1500	5750

1148

1150

1148 Crux type. Bare-headed bust left, with sceptre. R. Voided short cross with letters C, R, V, X, in angles. *B.M.C IIIa*	160	400
1149 Small Crux type. Reduced weight, small flans, sceptre inclined to bust such that the base penetrates drapery.	170	425
1150 Intermediate Small Cross type. RX at end of legend separate letters. *B.M.C I*	900	3000

1151

	F £	VF £
1151 Long Cross type. Bare-headed bust left. R. Voided long cross. *B.M.C IVa*	160	400

1152

1152 Helmet type. Armoured bust left in radiate helmet. *B.M.C VIII*...............	175	475
1153 As last but struck in gold.	45000	175000

1154

1154 Last Small Cross type. Diademed bust left, RX at end of legend ligated together as one letter-form. *B.M.C I*	150	375
1154A — —, similar but bust right..	250	700
1155 — —, similar but bust to edge of coin...	750	2250

1156

1156 Agnus Dei type. As illustration. *B.M.C X*...	9500	30000

Son of King Swein Forkbeard of Denmark, Cnut was acclaimed king by the Danish fleet in England in 1014 but was forced to leave; Cnut returned and harried Wessex in 1015. Æthelred II died in 1016 and resistance to the Danes was continued by his son Eadmund Ironside, for whom no coins are known, but upon the latter's death in 1016 Cnut became undisputed king. The following year Cnut consolidated his position by marrying Emma of Normandy, the widow of Æthelred II.

There is a high degree of regional variation in the style of dies, particularly in Quatrefoil type, for which readers are advised to consult the following paper: M.A.S. Blackburn and C.S.S. Lyon, 'Regional die production in Cnut's Quatrefoil issue' in *Anglo-Saxon Monetary History*, ed. M.A.S. Blackburn (Leicester: 1986), 223-72. Some quatrefoil coins have pellets or a cross added in the obverse or reverse fields. There is considerable weight fluctuation within and between the types.

Substantive types

1157

1158

1159

1160

		F	VF
		£	£
1157	Quatrefoil type (c.1017-23). Crowned bust left. *B.M.C. VIII*	170	425
1158	Pointed Helmet type (1024-1030). *B.M.C. XIV*	160	400
1159	Short Cross type (c.1029-1035/6). *B.M.C. XVI*	150	375
1159A	— —, similar but sceptre replaced with a banner	900	3250

Posthumous type

1160	Jewel Cross type. *B.M.C. XX*, style as 1163 in the name of Cnut.	850	3000

Type considered to have been struck under the auspices of his widow, Queen Emma of Normandy.

Harold was the illegitimate son of Cnut by Ælfgifu of Northampton and was appointed regent on behalf of his half-brother Harthacnut. Queen Emma of Normandy initially held Wessex for her son, Harthacnut, but by 1037 she had been driven from the country and Harold had been recognised as king throughout England. The principal issue was the Jewel Cross type which is also found in the name of Cnut and Harthacnut, cf. nos. 1160 and 1166.

1163   1165

		F	VF
		£	£
1162	Short Cross type (Autumn 1035). As 1159, but in the name of Harold. B.M.C. IIIa	1500	5000
1163	Jewel Cross type (c.1036-38). B.M.C. I	400	1200
1164	Fleur-de-Lis type (1038-40). Armoured and diademed bust left. R. Voided long cross, trefoil of pellets in each angle. B.M.C. V	375	1100
1165	— —, similar but fleur-de-lis between two pellets in each angle. B.M.C. V	350	1050

HARTHACNUT, 1035-1042

Although Harthacnut was the only legitimate son of Cnut and his legitimate heir, the political situation in Denmark prevented him from leaving for England until 1040, by which time Harold had secured the kingdom. Harold's death allowed Harthacnut to reclaim England without bloodshed, but he himself died after two years of sole rule. The main variety of Harthacnut is the Arm and Sceptre type from his sole reign. The Jewel Cross type from the early period is also found in the name of Cnut and Harold I, cf. nos. 1160 and 1163.

EARLY PERIOD (DURING REGENCY) 1035–7

1166	Jewel Cross type. As 1163, but in the name of Harthacnut. Diademed bust left. B.M.C. I	1000	3500

1167

1167	— —, similar but bust right. B.M.C I	950	3250

1168   1169

SOLE REIGN 1040–42

1168	Arm and Sceptre type. King's name given as 'Harthacnut.' Diademed bust left with sceptre in left hand, forearm visible across bust *B.M.C. II*	800	2500
1169	— —, Similar but king's name given as 'Cnut'.	650	1850

1170

1170	**Danish types.** Types exist in the name of Harthacnut other than those listed above and are Scandinavian in origin...	575	1750

EDWARD THE CONFESSOR, 1042-1066

Son of Æthelred II and Emma of Normandy, Edward spent twenty-five years in Normandy before he was adopted into the household of his half-brother Harthacnut in 1040. On the death of Harthacnut, Edward was acclaimed king. He is known by the title 'The Confessor' owing to his piety and he was canonised after his death. There is considerable weight fluctuation within and between the types, which is often unaffected by the smallness of the flan, rather the coin might be thicker to compensate.

Further reading: P. Seaby, 'The sequence of Anglo-Saxon types 1030–1050', *BNJ* 28 (1955-7), 111–46; T. Talvio, 'The design of Edward the Confessor's coins', in *Studies in Late Anglo-Saxon Coinage*, ed. K. Jonsson (Stockholm: 1990), 489–99. A. Freeman. *The Moneyer and the Mint in the Reign of Edward the Confessor: Parts 1 and 2*, (BAR) 1985.

1171   1172 (rev.)

1170A	Arm and Sceptre type (1042). *B.M.C. IIIa*	1500	5250
1171	Pacx type (1042–4). Diademed bust left. R. Voided long cross. *B.M.C. IV*	225	650
1172	— —, Similar but R. voided short cross. *B.M.C. V*..................................	250	750

1173

		F £	*VF* £
1173	Radiate/Small Cross type (1044–6). *B.M.C. I*	175	450

1174   1175

1174	Trefoil Quadrilateral type (1046–8). *B.M.C. III*	200	525
1175	Small flan type (1048–50). *B.M.C. II*	150	400
1176	Expanding Cross type (1050–53). Light issue, small flans; weight approx. 1.10-1.30g. *B.M.C. V*	210	575

1177

1177	— —. Heavy issue, large flans; weight approx. 1.40-1.70g. *B.M.C. V*.....	225	600
1178	— —, Similar but struck in gold	50000	200000

1179

1179	Pointed Helmet type (1053–6). Bearded bust right in pointed helmet. *B.M.C. VII*..	240	625
1180	— —, Similar but bust left.	1100	3500

F	*VF*
£	£

1181

1181 Sovereign/Eagles type (1056–9). King enthroned, holding orb. R. Cross,
eagles in angles *B.M.C. IX*.. 250 650

1182

1182 Hammer Cross type (1059–62). *B.M.C. XI* 200 575

1183

1183 Facing Bust/Small Cross type (1062–5). *B.M.C. XIII* 175 450

1184

1184 Pyramids type (1065–6). *B.M.C. XV* 200 525

1185

1185 Transitional Pyramids type (c.1065). *B.M.C. XIV* 2250 7500

Most York coins of this reign have an annulet in one quarter of the reverse.

Harold was the son of Earl Godwine of Wessex, who had dominated the royal court, and was brother-in-law to Edward the Confessor. Harold successfully repulsed an invasion of Harald Hardrada of Norway, but was himself killed in the Battle of Hastings after a reign of ten months.

Further reading: H. Pagan, 'The coinage of Harold II', in *Studies in Late Anglo-Saxon Coinage*, ed. K. Jonsson (Stockholm: 1990), 177–205.

1186   1187

		F	VF
		£	£
1186	Pax type. Crowned head left with sceptre. R. PAX across field. *B.M.C. I*	1750	5250
1187	— —, Similar but without sceptre. *B.M.C. Ia*	2000	5750
1188	— —, Similar but head right. *B.M.C. Ib*	3750	12500

Cnut, Short Cross type (S.1159) - WULNOTH ON WINC:
moneyer Wulnoth   *mint* Winchester

William, Paxs type (S.1257) - LIFINC ON WINCE
moneyer Lifinc   *mint* Winchester

Old English special letters found on Anglo-Saxon and Norman coins:

Letter	Name	Modern Equivalent
Æ	Ash	E
Ð	Eth	Th
Ϸ (Þ)	Wynn	W

In late Anglo-Saxon and Norman times coins were struck in the King's name at a large number of mints distributed in centres of population, and in times of emergency in places of refuge, across England and Wales. During the 10th century the use of a mint signature was sporadic but from the Reform type of Edgar the mint name is almost invariably given, usually in conjunction with that of the moneyer responsible, e.g. EDGAR ON BERCLE. At the peak, 71 mints struck the quatrefoil type of Cnut and 65 the PAXS type of William I and they provide a valuable insight into the economic and social structures of the period.

The output of the mints varied enormously and a dozen are exceptionally rare. Approximately 100,000 pennies survive, half of which emanate from the great centres of London, Canterbury, Lincoln, Winchester and York. At the other end of the scale a mint such as Rochester is known from about 500 coins, Derby from around 250, Guildford 100, Bedwyn 25, Horncastle 4 and Pershore 1. Many of these coins, particularly those from the great Scandinavian hoards, are in museum collections and are published in the Sylloge of Coins of the British Isles (SCBI) series.

There are too many type and mint combinations, over 1500 Saxon and 1000 Norman, to price each individually and our aim is to give an indication of value for the commonest Saxon and Norman type, in VF condition, for each of the 103 attested mints (excluding Baronial of Stephen's reign), and for a further 10 mints whose location or attribution is uncertain. The threshold VF price for a Norman coin exceeds that for a Saxon coin accounting for the difference in starting level. Prices for coins in lower grade would be less and there is a premium for the rarer types for each mint, but for many types, e.g. in the reigns of Harthacnut or Henry I, the value of the type itself far exceeds that of many of the constituent mints and a scarce mint is only worth a modest premium over a common one.

We also give the most characteristic mint signatures (often found abbreviated) and the reigns for which the mint is known. There are many pitfalls in identifying mints, not least that Saxon and Norman spelling is no more reliable than that of other ages and that late Saxon coins were widely imitated in Scandinavia. There is extensive literature and the specialist in this fascinating series can, for further details, consult J J North, *English Hammered Coinage Vol.1.*

Alf	—	Alfred the Great	Hd1	—	Harold I
EdE	—	Edward the Elder	HCn	—	Harthacnut
A'stn	—	Aethelstan	EdC	—	Edward the Confessor
Edm	—	Edmund	Hd2	—	Harold II
Edw	—	Eadwig	W1	—	William I
Edg	—	Edgar	W2	—	William II
EdM	—	Edward the Martyr	H1	—	Henry I
Ae2	—	Aethelred II	St	—	Stephen
Cn	—	Cnut			

Berkeley   Hastings

	SAXON VF £	NORMAN VF £
Axbridge (AXAN, ACXEPO) Edg, Ae2, Cn, HCn	5000	—
Aylesbury (AEGEL, AEEL), Ae2, Cn, EdC	4000	—
Barnstable (BARD, BEARDA) Edw, Edg, Ae2-Hd1, EdC, W1, St	1500	2000
Bath (BADAN) EdE-A'stn, Edw-EdC, W1-St	450	1200
Bedford (BEDAN, BEDEFOR) Edw-St	600	1000
Bedwyn (BEDEPIN) EdC, W1	2500	4000
Berkeley (BEORC, BERCLE) EdC	9500	—
Bramber (BRAN) St	—	3500
Bridport (BRYDI, BRIPVT) A'stn, Ae2, Cn, HCn, EdC-W1	1500	1750
Bristol (BRICSTO, BRVCSTO) Ae2-St	650	1000
Bruton (BRIVT) Ae2, Cn, HCn, EdC	2500	—
Buckingham (BVCIN) Edg, EdM-Hd1, HCn, EdC	3500	—
Bury St.Edmunds (EDMVN, S.EDM) EdC, W1, H1, St	1750	850
Cadbury (CADANBY) Ae2, Cn	9500	—
Caistor (CASTR, CESTR) EdM, Ae2, Cn.	5000	—
Cambridge (GRANTE) Edg-St	450	1200
Canterbury (DORO, CAENTPA, CNTL) Alf, A'stn, Edr, Edg-St	375	750
Cardiff (CIVRDI, CAIERDI) W1-H1, St, Mat	—	1500
Carlisle (CARD, EDEN) H1, St	—	900
Castle Rising (RISINGE) St (type II-VII)	—	2000
Chester (LEIGE, LEGECE, CESTRE) A'stn, Edm, Edg-St	500	1000
Chichester (CISSAN, CICEST) A'stn, Edg, Ae2-St	500	900
Christchurch (orig. Twynham) (TVEHAM, TPIN) W1, H1	—	3500
Cissbury (SIDESTEB, SIDMES) Ae2, Cn	3500	—
Colchester (COLN, COLECES) Ae2-St	450	900
Crewkerne (CRVCERN) Ae2, Cn, Hd1	3500	—
Cricklade (CROCGL, CRECCELAD, CRIC) Ae2-W2	1750	1750
Derby (DEORBY, DERBI) A'stn, Edm, Edg-St	1750	1750
Dorchester (DORCE, DORECES) Ae2-H1	1250	1500
Dover (DOFERA, DOFRN) A'stn, Edg, Ae2-St	375	900
Droitwich (PICC, PICNEH) EdC, Hd2	5000	—
Dunwich (DVNE) St	—	1500
Durham (DVNE, DVRHAM, DVNHO) W1-St	—	2250
Exeter (EAXA, EAXCESTRE, IEXECE) Alf, A'stn, Edw-St	450	900
Frome (FRO) Cn, HCn, EdC	4000	—
Gloucester (GLEAP, GLEPECE, GLOPEC) Alf, A'stn, Edg-St	500	900
Grantham (GRANTHA, GRE) Ae2	6500	—
Guildford (GYLD, GILDEFRI) EdM-W2	2000	3000
Hastings (HAESTINGPOR, AESTI) Ae2-St	500	1000
Hedon (HEDVN) St	—	4000
Hereford (HEREFOR, HRFRD) A'stn, Edg, Ae2-St	650	1000
Hertford (HEORTF, HRTFI, RET) A'stn, Edw-EdC, W1-H1	400	1500
Horncastle (HORN) EdM, Ae2	7000	—
Horndon (HORNIDVNE) EdC	9500	—
Huntingdon (HVNTEN, HVTD) Edg, Ae2-St	450	1000
Hythe (HIDEN, HIDI) EdC, W1, W2	4500	1750
Ilchester (GIFELCST, GIVELC, IVELCS) Edg, Ae2-St	1000	1750
Ipswich (GIPESWIC, GYPES) Edg-St	500	1000
Langport (LANCPORT, LAGEPOR) A'stn, Cn-EdC	2500	—
Launceston (LANSTF, LANSA, SANCTI STEFANI) Ae2, W1-H1	4500	3000
Leicester (LIHER, LEHRE, LEREC) A'stn, Edg, Ae2-St	600	1000
Lewes (LAEPES, LEPEEI, LAPA) A'stn, Edg-St	500	1000
Lincoln (LINCOLN, NICOLE) Edr, Edg-St	375	750
London (LVNDO, LVNDENE) Alf, A'stn, Edw-St	375	750
Louth (LVDE) Edm, Ae2	7000	—
Lydford (LYDANFOR) Edg-EdC	600	—
Lympne (LIMENE, LIMNA) A'stn, Edg-Cn	900	—
Maldon (MAELDVN, MIEL) A'stn, Edg, Ae2-Hd1, EdC-W2	500	1750
Malmesbury (MALD, MEALDMES, MELME) Edg, Ae2-W2, H1	2000	2500
Marlborough (MAERLEBI) W1, W2	—	5000
Melton Mowbray (MEDELTV) Ae2, Cn	6500	—
Milborne Port (MYLE) Ae2, Cn, EdC	6500	—

| | SAXON | NORMAN |
| | VF | VF |
	£	£
Newark (NEWIR, NIWOR) Edg-Cn	6500	—
Newcastle (CAST) St	—	2000
Newport (NIPANPO, NIPEPORT) Edw, Edg, EdC	4500	—
Northampton (HAMTVN, HMTI, NORHAM) Edw, Edg-St	500	850
Norwich (NORDPIC) A'stn-Edr, Edg-St	375	750
Nottingham (SNOTING) A'stn, Ae2-St	1250	1500
Oxford (OXNA, OCXEN, OXENFO) Alf, A'stn, Edr-St	500	900
Pembroke (PEI, PAN, PAIN) H1, St	—	3500
Pershore (PERESC) EdC	9500	—
Petherton (PEDR, PEDI) Cn, EdC	9000	—
Pevensey (PEFNESE, PEVEN) W1-St	—	2000
Reading (READIN, REDN) EdC	6000	—
Rhuddlan (RVDILI) W1	—	4000
Rochester (ROFEC, ROFSC) A'stn, Edg-H1	500	1500
Romney (RVMED, RVMNE) Ae2-H1	600	1250
Rye (RIE) St	—	3000
Salisbury (SEREB, SEARB, SALEB) Ae2-EdC, W1-St	450	900
Sandwich (SANDPI) EdC, W1-St	600	1250
Shaftesbury (SCEFTESB, CEFT, SAFTE) A'stn, Edg-St	500	900
Shrewsbury (SCROB, SCRVBS, SALOP) A'stn, Edg, Ae2-St	700	1250
Southampton (HAMPIC, HAMTVN) A'stn, Edw-Cn	600	1350
Southwark (SVDBY, SVDGE, SVDPERC) Ae2-St	375	750
Stafford (STAFFO, STAEF) A'stn, Edg, Ae2-Hd1, EdC, W1-St	750	1250
Stamford (STANFORD) Edg-St	375	800
Steyning (STAENIG, STENIC) Cn-W2, St	500	1000
Sudbury (SVDBI, SVBR) Ae2, Cn, EdC, W1-St	700	1000
Swansea (SVENSEI) St	—	3500
Tamworth (TOMPEARÐ, TAMPRÐ) A'stn, Edg-Hd1, EdC, W1-St	2000	2000
Taunton (TANTVNE) Ae2-St	1200	1250
Thetford (ÐEOTFOR, DTF, TETFOR) Edg-St	375	750
Torksey (TVRC, TORC) EdM-Cn	3000	—
Totnes (DARENT, TOTANES, TOTNES) A'stn, Edw-HCn, W2, H1	700	1750
Wallingford (PELINGA, PALLIG) A'stn, Edm, Edg, Ae2-H1	500	900
Wareham (PERHAM, PERI) A'stn, Edg-St	600	1250
Warminster (PORIME) Ae2-Hd1, EdC	3500	—
Warwick (PAERINC, PERPIC, PAR) A'stn (?), Edg-St	900	1250
Watchet (PECED, PICEDI, WACET) Ae2-EdC, W1-St	1750	2000
Wilton (PILTVNE) Edg-St	450	900
Winchcombe (WENCLES, PINCEL, PINCL) Edg, Ae2, Cn, HCn-W1	2500	2000
Winchester (PINTONIA, PINCEST) Alf, A'stn, Edw-St	375	750
Worcester (PIGER, PIHREC, PIREC) EdM, Ae2-St	600	1250
York (EBORACI, EFORPIC, EVERWIC) A'stn, Edm, Edg-St	375	800

Mints of uncertain identification or location

"Brygin" (BRYGIN) Ae2	3500	—
"Dyr/Dernt" (DYR, DERNE, DERNT) EdC (East Anglia)	1750	—
"Weardburh" (PEARDBV) A'stn, Edg	5000	—
Abergavenny (?) (FVNI) W1	—	4000
Gothabyrig (GEODA, GODABYRI, IODA) Ae2-HCn	3000	—
Eye (?) (EI, EIE) St	—	3000
Peterborough (?) (BVRI) W1, St	—	3500
Richmond, Yorks (?) (R1), St (type 1)	—	1750
St Davids (?) (DEVITVN) W1	—	3500
Wilton, Norfolk (?) (PILTV) Ae2 (LSC)	2750	—
Bamborough (BCI, CIB, OBCI) Henry of Northumberland	—	6000
Corbridge (COREB) Henry of Northumberland	—	6500

Aylesbury	Barnstaple	Cricklade	Dunwich
Exeter	Frome	Guildford	Horncastle
Ilchester	London	Milborne Port	Newark
Oxford	Pevensey	Rochester	Stafford

Torksey	Winchcombe	York

1. Launceston	13. Bath	25. Chichester	37. London	49. Huntingdon	61. Rhuddlan
2. Barnstaple	14. Marlborough	26. Steyning	38. Hertford	50. Bedford	62. Chester
3. Totnes	15. Wilton	27. Lewes	39. Maldon	51. Northampton	63. Shrewsbury
4. Exeter	16. Salisbury	28. Pevensey	40. Colchester	52. Warwick	64. Stafford
5. Watchet	17. Christchurch	29. Hastings	41. Ipswich	53. Worcester	65. Tamworth
6. Taunton	18. Abergavenny*	30. Romney	42. Sudbury	54. Winchcombe	66. Leicester
7. Bridport	19. Winchester	31. Hythe	43. Cambridge	55. Oxford	67. Derby
8. Dorchester	20. Bedwyn	32. Dover	44. Bury	56. Gloucester	68. Nottingham
9. Wareham	21. Malmesbury	33. Sandwich	45. Thetford	57. Hereford	69. Lincoln
10. Shaftesbury	22. Cricklade	34. Canterbury	46. Norwich	58. Cardiff	70. York
11. Ilchester	23. Wallingford	35. Rochester	47. Stamford	59. Pembroke	71. Durham
12. Bristol	24. Guildford	36. Southwark	48. Peterborough	60. St Davids*	72. Carlisle

Possible location of uncertain mint

William I maintained the Anglo-Saxon mint system and the practice of conducting frequent periodic recoinages by change of coin type. However, the twelfth-century witnessed a gradual transition from regional to centralised minting. Nearly seventy towns had moneyers operating under William I, but only thirty mint towns took part in the recoinage initiated by the Cross-and-Crosslets ('Tealby') coinage in 1158. Cut halfpennies and cut farthings were made during this period, but are scarce for all types up to BMC 13 of Henry I; cut coins are more frequently encountered for subsequent types.

Further reading: G.C. Brooke, *Catalogue of English Coins in the British Museum. The Norman Kings*, 2 volumes (London, 1916). (Abbr. BMC Norman Kings). I. Stewart, 'The English and Norman mints, c.600–1158', in *A New History of the Royal Mint,* ed. C.E. Challis (Cambridge, 1992), pp. 1–82.

WILLIAM I, 1066-1087

Duke William of Normandy claimed the throne of England on the death of his cousin Edward the Confessor. An important monetary reform occurred towards the close of the reign with the introduction of the *geld de moneta* assessed on boroughs. This may be seen as part of the raft of administrative reforms initiated by William I, which included the compilation of Domesday Book in 1086.

The date of the Paxs type is central to the absolute chronology of this and the subsequent reign. which is now widely accepted.

1250   1251

		F £	VF £
1250	**Penny**. *B.M.C*. 1: Profile left type.	575	1750
1251	*B.M.C*. 2: Bonnet type.	400	1200

1252   1253

1252	*B.M.C*. 3: Canopy type	525	1650
1253	*B.M.C*. 4: Two sceptres type.	450	1350

1254   1255

1254	*B.M.C*. 5: Two stars type.	400	1200
1255	*B.M.C*. 6: Sword type.	450	1350

1256   1257

		F	VF
		£	£
1256	*B.M.C.* 7: Profile right type (lead die struck examples exist from the Thames)	575	1750
1257	*B.M.C.* 8: Paxs type	325	900

WILLIAM II, 1087-1100

Second son of William I was killed while hunting in the New Forest. Five of the thirteen coin types in the name of 'William' have been assigned to the reign of William II, although it remains uncertain whether the Paxs type of his father continued into his reign.

1258   1259

1258	**Penny.** *B.M.C.* 1: Profile type.	1100	3250
1259	*B.M.C.* 2: Cross in quatrefoil type.	850	2250

1260   1261

1260	*B.M.C.* 3: Voided cross type	850	2250
1261	*B.M.C.* 4: Cross pattée and fleury type.	900	2400

1262
1262	*B.M.C.* 5: Cross fleury and piles type.	950	2500

Henry was the third son of William I. Administrative reforms and military action to secure Normandy dominated the king's work. After the death of his son in 1120 Henry sought to guarantee the throne for his daughter Matilda, widow of German Emperor Henry V.

The coin types continue to be numbered according to BMC Norman Kings (London, 1916), but the order 1, 2, 3, 4, 5, 6, 9, 7, 8, 11, 10, 12, 13, 14, 15 is now accepted as a working hypothesis for the reign. Greater uncertainty pertains to the chronology of the coin types. The reign coincided with a period of monetary crisis. Scepticism concerning the quality of coinage led to the testing of coins by the public, hindering their acceptance in circulation. In response the government ordered all coins mutilated at issue to force the acceptance of damaged coins. Thus, a few coins of type 6 and all of those of types 7–14 have an official edge incision or 'snick'. Round halfpennies were produced and as some are found snicked they can be dated to the period when official mutilation of the coinage was ordered. In 1124 there was a general purge of moneyers in England as the royal government attempted to restore confidence in the coinage.

Further reading: M.A.S. Blackburn, 'Coinage and currency under Henry I; A review', *Anglo-Norman Studies* 13 (1991), 49–81. M.M. Archibald and W.J. Conte, 'Five round halfpennies of Henry I. A further case for reappraisal of the chronology of types', *Spink's Numismatic Circular* 98 (1990), 232–6, M. Allen 'Henry I Type 14', *BNJ* 79 (2009), 72-171.

1263   1263A   1264

		F	VF
		£	£
1263	**Penny**. *B.M.C.* 1: Annulets type	525	1750
1263A	*B.M.C.* 2: Profile/cross fleury type	375	1100
1264	*B.M.C.* 3: Paxs type	350	1000

1265   1266

1265	*B.M.C.* 4: Annulets and piles type	375	1100
1266	*B.M.C.* 5: Voided cross and fleurs type	900	2750

1267   1268

1267	*B.M.C.* 6: Pointing bust and stars type	1000	3250
1268	*B.M.C.* 7: Facing bust/quatrefoil with piles type	500	1500

1269

1270

	F	VF
	£	£
1269 *B.M.C.* 8: Large profile/cross and annulets type	1100	3500
1270 *B.M.C.* 9: Facing bust/cross in quatrefoil type	900	2750

1271

1272

1271 *B.M.C.* 10: Facing bust/cross fleury type	325	900
1272 *B.M.C.* 11: Double inscription type	750	2250

1273

1274

1273 *B.M.C.* 12: Small profile/cross and annulets type	450	1350
1274 *B.M.C.* 13: Star in lozenge fleury type	450	1350

1275

1276

1275 *B.M.C.* 14: Pellets in quatrefoil type	300	900
1276 *B.M.C.* 15: Quadrilateral on cross fleury type	250	750

1277

1277A

1277 *Round halfpenny*. Facing head. R. Cross potent with pellets in angles	2000	5750
1277A — —, As last but reverse from penny die of type 9.	2500	7500

Stephen of Blois seized the English throne on the death of his uncle, Henry I, despite his oath to support Matilda, with whom he contended for power during his reign.

Substantive types BMC 1 and BMC 7 were the only nation-wide issues, the latter introduced after the conclusion of the final political settlement in 1153. The other substantive types, BMC 2 and BMC 6, were confined to areas in the east of England under royal control. In western England coinage was issued by or on behalf of the Angevin party (q.v. below). In areas without access to new dies from London, coinage was produced from locally made dies and initially based on the designs of regular coins of BMC 1. Particular local types were produced in the midlands and the north, associated with prominent magnates, in the king's name or occasionally in the name of barons. Entries contain references to the article by Mack (M).

Further reading: R.P. Mack, 'Stephen and the Anarchy 1135-54', *British Numismatic Journal* 35 (1966), 38–112. M.A.S. Blackburn, 'Coinage and currency', in *The Anarchy of King Stephen's Reign*, ed. E. King (Oxford, 1994), 145–205.

SUBSTANTIVE ROYAL ISSUES

1278

		F £	*VF* £
1278	**Penny.** *B.M.C.* 1: Cross Moline ('Watford') type (c.1136–45). Bust right holding sceptre..	325	900
1279	— —, Similar but obv. reads PERERIC or PERERICM	750	2750

1280

1280	*B.M.C.* 2: Voided cross and stars type (c.1145–50)	300	950

1281   1282

1281	*B.M.C.* 6: Cross and piles type (c.1150–54)	350	1100
1282	*B.M.C.* 7: Cross pommée (Awbridge) type (c.1154–58, largely posthumous)	275	900
	This type continued to be struck until 1158 in the reign of Henry II		

The types designated BMC 3, 4 and 5 are non-substantive, listed as 1300–1302.

● = Regular mints of Stephen.

⊕ = Mints striking irregular coins including Angevin.

+ = Mints striking regular and irregular coins.

N.B. Attribution to some of the towns shown is uncertain.

Roxburgh⊕   Bamborough⊕

Corbridge⊕   +Newcastle

+Carlisle

+Durham

York +

Hedon ●

Lincoln +

Chester ●

Derby   ⊕Newark

Stafford ●   ⊕ +Nottingham

Shrewsbury ●   Tutbury   Leicester   Stamford   Castle Rising ●

Tamworth +   +   Norwich +

  Peterborough ●

  +Huntingdon   +Thetford

Worcester ●   Warwick ●   Northampton +   +Bury   ⊕Eye   Dunwich ●

  ⊕Cambridge   Ipswich

Hereford +   Bedford   Sudbury +

  Colchester ●

+Gloucester

Cirencester⊕   +Oxford

⊕Cricklade

Swansea +   ⊕Malmesbury   ⊕Wallingford   London

Pembroke ●   Cardiff +   Southwark ●

Bristol ●   Bath ●   ⊕Marlborough   Canterbury +   ●Sandwich

⊕Trowbridge   ●Dover

Watchet ●   +Ilchester   ●Wilton   Rye ●

Wivelscombe⊕   Shaftesbury ●   Salisbury   +Winchester   Bramber ●   Lewes ●

Taunton   ⊕   Hastings ●

Sherborne   Southampton⊕   Chichester   Pevensey +

Exeter +   Dorchester   Wareham   Steyning

+Launceston

Wight ●

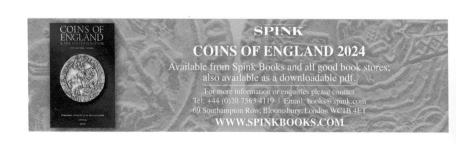

LOCAL AND IRREGULAR ISSUES OF THE CIVIL WAR

COINS STRUCK FROM ERASED DIES LATE 1130s – c.1145
The association of these coins with the Interdict of 1148 is erroneous. Some of the marks that disfigured the dies were probably cancellation marks, but the exigencies of the civil war required the re-use of the dies. Other defacements may well be an overtly political statement.

1283   1288

		F £	VF £
1283	As 1278, but obverse defaced with long cross. *East Anglian mints.* (M 137–47)	1000	3500
1284	— —, but king's bust defaced with cross. *Nottingham (M 149)*	1000	3500
1285	— —, but sceptre defaced with bar or cross. *Nottingham, Lincoln, Stamford.* (M 148, 150–54)	450	1500
1286	— —, but obverse legend erased. *Nottingham (M 157)*	650	2250
1286A	— —, but with defacement other than those noted above	450	1500

SOUTH EASTERN VARIANT

1287	As 1278, but king holds mace instead of sceptre. *Canterbury (M 158)*	1100	4000

EASTERN VARIANTS

1288	As 1278, but R. has roundels in centre, on cross limbs or in angles. *Suffolk mints (M 159–68)*	650	2250
1289	— —, but R. Plain cross, fleurs in angles. *Lincoln (M 169–73)*	575	2000
1290	— —, but R. Plain cross superimposed on cross moline *(M 174)*	525	1850
1290A	— —, but R. Quadrilateral over voided cross *(M 176)*	800	3000
1290B	— —, but cross penetrating legend to edge, fleurs inverted in angles. *Lincoln. (M 186–7)*	700	2500

SOUTHERN VARIANTS

1291   1295

1291	As 1278, but with large rosette of pellets at end of obverse legend *(M 184–5)*	525	1850
1292	— —, but with star at end of obverse legend *(M 187y)*	525	1850
1293	Bust r. or l., rosette in place of sceptre. R. As 1280, but solid cross. *(M 181–3)*	575	2000
1295	As 1278, but king wears collar of annulets. R. voided cross moline, annulet at centre. *Southampton. (M 207–212)*	425	1350

		F	VF
		£	£
1296	As 1278, but reverse cross penetrates legend with fleur-de-lis tips. *Leicester (M 177–8)*...	700	2250
1297	— —, but crude work. R. Voided cross, lis outward in angles. *Tutbury (M 179)*	850	3250

1298   1300

1298	— —, but crude work. R. Voided cross with martlets in angles. *Derby Tutbury (M 175)*	2500	8500
1299	— —, but R. plain cross with T-cross in each angle *(M 180)*...................	800	2750
1300	*B.M.C.* 3: Facing bust. R. Cross pattée, fleurs inwards. *Northampton and Huntingdon (?) (M 67–71)*...	800	2750

1301   1302

1301	*B.M.C.* 4: Lozenge fleury type. *Lincoln or Nottingham (M 72–5)*	450	1500
1302	*B.M.C.* 5: Bust half-right. R. Lozenge in Cross Moline with fleurs. *Leicester (M 76)*	1100	4500
1303	As 1280, but obverse legend ROBERTVS. *(M 269)*	3500	12500

NORTH-EASTERN AND SCOTTISH BORDER VARIANTS

1304	As 1278, but star before sceptre. R. Annulets at tips of fleurs *(M 188)* ...	750	2500
1305	— —, but voided cross penetrating legend to edge *(M 189–92)*...............	750	2500
1306	— —, but crude style *(M 276–9, 281–2)*..	850	2750
1307	— —, but R. Cross with cross pattée and crescent in angles *(M 288)*	1850	6000
	King David I of Scotland		
1308	As 1278, but obverse legend DAVID REX *(M 280)*	1850	6000
	Earl Henry of Northumberland (son of King David I of Scotland)		
1309	As 1278, but legend hENRIC ERL *(M 283–5)*..	2000	6500
1310	— —, Similar but reverse cross fleury *(M 286–7)*	2000	6500
1311	As 1307, but obverse legend NENCI:COM *(M 289)*	2500	7500

YORK ISSUES: THE ORNAMENTED GROUP ATTRIBUTED TO YORK (1140s)
King Stephen

| 1312 | As 1278, but obverse inscription NSEPEFETI, NSEPINEI or STIEFNER. R. ornamental letters WISÐGNOTA *(M 215–6)* .... | 1500 | 5000 |

1313   1315

	F £	VF £
1313 Flag type. As 1278, but lance with pennant before face, star right. R. As 1278, letters and four or eight ornaments in legend *(M 217)*	950	3500
1314 As 1278, but legend STEIN and pellet lozenge for sceptre-head *(M 218)*	950	3500
1314A King standing facing, holding sceptre and standard with triple pennon. R. Cross pattée, crescents and quatrefoils in angles, ornaments in legend.	4000	12500

King Stephen and Queen Matilda

1315 Two full-length standing figures holding sceptre. R. Legend of ornaments. *(M 220)*	4500	15000

1317   1320

Eustace Fitzjohn

1316 EVSTACIVS, knight standing with sword. R. Cross in quatrefoil, EBORACI EDTS or EBORACI TDEFL *(M 221-222)*	2750	10500
1317 − −, Similar but reverse legend ThOMHS FILIVS VLF *(M 223)*	3000	11000
1318 − −, Similar but reverse legend of ornaments and letters. *(M 224)*	2500	9000
1319 [EVSTA]CII. FII. IOANIS, lion passant right. R. Cross moline, ornaments in legend *(M 225)*	3500	12500
1320 EISTAOhIVS, lion rampant right. R. Cross fleury, ornaments in legend *(M 226)*	3250	12000

William of Aumale, Earl of York

1320A WILLELMVS, Knight stg. r. holding sword. R. Cross in quatrefoil. As 1316	4000	13500

1322

Rodbert III de Stuteville

1321 ROBERTVS IESTV, knight holding sword on horse right. R. as 1314. *(M 228)*	6000	20000
1321A Type as 1312, but obverse legend RODBDS[T DE?] *(M 227)*	3500	12500

Henry Murdac, Archbishop of York

1322 HENRICVS EPC, crowned bust, crosier and star before. R. similar to 1314 but legend STEPHANVS REX *(M 229)*	4000	13500

UNCERTAIN ISSUES

	F	VF
	£	£
1323 Obv. as 1278. R. Cross pattée with annulets in angles *(M 272)*	675	2500
1324 Obv. as 1275 (Henry I, *B.M.C.* 14), but reverse as last *(M 274 extr)*	900	3000
1325 Other miscellaneous types/varieties	650	1500

THE ANGEVIN PARTY

Matilda was the daughter of Henry I and widow of German Emperor Henry V (d.1125) and had been designated heir to the English throne by her father. Matilda was Countess of Anjou by right of her second husband Geoffrey of Anjou. Matilda arrived in England in pursuit of her inheritance in 1139 and established an Angevin court at Bristol and controlled most of south-western England. Matilda's cause was championed by her half-brother, Henry I's illegitimate son, Robert, Earl of Gloucester.

The initial phase of coinage in Matilda's name copied the designs of Stephen's BMC 1 and are dated to the early 1140s. The second type was only discovered in the Coed-y-Wenallt hoard (1980). A group of coins in the names of 'William' and 'Henry' and struck at the Angevin mints, particularly Hereford and Gloucester, are attributable, at least in part, to Earl William of Gloucester and Henry of Anjou (the future Henry II). Coins of Earl William, and his father Earl Robert, of the Lion type are now also known thanks to the discovery of the Box, Wiltshire hoard (1994). In addition to these great magnates a few minor barons placed their names on the coinage.

Further Reading: G. Boon, *Welsh Hoards 1979–81* (Cardiff, 1986). M.M. Archibald, 'The lion coinage of Robert Earl of Gloucester and William Earl of Gloucester', *British Numismatic Journal* 71 (2001), 71–86.

1326

Matilda (in England 1139–48)

1326 As 1278, but cruder style, MATILDI IMP or variant (M 230–40) *Bristol, Cardiff, Monmouth, Oxford and Wareham.*	2750	9000
1326A — —, MATILDI IMP or IM.HE.MA. R. Cross pattée over fleury (Coed-y-Wenallt hoard). *Bristol and Cardiff.*...	2850	9250
1326B — —, as last but triple pellets at cross ends (Coed-y-Wenallt hoard). *Bristol and Cardiff.*..	3000	9500

Henry de Neubourg

1326C Similar type to 1326A but HENRICI dE NOVOB (Coed-y-Wenallt hoard) *Swansea.*	3250	10000

Issues in the name 'Henry' and 'William'

1327 As 1278, but HENRICVS or HENRICVS REX *(M 241–5)*. *Hereford and Malmesbury.*	1750	6500
1327A As 1295, but HENRIC *(M 246)*. *Gloucester.*	1850	7000
1327B As 1326A, but HENNENNVS	1850	7000
1328 Obv. as 1278, but HENRICVS. R. Cross crosslet in quatrefoil *(M 254)*. *Gloucester.*	2000	7500

1329

1331

		F £	VF £

1329 — —, but HENRICVS or HENRICVS REX FVTVRVS R. Quadrilateral on cross fleury *(M 248–53). Hereford, Cirencester (?) and Ilchester (?)* 1750 6500

1330 Facing bust and stars, HENRICVS or HENRICVS RE. R. Quadrilateral on cross botonnée *(M 255–8). Bristol, Ilchester (?) and Sherborne (?)*........ 2250 7500

1331 — —, Quadrilateral, on voided cross botonnée *(M 259–61)* 2250 7500

1332 As 1329, but legend [WIL]LELM *(M 262)* 2500 8000

1333 As 1330, but legend WILLELM or variant *(M 263). Cirencester (?)* 2750 9000

1334 As 1331, but legend WILLELMVS *(M 264–8). Dorchester and Wareham* .. 2750 9000

Earl Robert of Gloucester (1121/22–1147)

1334A +ROB' COM' GLOC' lion passant right. R. Cross fleury 2500 8000

1334A* As 1278 but legend ROB COM GLO. R. Quadrilateral on cross fleury. *Shaftesbury.* 2750 9000

Earl William of Gloucester (1147-1183)

1334B +WILLEMVS, lion passant right. R. Cross fleury 2500 8000

Brian Fitzcount, Lord of Wallingford (?)

1335 As 1330, but legend B.R:C.I.T.B.R *(M 270)* 3750 13500

1336

Earl Patrick of Salisbury (?)

1336 Helmeted bust r. with sword, star behind. R. As 1329. *(M 271)*............... 3500 12500

MINTS HENRY II – EDWARD II (1158-1327)

Tealby (1158-80)

Short Cross (1180-1247)

Voided Long Cross (1247-7

New coinage (1279-1327).

HENRY II, 1154-1189

CROSS-AND-CROSSLETS ('TEALBY') COINAGE, 1158-1180

Coins of Stephen's last type continued to be minted until 1158. Then a new coinage bearing Henry's name replaced the currency of the previous reign which contained a high proportion of irregular and sub-standard pennies. The new Cross and Crosslets issue is more commonly referred to as the 'Tealby' coinage, as over 6000 of these pennies were discovered at Tealby, Lincolnshire, in 1807. Twenty-nine mints were employed in this re-coinage, but once the re-minting had been completed not more than a dozen mints were kept open. The issue remained virtually unchanged for twenty-two years apart from minor variations in the king's portrait. The coins tend to be poorly struck on irregular flans.

Cut coins occur with varying degrees of frequency during this issue, according to the type and local area.

Further reading: *A Catalogue of English Coins in the British Museum. The Cross-and-Crosslet ("Tealby") Type of Henry II.* (London: 1951) by D.F. Allen.

1337   1338   1339

		F £	VF £
1337	Class A (1158-c.1163). No hair, no collar. Mantle falls from chin as two parallel lines between which is a line of pellets.	150	450
1338	Class B (c.1162-c.1163). Similar, but mantle of two folds which meet at chin (various compositions).	160	475
1339	Class C (c.1163-c.1167). Curl of hair at temple. Jewelled collar, mantle of many folds, field between sometimes jewelled, as is cuff.	140	425

1340   1341

1340	Class D (c.1167-c.1170). Jewelled collar continues down shoulder unbroken. Single curl of hair at temple, folds of mantle horizontal	140	425
1341	Class E (c.1170-c.1174). Similar to 1340. Jewelled collar only. Folds of mantle rise from hand to top of shoulder.	140	425

1342

1342	Class F (c.1174-c.1180). Similar to 1341, but hair falls in long ringlets from temple.	125	375

Mints and Moneyers for the Cross-and-Crosslets (Tealby) Coinage

From F £

London: Accard (CD), Alwin (ABCDF), Edmund (ACDE), Geffrei (ACE), Godefrei (ACDEF), Godwin (BDE), Hunfrei (AC), Iohan (ACDEF), Lefwine (BCEF), Martin (ABC), Pieres (ACEF), Pieres Mer. (ABD), Pieres Sal. (AEF), Ricard (ABCD), Rodbert (AC), Swetman (ABC), Wid (A),   *125*

Canterbury: Alferg (A), Goldhavoc (ABCDEF), Goldeep (C), Lambrin (F), Raul (CDEF), Ricard (ABCDEF), Ricard Mr. (ABCDE), Rogier (ABCDEF), Rogier F. (A), Willem (C), Wiulf (ABCDEF),   *125*

Bedford: Arfin (A),   *Extremely Rare*

Bristol: Elaf (ACF), Rogier (ADEF), Tancard (ABD),   *250*

Bury St Edmunds: Henri (BDE), Raul (F), Willem (A),   *140*

Carlisle: Willem (ACDEF),   *140*

Chester: Andreu (A), Willem (AD),   *220*

Colchester: Alwin (AC), Pieres (CE),   *250*

Durham: Cristien (C), Iohan (B), Walter (A),   *180*

Exeter: Edwid (AC), Guncelin (AC), Rainir (BC), Ricard (A), Rogier (AD),   *220*

Gloucester: Godwin (A), Nicol (A), Rodbert (A), Sawulf (A),   *275*

Hereford: Driu (AC), Osburn (A), Stefne (A), [−]ward (A),   *250*

Ilchester: Adam (CDF), Reinard (A), Ricard (A), Rocelin (A),   *220*

Ipswich: Nicole (BCDEF), Robert (CEF), Turstain (CF),   *125*

Launceston: Willem (A),   *Extremely Rare*

Leicester: Ricard (A), Robert (A),   *250*

Lewes: Ricard (F),   *Extremely Rare*

Lincoln: Andreu (ABCDE), Godric (ABCD), Lanfram (ABCDF), Raulf (ABCDEF), Raven (ACF), Swein (ACD),   *140*

Newcastle: Willem (ACDEF),   *150*

Northampton: Ingeram (AC), Iosep (A), Pieres (A), Reimund (AC), Stefne (A), Waltier (AC), Warnier (AC),   *180*

Norwich: Gilebert (ABF), Herbert (ACD), Herbert R (A)., Hugo (ACF), Nicol (AC), Picot (ABC), Reiner (AD), Ricard (A),   *180*

Oxford: Adam (ADE), Aschetil (A), Rogier (A),   *220*

Pembroke: Walter (A),   *Extremely Rare*

Salisbury: Daniel (A), Levric (A),   *220*

Shrewsbury: Warin (A),   *Extremely Rare*

Stafford: Colbrand (AC), Willem (C),   *275*

Thetford: Siwate (ACD), Turstain (ACD), Willem (ACDF), Willem Ma (A), Willem De (A),   *140*

Wallingford: Fulke (A),   *Extremely Rare*

Wilton: Anschetil (A), Lantier (A), Willem (A),   *220*

Winchester: Herbert (AC), Hosbert (ACD), Ricard (AE), Willem (AC),   *140*

York: Cudbert (A), Gerrard (A), Godwin (AD), Griffin (AD), Herbert (ACD), Hervi (A), Iordan (A), Norman (A), Willem (A), Wulfsi (A),   *140*

Letters in brackets after moneyer's name indicate Class known to exist for the mint and moneyer combination

'SHORT CROSS' COINAGE OF HENRY II (1180-1189)

In 1180 a coinage of new type, known as the Short Cross coinage, replaced the Tealby issue. The new coinage is remarkable in that it covers not only the latter part of the reign of Henry II, but also the reigns of his sons Richard and John and on into the reign of his grandson Henry III, and the entire issue bears the name 'hЄNRICVS'. There are no English coins with the names of Richard or John. The Short Cross coins can be divided chronologically into various classes: ten mints were operating under Henry II and tables of mints, moneyers and classes are given for each reign.

The Publishers acknowledge the work of the late Prof. Jeffrey Mass for re-organising and updating the shortcross series.

Further reading: *Sylloge of Coins of the British Isles Vol 56. The J.P. Mass Collection of English Short Cross Coins 1180 to 1247*. London 2002.

1343	1343A

1344	1345

			F £	VF £
1343	Class 1a^1 - 1a^3. Small face, square E, and/or C, and/or round M, irregular number of curls		200	675
1343A	Class 1a^4 and 1a^5. Small face, seriffed X, round E and C, square M, irregular number of curls		125	400
1344	1b. Fine portrait, curls 2 left and 5 right, stop before REX on most coins		100	300
1345	1c. Portrait less finely shaped, irregular number of curls, normally no stop before REX		90	250

RICHARD I, 1189-1199

Pennies of Short Cross type continued to be issued throughout the reign, all bearing the name hЄNRICVS. The coins of class 4, which have very crude portraits, continued to be issued in the early years of the next reign. The only coins bearing Richard's name are from his territories of Aquitaine and Poitou in western France.

1346	1347	1348A	1348C

1346	2. Chin whiskers made of small curls, no side whiskers, almost always 5 pearls to crown, frequently no collar, sometimes RE/X	125	400
1347	3. Large or small face, normally 7 pearls to crown, chin and side whiskers made up of small curls	110	375

	F £	VF £
1348A 4a. Normally 7 pearls to crown, chin and side whiskers made up of small pellets, hair consisting of 2 or more non-parallel crescents left and right	95	325
1348B 4a* Same as last, but with reverse colon stops (instead of single pellets)	110	375
1348C 4b Normally 7 pearls to crown, chin and side whiskers made up of small pellets, single (or parallel) crescents as hair left and right, frequent malformed letters	95	325

JOHN, 1199-1216

'SHORT CROSS' COINAGE *continued*. All with name hϵNRICVS
The Short Cross coins of class 4 continued during the early years of John's reign, but in 1205 a re-coinage was initiated and new Short Cross coins of better style replaced the older issues. Coins of classes 5a and 5b were issued in the re-coinage in which sixteen mints were employed. Only two of these mints (London and Durham) were still working by the end of class 5. The only coins to bear John's name are the pennies, halfpence and farthings issues for Ireland.

1349	1350A	1350B
1351	1352	1354

1349	4c. Reversed S, square face at bottom, 5 pearls to crown, normally single crescents as hair left and right	110	375
1350A	5a1 Reversed or regular S, irregular curved lines as hair (or circular curls containing no pellets), cross pattée as initial mark on reverse, *London and Canterbury* only	200	650
1350B	5a2 Reversed S, circular curls left and right (2 or 3 each side) containing single pellets, cross pommée as initial mark on reverse	95	325
1350C	5a/5b or 5b/5a	80	275
1351	5b. Regular S, circular pelleted curls, cross pattée as initial mark on reverse	75	225
1352	5c. Slightly rounder portrait, letter X in the form of a St. Andrew's cross	70	210
1353	6a. Smaller portrait, with smaller letter X composed of thin strokes or, later, short wedges	75	225
1354	6b. Very tall lettering and long rectangular face	70	210

For further reading and an extensive listing of the English Short Cross Coinage see:
Sylloge of Coins of the British Isles. *The J. P. Mass Collection of English Short Cross Coins 1180-1247*

'SHORT CROSS' COINAGE *continued* (1216-47)

The Short Cross coinage continued for a further thirty years during which time the style of portraiture and workmanship deteriorated. By the 1220s minting had been concentrated at London and Canterbury, one exception being the mint of the Abbot of Bury St. Edmunds.

Halfpenny and farthing dies are recorded early in this issue; a few halfpennies and now farthings have been discovered. See nos 1357 D-E.

			F	VF
			£	£

		F	VF
1355 6c. Lettering now shorter, face narrow and triangular (also issued in the reign of John)		80	250
1355A 6c. orn. Various letters now ornamental in design, curls 3/3 left and right		100	350
1355B 6x. Canterbury mint only, RE/X, curls 2/2, nostril pellets outside nose...		475	1500
1355C 6d. Face less distinct in shape, N's containing a pellet along the crossbar		95	300

		F	VF
1356A 7a. Small compact face, letter A (rev. only) with top coming to a point under crossbar		45	150
1356B 7b. Letter A with square top, M appears as H (rev. only)		45	150
1356C 7c. Degraded portrait, letter A and M as in 7b, large lettering (rev. only)		40	125

		F	VF
1357A 8a. New portrait; letter X in shape of curule; cross pattée as initial mark on reverse (early style), or cross pommée (late style)		175	450
1357B 8b. Degraded portrait, wedge-shaped X, cross pommée as initial mark ..		65	175
1357C 8c. Degraded portrait, cross pommée X, cross pommée as initial mark ..		65	175
1357D Round **Halfpenny** in style of class 7, initial mark in shape of up-turned crescent, London mint only (dated to 1222)		2750	8500
1357E Round **Farthing** in style of class 7, initial mark in shape of up-turned crescent, London mint only (dated to 1222)		2500	7500

Mints and Moneyers for the Short Cross Coinage

Fine

Henry II:

London: Aimer (1a-b), Alain (1a-b), Alain V (1a-b), Alward (1b), Davi (1b-c),
Fil Aimer (1a-b), Gefrei (1c), Gilebert (1c), Godard (1b), Henri (1a-b),
Henri Pi (1a), Iefrei (1a-b), Iohan (1a-b), Osber (1b), Pieres (1a-c),
Pieres M (1a-b), Randvl (1a-b), Ravl (1b-c), Reinald (1a-b), Willelm (1a-b)   75
Carlisle: Alain (1b-c)   110
Exeter: Asketil (1a-b), Iordan (1a-b), Osber (1a-b), Ravl (1b), Ricard (1b-c),
Roger (1a-c)   100
Lincoln: Edmvnd (1b-c), Girard (1b), Hvgo (1b), Lefwine (1b-c), Rodbert (1b),
Walter (1b), Will. D.F. (1b), Willelm (1b-c)   90
Northampton: Filip (1a-b), Hvgo (1a-b), Ravl (1a-c), Reinald (1a-c), Simvn (1b),
Walter (1a-c), Willelm (1a-b)   85
Oxford: Asketil (1b), Iefrei (1b), Owein (1b-c), Ricard (1b-c), Rodbert (1b),
Rodbt. F. B. (1b), Sagar (1b)   95
Wilton: Osber (1a-b), Rodbert (1a-b), Iohan (1a)   100
Winchester: Adam (1a-c), Clement (1a-b), Gocelm (1a-c), Henri (1a),
Osber (1a-b), Reinier (1b), Rodbert (1a-b)   85
Worcester: Edrich (1b), Godwine (1b-c), Osber (1b-c), Oslac (1b)   100
York: Alain (1a-b), Efrard (1a-c), Gerard (1a-b), Hvgo (1a-c), Hunfrei (1a-b),
Isac (1a-b), Tvrkil (1a-c), Willelm (1a-b)   85

Richard I

London: Aimer (2-4a), Fvlke (4a-b), Henri (4a-b), Ravl (2), Ricard (2-4b),
Stivene (2-4b), Willelm (2-4b)   85
Canterbury: Goldwine (3-4b), Hernavd (4b), Hve (4b), Ioan (4b), Meinir (2-4b),
Reinald/Reinavd (2-4b), Roberd (2-4b), Samvel (4b), Simon (4b), Vlard (2-4b)   95
Carlisle: Alein (3-4b)   140
Durham: Adam (4a), Alein (4a-b), Pires (4b)   165
Exeter: Ricard (3)   150
Lichfield: Ioan (2)   4500
Lincoln: Edmvnd (2), Lefwine (2), Willelm (2)   115
Northampton: Giferei (4a), Roberd (3), Waltir (3)   125
Northampton or Norwich: Randvl (4a-b), Willelm (4a-b)   115
Shrewsbury: Ive (4a-b), Reinald/Reinavd (4a-b), Willem (4a)   190
Winchester: Adam (3), Gocelm (3), Osbern (3-4a), Pires (4a), Willelm (3-4a)   95
Worcester: Osbern (2)   250
York: Davi (4a-b), Efrard/Everard (2-4b), Hvgo/Hve (2-4a), Nicole (4a-b),
Tvrkil (2-4a)   95

John

London: Abel (5c-6b), Adam (5b-c), Beneit (5b-c), Fvlke (4c-5b), Henri (4c-5b/5a),
Ilger (5b-6b), Ravf (5c-6b), Rener (5a/b-5c), Ricard (4c-5b), Ricard B (5b-c),
Ricard T (5a/b-5b), Walter (5c-6b), Willelm (4c-5b), Willelm B (5a/b-5c),
Willelm L (5b-c), Willelm T (5b-c)   70
Canterbury: Goldwine (4c-5c), Hernavd/Arnavd (4c-5c), Hve (4c-5c), Iohan (4c-5c),
Iohan B (5b-c), Iohan M (5b-c), Roberd (4c-5c), Samvel (4c-5c), Simon (4c-5c)   75
Bury St Edmunds: Fvlke (5b-c)   115
Carlisle: Tomas (5b)   135
Chichester: Pieres (5b/a-5b), Ravf (5b/a-5b), Simon (5b/a-5b), Willelm (5b)   100
Durham: Pieres (5a-6a)   115
Exeter: Gileberd (5a-b), Iohan (5a-b), Ricard (5a-b)   100

Ipswich: Alisandre (5b-c), Iohan (5b-c)   85
Kings Lynn: Iohan (5b), Nicole (5b), Willelm (5b)   150
Lincoln: Alain (5a), Andrev (5a-5c), Hve (5a/b-5c), Iohan (5a), Ravf (5a/b-5b),
Ricard (5a-5b/a), Tomas (5a/b-5b)   75
Northampton: Adam (5b-c), Roberd (5b), Roberd T (5b)   85
Northampton or Norwich: Randvl (4c)   100
Norwich: Gifrei (5a/b-5c), Iohan (5a-c), Renald/Renavd (5a-c)   85
Oxford: Ailwine (5b), Henri (5b), Miles (5b)   95
Rochester: Alisandre (5b), Hvnfrei (5b)   110
Shrewsbury: Ive (4c)   750
Winchester: Adam (5a-c), Andrev (5b-c), Bartelme (5b-c), Henri (5a), Iohan (5a-c),
Lvkas (5b-c), Miles (5a-c), Ravf (5b-c), Ricard (5a-b)   75
York: Davi (4c-5b), Nicole (4c-5c), Renavd (5b), Tomas (5a/b-5b)   75

Henry III
London: Abel (6c-7a), Adam (7b-c), Elis (7a-b), Giffrei (7b-c), Ilger (6c-7b),
Ledvlf (7b-c), Nichole (7c-8c), Ravf (6c-7b), Ricard (7b), Terri (7a-b),
Walter (6b-c)   40
Canterbury: Arnold (6c/6x, 6x), Henri (6c-6c/d, 7a-c), Hivn/Ivn (6c-7b),
Iohan (6c-7c, 8b-c), Ioan Chic (7b-c), Ioan F. R. (7b-c), Nichole (7c, 8b-c),
Osmvnd (7b-c), Robert (6c, 7b-c), Robert Vi (7c), Roger (6c-7b),
Roger of R (7a-b), Salemvn (6x, 7a-b), Samvel (6c-d, 7a), Simon (6c-d, 7a-b),
Tomas (6d, 7a-b), Walter (6c-7a), Willem (7b-c, 8b-c), Willem Ta (7b-c)   40
Bury St Edmunds: Iohan (7c-8c), Norman (7a-b), Ravf (6c-d, 7a), Simvnd (7b-c),
Willelm (7a)   45
Durham: Pieres (7a)   90
Winchester: Henri (6c)   135
York: Iohan (6c), Peres (6c), Tomas (6c), Wilam (6c)   135

Irregular Local Issue
Rhuddlan (in chronological order)   105
Group I (c. 1180 – pre 1205) Halli, Tomas, Simond
Group II (c.1205 – 1215) Simond, Henricus

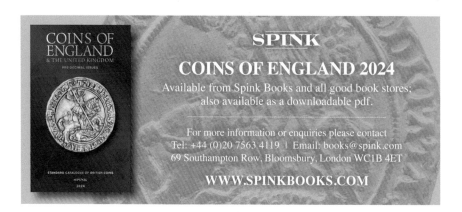

'LONG CROSS' COINAGE (1247-72)

By the middle of Henry's reign the Short Cross coinage in circulation was in a poor state and, in 1247, a new coinage was ordered with the cross on the reverse being extended to the edge of the coin in an attempt to prevent clipping. The earliest coins (1a) showed the names of the neither the mint nor the moneyer. Class 1b includes the name of the mint. From class 2 onwards all coins show the name of both the mint and the moneyer.

Following publication of the 1908 Brussels Hoard by Churchill and Thomas (2012) the classification of the Long Cross coinage was revised. This divided the Long Cross coinage into four phases: Phase I, 1247, Pre-provincial; Phase II, 1248-1250, Provincial when sixteen provincial mints, in addition to the main mints of London and Canterbury plus Bury St Edmunds were opened to facilitate the production and distribution of the new coins; Phase III, 1250-1272, The Post-provincial in which the mint of Durham re-opened operating intermittently; Phase IV, 1272-1280, Posthumous (see under Edward I on page 167) when the Long Cross coinage was continued in the name of Henry III through the first seven years of the reign of Edward I.

In Phases I and II the obverse features the King's head without a sceptre but during the Post-provincial phase, from class 4 onwards, the sceptre was re-introduced. No round Half-pennies or farthings were struck during the Long Cross coinage but cut halves and quarters were used in considerable numbers.

Mint marks feature on all coins from classes 1 to 4 inclusive and are an important aid to both chronology and identification. Five main varieties of mint mark exist.

1   2   3   4   5

Further reading: Ron Churchill and Bob Thomas, *The Brussels Hoard of 1908. The Long Cross Coinage of Henry III.* 2012. *The Voided Long-Cross Coinage 1247-1279* by Christopher R. Wren

THE LONG CROSS COINAGE, 1247-79

PHASE I, 1247 PRE-PROVINCIAL PHASE

1358   1359

		F	VF
		£	£
1358	Class 1a. Obv. hENRICVS REX. Rev. ANG LIE TER CI'. *mm* 1...........	475	1500
1359	Class 1b. Obv. hENRICVS REX ANG. Rev. LIE TER CI' LON (London),		
	CAN (Canterbury - scarce) or AED (Bury St Edmunds - very rare). *mm* 1.	75	200
1359A	Class 1a/1b and 1b/1a mules	325	1000
1360	Class 1b/2a mule. (London and Canterbury only)...................................	75	200

1361

1361	Class 2a. Obv. hENRICVS REX TERCI'. *mm* 2.		
	Rev. Moneyer & mint.	45	150

PHASE II, 1248-50 PROVINCIAL PHASE

1361A

	F £	VF £
1361A Class 2b. Long, narrow bust, curly X or straight limbed X. Rev. Moneyer & mint. *mm* 3.	40	135

1362   1362A   1362B

	F £	VF £
1362 Class 3a1. Obv. hENRICVS REX III. Class 2 bust. *mm* 3.	35	125
1362A Class 3a2. Bust altered, eyes are round comprising pellets in crescents; often with a colon after REX. *mm* 3.	35	125
1362B Class 3ab. Neat 3a-3b transitional bust. *mm* 3.	35	120

1363   1363A   1364

	F £	VF £
1363 Class 3b. Neat round bust; beard is three pellets either side of a large central pellet. *mm* 3.	30	110
1363A Class 3bc. Smaller bust with necklines (sometimes vestigal). ENR usually ligated. *mm* 4.	35	120
1364 Class 3c. Similar but coarser bust usually with necklines and a colon after REX. Eyes are round comprising pellets in annulets. *mm* 4.	30	110

PHASE III, 1250-72 POST-PROVINCIAL PHASE

1364A   1364B

	F £	VF £
1364A Class 3d1. Small neat bust generally with a pointed chin and neck lines. Most have a colon after REX. *mm* 4.	35	120
1364B Class 3d2. Larger more rounded bust resembling class 4 coins. Ball tailed letter R (R2). *mm* 4, with a few coins featuring *mm* 5.	35	120

| 1365 | 1365a | 1366 | 1366 detail |

	F £	VF £

1365 Class 4a. Bust similar to 3d2. King holds sceptre, crown has pellet ornaments.
Legend starts at 1 o'clock. *mm* 5. .... 125 450

1365A Class 4ab. As above but crown has end pellets and true central fleur. *mm* 5. 125 450

1366 Class 4b. As above but crown has true half fleurs and central fleur. *mm* 5. 250 750

| 1367 | 1367A | 1367B | 1367B detail |

1367 Class 5a1. Legend starts at 10 o'clock. Large round bust, round eyes and
half fleur at crown ends. No *mm*.. 150 525

1367A Class 5a2. As above but crown has end pellets. Some with the letter X
with one curved limb (Churchill/Thomas Class 5a3). 40 125

1367B Class 5a4. As above but with a jewelled crown.. 275 800

| 1368 | 1368A | 1368A detail |

1368 Class 5b1. Large oval bust, sometimes narrower with more pointed chin. Half
fleur crown ends. 150 525

1368A Class 5b2. As above but crown with end pellets. 30 110

| 1369 |

1369 Class 5c. Similar but with almond eyes or wedge tailed R., variety with
disjointed central fleur and/or no stalks... 30 110

		F £	VF £

1370 | Class 5d1. Completely new and very coarse bust with crude central fleur and half fleur ends often with unusual mint spellings. .... | 100 | 325

1370A | Class 5d2. As above but bust is more realistic and less crude................... | 70 | 175

1370B | Class 5d3. The "Beri" type; much neater and more pleasing. Central fleur has distinctly pointed ends. .... | 70 | 175

1371 | Class 5e. Bust similar to 5d3 (but Canterbury busts usually coarser) but with jewelled crown... | 150 | 525

1372 | Class 5f. New large and round bust similar to those from 5a to 5c with a double banded crown and a low central fleur. .... | 30 | 100

1373 | Class 5g. Similar bust but crown has thick single band with low central fleur. | 30 | 100

1374 | Class 5h. Similar but coarser with 'heavier' features and a more pointed chin. Crown fleur comprises three pellets often with one or more individual stalks, possibly posthumous.. | 65 | 200

1375

1375 | Gold Penny of 20 pence. As illustration. .... | 85000 | 325000

Only eight gold Pennies of Henry III are officially recorded from an original mintage estimated in excess of 80,000 coins. Their appearance for sale is infrequent in the extreme, and would likely attract global interest. The example illustrated was found at Hemyock, Devon in September 2021 and sold for a record £648,000 at Spink in January 2022. Copies are known and are frequently encountered.

Mints, Moneyers and Classes for the Long Cross Coinage

Question marks appear against certain sub classes eg Lincoln 3bc for Walter. In such cases, whilst the Brussels Hoard contained no specimens and whilst no specimen is known to Churchill and Thomas, it is thought feasible that coins of this sub-class were struck and examples may exist.

	Fine From £

London; Anonymous 1a, 1b, 1a/b, 1b/a.

Nicole (1b/2-5c2), Henri (3a1-5g), Davi (3d1-5f), Ricard (3d1/2-5g),

Note. Of the above four moneyers, only Nicole is known for class 4ab

Walter (5c2-5g), Willem (5c2-5g), Ion (5c3-5g), Thomas (5g), Robert (5g),

Renaud (5g-7), Phelip (7). 30

Note: Coins of 5a4 and 5d1 are not known for London and coins of 5d2 are excessively rare.

Canterbury: Anonymous 1b. Nicole (1b/2-5g), Gilbert (1b/2-3ab, 3b-5c, 5d3-5g),

Willem (1b/2, 2b-5g), Ion (4ab-5c, 5d2-5g), Robert/Roberd (5c-5d1, 5d3-5h)

Walter (5c-5g), Ambroci (5g), Alein (5g-5h), Ricard (5h), Roger (5h). 30

Note: No coin of class 2a is known for Willem but one may exist; coins of classes 4a, 4b, 5a1 and 5b1 are not known for any Canterbury moneyer and class 5a4 is known only for Nicole and Ion.

Bury St Edmunds: Ion (2a-3d2, 4ab, 5a2 and 5a3), Randulf (5b2-5c, 5d3, 5f), Renaud (5g),

Stephane (5g), Ion/Iohs (5g-7), Ioce (7). 30

Durham: Ricard (5a3, 5b2 & 5c), Roger (5g), Wilelm (5g), Roberd/Robert (6, 7).................. 55

Bristol: Elis (3ab, b, bc, c), Henri (3ab, b), Iacob (3ab, b, bc, c), Roger (3b, bc),

Walter (3ab, b, bc).. 65

Carlisle: Adam (3ab, b, bc), Ion (3ab, b, bc, c), Robert (3ab, b, bc), Willem (3ab, b). 85

Exeter: Ion (2b, 3a, a2, ab, b), Philip (2b, 3a, a2, ab, b), Robert (2b, 3a1, a2, ab, b),

Walter (2b2, 3a1, a2, ab, b).. 55

Gloucester: Ion (2b, 3a1, a2, ab, b, c), Lucas (2b2, 3a1, a2, ab, b, c),

Ricard (2b, 3a1, a2, ab, b, c), Roger (2b, 3a1, a2, ab, b, c)... 55

Hereford: Henri (3ab, b, c), Ricard (3ab, b, c), Roger (3ab, b, c), Walter (3ab, b, c). 75

Ilchester: Huge (3a2, ab, b, bc, c), Ierveis (3a2, ab, b, bc, c), Randvlf (3a2, ab, b, bc, c),

Stephe (3a2, ab, b, bc, c).. 75

Lincoln: Ion (2b, 3a1, a2, ab, b, bc, c), Ricard (2b, 3a1, a2, ab, b, bc, c),

Walter (2b, 3a1, a2, ab, b, bc, c), Willem (2b, 3a1, a2, ab, b, bc, c). 35

Newcastle: Adam (3ab, b, c), Henri (3ab, b, c), Ion (3ab, b, c), Roger (3ab, b, c). 45

Northampton: Lucas (2b, 3a1, a2, ab, b, bc, c), Philip (2b, 3a1, a2, ab, b, bc, c),

Tomas (2b, 3a1, a2, ab, b, bc, c), Willem (2b, 3a1, a2, ab, b, bc, c). 45

Norwich: Huge (2b, 3a1, a2, ab, b, bc, c), Iacob (2b, 3a1, a2, ab, b, bc, c),

Ion (2b, 3a, a2, ab, b, bc, c),Willem (2b, 3a1, a2, ab, b, bc, c). 45

Oxford: Adam (2b, 3a1, a2, ab, b, bc, c), Gefrei (2b, 3a1, a2, ab, b, bc, c),

Henri (2b, 3a1, a2, ab, b, bc, c), Willem (2b, 3a1, a2, ab, b, bc, c)................................... 45

Shrewsbury: Lorens (3ab, b, bc, c), Nicole (3ab, b, bc, c), Peris (3ab, b, bc, c),

Ricard (3ab, b, bc, c)... 75

Wallingford: Alisandre (3ab, b), Clement (3ab, b), Ricard (3ab, b), Robert (3ab, b). 75

Wilton: Huge (3ab, b, bc, c), Ion (3ab, b, bc, c), Willem (3ab, b, bc, c). 75

Winchester: Huge (2b, 3a1, a2, ab, b, bc, c), Iordan (2b, 3a1, a2, ab, b, bc, c),

Nicole (2b, 3a1, a2, ab, b, bc, c), Willem (2b, 3a1, a2, ab, b, bc, c). 45

York: Alain (2b, 3a1, a2, ab, b, bc), Ieremie (2b, 3a1, a2, ab, b, bc), Ion (2b, 3a1,

a2, ab, b, bc), Rener (2b, 3a1, a2, ab, b, bc), Tomas (3a2, ab, b, bc, c). 30

COINAGE IN THE NAME OF HENRY III 1272-1279

LONG CROSS COINAGE, 1247-79 *(continued)*

PHASE IV, POSTHUMOUS PHASE

These coins were struck between 1272 and 1279 during the reign of Edward I but they bear the name of Henry III. It is most likely that class 5h were also struck during these years but there are no means of separating the coins struck under Edward I from those struck before the death of Henry III; we have, therefore, included all coins of class 5h as being part of the Henry III Phase III.

The earliest coinage of Edward I, in the name of Henry III (Class 5i and 6), is of coarse style and was struck at London, Bury St. Edmunds and Durham only. Class 7, also only from these mints, is of neater style. In 1279 the Long Cross coinage was abandonned and a new coinage introduced.

Cut Halfpennies and Farthings also occur for this issue.

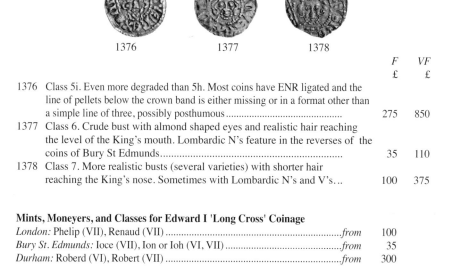

1376	1377	1378

	F £	VF £
1376 Class 5i. Even more degraded than 5h. Most coins have ENR ligated and the line of pellets below the crown band is either missing or in a format other than a simple line of three, possibly posthumous	275	850
1377 Class 6. Crude bust with almond shaped eyes and realistic hair reaching the level of the King's mouth. Lombardic N's feature in the reverses of the coins of Bury St Edmunds	35	110
1378 Class 7. More realistic busts (several varieties) with shorter hair reaching the King's nose. Sometimes with Lombardic N's and V's	100	375

Mints, Moneyers, and Classes for Edward I 'Long Cross' Coinage

London: Phelip (VII), Renaud (VII) ....*from*	100	
Bury St. Edmunds: Ioce (VII), Ion or Ioh (VI, VII) ....*from*	35	
Durham: Roberd (VI), Robert (VII) ....*from*	300	

NEW COINAGE (from 1279).

A major re-coinage was embarked upon in 1279 which introduced new denominations. In addition to the penny, halfpence and farthings were also minted and, for the first time, a fourpenny piece called a 'Groat', wt. 89 grs., (from the French *Gros*).

The groats, though ultimately unsuccessful, were struck from more than thirty obverse dies and form an extensive series with affinities to the pence of classes 1c to 3g. The chronology of this series has now been definitively established (see Allen, M. The Durham Mint, pp. 172-179).

As mint administration was now very much centralised, the practice of including the moneyer's name in the coinage was abandoned (except for a few years at Bury St. Edmunds). Several provincial mints assisted with the re-coinage during 1279-81, then minting was again restricted to London, Canterbury, Durham and Bury.

The provincial mints were again employed for a subsidiary re-coinage in 1300 in order to remint lightweight coins and the many illegal *esterlings* (foreign copies of the English pennies, mainly from the Low Countries), which were usually of poorer quality than the English coins.

1379A   1379E

	F £	VF £
1379A **Groat.** *London.* Variety a. (Fox 5). Small crowned bust within a quatrefoil of three lines, flowers in spandrels. Flat crown with pellet ornaments, drapery of two wedges with rosette below	2000	7250
1379B — b. (Fox 6). Larger face with flat hair. Unusual crescent crown carrying pearl ornaments, drapery with rosette in centre	1750	7000
1379C — c. (Fox 3). Similar face with bushy hair. Crown with plain band and pearl ornaments, drapery is foreshortened circle with rosette in centre ...	2000	7500
1379D — d. (Fox 7). New portrait with smaller pointed face, trefoils in spandrels. Crown with spearhead ornaments, drapery is segment of a circle with rosette in centre	2000	7500
1379E — e. (Fox 4). Larger oval face with bushy hair, flowers in spandrels. Crown with spearhead ornaments, thick curved drapery without rosette	1750	7000
1379F — f. (Fox 2). Quatrefoil of two lines. Broader face and shorter hair. Crown with spread side fleurs, drapery of two wedges, trefoil of pellets below .	1850	7250
1379G — f. (Fox 1). Quatrefoil of three lines. Drapery of two wedges, trefoil of pellets below	2100	8000
1379H — g. (Fox -). Quatrefoil of two lines. Crown with bifoliate side fleurs, drapery of two wedges with annulet (?) on breast, two annulets after ANG	2250	8500

Edward I groats were often mounted as brooches and gilt. Such specimens are worth considerably less

1381   1382   1383

	F £	VF £
1380 **Penny.** *London.* Class 1a. Crown with plain band, ЄDW RЄX; Lombardic Π on *obv;* pellet 'barred' S on rev. A with sloping top	375	1500
1381 — 1b. — ЄD RЄX; no drapery on bust, Roman N	1250	4500
1382 — 1c. — ЄDW RЄX; Roman N, normal or reversed; small lettering	60	175
1383 — 1d. — ЄDW R;—; large lettering and face	50	160

1384   1385   1386

1384 — — — Annulet below bust	125	450
1385 — 2a. Crown with band shaped to ornaments; usually broken left petal to central fleur portrait as ld. N usually reversed	35	110
1386 — 2b. — tall bust; long neck; N reversed	30	100

1388

1387 — 3a. Crescent-shaped contraction marks; pearls in crown, drapery is foreshortened circle with hook ends	40	135
1388 — 3b. — — drapery is segment of a circle, pearls in crown	40	135
1389 — 3c. — normal crown; drapery in one piece, hollowed in centre	30	90

1391   1392   1394

1390 — 3d. — — drapery in two pieces, broad face	30	90
1391 — 3e. — long narrow face (Northern mints)	30	90
1392 — 3f. — broad face, large nose, rougher work, late S first used	40	135
1393 — 3g. — Spread crown small neat bust, narrow face	30	80
1394 — 4a. Comma-shaped contraction mark, late S always used, C and Є open	30	90

1395   1396   1397

		F	*VF*
		£	£
1395	— 4b. Similar, but face and hair shorter	30	90
1396	— 4c. Larger face with more copious hair; nick to band of crown	35	125
1397	— 4d. Pellet at beginning of *obv.* and *rev.* legend	30	100
1398	— 4e. Three pellets on breast, ropy hair, pellet in *rev.* legend (no pellets on Bury or Durham)	35	125

1398   1399   1400

| 1399 | — 5a. Well spread coins, pellet on breast, face as 1398, A normally unbarred | 40 | 135 |
| 1400 | — 5b. Coins more spread, tall lettering, long narrow face, pellet on breast | 35 | 125 |

1401   1402   1403

1401	— 6a. Smaller coins, smaller lettering with closed E (from now on) initial cross almost plain, crown with wide fleurs, crude appearance	110	450
1402	— 6b. Initial cross pattée	70	250
1403	— 7a. Rose on breast (except Bury), short hair; almond-shaped eyes, double barred N	60	225

1404   1406   1406A

1404	— 7b. Rose on breast (London only) longer hair, new crown	65	240
1405	— 8a. Crown resembling 7b with central fleur usually broken	35	125
1406	— 8b. Similar to 1405 with wider drapery, top-tilted S	35	125
1406A	— 8c — — Crown with very arched band	40	135

1407

		F	VF
		£	£

1407 — 9a. Drapery of two wedges, pellet eyes, crown of 8a-b or new flatter one; often star on breast.. 30 90

1408 — 9b. Small coins; Roman N, normal, un-barred, or usually of pot-hook form; often star or (very rarely) pellet on breast. Some Durham coins are from locally made dies... 30 90

1408A – 9c. Larger crude lettering with barred A and abbreviation marks. (only found in combination with dies of 9b or 10ab, except Bury).......... 45 175

1409 - 10ab   1409B - 10ab

1409 — 10ab. ЄDWARD. Bifoliate crown (converted 9b or new taller one). Narrow incurved lettering... 25 85

1409A — 10ab. Similar with annulet on breast or a pellet each side of head and on breast 135 450

1409B — 10ab. ЄDWAR (rarely ЄDWR). Similar to 1409. A few early coins have the trifoliate crown of 9b.. 30 90

1410   1411

Crown 1	Crown 2	Crown 3	Crown 4	Crown 5

1410 — 10cf1. Crown 1 (Axe-shaped central fleur, wedge-shaped petals). ЄDWA from now on. Stub-tailed. R.. 25 85

1411 — 10cf2. Crown 2 (Well-shaped central lis, no spearheads). Spreading hair. 25 85

1413   1414

		F	*VF*
		£	£
1412	— 10cf3. Crown 3 (Left-hand arrowhead inclines to right). Early coins have the broken lettering of 10cf2; later have new lettering with round-backed Є.	25	85
1413	— 10cf4. Crown 4 (Neat with hooked petal to right-hand side fleur)......	30	100
1414	— 10cf5. Crown 5 (taller and more spread, right-hand ornament inclines to left). Later coins are on smaller flans.	25	85

Some of the coins of class 10cf3 (c.1307-9), and all of the coins of classes 10cf4 and 10cf5 (c.1309-10), were struck in the reign of Edward II.
For a more detailed classification of Class 10, see 'Sylloge of British Coins, 39, The J. J. North Collection, Edwardian English Silver Coins 1279-1351', The Classification of Class 10, c. 1301-10, by C. Wood.

Prices are for full flan, well struck coins.
The prices for the above types are for London. For coins of the other mints see following pages; types are in brackets, prices are for the commonest type of each mint.

Berwick Type 1   Type II   Type III   Type IV

		£	£
1415	*Berwick-on-Tweed*. (Blunt types I-IV) Local dies	35	120
1416	*Bristol*. (2; 3b; c, d; 3f, g; 9b)	30	90
1417	*Bury St. Edmunds*. Robert de Hadelie (3c, d, g; 4a, b, c)	50	175
1418	— Villa Sci Edmundi (4e; 5b; 6b; 7a; 8ab, 9a – 10 cf 5)	25	85
1419	*Canterbury*. (2; 3b-g; 4; 5; 7a; 7b; 9;10)	25	85
1420	*Chester*. (3g; 9b)	35	120
1421	*Durham*. Plain cross *mm* (9b; 10ab; 10cf 2-3; 10cf 5)	25	85
1422	— Bishop de Insula (2; 3b, c, e, g; 4a)	30	90
1423	— Bishop Bec (4b-e; 5b; 6b; 7b; 9a, 9b, 10) with *mm*. cross moline	30	90
1424	— — (4b) cross moline in one angle of *rev*	175	525
1425	*Exeter*. (9b)	35	120
1426	*Kingston-upon-Hull*. (9b)	40	135
1427	*Lincoln*. (3c, d, f, g)	30	90
1428	*Newcastle-upon-Tyne*. (3e; 9b; 10ab)	30	90
1429	*York*. Royal mint (2; 3b, c, d, e, f; 9b)	30	90
1430	— Archbishop's mint (3e, f; 9b). R. Quatrefoil in centre	30	100
1431	**Halfpenny,** *London*. Class 3b. ЄDWR ANGL DNS hYB, drapery composed of curved line with wedges above	60	175
1432	— 3c Drapery composed of two wedges	35	100

1434A

		F	VF
		£	£
1433	— 3g. New wide crown, thick-waisted S, drapery as 3b	35	100
1433A	— — 4c. Narrower crown, drapery of two unequal wedges	40	135
1433B	— — Similar, pellet before LON	50	150
1434	— 4e. Single-piece collar with (usually) three pellets on breast	60	175
1434A	— 6. Small face with short hair, large coarse crown, closed Є	65	185
1435	— 7. Larger face with square jaw, open Є, usually double-barred N	50	150
1436	— 8. Similar, new crown with straight sides	60	175
1437	— 10. ЄDWAR R ANGL DNS hYB, bifoliate or trifoliate crown, new waisted letters	40	110

The above prices are for London; halfpence of the mints given below were also struck.

1438	*Berwick-on-Tweed.* (Blunt types I, II and III)	100	325
1439	*Bristol.* Class 3c, 3g, 4c	50	150
1440	*Lincoln.* Class 3c	60	175
1441	*Newcastle.* Class 3e, single pellet in each angle of *rev.*	65	200
1442	*York.* Class 3c-e	50	150

1443A   1445

1443	**Farthing,** *London.* Class 1a. Base silver issue (6.65 grains), ЄDWARDVS RЄX. bifoliate crown with no intermediate jewels, inner circle. R. LONDONIЄNSIS, (rarely LONDRIЄNSIS),	75	250
1443A	— 1c. Similar trifoliate crown	50	175
1444	— 2. Smaller face, trifoliate crown with intermediate jewels	40	110
1445	— 3c. New tapering face, wide at top, crown with curved band	40	120
1445A	— 3de. Sterling silver issue (5.51 grains.) Є R ANGLIЄ bust (usually) to bottom of coin, no inner circle. R. LONDONIЄNSIS	40	135
1446	— 3g. Similar, new wide crown with curving side fleurs.	40	110
1446A	— 4de. Similar to 3de. R. CIVITAS LONDON	60	200
1446B	— 5. Similar, crude wide crown.	50	175
1447	— 6-7. New large face with wide cheeks, pellet or almond eyes	40	120
1448	— 8. Similar, small rounded face, tall crude crown	40	135
1449	— 9a. Є R ANGL DN, small tapering face, (a variety has the face of class 6-7)	50	175
1449A	— 9b. Small ugly face, usually wide crown with outwards-sloping sides..	60	200
1450	— 10 ЄDWARDVS REX (-, A, AN or ANG,) large bust within inner circle. *Type 1450 often appears on oval flans.*	40	110

It is now thought that the order of London Farthings is class 4de, 6-7, 5, 9a, 8, 9b

1446   1452

		F	*VF*
		£	£
1451	*Berwick-on-Tweed*. (Blunt type I, IIIb)...	150	525
1452	*Bristol*. Class 2, 3c, 3de	50	175
1453	*Lincoln*. Class 3de...	50	175
1453A	*Newcastle*. Class 3de, R NOVI CASTRI..	225	750
1454	*York*. Class 2, 3c, 3de	75	250

For further information see: *Farthings and Halfpennies, Edward I and II*, P. and B R Withers, 2001

EDWARD II, 1307-27

The coinage of this reign differs only in minor details from that of Edward I. No groats were issued in the years *c*. 1282-1351.

1458 (12a)   1459 (13)   1460 (14)

1461 (15a)   1462 (15b)   1463 (15c)

1455	**Penny,** *London*. Class 11a. Broken spear-head or pearl on l. side of crown; long narrow face, straight-sided N; round back to C and Є	30	110
1456	— 11b. — Є with angular back (till 15b), N with well-marked serifs (late)	30	110
1457	— 11c. — — A of special form	50	150
1458	— 12a. Central fleur of crown formed of three wedges; thick cross *mm*.	40	125
1458A	— 12b — Crown with diamond-shaped petals and cruciform central fleur; cross of four wedges *mm*	70	225
1458B	— 12c — Crown with heart-shaped petals; cross pattée *mm*	80	250
1459	— 13. Central fleur of crown as Greek double axe	40	125
1460	— 14. Crown with tall central fleur; large smiling face with leering eyes	40	125
1461	— 15a. Small flat crown with both spear-heads usually bent to l.; face of 14	40	125
1462	— 15b. — very similar, but smaller face...	40	125
1463	— 15c. — large face, large Є	45	135

Berwick Type V	Type VI	Type VII

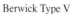

		F £	VF £
1464	*Berwick-on-Tweed.* (Blunt types V, VI and VII) Local dies except V	60	150
1465	*Bury St. Edmunds.* (11; 12; 13; 14; 15)..	30	110
1466	*Canterbury.* (11; 12a; 13; 14; 15)	30	110
1467	*Durham.* King's Receiver (11a), *mm.* plain cross......................................	30	120
1468	— Bishop Bec. (11a), *mm.* cross moline	30	120
1469	— Bishop Kellawe (11; 12a; 13), crozier on *rev.*	35	125
1470	— Bishop Beaumont (13; 14; 15), *mm.* lion with lis..............................	35	125
1471	*mm.* plain cross (11a, 14, 15c)	50	150

1472

1472	**Halfpenny,** *London.* Class 10-11, ЄDWARDVS REX (-, A, AN, ANG, ANGL or ANGLI,) bifoliate or trifoliate crown	60	185
1473	— *Berwick-on-Tweed.* (Blunt type V)	150	525

1474

1474	**Farthing,** *London.* Class 11, 13, ЄDWARDVS REX (-, A, AN, or AG), face with pellet eyes..	40	125
1475	— *Berwick-on-Tweed.* (Blunt type V)	175	575

During Edward's early years small quantities of silver coins were minted following the standard of the previous two reigns, but in 1335 halfpence and farthings were produced which were well below the .925 Sterling silver standard. In 1344 an impressive gold coinage was introduced comprising the Double Florin or Double Leopard valued at six shillings, and its half and quarter, the Leopard and the Helm. The design of the Florin was based on the contemporary gold of Philip de Valois of France.

The first gold coinage was not successful and it was replaced later the same year by a heavier coinage, the Noble, valued at 6s. 8d, i.e., 80 pence, half a mark or one third of a pound, together with its fractions. The Noble was lowered in weight in two stages over the next few years, being stabilised at 120 grains in 1351. With the signing of the Treaty of Bretigny in 1360 Edward's title to the Kingdom of France was omitted from the coinage, but it was resumed again in 1369.

In 1344 the silver coinage had been re-established at the old sterling standard, but the penny was reduced in weight to just over 20 grains and in 1351 to 18 grains. Groats were minted again in 1351 and were issued regularly henceforth until the reign of Elizabeth.

Subsequent to the treaty with France which gave England a cross-channel trading base at Calais, a mint was opened there in 1363 for minting gold and silver coins of English type. In addition to coins of the regular English mints, the Abbot of Reading also minted silver pence, halfpence and farthings with a scallop shell in one quarter of the reverse while coins from Berwick display one or two boar's or bear's heads.

There is evidence of re-use of dies at later periods, e.g. 3rd coinage halfpennies.

For further study of the English Hammered Gold Coinage see: *Sylloge of Coins of the British Isles, 47: The Herbert Schneider Collection Volume One*, by Peter Woodhead. 1996.

Mintmarks

✠	✠	✠	✚	♔	✠	✠	✚
6	1	2	3	74	4	5	7a

1334-51	Cross pattée (6)		1356	Crown (74)
1351-2	Cross 1 (1)		1356-61	Cross 3 (4)
1351-7	Crozier on cross end (76a, *Durham*)		1361-9	Cross potent (5)
1352-3	Cross 1 broken (2)		1369-77	Cross pattée (6)
1354-5	Cross 2 (3)			Plain cross (7a)

The figures in brackets refer to the plate of mintmarks in Appendix IV.

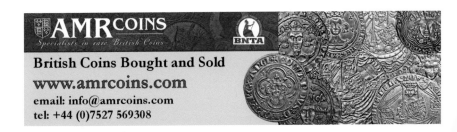

GOLD
(No gold coinage issued before 1344)

THIRD COINAGE, 1344-51, First period, 1344

1476	1477	1478

	F £	VF £

1476 **Double-florin (Double Leopard).** (=6s.; wt. 108 grs., 6.99g.). King enthroned
    beneath canopy; crowned leopard's head each side. ℞. Cross in quatrefoil   90000 350000
1477 **Florin.** Leopard sejant with banner l. ℞. Somewhat as last 40000 150000
1478 **Half-florin.** Helmet on fleured field. ℞. Floriate cross 20000 75000

Second period, 1344-46
1479 **Noble** (=6s. 8d., wt. 138.46 grs., 8.97g.). King stg. facing in ship with sword
    and shield. ℞. L in centre of royal cross in tressure 25000 90000
1479A **Half-noble.** Similar 8500 30000
1480 **Quarter-noble.** Shield in tressure. ℞. As last..   2500   9000

1481

1482

Third period, 1346-51
1481 **Noble** (wt. 128.59 grs., 8.33g.). As 1479, but Є in centre; large letters ...   3000 10000
1482 **Half-noble.** Similar 2250 8000
1483 **Quarter-noble.** As 1480, but Є in centre 575 1500

FOURTH COINAGE, 1351-77

Reference: L. A. Lawrence, *The Coinage of Edward III from 1351.*

Pre-treaty period, 1351-61. With French title.

		F	VF
		£	£
1484	**Noble** (wt. 120 grs., 7.77g.), series B (1351). Open Є and C, Roman M; *mm*. cross 1 (1)	1450	5500
1485	— — *rev*. of series A (1351). Round lettering, Lombardic M and N; closed inverted Є in centre	1650	6000
1486	C (1351-1352). Closed Є and C, Lombardic M; *mm*. cross 1 (1)	1350	5250
1487	D (1352-1353). *O.* of series C. R. *mm*. cross 1 broken (2)	2250	9000

1490   1498

1488	E (1354-1355). Broken letters, V often has a nick in r. limb; *mm*. cross 2 (3)	1350	5250
1489	F (1356). *mm*. crown (74)	1500	5750
1490	G (1356-1361). *mm*. cross 3 (4). Many varieties	1250	4500
1491	**Half-noble,** B. As noble with *rev*. of series A, but closed Є in centre not inverted	1000	3250
1492	C. *O.* as noble. *Rev*. as last	1100	3500
1493	E. As noble	1350	4500
1494	G. As noble. Many varieties	1000	3250
1495	**Quarter-noble,** B. Pellet below shield. R. Closed Є in centre	525	1250
1496	C. *O.* of series B. *Rev*. details as noble	650	1500
1497	E. *O.* as last. *Rev*. details as noble, pellet in centre	575	1350
1498	G. *mm*. cross 3 (4). Many varieties	475	1100

Transitional treaty period, 1361. French title omitted, replaced by that of Aquitaine on the noble and (rarely) on the half-noble, but not on the quarter-noble; irregular sized letters; *mm*. cross potent (5).

1499

1499	**Noble.** R. Pellets or annulets at corners of central panel	1350	5250

1504

			F	*VF*
			£	£
1500	**Half-noble.** Similar		850	2500
1501	**Quarter-noble.** Similar. Many varieties. Pellet and rarely Є in centre....		450	1100

Treaty period, 1361-69. Omits FRANC, new letters, usually curule-shaped X; *mm.* cross potent(5).

1502	**Noble.** *London.* Saltire or nothing before ЄDWARD..............................	1350	5000
1503	— Annulet before ЄDWARD (with, rarely, crescent on forecastle).........	1250	4750
1504	*Calais.* C in centre of *rev.,* flag at stern of ship	1350	5250
1505	— — without flag...	1400	5500

1506

1508

1506	**Half-noble.** *London.* Saltire before ЄDWARD	1000	3250
1507	— Annulet before ЄDWARD	1000	3250
1508	*Calais.* C in centre of *rev.,* flag at stern of ship	1250	4250
1509	— — without flag...	1350	4500
1510	**Quarter-noble.** *London.* As 1498. R. Lis in centre	425	1050
1511	— — annulet before ЄDWARD	450	1100
1512	*Calais.* R. Annulet in centre..	525	1350
1513	— — cross in circle over shield	475	1250
1514	— R. Quatrefoil in centre; cross over shield	575	1500
1515	— — crescent over shield..	725	1850

Post-treaty period, 1369-1377. French title resumed.

1516	**Noble.** *London.* Annulet before ЄD. R. Treaty period die......................	2250	8500
1517	— — — crescent on forecastle..	1500	5750
1518	— — post-treaty letters. R. Є and pellet in centre..............................	1350	5250
1519	— — — R. Є and saltire in centre...	2000	7500
1520	*Calais.* Flag at stern. R. Є in centre	1500	5750

1521

		F	VF
		£	£
1521	— — *Rev.* as 1518, with Є and pellet in centre	1350	5250
1522	— As 1520, but without flag. R. Є in centre	1750	7000
1523	**Half-noble.** *London*. *O*. Treaty die. *Rev.* as 1518	1850	7250
1524	*Calais*. Without AQT, flag at stern. R. Є in centre	1750	6750
1525	— — R. Treaty die with C in centre	2000	7500

SILVER

FIRST COINAGE, 1327-35 (0.925 fineness)

1526   1530

1526	**Penny.** *London*. As Edw. II; Fox class XVd with Lombardic n's	375	1250
1527	*Bury St. Edmunds*. Similar	475	1500
1528	*Canterbury; mm.* cross pattée with pellet centre	300	950
1529	— — three extra pellets in one quarter	275	900
1530	*Durham*. R. Small crown in centre	575	1850
1530A	*Reading*. R. Escallop in 2nd quarter	675	2000
1531	*York*. As 1526, but quatrefoil in centre of *rev;* three extra pellets in TAS quarter	185	625
1532	— — — pellet in each quarter of *mm*	200	650

1535   1537   1539

1534	— — — Roman N's on *obv*.	200	650
1535	*Berwick* (1333-1342, Blunt type VIII). Bear's head in one quarter of *rev.*	575	1850
1536	**Halfpenny.** *London*. Indistinguishable from EDWARD II (cf. 1472)	60	185
1537	*Berwick* (Bl. VIII). Bear's head in one or two quarters	125	475
1538	**Farthing.** *London*. Indistinguishable from those of EDWARD II (cf. 1474)	40	125
1539	*Berwick* (Bl. VIII). As 1537	110	450

1540   1542

	F £	VF £

SECOND COINAGE, 1335-43 (0.833 fineness)

1540 **Halfpenny.** *London.* ⲈDWARDVS RⲈX AN(G). Six-pointed star after AN and before LON. Bifoliate or trifoliate crown.	30	100
1540A — — New tall crown. Star of eight or six points after ANG and DON and before CIVI or none on rev.	35	110
1541 *Reading.* Escallop in one quarter, star before or after mint	200	675
1542 **Farthing.** *London.* A (N), six-pointed star after A (rarely omitted) and before LON, flat crown	50	150
1542A — ANG, star after ANG and before LON or after DON, tall crown	60	175

THIRD OR FLORIN COINAGE, 1344-51. Bust with bushy hair. (0.925 fine, 20 grs., 1.30g.)

1543   1544

Reverses: I. Lombardic n II. Roman N. III. Reversed N. IV. Reversed Double-barred N.

1543 **Penny.** Fox proposed 'Class XVI'. *London.* Class 1. ⲈDW, Lombardic N. Rev. I.	45	135
1544 — — Class 2, ⲈDWA, Lombardic N. Rev. I, II.	40	125
1545 — — Class 3. ⲈDW. Roman N. Rev. I, II, III.	40	125
1546 — — Class 4. ⲈDW. Reversed N. Rev. I, II, III, IV (doubtful)	40	125
1546A — Unusual types designated A to E.	60	175
1547 — Canterbury. Class 2. as 1544. Rev. I.	90	275
1548 — — Class 4. as 1546 Rev. I.	75	225
1549 *Durham,* Sede Vacante (possibly 1345 issues of Bishop Richard de Bury or Bishop Hatfield). A, ⲈDWR rev. No marks	45	135
1550 — — B, similar, ⲈDWAR R	50	160
1551 — Bp. Hatfield. C, similar, but pellet in centre of *rev.*	60	175
1552 — — — Crozier on *rev.*	60	175
1553 — — — — with pellet in centre of *rev.*	65	185
1554 — — D, ⲈDWARDVS RⲈX AIn, crozier on *rev.*	100	325

1555

1555 *Reading. obv.* as 1546. Ɍ. Escallop in one quarter	250	850
1555A — — ⲈDWARDVS RⲈX ANG. Rev. as 1555	300	1000
1556 *York. obv.* as 1546. Ɍ. Quatrefoil in centre	45	135

1557   1558

		F £	VF £
1557	**Halfpenny.** *London.* ЄDWARDVS RЄX	30	100
1558	— — ЄDWARDVS RЄX An.	35	110

1559   1561   1562

1559	— — as 1558 with pellet or small saltire each side of crown and/or in one reverse quarter	45	135
1560	— *Reading.* as 1557. Rev. Escallop in one quarter.	325	1000
1561	— — as 1558. Rev. as 1560.	350	1050
1562	**Farthing.** *London.* ЄDWARDVS RЄX	45	135
1562A	*Reading.* As S.1562. Rev. as 1560	375	1250
1562B	— — ЄDWARDVS RЄX An. Rev. as 1560	425	1350

FOURTH COINAGE, 1351-77

Reference: L. A. Lawrence, *The Coinage of Edward III from 1351.*
A large variety of mules exist between styles and issue.

Pre-treaty period, 1351-61. With French title.

1563   1565

1567

1563	**Groat** (=4d., 72 grs., 4.66g.). *London,* series B (1351). Roman M, open C and Є; *mm.* cross 1	160	575
1564	— — — crown in each quarter	3000	9500
1565	— C (1351-2). Lombardic M̄, closed Ꝿ and Є, R with wedge-shaped tail; *mm.* cross 1	75	250
1566	— D (1352-3). R with normal tail; *mm.* cross 1 or cross 1 broken (2)	85	300
1567	— E (1354-5). Broken letters, V often with nick in r. limb; *mm.* cross 2 (3)	70	225

		F	VF
		£	£
1568	— — — lis on breast	80	225
1569	— F (1356). *mm.* crown (74)	85	300

1570   1572

1570	— G (1356-61). Usually with annulet in one quarter and sometimes under bust, *mm.* cross 3 (4). Many varieties	75	250
1571	*York,* series D. As London	200	750
1572	— E. As London	90	300

1573   1581

1573	**Halfgroat.** *London,* series B. As groat	100	325
1574	— C. As groat	50	150
1575	— D. As groat	55	160
1576	— E. As groat	50	150
1577	— F. As groat	55	160
1578	— G. As groat	50	150
1579	— — — annulet below bust	55	160
1580	*York,* series D. As groat...	90	275
1581	— E. As groat	75	225
1582	— — — lis on breast	80	250
1583	**Penny.** *London.* Series A (1351). Round letters, Lombardic m and n, annulet in each quarter; *mm.* cross pattée	90	300

1584   1585   1591

1584	— C. Details as groat, but annulet in each quarter	40	135
1585	— D. Details as groat, but annulet in each quarter	50	160
1586	— E. Sometimes annulet in each quarter..	45	150
1587	— F. Details as groat...	45	150
1588	— G. Details as groat..	45	150

	F	VF
	£	£
1589 — — — annulet below bust	50	160
1590 — — — saltire in one quarter	60	175
1591 *Durham*, Bp. Hatfield. Series A. As 1583, but extra pellet in each quarter, VIL LA crozier DVRRЄM and VIL crozier LA DVRRЄM	90	275
1592 — C. Details as groat. �...		
1592 — C. Details as groat. Ɍ. Crozier, CIVITAS DVNЄLMIЄ	35	125
1593 — D — — —	40	140
1594 — E — — —	45	150
1595 — F — Ɍ. Crozier, CIVITAS DVRЄMЄ	40	140
1596 — G — — —	40	140
1597 — — — — — annulet below bust	45	150
1598 — — — — — saltire in one quarter	75	200
1599 — — — — — annulet on each shoulder	50	165
1600 — — — — — trefoil of pellets on breast	50	165
1601 — — — Ɍ. Crozier, CIVITAS DVRЄLMIЄ	70	200
1602 *York*, Royal Mint. Series D	40	135
1603 — — E	35	125
1604 — Archb. Thoresby. Series D. Ɍ. Quatrefoil in centre	40	135
1605 — — G —	35	125
1606 — — — annulet or saltire on breast	40	140

| | 1607 | | 1609 | | 1609A |

1607 **Halfpenny**. *London*. Series E. ЄDWARDVS RЄX A�␞	125	375
1608 — G, but with *obv.* of F (*mm.* crown). Annulet in one quarter	200	675
1609 **Farthing**. *London*. Series E. ЄDWARDVS RЄX	135	450
1609A — — Series G. Annulet in one quarter	150	525

Transitional treaty period, 1361. French title omitted, irregular sized letters; *mm.* cross potent (5).

1610 **Groat**. *London*. Annulet each side of crown	325	1250

| | 1611 | | 1612 | | 1615 |

1611 **Halfgroat**. Similar, but only seven arches to tressure	150	525
1612 **Penny,** *London*. Omits RЄX, annulet in two upper qtrs. of *mm*	135	500
1613 *York*, Archb. Thoresby. Similar, but quatrefoil enclosing pellet in centre of *rev.*	60	200
1614 *Durham*. Bp. Hatfield. Similar. Ɍ. Crozier, CIVITAS DORЄLMЄ	75	275
1615 **Halfpenny.** Two pellets over *mm.*, ЄDWARDVS RЄX Aⴭⴭ	225	750

Treaty period, 1361-69. French title omitted, new letters, usually 'Treaty' X, rarely curule chair X *mm*. cross potent (5).

		F	VF
		£	£
1616	**Groat,** *London*. Many varieties	85	300
1617	— Annulet before ЄDWARD	90	325
1618	— Annulet on breast	110	375

1617   1618

1619	*Calais*. As last	135	450

1620   1626

1620	**Halfgroat,** *London*. As groat	75	225
1621	— — Annulet before ЄDWARDVS	85	250
1622	— — Annulet on breast	90	275
1623	*Calais*. As last	125	400
1624	**Penny,** *London*. ЄDWARD АПGL R, etc	60	175
1625	— — — pellet before ЄDWARD	65	200
1626	*Calais*. Ꞧ. VILLA CALЄSIE	175	575
1627	*Durham*. Ꞧ. CIVITAS DVПЄLMIS	75	275
1628	— Ꞧ. Crozier, CIVITAS DVRЄMЄ	60	175
1629	*York*, Archb. Thoresby. Quatrefoil in centre of *rev.*, ЄDWARDVS DЄI		
	G RЄX АП	60	175
1630	— — — ЄDWARDVS RЄX АПGLI	40	140
1631	— — — — quatrefoil before ЄD and on breast	45	150
1632	— — — — annulet before ЄD	45	150
1633	— — — ЄDWARD АПGL R DПS HYB	60	175
1634	**Halfpenny.** ЄDWARDVS RЄX АП, pellet stops	40	135

1635   1636

1635	— Pellet before ЄD, annulet stops	40	135
1636	**Farthing.** ЄDWARDVS RЄX, pellet or no stops	200	750

Post-treaty period, 1369-77. French title resumed, X like St. Andrew's cross; *mm.* 5, 6, 7a.

1637   1639

		F	VF
		£	£
1637	**Groat.** Various readings, *mm.* cross pattée	125	400
1638	— — row of pellets across breast (chain mail)	300	900
1639	— row of annulets below bust (chain mail); *mm.* cross potent with four pellets	350	1100
1640	**Halfgroat.** Various readings	120	350

1641   1643

1640A	— Thin portrait of Richard II	150	525
1641	— row of pellets one side of breast (chain mail)	185	600
1642	**Penny,** *London.* No marks on breast	60	250
1643	— Pellet or annulet on breast	60	250
1644	— Cross or quatrefoil on breast	50	200
1645	*Durham,* Bp. Hatfield. *mm.* 7a, CIVITAS DVnOLM, crozier	45	175
1646	— — — — annulet on breast	45	185
1647	— — — — lis on breast	45	185
1648	*York.* Archb. Thoresby or Neville. R. Quatrefoil in centre	40	150
1649	— — — lis on breast	45	160
1650	— — — annulet on breast	40	150
1651	— — — cross on breast	45	175

1652

1652	**Farthing.** ЄDWARD RЄX ANGL, large head without neck	375	1250

For further reading see:
Halfpennies and Farthings of Edward III and Richard II. *Paul and Bente R. Withers, 2002.*

There was no change in the weight standard of the coinage during this reign and the coins evolve from early issues resembling those of Edward III to late issues similar to those of Henry IV.

There is no overall, systematic classification of the coins of Richard II but a coherent scheme for the gold coinage has been worked out and is published in the Schneider Sylloge (SCBI 47). This classification has been adopted here.

Reference: *Silver coinages of Richard II, Henry IV and V.* (B.N.J. 1959-60 and 1963).

Mintmark: cross pattée (6)

GOLD

		F	VF
		£	£
1653	**Noble,** *London*. Style of Edw. III. IA. Lis over sail	1850	6500

1654   1658

1654	— IB. Annulet over sail	1750	6000
1655	French title omitted. IIA. Crude style, saltire over sail. IIB. Fine style, trefoil over sail. IIC. Porcine style, no mark over sail	1650	5750
1656	French title resumed. IIIA. Fine style, no marks	1750	6000
1657	— IIIB. Lis on rudder. IIIC. Trefoil by shield	1750	6000
1658	Henry IV style. IVA. Escallop on rudder. IVB. Crescent on rudder	1850	6500
1659	*Calais*. With altered obverse of Edw. III, Edw. III lettering	2750	9500
1660	Style of Edw. III. IB. New lettering. Voided quatrefoil over sail	2000	7000

1661

1661	French title omitted. IIA. Crude style, no marks. IIB. Fine style, trefoil over sail. IIC. Porcine style, no marks	1750	5750
1662	French title resumed. IIIA. Fine style, no marks	1750	6000
1663	— IIIB. Lion on rudder. IIIC. Two pellets by shield	2000	7000

	F	VF
	£	£

1664 **Half-noble,** *London*. With altered *obv*. of Edw. III. Usually muled with
     rev. or altered *rev*. of Edw. III 2250 8000

1665   1673

		F	VF
1665	Style of Edw. III. IB. No marks or saltire over sail	1750	6500
1666	French title omitted. IIA. New style, no marks	1850	7000
1667	French title resumed. IIIA. No marks. IIIB. Lion on rudder	1750	6500
1668	Henry IV style. IVB. Crescent on rudder	2000	7500
1669	*Calais*. Mule with *obv*. or *rev*. of Edw. III	2250	8000
1670	Style of Edw. III. IB. Quatrefoil over sail	2000	7500
1671	Late style. French title. IIIA. No marks. IIIB. Saltire by rudder	1850	7000
1672	**Quarter-noble,** *London*. IA. R in centre of *rev*.	625	1500
1673	IB Lis in centre of *rev*.	575	1350
1674	— lis or cross over shield	675	1600

1675   1677

		F	VF
1675	IIIA. Pellet in centre of *rev*.	625	1500
1676	IIIB. Trefoil of annulets over shield or trefoils in spandrels	750	2000
1677	IVA. Escallop over shield	700	1750

SILVER

1680

	F	VF
	£	£
1678 **Groat.** I. Style of Edw. III, F *(i.e. et)* before FRANC, etc.	525	2250
1679 II. New lettering, retrograde Z before FRANC, etc.	375	1850
1680 III. Bust with bushy hair, 'fishtail' serifs to letters	450	2000
1681 IV. New style bust and crown, crescent on breast	950	3750

1682

	F	VF
1682 **Halfgroat.** II. New lettering; with or without French title	250	950
1683 III. As 1680	275	1000
1684 — — with *obv.* die of Edw. III (1640A)	300	1100
1685 IV. As 1681, with or without crescent on breast	600	1750
1686 **Penny,** *London.* I Lettering as 1678, RICARDVS RЄX AПGLIЄ	175	650
1688 — II. As 1679, Z FRAПC lis on breast	185	700

1688

	F	VF
1689 — III. As 1680, RICARD RЄX AПGLIЄ, fish-tail letters	200	750
1690 *York.* I. Early style, usually with cross or lis on breast, quatrefoil in centre of *rev*	75	325
1691 — II. New bust and letters, no marks on breast	75	325

1692

1692	— Local dies. Pellet above each shoulder, cross on breast, REX AnGLIE or AnGILIE	80	350
1693	— — — REX DNS ЄB	90	375
1694	— — — REX AnG FRAnC	100	400
1695	— III. As 1680, REX AnGL Z FRAnC (scallop after TAS)	90	375
1696	— IV. Very bushy hair, new letters, R. R in centre of quatrefoil.........	150	525
1697	*Durham.* Cross or lis on breast, DVnOLM	125	450

1698   1699

1698	**Halfpenny.** Early style. LONDON, saltire or annulet (rare) on breast	60	175
1699	Intermediate style. LOnDOn, no marks on breast	50	150
1700	Type III. Late style. Similar, but fishtail letters	50	150
1700A	Type IV. Short, stubby lettering	60	175

1701   1704A

1701	**Farthing.** Small bust and letters...	150	525
1703	Similar but no neck	150	525
1704	Rose in each angle of *rev.* instead of pellets	225	750
1704A	Large head with broad face as Henry IV	275	950

For further reading see:
Halfpennies and Farthings of Edward III and Richard II. P. and B. R. Withers, 2002.

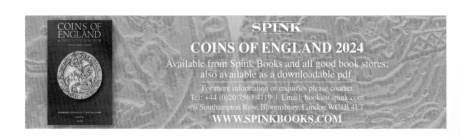

HENRY IV, 1399-1413

In 1412 the standard weights of the coinage were reduced, the noble by 12 grains and the penny by 3 grains, partly because there was a scarcity of bullion and partly to provide revenue for the king, as Parliament had not renewed the royal subsidies. As in France, the royal arms were altered, three fleur-de-lis taking the place of the four or more lis previously displayed.

Mintmark: cross pattée (6)

GOLD

HEAVY COINAGE, 1399-1412

1706   1707

		F	VF
		£	£
1705	**Noble** (120 grs., 7.77g.), *London*. Old arms with four lis in French quarters; crescent or annulet on rudder	6750	18500
1706	— New arms with three lis; crescent, pellet or no marks on rudder	6500	17500
1707	*Calais*. Flag at stern, old arms; crown on or to l. of rudder	7500	22500

1709

1708	— — new arms; crown or saltire on rudder	7000	20000
1709	**Half-noble,** *London*. Old arms	6750	18500
1710	— new arms	6500	17500
1711	*Calais*. New arms	7500	22500
1712	**Quarter-noble,** *London*. Crescent over old arms	1500	5250
1713	— — — new arms	1350	5000
1714	*Calais*. New arms. R. *Mm*. crown	1750	5750

1715

	F	VF
	£	£

LIGHT COINAGE, 1412-13

1715 **Noble** (108 grs., 6.99g.). Trefoil, or trefoil and annulet, on side of ship.
R. Trefoil in one quarter.. 1850 6500

1716 **Half-noble.** Similar, but always with annulet 2500 8500

1717

1717 **Quarter-noble.** Trefoils, or trefoils and annulets beside shield, lis above. R.
Lis in centre 950 2750

SILVER

HEAVY COINAGE, 1399-1412

1718	**Halfgroat** (36 grs., 2.33g.). Star on breast	2000	5500
1718A	— Muled with Edw. III (1640A) *obv.*...	750	2250
1719	**Penny,** *London.* Similar, early bust with long neck.................................	750	2500
1720	— later bust with shorter neck, no star on breast	675	2250

1722 1723 1725

1722	*York* Bust with broad face, round chin..	525	1500
1723	**Halfpenny.** Early small bust...	200	650
1724	— later large bust, with rounded shoulders, ...	225	700
1725	**Farthing.** Face without neck..	1000	3250

LIGHT COINAGE, 1412-13

1726   1732

	F £	VF £
1726 **Groat** (60 grs., 3.88g.). I. Pellet to l., annulet to r. of crown; altered die of Richard II	1350	6000
1727 New dies; II. Annulet to l., pellet to r. of crown, 8 or 10 arches to tressure	1250	5250
1728 — III. Similar but 9 arches to tressure	1100	4500
1729 **Halfgroat.** Pellet to l., annulet to r. of crown	900	3000
1730 Annulet to l., pellet to r. of crown	850	2750
1731 **Penny,** *London.* Annulet and pellet by crown; trefoil on breast and before CIVI	750	2250
1732 — — annulet or slipped trefoil before LON	850	2500
1733 — Pellet and annulet by crown	850	2500
1734 *York.* Annulet on breast. ꝶ. Quatrefoil in centre	450	1100
1735 *Durham.* Trefoil on breast, DVꞐOLM	425	1000

1737   1738

	F	VF
1737 **Halfpenny.** New dies; annulets by crown or neck, or no marks	225	700
1738 **Farthing.** Face, no bust; trefoil after RЄX	900	3000

For further information see:
Halfpennies and Farthings of Henry IV, V and VI. P. and B. R. Withers, 2003.

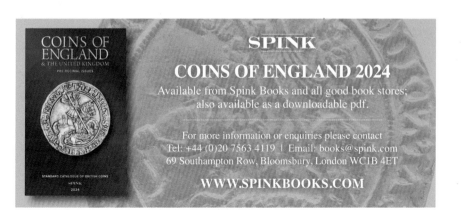

There was no change of importance in the coinage of this reign. There was, however, a considerable development in the use of privy marks which distinguished various issues, except for the last issue of the reign when most marks were removed. The Calais mint, which had closed in 1411, did not re-open until just before the end of the reign. There is now some uncertainty as to whether types A and B of Henry V should be given to Henry IV.

Mintmarks

Cross pattée (4)   Pierced cross with pellet centre (20)   Pierced cross (18).

GOLD

		F	VF
		£	£
1739	**Noble.** A. Quatrefoil over sail and in second quarter of *rev.* Short broad letters, no other marks	2250	7500
1740	— B. Ordinary letters; similar, or with annulet on rudder	1750	5750
1741	— C. Mullet by sword arm, annulet on rudder	1800	6000

1742   1744

1742	— — — broken annulet on side of ship	1600	5500
1743	—D. Mullet and annulet by sword arm, trefoil by shield, broken annulet on ship	1750	5750
1744	— E. Mullet, or mullet and annulet by sword arm, trefoil by shield, pellet by sword point and in one quarter, annulet on side of ship	1750	5750
1745	— — Similar, but trefoil on ship instead of by shield	1800	6000
1746	— F. Similar, but no pellet at sword point, trefoil in one quarter	1850	6500
1747	— G. No marks; annulet stops, except for mullet after first word	2000	7000
1748	**Half Noble.** B. As noble; Hen. IV *rev.* die	2250	7500
1749	— C. Broken annulet on ship, quatrefoil below sail	1500	4500
1750	— — Mullet over shield, broken annulet on *rev.*	1250	4000
1751	— F. Similar, but no annulet on ship, usually trefoil by shield	1350	4250
1752	— F/E. As last, but pellet in 1st and annulet in 2nd quarter	1500	4500

1753

1756

	F £	VF £
1753 — G. As noble, but quatrefoil over sail, mullet sometimes omitted after first word of *rev*.	1350	4250
1754 **Quarter Noble.** A. Lis over shield and in centre of *rev*. Short broad letters; quatrefoil and annulet beside shield, stars at corners of centre on *rev*.	675	1750
1755 — C. Ordinary letters; quatrefoil to l., quat. and mullet to r. of shield	625	1600
1756 — — — annulet to l., mullet to r. of shield	525	1350
1757 — F. Ordinary letters; trefoil to l., mullet to r. of shield	650	1650
1758 — G. — no marks, except mullet after first word	600	1500

SILVER

1759

1759 **Groat.** A. Short broad letters; 'emaciated' bust	750	2750
1760 — — muled with Hen. IV *obv*	900	4250
1761 — — muled with Hen. IV *rev*	750	3000

1762B   1767

1762 B. Ordinary letters; 'scowling' bust	275	950
1762A — — mullet in centre of breast	275	1000
1762B — — mullet to r. of breast	300	1250
1763 — — muled with Hen. IV	525	2000
1764 C. Normal 'frowning' bust	225	900
1765 — — mullet on r. shoulder	200	675
1766 — — R muled with Hen. IV	450	1750
1767 G. Normal 'frowning' bust; no marks	275	1000
1768 **Halfgroat.** A. As groat, but usually with annulet and pellet by crown	525	2000

		F	*VF*
		£	£
1769	B. Ordinary letters; no marks...	225	750
1770	— — muled with Hen. IV *obv*..	750	2750
1771	C. Tall neck, broken annulet to l. of crown..	150	475
1772	— — — mullet on r. shoulder	160	500

		F	*VF*
	1774 1775 1788		
1773	— — — mullet in centre of breast	150	475
1774	F. Annulet and trefoil by crown, mullet on breast	135	450
1775	G. New neat bust: no marks..	125	425
1776	**Penny.** *London*. Altered Hen. IV *obv*. with mullet added to l. of crown ..	650	2000
1777	— A. Letters, bust and marks as 1768	275	950
1778	— C. Tall neck, mullet and broken annulet by crown	50	175
1779	— D. Similar, but whole annulet	65	225
1780	— F. Mullet and trefoil by crown	65	225
1781	— G. New neat bust, no marks, DI GRA	70	240
1782	*Durham*. C. As 1778 but quatrefoil at end of legend	50	185
1783	— D. As 1779	50	185
1784	— G. Similar, but new bust. R. Annulet in one qtr.	60	200
1785	*York*. C. As 1778, but quatrefoil in centre of *rev*....................................	45	175
1786	— D. Similar, but whole annulet by crown	45	175
1787	— E. As last, but pellet above mullet	75	240
1788	— F. Mullet and trefoil by crown	45	175
1789	— — Trefoil over mullet to l., annulet to r. of crown.............................	70	225
1790	— G. Mullet and trefoil by crown (London dies)...................................	50	185

		F	*VF*
	1791 1796 1798		
1791	— — Mullet and lis by crown, annulet in one qtr. (usually local dies)....	45	175
1792	**Halfpenny.** A. Emaciated bust, annulets by crown	200	700
1793	— altered dies of Hen. IV..	275	850
1794	C. Ordinary bust, broken annulets by crown	40	135
1795	D. Annulets, sometimes broken, by hair...	45	150
1796	F. Annulet and trefoil by crown	45	150
1797	G. New bust; no marks, (usually muled with Henry VI annulet *rev*.)	60	200
1797A	**Farthing.** *London*. B. Very large head	750	2250
1798	— G. Small face with neck..	375	1350
1798A	*Calais*. G. as 1798, VILLA CALIS	900	3000

For further information see:
Halfpennies and Farthings of Henry IV, V and VI. P and B. R. Withers, 2003.

The supply of gold began to dwindle early in the reign, which accounts for the rarity of gold after 1426. The Calais mint had reopened just before the death of Henry V and for some years a large amount of coin was struck there. It soon stopped minting gold; the mint was finally closed in 1440. A royal mint at York was opened for a short time in 1423/4.

Marks used to denote various issues become more prominent in this reign and can be used to date coins to within a year or so.

Reference: C. A. Whitton, *The Heavy Coinage of Henry VI.* (B.N.J. 1938-41).

Mintmarks

⬦	✚	⚜	✚	✤	✳	✤	✳
136	7a	105	18	133	8	9	15

1422-7	Incurved pierced cross (136)	1422-34	Cross pommée (133)
1422-3	Lis (105, York)	1427-34	Cross patonce (8)
1422-60	Plain cross (7a, intermittently		Cross fleury (9)
	Lis (105, on gold)	1434-35	Voided cross (15)
1422-27	Pierced cross (18)	1435-60	Cross fleury (9)
1460	Lis (105, on rev. of some groats)		

For Henry VI (second reign 1470-71), restoration mintmarks see page 220.

GOLD

1799

		F	VF
		£	£

Annulet issue, 1422-c.1430

1799 **Noble.** *London.* Annulet by sword arm, and in one spandrel on *rev.;* trefoil stops on *obv.* with lis after hƐnRIC, annulets on *rev.,* with mullet after IhC .... | 1350 | 5000

1800 — Similar, but *obv.* from Henry V die.. | 2500 | 8000

1801 — As 1799, but Flemish imitative coinage .... | 1100 | 3750

1802

1802 *Calais.* As 1799, but flag at stern and C in centre of *rev* .... | 1750 | 6000

		F	VF
		£	£
1803	— — with h in centre of *rev.*	1450	5250
1804	*York*. As London, but with lis over stern..................................	1750	6000

1805

1805	**Half-noble.** *London*. As 1799..	1100	3500
1806	— Similar, but *obv.* from Henry V die....................................	1500	5000
1807	*Calais*. As noble, with C in centre of *rev.*...............................	1750	6000
1808	— — with h in centre of *rev.*	1600	5500
1809	*York*. As noble..	1750	6000
1810	**Quarter-noble.** *London*. Lis over shield; *mm.* large lis	450	1100
1811	— — — trefoil below shield	475	1200
1812	— — — pellet below shield	525	1350
1813	*Calais*. Three lis over shield; *mm.* large lis.............................	625	1500

1814

1819

1814	— Similar but three lis around shield	500	1250
1815	— As 1810, but much smaller *mm*...	475	1200
1816	*York*. Two lis over shield...	525	1350

Rosette-mascle issue, c.1430-31

1817	**Noble.** *London*. Lis by sword arm and in *rev.* field; stops, rosettes, or		
	rosettes and mascles..	2250	8000
1818	*Calais*. Similar, with flag at stern	2500	9000
1819	**Half-noble.** *London*. Lis in *rev.* field; stops, rosettes and mascles..........	2500	9500
1820	*Calais*. Similar, flag at stern; stops, rosettes	3500	12500
1821	**Quarter-noble.** *London*. As 1810; stops, as noble...................	1100	3500
1822	— without lis over shield...	1100	3500
1823	*Calais*. Lis over shield, rosettes r. and l., and rosette stops	1250	3750

Pinecone-mascle issue, c.1431-2/3

1824

		F £	VF £
1824	**Noble.** Stops, pinecones and mascles	2000	7500
1825	**Half-noble.** *O*. Rosette-mascle die. R. As last	3000	11000
1826	**Quarter-noble.** As 1810, but pinecone and mascle stops	1350	4000

1828

Leaf-mascle issue, c.1432/3-6

1827	**Noble.** Leaf in waves; stops, saltires with two mascles and one leaf	4000	15000
1828	**Half-noble.** (Fishpool hoard and Reigate hoard)	3500	12500
1829	**Quarter-noble.** As 1810; stops, saltire and mascle; leaf on inner circle of *rev.*	1250	3750

Leaf-trefoil issue, c.1436-8

1830	**Noble.** Stops, leaves and trefoils	3500	13500
1830A	**Half-noble.**	3250	12500
1831	**Quarter-noble.** Similar	1350	4000

Trefoil issue, 1438-43

1832	**Noble.** Trefoil to left of shield and in *rev.* legend	3500	13500

Leaf-pellet issue, 1445-54

1833	**Noble.** Annulet, lis and leaf below shield	4000	15000

Cross-pellet issue, 1454-61

1834	**Noble.** Mascle at end of *obv.* legend...	4500	17500

Muling exists in Henry VI coins spanning two or three issues. Full flan coins in the smaller denominations are difficult to find.

SILVER

Annulet issue, 1422-30

	1835		1836

				F	VF
				£	£
1835	**Groat.** *London.* Annulet in two quarters of *rev.*	....		90	275
1836	*Calais.* Annulets at neck. ℞. Similar	....		85	250
1837	— — no annulets on *rev.*	....		100	300

1838

1838	*York.* Lis either side of neck. ℞. As 1835	....	750	2500
1839	**Halfgroat.** *London.* As groat	....	50	160

	1840		1843

1840	*Calais.* As 1836	....	45	150
1841	— — no annulets on *rev.*	....	60	175
1843	*York.* As groat	....	1000	3500

1845

1844	**Penny.** *London.* Annulets in two qtrs.	....	45	140
1845	*Calais.* Annulets at neck. ℞. As above	....	40	130

		F £	VF £
1847	*York.* As London, but lis at neck	750	2500
1848	**Halfpenny.** *London.* As penny	30	100
1849	*Calais.* Similar, but annulets at neck	30	100

1850   1852

1850	*York.* Similar, but lis at neck	575	1750
1851	**Farthing.** *London.* As penny, but *mm.* cross pommée	175	650
1852	*Calais.* Similar, but annulets at neck	225	750
1852A	*York.* Similar, but lis at neck	675	2250

Annulet-trefoil sub-issue

1854   1855

1854	**Groat.** *Calais.* As 1836 but trefoil to l. of crown, R̈ trefoil after POSVI and only one annulet	110	325
1855	**Halfgroat.** *Calais.* Similar, usually a mule with annulet issue...............	75	225
1856	**Penny.** *Calais.* Similar, only one annulet on *rev*	125	400

Rosette-mascle issue, 1430-31. All with rosettes (early) or rosettes and mascles somewhere in the legends.

1858	**Groat.** *London.*..	110	325

1859   1861

1859	*Calais*..	85	250
1860	— mascle in two spandrels	90	275
1861	**Halfgroat.** *London.*	135	350

	1862	1870	1872	F £	VF £

1862	*Calais*..	60	175
1863	— mascle in two spandrels	65	185
1864	**Penny.** *London*...	150	525
1865	*Calais*..	45	150
1866	*York*. Archb. Kemp. Crosses by hair, no rosette	40	135
1867	— — Saltires by hair, no rosette..	50	150
1868	— — Mullets by crown	40	135
1869	*Durham*. Bp. Langley. Large star to l. of crown, no rosette, DVnOLMI	75	225
1870	**Halfpenny.** *London*.	40	125
1871	*Calais*..	35	110
1872	**Farthing.** *London*.	225	750
1873	*Calais. Mm*. cross pommée...	275	900

Pinecone-maSCle issue, 1431-32/3. All with pinecones and mascles in legends.

1874   1876

1874	**Groat.** *London*..	90	275
1875	*Calais*..	85	250
1876	**Halfgroat.** *London*.	70	200
1877	*Calais*..	60	175
1878	**Penny.** *London*...	75	225
1879	*Calais*..	50	150
1880	*York*. Archb. Kemp. Mullet by crown, quatrefoil in centre of *rev*.	50	160
1881	— — rosette on breast, no quatrefoil	50	160
1882	— — mullet on breast, no quatrefoil	60	185
1883	*Durham*. Bp. Langley. DVnOLMI...	70	200

1884   1886

	F £	VF £
1884 **Halfpenny.** *London.*	35	110
1885 *Calais.*................................	35	110
1886 **Farthing.** *London.*	200	650
1887 *Calais. Mm.* cross pommée................................	275	850

Leaf-mascle issue, 1432/3-6. Usually with a mascle in the legend and a leaf somewhere in the design.

1888 **Groat.** *London.* Leaf below bust, all appear to read DOnDOn	375	1100
1889 — — *rev.* of last or next coinage	250	750

1890   1892

1890 *Calais.* Leaf below bust, and usually below MЄVM	125	375
1891 **Halfgroat.** *London.* Leaf under bust, pellet under TAS and DON	175	575
1892 *Calais.* Leaf below bust, and sometimes on *rev*................................	150	475
1893 **Penny.** *London.* Leaf on breast, no stops on *rev*................................	100	325
1894 *Calais.* Leaf on breast and below SIЄ	110	350
1895 **Halfpenny.** *London.* Leaf on breast and on *rev*.	45	135
1896 *Calais.* Leaf on breast and below SIЄ	100	300

1897   1902

Leaf-trefoil issue, 1436-8. Mostly with leaves and trefoil of pellets in the legends.

1897 **Groat.** *London.* Leaf on breast	100	300
1898 — without leaf on breast................................	100	300
1899 *Calais.* Leaf on breast	250	750
1900 **Halfgroat.** *London.* Leaf on breast; *mm.* plain cross................................	95	300
1901 — *O. mm.* cross fleury; leaf on breast	85	250
1902 — — without leaf on breast................................	90	275
1902A *Calais.* leaf on breast, mule with leaf mascle *rev.*	200	675

	F	VF
	£	£
1903 **Penny.** *London*. Leaf on breast..	110	325
1903A *Calais.* Similar	275	750
1904 *Durham*. Bp. Neville. Leaf on breast. R. Rings in centre, no stops, DVnOLM	125	375

1905   1907

	F	VF
1905 **Halfpenny.** *London*. Leaf on breast	35	110
1906 — without leaf on breast...	40	120
1906A *Calais.* leaf on breast, mule with leaf mascle rev.	125	350
1907 **Farthing.** *London*. Leaf on breast; stops, trefoil and saltire on *obv.*........	300	950

Trefoil issue, 1438-43. Trefoil of pellets either side of neck and in legend, leaf on breast.

1910

	F	VF
1908 **Groat.** *London*. Sometimes a leaf before LON.	100	325
1909 — Fleurs in spandrels, sometimes extra pellet in two qtrs......................	110	350
1910 — Trefoils in place of fleurs at shoulders, none by neck, sometimes		
extra pellets...	110	350
1911 *Calais*..	275	850

1911A

	F	VF
1911A **Halfgroat.** *London*. Similar, but trefoil after DEUM and sometimes after		
POSVI Mule only with leaf trefoil *obv.*..	150	450
1911B — *Calais. Obv.* Similar to 1911, mule with leaf mascle *rev.*....................	325	1100
1911C **Penny.** *Calais.* Trefoils by neck, leaf on breast	475	1500
1912 **Halfpenny.** *London*.	35	120

1912A

	F	VF
1912A **Farthing.** *London*..	350	1250

Trefoil pellet issue, 1443-5

1913

		F £	VF £

1913   **Groat.** Trefoils by neck, pellets by crown, small leaf on breast; sometimes
extra pellet in two quarters   175   575

1915   1917

Leaf-pellet issue, 1445-54. Leaf on breast, pellet each side of crown, except where stated.

		F	VF
1914	**Groat.** ANGL; extra pellet in two quarters	90	300
1915	*Similar,* but ANGLI..	90	300
1916	— — trefoil in *obv.* legend	100	325
1917	Leaf on neck, fleur on breast, R often extra pellet in two quarters...........	85	275
1918	As last, but two extra pellets by hair..	225	750
1919	**Halfgroat.** As 1914 *mm.* Cross patonce	110	350
1920	Similar, but *mm.* plain cross, some times no leaf on breast, no stops.......	90	275
1921	**Penny.** *London.* Usually extra pellets in two quarters.............................	70	250
1922	— — pellets by crown omitted...	75	275
1923	— — trefoil in legend...	80	300
1924	*York,* Archb. Booth. R. Quatrefoil and pellet in centre	45	150
1925	— — two extra pellets by hair (local dies)...	45	150
1926	*Durham,* Bp. Neville. Trefoil in *obv.* legend. R. Two rings in centre of cross	70	200

1928

1930

		F	VF
1927	— — Similar, but without trefoil...	70	200
1928	**Halfpenny.** Usually extra pellet in two quarters	30	110
1929	— *mm.* plain cross	30	110
1930	**Farthing.** As last	300	975

Unmarked issue, 1453-4

1931   1935

		F	VF
		£	£
1931	**Groat.** No marks on *obv.;* two extra pellets on *rev.*	375	1250
1932	— four extra pellets on *rev.*	425	1350
1933	**Halfgroat.** As 1931	425	1350

Cross-pellet issue, 1454-61

1934	**Groat.** Saltire either side of neck, pellets by crown, leaf and fleur on breast, extra pellets on *rev.*	350	1100
1935	Saltire on neck, no leaf, pellets by crown, usually mullets in legend; extra pellets on *rev.*	125	375
1936	— Similar, but mascles in place of mullets on *obv.*	125	375
1937	— — pellets by hair instead of by crown	175	525
1938	**Halfgroat.** Saltire on neck, pellets by crown and on *rev.,* mullets in legend	375	1100

1940   1943   1944

1939	**Penny.** *London.* Saltire on neck, pellets by crown and on *rev.,* mascle(s), or mullet and mascle in legend	150	475
1940	*York.* Archb. Wm. Booth. Saltires by neck, usually leaf on breast, pellets by crown. R. Cross in quatrefoil in centre.	75	250
1941	*Durham.* Bp. Laurence Booth. Saltire and B or B only at neck, pellets by crown. R. Rings in centre	80	275
1942	**Halfpenny.** Saltires by neck, usually two extra pellets on *rev.*	45	135
1943	Similar, but saltire on neck, sometimes mullet after hЄnRIC	40	125
1944	**Farthing.** Saltire on neck, usually pellets by crown and on *rev.,* but known without either.	325	1100

For further information see:
Halfpennies and Farthings of Henry IV, V and VI. P. and B. R. Withers, 2003.

Lis-pellet issue, 1456-61

1945

1945	**Groat.** Lis on neck; pellets by crown. R. Extra pellets	250	800

EDWARD IV, First Reign, 1461-70

In order to increase the supply of bullion to the mint the weight of the penny was reduced to 12 grains in 1464, and the current value of the noble was raised to 8s. 4d. Later, in 1465, a new gold coin was issued, the Ryal or 'Rose Noble', weighing 120 grains and having a value of 10s. However, as 6s. 8d. had become the standard professional fee the old noble was missed, and a new coin was issued to take its place, the Angel of 80 grains.

Royal mints were set up in Bristol, Coventry, Norwich and York to help with the recoinage. The Coventry and Norwich mints were not open for long, but the York and Bristol mints remained open until 1471 and 1472 respectively.

Reference: C. E. Blunt and C. A Whitton, *The Coinage of Edward IV and Henry VI (Restored),* B.N.J. 1945-7.

Mintmarks

⚜	⬦	✚	✿	Y	✳	♛	†
105	9	7a	33	99	28	74	11

1461-4	Lis (105)	1467-70	Lis (105, *York*)
	Cross fleury (9)	1467-8	Crown (74) (often
	Plain cross (7a)		Sun (28) combined)
1464-5	Rose (33 and 34)	1468-9	Crown (74) (sometimes
1464-7	Pall (99, *Canterbury*)		Rose (33) combined)
1465-6	Sun (28)	1469-70	Long cross
1466-7	Crown (74)		fitchee (l.c.f) (11) (often
			Sun (28) combined)

GOLD

HEAVY COINAGE, 1461-4

1946

	F	VF
	£	£
1946 **Noble** (=6s. 8d., wt. 108 grs., 6.99g.). Normal type, but *obv.* legend commences at top left, lis below shield; *mm.*-/lis (Spink's sale May 1993)	5500	18500
1947 — Quatrefoil below sword arm; *mm.* rose/lis	6500	22500
1948 — R. Roses in two spandrels; *mm.* rose	7000	25000
1949 **Quarter-noble**	2250	6500

1950

	F £	VF £

LIGHT COINAGE, 1464-70

1950 **Ryal** or rose-noble (=10s., wt. 120 grs., 7.77g), *London*. As illustration. Large
fleurs in spandrels; *mm.* 33-74.. 1200 4250

1951 — — Small trefoils in spandrels; *mm.* 74-11 .... 1250 4500

1952

1952	— Flemish imitative coinage (mostly 16th cent. on a large flan).............	1100	4000
1953	*Bristol*. B in waves, large fleurs; *mm.* sun, crown	1500	5500
1954	— — small fleurs in spandrels; *mm.* sun, crown	1600	5750
1955	*Coventry*. C in waves; *mm.* sun..	2000	7250
1956	*Norwich*. � in waves; *mm.* sun, rose	2250	7500
1957	*York*. Є in waves, large fleurs in spandrels, *mm.* sun, lis	1500	5500
1958	— — small fleurs, *mm.* sun. lis	1600	5750
1959	**Half-ryal.** *London*. As 1950	1000	3250
1960	*Bristol*. B in waves; *mm.* sun, sun/crown..	1750	5000
1961	*Coventry*. C in waves; *mm.* sun...	5500	17500
1962	*Norwich*. Ⅱ in waves; *mm.* rose	4500	15000

1963   1965

	F	VF
	£	£

1963 *York*. Є in waves; *mm*. 28, 105, 33/105 .... 1100 3500
1963A Similar but lis instead of Є in waves (probably York)............................... 1350 4500
1964 **Quarter-ryal.** Shield in tressure of eight arcs, rose above. R. Somewhat
    as half ryal; *mm*. sun/rose 1750 5500
1965 Shield in quatrefoil. Є above, rose on l., sun on r.; *mm*. 33/28-74/33 ...... 625 1600
1966 — — sun on l., rose on r.; *mm*. 74-11 .... 675 1750

1967

1967 **Angel** (=6s. 8d., wt. 80 grs., 5.18g). St. Michael spearing dragon. R. Ship, rays of
    sun at masthead, large rose and sun beside mast; *mm*.-/33 .... 10000 40000
1968 — — small rose and sun at mast; *mm*.-/74 .... 12500 45000

SILVER

1969   1972

HEAVY COINAGE, 1461-4

1969 **Groat** (60 grs., 3.88g). Group I, lis on neck, pellets by crown; *mm*. 9, 7a,
    105, 9/105 .... 165 525
1970 — Lis on breast, no pellets; *mm*. plain cross, 7a/105 .... 175 575
1971 — — with pellets at crown; *mm*. plain cross.. 185 625
1972 II, quatrefoils by neck, crescent on breast; *mm*. rose 170 550
1973 III, similar but trefoil on breast; *mm*. rose 165 525

1974

1979

		F	VF
		£	£
1974	— — — eye in *rev.* inner legend, *mm.* rose	150	475
1975	— Similar, but no quatrefoils by bust..	200	675
1976	— — Similar, but no trefoil on breast	185	625
1977	IV, annulets by neck, eye after TAS; *mm.* rose	250	750
1978	**Halfgroat.** I, lis on breast, pellets by crown and extra pellets in two qtrs.; *mm.* 9, 7a..	525	2000
1979	II, quatrefoils at neck, crescent on breast; *mm.* rose	375	1100
1980	III, similar, but trefoil on breast, eye on *rev.*; *mm.* rose	325	950
1981	— Similar, but no mark on breast...	325	950
1982	IV, annulets by neck, sometimes eye on *rev.*; *mm.* rose...........................	375	1100
1983	**Penny** (15 grs.). *London.* I, marks as 1978, but mascle after RЄX; *mm.* plain cross	525	1750
1984	II, quatrefoils by neck; *mm.* rose	325	1000

1985   1991   1994

		F	VF
1985	III, similar, but eye after TAS; *mm.* rose..	350	1100
1986	IV, annulets by neck; *mm.* rose	450	1500
1987	*York,* Archb. Booth. Quatrefoils by bust, voided quatrefoil in centre of *rev.*; *mm.* rose	135	375
1988	*Durham. O.* of Hen. VI. R. DVΠOLIΠ	125	350
1988A	(ca.1461-c.1462). Local dies, mostly with rose in centre of *rev.*; *mm.* 7a, 33	45	150
1989	**Halfpenny.** I, as 1983, but no mascle..	85	275
1990	II, quatrefoils by bust; *mm.* rose	45	150
1991	— saltires by bust; *mm.* rose...	45	150
1992	III, no marks by bust; *mm.* rose	45	150
1992A	—saltires by bust, eye after TAS, *mm.* rose	135	525
1993	IV, annulets by bust; *mm.* rose..	70	325
1994	**Farthing.** I, pellets by crown, extra pellets on rev., with or without lis on breast	450	1350
1994A	II. saltires by bust; *mm.* rose	475	1400
1994B	III, no marks by bust; *mm.* rose	450	1350

LIGHT COINAGE, 1464-70. There is a great variety of groats and we give only a selection. Some have pellets in one quarter of the reverse, or trefoils over the crown; early coins have fleurs on the cusps of the tressure, then trefoils or no marks on the cusps, while the late coins have only trefoils.

		F £	VF £
1995	**Groat** (48 grs., 3.11g). *London*. Annulets at neck, eye after TAS; *mm*. 33 (struck from heavy dies, IV)	165	525
1996	— — Similar, but new dies, eye after TAS or DON	135	425
1997	— Quatrefoils at neck, eye; rose (heavy dies, III)	150	475
1998	— — Similar, but new dies, eye in *rev.* legend	135	425
1999	— No marks at neck, eye; *mm* rose	150	500
2000	— Quatrefoils at neck, no eye; *mm*. 33, 74, 28, 74/28, 74/33, 11/28	85	250

2001   2002

2001	— — — rose or quatrefoil on breast; *mm*. 33, 74/28	90	275
2002	— No marks at neck; *mm*. 28, 74, 11/28, 11	90	275
2003	— Trefoils or crosses at neck; *mm*. 11/33, 11/28, 11	85	250

2004   2014

2004	*Bristol*. B on breast, quatrefoils at neck; *mm*. 28/33, 28, 28/74, 74, 74/28	90	275
2005	— — trefoils at neck; *mm*. sun	100	325
2006	— — no marks at neck; *mm*. sun	175	575
2007	— Without B, quatrefoils at neck; *mm*. sun	150	450
	Bristol is variously rendered as BRESTOLL, BRISTOLL, BRESTOW, BRISTOW.		
2008	*Coventry*. C on breast, quatrefoils at neck, COVETRE; *mm*. 28/33, 28...	160	500
2009	— — Local dies, similar; *mm*. rose	185	600
2010	— — — as last, but no C or quatrefoils	200	650
2011	Norwich. N on breast, quatrefoils at neck, NORWIC or NORVIC, *mm*. 28/33, 28	125	350
2012	*York*. E on breast, quatrefoils at neck, EBORACI; *mm*. 28, 105/74, 105, 105/28	90	300
2013	— Similar, but without E on breast, *mm*. lis	125	375
2014	— E on breast, trefoils at neck; *mm*. 105/28, 105	135	400

2016   2035

		F	*VF*
		£	£
2015	**Halfgroat.** *London.* Annulets by neck (heavy dies); *mm.* 33	325	950
2016	— Quatrefoils by neck; *mm.* 33/-, 28/-, 74, 74/28	75	200
2017	— Saltires by neck; *mm.* 74, 74/28	80	225
2018	— Trefoils by neck; *mm.* 74, 74/28, 11/28	80	225
2019	— No marks by neck; *mm.* 11/28	100	275
2020	*Bristol.* Saltires or crosses by neck; *mm.* 33/28, 28, 74, 74/-..................	150	575
2021	— Quatrefoils by neck; *mm.* 28/-, 74, 74/-	135	525
2022	— Trefoils by neck; *mm.* crown	150	575
2023	— No marks by neck; *mm.* 74/28	175	625
2024	*Canterbury,* Archb. Bourchier (1464-7). Knot below bust; quatrefoils by neck; *mm.* 99/-, 99, 99/33, 99/28	70	185
2025	— — — quatrefoils omitted *mm.* 99	65	185
2026	— — — saltires by neck; *mm.* 99/-, 99/28	80	225
2026A	— — — trefoils by neck; *mm.* 99..	80	225
2027	— — — wedges by hair and/or neck; *mm.* 99, 99/–, 99/33, 99/28	70	185
2028	— — As 2024 or 2025, but no knot..	75	200
2029	— (1467-9). Quatrefoils by neck; *mm.* 74, 74/-	75	200
2030	— — Saltires by neck; *mm.* 74/-, 74	75	200
2031	— — Trefoils by neck; *mm.* 74, 74/-, 74/28, 33	70	185
2032	— No marks by neck; *mm.* sun..	95	275
2033	*Coventry.* Crosses by neck; *mm.* sun	900	2500
2034	*Norwich.* Quatrefoils or saltires by neck; *mm.* sun	750	2000
2035	*York.* Quatrefoils by neck; *mm.* sun, lis, lis/-	125	450
2036	— Saltires by neck; *mm.* lis	110	425
2037	— Trefoils by neck; *mm.* lis, lis/-	150	575
2038	— Є on breast, quatrefoils by neck; *mm.* lis/-	125	450
2039	**Penny** (12 grs., 0.77g.), *London.* Annulets by neck (heavy dies); *mm.* rose	325	950
2040	— Quatrefoils by neck; *mm.* 74, sun. crown	80	275
2041	— Trefoil and quatrefoil by neck; *mm.* crown.....................................	85	300
2042	— Saltires by neck; *mm.* crown	85	300
2043	— Trefoils by neck; *mm.* crown, long cross fitchée	95	325
2044	— No marks by neck; *mm.* long cross fitchée	135	425
2045	*Bristol.* Crosses, quatrefoils or saltires by neck, BRISTOW; *mm.* crown	350	1100
2046	— Quatrefoils by neck; BRI(trefoil)STOLL	375	1250
2047	— Trefoil to r. of neck BRISTOLL	375	1250
2048	*Canterbury,* Archb. Bourchier. Quatrefoils or saltires by neck, knot on breast; *mm.* pall	75	250
2049	— — Similar, but no marks by neck	75	250
2050	— — As 2048, but no knot...	80	275
2051	— — Crosses by neck, no knot	75	250
2052	— Quatrefoils by neck; *mm.* crown	150	475
2053	— King's Receiver (1462-4). Local dies, mostly with rose in centre of rev.; *mm.* 7a, 33..	45	160

		F	*VF*
		£	£
2054	— *Durham,* Bp. Lawrence Booth (1465-70). B and D by neck, B on *rev.; mm.* 33	60	180
2055	— — Quatrefoil and B by neck; *mm.* sun	50	165
2056	— — B and quatrefoil by neck; *mm.* crown	65	200
2057	— — D and quatrefoil by neck; *mm.* crown	60	180
2058	— — Quatrefoils by neck; *mm.* crown	50	165
2059	— — Trefoils by neck; *mm.* crown	60	180
2060	— Lis by neck; *mm.* crown	45	160
2061	*York,* Sede Vacante (1464-5). Quatrefoils at neck, no quatrefoil in centre of *rev.; mm.* sun, rose	65	200
2062	— Archb. Neville (1465-70). Local dies, G and key by neck, quatrefoil on *rev.; mm.* sun, plain cross	45	120

2063

		F	*VF*
2063	— — London-made dies, similar; *mm.* 28, 105, 11	50	160
2064	— — Similar, but no marks by neck; *mm.* large lis	60	180
2065	— — — Quatrefoils by neck; *mm.* large lis	65	200
2066	— — — Trefoils by neck; *mm.* large lis	60	180

2068   2077

		F	*VF*
2067	**Halfpenny,** *London.* Saltires by neck; *mm.* 34, 28, 74	40	135
2068	— Trefoils by neck; *mm.* 28, 74, 11	40	135
2069	— No marks by neck; *mm.* 11	50	175
2070	*Bristol.* Crosses by neck; *mm.* crown	125	400
2071	— Trefoils by neck; *mm.* crown	110	375
2072	*Canterbury.* Archb. Bourchier. No marks; *mm.* pall	85	275
2072A	— — Trefoils by neck, *mm.* pall	85	275
2073	— Saltires by neck; *mm.* crown	75	250
2074	— — Trefoils by neck; *mm.* crown	75	250
2074A	*Norwich.* Quatrefoils by neck., *mm.* Sun	300	950
2074B	— — Trefoils by neck; *mm.* crown	325	1000
2075	*York.* Royal mint. Saltires by neck; *mm.* lis/-, sun/-	75	250
2076	— — Trefoils by neck; *mm.* lis/-	65	225
2077	**Farthing,** *London.* ЄDWARD DI GRA RЄX, trefoils by neck, *mm.* crown	500	1500

Full flan coins are difficult to find in the smaller denominations.

For further information see:
Halfpennies and Farthings of Edward IV to Henry VII. P. and B. R. Withers, 2004; also *The English Long-Cross Pennies 1279-1489* by Christopher R. Wren

The coinage of this short restoration follows closely that of the previous reign. Only angel gold was issued, the ryal being discontinued. Many of the coins have the king's name reading hƐnRICV – another distinguishing feature is an R that looks like a B.

Mintmarks

Cross pattée (6)
Restoration cross (13)
Trefoil (44 and 45)

Rose (33, Bristol)
Lis (105)
Short cross fitchée (12)

GOLD

2078

		F	*VF*
		£	£
2078	**Angel,** *London.* As illus.; *mm.* -/6, 12, 105, none...................................	1850	6500
2079	*Bristol.* B in waves; *mm.* -/13, none...................................	3500	10500
2080	**Half-angel,** *London.* As 2078; *mm.* -/6, -/13, -/105...................................	4250	12000
2081	*Bristol.* B in waves; *mm.* -/13	6000	17500

SILVER

2082   2084   2089

2082	**Groat,** *London.* Usual type; *mm.* 6, 6/13, 6/105, 13, 13/6, 13/105, 13 /12	225	675
2083	*Bristol.* B on breast; *mm.* 13, 13/33, 13/44, 44, 44/13, 44/33, 44/12........	400	1250
2084	*York.* Ɛ on breast; *mm.* lis, lis/sun...................................	250	750
2085	**Halfgroat,** *London.* As 2082; *mm.* 13, 13/-...................................	350	1000
2086	*York.* Ɛ on breast; *mm.* lis	850	2500
2087	**Penny,** *London.* Usual type; *mm.* 6, 13, 12...................................	375	1100
2087A	*Bristol.* Similar; *mm.* 12...................................	575	1750
2088	*York.* G and key by neck; *mm.* lis	300	950
2089	**Halfpenny,** *London; mm.* 12, 13, ...	150	450
2090	*Bristol.* Similar; *mm.* cross...................................	375	1100

The Angel and its half were the only gold denominations issued during this reign. The main types and weight standards remained the same as those of the light coinage of Edward's first reign. The use of the 'initial mark' as a mintmark to denote the date of issue was now firmly established.

Mintmarks

33	105	12	55	44	55	28	56	17
30	37	6	18	19	20	31	11	38

1471-83	Rose (33, *York & Durham*)	1473-7	Cross pattée (6)
	Lis (105, *York*)		Pierced cross 1 (18)
1471	Short cross fitchee (12)	1477-80	Pierced cross and
1471-2	Annulet (large, 55)		pellet (19)
	Trefoil (44)		Pierced cross 2 (18)
	Rose (33, *Bristol*)		Pierced cross, central
1471-3	Pansy (30, *Durham*)		pellet (20)
1472-3	Annulet (small, 55)		Rose (33, *Canterbury*)
	Sun (28, *Bristol*)	1480-3	Heraldic cinquefoil (31)
1473-7	Pellet in annulet (56)		Long cross fitchee
	Cross and four pellets (17)		(11, *Canterbury*)
	Cross in circle (37)	1483	Halved sun and rose (38)
			(Listed under Ed. IV/V.)

GOLD

2091

2093

		F	VF
		£	£
2091	**Angel.** *London*. Type as illus.; *mm*. 12, 55, 56, 17, 18, 19, 31	1250	3750
2092	*Bristol*. B in waves; *mm*. small annulet	4500	15000
2093	**Half-angel.** As illus.; *mm*. 55, cross in circle, 19, 20/19, 31	950	3000
2094	King's name and title on rev.; *mm*. 12/-	1100	3250
2095	King's name and the title both sides; *mm*. 55/-	1100	3250

SILVER

2097

		F	*VF*
		£	£
2096	**Groat,** *London.* Trefoils on cusps, no marks by bust; *mm.* 12-37	85	250
2097	— — roses by bust; *mm.* pellet in annulet................................	225	850
2098	— Fleurs on cusps; no marks by bust; *mm.* 18-20....................................	85	250
2099	— — pellets by bust; *mm.* pierced cross	100	325
2100	— — rose on breast; *mm.* 31	90	300

2101

2107

2101	*Bristol.* B on breast no marks by bust; *mm.* 33, 33/55, 28/55, 55, 55/-, 28	200	675
2102	*York.* Є on breast no marks by bust; *mm.* lis...	250	800
2103	**Halfgroat,** *London.* As 2096; *mm.* 12-31	90	300
2104	*Bristol.* B on breast; *mm.* 33/12	450	1350
2105	*Canterbury.* Archb. Bourchier. As 2103; *mm.* 33, 11, 11/31, 31	60	200
2106	— C on breast; *mm.* rose..	50	175
2107	— — R. C in centre; *mm.* rose..	50	175
2108	— — R. Rose in centre; *mm.* rose	55	185
2109	*York.* No. Є on breast; *mm.* lis	325	1000
2110	**Penny,** *London.* No marks by bust; *mm.* 12-31	85	275
2111	*Bristol.* Similar; *mm.* rose	325	1000
2112	*Canterbury.* Archb. Bourchier. Similar; *mm.* 33, 11	85	275
2113	— C on breast; *mm.* rose..	100	350
2114	*Durham,* Bp. Booth (1471-6). No marks by neck; *mm.* 12, 44..................	35	140

2115

2116

2115	— — D in centre of *rev.;* B and trefoil by neck; *mm.* 44, 33, 56.............	35	140
2116	— — — two lis at neck; *mm.* rose..	45	150
2117	— — — crosses over crown, and on breast; *mm.* rose............................	45	150
2118	— — — crosses over crown, V under CIVI; *mm.* rose, pansy.................	45	150
2119	— — — B to l. of crown, V on breast and under CIVI.............................	40	140

		F	VF
		£	£
2120	— — — As last but crosses at shoulders	40	140
2121	— — R. D in centre; *mm*. rose	45	150
2122	— Bp. Dudley (1476-83). V to r. of neck; as last	45	150

2123   2125   2131

		F	VF
2123	— — D and V by neck; as last, but *mm*. 31	40	140

Nos. 2117-2123 are from locally-made dies.

		F	VF
2124	*York,* Archb. Neville (1471-2). Quatrefoils by neck. R. Quatrefoil; *mm*. 12 (over lis)	75	250
2125	— — Similar, but G and key by neck; *mm*. 12 (over lis)	40	140
2126	— Neville suspended (1472-5). As last, but no quatrefoil in centre of *rev.*	65	200
2126A	— — no marks by bust, similar; *mm*. annulet	75	225
2127	— — No marks by neck, quatrefoil on *rev.; mm*. 55, cross in circle, 33..	40	140
2128	— — Similar but Є and rose by neck; *mm*. rose	40	140
2129	— Archb. Neville restored (1475-6). As last, but G and rose	45	150
2130	— — Similar, but G and key by bust	40	135
2131	— Sede Vacante (1476). As 2127, but rose on breast; *mm*. rose	60	175
2132	— Archb. Lawrence Booth (1476-80). B and key by bust, quatrefoil on *rev.; mm*. 33, 31	40	140
2133	— Sede Vacante (1480). Similar, but no quatrefoil on rev.; *mm*. rose	60	175

2134   2140

		F	VF
2134	— Archb. Rotherham (1480-3). T and slanting key by neck, quatrefoil on *rev.; mm*. 33	40	140
2135	— — — Similar, but star on breast	60	175
2136	— — — Star on breast and to r. of crown	65	200
2137	**Halfpenny**, *London*. No marks by neck; *mm*. 12-31	35	110
2138	— Pellets at neck; *mm*. pierced cross	40	135
2139	*Canterbury* (Archbishop Bourchier). C on breast and in centre of *rev.; mm*. rose	110	350
2140	— C on breast only; *mm*. rose	90	275
2141	— Without C either side; *mm*. 11	100	300
2142	*Durham*, Bp. Booth. No marks by neck. R. DЄR ĀM, D in centre; *mm*. rose	250	800
2142A	— — Lis either side of neck. R. with or without D in centre	275	900
2142B	— — B to l. of crown, crosses at shoulders. R. with or without D. in centre; *mm*. rose	275	900
2143	— — — Bp. Dudley V to l. of neck; as last	250	800

Full flan coins are very difficult to find in the small denominations.

On 12th February 1483, the prolific cinquefoil coinage of Edward IV came to an end and an indenture between the king and the new master of the mint, Bartholomew Reed, saw the introduction of the sun and rose mintmark.

Edward IV died on 9th April 1483, but the sun and rose coinage continued, essentially unaltered, through the short reign of Edward V and into the reign of Richard III, ending with the indenture of 20th July 1483, with Robert Brackenbury, who had been Richard's ducal treasurer, and the introduction of the boar's head mintmark.

New dies prepared after the accession of Richard III on 26th June 1483, bear his name but coins of the sun and rose coinage struck under Edward IV and Edward V can only be distinguished by arranging the dies in sequence. This is possible for the angels (Schneider Sylloge, SCBI 47, p.41) but has not yet been achieved for the silver coinage.

Mintmark: Halved sun and rose.

GOLD

2144A

		F	*VF*
		£	£
2144 **Angel.** Type As 2091, reading EDWARD DEI GRA (Edward IV)		5750	17500
2144A — Similar but reading EDWARD DI GRA (Edward V)		15000	45000
2145 **Half-angel.** As 2093 (probably Edward IV)		6500	18500

SILVER

2146

2146 **Groat.** *London,* pellet below bust, reading EDWARD or EDVARD	1350	4500
2146A — — No pellet below, reading EDWARD or EDWRD	1250	4250
2147 **Penny.** *London* As 2110	2250	6500
2148 **Halfpenny.** *London* As 2137	375	950

Richard's coinage follows the pattern of previous reigns. The portrait on the silver denominations remains stylised, though increasingly distinctive. It can be divided into three types according to mintmark. Type 1, the first sun and rose coinage, lasted 24 days to 20th July 1483. Type 2, the boar's head coinage, was issued until about June 1484. Type 3, the second sun and rose coinage, was struck until the end of the reign (Schneider Sylloge, SCBI 47, pp. 41-2).

It is evident that coin dies were stored in a 'loose-box' system which led to extensive muling between types. As an interim measure, after the indenture of 20th July 1483, at least eleven existing sun and rose obverse dies, both gold and silver, were overpunched with the boar's head mark. The seven overpunched groat dies included four Edward IV/V dies, then still in use, and three dies of Richard III type 1.

Mintmarks

| SR1 | BH1 | BH2 | SR2 | SR3 | 105 | 33 |

Halved sun and rose, 1, 2 and 3.
Boar's head, 1 (62) 2 (63).
Lis (105, *Durham*)
Rose only (33).

GOLD

2150   2152

		F	VF
		£	£
2149	**Angel.** 1. Reading RICARD. R. R and rose by mast; *mm.* sun and rose 1	8000	22500
2150	— 2a. Reading EDWARD. R. E and rose or R and rose by mast; *mm.* boar's head 1 over sun and rose 1/sun and rose 1	8500	25000
2151	— 2b. Reading RICARD. R. R and rose by mast; mm. boar's head 1 over sun and rose 1/sun and rose 1, boar's head 1, boar's head 2 (often muled)	7500	20000
2152	— 3. Reading RICARD or RICAD; *mm.* sun and rose 2	6500	18500

2153

| 2153 | **Half-angel.** 2b. R. R and rose by mast; *mm.* boar's head 1 | 9500 | 35000 |

SILVER

2154   2155

		F £	VF £

2154 **Groat.** 1. *London*. Reading RICARD; *mm*. sun and rose 1 .... 950 | 2750
2155 — 2a. Reading EDWARD; *mm*. boar's head 1 over sun and rose 1/sun and rose 1 | 1350 | 4000

2156 - BH2   2158 - SR3

2156   — 2b. Reading RICARD; *mm*. boar's head 1 over sun and rose 1/sun
and rose 1, boar's head 1, boar's head 2 (often muled) .... 1100 | 3250
2157   — 3. *mm*. sun and rose 2, sun and rose 3 .... 850 | 2500
2158   — — Pellet below bust, *mm*. sun and rose 2, sun and rose 3 .... 900 | 2750
2159   *York*. 3. *mm*. sun and rose 2/- .... 2250 | 6500

2161   2164   2166

2160 **Halfgroat.** *London*. 2a. Reading EDWARD; *mm*. boar's head 1 over sun
and rose 1/- .... 2500 | 7500
2161   — 2b. Reading RICARD; *mm*. boar's head 2/- .... 2000 | 6000
2162   — 3. *mm*. sun and rose 2, sun and rose 2/- .... 1750 | 5500
2163   — — Pellet below bust; *mm*. sun and rose 2 .... 2000 | 6000
2164 **Penny.** *London*. 2a. Reading EDWARD; *mm*. boar's head 1 over sun
and rose 1/- .... 2500 | 7000
2165   — 2b. Reading RICARD; *mm*. boar's head 1/- .... 2250 | 6500
2166   *York*. Archb. Rotherham. T and upright key at neck. R. Quatrefoil in centre;
mm. boar's head 1/- .... 575 | 1350
2167   — — *mm*. rose/- .... 450 | 1200
2168   — No marks at neck; *mm*. sun and rose 2/- .... 625 | 1500

2169   2171

2169   *Durham*. Bp. Sherwood. S on breast. R. D in centre; *mm*. lis/-................ 400 | 1100
2170 **Halfpenny.** *London*. 2b. No marks by neck; *mm*. boar's head 1/- .... 375 | 1000
2171   — 3. *mm*. sun and rose 2/- .... 350 | 950
2171A **Farthing.** *London*. 3. *mm*. sun and rose 2/-... 1750 | 4500

HENRY VII, 1485-1509

For the first four years of his reign Henry's coins differ only in name and mintmark from those of his predecessors, but from 1489 radical changes were made in the coinage. On the Groat and subsequently on the lesser denominations the traditional open crown was replaced with an arched imperial crown. Though the pound sterling had been a denomination of account for centuries, a pound coin had never been minted. Now a magnificent gold pound was issued, and, from the design of the king enthroned in majesty, was called a 'Sovereign'. A small simplified version of the Sovereign portrait was at the same time introduced on the silver pence. The reverse of the gold 'Sovereign' had the royal arms set in the centre of a Tudor rose. A few years later the angel was restyled and St. Michael, who is depicted about to thrust Satan into the Pit with a cross-topped lance, is no longer a feathered figure but is clad in armour of Renaissance style. A gold ryal of ten shillings was also minted again for a brief period.

The other major innovation was the introduction of the shilling (testoon) in the opening years of the 16th century. It is remarkable for the very fine profile portrait of the king which replaces the representational image of a monarch that had served on the coinage for the past couple of centuries. This new portrait was also used on groats and halfgroats but not on the smaller denominations.

Mintmarks

39	41	40	42	33	11	7a	123

105	76b	31	78	30	91	43	57

85	94	118	21	33	53

1485-7	Halved sun and rose (39)	1495-8	Pansy (30)
	Lis upon sun and rose (41)		Tun (123, *Canterbury*)
	Lis upon half rose (40)		Lis (105, York)
	Lis-rose dimidiated (42)	1498-9	Crowned leopard's head (91)
	Rose (33, *York*)		Lis issuant from rose (43)
1487	Lis (105)	1499-1502	Tun (123, *Canterbury*)
	Cross fitchée (11)		Anchor (57)
1487-8	Rose (33)	1502-4	Greyhound's head (85)
	Plain cross (7a, *Durham*)		Lis (105, profile issue only)
1488-9	No marks		Martlet (94, *York*)
1489-93	Cinquefoil (31)	1504-5	Cross-crosslet (21)
	Crozier (76b, *Durham*)	1504-9	Martlet (94, (*York, Canterbury*)
1492	Cross fitchée (11, gold only)		Rose (33, *York* and
1493-5	Escallop (78)		*Canterbury*)
	Dragon (118, gold only)	1505-9	Pheon (53)
	Lis (105, *Canterbury and York*		
	Tun (123, *Canterbury*)		

GOLD

	F £	VF £
2172 **Sovereign** (20s; wt. 240 grs., 15.55g). Group I. Large figure of king sitting on backless throne. ℞. Large shield crowned on large Tudor rose. *mm*. 31 ..	125000	500000
2173 — Group II. Somewhat similar but throne has narrow back, lis in background. ℞. Large Tudor rose bearing small shield. *mm*. -/11	100000	375000

2174

	F £	VF £
2174 — III. King on high-backed very ornamental throne, with greyhound and dragon on side pillars. ℞. Shield on Tudor rose; *mm*. dragon	50000	175000
2175 — IV. Similar but throne with high canopy breaking legend and broad seat, *mm*. 105/118, (also with no *obv*. i.c. *mm*. 105/118, very rare)	45000	150000
2176 — Narrow throne with a portcullis below the king's feet (like Henry VIII); *mm*. 105/21, 105/53	40000	135000
2177 **Double-sovereign** and **Treble-sovereign** from same dies as 2176. These piedforts were probably intended as presentation pieces *mm*. 105/21, 105/53	125000	450000

2178

	F £	VF £
2178 **Ryal** (10s.). As illustration: *mm*. -/11	35000	135000
2179 **Angel** (6s. 8d). I. Angel of old type with one foot on dragon. ℞. PЄR CRVCЄM. etc., *mm*. 39, 40, (also muled both ways)...............................	1750	6500
2179A — With Irish title, and legend over angel head. mm. 33/-........................	2000	7500
2180 — — Name altered from RICARD? and h on *rev*. from ℞. mm. 41/39, 41/40, 41/-, 39/?	2250	8000

2181   2183

2187

		F	VF
		£	£
2181	II. As 2179, but *mm*. none. 31/-.	1500	5500
2181A	II/III mule. *mm*. 31/78, Ɍ. PER CRUC or AVTEM TRANS	1750	6500
2182	As 2181. Ɍ. IhC AVTEM TRAnSIEnS etc.; *mm*. none, 31/-	2250	8000
2183	III. New dies, angel with both feet on dragons; (large straight lettering) *mm*. 78-85 except 91 (many mules exist)	1100	3500
2183A	— Angel with very small wings. *mm*. escallop	1350	4500
2184	— — Ɍ. IhC AVTEM TRAnSIEnS, etc.; *mm*. escallop	2000	7500
2185	IV. Small square lettering; *mm*. 85 (also muled with 2183)	1250	4000
2186	— Tall thin lettering; *mm*. 21 (also muled with 2185 obv.)	1250	4000
2187	V. Large crook-shaped abbreviation after hEnRIC; *mm*. 21 and 53 (combinations and mules exist)	1100	3750
2188	**Half-angel or angelet.** I. *Mm*. 39, 41, (old dies RIII altered)	2250	8000
2189	III. Angel with both feet on dragon: *mm*. 30, 57/30, 30/85	1200	3750
2190	IV. Small square lettering; *mm*. rose *mm*. -/85	1100	3500
2191	— *Obv*. as last. Ɍ. Tall thin lettering; *mm*. 33/21	1200	3750
2192	V. As angel; *mm*. pheon, cross-crosslet	1000	3250

SILVER

Facing bust issues. Including 'Sovereign' type pennies.

| 2193 | **Groat.** I. Open crown; *mm*. 40 (rose on bust), 39-42 and none (combinations) | 135 | 450 |

2194   2195

| 2194 | — — crosses or saltires by neck, 41, 40, 105-33 and none (combinations) | 150 | 525 |
| 2195 | IIa. Large bust with out-turned hair, crown with two plain arches; *mm*. none, 31, 31/-, 31/78 | 110 | 350 |

| | 2198A | 2199 | 2201 |

	F	VF
	£	£
2196 — — similar but crosses by neck; *mm.* none, -/105	125	375
2197 — — R. Portcullis over long cross; *mm.* -/lis	3750	12500
2198 IIIa. Bust as IIa. Crown with two jewelled arches, *mm.* 31	300	850
2198A IIIb. Similar, but new bust with realistic hair *mm.* 78, 30	110	350
2199 IIIc. Bust as IIIb, but crown with one plain and one jewelled arch, *mm.* 30-21 and none	100	325
2199A IIId. As last, but plainer letters. mm 57, 85, 33 and none	110	350
2200 IVa. Wide single arch crown; arch is single or double bar with 4 crockets; *mm.* 85, 85/33, 21	135	450
2201 IVb. — Similar, but arch is double bar with 6 uprights or crockets as jewels; *mm.* 85, 21/85, 21	150	500
2202 **Halfgroat,** *London.* I. Open crown, tressure unbroken; *mm.* 40/-, 40/39 (R. III mule)	350	1250
2203 — IIIa. Double arched crown, rosettes on tressure; mm. escallop	175	650
2204 — IIIb. Similar, nothing on tressure. R. Lozenge panel in centre; *mm.* lis	65	225
2205 — — Similar, but also with lis on breast; mm. lis.................................	70	250
2206 — IIIc. Unarched crown with tressure broken. R. Lozenge panel in centre; *mm.* lis	65	200
2206A — — — Similar but smaller dies and much smaller lettering	70	225

2208

| 2207   *Canterbury,* Archb. Morton. I. Open crown, crosses by neck. R. M in centre; *mm.* tun/- .... | 75 | 250 |
| 2208   — — II. Similar, but double-arched crown; no *mm.* .... | 75 | 250 |

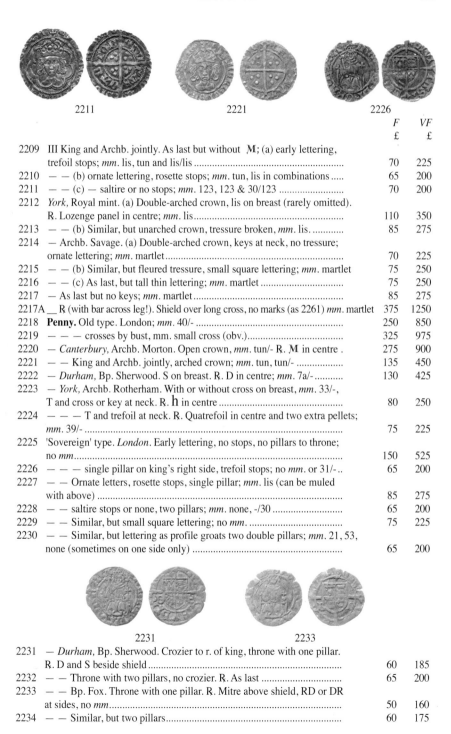

		2211		2221		2226	

		F £	VF £
2209	III King and Archb. jointly. As last but without M; (a) early lettering, trefoil stops; *mm*. lis, tun and lis/lis	70	225
2210	— — (b) ornate lettering, rosette stops; *mm*. tun, lis in combinations	65	200
2211	— — (c) — saltire or no stops; *mm*. 123, 123 & 30/123	70	200
2212	*York,* Royal mint. (a) Double-arched crown, lis on breast (rarely omitted). R. Lozenge panel in centre; *mm*. lis...	110	350
2213	— — (b) Similar, but unarched crown, tressure broken, *mm*. lis.	85	275
2214	— Archb. Savage. (a) Double-arched crown, keys at neck, no tressure; ornate lettering; *mm*. martlet..	70	225
2215	— — (b) Similar, but fleured tressure, small square lettering; *mm*. martlet	75	250
2216	— — (c) As last, but tall thin lettering; *mm*. martlet	75	250
2217	— As last but no keys; *mm*. martlet	85	275
2217A	__ R (with bar across leg!). Shield over long cross, no marks (as 2261) *mm*. martlet	375	1250
2218	**Penny.** Old type. London; *mm*. 40/-	250	850
2219	— — — crosses by bust, mm. small cross (obv.).....................................	325	975
2220	— *Canterbury,* Archb. Morton. Open crown, *mm*. tun/- R. M in centre .	275	900
2221	— — King and Archb. jointly, arched crown; *mm*. tun, tun/-	135	450
2222	— *Durham,* Bp. Sherwood. S on breast. R. D in centre; *mm*. 7a/-	130	425
2223	— *York,* Archb. Rotherham. With or without cross on breast, *mm*. 33/-, T and cross or key at neck. R. h in centre	80	250
2224	— — — T and trefoil at neck. R. Quatrefoil in centre and two extra pellets; *mm*. 39/-	75	225
2225	'Sovereign' type. *London.* Early lettering, no stops, no pillars to throne; no *mm*...	150	525
2226	— — — single pillar on king's right side, trefoil stops; no *mm*. or 31/-..	65	200
2227	— — Ornate letters, rosette stops, single pillar; *mm*. lis (can be muled with above)	85	275
2228	— — saltire stops or none, two pillars; *mm*. none, -/30	65	200
2229	— — Similar, but small square lettering; no *mm*.	75	225
2230	— — Similar, but lettering as profile groats two double pillars; *mm*. 21, 53, none (sometimes on one side only)	65	200

	2231		2233	

		F	VF
2231	— *Durham,* Bp. Sherwood. Crozier to r. of king, throne with one pillar. R. D and S beside shield	60	185
2232	— — Throne with two pillars, no crozier. R. As last	65	200
2233	— — Bp. Fox. Throne with one pillar. R. Mitre above shield, RD or DR at sides, no *mm*..	50	160
2234	— — Similar, but two pillars...	60	175

2235   2239   2244A

2245   2249   2250

		F	VF
		£	£
2235	*York,* Archb. Rotherham. Keys below shield; early lettering, trefoil stops, no pillars to throne, no *mm.*	70	225
2236	— — — single pillar	65	200
2237	— — — — ornate lettering, rosette or no stops,	65	200
2238	— — — two pillars sometimes with crosses between legs of throne	65	200
2239	**Halfpenny,** *London.* I. Open crown; *mm.* 40, 42	50	175
2240	— — — trefoils at neck; no *mm.,* rose	60	185
2241	— — — crosses at neck; *mm.* rose, cross fitchée	45	150
2242	— II. Double arched crown; *mm.* cinquefoil, none	35	100
2243	— — — saltires at neck; no *mm*	35	100
2244	— IIIa. Crown with single arch, ornate lettering; no *mm.,* pansy	30	90
2244A	— IIIb. Similar but with rosette stops; *mm.* none, rose, lis	40	110
2245	— IIIc. Much smaller portrait; *mm.* pheon, lis, none	30	90
2246	*Canterbury,* Archb. Morton. I. Open crown, crosses by neck; R. M in centre	110	350
2247	— — II. Similar, but arched crown, saltires by bust; *mm.* profile eye (82)	100	325
2247A	— — — no marks at neck	95	300
2248	— III. King and Archb. Arched crown; *mm.* lis, none	50	175
2249	*York,* Archb. Savage. Arched crown, key below bust to l or r. *mm.* martlet	125	375
2250	**Farthing,** *London.* hЄnRIC DI GRA RЄX (A), arched crown	575	1500

*No.s 2239-49 have *mm.* on *obv.* only.

Profile issue

2251	**Testoon** (ls.). Type as groat. hЄnRIC (VS); *mm.* lis	15000	40000
2252	— hЄnRIC VII; *mm.* lis	16000	45000

2253   2254

2253	— hЄnRIC SЄPTIM; *mm.* lis	17500	52500
2254	**Groat,** *Tentative issue* (contemporary with full-face groats). Double band to crown, hЄnRIC VII; *mm.* 85, 21	325	1200

	F	VF
	£	£
2254A — — — experimental types; *mm*. none, 105/-, -/105, 105/85, 105.	475	1500
2255 — — — tressure on *obv*.; *mm*. cross-crosslet..	2250	8500
2256 — — hɛnRIC (VS); *mm*. 105, -/105, 105/ 85, none	525	1750
2257 — — hɛnRIC SɛPTIM; *mm*. -/105...	2000	7500

2258

2258 *Regular issue*. Triple band to crown; *mm*. 21, 53 (both *mm*.s may occur on *obv*. or *rev*. or both)..	175	500
2259 **Halfgroat,** *London*. As last; *mm*. 105, 53/105, 105/53, 53......................	125	375
2260 — — no numeral after King's name, no *mm*., -/lis.................................	575	1750
2261 *Canterbury,* King and Archb. As London, but *mm*. 94, 33, 94/33	110	325

2262   rev. enlarged   2263

2262 *York,* Archb. Bainbridge. As London, but two keys below shield; *mm*. 94, 33, 33/94	100	300
2263 — — XB beside shield; *mm*. rose/martlet	225	750
2263A — — Similar but two keys below shield *mm*. rose(?)/martlet	275	900

Henry VIII is held in ill-regard by numismatists as being the author of the debasement of England's gold and silver coinage; but there were also other important numismatic innovations during his reign. For the first sixteen years the coinage closely followed the pattern of the previous issues, even to the extent of retaining the portrait of Henry VII on the larger silver coins.

In 1526, in an effort to prevent the drain of gold to continental Europe, the value of English gold was increased by 10%, the sovereign to 22s. 0d. and the angel to 7s. 4d., and a new coin valued at 4s. 6d.—the Crown of the Rose—was introduced as a competitor to the French *écu au soleil*. The new crown was not a success and within a few months it was replaced by the Crown of the Double Rose valued at 5s but made of gold of only 22 carat fineness, the first time gold had been minted below the standard 23c. At the same time the sovereign was again revalued to 22s. 6d. and the angel to 7s. 6d., with a new coin, the George Noble, valued at 6s. 8d. (one-third pound).

The royal cyphers on some of the gold crowns and half-crowns combine the initial of Henry with those of his queens: Katherine of Aragon, Anne Boleyn and Jane Seymour. The architect of this coinage reform was the chancellor, Cardinal Thomas Wolsey, who besides his other changes had minted at York a groat bearing his initials and cardinal's hat in addition to the other denominations normally authorised for the ecclesiastical mints.

When open debasement of the coinage began in 1544 to help finance Henry's wars, the right to coin of the archbishops of Canterbury and York and of the bishop of Durham was not confirmed. Instead, a second royal mint was opened in the Tower as in subsequent years were six others, at Southwark, York, Canterbury, Bristol, Dublin and Durham House in the Strand. Gold, which fell to 23c. in 1544, 22c. in 1545, and 20c. in 1546 was much less debased than silver which declined to 9oz 2dwt. in 1544, 6oz 2dwt. in 1545 and 4oz 2dwt. in 1546. At this last standard the blanched silver surface of the coins soon wore away to reveal the copper alloy beneath which earned for Henry the nickname 'Old Coppernose'.

Mintmarks

| 53 | 69 | 70 | 108 | 33 | 94 | 73 | 11 |

| 105 | 22 | 23 | 30 | 78 | 15 | 24 | 110 |

| 52 | 72a | 44 | 8 | 65a | 114 | 121 | 90 |

| 36 | 106 | 56 | S | E | 116 | 135 |

1509-26	Pheon (53)	1509-14	Martlet (94, *York*)
	Castle (69)	1509-23	Radiant star (22, *Durham & York*)
	Castle with H (70, gold)	1513-18	Crowned T (135, Tournai)
	Portcullis crowned (108)	1514-26	Star (23, *York & Durham*)
	Rose (33, *Canterbury*)		Pansy (30, *York*)
	Martlet (94, *Canterbury*)		Escallop (78, *York*)
	Pomegranate (73, but broader, *Cant.*)		Voided cross (15, *York*)
	Cross fitchée (11, *Cant.*)	1523-26	Spur rowel (24, *Durham*)
	Lis (105, *Canterbury, Durham*)		

1526-44	Rose (33)	1526-32	Cross patonce (8, *Cant.*)
	Lis (105)		T (114, *Canterbury*)
	Sunburst 110)		Uncertain mark (121,
	Arrow (52)		*Canterbury*)
	Pheon (53)	1529-44	Radiant star (22, *Durham*)
	Lis (106)	1530-44	Key (90, *York*)
	Star (23, *Durham*)	1533-44	Catherine wheel (36,
1526-9	Crescent (72a, *Durham*)		*Canterbury*)
	Trefoil (44 variety,	1544-7	Lis (105 and 106)
	Durham)		Pellet in annulet (56)
	Flower of eight petals and		S (Southwark)
	circle centre (*Durham*)		Є or E (Southwark)
1526-30	Cross (7a, sometimes	1546-7	WS monogram (116, *Bristol*)
	slightly voided, *York*)		
	Acorn (65a, *York*)		

GOLD

FIRST COINAGE, 1509-26

2265

		F	VF
		£	£
2264	**Sovereign** (20s; wt. 240grs., 15.55g.). Similar to last sov. of Hen. VII; *mm*. 108	13500	50000
2264A	**Ryal** (10s.) King in ship holding sword and shield. R. Similar to 1950, *mm*.-/108	*Extremely rare*	
2265	**Angel** (6s. 8d.). As Hen. VII, but hЄnRIC? VIII DI GRA RЄX, etc.; *mm*. 53, 69, 70, 70/69, 108, R. May omit h and rose, or rose only; *mm*. 69, 108	1250	4250
2266	**Half-angel.** Similar (sometimes without VIII), *mm*. 69, 70, 108/33, 108	1000	3250

SECOND COINAGE, 1526-44

2267

2267	**Sovereign** (22s. 6d; wt. 240grs., 15.55g.). As 2264, R. single or double tressure *mm*. 110, 105, 105/52	15000	55000
2268	**Angel** (7s. 6d.). As 2265, hЄnRIC VIII D(I) G(RA) R(ЄX) etc,; *mm*. 110, 105	1750	6000

		F	VF
		£	£
2269	**Half-angel.** Similar; *mm*. lis	1850	6500

2270   2272

2270	**George-noble** (6s. 8d.). As illustration; *mm*. rose	11000	42500
2270A—	Similar, but more modern ship with three masts, without initials hR. R.		
	St. George brandishing sword behind head..	13500	52500
2271	**Half-George-noble.** Similar to 2270 *mm* rose, lis................................	15000	60000
2272	**Crown of the rose** (4s. 6d., 23 c. 3 $^1/_2$ gr.). As illustration; *mm*. rose,		
	two legend varieties	7500	25000
2273	**Crown of the double-rose** (5s., 22 c). Double-rose crowned, hK (Henry and		
	Katherine of Aragon) both crowned in field. R. Shield crowned; *mm*. rose	1000	3750

2274   2285

2274	— hK both sides; *mm*. rose/lis, lis, arrow	1100	4000
2275*	— hK/hA or hA/hK; *mm*. arrow...	3750	15000
2276*	— hR/hK or hI/hR; *mm*. arrow	1350	5250
2277	— hA (Anne Boleyn); *mm*. arrow	5000	20000
2278	— hA/hR; *mm*. arrow..	3750	15000
2279	— hI (Jane Seymour); *mm*. arrow	1250	4500
2280*	— hK/hI; *mm*. arrow	1750	6000
2281	— hR/hI; *mm*. arrow	1350	5250
2282	— hR (Rex); *mm*. arrow..	1100	4250
2283	— — *mm*. pheon	1200	4500
2284	**Halfcrown.** Similar but king's name henric 8 on *rev.*, no initials; *mm*. rose	1500	5250
2285	— hK uncrowned on *obv.; mm*. rose..	1100	3500
2286	— hK uncrowned both sides; *mm*. rose/lis, lis, arrow	1100	3500
2287	— hI uncrowned both sides; *mm*. arrow	1250	4500
2288	— hR uncrowned both sides; hIB REX; *mm*. pheon	1500	5250

*The hK initials may on later coins refer to Katherine Howard (Henry's fifth wife).

THIRD COINAGE, 1544-7

2291

	F	VF
	£	£

2289 **Sovereign,** I (20s., Wt. 200 grs., 12.96g., 23 ct.). Large module, similar to 2291 but king with large head; *mm*. lis 45000 175000

2290 II (20s., wt. 200 or 192 grs., 23, 22 or 20 ct.). *Tower*. As illustration; *mm*. lis, pellet in annulet/lis 8500 30000

2291 — *Southwark*. Similar; *mm*. S, Є/S 8000 27500

2292 — — Similar but Є below shield; *mm*. S/Є 9000 32500

2293 — *Bristol*. As London but *mm*. WS/- 13500 50000

2294

2303

2294 **Half-sovereign** (wt. 100 or 96 grs., 6.22g.), *Tower*. As illus.; *mm*. lis, pellet in annulet 1250 3750

2295 — Similar, but with annulet on inner circle (either or both sides)........ 1350 4000

2296 *Southwark*. *mm*. S 1350 4000

2297 — Є below shield; *mm*. S, Є, S/Є, Є/S, (known without sceptre; *mm*. S) 1250 3750

2298 *Bristol*. Lombardic lettering; *mm*. WS, WS/- 4500 13500

2299 **Angel** (8s., 23 c). Annulet by angel's head and on ship, hЄnRIC' 8; *mm*. lis 1350 4500

2300 — Similar, but annulet one side only or none 1350 4500

2300A— Similar, but three annulets on ship, *mm*. lis 1750 6000

2301 **Half-angel.** Annulet on ship; *mm*. lis.. 1100 3500

2302 — No annulet on ship; *mm*. lis.. 1200 3750

2303 — Three annulets on ship; *mm*. lis.. 1350 4500

2304   2309

		F	VF
		£	£
2304	**Quarter-angel** Angel wears armour; *mm.* lis	1100	3250
2304A	— Angel wears tunic; *mm.* lis	1100	3500
2305	**Crown,** *London.* Similar to 2283, but hɛnRIC' 8 ; Lombardic lettering; *mm.* 56	1000	3250
2306	— without RVTILAnS; *mm.* 56..	1100	3500
2307	— — — with annulet on inner circle	1200	3750
2307A	— King's name omitted. DEI GRA both sides, *mm.* 56	1500	5000
2308	— *Southwark.* As 2306; *mm.* S, Ɛ, E/S, Ɛ/-, Ɛ/Ɛ	1100	3500
2309	*Bristol.* hɛnRIC VIII. ROSA etc. R. D G, etc.; *mm.*-/WS	1200	4000
2309A	— — with initials H R transposed on rev...............................	1350	4500
2310	— Similar but hɛnRIC(VS) 8 R. DƐI) G(RA); *mm.* -/WS, WS	1250	4250
2311	**Halfcrown,** *London.* Similar to 2288; *mm.* 56, 56/-................	800	2500
2312	— — with annulet on inner circle *mm.* 56................................	850	2750
2313	*Southwark.* As 2311; *mm.* S	900	3000
2314	— *O.* hɛnRIC 8 ROSA SINƐ SPIn. R. DƐI GRA, etc.; *mm.* Ɛ	950	3250
2315	*Bristol. O.* RVTILAnS, etc. R. hɛnRIC 8; *mm.* WS/-...........................	1100	3750

For other gold coins in Henry's name see page 221-2.

SILVER

2316   2322

		F	VF
2316	**Groat.** Portrait of Hen. VII. *London mm.* 53, 69, 108, 108 over 135.......	175	500
2317	— *Tournai; mm.* crowned T. R. CIVITAS TORnACɛn*, dated 1513 ...	1100	4500
2318	**Halfgroat.** Portrait of Hen. VII. London; *mm.* 108, 108/-..........	175	575
2319	— *Canterbury,* Archb. Warham. POSVI *rev.; mm.* rose	225	700
2320	— — — WA above shield; *mm.* martlet	150	525
2321	— — — WA beside shield; *mm.* cross fitchee............................	150	525
2322	— — CIVITAS CAnTOR *rev.,* similar; *mm.* 73, 105, 11/105	110	350
2323	— *York,* POSVI *rev.,* Archb. Bainbridge (1508-14). Keys below shield;		
	mm. martlet	125	400
2324	— — — XB beside shield no keys; *mm.* martlet	135	500
2325	— — — Archb. Wolsey (1514-30). Keys and cardinal's hat below shield;		
	mm. 94, 22..	275	850
2326	— — CIVITAS ƐBORACI *rev.* Similar; *mm.* 22, 23, 30, 78, 15, 15/78..	110	350
2327	— — As last with TW beside shield; *mm.* voided cross................	135	500
2327A	— *Tournai.* As 2317..	950	3250

*Non-portrait groats and half-groats exist of this mint, captured during an invasion of France in 1513. (Restored to France in 1518.)

	2328	2332	2334	2336	

		F	VF
		£	£
2328	**Penny,** 'Sovereign' type, *London; mm.* 69, 108 /-, 108/108	65	185
2329	— *Canterbury.* WA above shield; *mm.* martlet..	200	650
2330	— — — WA beside shield; *mm.* 73/-	110	350
2331	— *Durham,* Bp. Ruthall (1509-23). TD above shield; *mm.* lis.................	60	175
2332	— — — TD beside shield; above or below horizontal line *mm.* lis, radiant star	60	175
2333	— — Bp. Wolsey (1523-9). DW beside shield, cardinal's hat below; *mm.* spur rowel	250	800
2334	**Halfpenny.** Facing bust, henRIC DI GRA REX (AGL). *London; mm.* 69, 108/-	45	150
2335	— *Canterbury.* WA beside bust; *mm.* 73/-, 11	100	325
2335A	— *York.* Key below bust, *mm.* star, escallop..	125	375
2336	**Farthing.** *mm.* 108/-, henRIC DI GRA REX, portcullis.		
	R. CIVITAS LONDON, rose in centre of long cross	350	900

SECOND COINAGE, 1526-44

	2337A	2337D	

2337	**Groat.** His own young portrait. *London;* Laker bust A, large renaissance-style bust, crown arch breaking inner circle. Roman/Roman lettering, roses in cross-ends; *mm.* rose	900	3250
2337A	— — Laker bust A1 but with Roman/Lombardic lettering, saltires in cross-ends; *mm.* rose	450	1500
2337B	— —Laker bust A2 but withLombardic/Lombardic lettering, roses in cross-ends; *mm.* rose	575	2000
2337C	— — Laker bust A3 but with Lombardic/Lombardic lettering, saltires in cross-ends; *mm.* rose	275	950
2337D	— Laker bust B, smaller face with pointed nose, crown arch does not break inner circle. Lombardic lettering; *mm.* rose	150	500

	2337E	

2337E	— Laker bust D, larger squarer face with roman nose, fluffy hair, crown arch does not break inner circle. Lombardic lettering; *mm.* 33, 105, 110, 52, 53 (sometimes muled)...	135	450

		F	VF
		£	£
2338	— — with Irish title HIB; reads hЄnRIC 8; *mm.* 53, 105, 53/105, 105/53,	325	1100
2339	— *York*, Archb. Wolsey. TW beside shield, cardinal's hat below; *mm.*		
	voided cross, acorn, muled (both ways)	175	525
2340	— — — omits TW; *mm.* voided cross	750	2500

2341   2343   2345

2341	**Halfgroat.** *London;* type as groats, Lombardic lettering both sides.		
	mm. rose to arrow or none (sometimes muled)..	90	275
2341A	— — Mainly Roman letters on obv. or on both sides, *mm.* rose	135	450
2342	As 2341 with Irish title HIB; *mm.* pheon...	525	1750
2343	— *Canterbury*, Archb. Warham (—1532). R̃. CIVITAS CAnTOR, WA		
	beside shield; *mm.* 121, 121/-, 121/33, 8, 8/T, T.......................................	80	250
2344	— — — nothing by shield; *mm.* 121/-...	90	300
2345	— — Archb. Cranmer (1533—). TC beside shield; *mm.* 36, 36/-............	85	275
2346	— *York*, Archb. Wolsey (—1530). R̃. CIVITAS ЄBORACI, TW		
	beside shield, hat below; *mm.* 15/-, 15...	85	275
2347	— — Sede Vacante (1530/1). No marks; *mm.* key...................................	90	300
2348	— — Archb. Lee (1531-44). EL or LE beside shield; *mm.* key	80	250

2349   2358   2362

2349	**Penny.** 'Sovereign' type h . D . G . ROSA SInЄ SPInA, *London;*		
	mm. rose to arrow (*obv.* only), *mm.* lis both sides............................	65	200
2350	— *Canterbury*. WA beside shield; *mm.* 121/-, 8/-, T/-............................	150	525
2351	— — TC beside shield; *mm.* 36/-	200	675
2352	— *Durham*, Bp. Wolsey (—1529). TW beside shield, hat below; *mm.* 23,		
	23/44, 23/-, 72a/-, 44, 44/-, 72a/44 (muled with 2333 *obv.*, *mm.* 24/44)..	50	175
2353	— — Sede Vacante (1529-30). No marks; *mm.* 23/-, 22/-........................	65	200
2354	— — Bp. Tunstall (1530—). CD beside shield; *mm.* 23, 23/-, 22/-, 22 ...	50	175
2355	— *York*. EL beside shield; *mm.* key/-..	450	1350
2356	**Halfpenny.** Facing bust, h D G ROSA SIЄ SPIA. *London;* sometimes		
	annulet in centre of rev. *mm.* rose to arrow, arrow/-	45	150
2357	— *Canterbury*. WA beside bust; *mm.* 121/-, 8/-, T/-..............................	150	450
2358	— — TC beside bust; *mm.* 36/-...	45	150
2359	— *York*. TW beside bust; *mm.* acorn/-...	110	350
2359A	— — —; key below bust	135	450
2360	— — Sede Vacante. Key below bust; *mm.* 15/-......................................	75	250
2361	— — EL or LE beside bust; *mm.* key/-..	45	150
2362	**Farthing.** *O*. RVTILANS ROSA, portcullis; *mm.* 105/-, 110/-. R̃.		
	DEO GRACIAS, long cross with pellet in each angle	325	800
2363	— — *mm.* arrow/- R̃. DEO GRACIAS, rose on long cross	375	950
2363A	— *Canterbury*. O. Similar. R̃. Similar. *mm.* 36/-	975	3000

2364

	F	VF
	£	£

THIRD COINAGE, 1544-7 (Silver progressively debased. 9oz (2dwt), 6oz (2dwt) 4oz (2dwt)).

2364	**Testoon.** *Tower.* hϵnRIC'. VIII, etc. Ɍ. Crowned rose between crowned h and R.POSVI, etc.; *mm.* lis, lis and 56, lis/two lis	2000	7500
2365	— hϵnRIC 8, *mm.* 105 and 56, 105/56, 105 and 56/56, 56	1250	5250
2366	— — annulet on inner circle of rev. or both sides; *mm.* pellet in annulet	1350	5500

2367

2367	— *Southwark.* As 2365. Ɍ. CIVITAS LOnDOn; *mm.* S, ϵ, S/ϵ, ϵ/S	1250	5250
2368	— *Bristol. mm.*-/WS monogram. (Tower or local dies.)..........................	1500	6000

2369 Bust 1   2374 Bust 3

2369	**Groat.** *Tower.* As ill. above, busts 1, 2, 3; *mm.* lis/-, lis.............................	125	575
2369A	Bust 1, Ɍ. As second coinage; i.e. saltires in forks; *mm.* lis	175	750
2370	Bust 2 or 3 annulet on inner circle, both sides or rev. only	135	625
2371	*Southwark.* As 2367, busts 1, 2, 3, 4; no *mm.* or lis/-; S or S and ϵ or ϵ in forks	135	625
2372	*Bristol. Mm.*-/WS monogram, Bristol bust and Tower bust 2 or 3	130	600
2373	*Canterbury.* Busts 1, 2, (2 var); no *mm,* or lis/–	135	625
2374	*York.* Busts 1 var., 2, 3, no *mm*...	130	600

2377   2384

		F	*VF*
		£	£
2375	**Halfgroat.** *Tower.* As 2365, bust 1; *mm.* lis, none	85	350
2376	*Southwark.* As 2367, bust 1; no *mm.*; S or Є and S in forks	110	425
2377	*Bristol. Mm.*-/WS monogram	80	325
2378	*Canterbury.* Bust 1; no *mm.*	70	275
2379	*York.* Bust 1; no *mm.*	85	350
2380	**Penny.** *Tower.* Facing bust; no *mm.* or lis/-	65	250
2381	*Southwark.* Facing bust; *mm.* S/-, Є/-, -/Є	100	350
2382	*Bristol.* Facing bust; no *mm.* (Tower dies or local but truncated at neck)	70	275
2383	*Canterbury.* Facing bust; no *mm.*	60	225
2384	*York.* Facing bust; no *mm.*	65	250

2385   2388A

2385	**Halfpenny.** *Tower.* Facing bust; pellet in annulet in *rev.* centre, no *mm.* or lis/-	80	225
2386	*Bristol.* Facing bust; no *mm.*	100	325
2387	*Canterbury.* Facing bust; no *mm.*, (some read H 8)	70	200
2388	*York.* Facing bust; no *mm.*	60	175
2388A	**Farthing** *obv.* Rose. R. Cross and pellets	975	3000

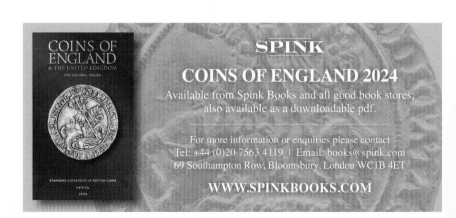

These coins were struck during the reign of Edward VI but bear the name and portrait of Henry VIII, except in the case of the half-sovereigns which bear the youthful head of Edward.

Mintmarks

56	105	52	K	E	116

66	115	33	122	t	94

GOLD

	F	VF
	£	£
2389 **Sovereign** (20 ct.), *London*. As no. 2290, but Roman lettering; *mm*. lis..	11000	40000
2390 — *Bristol*. Similar but *mm*. WS	15000	60000

2391

2393

2391 **Half-sovereign.** As 2294, but with youthful portrait with sceptre. *Tower*;		
mm. 52, 105, 94 (various combinations)	1250	3750
2391A — Similar but no sceptre; *mm*. 52, 52/56	1350	4000
2392 — — — K below shield; *mm*.-/K, none,. E/-	1350	4000
2393 — — — grapple below shield; *mm*. 122, none, 122/-, -/122.	1350	4000
2394 — *Southwark. Mm*. E, E/-, -/E, Є /E. Usually Є or E (sometimes retro-		
grade) below shield (sceptre omitted; *mm*. -/E)	1250	3750
2394A — — — Ɍ. As 2296; *mm*.-/S	1500	4500

2395

		F	VF
		£	£
2395	**Crown.** Similar to 2305. *London; mm.* 52, 52/-, -/K, 122, 94, ...	1050	3250
2396	— Similar but transposed legends without numeral; *mm.* -/arrow	1100	3500
2396A	— As 2395, but omitting RVTILANS; *mm.* arrow	1100	3500
2396B	Similar, but RVTILANS both sides; *mm.* arrow	1350	4000
2397	— *Southwark.* Similar to 2396; *mm.* E	1250	3750
2398	— — King's name on *obv.; mm.* E/-, -/E................................	1100	3500
2399	**Halfcrown.** Similar to 2311. *London; mm.* 52, K/-, 122/-, 94, -/52	800	2750
2399A	As last but E over h on *rev., mm.* 56/52...................................	1100	4000
2399B	As 2399 but RVTILANS etc. on both sides, *mm.* arrow	950	3250
2400	— *Southwark. mm.* E, E/-, -/E	750	2500

SILVER

AR (4oz .333)

2401	**Testoon.** *Tower.* As 2365 with lozenge stops one side; -/56, 56...........	2500	9500

2403 Bust 4   2403 Bust 6

Some of the Bristol testoons, groats and halfgroats with WS monogram were struck after the death of Henry VIII but cannot easily be distinguished from those struck during his reign.

2403	**Groat.** *Tower.* Busts 4, 5, 6 (and, rarely, 2). ℞. POSVI, etc.; *mm.* 105-94 and none (frequently muled)..	125	575
2404	— *Southwark.* Busts 4, 5, 6. ℞. CIVITAS LONDON; no *mm.* -/E; lis/-, -/lis, K/E; roses or crescents or S and Є in forks, or rarely annulets	110	500
2405	— *Durham House.* Bust 6. ℞. REDDE CVIQUE QVOD SVVM EST; *mm.* bow..	275	850
2406	— *Bristol. mm.* WS on *rev.* Bristol bust B, Tower bust 2 and 3	125	575
2407	— — *mm.* TC on *rev.* Similar, Bristol bust B	135	650
2408	— *Canterbury.* Busts 5, 6; no *mm.* or rose/-	100	475
2409	— *York.* Busts 4, 5, 6; no *mm.* or lis/-, -/lis..	110	550

2411   2416

		F £	VF £
2410	**Halfgroat.** Bust 1. *Tower*. POSVI, etc.; *mm*. 52, 52/-, 52/K , -/K, 52/122, 122, -/122	95	400
2411	— *Southwark*. CIVITAS LONDON; *mm*. E, -/E, none, 52/E, K/E	60	225
2412	— *Durham House*. Ɍ. REDD, etc.; *mm*. bow, -/bow	575	2000
2413	— *Bristol*. Mm. WS on *rev*.	80	350
2414	— — *mm*. TC on *rev*.	95	400
2415	— *Canterbury*. No *mm*. or t/-, -/t,	60	200
2416	— *York*. No *mm*., bust 1 and three-quarter facing	75	300

2417   2418

2417	**Penny.** *Tower*. CIVITAS LONDON. Facing bust; *mm*. 52/-, -/52, -/K, 122/-, -/122, none	60	225
2418	— — three-quarter bust; no *mm*.	60	225
2419	— *Southwark*. As 2417; *mm*. E, -/E	65	250
2420	— *Durham House*. As groat but shorter legend; *mm*. -/bow	525	1500

2421   2426   2428

2421	— *Bristol*. Facing busts, as 2382 but showing more body, no *mm*	85	325
2422	— *Canterbury*. Similar to 2417	60	225
2423	— — three-quarter facing bust; no *mm*.	65	250
2424	— *York*. Facing bust; no *mm*	60	225
2425	— — three-quarter facing bust; no *mm*.	75	300
2426	**Halfpenny.** *Tower*. mm 52?, none	50	160
2427	— *Canterbury*. No *mm*., sometimes reads H8	60	175
2428	— *York*. No *mm*.	50	160

The 4 oz. 2.5dwt coins of Henry VIII and those issued under Edward in 1547 and 1548 caused much disquiet, yet at the same time government was prevented by continuing financial necessity from abandoning debasement. A stratagem was devised which entailed increasing the fineness of silver coins, thereby making them appear sound, while at the same time reducing their weight in proportion so that in practice they contained no more silver than hitherto. The first issue, ordered on 24th January 1549, at 8 oz.2 dwt. fine produced a shilling which, at 60 gr., was so light that it was rapidly discredited and had to be replaced in April by another at 6 oz. 2 dwt. Weighing 80 gr., these later shillings proved acceptable.

Between April and August 1551 the issue of silver coins was the worst ever – 3 oz. 2dwt. fine at 72s per lb. before retrenchment came in August, first by a 50% devaluation of base silver coin and then by the issue of a fine standard at 11oz. 1dwt. 'out of the fire'. This was the equivalent of 11oz.3dwt. commixture, and means that since sterling was only 11oz. 2dwt., this issue, which contained four new denominations – the crown, halfcrown, sixpence and threepence – was in effect the finest ever issued under the Tudors.

Some base 'pence' were struck in parallel with the fine silver, but at the devalued rate, they and the corresponding 'halfpence' were used as halfpence and farthings respectively.

The first dates on English coinage appear in this reign, first as Roman numerals and then on the fine issue crowns and halfcrowns of 1551-3, in Arabic numerals.

Mintmarks

66	52	35	115	E	53	122

t	T	111	Y	126	94	91A

92	105	y	97	123	78	26

1547-8	Arrow (52)		
	E (Southwark)		
1548-50	Bow (66, *Durham House*)	1550	Martlet (94)
1549	Arrow (52)	1550	Leopard's head (91A)
	Grapple (122)	1550-1	Lion (92)
	Rose (35, *Canterbury*)		Lis (105, *Southwark*)
	TC monogram (115, *Bristol*)		Rose (33)
	Pheon (53)	1551	Y or y (117, *Southwark*)
	t or T (*Canterbury*)		Ostrich's head (97, gold only)
1549-50	Swan (111)	1551-3	Tun (123)
	Roman Y (*Southwark*)		Escallop (78)
1549-50	6 (126 gold only)	1552-3	Pierced mullet (26, *York*)

GOLD

First period, Apr. 1547-Jan. 1549

2430

		F	*VF*
		£	£
2429	**Half-sovereign** (20 c). As 2391, but reading EDWARD 6. Tower; *mm.* arrow	3000	9500
2430	— *Southwark* (Sometimes with E or Є below shield); *mm.* E...............	2500	7500
2431	**Crown.** RVTILANS, etc., crowned rose between ER both crowned. ℞. EDWARD 6, etc., crowned shield between ER both crowned; *mm.* arrow, E over arrow/-	2750	8500
2431A	— *Obv.* as last. ℞. As 2305, *mm.* 52/56	2500	7500
2432	**Halfcrown.** Similar to 2431, but initials not crowned; *mm.* arrow	1750	5000
2432A	—*Southwark.* Similar. *mm.* –/E	1750	5000

Second period, Jan. 1549-Apr. 1550

2433

2433	**Sovereign** (22 ct). As illustration; *mm.* arrow, –/arrow, Y, ...	7500	22500
2434	**Half-sovereign.** Uncrowned bust. *Tower.* TIMOR etc., MDXLIX on *obv. mm.* arrow..	5250	15000

2435

| 2435 | — — SCVTVM, etc., as illustration; *mm.* arrow, **6,** Y............................ | 3250 | 9000 |

| | F | VF |
| | £ | £ |

2436 — *Durham House*. Uncrowned, 1/2 length bust with MDXLVIII at end of
obv. legend; *mm*. bow; SCVTVM etc. 10000 32500
2437 — Normal, uncrowned bust. LVCERNA, etc., on *obv*.; *mm*. bow 8500 25000
2437A — Normal, uncrowned bust. SCVTVM, etc. but with *rev*. as 2440, *mm*. bow 6750 20000

2438   2441

2438 — *London, Southwark*. Crowned bust. EDWARD VI, etc. R̶. SCVTVM, etc.;
mm. 52, 122, 111/52, 111, Y, 94 .... 3000 8500
2439 — *Durham House*. Crowned, half-length bust; *mm*. bow 10000 32500
2440 — — King's name on *obv*. and *rev*.; *mm*. bow (mule of 2439/37) 11000 35000
2441 **Crown.** Uncrowned bust, as 2435; *mm*. 6, Y, 52/-, Y/- 4500 13500
2442 — Crowned bust, as 2438; *mm*. 52, 122, 111, Y (usually *obv*. only)........ 3500 11000
2443 **Halfcrown.** Uncrowned bust; R̶. As 2441, *mm*. arrow, Y, Y/-, 52/- 4000 12000
2444 — Crowned bust, as illus. above; *mm*. 52, 52/111, 111, 122, Y, Y/- 2250 7000
2445 — Similar, but king's name on *rev*., *mm*. 52, 122.................................... 2500 8000

Third period, 1550-3, Fine Gold (23 ct.)
2446 **Sovereign** (30s., 240grs., 15.55g.). King on throne; *mm*. 97, 123 .... 35000 125000

2444   2448

2447 **Double sovereign.** From the same dies, *mm*. 97 .... 100000 400000
2448 **Angel** (10s.). As illustration; *mm*. 97, 123.. 12500 40000
2449 **Half-angel.** Similar, *mm*. 97 .... 13500 45000

2450

	F	VF
	£	£

Crown Gold (22 ct.)

2450 **Sovereign**. (=20s., 174.6 grs., 11.31g.). Half-length
figure of king r., crowned and holding sword and orb. ℞. Crowned shield
with supporters; *mm*. y, tun .... | 7500 | 22500

2451

2451 **Half-sovereign**. As illustration above; *mm*. y, tun	2750	8500
2452 **Crown**. Similar, but *rev.* SCVTVM etc., *mm*. y, tun	4500	13500
2453 **Halfcrown**. Similar, *mm*. tun, y..	4000	12500

*Small denominations often occur creased or straightened.

SILVER

First period, Apr. 1547-Jan. 1549

2454   2455

2454 **Groat**. Crowned bust r. *Tower*. ℞. Shield over cross, POSVI, etc.; *mm*. arrow	850	4500
2455 — As last, but EDOARD 6, *mm*. arrow..	950	5000
2456 *Southwark*. *Obv*. as 2454. ℞. CIVITAS LONDON; *mm*.-/E or none, sometimes S in forks..	850	4500
2457 **Halfgroat**. *Tower*. *Obv*. as 2454; *mm*. arrow	675	2500
2458 *Southwark*. As 2456; *mm*. arrow, E on reverse only	625	2200

2459   2462

		F £	VF £
2459	*Canterbury*. Similar. No *mm*., reads EDOARD or EDWARD (rare)	525	1650
2460	**Penny**. *Tower*. As halfgroat, but E.D.G. etc. ℞. CIVITAS LONDON; *mm*. arrow	575	1750
2461	*Southwark*. As last, but *mm*. -/E...	675	2000
2462	*Bristol*. Similar, but reads ED6DG or E6DG no *mm*.................................	575	1750
2463	**Halfpenny**. *Tower*. O. As 2460, *mm*. E (?). ℞. Cross and pellets	650	1850
2464	*Bristol*. Similar, no *mm*. but reads E6DG or EDG....................................	750	2250

Second period, Jan. 1549-Apr. 1550

At all mints except Bristol, the earliest shillings of 1549 were issued at only 60 grains but of 8 oz. 2 dwt standard. This weight and size were soon increased to 80 grains, (S.2466 onwards), but the fineness was reduced to 6 oz. 2 dwt so the silver content remained the same. Dies, mm G were prepared for a coinage of 80gr shillings at York, but were not used. Coins from the *mm* are found suitably overmarked, from other mints, S.2466-8. The shilling bust types are set out in *J. Bispham 'The Base Silver Shillings of Edward VI; BNJ 1985.*

Bust 1   2465A   Bust 2

First Issue, 60 grs., 3.88g., 8oz. 2 dwt.

2465	**Shilling**. *Tower*. Broad bust with large crown. *Obv*. TIMOR etc. MDXLIX. ℞. Small, oval garnished shield dividing ER. EDWARD VI etc., *mm*. 52, no *mm*, Bust 1; *mm*, –/52, Bust 2 (very rare)	375	1750
2465A	*Southwark*. As last, Bust 1, *mm*. Y, EY/Y	375	1750
2465B	*Canterbury*. As last, Bust 1, *mm*. -/rose	425	1850

2465C

2465C	*Durham House*. Bust with elaborate tunic and collar TIMOR etc. MDXLIX. ℞. Oval shield, very heavily garnished in different style. EDWARD VI etc., *mm*. bow (2469)	475	2000

Second Issue, debased, 80 grs., 5.18g., 6oz. 2 dwt.

Bust 3

Bust 4

Bust 5

2466C

2468

2472

	F	VF
	£	£
2466 *Tower.* Tall, narrow bust with small crown. *Obv.* EDWARD VI etc. MDXLIX or MDL. R. As 2465 but TIMOR etc., Busts 3, 4 and 5, *mm.* 52-91a (frequently muled)	225	950
2466A — *Obv.* as last, MDXLIX. R. Heavily garnished shield, Durham House style, Bust 3 *mm.* grapple	525	2250
2466B *Southwark.* As 2466, Busts 3, 4 and 5 *mm.* Y, Y/swan	225	950
2466C — — — Bust 4; R. as 2466A. *mm.* Y	525	2250
2467 *Bristol. Obv.* similar to 2466, Bust 3 or local die R. Shield with heavy curved garniture or as 2466, *mm.* TC, or TC over G	1250	5000
2468 *Canterbury.* As 2466, Bust 3 and 4 *mm.* T, T/t, t/T, t or t over G	275	1250
2470 *Durham House.* Bust as 2465C. INIMICOS etc., no date. R. EDWARD etc.	350	1500
2472 — Bust similar to 2466. EDWARD VI etc. R. INIMICOS etc.	225	1000
2472A — As last but legends transposed	350	1500
2472B *Tower.* Elegant bust with extremely thin neck. Bust 6, R. As 2466, *mm.* martlet	525	2250
2472C *Southwark.* As last, Bust 6, *mm.* Y	275	1250

For coins of Edward VI countermarked, see p. 236

Third period, 1550-3

Very base issue (1551) ca. 70grs., ca. 4.88g., 3oz. 2 dwt.

2473 Bust 6   2474   2476

			F	VF
			£	£
2473	**Shilling**, *Tower*. As 2472B. MDL or MDLI, *mm*. lion, rose, lion/rose		250	1100
2473A	*Southwark*. As last, *mm*. lis/Y, Y/lis, lis		250	1100
2474	**Base Penny**. *London. O.* Rose. ℞. Shield; *mm*. escallop (*obv.*)................		75	275
2475	— — *York*. *Mm*. mullet (*obv.*) as illustration		70	250
2476	**Base Halfpenny**. As penny, but single rose		450	1750

* The base penny and halfpenny were used as halfpenny and farthing respectively.

Note: Irish very base shillings exist which are all dated MDLII, a date that does not occur for English issued shillings.

Fine silver issue, (1551-3) 460grs., 30g., 11oz. 3 dwt.

2478

2478	**Crown**. King on horseback with date below horse. ℞. Shield on cross; *mm*. y. 1551; tun, 1551-3 (1553, wire line inner circle may be missing) .	1250	4000

2479

2479	**Halfcrown**. Walking horse with plume; *mm*. y, 1551	650	2250
2480	Galloping horse without plume; *mm*. tun, 1551-3	750	2500

2482

2483   2484

		F	VF
		£	£
2481	Large walking horse without plume; *mm.* tun, 1553	1750	5750
2482	**Shilling**. Facing bust, rose l., value XII r. *mm.* y, tun (several bust varieties)	160	625
2483	**Sixpence**. *London*. Similar value VI, as illustration; *mm.* y/-, -/y, y, tun (bust varieties)	175	650
2484	*York*. As last, but rev. reads CIVITAS EBORACI; *mm.* mullet..............	350	1500

2485   2486

| 2485 | **Threepence**. *London*. As sixpence, but value III; *mm.* tun .... | 275 | 1100 |
| 2486 | *York*. As 2484, but III by bust .... | 650 | 2500 |

2487   2487A

| 2487 | **Penny**. 'Sovereign' type; *mm.* tun .... | 1250 | 4750 |
| 2487A | **Farthing**. *O*. Portcullis, R Cross and Pellets .... | 1500 | 5250 |

SPINK

LONDON
1666

THE COINS OF ENGLAND COLOURING BOOK

SPINK BOOKS ARE PROUD TO PRESENT THE FIRST EVER
COINS OF ENGLAND COLOURING BOOK
A COLOURING BOOK FOR ALL AGES

22 FULL PAGE ILLUSTRATIONS
FILLED WITH A SELECTION OF OUR NATION'S MOST BEAUTIFUL COIN DESIGNS
EACH COLOURING DESIGN IS ACCOMPANIED BY A SHORT PAGE OF HISTORICAL CONTEXT

ISBN: 978-1-912667-40-6
RRP: £6.99

Mary brought English coins back to the sterling standard and struck all her gold coins at the traditional fineness of 0.995. The mintmarks usually appear at the end of the first or second word of the legends.

Pomegranate   Halved rose and castle

GOLD

2488

	F £	VF £
2488 **'Fine' Sovereign** (30s.). Queen enthroned. ℞. Shield on rose, MDLIII, MDLIIII and undated, *mm*. pomegranate, half-rose (or mule)	12500	40000

2489

2489 **Ryal** (15s.). As illus, MDLIII. ℞. As 1950 but A DNO etc. *mm*. pomegranate/-	35000	110000

2490

		F	*VF*
		£	£
2490	**Angel** (10s.). Class I, annulet stops; *mm*. pomegranate	2500	7500
2490A	— Class II, pellet stops, *mm*. pomegranate (often muled with class I reverse)	2750	8000
2490B	— Class III, pellet stops, large Roman letters, *mm*. half-rose and castle .	3500	9000
2491	**Half-angel**. Similar; *mm*. pomegranate, pomegranate/-	6500	17500

SILVER

2492

2492	**Groat**. Crowned bust l. ℞. VERITAS, etc.; *mm*. pomegranate, pomegranate/-	175	650
2493	**Halfgroat**. Similar	900	3250

2494

2494	**Penny**. Similar, but M. D. G. ROSA, etc.	750	2750
2495	— As last. ℞. CIVITAS LONDON; no *mm*	750	2750

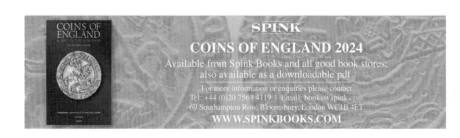

The groats and smaller silver coins of this period have Mary's portrait only, but the shillings and sixpences show the bust of the queen's husband, Philip of Spain.

Mintmarks

Lis (105   Half-rose and castle

GOLD

2496A

		F	VF
		£	£
2496	**Angel**. As illustration; wire line inner circles, calm sea, *mm*. lis	7500	22500
2496A	— — New-style, large wings, wire line i.c.	8500	25000
2496B	— — As above but beaded i.c.	9500	27500
2497	**Half-angel**. Similar to 2496	15000	45000

SILVER

2497A

2497A	**Halfcrown (Pattern)**. As illustration. Bust of Philip r., crown above, date 1554 below. R. Bust of Mary l. crown and date 1554 above, without mark of value, no *mm*...	13500	40000
2498	**Shilling**. Busts face-to-face, full titles, undated, no *mm*.	500	2250
2499	— — — also without mark of value	525	2500

2500

		F	VF
		£	£
2500	— — 1554	525	2500
2501	— English titles only 1554, 1555	575	2750
2501A	— — undated	675	3000
2502	— — without mark of value, 1554, 1555 (rare)	600	2850
2503	— — date below bust, 1554, 1555	3750	13500
2504	— — As last, but without ANG., 1555	4500	15000

2505   2506

2505	**Sixpence**. Similar. Full titles, 1554 (and undated?)	375	1750
2506	— English titles only, 1555 (no *mm*., rare), 1557 (*mm*. lis, rounder garnishing)	350	1600
2506A	— As last but heavy beaded i.c. on obv. 1555. (Irish 4d. obv. mule)	450	2000
2507	— — date below bust, 1554, 1557 (very rare)	1100	4500

2508   2510A

2508	**Groat**. Crowned bust of Mary 1. ℞. POSVIMVS etc. (several legend vars.); *mm*. lis	200	750
2509	**Halfgroat**. Similar, but POSVIM, *mm*. lis	575	2250
2510	**Penny**. Similar to 2495, but P. Z. M. etc.; *mm*. lis	375	1500
2510A	**Base penny**, but P. Z. M . etc.; *mm*. halved rose and castle or castle/–, (used as a halfpenny)	90	325

Elizabeth's coinage is particularly interesting on account of the large number of different denominations issued. 'Crown' gold coins were again issued as well as the 'fine' gold denominations. In 1560 the base shillings of Edward VI's second and third coinages were called in and countermarked for recirculation at reduced values. Smaller debased coins were also devalued but not countermarked. The old debased groat became a three halfpence and other coins in proportion. The normal silver coinage was initially struck at 0.916 fineness as in the previous reign but between 1560 and 1577 and after 1582 the old sterling standard of 0.925 was restored. Between 1578 and 1582 the standard was slightly reduced and the weights were reduced by 1/32nd in 1601. Gold was similarly reduced slightly in quality 1578-82, and there was a slight weight reduction in 1601.

To help alleviate the shortage of small change, and to avoid the expense of minting an impossibly small silver farthing, a threefarthing piece was introduced to provide change if a penny was tendered for a farthing purchase. The sixpence, threepence, threehalfpence and threefarthings were marked with a rose behind the queen's head to distinguish them from the shilling, groat, half-groat and penny.

Coins of exceedingly fine workmanship were produced in a screw press introduced by Eloye Mestrelle, a French moneyer, in 1561. With parts of the machinery powered by a horse-drawn mill, the coins produced came to be known as 'mill money'. Despite the superior quality of the coins produced, the machinery was slow and inefficient compared to striking by hand. Mestrelle's dismissal was engineered in 1572 and six years later he was hanged for counterfeiting.

Mintmarks

1ST ISSUE	2ND ISSUE		3RD & 4TH ISSUES				
106	21	94	23	53	33	107	92
			74	71	77	65b	27

5TH ISSUE			6TH ISSUE				
7	14	113	60	54	79	72b	86

7TH ISSUE							
1	2		123	124	90	57	0

First Issue			Lis (106, milled)		1584-6	Escallop (79)
1558-60	Lis (106)	1569-71	Castle (71)		1587-9	Crescent (72b)
Second Issue		1572-3	Ermine (77)		1590-2	Hand (86)
1560-1	Cross crosslet (21)	1573-4	Acorn (65b)		1592-5	Tun (123)
	Martlet (94)	1573-8	Eglantine (27)		1594-6	Woolpack (124)
Third & Fourth Issue		Fifth Issue			1595-8	Key (90)
1560-6	Star (23, milled)	1578-9	Greek cross (7)		1598-1600	Anchor (57)
1561-5	Pheon (53)	1580-1	Latin cross (14)		1600	0
1565	Rose (33)	1582	Sword (113)		Seventh Issue	
1566	Portcullis (107)	Sixth Issue			1601-2	1
1566-7	Lion (92)	1582-3	Bell (60)		1602	2
1567-70	Coronet (74)	1582-4	A (54)			

N.B. *The dates for* mms *sometimes overlap. This is a result of using up old dies, onto which the new mark was punched.*

GOLD

HAMMERED COINAGE
First to Fourth issues, 1559-78. ('Fine' gold of 0.994. 'Crown' gold of 0 .916 fineness. Sovereigns of 240 grs., 15.55g.). Mintmarks; lis to eglantine.

	F	VF
	£	£

2511   **'Fine' Sovereign** (30 s.) Queen enthroned, tressure broken by throne,
reads Z not ET, no chains to portcullis. R. Arms on rose; *mm*. lis............ 17500 65000

2512

2512   — — Similar but ET, chains on portcullis; *mm*. crosslet 11000 35000

2513

2513   **Angel**. St. Michael. R. Ship. Wire line inner circles; *mm*. lis.................. 2250 7000
2513A — Similar, but beaded i.c. on *obv*., *mm*. lis 2500 8000
2514   — — Similar, but beaded inner circles; ship to r.; *mm*. 106, 21, 74, 27,.. 1750 5500
2515   — — — Similar, but ship to l.; *mm*. 77-27 .... 1850 6000
2516   **Half Angel**. As 2513, wire line inner circles; *mm*. lis 4000 12500
2516A — As last, but beaded i.c.s, legend ends. Z.HIB 2250 7500

2517

2517   — As 2514, beaded inner circles; *mm*. 21, 74, 77-27 .... 1250 4000
2518   **Quarter Angel**. Similar; *mm*. 74, 77-27.. 1100 3500
2519   **Half Pound** (10 s.) Young crowned bust l. R. Arms. Wire line inner
circles; *mm*. lis 7500 25000

2520

		F	VF
		£	£
2520	— Similar, but beaded inner circles; *mm.* 21, 33-107	1850	6000
2520A	— Smaller bust; *mm.* lion	3000	9500
2520B	— Broad bust, ear visible; *mm.* 92, 74, 71	2250	7000
2521	**Crown**. As 2519; *mm.* lis	6000	18500
2522	— Similar to 2520; *mm.* 21, 33-107	1350	4500
2522A	— Similar to 2520B; *mm.* 74, 71, 92	1500	5000

2523   2524

2523	**Half Crown**. As 2519; *mm.* lis	4500	13500
2524	— Similar to 2520; *mm.* 21, 33-107 (2 busts)	1250	4000
2524A	— Similar to 2520B; *mm.* 107-71	1350	4250

Fifth Issue, 1578-82 (`Fine' gold only of 0.992). *Mms* Greek cross,
Latin cross and sword.

2525	**Angel**. As 2514; *mm.* 7, 14, 113	1750	5500
2526	**Half Angel**. As 2517; *mm.* 7, 14, 113	1350	4500
2527	— Similar, but without E and rose above ship; *mm.* latin cross	1750	6000
2528	**Quarter Angel**. As last; *mm.* 7, 14, 113	1050	3250

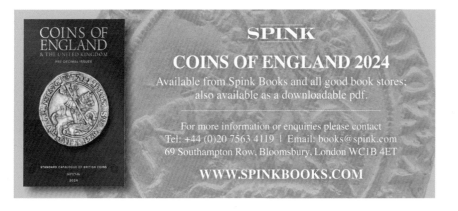

Sixth Issue, 1583-1600 (`Fine' gold of 0.995, `crown' gold of 0.916; pound of 174.5 grs. wt.).
Mintmarks: bell to **O**.

2529

		F	*VF*
		£	£
2529	**Sovereign** (30 s:). As 2512, but tressure not normally broken by back of throne; *mm*. 54-123	10000	30000

2530

| 2530 | **Ryal** (15 s.). Queen in ship. Ŗ. Similar to 1950; *mm*. 54-86 (*rev.* only) .. | 22500 | 65000 |

Note: Contemporary imitations of the Elizabeth Ryal are known for the Low Countries.

2531

| 2531 | **Angel**. As 2514; *mm*. 60-123, 90-**O** | 1600 | 5250 |
| 2532 | **Half Angel**. As 2517; *mm*. 60-86, 90-57 | 1250 | 4000 |

2535

		F	VF
		£	£
2533	**Quarter Angel**. As 2518; *mm.* 60-123, 90-57/–	1000	3000
2534	**Pound** (20 s.). Old bust l., with elaborate dress and profusion of hair; *mm.*,		
	lion and tun/tun, 123-**O**	6500	17500
2535	**Half Pound**. Similar; *mm.* tun	4750	15000
2535A	— Similar but smaller bust with less hair; *mm.* 123-**O**	4250	13500

2536

2536	**Crown**. Similar to 2534; *mm.* 123-90. **O**	2750	8500
2537	**Half Crown**. Similar; *mm.* -/123, 123-0, **O**	1750	5250

Seventh Issue, 1601-3 ('Fine' gold of 0.994, 'crown' gold of 0.916; Pound of 172 gr.). Mintmarks: **1** and **2**

2538	**Angel**. As 2531; *mm.* **1, 2**	2750	9500
2539	**Pound**. As 2534; *mm.* **1, 2**	7500	22500
2540	**Half Pound**. As 2535A; *mm.* **1, 2**	8000	25000
2541	**Crown**. As 2536; *mm.* **1, 2**	3500	10500
2542	**Half Crown**. As 2537; *mm.* **1, 2**	3000	9000

MILLED COINAGE, 1561-70

2543

2543	**Half Pound**. Crowned bust l.; *mm.* star, lis	4250	12500
2544	**Crown**. Similar; *mm.* star, lis	4500	13500
2545	**Half Crown**. Similar; *mm.* star, lis	5000	15000

For further details on the Gold milled coinage, *see* D. G. Borden & I.D. Brown *'The milled coinage of Elizabeth I'*. BNJ 53, 1983

SILVER
HAMMERED COINAGE
Countermarked Edward VI base shillings (1560)

2546   2547

		Fair	*F*
		£	£
2546	**Fourpence-halfpenny**. Edward VI 2nd period 6oz and 8oz shillings .... cmkd on obv. with a portcullis; *mm*. 66, –/33, 52, t, 111, Y and 122	750	3500
2547	**Twopence-farthing**. Edward VI 3rd period 3 oz. shillings .... countermarked on obverse with a seated greyhound; *mm*. 92. 105, 35 and 87	1250	4500
N.B.	*Occasionally the wrong countermark was used*		

First Issue, 1559-60 (.916 fine, shillings of 96 grs., 6.22g.)

2549   2551

1A   1B   1D   2A   2B

		F	*VF*
		£	£
2548	**Shilling**. Without rose or date. ELIZABET(H), wire line inner circles, pearls on bodice, busts 1A, and 1B; *mm*. lis.	600	3000
2549	— Similar, ELIZABETH, wire line and beaded inner circles, busts 1A, 1D, 2A and 2B; *mm*. lis..	250	1250

			F	VF
1F	1E 2550 only	1G	£	£
2550	**Groat**. Without rose or date, wire line or no inner circle, (busts 1F and 1E); *mm*. lis		175	750
2551	— Similar, wire line and beaded inner circles, bust 1F; *mm*. lis...........		125	450
2551A	— — Small bust 1G and shield (from halfgroat punches); *mm*. lis......		135	575

2551A		2552	2553	
2552	**Halfgroat**. Without rose or date, wire line inner circles; *mm*. lis		175	750
2553	**Penny**. Without rose or date, wire line inner circles; *mm*. lis		450	1750
2554	— Similar but dated 1558 on *obv*.; *mm*. lis...		1350	5000
2554A	— Similar to 2553, but wire line and beaded inner circles.; *mm*. lis		525	2000

Second Issue, 1560-1 (0.925 fineness, shilling of 96 grs., 6.22g.)

2555

2557 2558

3A 3B 3C 3J

	F	VF
	£	£
2555 **Shilling**. Without rose or date, beaded inner circles. ET instead of Z busts 3A, 3B, 3C and 3J; *mm*. 21, 94	150	600
2555A — large bust with pearls on bodice as 2548; *mm*. 21, bust 1A, 94, bust 1B	175	750
2556 **Groat**. Without rose or date, bust as 2551; *mm*. 21, 94	100	350
2557 **Halfgroat**. Without rose or date; *mm*. 21, 94..	75	275
2558 **Penny**. Without rose or date (three bust varieties); *mm*. 21, 94............	50	175

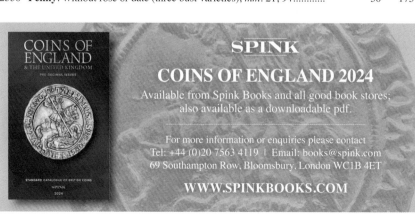

Third and Fourth Issues, 1561-77 (Same fineness and weight as last)

2559 2561 2561B

	F £	VF £

2559 **Sixpence**. With rose and date, large flan (inner beaded circle 19mm), large bust 3D with hair swept back, 1561; *mm*. pheon 150 650
2560 — Similar, small bust 1F, 1561; *mm*. pheon 90 400

3D 2559 only 1F 2560 3E 2561B only

2562 4B 2562

2561 — Smaller flan (inner beaded circle 17.5mm). Small bust 1F, 1561-6; *mm*. 53-107 80 325
2561B — Similar, very large bust 3E, 1563-5; *mm*. pheon 110 450
2562 — Intermediate bust 4B, ear shows, 1566-73; *mm*. 92-77 ...... 80 325
2562A — Similar, without date; *mm*. lion, coronet, ermine 1250 4000

2563 5A 2563 2565

2563 — Larger bust 5A, 1573-7; *mm*. 77-27 ...... 80 325
2564 **Threepence**. With rose and date 1561, large flan (inner circle 15mm.); *mm*. pheon 80 325
2565 — smaller flan (inner circle 14mm.). Regular bust, 1561-7; *mm*. 53-92 . 90 350

2566   2567

	F	VF
	£	£
2566 — taller bust, ear shows, 1567-77; *mm*. 74-27	75	300
2566A — Similar, without rose, 1568; *mm*. coronet	525	1500
2567 **Halfgroat**. Without rose or date; *mm*. 107-71	80	300
2568 **Threehalfpence**. With rose and date 1561, large flan (inner circle 12.5mm.) *mm*. pheon	85	325
2569 — — Smaller flan (inner circle 10.5-11.5mm.); 1561-2, 1564-78; *mm*. 53-27	50	225

2570   2571

	F	VF
2570 **Penny**. Without rose or date; *mm*. 33-71, 65b, 27	60	200
2571 **Threefarthings**. With rose and date 1561-2, 1564, 1567, 1568, 1572-7; *mm*. 53, 74, 77-27	75	275

Fifth Issue, 1578-82 (0.921 fineness, "shilling" of 95.6 grs., 6.19g.)

2572   2573

	F	VF
2572 **Sixpence**. As 2563, 1578-82; *mm*. 7-113..	75	300
2573 **Threepence**. As 2566, 1578-82; *mm*. 7-113	70	275

2574   2575

	F	VF
	£	£
2574 **Threehalfpence**. As 2569, 1578-9, 1581-2; *mm.* 7-113	65	275
2575 **Penny**. As 2570; *mm.* 7-113	50	200
2576 **Threefarthings**. As 2571, 1578-9, 1581-2; *mm.* 7-113	110	350

Sixth Issue, 1582-1600 (0.925 fineness, shilling of 96 grs., 6.22g.)

2577

2578   2581

6A   6B   6C

2577 **Shilling**. Without rose or date, ELIZAB; busts 3B and 6A ear concealed, *mm.* 60-72b. Bust 6B. Ear shows, *mm.* 79-**0** (mules occur)	125	575
2578 **Sixpence**. As 2572, ELIZABETH, 1582, 1583 *mm.* bell	110	400
2578A — Similar, ELIZAB, 1582-1589; *mm.* 60-72b	90	375
2578B — Similar, but bust 6C 1589-1600, *mm.* 72b-**0**	90	375
2579 **Halfgroat**. Without rose or date, two pellets behind bust. R. CIVITAS LONDON; *mm.* 60-**0** (*mm.* bell sometimes without pellets or with ··/II).	45	150
2580 **Penny**. Without rose or date. R. CIVITAS LONDON; *mm.* 60-**0**; 90-**0** on obv only	60	200
2581 **Halfpenny**. Portcullis. R. Cross and pellets; *mm.* none, 54-**0**	50	175

Seventh Issue, 1601-2 (0.925 fineness, shilling of 92.9 grs., 6.02)

2582

		F	VF
		£	£
2582	**Crown**. As illustration, *mm.* **1**	1850	4750
2582A	– Similar, *mm.* **2**	3750	15000

2583

2583	**Halfcrown**. As illustration, *mm.* **1**	1100	3250
2583A	– Similar, *mm.* **2**	3000	12500
2584	**Shilling**. As 2577; bust 6B *mm.* **1, 2**	135	600
2585	**Sixpence**. As 2578B, 1601-2; *mm.* **1, 2**	85	350
2586	**Halfgroat**. As 2579, *mm.* **1, 2**	50	175
2587	**Penny**. As 2580, *mm.* **1, 2**	65	250

2588

2588	**Halfpenny**. As 2581, *mm.* **1, 2**	50	175

MILLED COINAGE 1561-71

2589	**Shilling**. Without rose or date; *mm*. star. Plain dress, large size (over 31 *mm*.)	1250	3750
2590	— decorated dress, large size	475	1500
2591	— — intermediate size (30-31 *mm*.)	375	1350
2592	— — small size (under 30 *mm*.)	325	1250

2593

2593	**Sixpence**. Small bust, large rose. R. Cross fourchee, 1561 *mm*. star	175	675

2594

2594	Tall narrow bust with plain dress, large rose, 1561-2; *mm*. star	160	650

2595

2595	— similar, but decorated dress, 1562	150	625

2596

2596	Large broad bust, elaborately decorated dress, small rose, 1562; *mm*. star	140	575
2597	— — cross pattée on *rev*., 1562, 64 *mm*. star	175	675
2598	— similar, pellet border, 1562-4	175	675
2598A	Bust with low ruff, raised rim, 1564, 1566 (both overdates)..................	200	800

2599

| | *F* | *VF* |
| | £ | £ |

2599 Small bust, 1567-8, R. As 2593; *mm*. lis 140   575

2600

2600 Large crude bust breaking legend; 1570, *mm*. lis; 1571/0, *mm*. castle
      (over lis).. 575   2000

2601

2601	**Groat**. As illustration...	325	1250
2602	**Threepence**. With rose, small bust with plain dress, 1561	450	1750
2603	Tall narrow decorated bust with medium rose, 1562...............................	175	750
2604	Broad bust with very small rose, 1562	225	1000
2605	Cross pattée on *rev*., 1563, 1564/3...	575	2250

2606

| 2606 | **Halfgroat**. As groat .... | 250 | 1000 |
| 2607 | **Threefarthings**. E . D . G . ROSA, etc., with rose. R. CIVITAS LONDON, shield with 1563 above .... | 3750 | 9500 |

Further reading:
The Hammered Silver Coins produced at the Tower Mint during the reign of Elizabeth I.
I. D. Brown, C. H. Comber and W. Wilkinson. 2006.
The Milled Coinage of Elizabeth I. D. G. Borden and I. D. Brown. *BNJ* 53, 1983

EAST INDIA COMPANY TRADE COINAGE - 'Portcullis money'

Trade coins of 8, 4, 2, and 1 Testerns were coined at the Tower Mint in 1600/1 for the first voyage of the incorporated 'Company of Merchants of London Trading into the East Indies'. The coins bear the royal arms on the obverse and a portcullis on the reverse and have the *mm*. **O**. They were struck to the weights of the equivalent Spanish silver 8, 4, 2 and 1 reales.

2607A

	F	VF
	£	£
2607A Eight testerns	6000	17500

2607B

2607B Four testerns .	2750	8000

2607C

2607D

2607D

2607C Two testerns..	2250	7000
2607D One testern..	2000	5500

THE HOUSE OF STUART 1603-49

JAMES I, 1603-25

With the accession of James VI of Scotland to the English throne, the royal titles and coat of arms are altered on the coinage; on the latter the Scottish rampant lion and the Irish harp now appear in the second and third quarters. In 1604 the weight of the gold pound was reduced and the new coin became known as the 'Unite'. Fine gold of 0·979 and crown gold of 0·916 fineness were both issued, and a gold four-shilling piece was struck 1604-19. In 1612 all the gold coins had their values raised by 10%; but in 1619 the Unite was replaced by a new, lighter 20s. piece, the 'Laurel', and a lighter rose-ryal, spur-ryal and angel were minted.

In 1613 the king granted Lord Harington a licence to coin farthings of copper as a result of repeated public demands for a low value coinage; this was later taken over by the Duke of Lennox. Towards the end of the reign coins made from silver sent to the mint from the Welsh mines had the Prince of Wales's plumes inserted over the royal arms.

Mintmarks

125	105	33	79	84	74	90

60	25	71	45	32	123	132

72b	7a	16	24	125	105	46

First coinage		1609-10	Key (90)		1618-19	Plain cross (7a)
1603-4	Thistle (125)	1610-11	Bell (60)		1619	Saltire cross (16,
1604-5	Lis (105)	1611-12	Mullet (25)			gold)
		1612-13	Tower (71)			
Second coinage		1613	Trefoil (45)		Third coinage	
1604-5	Lis (105)	1613-15	Cinquefoil (32)		1619-20	Spur rowel (24)
1605-6	Rose (33)	1615-16	Tun (123)		1620-1	Rose (33)
1606-7	Escallop (79)	1616-17	Book on lectern (132)		1621-3	Thistle (125)
1607	Grapes (84)				1623-4	Lis (105)
1607-9	Coronet (74)	1617-18	Crescent (72b, gold)		1624	Trefoil (46)

GOLD

FIRST COINAGE, 1603-4 (Obverse legend reads D' . G' . ANG : SCO : etc.)

		F	VF
		£	£
2608	**Sovereign** (20s; 171.9 grs., 11.14g.). King crowned r., half-length, first bust with plain armour. R. EXVRGAT, etc.; *mm*. thistle	6500	18500
2609	— second bust with decorated armour; *mm*. thistle, lis...........................	7500	20000

2610   2611

2610	**Half-sovereign**. Crowned bust r. R. EXVRGAT, etc.; *mm*. thistle	8500	25000
2611	**Crown**. Similar. R. TVEATVR, etc.; *mm*. 125, 105/125	3500	10000
2612	**Halfcrown**. Similar; *mm*. thistle, lis...	1500	5250

N.B. *The Quarter-Angel of this coinage is considered to be a pattern (possibly a later strike), although coin weights are known.*

SECOND COINAGE, 1604-19 (Obverse legend reads D' G' MAG : BRIT : etc.)

2613

2613	**Rose-ryal** (30s., 33s. from 1612; 213.3 grs., 13.83g.) (Fine gold, 23 ct.). King enthroned. R. Shield on rose; *mm*. 33-90, 25-132	6000	17500

2614

		F £	VF £
2614	**Spur ryal** (15s., 16s. 6d. from 1612). King in ship; *mm*. 33, 79, 74, 25-32, 132	10000	37500
2615	**Angel** (10s., 11s. from 1612). Old type but larger shield; *mm*. 33-74, 60-16...	1850	6000
2616	— — pierced for use as touch-piece	750	2000
2617	**Half-angel** (5s., 5s. 6d. from 1612; 154.8 grs., 10.03 g.) (Crown gold, 22 ct.). Similar; *mm*. 71-132, 7a, 16	4500	13500
2618	**Unite** (20s., 22s. from 1612). Half-length second bust r. R. FACIAM etc.; *mm*. lis or rose..	1250	3750

2619

2619	— fourth bust; *mm*. rose to cinquefoil...	1100	3250
2620	— fifth bust; *mm*. cinquefoil to saltire..	1000	2750
2621	**Double-crown**. Third bust r. R. HENRICVS, etc.; *mm*. lis or rose	750	2250

2623

2622	Fourth bust; *mm*. rose to bell	650	2000
2623	Fifth bust; *mm*. key, mullet to saltire	650	2000

2624   2627

		F £	VF £
2624	**Britain crown**. First bust r.; *mm*. lis to coronet	375	950
2625	Third bust; *mm*. key to cinquefoil..	350	900
2626	Fifth bust; *mm*. cinquefoil to saltire...	350	900
2627	**Thistle crown** (4s.). As illus.; *mm*. lis to plain cross	450	1250
2628	— IR on only one side or absent both sides; *mm*. 79, 74, 71-123	500	1350
2629	**Halfcrown**. I' D' G' ROSA SINE SPINA. First bust; *mm*. lis to key	350	850
2630	Third bust; *mm*. key to trefoil, trefoil/tower	400	900
2631	Fifth bust; *mm*. cinquefoil to plain cross	350	850

THIRD COINAGE, 1619-25

2632	**Rose-ryal** (30s.; 194.2 grs., 12.58 g.) (Fine gold, 23 ct.). King enthroned. R. XXX above shield; lis, lion and rose emblems around; *mm*. 24, 125, 105	8000	25000
2633	Similar but plain back to throne; *mm*. trefoil...	10000	30000

2634

2634	**Spur-ryal** (15s.). As illus. R. Somewhat like 2614, but lis are also crowned. *mm*. 24-125, 46	13500	50000

2635

2635	**Angel** (10s.) of new type; *mm*. 24-46	2000	6500
2636	— pierced for use as touch-piece...	750	2000

2637   2638

	F	VF
	£	£

2637 **Laurel** (20s.; 140.5 grs., 9.10 g.) (Crown gold, 22 ct.). First (large) laur.
bust l.; *mm*. 24, 24/- 1250 4000

2638 Second, medium, square headed bust, `SS' tie ends; *mm*. 24, 33 .... 950 3250

2638A Third, small rounded head, ties wider apart; *mm*. 33, 105, 125................. 900 3000

2638B Fourth head, very small ties; *mm*. 105, 46 .... 900 3000

2638C Fourth head variety, tie ends form a bracket to value; *mm*. lis 950 3250

2639

2639 Fifth, small rather crude bust; *mm*. trefoil 2500 8500

2641A   2642A

2640 **Half-laurel**. First bust; *mm*. spur rowel... 800 2250

2641 — As 2638A; *mm*. rose.. 900 2750

2641A — As 2638B; *mm*. 33-46, 105/-.. 700 2000

2642 **Quarter-laurel**. Bust with two loose tie ends; *mm*. 24-105 .... 425 1000

2642A Bust as 2638C; *mm*. 105, 46, 105/46 .... 375 900

2642B As last but beaded, i.c. on *rev*. or both sides; *mm*. 105, 46...................... 450 1100

Rev. mm. on ¹/₂ and ¹/₄ laurels normally follows REGNA.

SILVER

2644

FIRST COINAGE, 1603-4

		F	VF
2643	**Crown**. King on horseback. R. EXVRGAT, etc., shield; *mm*. thistle, lis.	1350	4000
2644	**Halfcrown**. Similar	1500	5000

2645   2646

		F	VF
2645	**Shilling**. First bust, square-cut beard. R. EXVRGAT, etc.; *mm*. thistle ...	110	600
2645A	— transitional bust, nape of neck shows above broad collar, crown similar to first bust, shoulder armour as second bust, *mm*. thistle	135	650
2646	— Second bust, beard appears to merge with collar; *mm*. thistle, lis	85	350

2647   2648

		F	VF
2647	**Sixpence**. First bust; 1603; *mm*. thistle	90	425
2648	Second bust; 1603-4; *mm*. thistle, lis	70	325

2649   2650   2651

		F	VF
2649	**Halfgroat**. First bust, II behind head; *mm*. thistle, lis	40	150
2650	**Penny**. First bust I behind head; *mm*. thistle	110	400
2650A	— Second bust; *mm*. thistle, lis	40	135
2651	**Halfpenny**. As illustration; *mm*. thistle, lis	40	125

SECOND COINAGE, 1604-19

2652

		F £	VF £
2652	**Crown**. King on horseback. ℞. QVAE DEVS, etc. *rev.* stops; *mm.* 105-84	1250	4000
2653	**Halfcrown**. Similar; *mm.* 105-79	1750	6000
2654	**Shilling**. Third bust, beard cut square and stands out (*cf.* illus. 2657); *mm.* lis, rose	90	400
2655	— Fourth bust, armour plainer (*cf.* 2658); *mm.* 33-74, 90 over 74, or 60 over 74	80	375

2656

		F	VF
2656	— Fifth bust, similar, but hair longer; single-arched crown, *mm.* 74; higher double-arched crown, *mm.* 74 (rare), 90-7a	95	425

2657   2658

		F	VF
2657	**Sixpence**. Third bust; 1604-6; *mm.* lis, rose, escallop	75	350
2658	— Fourth bust; 1605-16; *mm.* rose to book, 90/60, 25/60	75	350
2658A	— Fifth bust, 1618; *mm.* plain cross	900	3000

2659

		F	VF
		£	£
2659	**Halfgroat**. As illus. but larger crown on *obv*.; *mm*. lis to coronet............	35	120
2660	— — Similar, but smaller crown on *obv*.; *mm*. coronet to plain cross......	35	120
2660A	As before, but TVEATVR legend both sides; *mm*. plain cross over book	50	175
2661	**Penny**. As halfgroat but no crowns; *mm*. 105-32,7a and none, -/84, 32/-	35	120
2662	— As before but TVEATVR legend both sides; *mm*. mullet....................	50	175
2663	**Halfpenny**. Rose, Ꝛ Thistle (with *mm*.) 105-25, 32; all *mm*s on rev. only	40	125

THIRD COINAGE, 1619-25

| 2664 | **Crown**. As 2652, with plain or grass ground line, colon stops on *obv*., no stops on *rev*.; *mm*. 33-46 .... | 950 | 2250 |

2665

| 2665 | — — plume over shield; *mm*. 125-46 .... | 1250 | 3750 |

2667

| 2666 | **Halfcrown**. As 2664 with plain or grass ground line; all have bird-headed harp; *mm*. 33-46.. | 300 | 1000 |
| 2666A | — — Similar but no ground line; *mm*. rose... | 1250 | 4000 |

2668

2669

		F	VF
		£	£
2667	— — Plume over shield; groundline *mm*. 125-46	575	1750
2668	**Shilling**. Sixth (large) bust, hair longer and very curly; *mm*. 24-46	95	450
2669	— — plume over shield; *mm*. 125-46	250	950

2670

2672

2673

2670	**Sixpence**. Sixth bust; 1621-4; *mm*. 33-46; 1621/0, *mm*. rose	80	375
2671	**Halfgroat**. As 2660 but no stops on *rev*.; *mm*. 24-46 and none, 105 and 46,		
	46/- *mm*. 24 with *rev*. stops known	30	110
2671A	Similar but no inner circles; *mm*. lis, trefoil over lis	35	120
2672	**Penny**. As illus.; *mm*. 24, 105, two pellets, none, trefoil, ...	30	90
2672A	— Similar but without inner circles on one or both sides; *mm*. lis, two		
	pellets	30	95
2673	**Halfpenny**. As 2663, but no *mm*.	25	90

COPPER

For further details see Tim Everson, *The Galata Guide to the Farthing Tokens of James I and Charles I*

Farthings

2674

2675

2674	Harington Type 1a small size, (originally tinned surface). Mintmark on cushion		
	of crown, *Mintmarks*: A, B, C, D, F, S, Ermine, Millrind, Pellet.	40	100
2675	— — 1b small size. Mintmark replaces central jewel on circlet of crown mm:		
	Trefoil, Crescent, Mullet, or omitted (unmodified)	30	50
2675A	— — 1c small size. Mintmark below crown, *mm*: :<	40	100

2676

	F	VF
	£	£
2676 — — 2 normal size. Mintmark on reverse only, *mm*: Cinquefoil, Cross saltire, Lis, Mullet, Trefoil..	20	40
2676A — — 3, large crown and harp, mintmark on reverse only, *mm* Martlet ...	30	70
2677 Lennox Type 1, mintmark on reverse only; *mm*: Bell, Tower	35	70

2678   2679

2678 — — 2, mintmark both sides, *mm*: Flower, Fusil.....................................	10	30
2679 — — 3, mintmark on obverse only, *mm*: Annulet, Coronet, Cross flory fitchée, Cross patée fourchée, Dagger, Eagle's head, Fusil, Key (horizontal), Lion passant, Quatrefoil, Rose (double), Roundel, Thistlehead, Trefoil, Tun, Turtle, Woolpack...	10	30
2679A Contemporary counterfeits of Lennox Type 3, *mm*: A, Annulet, Coronet, Crescent, Cross (plain or patée), Dagger, Fusil, Key, Mascle, Roundel, Star (pierced), Stirrup, Trefoil, Triangle, Triangle with pellet below, Tun	10	25

2680

2680 — — 4, as 3 but with larger, 9 jewel, crowns, *mm*: A, Dagger, Fusil, Lion rampant, Lis (three), Mascle, Stirrup, Trefoil, Triangle............................	10	30
2680A Contemporary forgeries of Lennox Type 4, *mm* A, Annulet, Dagger, Fusil, Lis, Mascle, Pellets (four), Tun, ...	10	25
2681 — — 5, oval flan, legend starts at bottom left, *mm* Cross patée	60	120

Lennox Type 5, the oval farthings, were issued for use in Ireland

Numismatically, this reign is one of the most interesting. Some outstanding machine-made coins were produced by Nicholas Briot, a French die-sinker, but they could not be struck at sufficient speed to supplant hand-hammering methods, and the weights often had to be adjusted by blank filing. In 1637 a branch mint was set up at Aberystwyth to coin silver extracted from the Welsh mines and dies supplied from Tower Mint. After the king's final breach with Parliament the parliamentary government continued to issue coins at London with Charles's name and portrait until the king's trial and execution. The coinage of copper farthings continued to be manufactured privately under licences held first by the Duchess of Richmond and, lastly, by Lord Maltravers. Parliament took control of the Token House in 1643, and production ceased the following year.

During the Civil War coins were struck at a number of towns to supply coinage for those areas of the country under Royalist control. Many of these coins have an abbreviated form of the 'Declaration' made at Wellington, Shropshire, Sept., 1642, in which Charles promised to uphold the Protestant Religion, the Laws of England and the Liberty of Parliament. Amongst the more spectacular pieces are the gold triple unites and the silver pounds and half-pounds struck at Shrewsbury and Oxford, and the emergency coins, some made from odd-shaped pieces of silver plate during the sieges of Newark, Scarborough, Carlisle and Pontefract.

Mintmarks

105	10	96	71	57	88	101	35
87	107	60	70	123	57	119a	23
119b	98	112	81	120	109		

Tower Mint under Charles I

1625	Lis (105)	1633-4	Portcullis (107)
1625-6	Cross Calvary (10)	1634-5	Bell (60)
1626-7	African head (96)	1635-6	Crown (75)
1627-8	Castle (71)	1636-8	Tun (123)
1628-9	Anchor (57)	1638-9	Anchor (57)
1629-30	Heart (88)	1639-40	Triangle (119a)
1630-1	Plume (101)	1640-1	Star (23)
1631-2	Rose (35)	1641-3	Triangle in circle
1632-3	Harp (87)		(119b)

Tower Mint under Parliament

1643-4	P in brackets (98)
1644-5	R in brackets (112)
1645	Eye (81)
1645-6	Sun (120)
1646-8	Sceptre (109)

Mint mark no. 57 maybe upright, inverted, or horizontal to left or right.

| 59 | B | 58var | 58 |

Briot's Mint

1631-2	Flower and B (59)	1638-9	Anchor (57)
1632	**B**		Anchor and B (58)
			(B upright or on side)
			Anchor and Mullet (58v)

61	104	35	92	103	6	65b	71
89	91*var*	131	84	94*var*	64	93	34
102	67	127	128	129	25	83	100
	134	71	A	B	75		

Provincial and Civil War Mints

1638-42	Book (61, *Aberystwyth*)	1643-4	Boar's head (64 *Worcs.* or *Shrews.*)
1642	Plume (104, *Shrewsbury*)		Lion rampant (93, *Worcs.* or *Shrews.*)
	Pellets or pellet (*Shrewsbury*)		Rosette (34, *Worcs.* or *Shrews.*)
1642-3	Rose (35, *Truro*)	1643-5	Plume (102, *Bristol*)
	Bugle (134, *Truro*)		Br. (67, *Bristol*)
1642-4	Lion (92, *York*)		Pellets (*Bristol*)
1642-6	Plume (103, *Oxford*)		Rose (35, *Exeter*)
	Pellet or pellets (*Oxford*)		Rosette (34, *Oxford*)
	Lis (105, *Oxford*)	1643-6	Floriated cross (127, *Oxford*)
1643	Cross pattee (6, *Bristol*)	1644	Cross pattee (6, *Oxford*)
	Acorn (65b, *Bristol*)		Lozenge (128, *Oxford*)
	Castle (71, *Worcester* or *Shrewsbury*)		Billet (129, *Oxford*)
	Helmet (89, *Worcester* and *Shrewsbury*)		Mullet (25, *Oxford*)
1643-4	Leopard's head (91 var. *Worcester*)	1644-5	Gerb (83, *Chester*)
	Two lions (131, *Worcester*)		Pear (100, *Worcester*)
	Lis (105, *Worcs.* or *Shrews.*)		Lis (105, *Hereford?*)
	Bunch of grapes (84, *Worcs.* or *Shrews.*)		Castle (71, *Exeter*)
	Bird (94 var., *Worcs.* or *Shrews.*)	1645-6	Plume (102, *Ashby, Bridgnorth*)
		1645	A (*Ashby*)
		1646	B (*Bridgnorth*)
		1648-9	Crown (75, *Aberystwyth Furnace*)

GOLD COINAGE

TOWER, UNDER THE KING (1625-42), AND UNDER PARLIAMENT (1642-9)

For bust varieties on Tower Mint Gold see H. Schneider BNJ 1955-61

Numbers in brackets following each entry refer to numbers employed in previous editions of this catalogue

		F	VF
		£	£
2682	**Angel**. St. Michael slaying dragon, no mark of value. R. Three masted ship, royal arms on mainsail; mm. lis, cross calvary	5500	20000
2682A	— — — pierced for use as touch-piece (2683)	1750	6500
2683	— X in field to right of St. Michael; m.m. African head, castle, anchor, heart, castle and African head/castle, anchor and castle/anchor (2684)	3750	13500
2683A	— — — pierced for use as touch-piece (2685)	1000	3500
2684	— X in field to left of St. Michael; mm. African head, heart, rose, harp, portcullis, bell, crown, tun, anchor, triangle, star, triangle-in-circle (2686)	3000	10000
2684A	— — — pierced for use as touch-piece (2687)	950	3000

2685

2685	**Unite**. Group A, first bust, in coronation robes, bust 1, high double-arched crown. R. Square-topped shield, plain or elaborate garnishing; mm. lis (2688, 2688A)	1250	3500
2686	— — bust 1a, flatter single-arched crown; mm. lis, cross calvary (2689, 2689A)	1350	3750
2687	Group B, second bust, in ruff, armour and mantle. R. Square-topped shield; m.m. cross calvary, African head, castle, anchor, heart (2690)	1200	3250

2688

2688	— — more elongated bust, usually dividing legend, mm. anchor, heart, plume (2690A)	1200	3250
2689	— — anchor below bust; mm. (2691)	2500	7500
2689A	Group B/C mule. R. Oval shield with CR at sides; mm. plume (2691A)	1500	5000
2690	Group C, third bust, shorter with heavier armour. R. Oval shield with CR at sides; mm. plume, rose (2692)	1250	3500
2691	Group D, fourth bust, with falling lace collar, bust 4, large bust with jewelled crown. R. Oval shield with CR at sides; mm. harp, portcullis (2693)	1250	3500
2692	— — bust 5, smaller bust, unjewelled crown; mm. portcullis, bell, crown, tun, anchor, triangle, star (2693A)	1250	3500

		F	*VF*
		£	£
2693	— — — (under Parliament); mm. (P), (P)/- (2710)	1750	5000
2694	Group F, sixth 'Briot's' bust, with stellate lace collar. R. Oval shield with CR at sides, mm. triangle, star, triangle-in-circle (2694).........................	1500	4500
2695	— — (under Parliament); mm. (P), (R) (2711)	1750	5000

2696

| 2696 | Group G, (under Parliament), seventh bust, smaller collar; mm. eye, sun, sceptre (2712)... | 2250 | 6500 |

2697   2699

2697	**Double-crown.** Group A, first bust, in coronation robes, bust 1, high double-arched crown, both arches jewelled. R. Square-topped shield; mm. lis (2696)	850	2750
2698	— — bust 1a, flatter crown, outer arch only jewelled; m.m. lis, cross calvary (2696A)...	800	2500
2699	Group B, second bust, in ruff, armour and mantle, bust 2. R. Square-topped shield; mm. cross calvary, African head, castle, anchor (2697)...............	675	2000
2700	— — busts 3-4, more elongated bust, usually dividing legend; mm. anchor, heart, plume (2697A)	725	2250
2700A	Group B/C mule, elongated bust dividing legend. R. oval shield, *mm.* plume	950	3000
2701	Group C, third bust, bust 5. R. Oval shield with CR at sides; mm. plume, rose (2698)...	900	2750
2702	Group D, fourth bust, with falling lace collar, bust 6, large bust with jewelled crown. R. Oval shield with CR at sides; mm. harp, crown (2699)	950	3000
2703	— — bust 7, smaller head, inner or both arches of crown unjewelled; mm. harp, portcullis, bell, crown, tun, anchor (2699A-C)..	900	2750
2703A	— — — Group Da, (under Parliament), re-cut Group D bust punches; m.m. eye (2713)...	1500	4500
2704	Group E, fifth bust, 'Aberystwyth' bust, bust 8, double-arched crown. R. Oval shield with CR at sides; m.m. anchor (2700)..	1400	4250
2705	— — bust 9, smaller 'Aberystwyth' bust, single-arched crown; m.m. anchor, triangle (2700A)..	1350	4000
2705A	— — — Group Ea, (under Parliament), re-cut bust 9; m.m. sun, sceptre (2714)	1500	4500
2706	Group F, sixth 'Briot's' bust, with stellate lace collar, bust 10. R. Oval shield with CR at sides; mm. triangle, star, triangle-in-circle (2701)	950	3000

		F	VF
		£	£
2707	— — (under Parliament); mm. (P), (R) (2715)	1100	3250
2708	Group H, (under Parliament), bust 11, dumpy crude bust, single flat-arched crown; mm. sun (2716)...............	1750	6000

2710   2715

2709	**Crown**. Group A, first bust, in coronation robes, bust 1 var, tall narrow bust, double-arched crown. ℞. Square-topped shield; mm. lis (2703)	450	1350
2710	— bust 1, broader, less angular bust; m.m. lis, cross calvary (2703A) ...	525	1500
2711	Group B, second bust, in ruff, armour and mantle, bust 2. ℞. Square-topped shield; mm. cross calvary, African head, castle (2704)...........................	425	1250
2712	— — bust 3, narrower; more elongated bust; m.m. anchor, heart, plume (2704A)...............	375	1100
2713	— — — anchor below bust; mm. anchor (2704B)...............	850	2500
2713A	Group B/C mule. ℞. Oval shield with CR at sides; mm. plume, rose (2705)	450	1350
2714	Group C, third bust, bust 4. ℞. Oval shield with CR at sides; mm. plume (2706)...............	525	1500
2715	Group D, fourth bust, with falling lace collar, busts 5, 7. ℞. Oval shield with CR at sides; m.m. harp, -/harp, portcullis, portcullis/bell, bell, crown, tun, anchor, triangle, star/triangle, star, triangle-in-circle (2707)	425	1250
2716	— — (under Parliament), bust 5, jewelled crown; m.m. (P), (R), eye, sun (2717)...............	525	1500
2716A	— — (under Parliament), bust 6, unjewelled crown; m.m. eye, sun, sceptre (2717A)...............	575	1650
2717	Group E, fifth bust, small 'Aberystwyth' bust, bust 8. ℞. Oval shield with CR at sides; mm. anchor (2708)	750	2250
2721C	— Group F, sixth 'Briot's' bust, bust 9, only known as Briot/hammered mule (see 2721C below)	1750	5000

NICHOLAS BRIOT'S COINAGES, 1631-2 and 1638-9
MILLED ISSUES, 1631-2

2718	**Angel**. Type somewhat as Tower but smaller and neater; *mm*. -/B	15000	45000

2719

2719	**Unite**. As illustration. ℞. FLORENT etc.; *mm*. flower and B/B	6500	18500
2720	**Double-crown**. Similar but X. ℞. CVLTORES, etc. *mm*. flower and B/B	2750	8500

2720A Similar but King's crown unjewelled: *mm*. flower and B/B, B 3000   9000
2721   **Crown**. Similar; *mm*. B 7000 20000

BRIOT'S HAMMERED ISSUES, 1638-9

2721A **Unite**. Briot's (sixth) bust, large lace collar. R. FLORENT etc., Briot's
       square-topped shield dividing crowned C R; *mm*. anchor 8000 25000
2721B **Double-crown**. Briot's bust, similar. R. CVLTORES etc., square-topped
       shield dividing crowned C R; *mm*. anchor.. 3000   8500
2721C **Crown**. Briot's bust, similar. R. CVLTORES etc., oval shield dividing
       crowned C R (a Briot hammered issue/Tower mule); *mm*. anchor.......... 1750   5000

GOLD COINAGES

PROVINCIAL ISSUES AND COINAGES OF THE ENGLISH CIVIL WAR, 1642-9
CHESTER, 1644

2722   **Unite**. As Tower. Somewhat like a crude Tower sixth bust. R. Crowned,
       oval shield, crowned CR, *mm*. plume 35000 125000

SHREWSBURY, 1642 (See also 2749)

2723   **Triple unite**, 1642. Half-length figure l holding sword and olive-branch;
       mm.: R. EXVRGAT, etc., around RELIG PROT, etc., in two wavy lines.
       III and three plumes above, date below 85000 300000

2727

	F	VF
	£	£

OXFORD, 1642-6

		F	VF
2724	**Triple unite**. As last, but *mm*. plume, tall narrow bust, 1642..................	13500	40000
2725	Similar, 1643	20000	65000
2725A	Large bust of fine style. King holds short olive branch; *mm*. small lis	60000	175000
2726	As last, but taller bust, with scarf behind shoulder, 1643, *mm*. plume	15000	45000
2727	Similar, but without scarf, longer olive branch, 1643	13500	42500
2728	Similar, but OXON below 1643, rosette stops	25000	75000
2729	Smaller size, olive branch varies, bust size varies, 1644 OXON	17500	50000
2730	— Obv. as 2729, 1644 / OX	18500	55000

2735

2731	**Unite**. Tall thin bust. ℞. 'Declaration' in two wavy lines, 1642; *no mm*...	4500	15000
2732	— ℞. 'Declaration' in three lines on continuous scroll, 1642-3	5000	17500
2733	Tall, well-proportioned bust. ℞. Similar, 1643, no *mm*...........................	6000	20000
2734	Shorter bust, king's elbow not visible. ℞. Similar, 1643; *mm*. plume/-	4000	12500
2735	Similar but longer olive branch curving to l. 1644 / OX; *mm*. plume	4250	13500
2735A	Similar, but dumpy bust breaking lower i.c., small flan	5000	17500
2736	Tall bust to edge of coin. ℞. Similar, 1643	9000	30000
2737	As 2734. ℞. 'Declaration' in three straight lines, 1644 / OX (as shilling *rev*. S2971)..	7500	25000
2738	Similar to 2734, but smaller size; small bust, low olive branch. 1645	6000	20000
2739	— ℞. Single plume above 'Declaration', 1645-6 / OX; *mm*. plume, rosette, none	5500	18500
2740	**Half-unite**. 'Declaration' in three straight lines, 1642	4500	15000
2741	'Declaration' on scroll; *mm*. plume; 1642-3	4000	13500

2742

		F £	*VF* £
2742	Bust to bottom of coin, 1643; Oxford plumes	3500	11000
2743	— 1644 / OX. Three Shrewsbury plumes (neater work)	5000	16000

BRISTOL, 1643-5
| 2744 | **Unite.** Somewhat as 2734; Two busts known. *mm.* Br. or Br/ plumelet.;
1645 .... | 25000 | 90000 |
| 2745 | **Half-unite.** Similar 1645 .... | 15000 | 50000 |

TRURO, 1642–3
| 2745A | **Half-Unite.** Crowned bust l. (similar to Tower 4th bust). R.
CVLT, etc., crowned shield.. | 17500 | 60000 |

EXETER, 1643–5
| 2746 | **Unite.** *obv.* sim. to early Oxford bust. R. FLORENT, etc., crowned oval
shield between crowned CR, *mm*. rose .... | 22500 | 85000 |
| 2747 | — R. CVLTORES, etc., similar but no CR .... | 22500 | 85000 |

WORCESTER, 1643-4
| 2748 | **Unite.** Crude bust R. FLORENT, etc., double annulet stops, crowned oval
shield, lion's paws on either side of garniture, no *mm*............................... | 25000 | 90000 |

SALOPIA (SHREWSBURY) , 1644
| 2749 | **Unite.** *Obv.* bust in armour. R. Cr. shield, crowned CR. *mm*. lis/- .... | 35000 | 120000 |

COLCHESTER BESIEGED, 1648
| 2750 | **Ten Shillings** Gateway of castle between CR; below OBS COL 16 S/X 48.
Uniface – now considered a later concoction .... | | |

PONTEFRACT BESIEGED, 1648-9. After the death of Charles I, in the name of Charles II
| 2751 | **Unite.** DVM : SPIRO : SPERO around CR crowned. CAROLVS :
SECVꟼDVS : 16 48, castle, OBS on l., PC above. .... | 80000 | 275000 |
| 2752 | **Unite.** CAROL : II, etc., around HANC : DEVS, etc. R. POST : MORTEM,
etc.,around castle. *Octagonal*... | 75000 | 250000 |

SILVER COINAGES

TOWER, UNDER THE KING (1625-42), AND UNDER PARLIAMENT (1642-9)
2753	**Crown**. Group I, first horseman, type 1a, king on horseback left, horse caparisoned with plume on head and crupper. R. Square-topped shield over long cross fourchee; mm. lis, cross calvary	950	3000
2754	— — 1b. R. Plume above shield, no cross fourchee; mm. lis, cross calvary, castle..	2250	8000
2755	Group II, second horseman, type 2a, smaller horse, plume on head only, cross on housing. R. Oval shield over cross fourchee, CR above; mm. harp	750	2500
2756	— — 2b1. R. Plume between CR above shield, no cross fourchee; mm. plume, rose...	1000	3500
2757	— — 2b2. R. Plume between CR, cross fourchee; mm. harp	1250	4000

2758

	F	VF
	£	£

2758 Group III, third horseman, type 3a, horse without caparisons, sword upright.
R. Oval shield without CR; mm. bell, crown, tun, anchor, triangle, star.. | 950 | 3000

2759 — — 3b. R. Plume above shield; mm. portcullis, crown, tun .... | 1100 | 3750

2760 'Briot's' horseman with groundline, lozenge stops on obverse; mm. triangle
in circle .... | 8500 | 25000

2761 Group IV, (under Parliament), fourth horseman, type 4, foreshortened horse
R. Oval shield; mm. (P), (R), eye, sun .... | 1000 | 3250

2762 Group V, (under Parliament), fifth horseman, type 5, tall spirited horse;
mm. sun.. | 1250 | 4000

2763   2769

2763 **Halfcrown**. Group I, first horseman, type 1a1, horse caparisoned with plume
on head and crupper, rose on housings, ground-line. R. Square-topped shield
over long cross fourchee; mm. lis.. | 525 | 2250

2764 — — 1a2. No rose on housings, no ground-line; mm. lis, cross calvary | 325 | 1250

2765 — — — ground-line; mm. lis.. | 475 | 2000

2766 — — 1a3. No rose on housings, no ground-line. R. No long cross, heavy or light
garnishing to shield; mm. cross calvary*, African head, castle................ | 375 | 1500

2767 — — — 1b. R. Plume above shield, heavy or light garnishing; mm. lis, cross
calvary*, African head, castle, anchor .... | 750 | 3000

2768 Group II, second horseman, type 2/1b, plume on horse's head only, rose on
housings. R. Plume over shield; mm. heart, plume .... | 1100 | 4250

2769 — — 2a. Smaller horse, cross on housings. R. Oval shield with CR above
(CR divided by rose (very rare), lis over rose (rare), or lis); mm. plume,
rose, plume/rose .... | 175 | 575

2770 — — — 2b. R. Plume between CR above shield; mm. plume, rose........ | 325 | 1250

2773

		F £	VF £
2771	— — 2c. R. Oval draped shield with CR at sides; mm. harp, portcullis, portcullis/harp	150	425
2772	— — — 2d. R. Plume above shield; mm. harp	1350	5750
2773	Group III, third horseman, type 3a1, no caparisons on horse, scarf flying from king's waist. R. Oval garnished shield; mm. bell, bell/crown, crown, tun, triangle	125	350
2774	— — — 3b. R. Plume above shield; mm. portcullis, bell, crown, tun	225	700
2775	— — 3a2. King wears cloak flying from shoulder. R. Oval garnished shield; mm. tun, anchor, triangle, star, triangle-in-circle	125	350

2776   2779

2776	— — — — rough ground under horse; mm. triangle, star	110	325
2777	— — horseman of finer style, short busy tail, cloak like arrowhead behind shoulder, no ground below; mm. triangle, star	160	525
2778	— — 3a3, (under Parliament), no ground, cruder workmanship; mm. (P), (R), eye, sun	95	300
2779	Group IV, fourth horseman, type 4, foreshortened horse. R. Oval garnished shield; mm. star, triangle in circle	95	300
2779A	— — (under Parliament); mm. (P)	225	700
2779B	— —, transitional type 4/5, mm. sun	175	575
2780	Group V, (under Parliament), fifth horseman, type 5, tall spirited horse. R. Oval garnished shield; mm. sun, sceptre	125	350

* Light weight half crowns (204 grains) exist of No. 2766 and 2767, mm. cross calvary

2781   2782

		F	VF
		£	£
2781	**Shilling**. Group A, first bust, type 1, in coronation robes, bust 1, high double-arched crown, both arches jewelled. R. Square-topped shield over cross fourchee (Sharp A1/1); mm. lis	125	525
2782	— — bust 2, larger crown, outer arch only jewelled (Sharp A2/1-2); mm. lis*, cross calvary*	135	575
2783	— — — 1b1. R. Plume above shield, no cross fourchee (Sharp A2/3); mm. lis, cross calvary	900	3500
2784	Group B, second bust, type 1a, in ruff, armour and mantle. R. Square-topped shield over cross fourchee (Sharp B1-5/1); mm. cross calvary*, African head, castle	125	475
2785	— — 1b2. R. Plume above shield, no cross fourchee (Sharp B1-5/2); mm. cross calvary*, African head, castle, anchor, heart, plume	275	1000
2786	— — 1b3. R. Plume above shield, cross fourchee (Sharp B2/3); mm. African head	1750	5750
2787	Group C, third bust, type 2a, with more visible armour. R. Oval garnished shield with CR above (Sharp C1/1, C2/1-3); mm. plume, rose	120	450
2788	— — 2b. R. Plume above shield (Sharp C1/4, C2/4-6, C3/5); mm. plume, rose	250	900
2789	Group D, fourth bust, type 3.1, with falling lace collar, inner circles. R. Garnished oval shield with CR at sides (Sharp D1-6/1); mm. harp, portcullis	125	350
2790	— — — 3.2. R. Plume above shield (Sharp D1- 3/2); mm. harp	800	3000

2791

2791	— — 3a, no inner circles. R. Round garnished shield, no CR (Sharp E1/1-2, E2/1-2; E3/2); mm. bell, crown, tun	90	275
2792	— — — rare bust varieties, no inner circles: (a) large crude bust (Sharp E4/2); mm. tun; (b) neat 'Aberystwyth' bust (Sharp E5/2); mm. tun	100	300
2793	— — 3b. R. Plume above shield (Sharp E1-2/3); mm. bell, crown, tun	120	425

* Light weight shillings (81.75 grains) exist of No. 2782, mm. lis, cross calvary over lis; No. 2784, mm. cross calvary; and No. 2785 mm. cross calvary
See Sharp BNJ 1977 for shilling bust varieties including fine work coins. See also Holt, Hulett and Lyle, BNJ 2014.

2794   2797

		F £	VF £
2794	Group E, fifth "Aberystwyth" bust, type 4.2, double-arched crown, small or large XII. R. Square-topped shield over cross moline (Sharp F1/1); mm. tun, anchor	95	300
2795	— — 4.1, larger bust, single-arched crown, small or large XII (Sharp F2/1); mm. tun, anchor	100	325
2796	— — 4.3, smaller bust, single-arched crown, large XII (Sharp F3/1-2); mm. tun, anchor, triangle	90	275
2797	— — 4.1var., larger bust with rounded shoulder, large XII (Sharp F5/1-2); mm. anchor, triangle	90	275
2798	— — rare bust varieties : (a) small 'Aberystwyth' bust, double-arched crown (Sharp F4/1); mm. anchor (to right); (b) small 'Briot's' bust, with stellate lace collar, single-arched crown (Sharp F6/1-2); mm. triangle; (c) small 'Aberystwyth' bust, single-arched crown (Sharp F7/2); mm. triangle-in-circle	200	650
2799	Group F, sixth large 'Briot's' bust, type 4.4, with stellate lace collar, double-arched crown. R. Square-topped shield over cross moline (Sharp G 1/1-2); mm. triangle, star, triangle-in-circle	70	200

2800   2803

		F £	VF £
2800	— — — (under Parliament) (Sharp G1-2/2); mm. (P), (R), eye, sun	70	200
2801	— — 4.4 var., (under Parliament), small thin bust, 'nick' below truncation (Sharp G3/2); mm. sun	375	1350
2802	Group G, (under Parliament), seventh bust, type 4.5, tall coarse narrow bust. R. Square-topped shield over cross moline (Sharp H1/1); mm. sun, sceptre.	120	375
2803	— — 4.6, shorter slim better proportioned bust (Sharp H2/2); mm. sceptre	125	400
2804	— — — short broad bust (Sharp H3/2); mm. sceptre	135	500

2805   2810

		F £	VF £
2805	**Sixpence**. Group A, first bust, in coronation robes, type 1, small bust, double-arched crown. R. Square-topped shield over cross fourchee, date above; 1625, mm. lis..................	125	425
2806	— — broader bust, larger crown; 1625, mm. lis, cross calvary*; 1626, mm. cross calvary*	135	450
2807	Group B, second bust (several varieties), type 1a1, in ruff, armour and mantle. R. Square-topped shield over cross fourchee, date above; 1625, mm. cross calvary; 1626, mm. cross calvary*, African head; 1627, mm. African head, castle; 1628, mm. castle, anchor; 1629, mm. anchor, heart......................	175	600
2808	— — 1a2. R. No cross fourchee; 1630, mm. heart, plume	525	1650
2809	Group C, third bust, type 2a. R. Oval garnished shield with CR above; mm. plume, rose..........................	100	350
2810	— — 2b. R. Plume above shield; mm. plume, rose, plume/rose............	175	575

2811   2814   2819

		F £	VF £
2811	Group D, fourth bust, type 3, with falling lace collar, inner circles, (medium, large and small bust). R. Oval garnished shield with CR at sides; mm. harp, portcullis	85	300
2812	— — — omits C R by shield; mm. portcullis	150	525
2813	— — — 3a, no inner circles (type 3/3a mules exist); mm. bell, crown, tun .	75	250
2814	Group E, fifth 'Aberystwyth' bust, type 4.1, double-arched crown, small or large VI. R. Square-topped shield over cross moline; mm. tun, anchor .	85	300
2815	— — — R. Lyre cross-ends; mm. tun	325	1250
2816	— — 4.2, single-arched crown; mm. tun, anchor, triangle	70	240
2817	Group F, sixth 'Briot's' bust, type 4.3, with stellate lace collar. R. Square-topped shield over cross moline; mm. triangle, star, triangle-in-circle	65	225
2818	— — (under Parliament); mm. (P), (R)	90	325
2819	Group G, (under Parliament), late 'Aberystwyth' bust with riveted shoulder, type 4.4. R. Square-topped shield over cross moline; mm. (P), (R), eye, sun, sceptre	85	300

* Light weight sixpences (40.85 grains) exist of No. 2806, 1625, mm. cross calvary, 1626, mm. cross calvary; and No. 2807, 1626, mm. cross calvary

		F £	VF £
2820	— — 4.5, squat bust of crude style; mm. eye, sun (over eye)	150	525
2821	— — 4.5 var., small 3a type bust, double-arched crown, inner circle both sides; mm. sun (over eye)	275	950

2822   2824   2832

		F	VF
2822	**Halfgroat**. Group A, without bust, crowned rose each side, type 1, inner circles on one or both sides;mm. lis, lis/-, cross calvary, castle, none......	35	125
2823	— — 1a, without inner circles; mm. African head, castle, anchor, heart, plume	35	125
2824	Group B, second bust, type 2a, in ruff and mantle. R. Oval shield; mm. plume, rose...	40	135
2825	— — 2b. R. plume above shield; mm. plume, plume/-, rose	50	175
2826	Group C, third bust, more armour, crown breaks inner circle; mm. plume, rose..	45	150
2827	— — R. Plume above shield; mm. plume	60	200
2828	Group D, fourth bust, type 3.1, no inner circles. R. Oval shield dividing C R; mm. harp, portcullis crown	30	120
2829	— — — — 3.2-4, inner circle on one or both sides; mm. harp, portcullis, ../harp (2811-13)	30	120
2830	— — — 3.5-6. R. Oval shield, no C R, no inner circle or obv. only; mm. harp, portcullis	40	135
2831	— — 3a1. R. Rounder shield, no inner circles; mm. bell, crown, tun, anchor, triangle	30	110
2832	— — 3a2-3, inner circles on obverse or both sides; mm. anchor, triangle, star, triangle-in-circle	35	125
2833	— — — (under Parliament), type 3a3, inner circles both sides; mm. (P)/triangle-in-circle, (P), (R), eye, sun, sceptre	30	120
2834	Group E, fifth 'Aberystwyth' bust, types 3a4-5, no inner circles or on reverse only; mm. anchor (2819-20)	50	175
2835	— — 3a6, very small bust (from penny puncheon), no inner circles; mm. anchor	60	200
2836	Group G, (under Parliament), seventh bust, type 3a7, older bust with pointed beard; mm. eye, sun, sceptre..	30	110

2838

		F	VF
2837	**Penny**. Group A, without bust, rose each side, type 1, inner circles; mm. lis, African head, one or two pellets	35	100
2838	— — 1a, no inner circles; mm. lis, anchor, one or two pellets	30	95
2839	— — 1b, inner circle on reverse; mm. African head/two pellets	45	150
2840	Group B, second bust, type 2, in ruff and mantle. R. Oval shield, inner circles; mm. plume, plume/rose, rose	40	135
2841	— — 2.1, no inner circles; mm. plume, rose...	40	125
2842	Group C, third bust, type 2a1, more armour visible, no inner circles; mm. plume, plume/rose, rose...	35	110

	F £	VF £
2843 — — 2a2-4, inner circles on obverse, both sides or reverse; mm. plume, rose	35	110
2844 Group D, fourth bust, type 3.1, with falling lace collar. R. CR by shield, no inner circles; mm. harp, one or two pellets	30	95

2845

	F £	VF £
2845 — — — 3.2, no C R by shield, no inner circles; mm. harp, portcullis, pellets, none	30	95
2846 — — — 3.3-4, inner circles on obverse or reverse; mm. harp, two pellets	30	100
2847 — — 3a1, shield almost round with scroll garniture, no inner circles; mm. bell, triangle, one to four pellets, none	25	90
2848 — — 3a1 var., inner circle on one or both sides; mm. triangle/two pellets	35	110
2849 Group E, fifth 'Aberystwyth' bust, type 3a3, inner circle on obverse or none; mm. triangle, anchor, one or two pellets, none	30	95
2850 Group G, (under Parliament), seventh bust, type 3a2, older bust, inner circle on obverse only; mm. one or two pellets	35	110

2851

	F £	VF £
2851 **Halfpenny**. Rose each side, no legend or mm	25	90

NICHOLAS BRIOT'S COINAGE, 1631-9

FIRST MILLED ISSUE, 1631-2

	F £	VF £
2852 **Crown**. King on horseback. R. Crowned shield between CR crowned; *mm*. flower and B / B	1350	4000

2853	2855	

	F £	VF £
2853 **Halfcrown**. Similar	850	2250
2854 **Shilling**. Briot's early bust with falling lace collar. R. Square-topped shield over long cross fourchee; R. Legend starts at top or bottom (extr. rare) *mm*. flower and B/B, B	575	1500
2855 **Sixpence**. Similar, but VI behind bust; *mm*. flower and B/B, flower and B/-	250	650

2856	2856A

	F	VF
	£	£

2856 **Halfgroat**. Briot's bust, B below, II behind. R̟. IVSTITIA, etc., square-
topped shield over long cross fourchee 110   275

2856A Pattern halfgroat. Uncrowned bust in ruff r. R̟. crowned, interlocked Cs.
(North 2687). (Included because of its relatively regular appearance.) ... 100   275

2857 **Penny**. Similar, but I behind bust, B below bust; position of legend may vary 100   250

SECOND MILLED ISSUE, 1638-9

2859

2858 **Halfcrown**. As 2853, but *mm.* anchor and B.. 800   2250

2859 **Shilling**. Briot's late bust, the falling lace collar is plain with broad lace
border, no scarf. R̟. As 2854 but cross only to inner circle; *mm.* anchor and
B, anchor or muled 300   850

2860 **Sixpence**. Similar, but VI; *mm.* anchor, anchor and mullet/anchor.......... 175   525
The last two often exhibit flan reduction marks.

HAMMERED ISSUE, 1638-9

2861 **Halfcrown**. King on Briot's style horse with ground line. R̟. Square-topped
shield; *mm.* anchor, triangle over anchor. Also muled with Tower *rev*..... 900   2250

2862 **Shilling**. Briot's first hammered issue, Sim. to 2859; R̟. Square-topped
shield over short cross fleury, contraction stops on *obv.,* pellet stops
rev. mm. anchor 1350   4500

2862A — Briot's second hammered issue. As 2862 but lozenge stops both sides.
mm. anchor, triangle over anchor or triangle 350   1000

2862B Tower, Group E, obv. type 4.1 var. (S.2797) above R̟. as Briot's 1st or 2nd
hammered issue; mm. Δ over anchor... 575   1750

2862C Tower, Group F, obv. type 4.4 (S.2799 above) R̟. as Briot's 2nd hammered
issue; mm Δ/Δ over anchor. 425   1250

YORK, 1643-4. *Mm. Lion*

2867

		F £	VF £
2863	**Halfcrown**. 1. Ground-line below horse. R. Square-topped shield between CR	625	2250
2864	— 2. — R. Oval shield as Tower 3a, groundline grass or dotted	525	2000
2865	— 3. No ground-line. R. Similar	525	2000
2866	— 4. As last, but EBOR below horse with head held low. Base metal, often very base (*These pieces are contemporary forgeries*)	125	325
2867	— 5. Tall horse, mane in front of chest, EBOR below. R. Crowned square-topped shield between CR, floral spray in legend	450	1500

2868

		F	VF
		£	£
2868	— 6. As last, but shield is oval, garnished (*rev.* detail variations)	350	1100
2869	— 7. Similar, but horse's tail shows between legs. R. Shield as last, but with lion's skin garniture, no CR or floral spray	350	1100

2870   2872

2870	**Shilling**. 1. Bust in scalloped lace collar similar to 3^1. R. EBOR above square-topped shield over cross fleury	275	850
2871	— 2. Similar, but bust in plain armour, mantle; coarse work	350	1100
2872	— 3. Similar R. EBOR below oval shield	350	1100
2873	— 4. — Similar, but crowned oval shield (*obv.* finer style)	250	750
2874	— 5. — As last, but lion's skin garniture	250	750
2875	**Sixpence**. *Obv.* Sim. to 2870. Crowned oval shield	325	950

2876   2877

2876	— — Crowned CR at sides	275	850
2877	**Threepence**. As type 1 shilling, but III behind bust. R. As 2870	125	300

ABERYSTWYTH, 1638/9-42. *Mm*. book.
Plume 1=with coronet and band. Plume 2=with coronet only

2878

		F	VF
		£	£
2878	**Halfcrown**. Horseman similar to 2773, but plume 2 behind. R. Oval garnished shield with large plume above. *Obv.* plume 2, *rev.* plume 1.....	1750	6000
2879	— Similar to 2774, plume 1 behind King, ground below horse. *Obv.* squat plume 1, *rev.* plume 1	1850	6500
2880	As 2773 but more spirited horse, no ground. FRAN ET HIB, plume 2/1	1750	6000

2881

2881	**Shilling**. Bust with large square lace collar, plume 2 before, small XII. R. As Tower 3b.............................	650	2250
2882	— inner circle on *rev*.	575	2000
2883	As 2881, but large plume 1 or 2, large XII, inner circles, large or small shield	575	2000

2884   2886

2884	As last, but small narrow head, square lace collar, large or square plume	625	2250
2885	Small Briot style face, small crown, plume 2, large shield	850	2750
2885A	**Sixpence**. *Obv.* as Tower bust 3a, plume before. R. as 2889; inner circles both sides, *mm.* book (*obv.* only).............................	675	2250
2886	Somewhat as 2881, but double-arched crown, small VI; no inner circles	275	900
2887	Similar to 2886, but single arched crown, plume 2, inner circle *obv.* Large VI	325	1000
2888	Similar, but with inner circles both sides................................	350	1100
2889	— — *Rev*. with small squat-shaped plume above, sometimes no *rev. mm*.	300	950

		F £	VF £
2890	Bust as the first Oxford sixpence; with crown cutting inner circle	450	1500

		2891	2894		
2891	**Groat**. Large bust, lace collar, no armour on shoulder. Crown breaks or touches inner circle. Ř. Shield, plume 1 or 2			100	300
2892	— Similar, armour on shoulder, shorter collar. Ř. Similar			110	325
2893	— Smaller, neater bust well within circle. Ř. Similar			100	300
2894	**Threepence**. Small bust, plume 2 before. Ř. Shield, plume 1 or 2 above, *obv.* legend variations..			90	275
2895	— Similar, but crown cuts i.c. squat pl. on *obv.*, Ř. Pl. 2, *obv.* legend variations..			95	300
2900	**Halfgroat**. Bust as Tower type 3. Ř. Large plume. No inner circles, *mm.* pellet/book,book			125	450
2900A	Bust as 2886. Ř. As last, no inner circle			110	400

		2901	2903	2907		
2901	Bust with round lace collar; single arch crown, inner circles, colon stops				90	275
2902	After Briot's bust, square lace collar: inner circles...................................				80	250
2903	**Penny**. As 2901; CARO; no inner circles				110	375
2904	As 2901; CARO; inner circles				100	350
2905	As last but reads CAROLVS; inner circles...				120	400
2906	*Obv.* similar to 2890, tall narrow bust, crown touches inner circle				125	425
2907	**Halfpenny**. No legend. *O.* Rose. Ř. Plume				350	1100

ABERYSTWYTH-FURNACE, 1648/9. *Mm.* crown

		F	VF
		£	£
2908	**Halfcrown**. King on horseback. R. Sim. to 2878..................................	3000	9000
2909	**Shilling**. Aberystwyth type, but *mm.* crown	6500	18500
2910	**Sixpence**. Similar	1750	4500

2911

2913

2911	**Groat**. Similar	300	850
2912	**Threepence**. Similar..	450	1350
2913	**Halfgroat**. Similar. R. Large plume	425	1250
2914	**Penny**. Similar...	1100	3500

UNCERTAIN MINTS

2915

2915	**Halfcrown**. As illustration, (Hereford?) dated 1645 or undated	4000	12500
2915A	**Halfcrown.** (Compton House) Scarf with long sash ends. CH (Chirk castle?) below horse. R. Oval shield 1644	5250	17500
2915B	— — R. Crowned oval shield, lion paws	4750	15000

SHREWSBURY, 1642. Plume without band used as *mm.* or in field.

2917	**Pound**. King on horseback, plume behind, from the puncheon of Tower grp. 3 crowns. R. Declaration between two straight lines, XX and three Shrewsbury plumes above, 1642 below; *mm.* pellets, pellets/-	8000	25000
2918	Similar, but Shrewsbury horse walking over pile of arms; no *mm.*, pellets	6500	18500
2919	As last, but cannon amongst arms and only single plume and XX above Declaration, no *mm.*..	8500	25000
2920	**Half-pound**. As 2917, but X; *mm.* pellets	3000	8500
2921	Similar, but only two plumes on *rev.*; *mm.*, pellets...................................	4500	12500
2922	Shrewsbury horseman with ground-line, three plumes on *rev.*; *mm.*, none, pellets/-	2250	5500
2923	— with cannon and arms or arms below horse; *mm.* pellets/-..................	2750	6750

	F	VF
	£	£
2924 — no cannon in arms, no plume in *obv.* field; *mm.* plume/pellets, plume/-	1750	5000
2925 **Crown**. Aberystwyth horseman from the puncheon of a Tower halfcrown no ground line	22500	75000

2926

2926 Shrewsbury horseman with ground-line; *mm.* -/pellets, pellets/-, none ...	1750	5500
2927 **Halfcrown**. *O*. From Aberystwyth die; (S2880); *mm.* book. R. Single plume above Declaration, 1642	4750	15000
2928 Sim. to Aberystwyth die, fat plume behind. R. Three plumes above Declaration; *mm.* pellets, pellets/-	1350	4500
2929 Shrewsbury horseman, no ground line. R. As 2927, single plume, no *mm.*	1750	5500
2929A — — R. As 2933	1500	4750

2930

2930 — R. 2: plume; 6, above Declaration	3750	12000
2931 — with ground-line. R. Similar	3750	12000
2932 — — R. As 2927, single plume	1750	5500
2933 — — R. Three plumes above Declaration; *mm.* none or pellets	1350	4500
2933A — — R. Aberystwyth die, plume over shield; *mm.* -/book......................	4750	15000
2934 As 2933 but no plume behind king; *mm.* plume/pellets	1250	4000

2935

		F	VF
		£	£
2935	**Shilling**. *O*. From Aberystwyth die; S2885 *mm*. book. ℞. Declaration type	2500	7500
2936	*O*. From Shrewsbury die. ℞. Similar	5000	15000

OXFORD, 1642-6. *Mm.* usually plume with band, except on the smaller denominations when it is lis or pellets. There were so many dies used at this mint that we can give only a selection of the more easily identifiable varieties.

For many years Oxford Halfcrowns and Shillings have been catalogued according to Morrieson obverse die varieties. In many cases, these are very small and difficult to identify. We have, therefore, simplified the obverse classification and used the available space to expand the listing of the more interesting reverse varieties.

2943

2937	**Pound**. Large horseman over arms, no exergual line, fine workmanship. ℞. Three Shrewsbury plumes and XX above Declaration, 1642 below; *mm*. plume/pellets..	12500	40000
2938	— Similar, but three Oxford plumes, 1643; *mm*. as last............................	9500	30000
2939	Shrewsbury horseman trampling on arms, exergual line. ℞. As last, 1642	5000	15000
2940	— — cannon amongst arms, 1642-3; *mm*. similar	4750	13500
2941	— as last but exergue is chequered, 1642; *mm*. similar............................	8000	22500
2942	Briot's horseman, 1643; *mm*. similar..	9500	30000
2943	*O*. As 2937. ℞. Declaration in cartouche, single large plume above, 1644 OX below..	22500	65000

	F	VF
	£	£

2944 **Half-pound**. Shrewsbury horseman over arms, Oxford plume behind.
R. Shrewsbury die, 1642; mm. plume/- .... | 1750 | 5500

2945 — R. Three Oxford plumes above, 1642; mm. plume/- .... | 1500 | 4500

2945A — — 1643; *mm*. plume/- .... | 1600 | 4750

2946 **Crown.** Shrewsbury die with groundline. R. Three Oxford plumes,
1642; no mm. .... | 1750 | 5500

2946A — — 1643; no *mm*. .... | 1650 | 5250

2947 Oxford horseman, grass below. R. Three Oxford plumes, 1643; *mm*. plume/- | 1850 | 6000

2948

2948 Rawlins' crown. King riding over a view of the city. R. Floral scrolls
above and below Declaration, date in script, 1644 OXON; *mm*.
floriated cross/- *(Electrotypes and copies of this coin are common)*........ | 45000 | 135000

2949 **Halfcrown.** *O*. Shrewsbury die with groundline, plume behind. R.
Oxford die, declaration in two lines, three Oxford plumes above,
1642 below; no *mm*.. | 1350 | 4500

2950 — no plume behind. R. as last, 1642; *mm*. plume/- .... | 1000 | 3000

2951 Shrewsbury horseman with groundline, Oxford plume behind. R.
Shrewsbury die, 1642; *mm*. plume/- .... | 1250 | 4000

2952 — R. Three Oxford plumes, 1642; *mm*. plume/- .... | 500 | 1500

2953 — — without groundline, 1642; *mm*. plume/- .... | 500 | 1500

2954		2955

2954 Oxford horseman without groundline, 1643; *mm*. plume/- .... | 450 | 1350

2954A — — R. Shrewsbury die, 1642; *mm*. plume/- or no *mm*. .... | 1250 | 4000

2955 — with groundline. R. Three Oxford plumes, 1643; *mm*. plume/- .... | 475 | 1400

2956 Briot horseman, grassy, rocky or uneven ground. R. Three Oxford plumes,
1643; *mm*. plume/-, plume & rosette/- .... | 400 | 1200

2957 — — 1643 OX; *mm*. plume/rosette, rosette .... | 425 | 1250

		2961		2965A	
				F	VF
				£	£

		F £	VF £
2958	— — 1644 OX; *mm.* plume/-	450	1350
2958A	— — lozenges by OX, 1644 OX; *mm.* plume/-	425	1250
2959	— — 1645 OX; *mm.* plume/-, plume/rosette	425	1250
2959A	— — pellets by date, 1645 OX; *mm.* plume/-	500	1500
2960	— — 1646 OX; *mm.* plume/-	425	1250
2961	— — pellets or annulets by plumes and date, 1646 OX; *mm.* plume/- ...	500	1500
2962	— R. Large central plume and two Oxford plumes, 1643; *mm.* plume/-	450	1350
2963	— — 1643 OX; *mm.* plume/-, rosette/-, plume & rosette/rosette, plume & rosette/-	425	1250
2964	— — rosettes by OX, 1643 OX; *mm.* rosette/-, plume & rosette/-	500	1500
2965	— — plain, pellets or lozenges by plumes and/or OX, 1644 OX; *mm.* plume/- plume/rosette, rosette	375	1100
2965A	— — date in script, 1644 OX; *mm.* plume/-	425	1250
2966	— — rosettes by plumes and date, 1644 OX; *mm.* plume & rosette/rosette	600	1750
2967	— — small plumes by date, 1644 OX; *mm.* plume & rosette/-, rosette ..	650	1850
2968	— R. Large central plume and two small Shrewsbury plumes, lozenges in field, date in script, 1644 OX; *mm.* plume/rosette	650	1850
2969	— — small plumes by date, pellets by OX, 1644 OX; *mm.* plume/-	750	2250

2971

2970	**Shilling.** *O.* Shrewsbury die. R. Declaration in three lines, three Oxford plumes above, 1642; *mm.* plume/-	2250	6500
2971	Oxford bust (small). R. Three Oxford plumes, 1642; *mm.* Oxford plume/-,	375	1250
2972	Oxford bust (small or large). R. Three Oxford plumes, 1643; *mm.* Oxford plume/-, Oxford plume/rosette	400	1350
2972A	— — pellets by date, 1644; *mm.* plume/-	450	1500
2972B	— — 1644 OX; mm. plume/rosette	450	1500
2973	— R. Oxford and two Shrewsbury plumes, lozenges by date, 1644 OX; *mm.* plume/-	550	1750
2974	— R. Three Shrewsbury plumes, 1643; *mm.* plume/-	400	1350

	F	VF
	£	£

2975 Fine Oxford bust. Ɍ. Three Oxford plumes, lozenges in field, 1644
OX; *mm*. Shrewsbury plume/- 425 1400

2975A — — large date in script, 1644 OX; *mm*. plume/- 450 1500

2976 — 1645 OX; *mm*. plume/- 3000 9000

2976A — Ɍ. Oxford and two Shrewsbury plumes, 1644 OX; *mm*. plume/- 550 1750

2977 — Ɍ. Three Shrewsbury plumes, 1644 OX; *mm*. plume/- 425 1400

2978 — — annulets or pellets at date, 1646; *mm*. plume/floriated cross,
plume/- 425 1400

2979

2979 Rawlins' die. Fine bust with R. on truncation. Ɍ. Three Oxford plumes,
rosettes or lozenges by plumes, lozenges by date, 1644 OX; *mm*.
Shrewsbury plume/rosette, Shrewsbury plume/- 1250 4000

2979A — — pellets by date, no OX, 1644; *mm*. plume/- 1350 4250

2979B — Ɍ. Oxford and two Shrewsbury plumes, 1644 OX; *mm*. plume/- 1500 4500

2980A

2980 **Sixpence.** O. Aberystwyth die Ɍ. Three Oxford plumes, 1642; *mm*. book/- 350 950

2980A — — 1643; *mm*. book/- 325 900

2981 — Ɍ. Three Shrewsbury plumes, 1643; *mm*. book/- 300 850

2982 — Ɍ. Shrewsbury plume and two lis, 1644 OX (groat rev. die); *mm*. book/- 750 2250

2983 **Groat.** *O*. Aberystwyth die. Ɍ. Shrewsbury plume and two lis, 1644 OX;
mm. book/- 350 1000

2984 — Ɍ. Three Shrewsbury plumes, 1644 OX; mm. book/- 425 1250

2985

2985 Oxford bust within inner circle. R. As 2983, 1644 OX; mm. floriated cross/- 275 850

2988   2990

	F	VF
	£	£
2985A — R. Three Shrewsbury plumes, 1644 OX; *mm*. floriated cross/-	425	1250
2985B — R. Single plume, 2 scrolls and OX monogram over Decl, 1645; *mm*. floriated cross/-	525	1500
2986 Large bust to top of coin. R. As 2983, 1644 OX; *mm*. lis/-	375	1100
2987 Large bust to bottom of coin. R. As 2983, 1644 OX; no *mm*.	375	1100
2988 — R. Single plume, 2 scrolls and OX monogram over Decl, 1645; no *mm*.	325	950
2989 Rawlins' die, no inner circle, R on shoulder. R. As 2983, 1644 OX; no *mm*.	525	1500
2990 — R. Single plume, Declaration in cartouche, 1645; no *mm*.	375	1100
2991 — — 1646/5; no mm.	375	1100
2992 **Threepence.** *O*. Aberystwyth die. R. Three lis over Declaration, 1644 OX; *mm*. book/-	375	900
2993 Rawlins; die, R below shoulder. R. Aberystwyth die, oval shield; *mm*. lis/book	375	900
2994 — R. Three lis over Declaration, 1644; *mm*. lis/-	175	525

2994   3000

2995 Crown breaks inner circle, no R. R. Three lis, 1646/4; *mm*. lis/-	185	550
2996 **Halfgroat.** Small bust, beaded or wireline inner circle. R. Large plume in field; *mm*. mullet/lis, lis, -/lis, plain cross/-, plain cross/lis	150	450
2997 — R. Three lis over Delcaration, 1644 OX; *mm*. lis	175	500
2998 **Penny.** *O*. Aberystwyth die, CARO. R. Small plume in field; *mm*. book/-	200	650
2999 Aberystwyth die, CAROLVS; R. Large plume; *mm*. book/-	225	750
3000 Rawlins' die, CARO. R. Small plume; *mm*. lis/mullet, lis/-	275	950
3001 Broad bust, CAROL. R. Small plume; *mm*. lis	250	850
3002 — R. Three lis over Declaration, 1644; *mm*. lis	1250	3500

BRISTOL, 1643-5. *Mm*. usually plume or Br., except on small denominations

3003 **Halfcrown.** *O*. Oxford die with or without ground-line. R. Declaration, three Bristol plumes above, 1643 below, *mm*. plume/- or plume/cross	675	2000
3004 — Obv. as above. R as above, but *mm*. Br. 1643	750	2250
3005 King wears unusual flat crown, *obv. mm*. acorn? between four pellets. R. As 3003, 1643	600	1750
3006 — Obv. as above. R as 3004, *mm*. Br., 1643-4	525	1600
3007 Shrewsbury plume behind king. R. As last	500	1500
3008 — Obv. as above. R as 3004 but Br below date instead of as *mm*. 1644	525	1600

3009

		F	VF
		£	£
3009	— Obv. as 3007 but Br below horse. R as above but 1644-5	500	1500
3010	— Obv. as above. R as 3004, *mm*. Br. and Br. below date, 1644-5	600	1750
3011	**Shilling**. *O*. Oxford die. R. Declaration, 1643, 3 crude plumes above, no *mm*.	750	2250

3012   3014

3012	— — R Similar, but *mm*. Br., 1643-4, less crude plumes	600	1750
3013	—Obv. Coarse bust. R. As 3011, *mm*., plume /- 1643	1750	6000
3014	— — Coarse bust, R. as 3012, *mm*. Br, but 1644	675	2000

3016A   3017

3015	Obv. Bust of good style, plumelet before face. R. As 3012 *mm*. Br. but 1644-5	550	1600
3016	— — R.as 3012, 1644, but Br below date instead of *mm*.	600	1750
3016A	— — R as 3012, 1644 but plume and plumelet either side	500	1500
3017	—Obv. Taller bust with high crown, no plumelets before, *mm*. Br. on its side. R As 3016 Br.below 1644-5	800	2500
3018	—Obv. As 3017 but no *mm*. R as above but *mm*. Br., no Br. below 1644-5	900	2750
3018A	— — R as above but plume and plumelets, 1645	1000	3000
3019	**Sixpence**. Small bust, nothing before. R. Declaration surrounded by CHRISTO etc., 1643; *mm*. /Br.	900	2500

3020 3022

	F	VF
	£	£
3020 Fine style bust. Plumelet before face, 1644; *mm.* ./Br. (on its side)	450	1250
3021 **Groat**. Bust l. R. Declaration, 1644	275	900
3022 — Plumelet before face, 1644	250	800
3023 — Br. below date, 1644	225	700
3023A — Similar, but larger bust and more spread plume before. Mm. pellet/Br;		
nothing below 1644	250	800

3024 3026 3027

3024 **Threepence**. *O.* As 2992. Aberystwyth die; *mm.* book. R. Declaration, 1644	350	1000
3025 Bristol die, plume before face, no *mm.*, 1644	500	1500
3026 **Halfgroat**. Br. in place of date below Declaration	325	950
3027 **Penny**. Similar bust, I behind. R. Large plume with bands.....................	800	2500

This penny may belong to the late declaration issue. It has the same reverse plume punch as 3044.

LATE 'DECLARATION' ISSUES, 1645-6

After Bristol surrendered on 11th September 1645, many of the Royalist garrison returned unsearched to Oxford and the Bristol moneyers appear to have continued work, using altered Bristol dies and others of similar type bearing the marks A, B and plume. Ashby de la Zouch was reinforced from Oxford in September 1645 and, following its fall on 28th February 1646, Royalist forces marched to Bridgnorth-on-Severn, holding out until 26th April 1646. Mr Boon suggested (cf. SCBI 33, p. xli) that Ashby and Bridgnorth are plausible mint sites and the most likely candidates for the A and B marked issues, if these do indeed represent fixed mint locations.

ASHBY DE LA ZOUCH, 1645

3028 **Halfcrown**. Horseman of Bristol type, A below. R. Altered Bristol die. A		
(over Br) below date, 1645; *mm.* plume/A (over Br)	4500	13500
3029 - - R. A below date (new die), 1645; *mm.* plume/A	4500	13500
3030 - - R. Nothing below date 1645; *mm.* plume/A...	4000	12500
3031 **Shilling**. Crowned bust left. R. Declaration type, A below date, 1645; mm.		
plume/A	2250	7000

3032

		F	*VF*
		£	£

3032 - plumelet before face, 1645; *mm.* plume/A 2000 6500

3033 **Sixpence.** Bust of Bristol style, plumelet before face. R. Declaration type,
1645; *mm.* A (on its side)/- 1750 5250

3034 **Groat.** Similar, plumelet before face, 1645; *mm.* A (on its side)/- 1600 4750

3035 **Threepence.** Similar, plumelet before face. R. Single plumelet above
Declaration, 1645; no *mm.* 1100 3250

BRIDGNORTH-ON-SEVERN, 1646

3036 **Halfcrown.** Horseman of Bristol type, A below (same die as 3028-30). R.
Scroll above Declaration, B below, 1646; *mm.* plume/A 5250 15000

3036A- - R. Nothing below date, 1646; *mm.* plume/- 3750 11000

3037

3037 - plumelet (over A) below horse (same die as 3028-30 recut). R. Nothing
below date, 1646; *mm.* plume, plume/- 1750 4750

3038 - - plumelet below date, 1646; *mm.* plume 1750 4750

3039 **Shilling.** Crowned bust left, plumelet before face (same die as 3032). R.
Scroll above Declaration, 1646; *mm.* plume/plumelet 850 2500

3039A- Bristol obverse die, nothing before face. R. Scroll above Declaration, 1646;
2000 *mm.* Br/- 1750 5250

3040 - - plume before face (altered die of 3039A), 1646; *mm.* plumelet (over
Br)/- 900 2750

3041   3042

	F	VF
	£	£
3041 **Sixpence.** Crowned bust left, plume before face. R. Scroll above Declaration, 1646; *mm*. B/-	325	950
3042 **Groat.** Similar, plumelet before face, 1646; *mm*. plumelet, plumelet/-	300	900
3043 **Threepence.** Similar, plumelet before face. R. Single plume above Declaration, 1646; *mm*. plumelet/-	275	850
3044 **Halfgroat.** Crowned bust left, II behind. R. Large plume with bands dividing date, 1646; no *mm*	675	2000

3045   3047

TRURO, 1642-3. *Mm*. rose except where stated

3045 **Crown.** King on horseback, head in profile, sash flies out in two ends. R. CHRISTO, etc., round garnished shield	675	1750
3046 **Halfcrown.** King on walking horse, groundline below, R. Oblong shield, CR above, *mm*. bugle/–	4500	13500
3047 Galloping horse, king holds baton. R. Oblong shield, CR at sides	3750	12500
3048 Walking horse, king holds sword. R. Similar	1000	3500
3049 — R. Similar, but CR above	1100	3750
3050 Galloping horse, king holds sword. R. Similar, but CR at sides	1350	4500
3051 — R. Similar, but CR above	1650	5250
3052 Trotting horse. R. Similar, but CR at sides	1000	3500
3053 **Shilling.** Small bust of good style. R. Oblong shield	4500	13500

EXETER, 1643-6. Undated or dated 1644-5 *Mm*. rose except where stated

3054 **Half-pound.** King on horseback, face towards viewer, sash in large bow. R. CHRISTO, etc., round garnished shield. Struck from crown dies of 3055 on a thick flan	9500	27500
3055 **Crown.** King on horseback, sash in large bow. R. Round garnished shield	575	1600

		F	VF
		£	£
3056	— Shield garnished with twelve even scrolls	650	1850
3057	As 3055, R̟ Date divided by *mm*. 16 rose 44	625	1750
3058	— R̟ Date to l. of *mm*. 1644	575	1600
3059	— *mm*: rose/Ex, 1645	625	1750
3060	King's sash flies out in two ends; *mm*. castle/rose, 1645	650	1850
3061	— *mm*. castle/Ex, 1645	600	1650
3062	— *mm*. castle, 1645	525	1400
3063	**Halfcrown**. King on horseback, sash tied in bow. R̟. Oblong shield CR at sides	1250	4000
3064	— R̟. Round shield with eight even scrolls	325	900

3065

| 3065 | — R̟. Round shield with five short and two long scrolls .... | 275 | 750 |
| 3066 | — R̟. Oval shield with angular garnish of triple lines .... | 750 | 2250 |

3067

3067	Briot's horseman with lumpy ground. R̟. As 3064	400	1250
3068	— R̟. As 3065	350	950
3069	— R̟. As 3066	750	2250
3070	— R̟. As 3065, date to l. of *mm*. 1644	475	1500

3071

| 3071 | King on spirited horse galloping over arms. R̟. Oval garnished shield, 1642 in cartouche below .... | 5000 | 15000 |

				F	VF
				£	£
3072	— R. As 3070, date to 1. of *mm*. 1644-5			6000	20000
3073	— R. *mm*. castle, 1645			6500	22500
3074	Short portly king, leaning backwards on ill-proportioned horse, 1644, 16 rose 44			1100	3500
3075	Horse with twisted tail, sash flies out in two ends R. As 3064			650	2000

3076

3076	— R. As 3070, date divided by *mm*. 16 rose 44, or date to 1. of *mm*. 1644-5	550	1650
3077	— R. *mm*. castle, 1645	600	1750
3078	— R. *mm*. Ex, 1645	600	1750
3079	— R. Declaration type; *mm*. Ex. 1644-5	2750	8500
3080	— R. Similar, Ex also below declaration, 1644	2500	7500
3081	**Shilling.** Large Oxford style bust. R. Round shield with eight even scrolls	1750	6000
3082	— R. Oval shield with CR at sides	2250	7500
3083	Normal bust with lank hair. R. As 3081	950	2750
3083A	— R. As 3082	1650	5500
3084	— R. Round shield with six scrolls	800	2500

3085

3085	— R. Similar, date 1644, 45 to left of rose *mm*. 16 rose 44 (rare), 1644 to right of rose (very rare)	450	1200
3086	— R. Declaration type, 1645	1750	6000

3087A

3087	**Sixpence.** Similar to 3085, large bust and letters 1644 rose	425	1250
3087A	— Smaller bust and letters from punches used on 3088, small or large VI, 16 rose 44	425	1250

	F £	VF £
3088 **Groat**. Somewhat similar but 1644 at beginning of *obv.* legend..............	175	475

3089		3092
3089 **Threepence**. Similar. R. Square shield, 1644 above	175	525
3090 **Halfgroat**. Similar, but II. R. Oval shield, 1644	275	700
3091 — R. Large rose, 1644...	300	750
3092 **Penny**. As last but I behind head	350	950

WORCESTER, 1644-45

	F	VF
3093 **Halfcrown**. King on horseback l., W below; *mm.* two lions. R. Declaration type 1644 altered from 1643 Bristol die; *mm.* pellets..............................	2250	7500
3094 — R. Square-topped shield; *mm.* helmet, castle	1250	4750
3095 — R. Oval shield; *mm.* helmet...	1350	5000

3096

	F	VF
3096 Similar but grass indicated; *mm.* castle. R. Square-topped shield; *mm.* helmet or pellets..	1100	4000
3097 — R. Oval draped shield, lis or lions in legend	1200	4250
3098 — R. Oval shield CR at sides, roses in legend	1250	4500
3099 — R. FLORENT etc., oval garnished shield with lion's paws each side .	1350	5000
3100 Tall king, no W or *mm.* R. Oval shield, lis, roses, lions or stars in legend	1000	3750
3101 — R. Square-topped shield; *mm.* helmet	1100	4000
3102 — R. FLORENT, etc., oval shield; no *mm.*..	1350	5000
3103 Briot type horse, sword slopes forward, ground-line. R. Oval shield, roses in legend; *mm.* 91v, 105, none (combinations)	1200	4250
3104 — Similar, but CR at sides, 91v/-...	1250	4500
3105 Dumpy, portly king, crude horse. R. As 3100; *mm.* 91v, 105, none	1100	4000

3106

	F	*VF*
	£	£
3106 Thin king and horse. R. Oval shield, stars in legend; *mm*. 91v, none......	1100	4000

WORCESTER OR SALOPIA (SHREWSBURY), 1643-4

3107 **Shilling**. Bust of king l., adequately rendered. R. Square-topped shield; *mm*. castle	2750	9000
3108 — R. CR above shield; *mm*. helmet and lion	2750	9000
3109 — R. Oval shield; *mm*. lion, pear	2250	7500
3110 — Bust a somewhat crude copy of last (two varieties); *mm*. bird, lis. R. Square-topped shield with lion's paws above and at sides; *mm*. boar's head, helmet..	2400	8500

3108

3111 — — CR above	2250	8000
3112 — R. Oval shield, lis in legend; *mm*. lis	1750	6000
3113 — R. Round shield; *mm*. lis, 3 lis	1750	6000
3114 Bust r.; *mm*. pear/-, pear/lis. R. draped oval shield with or without CR. (Halfcrown reverse dies)..	4500	13500
3115 **Sixpence**. As 3110; *mm*. castle, castle/boar's hd	1500	5250

3116   3117

3116 **Groat**. As 3112; *mm*. lis/helmet, rose/helmet...	675	2000
3117 **Threepence**. Similar; *mm*. lis	400	1100
3118 **Halfgroat**. Similar; *mm*. lis (*O*.) various (*R*.)...	450	1250

	F £	*VF* £

SALOPIA (SHREWSBURY), 1644

3119 **Halfcrown**. King on horseback l. SA below; *mm*. lis. ℞. (*mm*. lis, helmet,
lion rampant, none). Cr. oval shield; CHRISTO etc. *mm*. helmet 6000 17500
3120 — ℞. FLORENT, etc., crowned oval shield, no *mm*. 6000 17500
3121 — SA erased or replaced by large pellet or cannon ball; *mm*. lis in legend,
helmet. ℞. As 3119.. 3000 9000
3122 Tall horse with mane blown forward, nothing below; *mm*. lis. ℞.
Large round shield with crude garniture; *mm*. helmet 1350 5000
3123 — ℞. Uncrowned square-topped shield with lion's paw above and at sides;
mm. helmet... 1500 6000
3124 — ℞. Small crowned oval shield; *mm*. various 1100 4000

3125

3125 — ℞. As 3120 .... 1200 4500
3126 Finer work with little or no mane before horse. ℞. Cr. round or oval shield 1750 6500
3127 Grass beneath horse. ℞. Similar; *mm*. lis or rose 1750 6500
3128 Ground below horse. ℞. As 3120... 2250 7500

HARTLEBURY CASTLE (WORCS.), 1646

3129

3129 **Halfcrown**. *O. Mm*. pear. ℞. HC (Hartlebury Castle) in garniture below
shield; *mm*. three pears 1750 5250

CHESTER, 1644

3130

		F	*VF*
		£	£
3130	**Halfcrown**. As illus. ℞. Oval shield; *mm.* three gerbs and sword	1350	5000
3131	— Similar, but without plume or CHST; ℞. Cr. oval shield with lion skin; *mm.* prostrate gerb; -/cinquefoil, ⁻/⫶	1200	4500
3132	— ℞. Crowned square-topped shield with CR at sides both crowned *rev.*; *mm.* cinquefoil (these dies were later crudely recut)	2750	9000
3133	As 3130, but without plume or CHST. ℞. Declaration type, 1644 *rev.*; *mm.* plume	1500	5250
3133A	**Shilling**. Bust l. ℞. Oval garnished shield; *mm.* ∴ (obv. only)	6000	17500
3133B	— ℞. Square-topped shield; *mm.* as last	6500	20000
3133C	— ℞ . Shield over long cross	6000	17500
3134	**Threepence**. ℞. Square-topped shield; *mm.*-/ prostrate gerb	1500	4500

WELSH MARCHES? 1644

3135

| 3135 | **Halfcrown**. Crude horseman, l. ℞. Declaration of Bristol style divided by a dotted line, 3 plumes above, 1644 below .... | 2250 | 7500 |

CARLISLE, 1644-5

| | | 3137 | | | 3139 |

		F £	VF £
3136	**Three shillings**. Large crown above C R between rosettes III. S below. rev. OBS . CARL / . 1645, rosette below	13500	32500
3137	Similar but :- OBS :/-: CARL :./.1645, rosette above and below	12500	27500
3138	**Shilling**. Large crown above C R between trefoil of pellets, XII below. *rev.* as 3137	8000	18500
3139	R. Legend and date in two lines	8500	20000

Note. *(3136-39) Round or Octagonal pieces exist.*

NEWARK, 1645-6

| | | 3140 | | | 3142 |

		F £	VF £
3140	**Halfcrown**. Large crown between CR ; below, XXX. *rev.* OBS / NEWARK / 1645	1350	3750
3140A	— Similar 1646	1250	3250
3141	**Shilling**. Similar but crude flat shaped crown, NEWARKE, 1645	1350	3500
3142	Similar but normal arched crown, 1645	1000	2250
3143	— NEWARK, 1645 or 1646	900	2000

3144   3146

		F	VF
		£	£
3144	**Ninepence.** As halfcrown but IX, 1645 or 1646	800	1850
3145	— NEWARKE, 1645...	850	2000
3146	**Sixpence.** As halfcrown but VI, 1646......................................	1250	3000

PONTEFRACT, June 1648-March 1649. Before execution of Charles I

3147 **Two shillings** (lozenge shaped). DVM : SPIRO : SPERO around CR crowned.
       ℞. Castle surrounded by OBS, PC, sword and 1648, weight: c.9-10g. ...   12500 35000

3148

| 3148 | **Shilling** (lozenge shaped, octagonal or round). Similar.......................... | 3250 | 7500 |
| 3149 | — Similar but XII on r. dividing PC .... | 3000 | 7000 |

After the execution of Charles I (30 Jan. 1649), in the name of Charles II

3150

3150 **Shilling** (octagonal). *O*. As last. ℞. CAROLVS : SECVИDVS : 1648, castle
       gateway with flag dividing PC, OBS on l., cannon   protrudes on r.   3000 7000
3151 CAROL : II : etc., around HANC : DE / VS : DEDIT 1648. ℞. POST :
       MORTEM : PATRIS : PRO : FILIO around gateway etc. as last 3500 8000

SCARBOROUGH, July 1644-July 1645*

3152

3156

3166

		VF
Type I. Large Castle with gateway to left, SC and value Vs below		
3152	**Crown.** (various weights)	65000
Type II. Small Castle with gateway, no SC, value punched on flan		
3153	**Five shillings and eightpence.**..	60000
3154	**Crown.** Similar...	85000
3155	**Three shillings.** Similar	50000
3156	**Two shillings and tenpence.** Similar	45000
3157	**Two shillings and sevenpence.** Similar	45000
3158	**Halfcrown.** Similar	55000
3159	**Two shillings and fourpence.** Similar	45000
3162	**One shilling and sixpence.** Similar to 3159..........................	37500
3163	**One shilling and fourpence.** Similar	37500
3164	**One shilling and threepence.** Similar....................................	37500
3165	**Shilling.** Similar	45000
3166	**Sixpence.** Similar	35000
3167	**Groat.** Similar	27500

*No research has been done on this complicated series for many years but a detailed overview was set out in the 'Slaney' catalogue, Spink auction 229, 14th May 2015.

VF

UNCERTAIN CASTLE

Type III. Castle gateway with two turrets, value punched below

3168	**Two shillings and twopence**	15000
3169	**Two shillings.** Castle punched twice......................................	15000
3170	**One shilling and sixpence.** Similar to 3168...........................	13500
3171	**One shilling and fourpence.** Similar	13500
3172	**One shilling and threepence.** Similar...................................	13500
3173	**One shilling and twopence.** Similar......................................	12500
3174	**One shilling and one penny.** Similar.....................................	12500
3175	**Shilling.** Similar	13500
3176	**Elevenpence.** Similar...	12000
3177	**Tenpence.** Similar..	12000
3178	**Ninepence.** Similar..	12000
3178A	**Eightpence.** Similar	10000
3179	**Sevenpence.** Similar..	10000
3180	**Sixpence.** Similar	12500

COPPER

For further details see Tim Everson, *The Galata Guide to the Farthing Tokens of James I and Charles I*

Farthings

3182   3183

		F £	VF £
3181	Richmond 1a, colon stops, CARO over IACO, five jewel crowns on obverse, mm on obverse only; *mm*: Coronet, Crescent with mullet.	20	50
3182	—— 1b, colon stops, CARO over IACO, nine jewel crowns on obverse, *mm*: Dagger, Mascle	20	50
3183	—— 2 CARO, colon stops, *mm* on obverse only; *mm*: Lombardic A, Lombardic A with pellet below, Annulet, Annulet with pellet within, Bell, Book, Castle, Cinquefoil, Crescent (large and small), Cross (pellets in angles), Cross calvary, Cross patée, Cross patée fitchée, Cross patonce, Cross patonce in saltire, Cross saltire, Dagger, Ermine, Estoile (pierced), Eye, Fish hook, Fleece, Fusil, Fusils (two), Halberd, Harp, Heart, Horseshoe, Key (vertical), Leaf, Lion passant, Lis (large), Lis (demi), Lis (three), Martlet, Mascle with pellet within, Nautilus, Pike-head, Rose (single), Shield, Star, Tower, Trefoil, Tun, Woolpack, Woolpack over Crescent.	10	30
3183A	—— CARA farthings (Contemporary forgeries manufactured from official punches. Usually F for E in REX), mm on obverse only; *mm*: Annulet, Coronet, Cross patée fourchée, Dagger, Fusil, Key, Mascle, Trefoil, Tun	150	300
3183B	—— Contemporary forgeries of Richmond Type 2, mm: Lombardic A, Annulet, Annulet with saltire within, Barbell and pellets, Cross (pellets in angles), Cross patée, Cross patonce, Cross patonce in saltire, Cross saltire, Dagger, Fusil, Heart, Horseshoe, Key (horizontal), Lis (large), Lis, Lis demi, Lis (three), Lis (two), Mascle, Mascle with pellet within, Rose, Star, Thistlehead, Tower, Triangle, Triangle (inverted), Tun..	5	15

3184

3185

		F £	*VF* £
3184	— — 3, apostrophe stops, eagle-headed harp, mm on obverse only; *mm*: Lion rampant, Trefoil..........................	10	24
3185	— — 4, beaded harp, *mm* Rose (double) on obverse only.	15	35
3186	— — 5, scroll-fronted harp, 5 jewels on circlet, *mm* Rose (double) on obverse only.........................	15	35
3187	— — 6, scroll-fronted harp, 7 jewels on circlet, *mm* Rose (double) on obverse only.........................	15	35

3187A

3187A	Type 6 on an uncut square flan.	400	900
	— Longer strips of two to twelve farthings also exist............................	*Extremely Rare*	

3188   3189   3193

3188	— — 7, oval flans, CARO over IACO, legend starts bottom left, *mm* Cross patée on one or both sides..................	50	100
3189	— — 8, CARO, colon stops, mm on obverse only, *mm* Lis (demi)	50	100
3190	— — 9, mm on reverse only; *mm*: Martlet, Millrind.	50	100

3195   3196

3191	— — 10a, mm on both sides; *mm*: Crescent	50	100
3192	— — 10b, upright mm both sides, *mm* Goutte..	50	100
3193	— — 10c, mm both sides, between sceptre handles on obverse, *mm* 9 ...	35	75
3194	— — 11, apostrophe stops, *mm* Rose (double) on both sides.	60	125
3194A	— — 11/10b mule, *mm* Rose (double)/Goutte	50	150
3195	— — 12, *mm* Rose (double) on obverse only...	45	90
3196	Transitional Issue Farthings, double arched crowns, mm on obverse only; *mm*: Harp, Quatrefoil..........................	20	50

	F	VF
	£	£

3197 Maltravers Type 1, inner circles, mm on obverse only; *mm*: Rose (double), Woolpack 50 100

3197A Counterfeits of Maltravers Type 1, *mm*: Bell, Lis, Tun, Woolpack 15 35

3198 — — 2, mm both sides; *mm*: Bell, Lis (large), Lis (small), Martlet, Rose (double), Woolpack.. 15 35

3198A Counterfeits of Maltravers Type 2, *mm*: Bell, Cross patée, Harp, Lis (small), Mascle, Star, Woolpack 15 35

3199   3199   3200

3199 — — 3, different mm on each side; *mm*: Woolpack/Rose (double), Martlet/ Bell, Woolpack/Portcullis, Lis/Portcullis, Harp/Bell, Harp/Billet............ 15 35

3199A Counterfeits of Maltravers Type 3, *mm*: Bell/Cross patée fitchée, Bell/ Woolpack, Cross patée fitchée/Bell, Tun/Bell, Woolpack/Lis.................. 15 35

3200 Maltravers Oval Type 4, no inner circles, legend starts bottom left, mm Lis (large) on both sides.. 75 150

Richmond Types 7 to 12 and Maltravers Type 4, 3188 to 3195 and 3200, the oval farthings, were issued for use in Ireland.

            3201   3202   3203

(There is frequent muling between types in the Rose Farthing sequence)

3201 Rose Type 1, large double-arched crowns, sceptres within inner Circle, BRIT, mm on obv. or rev. or both; *mm*: Lis, Martlet 45 90

3202 — — 2, similar but small crowns and sceptres just cross inner circle, BRIT, mm on obverse only or both sides, *mm* Lis 30 75

3203 — — 3, similar but crowns with pointed sides and sceptres almost to outer circle, BRIT, *mm* Lis, Cross patée, Mullet, Crescent................................ 15 35

            3204   3206   3207

3204 - - Mules of Type 3 with Types 4a and 4b, *mm* Lis, Mullet, Crescent........ 15 35

3205 - - 4a Single arched crowns, Long legends with CAROLVS, MAG, FRAN and HIB, *mm*: Lis, Mullet, Crescent. 10 25

3206 — — 4b Single arched crowns, Short legends with CAROLV, MA, FRA and HI, *mm*: Mullet, Crescent.. 10 25

3206A Counterfeits of Rose type 4, *mm* Crescent.. 20 45

3207 — — 5, sceptres below crown, *mm* Mullet on both sides 35 75

The Rose farthings were also authorised for use in Ireland but do not seem to have reached there.

The coins struck during the Commonwealth have inscriptions in English instead of Latin as a truer expression of Protestantism. St. George's cross and the Irish harp take the place of the royal arms. The silver halfpenny was issued for the last time. Coins with *mm.* anchor were struck during the protectorship of Richard Cromwell.

Mintmarks

1649-57 Sun   1658-60 Anchor

GOLD

3208

	F	VF
	£	£

3208 Unite. As illustration; *mm.* sun,

1649	3000	9000
1650	2750	8000
1651	2500	7000
1652	2750	8000
1653	2500	7000
1654	2600	7500
1655	4250	10000
1656	3000	8500
1657	3000	8500

3209 Similar, *mm.* anchor,

| 1658 | 13500 | 35000 |
| 1660 | 12000 | 30000 |

3210

3210 Double-crown. Similar; but X; *mm.* sun,

1649	2500	7500
1650	2250	6500
1651	2000	6250

	F	VF
	£	£
1652	2500	7000
1653	2000	6250
1654	2500	7000
1655	4000	12000
1656	3500	10500
1657	4000	12000

3212

		F	VF
3211	Similar, *mm*. anchor, 1660	7500	20000
3212	**Crown.** Similar, but V; *mm*. sun,		
1649		2000	6000
1650		1650	5000
1651		1650	5000
1652		1600	4750
1653		1500	4500
1654		1750	5500
1655		3500	8500
1656		3500	8500
1657		3000	7500

Numerous overstruck dates exist in this series.

		F	VF
3213	Similar *mm*. anchor,		
1658		6000	15000
1660		7000	17500

SILVER

		F	VF
3214	**Crown.** Same type; *mm*. sun,		
1649		7500	18500
1651		3000	7500
1652		1350	3500
1653		1250	3000
1654		1750	5000
1656		1500	3500

3215

		F	VF
		£	£

3215 Halfcrown. Similar; *mm.* sun,

1649	900	3000
1651	450	1250
1652	450	1250
1653	375	950
1654	425	1200
1655	1750	4500
1656	400	1000
1657	2000	5500

3216 Similar, *mm.* anchor

1658	1750	4500
1659	4500	12000
1660	1750	4500

3217 rev

3217 Shilling. Similar; *mm.* sun,

1649	450	1250
1651	275	700
1652	275	700
1653	275	700
1654	275	700
1655	400	1000
1656	275	700
1657	900	2250

	3218 obv	3219

3218   Similar, *mm*. anchor

1658	 1000	2500
1659	 3500	9500
1660	 1000	2500

3219 **Sixpence**. Similar; *mm*. sun,

1649	 325	900
1651	 250	700
1652	 225	650
1653	 250	700
1654	 275	750
1655	 700	2000
1656	 250	700
1657	 750	2000

3220 Similar; *mm*. anchor,

1658	 750	2000
1659	 1850	5500
1660	 750	2000

3221	3222

3221 **Halfgroat**. 70	175
3222 **Penny**. Similar, but I above shields 60	150

3223

3223 **Halfpenny**. 50	135

Oliver Cromwell, 'the Great Emancipator' was born on 25th April 1599 in Huntingdon. He married Elizabeth Bourchier in August 1620 and had nine children, seven of whom survived infancy. The Protectorate was established on 16th December 1653, with work on the production of portrait coins authorised in 1655. Although often referred to as patterns, there is in fact nothing to suggest that the portrait coins of Oliver Cromwell were not *intended* for circulation. Authorised in 1656, the first full production came in 1657 and was followed by a second more plentiful one before Cromwell's death on 3rd September 1658. All coins were machine made, struck from dies by Thomas Simon (1618-1665) in the presses of the Frenchman, Pierre Blondeau. Later, some of Simon's puncheons were sold in the Low Countries and an imitation Crown was made there. Other Dutch dies were prepared and some found their way back to the Mint, where in 1738 it was decided to strike a set of Cromwell's coins. Shillings and Sixpences were struck from the Dutch dies, and Crowns from new dies prepared by John Tanner. Dutch and Tanner Halfbroads were also made. Oliver was succeeded as Lord Protector by his son Richard for whom no coins were struck.

GOLD

	F	VF	EF
	£	£	£

3224 **Fifty shillings**. Laur. head l. R. Crowned Shield of the Protectorate, die axis ↑↓ 1656 from the same dies as the Broad 45000 110000 350000
Lettered edge PROTECTOR · LITERIS · LITERÆ · NUMMIS · CORONA · ET · SALUS

3225
1656 gold Broad

3225 **Broad**. of Twenty Shillings. Laur. head l. R. Crowned Shield of the Protectorate, but grained edge die axis ↑↓ 1656. .... 9500 22500 65000

SILVER

3226
1658 Crown 8 over 7 - Die flawed drapery

				F	VF	EF
3226	**Crown**. Dr. bust l. R. Crowned shield, 1658/7. Lettered edge ↑↓			2000	4250	10500
3226A	**Crown**. Dutch copy, similar with A И G legend 1658			2400	6250	18500
3226B	**Crown**. Tanner's copy (struck 1738) dated 1658			2500	6500	20000

	F £	VF £	EF £
3227 **Halfcrown.** Dr. bust l. ℞. Crowned shield 1656 HI type legend, lettered edge, die axis ↑↓	3500	9500	22500

3227A
1658 Halfcrown with HIB obverse legend

	F £	VF £	EF £
3227A **Halfcrown.** Similar, 1658 HIB type legend, lettered edge, die axis ↑↓	1350	2750	6000

3228
1658 Shilling

	F £	VF £	EF £
3228 **Shilling.** Dr. bust l. ℞. Crowned shield, grained edge, 1658 die axis ↑↓	1250	2500	5250
3229 **Sixpence.** Similar 1658 die axis ↑↓	30000	—	—
3229A Dutch copy	2000	4750	10500

COPPER

3230
Copper Farthing

	F £	VF £	EF £
3230 **Farthing.** Dr. bust l. ℞. CHARITIE AND CHANGE, shield ↑↓	3750	15000	32500

There are also other reverse types for this coin, and an obverse with mullet on top.

CHARLES II, 1660-85

Charles II was born at St James Palace on 29th May 1630. He spent a long exile in France and returned after the fall of the Protectorate in 1660. The Restoration commenced and he married Catherine of Braganza, but he bore no legitimate successor. Charles II died on 6th February 1685.

For the first two years after the Restoration the same denominations, apart from the silver crown, were struck as were issued during the Commonwealth although the threepence and fourpence were soon added. Then, early in 1663, the ancient hand hammering process was finally superceded by the machinery of Blondeau.

For the emergency issues struck in the name of Charles II in 1648/9, see the siege pieces of Pontefract listed under Charles I, nos. 3150-1.

HAMMERED COINAGE, 1660-2

Mintmark: Crown.

GOLD

3301

	F £	VF £

First issue. Without mark of value; *mm.* crown on *obv.* only

3301 **Unite** (20s.). Type as illustration 4000   12000

3302   3303

3302 **Double-crown**. As illustration...3000   8500
3303 **Crown**. Similar 2750   8000

3304

		F	VF
		£	£

Second issue. With mark of value; *mm*. crown on *obv*. only

3304 **Unite.** Type as illustration 3000   8500

3305

3305 **Double-crown.** As illustration 2500	7500
3306 **Crown.** Similar 3500	10000

SILVER

3307

First issue. Without inner circles or mark of value; *mm*. crown on *obv*. only

3307 **Halfcrown.** Crowned bust, as 3308 1850   7500

3308

	F	VF
	£	£
3308 **Shilling**. Similar. (Also known with smaller harp on reverse.) 750		2750

3309

3309 **Sixpence**. Similar.. 450	1750
3310 **Twopence**. Similar... 70	225
3311 **Penny**. Similar 50	135
3312 As last, but without mintmark 60	150

3313

Second issue. Without inner circles, but with mark of value; *mm*. crown on *obv*. only

3313	**Halfcrown**. Crowned bust 1750	7000
3314	**Shilling**. Similar 1100	3500
3315	**Sixpence**. Similar 1350	4500

3316

	F	VF
	£	£

3316 **Twopence**. Similar, but mm. on obv. only 150 525

3317 Similar, but mm. both sides (machine made)..60 175

3318 Bust to edge of coin, legend starts at bottom l. (machine made, single arch
crown) 60 175

3319 **Penny**. As 3317...85 250

3320 As 3318 (single arch crown) 70 200

3321

Third issue. With inner circles and mark of value; *mm.* crown on both sides

3321 **Halfcrown**. Crowned bust to i.c. (and rarely to edge of coin) 275 1250

3322 **Shilling**. Similar, rarely *mm.* crown on *obv.* only. (Also known with
smaller harp on reverse.) 150 650

3323 **Sixpence**. Similar...135 525

3324 **Fourpence**. Similar..50 150

3325 **Threepence**. Similar..40 110

3326

3326 **Twopence**. Similar..35 100

3327 **Penny**. Similar..30 90

Grading of Early and Later Milled Coinage

Milled coinage refers to coins that are struck by dies worked in a mechanical coining press. The early period is defined from the time of the successful installation of Peter Blondeau's hand powered machinery at the mint, initiated to strike the first portrait coins of Oliver Cromwell in 1656, continuing until the advent of Matthew Boulton's steam powered presses from 1790. The coinage of this early period is therefore cruder in its execution than the latter. When pricing coins of the early peiod, we only attribute grades as high as extremely fine, and as high as uncirculated for the latter period. Most coins that occur of the early period in superior grades than those stated, in particular copper coins retaining full original lustre, will command considerably higher prices, due to their rarity. We suggest the following definitions for grades of preservation:

Milled Coinage Conditions

Proof   A very carefully struck coin from specially prepared dies, to give a superior definition to the design, with mirror-like fields. Occurs occasionally in the Early Milled Coinage, more frequently in the latter period. Some issues struck to a matt finish for Edward VII.

FDC   *Fleur-de-coin*. Absolutely flawless, untouched, without wear, scratches, marks or hairlines. Generally applied to proofs.

UNC   *Uncirculated*. A coin in as new condition as issued by the Mint, retaining full lustre or brilliance but, owing to modern mass-production methods of manufacture and storage, not necessarily perfect.

EF   *Extremely Fine*. A coin that exhibits very little sign of circulation, with only minimal marks or faint wear, which are only evident upon very close scrutiny.

VF   *Very Fine*. A coin that exhibits some wear on the raised surfaces of the design, but really has only had limited circulation.

F   *Fine*. A coin that exhibits considerable wear to the raised surfaces of the design, either through circulation, or damage perhaps due to faulty striking

Fair   *Fair*. A coin that exhibits wear, with the main features still distinguishable, and the legends, date and inscriptions still readable.

Poor   *Poor*. A coin that exhibits considerable wear, certainly with milled coinage of no value to a collector unless it is an extremely rare date or variety.

Examples of Condition Grading

Early Milled

Gold A̸V   Silver Æ̸R   Copper Æ

Extremely Fine

Early Milled *continued*

Gold A̸V   Silver Æ̸R   Copper Æ

Very Fine

Fine

George III   *James II*   *George II*
Guinea   *Crown*   *old head Halfpenny*

Later Milled

Gold A̸V   Silver Æ̸R   Copper Æ

Uncirculated

Gold Ν   Silver Ρ   Copper Æ

Extremely Fine

Very Fine

Fine

Victoria
Jubilee head Sovereign

George IV
laureate bust Crown

Victoria
Young head Halfpenny

MILLED COINAGE, 1662-85

Early in 1663, the ancient hand hammering process was finally superceded by the machinery of Blondeau. John and Joseph Roettier, two brothers, engraved the dies with a safeguard against clipping, the larger coins were made with the edge inscribed DECVS ET TVTAMEN and the regnal year. The medium-sized coins were given a grained edge.

The new gold coins were current for 100s., 40s., 20s. and 10s., and they came to be called 'Guineas' as the gold from which some of them were made was imported from Guinea by the Africa Company (whose badge was the Elephant and Castle). It was not until some years later that the Guinea increased in value to 21s. and more. The Africa Co. badge is also found on some silver and so is the plume symbol indicating silver from the Welsh mines. The four smallest silver denominations, though known today as 'Maundy Money', were actually issued for general circulation: at this period the silver penny was probably the only coin distributed at the Royal Maundy ceremonies. Though never part of the original agreement, smaller coins were eventually also struck by machinery.

A good regal copper coinage was issued for the first time in 1672, but later in the reign, farthings were struck in tin (with a copper plug) in order to help the Cornish tin industry.

Engravers and designers: John Roettier (1631-1700), Thomas Simon (1618-1665)

GOLD

3328
1672 First bust type Five-Guineas

		F	VF	EF
		£	£	£

3328 Five Guineas. First laur. bust r., pointed trun., regnal year on edge in words, die axis ↑↓
(e.g. 1669=VICESIMO PRIMO), ℞. Crowned cruciform shields, sceptres in angles

		F	VF	EF
1668	VICESIMO	9000	27500	110000
1668	V. PRIMO	9500	30000	115000
1669	V. PRIMO	8500	25000	100000
1670	V. SECVNDO	8000	22500	95000
1670	V. Similar proof *FDC* £300000			
1671	V. TERTIO	9500	30000	115000
1672	V. QVARTO	9000	27500	110000
1673	V. QVINTO	8500	25000	100000
1674	V. QVINTO	10000	35000	125000
1674	V. SEXTO	9500	30000	115000

3328A Five Guineas. First bust. Similar hair of different style. Shorter ties

		F	VF	EF
1674	QVINTO	10000	35000	125000
1675	V. SEPTIMO	9000	27500	110000
1676	V. SEPTIMO	9000	27500	110000
1676	V. OCTAVO	9000	27500	110000
1677	V. NONO	8500	25000	100000
1678/7	TRICESIMO	9000	27500	110000

		F £	VF £	EF £
3329	**Five Guineas.** First bust with elephant below, similar die axis ↑↓			
1668	VICESIMO 8000	22500	95000
1669	V. PRIMO 10000	32500	125000
1675	V. SEPTIMO 10000	32500	125000
1677/5	V. NONO 12500	35000	135000

3330
1676 Five-Guineas with elephant and castle provenance mark

		F	VF	EF
3330	**Five Guineas.** First bust with elephant and castle below, similar die axis ↑↓			
1675	V. SEPTIMO 12500	35000	135000
1676	V. OCTAVO 9500	30000	115000
1677	V. NONO 10000	32500	125000
1678/7	– TRICESIMO 10000	32500	125000
3331	**Five Guineas.** Second laur. bust r., rounded trun. similar die axis ↑↓			
1678/7	TRICESIMO 9000	27500	110000
1679	T. PRIMO 8000	22500	95000
1680/79	T. SECVNDO 9000	27500	110000
1681	T. TERTIO 9000	27500	110000
1682	T. QVARTO 8000	22500	95000
1683	T. QVINTO 8000	22500	95000
1683/2	T.QVINTO 9000	25000	105000
1684	T. SEXTO 8000	22500	95000
3332	**Five Guineas.** Second laur. bust r., with elephant and castle below, similar die axis ↑↓			
1680/79	T.SECVNDO 9750	32500	120000
1681	T. TERTIO 9750	32500	120000
1682	T. QVARTO 9500	30000	115000
1683	T. QVINTO 9750	32500	120000
1684	T. SEXTO 9000	27500	110000

3333

1664 First bust type Two Guineas

	F	VF	EF
	£	£	£

3333　Two Guineas. First laur. bust r., pointed trun. R. Crowned cruciform shields, sceptres in angles, die axis ↑↓

1664	 3000	7500	28500
1665	.... *Extremely rare*		
1669	.... *Extremely rare*		
1671	 7500	20000	—
1673	 12500	—	—

3334

1664 Two Guineas with elephant only below

3334　Two Guineas. First bust with elephant below, similar die axis ↑↓

1664	 2750	7250	27500

3335

1675 Two Guineas - second bust

3335　Two Guineas. Second laur. bust r., rounded trun, similar die axis ↑↓

1675	 3500	8500	37500
1676	 3250	8000	35000
1677	 3250	8000	35000
1678/7	 3250	8000	35000
1679	 3250	8000	35000
1680	 4500	10000	42500

		F	VF	EF
		£	£	£
1681		3250	8000	35000
1682		3250	8000	35000
1683		3250	8000	35000
1684		3750	8500	37500

3336 Two Guineas. Second bust with elephant and castle below, similar die axis ↑↓

		F	VF	EF
1676		3750	9000	40000
1677				*Extremely rare*
1678		3750	9000	40000
1682		3750	9000	40000
1683		4500	11000	45000
1684		3750	9000	40000

3337 Two Guineas. Second bust with elephant only below, die axis ↑↓

		F	VF	EF
1678				*Extremely rare*

3337A   3339

1663 Guinea first bust, elephant below

3337A Broad of 20s. Laur. and dr. bust r. R. Crowned shield of arms
(approx. 3400 issued), die axis ↑↓

		F	VF	EF
1662		3250	8500	25000

3338 Guinea. First laur. bust r., R. Crowned cruciform shields, die axis ↑↓

| 1663 | | 7500 | 22500 | 75000 |

3339 Guinea. First bust with elephant below, similar die axis ↑↓

| 1663 | | 6500 | 20000 | 60000 |

3340 Guinea. Second laur. bust r.,similar die axis ↑↓

| 1663 | | 6000 | 17500 | 50000 |
| 1664 | | 3000 | 9000 | 32500 |

3341   3342   3342A

1664 Guinea second bust elephant below   1666 Guinea - third bust

3341 Guinea. Second bust with elephant below, similar die axis ↑↓

		F	VF	EF
1664		4500	13500	47500

3342 Guinea. Third laur. Bust r., forward slanting 'tall' leaves, similar die axis ↑↓

1664		1850	4750	16500
1665		1750	4500	16000
1666		1750	4500	16000
1667		2500	6000	—

	F	*VF*	*EF*
	£	£	£
3342A Guinea. Third laur. Bust variety r. two straight 'short' leaves, similar die axis ↑↓			
1667	1750	4500	16000
1668	1600	4000	15000
1669	1750	4500	16000
1670	1750	4500	16000
1671	1750	4500	16000
1672	1850	5000	16500
1673	2000	5500	17500
3343 Guinea. Third laur. bust r., with elephant below, similar die axis ↑↓			
1664	2250	6500	22500
1665	2250	6500	22500
1668	*Extremely rare*		

3344

1679 Guinea - Fourth bust

3345

1682 - Fourth bust - elephant below

3344 Guinea. Fourth laur. bust r., rounded trun. similar die axis ↑↓			
1672	1350	3250	13500
1673	1300	3000	13000
1674	1350	3250	13500
1675	1350	3250	13500
1675 CRAOLVS error	4500	12500	—
1676	1300	3000	13000
1676/4	1350	3250	13500
1677	1250	2850	12500
1677 GRATIR error	4500	—	—
1677 CAROLVS error	1350	3250	13500
1678	1300	3000	13000
1679	1250	2850	12500
1679 'O' over 'o' on its side and R of FRA over A	1300	3000	13000
1680	1250	2850	12500
1680/79	1350	3250	13500
1681	1300	3000	13000
1682	1300	3000	13000
1682 rev.@90° axis	1350	3250	13500
1683	1250	2850	12500
1684	1350	3250	13500
3345 Guinea. Fourth laur. bust r., with elephant and castle below, similar die axis ↑↓			
1674	*Extremely rare*		
1675	2250	6500	18500
1676	2250	6500	18500
1677	2250	6500	18500
1677 GRATIR error	4500	—	—
1678	2250	6500	18500

		F	VF	EF
		£	£	£
1679		2400	7000	20000
1680		2400	7000	20000
1681		2400	7000	20000
1682		2250	6500	18500
1683		2250	6500	18500
1684		2500	7500	22500

3346 Guinea. — — with elephant below bust, similar die axis ↑↓

1677/5				*Extremely rare*
1678		7500	20000	—

3347
1669 Half-Guinea, first bust

3348
1684 Half-Guinea, second bust

3347 Half-Guinea. First laur. bust r., pointed trun.R. Crowned cruciform shields, sceptres in angles die axis ↑↓

1669		950	2500	9500
1670		900	2350	9000
1671		1250	3250	12500
1672		1000	2750	10000

3348 Half-Guinea. Second laur. bust r., rounded trun. similar die axis ↑↓

1672		900	2350	9000
1673		950	2500	9500
1674		1000	3000	11000
1675		900	2350	9000
1676		900	2350	9000
1676/4		950	2500	9500
1677		950	2500	9500
1678		1000	2750	10000
1678/7		950	2500	9500
1679		900	2350	9000
1680		950	2500	9500
1681		1000	2750	10000
1682		950	2500	9500
1683		950	2500	9500
1684		950	2500	9500

3349 Half-Guinea. Second bust with elephant and castle below, similar die axis ↑↓

1676		1650	6000	—
1677		1350	5000	12500
1678/7		1350	5000	12500
1680		1650	6000	—
1681		1650	6000	—
1682		1350	5000	12500
1683				*Extremely rare*
1684		1350	5000	12500

SILVER

3350 - 1662 Crown, first type, rose below bust

	F £	VF £	EF £
3350 Crown. First dr. bust r., rose below, numerous varieties in length and style of hair ties. R. Crowned cruciform shields, interlinked C's in angles edge undated, die axis ↑↓			
1662 225		1250	12500
3350A Crown. — — Similar, die axis ↑↑			
1662 275		1350	—
3350B Crown. — striped cloak to drapery,			
1662 similar die axis ↑↓ 375		1750	—
3350C Crown. — — II of legend at 12 o'clock, similar die axis ↑↓			
1662 2500		—	—
3351 Crown. — — edge dated, similar die axis ↑↓ or ↑↑			
1662 250		1350	13500
3352 Crown. — legend re-arranged no rose, edge dated, similar die axis ↑↓			
1662 250		1350	13500
3353 Crown. — — edge not dated, similar die axis ↑↓			
1662 225		1250	12500
3354 Crown. — — shields altered, 1663, similar regnal year on edge in Roman figures			
ANNO REGNI XV die axis ↑↓ 185		1100	11000
1663 no stops on revers 200		1250	12500
1663 edge not dated, as 3350 ....*Extremely rare*			

3354A

3354A Pattern 'Petition' Crown, 1663 by Thomas Simon. Laur. Bust r. of fine style in high relief, *Simon* below, edge inscription of Simon's 'petition': THOMAS SIMON. MOST HVMBLY. PRAYS. YOVR MAJESTY etc., etc......47500   175000   525000

	F	VF	EF
	£	£	£

3354B Pattern 'Reddite' Crown, 1663, by Thomas Simon, struck from the same dies, edge
inscription: REDDITE. QVAE. CESARIS etc., etc. 27500   90000   375000

3355   **Crown.** Second dr. bust r. smaller than first bust and with curving tie to wreath. Regnal
year on edge in Roman figures (e.g. 1664 = XVI), die axis ↑↓

1664 edge XVI	200	1000	8750
1664 Proof *FDC* Fine work £95000			
1665 XVI	2250	—	—
1665/4 XVII	2500	—	—
1665 XVII	2000	5750	—
1666 XVIII	275	1100	9500
1666 XVIII RE·X	325	1200	11000
1667 XVIII	4500	—	—

3356   **Crown.** Second bust elephant below, similar, die axis ↑↓

1666 XVIII	1200	4500	22500
1666 XVIII RE·X	1250	4750	—

3357

1668 Crown - second bust

3357   **Crown.** Second bust, similar, Regnal year on edge in words (e.g. 1667= DECIMO NONO)
die axis ↑↓

1667 D. NONO	200	850	8500
1667 — AN.· REG.·	200	850	8500
1668 VICESIMO	185	750	8000
1668 — error edge inverted	450	—	—
1668/7 VICESIMO	200	850	8500
1668/5 VICESIMO	450	—	—
1669 V· PRIMO	350	1350	—
1669/8 V· PRIMO	375	1500	—
1670 V. SECVNDO	200	850	8500
1670/69 V. SECVND	275	950	9500
1671 V· TERTIO	175	725	8000
1671 — T/R in ET	250	900	—
1671 — ET over FR	275	1000	—

3358
Third bust Crown

| | F | VF | EF |
| | £ | £ | £ |

3358 Crown. Third dr. bust r. much larger and broader than second bust, tie nearly straight. From end of tie to top of nose is 20mm. R.Similar die axis ↑↓

1671 V. TERTIO	185	750	8000
1671 V. QVARTO	450	1350	—
1672 V. QVARTO	185	750	8000
1673 V. QVARTO			Extremely rare
1673 V. QVINTO	185	750	8000
1673 B/R in BR	250	900	—
1673/2 V. QVINTO	200	850	8500
1674 V. SEXTO			Extremely rare
1675/3 V. SEPTIMO	700	2750	—
1675 —	800	3250	—
1676 V. OCTAVO	185	750	8000
1676 OCCTAVO	200	850	8500
1677 V. NONO	185	750	8000
1677/6 V. NONO	185	750	8000
1678/7 TRICESIMO	275	1100	10000
1679 T. PRIMO	185	750	8000
1680/79 T. SECVNDO	250	900	9000
1680 T. SECVNDO	200	850	8500

3359
Fourth bust Crown

3359 Crown. Fourth dr. bust r. still larger, with older features and more pointed nose. From end of tie to tip of nose is 21mm. R.Similar die axis ↑↓

| 1679 T. PRIMO | 225 | 750 | 7500 |
| 1679 HIBR·EX | 425 | 1750 | — |

	F	VF	EF
	£	£	£
1680 T. SECVNDO 225		750	7500
1680/79 T. SECVNDO 275		850	8500
1681 T. TERTIO 225		750	7500
1682/1 T. QVARTO 225		750	7500
1682 T. QVARTO 250		800	8000
1682/1 QVRRTO error 275		825	8250
1683 T. QVINTO..425		1350	—
1684 T. SEXTO 350		1000	9500
3360 **Crown.**— elephant and castle below bust, die axis ↑↓			
1681 T. TERTIO 6000		16500	—

3361
First bust Halfcrown

3362
Second bust Halfcrown

3361 Halfcrown. First dr. bust r. R. Crowned cruciform shields, interlinked C's in angles, regnal year on edge in Roman figures die axis ↑↓

1663 XV 225		1000	6500
1663 XV V/S in CAROLVS 300		1200	7000
1663 XV A/T in GRATIA..300		1200	7000
1663 XV no stops on obverse..250		1100	6750
3362 Halfcrown. Second dr. bust r., similar die axis ↑↓			
1664 XVI 325		1250	7500
3363 Halfcrown. Third dr. bust r., similar die axis ↑↓			
1666/4 XVIII 1250		4250	—

3364
Third bust, elephant below Halfcrown

3364 Halfcrown. Third bust elephant below, die axis ↑↓

1666 XVIII 1100		3750	—

3365 - 1670 Halfcrown, third bust

MRG for MAG var

	F	VF	EF
	£	£	£

3365 Halfcrown. Third dr. bust r. regnal date on edge in words (eg. 1667=DECIMO NONO) ↑↓

	F	VF	EF
1667/4 D. NONO	4500	—	—
1668/4 VICESIMO	350	1350	—
1669/4 V. PRIMO	300	1100	—
1669 V. PRIMO	325	1250	—
1669 — R/I in PRIMO	350	1350	—
1670 V. SECVNDO	140	575	4250
1670 – MRG for MAG	225	850	—
1670 V/S CAROLVS	200	750	—
1670 E/R in ET	250	900	—

3366
1671 Halfcrown third bust variety

3366 Halfcrown. Third bust variety r. R. Similar die axis ↑↓

	F	VF	EF
1671 V. TERTIO	140	575	4250
1671 A/R in MAG	225	750	—
1671/0 V. TERTIO	175	625	4500
1672 V. TERTIO			Extremely rare
1672 V. QVARTO	140	575	4250

3367
Fourth bust Halfcrown

	F	VF	EF
	£	£	£

3367 Halfcrown. Fourth dr. bust r. R. Similar die axis ↑↓

	F	VF	EF
1672 V. QVARTO	150	575	4250
1673 V. QVINTO	150	575	4250
1673 — A/R in FRA	200	675	—
1673 — B/R in BR	200	675	—
1673 — FR/M in FRA	200	675	—
1674 V. SEXTO	175	625	4500
1674/3 V. SEXTO	225	750	—
1675 V. SEPTIMO	150	575	4250
1675 — Retrograde 1	175	625	4500
1676 V. OCTAVO	140	550	4000
1676 R/T in BR	225	750	—
1676 — Retrograde 1	150	575	4250
1676 F/H in FRA	200	675	—
1677 V. NONO	140	550	4000
1677 F/H in FRA	225	750	—
1678 TRICESIMO	250	900	5250
1679 T. PRIMO	140	550	4000
1679 — DECNS error	175	625	4500
1679 — DNCVS error	180	650	—
1679 — PRICESIMO	175	625	4500
1680 T. SECVNDO	150	575	4250
1680 T. SECVNCIO error	185	650	4750
1681 T. TERTIO	250	900	5250
1681/0 —	300	1100	—
1682 T. QVARTO	175	625	4500
1682/79 T. QVARTO	250	950	—
1683 T. QVINTO	140	550	4000
1684/3 T. SEXTO	400	1350	—

3369 - Plume in centre

	F	VF	EF
	£	£	£
3368 Halfcrown. Fourth bust plume below, R. Similar die axis ↑↓			
1673 V. QVINTO	7000	18500	—
1683 T. QVINTO	8500	22500	—
3369 Halfcrown.— plume below bust and in centre of *rev.*, die axis ↑↓			
1673 V. QVINTO	9500	25000	—

3370
Elephant and Castle below bust

	F	VF	EF
3370 Halfcrown.— elephant and castle below bust, die axis ↑↓			
1681 T. TERTIO	4500	13500	35000

SHILLINGS

First bust   First bust variety   Second bust   Third bust

First bust   First bust variety   First and first bust   Second bust
                                                variety, double top leaf   single top leaf

3371 - First bust   3372

	F	VF	EF
	£	£	£

3371 Shilling. First dr. bust r.R. Crowned cruciform shields interlinked C's in angles edge milled,

1663 die axis ↑↑ (en medaille)	135	600	—
1663 die axis ↑↓ as usual	125	450	3000
1663 GARTIA error, die axis ↑↓	1250	3000	—
1663 Transposed shields of Scotland and Ireland, die axis ↑↓	250	900	—
1663 A over G in FRA, die axis ↑↓	375	—	—

3372 Shilling. First bust variety r. similar die axis ↑↓

1663	125	450	3000
1666	6250	17500	—
1668	675	2500	—
1669/6	4500	—	—

3373 Shilling. First bust variety r. elephant below bust, die axis ↑↓

1666	1000	3250	12000

3374   3375 - Second bust shilling

3374 Shilling. Guinea head, elephant below bust, die axis ↑↓

1666	4250	10000	—

3375 Shilling. Second dr. bust r. similar die axis ↑↓

1666	3000	8500	—
1668	135	450	2750
1668/7	175	650	3250
1669			*Extremely rare*
1670	225	800	3750
1671	225	800	3750
1672	225	800	3750
1673	225	800	3750
1673/2	275	900	4250
1674	275	900	4250
1674/3	250	850	4000
1675	250	850	4000
1675/4	250	850	4000
1676	175	650	3250
1676/4	225	800	3750
1676/5	200	750	3500
1677	175	650	3250

	F	VF	EF
	£	£	£
1678	.225	800	3750
1678/7	.250	850	4000
1679	.200	750	3500
1679/7	.225	800	3750
1680	.1350	4000	10500
1680/79	.1500	4500	—
1681	.575	1500	—
1681/0	.675	1750	—
1682/1	.1350	4500	—
1683	.1350	4500	—

The 1668 shilling is also known with large 6's in the date

3376 - Plume both sides shilling of 1671

3376 Shilling. Second Bust — plume below bust and in centre of *rev*. similar die axis ↑↓

1671	.800	2750	6500
1673	.900	3000	7000
1674	.800	2750	6500
1675	.900	3000	7000
1676	.900	3000	7000
1679	.850	2850	6750
1680/79	.1750	5000	—

3378
1679 Shilling - plume on obverse only

	F £	VF £	EF £
3377 Shilling. — Plume *rev.* only, similar die axis ↑↓			
1674 2000		6500	—
3378 Shilling. — Plume *obv.* only similar die axis ↑↓			
1677 2500		7500	—
1679 2000		6500	—
3379 Shilling. — elephant and castle below bust, die axis ↑↓			
1681/0 5250		15000	—

3380   3381
Third bust Shilling   1684 Shilling - fourth bust

3380 Shilling. Third dr. (large) bust r. similar die axis ↑↓			
1674 1000		3500	9500
1675/3 750		2750	7500
1675/4 850		3000	8500
3381 Shilling. Fourth dr. (large) bust r., older features, similar die axis ↑↓			
1683 300		1100	4500
1684 300		1100	4500

3382
1677 Sixpence

3382 Sixpence. Dr. bust r. R. Crowned cruciform shields, interlinked C's in angles die axis ↑↓			
1674 75		240	800
1675 80		250	850
1675/4 80		250	850
1676 95		300	950
1676/5 90		275	900

	F	VF	EF
	£	£	£
1677	75	240	800
1678/7	80	250	850
1679	85	275	900
1680	100	325	1000
1681	75	240	800
1682	100	325	1000
1682/1	90	300	950
1683	75	240	800
1684	80	250	850

3383
Undated Fourpence

3384 -
1678 Fourpence

3383 Fourpence. Undated. Crowned dr. bust l. to edge of coin, value
behind. R. Shield, die axis ↑↓ 20   50   120

3384 Fourpence. Dated. Dr. bust r. R. Crowned four interlinked Cs quartered emblems die axis ↑↓

1670	20	45	125
1671	18	40	110
1672/1	22	48	125
1673	18	40	100
1674	18	40	100
1674/4 sideways	20	40	150
1674 7 over 6	18	40	100
1675	18	40	100
1675/4	18	45	120
1676	18	40	100
1676 7 over 6	18	45	135
1676/5	18	45	120
1677	15	32	95
1678	18	45	120
1678/6	18	40	100
1678/7	18	40	100
1679	10	20	70
1680	12	22	80
1681	15	40	95
1681 B/R in HIB	18	38	150
1681/0	15	32	115
1682	18	40	110
1682/1	18	40	115
1683	18	40	110
1684	20	40	120
1684/3	20	40	110

3386
1678 Threepence

	F	VF	EF
	£	£	£
3385 **Threepence.** Undated. As 3383, die axis ↑↓ 14		35	110
3386 **Threepence.** Dated. Dr. bust r. R. Crowned three interlinked C's, die axis ↑↓			
1670 12		25	90
1671 10		22	80
1671 GRⱯTIA 18		38	150
1671 GRⱯTIA 12		28	100
1672/1 10		22	90
1673 10 22		80	—
1674 12 25		90	—
1675 15 30		95	—
1676 10 22		85	—
1676/5 12 28		100	—
1676 ERA for FRA 12		38	175
1677 15 30		100	—
1678 12 25		100	—
1678 on 4d flan 12		25	125
1679 10 20		60	—
1679 O/A in CAROLVS 15		38	150
1680 12 25		85	—
1681 14 22		90	—
1681/0 12 30		100	—
1682 15 30		105	—
1682/1 15 32		95	—
1683 15 30		105	—
1684 15 30		105	—
1684/3 15 32		95	—

3388
1678 Twopence

	F	VF	EF
3387 **Twopence.** Undated. As 3383 (double arch crown)			
die axis ↑↓ 12		30	90
3388 **Twopence.** Dated. Dr. bust r. R. Crowned pair of linked C's, die axis ↑↓			
1668 die axis ↑↑ 15		30	100
1670 10		22	75
1671 10		20	65
1672/1 10		20	65
1672/1 GRⱯTIⱯ 13		38	165

	F	VF	EF
	£	£	£
1673	12	25	80
1674	10	20	65
1675	12	25	80
1676	10	20	75
1677	12	25	75
1678	15	35	95
1678/6	13	28	100
1679	10	20	65
1679 HIB over FRA	13	38	150
1680	10	20	70
1680/79	13	28	85
1681	10	20	70
1682/1	13	28	80
1682/1 ERA for FRA	13	38	150
1684	13	28	75
1683	10	22	70
1683/2	13	28	70

3390
1678 Penny

3389 Penny. Undated. As 3383 (double arch crown)
die axis ↑↓	12	35	110

3390 Penny. Dated. Dr. bust r. R. Crowned C die axis ↑↓

1670	12	30	105
1671	12	30	105
1672/1	12	30	105
1673	12	30	105
1674	14	35	120
1674 ƆRATIA error	18	40	175
1675	12	30	105
1675 ƆRATIA error	18	40	175
1676	22	50	145
1676 ƆRATIA error	15	40	175

	F	VF	EF
	£	£	£
1677 12	30	105
1677 ƆRATIA error 15	40	175
1678 24	55	145
1678 RATIA error 12	50	185
1679 24	55	145
1680 12	30	105
1680 on 2d flan .... *Extremely rare*
1681 22	65	170
1682 22	50	140
1682/1 18	40	145
1682 ERA for FRA 18	40	150
1683/1 13	35	110
1684 24	50	145
1684/3 24	50	150
3391 Maundy Set. Undated. The four coins 100	225	575
3392 Maundy Set. Dated. The four denominations. Uniform dates
1670 100	275	650
1671 90	200	550
1672 95	250	600
1673 80	200	550
1674 90	210	600
1675 90	225	600
1676 100	250	700
1677 90	225	675
1678 115	300	800
1679 90	225	650
1680 .,...85	200	600
1681 100	300	650
1682 90	250	725
1683 80	200	750
1684 100	275	775

COPPER AND TIN

3393
1675 Halfpenny

3393 Copper Halfpenny Cuir. bust l. R. Britannia seated l. date in ex., die axis ↑↓

1672 60	350	1400
1672 CRAOLVS error .... *Extremely rare*
1673 50	330	1200
1673 CRAOLVS error 225	—	—

	Fair	F	VF	EF
	£	£	£	£
1673 no stops on obv.				*Extremely rare*
1673 no rev. stop..		90	500	—
1675		60	350	1400
1675 no stops on obv.		90	500	—
1675/3		165	600	—

3394
1672 Farthing

3394   Copper **Farthing.** Cuir. bust l. R. Britannia seated l. date in ex., die axis ↑↓

	Fair	F	VF	EF
1672		45	265	825
1672 Rev. loose drapery		65	325	1000
1672 no stops on obv.		65	325	1000
1672 RO/OL on obv...		90	450	—
1672 die axis ↑↑		65	325	1000
1673		50	275	825
1673 CAROLA error		150	550	—
1673 O/sideways O..		75	325	1100
1673 BRITINNIA error		225	—	—
1673 no stops on obv.		165	—	—
1673 no rev. stop..		165	—	—
1674		55	300	900
1674 'O' for 'C' in CAROLVS...................................		100	500	—
1675		50	275	825
1675 no stop after CAROLVS		165	—	—
1679		55	300	900
1679 no rev. stop..		65	325	1100

3395
Tin Farthing

Prices for tin coinage based on corrosion free examples, and in the top grades with some lustre

3395   Tin **Farthing.** Somewhat similar, but with copper plug, edge inscribed NUMMORVM
FAMVLVS, and date on edge only die axis ↑↓

1684	various varieties of edge................55	250	900	3600
1685	.... *Extremely rare*			

James II, brother of Charles II, was born on 14th October 1633; he married Anne Hyde with whom he produced 8 children. He lost control of his subjects when the loyalist Tories moved against him over his many Catholic appointments. Parliament invited his protestant daughter Mary with husband William of Orange to be joint rulers. James II abdicated and died in exile in France.

During this reign the dies continued to be engraved by John Roettier (1631-1700), the only major difference in the silver coinage being the ommission of the interlinked C's in the angles of the shields on the reverses. The only provenance marked silver coin of this reign is the extremely rare plume on reverse 1685 Shilling. The elephant and castle provenance mark continues to appear on some of the gold coins of this reign. Tin halfpence and farthings provided the only base metal coinage during this short reign. All genuine tin coins of this period have a copper plug.

GOLD

	F £	VF £	EF £
3396 Five Guineas. First laur. bust l., R. Crowned cruciform shields sceptres misplaced in angles smaller crowns date on edge in words (e.g. 1686 = SECVNDO) die axis ↑↓			
1686 SECVNDO	9500	22500	105000
3397 Five Guineas. First laur bust l. R. similar bust sceptres normal. die axis ↑↓			
1687 TERTIO	10000	24000	110000
1688 QVARTO	10000	24000	110000

3397A
1687 Five Guineas, second bust

3397A Five Guineas. Second laur. bust l. R. similar die axis ↑↓			
1687 TERTIO	9000	20000	95000
1688 QVARTO	9000	20000	95000

3398
1687 Five Guineas, first bust, elephant and castle below

	F	VF	EF
	£	£	£
3398 **Five Guineas.** First laur. bust l. Elephant and castle below R. Similar die axis ↑↓			
1687 TERTIO 10000		24000	110000
1688 QVARTO 11000		25000	115000

3399
Two Guineas

3399 **Two Guineas.** Laur. bust l. R. Crowned cruciform shields, sceptres in angles, edge milled, die axis ↑↓			
1687 5250		13500	50000
1688/7 5250		13500	50000
3400 **Guinea.** First laur. bust l. R. Crowned cruciform shields, sceptres in angles, edge milled, die axis ↑↓			
1685 1450		3750	14500
1686 1500		4000	15000
1686 B/I in HIB 1600		4250	16000
1686/5 1600		4250	16000
3401 **Guinea.** First bust elephant and castle below R. similar die axis ↑↓			
1685 2250		5250	17500
1686 5250		—	—

3402
1688 Guinea, second bust

	F	VF	EF
	£	£	£

3402 Guinea. Second laur. bust l. R. similar die axis ↑↓

		F	VF	EF
1686	....	1450	3750	14500
1687	....	1450	3750	14500
1687/6	....	1500	3850	15000
1688	....	1450	3750	14500

3403

3403 Guinea. Second bust elephant and castle below R. similar die axis ↑↓

1686	....	2750	6000	18500
1687	....	2500	5750	18000
1688	....	2500	5750	18000

3404

3404 Half-Guinea. Laur. bust l. R. Crowned cruciform shields sceptres in angles, edge milled
die axis ↑↓

1686		....	1000	3000	10000
1686	OBV/BVS	....	1050	3250	10500
1687		....	1000	3000	10000
1688		....	1000	3000	10000

3405 Half-Guinea. Laur bust with elephant and castle below, R. similar die axis ↑↓

1686	....	1250	4750	12500

SILVER

3406
1686 Crown, first bust

	F	VF	EF
	£	£	£

3406 Crown. First dr. bust, l. regnal year on edge in words (e.g. 1686 = SECVNDO) die axis ↑↓

1686 SECVNDO	325	1350	8500
1686 — No stops on obverse	350	1500	9000

3407
1687 Crown, second bust

3407 Crown. Second dr. bust l. narrower than first bust. R. Crowned cruciform shields edge inscribed in raised letters die axis ↑↓

1687 TERTIO	250	750	7000
1688 QVARTO	275	850	7500
1688/7 QVARTO	300	950	8000

3408	1st bust	2nd bust
1686 Halfcrown, first bust	Halfcrown hair ties	

	F £	VF £	EF £

3408 Halfcrown. First laur and dr. bust, l. regnal year on edge in words
(e.g. 1685 = PRIMO) die axis ↑↓

	F	VF	EF
1685 PRIMO	200	675	7000
1686 SECVNDO	190	650	6750
1686/5 —	250	750	7500
1686 TERTIO V over S or B in JACOBVS	225	725	7250
1686 TERTIO	225	725	7250
1687 TERTIO	200	675	7000
1687/6 —	250	750	7500
1687 — 6 over 8	300	950	—
1687 A/R in GRATIA	275	850	7500

3409 Halfcrown. Second laur and dr. bust l. R. Crowned cruciform shields
edge inscribed in raised letters die axis ↑↓

	F	VF	EF
1687 TERTIO	225	725	7250
1688 QVARTO	200	675	7000

3410
1687 Shilling

3410 Shilling. Laur and Dr. bust l. R. Crowned cruciform shields die axis ↑↓

	F	VF	EF
1685	240	550	3500
1685 no stops on rev.	275	650	3750
1686	240	550	3500
1686/5	325	750	4000
1686 V/S in JACOBVS	275	650	3750
1686 G/A in MAG	275	650	3750
1687	275	650	3750
1687 G/A in MAG	325	750	4000
1687/6	240	550	3500
1687/6 G/A in MAG	250	600	3600
1688	325	750	4000
1688/7	275	650	3750

3411 Shilling. Similar, plume in centre of *rev.*, die axis ↑↓

	F	VF	EF
1685	12500	32500	—

3412   3413
1686 Sixpence, early shields, indented tops   1687 Sixpence, later shields

	F	VF	EF
	£	£	£

3412   Sixpence. Laur and dr. bust l. R. Early type crowned cruciform shields die axis ↑↓

1686	150	425	1350
1687	185	500	1600
1687/6	175	475	1500

3413   Sixpence. Similar R. Late type shields die axis ↑↓

1687	150	425	1400
1687/6	200	525	1650
1687 Later/early shields	185	500	1600
1688	160	450	1500

3414	3415	3416	3417
Fourpence	Threepence	Twopence	Penny

3414   Fourpence. Laur. head l. R. IIII Crowned die axis ↑↓

1686	15	30	100
1686 Date over crown	18	30	110
1687/6	15	25	100
1687 8 over 7	18	30	110
1688	22	45	145
1688 1 over 8	25	55	150
1688/7	22	45	140

3415   Threepence. Laur. head l. R. III Crowned die axis-↑↓

1685	12	30	95
1685 Groat flan	35	80	165
1686	12	35	100
1686 4d obv. die	18	40	120
1687	12	32	100
1687/6	12	32	100
1688	22	55	145
1688/7	25	55	140

3416   Twopence. Laur. head l. R. II Crowned die axis ↑↓

1686	15	35	90
1686 IΛCOBVS	18	35	1150
1687	12	32	85
1687 ERA for FRA	25	45	150
1688	18	40	13
1688/7	18	40	120

	Fair £	F £	VF £	EF £
3417 Penny. Laur. head l. R. I Crowned die axis ↑↓				
1685	15		30	100
1686	20		40	1100
1687	20		40	1100
1687/6	20		40	110
1687/8	25		50	130
1688	25		55	14
1688/7	25		55	13
3418 Maundy Set. As last four. Uniform dates				
1686	100		300	575
1687	100		300	575
1688	175		350	750

TIN

3419
Tin Halfpenny

Prices for tin coinage based on corrosion free examples, and in the top grades with some lustre

3419 Halfpenny. Laur. and dr. bust r. R. Britannia seated l. date on edge die axis ↑↓

1685	various varieties of edge.............100	250	775	3850
1686	110	275	825	4200
1687	90	300	775	3850

3420
Cuirassed bust Tin Farthing

3420 Farthing. Laur. and Cuir. bust r. R. Britannia seated l. date on edge die axis ↑↓

1684	....*Extremely rare*			
1685	various varieties of edge...............65	195	700	3000
1686	two varieties of edge 80	225	775	3250
1687	.... *Extremely rare*			
3421 Farthing. Dr. bust r.; date on edge, 1687 various varieties				
of edge ↑↓ 100		250	875	3750

Mary Stuart was born on 30th April 1662, and married William of Orange as part of Charles II's foreign policy. She eventually became William's loyal servant but bore him no children. The Bill and the Claim of Rights were both passed in 1689 and curbed the Royal and Prerogative rights of Monarchs. Mary died from smallpox on 28th December 1694.

Due to the poor state of the silver coinage, much of it worn hammered coin, the Guinea, which was valued at 21s. 6d. at the beginning of the reign, circulated for as much as 30s. by 1694. The elephant and elephant and castle provenance marks continue on some gold coin. The tin Halfpennies and Farthings were replaced by copper coins in 1694. The rampant Lion of Nassau is now placed as an inescutcheon on the centre of the royal arms. The WM monogram appears in the angles of the silver coins of this reign.

Engravers and designers: George Bower (d.1689), Henry Harris (d.1704), John Roettier (1631-1700), James Roettier (1663-1698), Norbert Roettier (b.1665)

GOLD

3422
Five Guineas

	F £	VF £	EF £
3422　Five Guineas. Conjoined busts r. regnal year on edge in words (e.g. 1691 = TERTIO) ↑↓			
1691 TERTIO	8500	22500	120000
1692 QVARTO	8500	22500	120000
1692 QVINTO	10000	25000	130000
1693 QVINTO	8500	22500	120000
1694/2 SEXTO	10000	25000	130000
1694 SEXTO	9000	24000	125000

3423
Elephant and castle below busts

3423 Five Guineas. Conjoined busts, elephant and castle below, R. Crowned shield of arms
die axis ↑↓

1691 TERTIO	9000	24000	125000
1692 QVARTO	9000	24000	125000
1693 QVINTO	9500	25000	130000
1694/2 SEXTO	10000	26000	135000
1694 SEXTO	9500	25000	130000

3424
1694 Two Guineas

3424 Two Guineas. Conjoined busts r. R. Crowned shield of arms, Lion of Nassau at centre
die axis ↑↓

1693	3500	12000	45000
1694/3	3500	12000	45000

3425 Two Guineas. Conjoined busts, elephant and castle below, R. similar die axis ↑↓

1691			*Extremely rare*
1693	5750	16500	—
1694/3	4500	13500	52500

3426   3427

1689 Guinea, later harp   1689 Elephant and castle below busts

	F £	VF £	EF £
3426 Guinea. Conjoined busts r. R. Crowned shield of arms Lion of Nassau at centre die axis ↑↓			
1689 Early slanting harp with base of harp in line with X of REX	1750	5000	16000
1689 Later upright harp with base of harp in line with R of REX	1750	5000	16000
1689 MVS over EL	2000	5250	16500
1690	2000	5250	16500
1690 FT for ET obv	2200	5500	17500
1690 D/G in DEI	2200	5500	17500
1690 GVLIFLMVS	2250	5500	17500
1691	2000	5250	16500
1692	2000	5250	16500
1693	2000	5250	16500
1694	2000	5250	16500
1694/3	2000	5250	16500
3427 Guinea. Conjoined busts elephant and castle below R. Similar die axis ↑↓			
1689	2200	5500	17500
1689 G of REGINA over E	2250	6000	18000
1690	3250	8000	—
1691	2250	6000	18000
1692	2400	6250	18500
1693	3250	8000	—
1694	2400	6250	18500
1694/3	2500	6500	19000
3428 Guinea. Conjoined busts elephant only below, R. Similar die axis ↑↓			
1692	2600	6750	20000
1693	2750	7000	22500

3429

1689 Half-Guinea, first busts, first shield

3429 Half-Guinea. First busts r. R. First Crowned shield of arms die axis ↑↓

1689	1050	3250	10500

3430
1690 Half-Guinea, second busts, second shield

	F £	VF £	EF £
3430 Half-Guinea. Second busts r. R. Second Crowned shield of arms die axis ↑↓			
1690	1050	3250	11000
1691	1050	3250	11000
1692	1100	3400	11500
1693	1250	3750	—
1693/2	825	3750	—
1694	1050	3250	10500
3431 Half-Guinea. Second busts elephant and castle below, R. Second shield of arms die axis ↑↓			
1691	1350	4250	13500
1692	1350	4250	13500
3432 Half-Guinea. Second busts elephant only below, R. Second shield of arms die axis ↑↓			
1692	1500	4500	—

SILVER

3433
Crown

3433 Crown. Conjoined busts r. regnal year on edge in words (e.g. 1691 = TERTIO)
die axis ↑↓

1691 TERTIO	600	2000	8500
1691 I/E in legend	650	2100	8750
1691 TERTTIO	650	2250	9000
1692 QVARTO	600	2000	8500
1692/ ꝅ QVARTO	625	2250	9000
1692/ ꝅ QVINTO	600	2000	8500

Caul frosted →   ← Caul not frosted

Pearls →   ← No Pearls

Interior frosted ↗   ↖ Interior not frosted

3434
1689 Halfcrown - first reverse

3435
1689 Halfcrown - second reverse

	F £	VF £	EF £
3434 Halfcrown. First busts, r. R. First crowned shield, 1689 PRIMO R. Crown with caul and interior frosted, with pearls edge inscribed die axis ↑↓	140	425	3250
1689— 2nd L/M in GVLIELMVS	150	450	3500
1689 — 1st V/A in GVLIELMVS, only caul frosted	160	475	3500
1689 — — interior also frosted, no pearls	150	450	3500
1689 Caul only frosted, pearls	140	425	3250
1689 — no pearls	150	450	3500
1689 No frosting, pearls	140	425	3250
1689 No stops on obverse	225	650	4500
1689 FRA for FR	200	625	4250
3435 Halfcrown. First busts r. R. Second crowned shield die axis ↑↓			
1689 PRIMO R. Caul and interior frosted with pearls	140	425	3250
1689 — — no pearls	150	450	3500
1689 Caul only frosted pearls	140	425	3250
1689 interior frosted, no pearls	185	550	4000
1689 Caul only frosted, no pearls	185	550	4000
1689 no frosting, pearls	140	425	3250
1689 no frosting, no pearls	140	425	3250
1690 SECVNDO —	185	550	4000
1690 — GRETIA error with second V of GVLIELMVS struck over S	375	1000	5500
1690 TERTIO	200	625	4250

3436
Halfcrown, second busts, third reverse

	F	VF	EF
	£	£	£

3436 Halfcrown. Second busts r. R. Crowned cruciform shields, WM monogram in angles
 die axis ↑↓

1691 TERTIO	.200	625	4250
1692 QVARTO	.200	625	4250
1692 R/G in REGINA also showing H/B in HI	.250	675	4500
1692 QVINTO	.275	725	4750
1693 QVINTO	.175	525	3750
1693 3/inverted 3	.185	550	4000
1693 inverted 3	.350	950	5250

3437	3438
Shilling	Sixpence

3437 Shilling. Conjoined busts r. R. Crowned cruciform shields, WM monogram in
 angles die axis ↑↓

1692	.200	625	3000
1692 inverted 1	.225	675	3250
1692 RE/ET on R	.225	675	3250
1692 A of GRATIA over T and T over I	.250	750	3500
1693 9/0	.250	750	3500
1693	.200	625	3000

3438 Sixpence. Conjoined busts r. R. Crowned cruciform shields, WM monogram in
 angles die axis ↑↓

1693	.175	425	1350
1693 inverted 3	.225	575	1750
1694	.185	475	1500

	3439	3440
	Groat, first busts	Groat, Second busts

	F	VF	EF
	£	£	£

3439 Fourpence. First busts, r. no tie to wreath. R. Crowned 4 die axis ↑↓

	F	VF	EF
1689 GV below bust	15	30	80
1689 G below bust	15	30	80
1689 stop befor G	15	30	80
1689 berries in wreath	15	30	80
1689 GVLEELMVS	65	200	–
1689 I over first E in GVLEELMVS corrected die for above	65	200	–
1690	20	50	110
1690 6 over 5	20	55	120
1691	20	45	130
1691/0	20	40	120
1694	20	60	160

3440 Fourpence. Second busts r. tie to wreath. R. Crowned 4 die axis ↑↓

	F	VF	EF
1692	30	90	180
1692/1	25	65	165
1692 MAR•IA			*Extremely rare*
1693	35	100	280
1693/2	35	100	280
1694	30	95	200
1694 small lettering	30	95	200

3441 Threepence. First busts, r. no tie to wreath. R. Crowned 3 die axis ↑↓

	F	VF	EF
1689	15	30	75
1689 No stops on rev.	20	40	110
1689 LMV over MVS	20	40	110
1689 Hyphen stops on rev.	20	40	100
1690	20	50	105
1690 6 over 5	20	50	10
1690 Large lettering	20	50	105
1690 9 over 6	20	50	105
1691	100	220	450

3442 Threepence. Second busts, r. tie to wreath R. Crowned 3 die axis ↑↓

	F	VF	EF
1691	40	130	220
1692 G below bust	25	65	140
1692 GV below bust	25	65	140
1692 GVL below bust	25	65	140
1693 G below bust	20	55	140
1693/2 G below bust	20	55	140
1693 GV below bust	20	55	140
1694 G below bust	20	55	140
1694 — MΛRIΛ error	24	60	170
1694 GV below bust	20	55	140
1694 GVL below bust	20	55	140

	F £	VF £	EF £
3443 Twopence. Conjoined busts r. R. Crowned 2 die axis ↑↓			
1689	18	40	90
1691	18	45	110
1692	20	45	120
1693	15	42	115
1693/2	18	42	115
1693 GV below bust	18	42	115
1694	20	45	120
1694/3	18	45	120
1694/3 no stop after DG	18	45	120
1694 MARLA error	35	65	27
1694 HI for HIB	20	45	120
1694 GVLI below bust	20	45	12
1694 GVL below bust	20	45	120

3444
Penny

3445
Legend intruded

	F £	VF £	EF £
3444 Penny. Legend continuous over busts, R. Crowned 1 die axis ↑↓			
1689	225	425	800
1689 GVIELMVS error	250	525	1000
1689 MARIΛ	250	450	850
3445 Penny. Legend broken by busts, R. Crowned 1 die axis ↑↓			
1690	28	55	125
1691/0	35	60	135
1692	45	85	200
1692/1	35	80	180
1693	35	60	130
1694 date spread	22	50	120
1694 no stops on obv.	22	55	120
1694 HI for HIB	28	60	190
1694 — 9/6	25	55	135

3446
Maundy Set

	F £	VF £	EF £
3446 Maundy Set. The four denominations. Uniform dates			
1689	375	750	1500
1691	175	425	1000
1692	160	400	975
1693	180	475	1100
1694	145	375	950

TIN AND COPPER

3447
Tin Halfpenny first busts

	Fair	F	VF	EF
	£	£	£	£

Prices for tin coinage based on corrosion free examples, and in the top grades with some lustre

3447 Tin **Halfpenny.** Small dr. busts r.; date on edge ↑↓

1689 925   1800   —   —

— — — obv. with star stops 1689 .... *Extremely rare*

3448   3451
Tin Halfpenny cuirassed busts   Tin Farthing

3448 Tin **Halfpenny.** — Large cuir. busts r.; R. Britannia seated L. date only on edge, die axis ↑↓

1690 various edge varieties 80   190   800   3250

3449 Tin **Halfpenny.** Similar date in ex. and on edge die axis ↑↓

1691 various edge varieties 70   175   700   2750

1691 in ex. 1692 on edge..*Extremely rare*

1692 70   175   700   2750

3450 Tin **Farthing.** Small dr. busts r. R. Britannia seated l. die axis ↑↓

1689 275   700   2250   —

1689, in ex. 1690 on edge..*Extremely rare*

3451 Tin **Farthing.** Large cuir. busts r. R. Britannia seated l.die axis ↑↓

1690, in ex. 1689 on edge..*Extremely rare*

1690 various edge varieties 55   175   700   3000

1691 various edge varieties 55   175   700   3000

1692 70   190   750   3000

3452
1694 Halfpenny

	F	VF	EF
	£	£	£

3452   Copper **Halfpenny,** Conjoined busts r. R. Britannia die axis ↑↓

1694	75	275	1150
1694 GVLIEMVS error	200	600	—
1694 MVRIA error	225	650	—
1694 MΛRIΛ error	150	525	—
1694 BRITΛNNI/Λ	175	550	—
1694 no rev. stop	150	525	—
1694 GVLEELMVS	250	625	—

3453
1694 Farthing

3453   Copper **Farthing**, Conjoined busts r. R. Britannia die axis ↑↓

1694	65	275	1000
1694 MΛRIΛ error	175	500	—
1694 no stop after MΛRIΛ	100	415	—
1694 — BRITΛNNIΛ	125	415	—
1694 no stop on rev.	100	350	—
1694 no stop on obv.	100	350	—
1694 GVLIELMS, BRITΛNNIΛ errors	225	525	—
1694 BRITΛNNIΛ	150	475	—
1694 Broad heavier flan 25.5mm	200	500	—

WILLIAM III, 1694-1702

William of Orange was born on 4th November 1650. He married Mary Stuart under Charles II's foreign policy and was invited to England by Parliament, where he proceeded to supress the Jacobites. The Bank of England was founded during this reign, and William ruled alone and without issue after Mary's death until his own demise on 8th March 1702 following a serious fall from his horse.

In 1696 a great re-coinage was undertaken to replace the hammered silver that made up most of the coinage in circulation, much of it being clipped and badly worn. Branch mints were set up at Bristol, Chester, Exeter, Norwich and York to help with the re-coinage. For a short time before they were finally demonetised, unclipped hammered coins were allowed to circulate freely provided they were officially pierced in the centre. Silver coins with roses between the coats of arms were made from silver obtained from the West of England mines. The elephant and castle provenance mark continues on some guineas and half-guineas.

Engravers and designers: Samuel Bull (d.c.1720), John Croker (1670-1740), Henry Harris (d.1704), John Roettier (1663-1698).

GOLD

3454
1699 Five Guineas, first bust

	F	VF	EF
	£	£	£
3454 Five Guineas. First laur. bust r. regnal year on edge in words (e.g. 1699 = UNDECIMO) ↑↓			
1699 UNDECIMO...9500		24000	110000
1700 DVODECIMO...9500		24000	110000

3455
Elephant and castle below first bust

3455 Five Guineas. First bust elephant and castle below			
1699 UNDECIMO...10000		25000	120000

3456
1701 Five Guineas 'Fine Work'

	F £	VF £	EF £

3456 Five Guineas. Second laur. bust r. ('fine work'), R. Crowned cruciform shields Plain or ornamental sceptres DECIMO TERTIO die axis ↑↓

1701*	8500	22500	95000

3457
'Fine work' Two Guineas

3457 Two Guineas. ('fine work'), Laur. bust r. similar die axis ↑↓

1701	3750	10000	42500

3458
1695 Guinea, first bust

3458 Guinea. First laur. bust r. R. Crowned cruciform shields, sceptres in angles die axis ↑↓

1695 large and small lis in French arms	1250	3250	10500
1695 M over V in GVLIELMVS in error	1350	3500	12500
1696	1400	3750	12500
1697	1400	3750	12500

3459 Guinea. First bust elephant and castle below R. Similar die axis ↑↓

1695	2250	6500	20000
1696			Extremely rare

* Beware of low grade counterfeits

3460	3463
Guinea, second bust	Narrow crowns

	F	VF	EF
	£	£	£

3460 Guinea. Second laur. bust r. R. Similar with human-headed harp in Irish arms. die axis ↑↓

1697	1400	3750	12500
1698	1250	3250	10500
1699	1500	4250	13500
1700 large or small lions in arms	1250	3250	10500

3461 Guinea. Second bust elephant and castle below. R. Similar die axis ↑↓

1697	3000	8500	—
1698	2250	6500	20000
1699	.... *Extremely rare*		
1700	2750	8000	—

3462 Guinea. Second laur. bust. r. R. Similar with human-headed harp.
Large lettering and large date, die axis ↑↓

| 1698 | ....1350 | 3500 | 12000 |

3463 Guinea. — R. Narrow crowns, plain or ornamented sceptres, axis ↑↓

| 1701 | ....1250 | 3250 | 10000 |

3464 Guinea. Second bust elephant and castle below, die axis ↑↓

| 1701 | .... *Extremely rare* | | |

3465 Guinea. Third laur. bust r. ('fine work'), R. Similar die axis ↑↓

| 1701 | ....4500 | 12500 | 35000 |

3466	3468
1695 Half-Guinea, early harp	Later harp

3466 Half-Guinea. Laur. bust r. R. With early harp, die axis ↑↓

| 1695 | ....700 | 1850 | 6250 |

3467 Half-Guinea. Laur. bust elephant and castle below. R. With early harp, die axis ↑↓

| 1695 | ....1250 | 3250 | 10000 |
| 1696 | ....900 | 2750 | 7500 |

3468 Half-Guinea. Laur. bust r. R. Crowned cruciform shields, sceptres in angles
with late harp, die axis ↑↓

1697	1100	3000	9000
1698	700	1850	6250
1699	.... *Extremely rare*		
1700	800	2250	6750
1701	750	2000	6500

3469 Half-Guinea. Laur. bust elephant and castle below, die axis ↑↓

| 1698 | ....1250 | 3250 | 9500 |

SILVER

First harp

3470
Crown - first bust - round collar

	F	VF	EF
	£	£	£

3470 Crown. First dr. bust, r. with curved breast plate or drapery. R.First harp, regnal year on edge in words (e.g. 1696 = OCTAVO) ↑↓

	F	VF	EF
1695 SEPTIMO 120	400	4000
1695 SEPTIMO cinquefoils for crosses on edge 200	575	—
1695 OCTAVO 120	375	3750
1695 TVTA·EN error 225	650	—
1695 plain edge proof *FDC* £32500		
1696 OCTAVO 110	325	3500
1696 No stops on obverse...225	650	4500
1696 G/D IN GRA...200	575	4250
1696 — no stops 200	575	4250
1696/5 185	550	4250
1696 GEI for DEI...675	2250	—
1696 — no stops 750	2500	—
1696 plain edge proof *FDC* £35000		

Second harp

3471
1696 Crown, second bust - hair across breast

3471 Crown. Second dr. bust r. with two locks of hair across the bust and no hair below the truncation. R. Second harp (hair across breast), 1696 (two varieties) die axis ↑↓
OCTAVO ....*Each unique*

3472
Third bust, straight breastplate

	F	VF	EF
	£	£	£

3472 Crown. Third dr. bust, r. Easily distinguished by the straight breast plate or drapery. ℞. First harp, die axis ↑↓

1696 OCTAVO	120	400	4000
1696 TRICESIMO			*Extremely rare*
1696 plain edge proof *FDC* £27500			

3473 Crown. Similar, ℞. Second harp, die axis ↑↓

1697 NONO	3250	12500	45000

Third harp

3474
1700 Crown, third bust variety

3474 Crown. Third bust variety r. of same general style but dies have been recut and hair varied a little. Tie is slightly longer and thinner than normal third bust. ℞. Third harp with scroll front and back, ↑↓

1700 DVODECIMO	120	375	3750
1700 DECIMO. TERTIO	150	450	4250

3475 Halfcrown. First bust r. ℞. Small shields,

1696 die axis ↑↓ OCTAVO	100	275	2000
— — 1696 DECɅS error	110	325	2250

3476 Halfcrown. B (*Bristol*) below First bust,

die axis ↑↓ 1696 OCTAVO	110	325	2250
— 1696 B Similar proof *FDC* £17500			

3477
Chester Mint

3478
Exeter Mint

	F £	VF £	EF £
3477 Halfcrown. C (*Chester*) below first bust, die axis ↑↓			
1696 OCTAVO 175	525	2500
3478 Halfcrown. E (*Exeter*) below first bust, die axis ↑↓			
1696 OCTAVO 200	575	2750
3479 Halfcrown. N (*Norwich*) below first bust, die axis ↑↓			
1696 OCTAVO 175	525	2500
3480 Halfcrown. y (*York*) below first bust, die axis ↑↓			
1696 OCTAVO 185	550	2600

3480
1696 Halfcrown - York Mint

3481
1696 Halfcrown, large shield
reverse with early harp

	F £	VF £	EF £
3481 Halfcrown. First bust r. ℞. Large shield, early harp, die axis ↑↓			
1696 OCTAVO 100	275	2000
1696 Proof plain edge *FDC* £15000			
3482 Halfcrown. — B (*Bristol*) below bust, die axis ↑↓			
1696 OCTAVO 110	325	2250
3483 Halfcrown. — C (*Chester*) below bust, die axis ↑↓			
1696 OCTAVO 185	550	2600
3484 Halfcrown. — E (*Exeter*) below bust, die axis ↑↓			
1696 OCTAVO...175	525	2500
3485 Halfcrown. — N (*Norwich*) below bust, die axis ↑↓			
1696 OCTAVO...375	1250	—
3486 Halfcrown. — y (*York*) below bust, die axis ↑↓			
1696 OCTAVO...120	350	2400
— — die axis ↑↓ 1696 y (*York*), Scots Arms at date 1000	—	—
— die axis ↑↓ y over E 1696...225	850	—

3487   3489
Large shields, ordinary harp   Chester Mint Halfcrown, large shields

	F	VF	EF
	£	£	£
3487 Halfcrown. First bust r. R. Large shields, ordinary harp die axis ↑↓			
1696 OCTAVO 200	625	3000
1697 NONO..90	225	1500
1697 — GRR for GRA...450	—	—
1697 G/A in MAG 350	—	—
1697/6 — 135	450	2500
1697 Proof plain edge *FDC* £15000			
3488 Halfcrown. — B (*Bristol*) below first bust, die axis ↑↓			
1697 NONO..125	375	2250
1697 proof on thick flan *FDC* .... *Extremely rare*		
1697 — no stops on reverse 150	475	2500
3489 Halfcrown. — C (*Chester*) below first bust, similar die axis ↑↓			
1696 OCTAVO 200	625	3000
1697 NONO..150	475	2500

3490
Exeter Mint Halfcrown, large shields

3490 Halfcrown. — E (*Exeter*) below first bust, similar die axis ↑↓			
1696 OCTAVO 175	525	2500
1696 NONO..450	—	—
1697 OCTAVO 475	—	—
1697 NONO..110	325	2250
1697 E over C or B under bust 200	600	—

3491
Norwich Mint Halfcrown, large shields

	F	VF	EF
	£	£	£

3491 Halfcrown. — N *(Norwich)* below first bust, similar die axis ↑↓

1696 OCTAVO	375	1250	—
1697 OCTAVO	250	950	—
1697 NONO...	150	525	2500
1697 — Scots Arms at date	1000	—	—

3492 Halfcrown. — — y *(York)* below first bust, similar die axis ↑↓

1697 NONO..	100	275	2000
1697 OCTAVO	350	—	—

3493 Halfcrown. Second dr. bust r. (hair across breast), die axis ↑↓

1696 OCTAVO .... *Unique*

3494
1700 Halfcrown, modified large shields

3494 Halfcrown. First dr. bust R. Modified large shields die axis ↑↓

1698 OCTAVO	475	1500	—
1698 DECIMO	85	225	1500
1698/7 —	250	950	—
1698 UNDECIMO...	350	1000	—
1699 UNDECIMO...	150	525	2500
1699 — Inverted A's for V's on edge	175	600	—
1699 — Scots Arms at date	900	—	—
1699 — Lion of Nassau inverted...........................	525	1500	—
1700 DVODECIMO...	90	250	1650
1700 D. TERTIO	100	275	1750
1700 — DECⱯS error	110	300	1850
1701 D. TERTIO	90	250	1650
1701 — no stops on reverse	150	525	2500

3495
1701 Halfcrown, elephant and castle below bust

	F	VF	EF
	£	£	£
3495 Halfcrown. – elephant and castle below bust, die axis ↑↓			
1701 D. TERTIO 3000		9000	—

3496
1701 Halfcrown, plumes on reverse

3496 Halfcrown. – ℞. Plumes in angles, die axis ↑↓			
1701 D. TERTIO 300		900	5250

SHILLINGS

First bust	**Third bust**	**Third bust variety**
This bust is distinctive in having the hair turned outwards above and below the crown of the head	This is rather like the first bust but the hair at the back all turns downwards and inwards	Tie thicker, more hair below bust, more aquiline profile and coarser features

	F	VF	EF
	£	£	£

3497 Shilling. First dr. bust r. R. Crowned cruciform shields edge milled die axis ↑↓

	F	VF	EF
1695 45	125	725
1695 E of ET over H...60	150	850
1696 40	120	700
1696/5 and GVLICLMVS 475	—	—
1696 no stops on reverse 100	350	—
1696 MAB for MAG error 650	—	—
1696 GVLIEMVS error...575	—	—
1696 GVLIELMVS error 85	325	—
1696 GⱯLIELMVS error 110	375	—
1696 GVLELMVS 675	—	—
1696 2nd L over M 125	400	—
1696-1669 error date 1000	3000	—
1697 40	120	700
1697 E/A in DEI 275	900	—
1697 GRI for GRA error...575	—	—
1697 Arms of Scot/Ireland transposed 750	—	—
1697 Irish Arms at date...950	—	—
1697 no stops on reverse 110	375	—
1697 GVLELMVS error..575	—	—
1697 GVLIELMⱯS error 100	350	—
1697 L/M in legend 125	400	—

3498
Bristol Mint

3499
1696 Chester Mint Shilling

	F £	VF £	EF £
3498 Shilling. Similar B *(Bristol)* below bust die axis ↑↓			
1696	80	275	1350
1696 GⱯLIELMVS error and large G in MAG	90	300	1500
1696 small x in REX	*Scarce variety*		
1697	75	250	1250
3499 Shilling. Similar C *(Chester)* below bust die axis ↑↓			
1696	90	300	1500
1696 R/V in GRA	175	575	2500
1696 thick flan proof *FDC*	*Extremely rare*		
1697	90	300	1500

3500

3500 Shilling. Similar E *(Exeter)* below bust die axis ↑↓			
1696	90	300	1500
1697 E over N	135	475	—
1697	125	450	1850
3501 Shilling. Similar N *(Norwich)* below bust die axis ↑↓			
1696	110	325	1350
1697 no stops on obv.	135	425	1750
1697	110	325	1350
3502 Shilling. Similar y *(York)* below bust die axis ↑↓			
1696 Also known with no stop after GVLIELMVS	90	250	1250
1696	100	325	—
1697	90	250	1250
1697 Arms of France/Ireland transposed	1250	—	—
1697 Arms of Scotland/Ireland transposed	1250	—	—
3503 Shilling. Similar Y *(York)* below bust die axis ↑↓			
1696	110	350	1650
1697 Y over Ⱥ	375	1250	—
1697	175	575	—
3504 Shilling. Second dr. bust r. (hair across breast), similar die axis ↑↓			
1696	*Unique*		

	3505	3513

Third bust variety   Chester Mint, Third bust variety

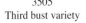

	F	VF	EF
	£	£	£
3505 Shilling. Third dr. bust r., similar die axis ↑↓ 1697..40		120	700
3506 Shilling. Similar B (*Bristol*) below bust, die axis ↑↓			
1697 125		375	1650
3507 Shilling. Similar C (*Chester*) below bust die axis ↑↓			
1696 225		575	2250
1697 small or large lettering 125		375	1650
1697 FR.A error 175		525	2000
1697 no stops on reverse 175		525	2000
1697 Arms of Scotland at date 1500		—	—
3508 Shilling. Similar E (*Exeter*) below bust, die axis ↑↓			
1696 2250		—	—
1697 125		375	1650
3509 Shilling. Similar N (*Norwich*) below bust, die axis ↑↓			
1697 135		425	1750
3510 Shilling. Similar y (*York*) below bust die axis ↑↓			
1696 900		—	—
1697 110		325	1350
3511 Shilling. Third bust variety r. similar die axis ↑↓			
1697 GⱯLIELMVS error 125		375	—
1697 50		150	900
1697 GVLIELMⱯS error 125		375	—
1698 110		325	1350
1698 plain edge proof *FDC* £10000			
3512 Shilling. Similar B (*Bristol*) below bust, die axis ↑↓			
1697 225		575	2250
3513 Shilling. Similar C (*Chester*) below bust, die axis ↑↓			
1697 250		675	—
1697 thick flan ....*Extremely rare*			
3514 Shilling. Similar R. Plumes in angles, die axis ↑↓			
1698 325		950	4250

Third bust   **Fourth bust**   **Fifth bust**

3515
Fourth bust

3516
Fifth bust

	F	VF	EF
	£	£	£
3515 Shilling Fourth dr. bust ('flaming hair') r. similar die axis ↑↓			
1698 275		900	4000
1698 No stops on reverse 325		950	4250
1698 plain edge proof *FDC* £13500			
1699 225		750	3250
1699 plain edge proof *FDC* ....*Extremely rare*			
3516 Shilling. Fifth dr. bust (hair high) r. similar die axis ↑↓			
1699 135		425	1750
1699 Plain edge proof £12500			
1700 40		120	675
1700 no stops on rev 60		150	850
1700 Circular small O's in date 45		125	700
1700 no stop after DEI 65		160	900
1700 Tall O's no stops on reverse 60		150	850
1701 small or large lions 110		325	1350
1701 DEI/GRA 475		—	—

3517
1701 Shilling, plumes on reverse

3518
1699 Shilling, roses on reverse

3517 Shilling. Similar R. Plumes in angles die axis ↑↓			
1699 200		700	2750
1701 200		700	2750
3518 Shilling. Similar R. Roses in angles, die axis ↑↓			
1699 475		1500	5750
3519 Shilling. Similar plume below bust, die axis ↑↓			
1700 6000		17500	—

SIXPENCES

First bust

Third bust

**Early harp
large crown**

**Later harp
small crown**

3520
First bust Sixpence, French arms at date

	F £	VF £	EF £
3520 Sixpence. First dr. bust r. R. Crowned cruciform shields, large crowns, edge milled, early harp, die axis ↑↓			
1695	30	70	325
1696	25	60	300
1696 Heavy flan	850	—	—
1696 French Arms at date	525	—	—
1696 GVLIELMⱯS	35	95	400
1696 Scots Arms at date	350	—	—
1696/5	35	95	400
1696 no stops on obverse	45	125	525
1696 DFI for DEI	45	125	—
3521 Sixpence. Similar B *(Bristol)* below bust, die axis ↑↓			
1696	30	90	350
— — 1696 B over E	40	95	400
3522 Sixpence. Similar C *(Chester)* below bust, die axis ↑↓			
1696	40	100	425

3523   3525
1696 York Mint sixpence, early harp, first bust

3523 Sixpence. Similar E *(Exeter)* below bust, die axis ↑↓			
1696	45	110	450
3524 Sixpence. Similar N *(Norwich)* below bust, die axis ↑↓			
1696	40	100	425
3525 Sixpence. Similar y *(York)* below bust, die axis ↑↓			
1696	30	80	350

	F	VF	EF
	£	£	£
3526 Sixpence. Similar Y *(York)* below bust, die axis ↑↓			
1696 30	90	375
1696 no stops on obverse 45	110	450
3527 Sixpence. Similar R. Later harp, large crowns, die axis ↑↓			
1696 45	110	450
1696 no stops on obverse 65	175	—
3528 Sixpence. — — — B *(Bristol)* below bust, similar die axis ↑↓			
1696 60	150	575
1696 no stops on obv. 75	175	625
1697 40	110	425
3529 Sixpence. — — — C *(Chester)* below bust, similar die axis ↑↓			
1697 100	250	750
3530 Sixpence. — — — E *(Exeter)* below bust, similar die axis ↑↓			
1697 40	100	425
3531 Sixpence. — — R. small crowns, similar die axis ↑↓			
1696 40	110	450
1697 30	80	350
1697 GVLIELMVS 50	125	—
1697 Arms of France/Ireland transposed.........................350	—	—

3532
Bristol Mint Sixpence, small crowns

	F	VF	EF
3532 Sixpence. — — — B *(Bristol)* below bust, similar die axis ↑↓			
1696 45	125	475
1696 no stops on O 75	175	575
1697 30	80	350
1697 B over E...40	90	375
3533 Sixpence. — — — C *(Chester)* below bust, similar die axis ↑↓			
1696 90	225	650
1697 40	95	400
1697 Irish shield at date.......................................300	900	—
1697 Plain edge 150	375	1100
3534 Sixpence. — — — E *(Exeter)* below bust, similar die axis ↑↓			
1697 40	100	425
1697 E over B...45	110	450
3535 Sixpence. — — — N *(Norwich)* below bust, similar die axis ↑↓			
1696 80	185	575
1697 GVLIEMVS 125	475	—
1697 45	110	425
3536 Sixpence. — — — y *(York)* below bust, similar die axis ↑↓			
1697 45	110	425
1697 Irish shield at date.......................................225	675	—

	3537		3538	

Second bust Sixpence

Sixpence, third bust,
later harp, large crowns

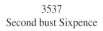

	F	VF	EF
	£	£	£
3537 Sixpence. Second dr. bust r. R. Similar die axis ↑↓			
1696 275		725	2250
1696 hair across breast *(as 3471)* ....*Extremely rare*			
1696 GVLELMVS 325		800	2500
1697 175		650	2000
1697 GVLIELMⱯS 225		700	2200
1697 G/I in GRA 200		675	2100
1697 GVLIEMVS 250		750	2250
1697 GR/DE in GRA...225		700	2250
3537A Sixpence. Third dr. bust, r. early harp, large crowns. E *(Exeter)* below bust			
1696 275		850	—
3537B Sixpence. — — — Y *(York)* below bust, similar die axis ↑↓			
1696 300		950	—
3538 Sixpence. Third dr. bust, r., R. Later harp, large crowns, similar die axis ↑↓			
1697 25		70	325
1697 GVLIEIMVS 35		80	350
1697 GⱯLIELMVS 40		90	375
1698 40		90	400
1699 90		225	675
1700 35		80	375
1701 70		175	575
3539 Sixpence.— — B *(Bristol)* below bust, similar die axis ↑↓			
1697 60		150	525
1697 IRA for FRA 80		200	—

3540
Chester Mint Sixpence, third bust

	F	VF	EF
3540 Sixpence.— — C *(Chester)* below bust, similar die axis ↑↓			
1697 90		225	650
3541 Sixpence.— — E *(Exeter)* below bust, similar die axis			
1697 90		225	675

3545   3547
York Mint Sixpence - Y provenance mark   Sixpence, roses on reverse

	F	VF	EF
	£	£	£
3542 Sixpence. Third dr. bust, r. R. Small crowns, similar die axis ↑↓			
1697 30	75	350
1697 D/F in DEI 80	200	625
1697 G/D in GRA 70	175	600
3543 Sixpence.— — C *(Chester)* below bust, similar die axis ↑↓			
1697 60	150	575
3544 Sixpence.— — E *(Exeter)* below bust, similar die axis ↑↓			
1697 50	125	475
3545 Sixpence.— — Y *(York)* below bust, similar die axis ↑↓			
1697 45	120	450
3546 Sixpence.— — R. Plumes in angles, similar die axis ↑↓			
1698 100	300	900
1699 100	300	900
3547 Sixpence.— R. Roses in angles, similar die axis ↑↓			
1699 120	325	1000
1699 GⱯLIELMVS 135	375	—

3548   3549
1700 Sixpence, plume below bust   1699 Groat or Fourpence

	F	VF	EF
3548 Sixpence.— plume below bust, R. Similar die axis ↑↓			
1700 2250	6500	17500
3549 Fourpence. Laur. and dr. bust r. R. 4 Crowned die axis ↑↓			
1697 ....*Unique*		
1698 28	60	190
1699 25	50	145
1700 25	50	165
1701 30	65	190
1702 20	45	90
3550 Threepence. Laur. and dr. bust r. R. 3 Crowned die axis ↑↓			
1698 20	40	110
1699 25	50	140
1700 22	45	130
1701 GBA for GRA 24	45	150
1701 small lettering 20	40	110
1701 large lettering 20	40	110

	F	VF	EF
	£	£	£
3551 Twopence. Laur. and dr. bust r. ℞. Crown to edge of coin, large figure 2 die axis ↑↓			
1698 25		50	135
3551A Twopence. Laur. and dr. bust r. ℞ Crown within inner circle of legend, smaller figure 2, die axis ↑↓			
1698 25		45	125
1699 18		30	95
1700 18		30	95
1701 18		30	95
3552 Penny. Laur. and dr. bust r. ℞. 1 Crowned die axis ↑↓			
1698 25		45	135
1698 IRA for FRA error 25		45	125
1698 HI.BREX error 25		45	125
1699 40		80	225
1700 35		70	165
1701 25		45	120

3553 - 1701 Maundy Set

3553 Maundy Set. The four denominations. Uniform dates

	F	VF	EF
1698 125		300	775
1699 175		400	925
1700 165		375	825
1701 125		300	75

COPPER

3554
Halfpenny

	F	VF	EF
	£	£	£

3554 Halfpenny. First issue. Laur. and cuir. bust r. ℞. Britannia with r. hand raised die axis ↑↓

1695	...45	210	1150
1695 BRITANNIA error	...200	—	—
1695 no stop on rev.	...60	275	—
1695 no stops on obv.	...60	275	—
1696	...35	175	1000
1696 GVLIEMVS, no rev. stop	...300	—	—
1696 TERTVS error	...275	—	—
1697	...35	175	950
1697 all stops omitted	...225	—	—
1697 I/E in TERTIVS	...225	—	—
1697 GVLILMVS, no rev. stop	...300	—	—
1697 no stop after TERTIVS	...50	275	—
1698	...45	210	1150

3555 Halfpenny. Second issue. Laur. and cuir. bust r. ℞. Britannia, date in legend die axis ↑↓

1698 Stop after date	...35	200	1050
1699 no stop after date	...30	165	1000
1699 BRITANNIA error	...225	—	—
1699 GVLIEMVS error	...225	—	—
1699 BRITAN IA error	...225	—	—

3556

3556 Halfpenny. Third issue. Laur. and cuir. bust r. ℞. Britannia, date in exergue, die axis ↑↓

1699	...35	175	950
1699 stop after date	...225	—	-
1699 BRITANNIA error	...100	380	—
1699 GVILELMVS error	...275	—	—
1699 TERTVS error	...275	—	—

	F	VF	EF
	£	£	£
1699 — no rev. stop	150	—	—
1699 no stops on obv.	85	380	—
1699 no stop after GVLIELMVS	85	325	—
1700	35	175	950
1700 no stops on obv.	100	350	—
1700 no stop after GVLIELMVS	100	350	—
1700 BRITANNIA error	40	175	950
1700 — no stop after	45	195	1000
1700 GVLIELMS	100	350	—
1700 GVLIEEMVS	65	250	1200
1700 GVLIEEMVS	65	250	1200
1700 TER TIVS	45	195	1000
1700 I/V in TERTIVS	225	—	—
1701	40	175	950
1701 BRITANNIA	50	225	1050
1701 — no stops on obv.	225	—	—
1701 — inverted A's for V's	60	250	1050

3557	3558
1696 Farthing date in exergue	1699 Farthing date in legend

3557 Farthing. First issue Laur. and cuir. bust r. R. Britannia l. die axis ↑↓

	F	VF	EF
1695	40	250	950
1695 GVLIELMV error	200	—	—
1696	35	210	900
1697	30	175	825
1697 GVLIELMS error	250	—	—
1697 TERTIV error	250	—	—
1698	200	625	—
1698 B/G on rev.	325	—	—
1699	35	240	900
1699 GVLILEMVS•	175	450	—
1700	30	155	775
1700 RRITANNIA	225	—	—

3558 Farthing. Second issue. Laur. and cuir. bust r. R. Britannia date at end
of legend die axis ↑↓

	F	VF	EF
1698 Stop after date	45	275	1000
1699 no stop after date	50	300	1050
1699 no stop after GVLIELMVS	125	—	—
1699 — No stop before or after			*Extremely rare*
1699 BRITANNIA	225	—	—
1699 BRITANNIA	225	—	—

Anne, the second daughter of James II, was born on 6th February 1665 and as a protestant succeeded to the throne on William III's death. Anne married Prince George of Denmark and produced 17 children, sadly none surviving to succeed to the throne. Anne died on 1st August 1714.

The Act of Union of 1707, which effected the unification of the ancient kingdoms of England and Scotland into a single realm, resulted in a change in the royal arms—on the Post-Union coinage the English lions and Scottish lion are emblazoned per pale on the top and bottom shields. After the Union the rose in the centre of the reverse of the gold coins is replaced by the Garter star.

Following a successful Anglo-Dutch expedition against Spain, bullion seized in Vigo Bay was sent to be minted into coin, and the coins made from this metal had the word VIGO placed below the Queen's bust. The elephant and castle provenance mark continues on some guineas in the Post-Union period.

Engravers and designers: Samuel Bull (d.c1720), Joseph Cave (d.c1760), James Clerk, John Croker (1670-1741), Godfrey Kneller (1646-1723)

GOLD
PRE-UNION WITH SCOTLAND 1702-07

3560
1705 Pre-Union Five Guineas

The shields on the reverse are Pre-Union type.

	F £	VF £	EF £
3560 Five Guineas. Dr. bust l, regnal year on edge in words (e.g. 1705 = QVARTO) die axis ↑↓			
1705 QVARTO	15000	40000	200000
1706 QVINTO	13500	35000	175000
3561 Five Guineas. Similar VIGO below bust, die axis ↑↓			
1703 (Three varieties) SECVNDO	65000	175000	650000

3562
1705 Pre-Union Guinea

3563
1703 VIGO Guinea

	F £	VF £	EF £
3562 Guinea. Dr. bust l. R. Crowned cruciform shields sceptres in angles die axis ↑↓			
1702	2250	6500	22500
1702 plain edge proof £40000			
1705	2500	7500	25000
1706	2500	7500	25000
1707	2400	7000	24000
3563 Guinea. Similar with VIGO below bust, die axis ↑↓			
1703	25000	65000	150000

3564
Pre-Union Half-Guinea

3565
VIGO Half-Guinea

3564 Half-Guinea. Dr bust l. R. Crowned cruciform shields sceptres in angles die axis ↑↓			
1702	1750	5250	16500
1705	1500	4750	15000
3565 Half-Guinea. Similar with VIGO below bust			
1703	13500	42500	90000

POST UNION WITH SCOTLAND 1707-14

3566
1706 Post-Union Five Guineas

The shields on the reverse are changed to Post-Union type die axis ↑↓

3566 Five Guineas. Dr. bust l., regnal year on edge in words			
1706 QVINTO	9500	22500	110000

3567
1709 - Narrow shields

3568
1711 - Broad shields

	F £	VF £	EF £
3567 **Five Guineas.** Similar R. Narrower shields, tall narrow crowns, larger rev. lettering, die axis ↑↓			
1709 OCTAVO	10000	24000	120000
3568 **Five Guineas.** New bust l. R. Broader shields edge inscribed die axis ↑↓			
1711 DECIMO	10000	24000	120000
1713 DVODECIMO	11000	25000	125000
1714/3 D. TERTIO	12000	27500	130000
1714 D. TERTIO	11000	25000	125000

3569
1713 Two Guineas

3569 **Two Guineas.** Dr. bust l.R. Crowned cruciform shields sceptres in angles edge milled die axis ↑↓			
1709	2500	10000	42500
1711	2250	9000	40000
1713	2500	10000	42500
1714/3	2750	11000	45000
3570 **Guinea.** First dr. bust l. R. Crowned cruciform shields sceptres in angles edge milled die axis ↑↓			
1707	1500	3750	17500
1708	1500	3750	17500

3571
1708 Guinea, first bust,
elephant and castle below

3574
1713 Guinea, third bust

3571 Guinea. First dr. bust l. elephant and castle below, R. Similar die axis ↑↓

1707		3750	11000	30000
1708				*Extremely rare*

3572 Guinea. Second* dr. bust l. R. Similar die axis ↑↓

1707		1500	3750	17500
1708		1300	3250	16000
1709		1300	3250	16000

3573 Guinea. Second bust elephant and castle below R. Similar die axis ↑↓

1708		4000	12500	35000
1709	1	3250	10000	25000

3574 Guinea. Third* dr. bust l. R. Similar die axis ↑↓

1710		1250	3000	15500
1711		1250	3000	15500
1712		1250	3000	15500
1713/1		1350	3250	16000
1713		1100	2750	15000
1714		1100	2750	15000
1714 GRATIΛ		1350	3250	16000

3575
1710 Half-Guinea

3575 Half-Guinea. Dr. bust l. R. Crowned cruciform shields, sceptres in angles,
edge milled die axis ↑↓

1707		850	2500	8000
1708		875	2750	8250
1709		875	2750	8250
1710		750	2000	7250
1711		800	2250	7500
1712		875	2750	8250
1713		800	2250	7500
1714		800	2250	7500

* There is a small difference between the 2nd and 3rd busts in the facial profile and eye.

SILVER

PRE UNION WITH SCOTLAND

3576
1703 VIGO Crown

The shields on the reverse are Pre-Union type.

	F	VF	EF
	£	£	£

3576   Crown. VIGO below dr. bust, l., regnal year on edge in words (e.g. 1703 = TERTIO)
   die axis↑↓
   1703 TERTIO 650   1750   13500

3577   3578
1705 Crown, plumes on reverse   1707 Pre-Union crown, roses and plumes

3577   Crown. Dr bust l. ℞. Plumes in angles, die axis ↑↓
   1705 QVINTO 850   2750   17500
3578   Crown. ℞. Similar Crowned cruciform shields Roses and plumes in angles die axis ↑↓
   1706 QVINTO 400   1200   6250
   1707 SEXTO 350   900   5250

3579
1703 Halfcrown, plain below bust

	F	VF	EF
	£	£	£

3579   Halfcrown. Dr. bust l. R. Similar Regnal year on edge in words die axis ↑↓

1703 TERTIO 750   2250   9500

3580
1703 VIGO Halfcrown

3580   Halfcrown. Similar VIGO below bust, die axis ↑↓

1703 TERTIO 175   575   4250

3581
Halfcrown, plumes on reverse

3581   Halfcrown. Dr. bust l. R. Plumes in angles, similar die axis ↑↓

1704 TERTIO 225   850   5000
1705 QVINTO 200   750   4500

3582
Halfcrown, Pre-Union,
roses and plumes

3583
Shilling

	F	VF	EF
	£	£	£

3582 Halfcrown. Dr. bust l. R. Roses and plumes in angles, similar die axis ↑↓
1706   QVINTO..175   475   3000
1707 SEXTO 150   425   2750

First bust   **Second bust**

3583 Shilling. First dr. bust l. R. Similar die axis↑↓
1702 120   375   2250
3584 Shilling. Similar R. Plumes in angles, die axis ↑↓
1702 125   425   2500
3585 Shilling. First dr. bust VIGO below, die axis ↑↓
1702 120   375   2250
1702 :ANNA...225   625   3000

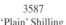

3586
1703 VIGO Shilling

3587
'Plain' Shilling

3586 Shilling. Second dr. bust, l. VIGO below R. Similar, die axis ↑↓
1703 110   350   2000
3587 Shilling. Similar R. Crowned cruciform shields, angles plain, die axis ↑↓
1704 750   2500   —
1705 250   750   3500
3588 Shilling. Second dr. bust l. R. Plumes in angles die axis ↑↓
1704 175   525   2750
1705 125   425   2500

	F	VF	EF
	£	£	£

3589 Shilling. Second dr. bust l. R. Roses and plumes in angles die axis ↑↓

1705	125	425	2500
1707	175	525	2750

3590 Sixpence. Dr. bust l. VIGO below dr. bust, l. die axis ↑↓

1703	40	150	675

3591 Sixpence. Dr bust l., R. Angles plain, die axis ↑↓

1705	65	225	900

3592 Sixpence. Similar R. Early shields, plumes in angles, die axis ↑↓

1705	50	175	750

3593
1705 Plumes Sixpence

Early Shield

Late Shield

3593 Sixpence. Similar R. Late shields, plumes in angles, die axis ↑↓

1705	60	185	800

3594 Sixpence. Similar R. Crowned cruciform shields Roses and plumes in angles die axis ↑↓

1705	60	185	800
1707	50	175	750

3595
Groat or fourpence, first bust

3595C
Groat or Fourpence, second bust

3595 Fourpence. First dr. bust l. small face, curls at back of head point downwards.
R Small crown above the figure 4 die axis ↑↓

1703	20	50	150
1704	15	30	75

3595A Fourpence. Second dr. bust l. larger face, curls at back of head point upwards die axis ↑↓

1705	40	95	200
1706	15	30	85
1708	18	38	95
1709	15	40	100
1710	12	25	70

3595B –Fourpence. Similar R Large crown with pearls on arch, larger serifs on the
figure 4 die axis ↑↓

1710	12	25	75
1713	15	30	80

3595C Fourpence. Second dr. bust l., but with re-engraved hair R. Crowned 4 die axis ↑↓

1710	12	25	75
1713	15	30	80

		F	VF	EF
		£	£	£

3596 Threepence. First dr. bust l., broader, tie riband pointing outwards. R. Crowned 3 die axis ↑↓

17037 above crown 18	45	130	1703 7 not above crown18	45	130

3596A Threepence. Second dr. bust l., taller and narrow, tie riband pointing inwards die axis ↑↓

1704 18	40	100	1706 15	35	105
1705 18	45	130			

3596B
Threepence, third bust

3596B Threepence. Third larger more finely engraved dr. bust l. R. Crowned 3, die axis ↑↓

1707	15	30	75
1708	15	35	105
1708/7	15	35	105
1709	15	35	105
1710	12	28	85
1713	15	35	100
1713 mule with 4d obv. die	20	42	150

3597 Twopence. First dr. bust l., as fourpence, R. Crown to edge of coin, small figure 2 die axis ↑↓

1703	22	50	105
1704	20	40	80
1704 No stops on obv.	22	50	110
1705	25	55	12
1706	20	40	95
1707	20	40	80

3597A Twopence. Second dr. bust l., as fourpence, R Crown within inner circle of legend, large figure 2 die axis ↑↓

1708	20	40	85
1709	25	50	115
1710	18	35	80
1713	20	40	85

3598 Penny. Dr. bust l. R. Crowned 1 die axis ↑↓

1703	25	50	125
1705	22	45	105
1706	22	45	105
1708	20	30	45
1709	20	40	90
1710	60	120	230
1713/0	30	55	135

3599
1713 Maundy Set

3599 Maundy Set. The four denominations. Uniform dates

1703	125	300	750
1705	150	300	750
1706	125	250	650
1708	300	450	950
1709	125	250	650
1710	150	300	750
1713	125	250	650

POST UNION WITH SCOTLAND, 1707-14

The shields on the reverse are changed to the Post-Union types. The Edinburgh coins have been included here as they are now coins of Great Britain.

3600 Crown. Second dr. bust, l. E (Edinburgh) below, R. Crowned cruciform shields regnal
year on edge in words, die axis ↑↓ (e.g. 1708 = SEPTIMO)

1707 SEXTO	250	650	4500
1707 SEPTIMO	2000	—	—
1708 SEPTIMO	300	800	5500
1708/7 SEPTIMO	325	825	5750

3601
Crown, second bust, plain reverse

3601 Crown. Second dr. bust l. R. Crowned cruciform shields, angles plain die axis ↑↓

1707 SEPTIMO	275	750	5250
1708 SEPTIMO	275	750	5250

3602 Crown. Similar R. Plumes in angles, die axis ↑↓

1708	SEPTIMO..300	800	5500
1708 — BR for BRI	....*Extremely rare*		

3603
1713 Crown, third bust, roses and plumes

	F £	VF £	EF £
3603 Crown. Third dr. bust. l. R. Roses and plumes			
1713 DVODECIMO 275		750	5250

3604
1708 Halfcrown, Post-Union

3604 Halfcrown. Dr. bust R. Plain, regnal year on edge in words (e.g. 1709 = OCTAVO), die axis ↑↓

	F	VF	EF
1707 SEPTIMO 125		375	2250
1707 no stops on reverse 200		750	—
1708 SEPTIMO 125		375	2250
1709 OCTAVO 125		375	2250
1713 DVODECIMO 140		425	2500

3605

3605 Halfcrown. Dr. bust E below R. Crowned cruciform shields die axis ↑↓

	F	VF	EF
1707 SEXTO 125		375	2250
1707 SEPTIMO 450		1750	—
1708 SEPTIMO 135		400	2500
1709 OCTAVO 350		1250	—

3606	3607
1708 Halfcrown, plumes on reverse	1714 Halfcrown, roses and plumes

	F £	VF £	EF £
3606 Halfcrown. Similar R. Plumes in angles, die axis ↑↓			
1708 SEPTIMO	140	425	2500
3607 Halfcrown. Similar R. Roses and plumes in angles die axis ↑↓			
1710 NONO	140	425	2500
1712 UNDECIMO	125	375	2250
1713 DVODECIMO	135	400	2400
1714 D. TERTIO	135	400	2400
1714/3 D. TERTIO	175	475	2750

3608	3609
1707 Edinburgh Mint Shilling, second bust	1708 E* Shilling

	F	VF	EF
3608 Shilling. Second dr. bust, l. E *(Edinburgh)* below, R. Crowned cruciform shields die axis ↑↓			
1707	135	450	2250
1707 no stops on reverse	375	950	—
1707 Plain edge proof *FDC* £15000			
1708	225	675	3000
3609 Shilling. Similar E* *(Edinburgh)* below bust die axis ↑↓			
1707	225	675	3000
1708	175	575	2750
1708/7	625	—	—
1708 no rays to garter star	750	—	—
3609A Shilling. Similar E* *(Edinburgh)* local dies die axis ↑↓			
1707	525	1750	—
1708	575	2000	9500

Third bust   **Fourth bust**

3610
Shilling, third bust

3611
Shilling, plumes on reverse

	F	VF	EF
	£	£	£
3610 Shilling Third dr. bust. l. R. Crowned cruciform shields, angles Plain, die axis ↑↓			
1707	50	175	850
1708	40	150	675
1709	40	150	675
1711	125	375	1750
3611 Shilling. Third dr. bust. l. R. Plumes in angles die axis ↑↓			
1707	110	350	1350
1708	100	325	1250
3612 Shilling. Third dr. bust. E below R. angles plain die axis ↑↓			
1707	100	325	1250
1708	135	450	2000
1708/7	175	575	—
3613 Shilling. Second dr. bust l. R. Roses and plumes, die axis ↑↓			
1708	135	450	2000

3614
1708 Shilling, roses and plumes

3614 Shilling. Third dr. bust l. R. Crowned cruciform shields Roses and plumes die axis ↑↓			
1708	125	350	1500
1710	100	325	1250

3615	3620	3623
Edinburgh bust – E* Shilling	Edinburgh Mint Sixpence	1707 Sixpence, plumes on reverse

	F £	VF £	EF £
3615 Shilling. 'Edinburgh' bust, E* below, R. Crowned cruciform shields die axis ↑↓			
1707 750	—	—	
1708 225	750	2500	
1709 225	750	2500	
3616 Shilling. — E below, R. Similar die axis ↑↓			
1709 525	1750	—	
3617 Shilling. Fourth dr. bust. l. R. Roses and plumes die axis ↑↓			
1710 125	375	1750	
1710 plain edge proof *FDC* ....*Extremely rare*			
1712 100	300	1250	
1713/2 125	350	1500	
1714ˈ 100	300	1250	
1714/3 125	375	1750	
3618 Shilling. Similar, R. angles plain, die axis ↑↓			
1711 45	150	675	
1711 plain edge proof *FDC* ....*Extremely rare*			
3619 Sixpence. Normal dr. bust. l. R. angles plain die axis ↑↓			
1707 40	135	525	
1707 BR. FRA error 475	—	—	
1708 40	135	525	
1711 35	100	375	
1711 Large Lis 35	110	400	
3620 Sixpence. Normal dr. bust E *(Edinburgh)* below R. Similar die axis ↑↓			
1707 45	140	625	
1707 Proof *FDC* £6500			
1708/7 75	225	850	
1708 60	185	725	
3621 Sixpence. Normal dr. bust E* *(Edinburgh)* below, R. Similar die axis ↑↓			
1708 60	185	725	
1708/7 70	200	800	
3622 Sixpence. 'Edinburgh' bust, l. E* below, R. Similar die axis ↑↓			
1708 75	225	850	
3623 Sixpence. Normal dr. bust. l. R. Plumes in angles die axis ↑↓			
1707 45	140	575	
1708 50	175	675	
3624 Sixpence. Similar R. Roses and plumes in angles, die axis ↑↓			
1710 60	185	750	

COPPER

3625
1714 Pattern Farthing

3625 Farthing. Dr. bust l. R. Britannia
1714 pattern only, die axis ↑↓ 325   650   1350

GEORGE I, 1714-27

George I was born on 28th May 1660 son of Ernest, Elector of Hanover and Sophia, grandaughter of James I, and inherited the English Throne as Parliament considered him a better alternative than James Edward Stuart – Anne's half-brother. He was, however, thoroughly German, did not want to learn English and spent over half his reign in Germany. He brought two mistresses with him to England while his wife ironically languished in a German prison on a charge of adultery. His reign created a government that could run independently of the King. The office of Prime Minister was created in 1721. He also kept England out of war for his entire reign, and he died on 11th June 1727.

The coins of the first of the Hanoverian kings have the arms of the Duchy of Brunswick and Luneberg on one of the four shields, the object in the centre of the shield being the Crown of Charlemagne. The King's German titles also appear, in abbreviated form, and name him 'Duke of Brunswick and Luneberg. Arch-treasurer of the Holy Roman Empire, and Elector', and on the Guinea of 1714, 'Prince Elector'. A Quarter-Guinea was struck for the first time in 1718, but it was of an inconvenient size, and the issue was discontinued. The elephant and castle provenance mark continues on some guineas and half-guineas, but today are rarely seen.

Silver coined from bullion supplied to the mint by the South Sea Company in 1723 shows the Company's initials S.S.C.; similarly Welsh Copper Company bullion has the letters W.C.C. below the King's bust; and plumes and an interlinked CC in the reverse angles. Roses and plumes together on the reverse indicate silver supplied by the Company for Smelting Pit Coale and Sea Coale.

Engravers and Designers: Samuel Bull (d.c.1720), John Croker (1670-1741), John Rudulf Ochs Snr, (1673-c.1748), Norbert Roettier (b.1665)

Prime Minister: Sir Robert Walpole (1676 – 1745) –Whig, 1721-42

GOLD

3626
1717 Five Guineas

	F £	VF £	EF £
3626 Five Guineas. Laur. head r. regnal year on edge in words (e.g. 1717 = TERTIO) die axis ↑↓			
1716 SECVNDO	11000	25000	125000
1717 TERTIO	12500	30000	140000
1717 Variety O for D on edge exits			
1720 SEXTO	12500	30000	140000
1726 D. TERTIO	11000	25000	125000
1726 Variety И for N on edge exists			

3627
Two Guineas

| | F | VF | EF |
	£	£	£

3627 Two Guineas. Laur. head r. R. Crowned cruciform shields, sceptres in angles,
   edge milled, die axis ↑↓

1717	2750	9000	37500
1720	2750	9000	37500
1720/17	3250	9500	40000
1726	2500	7500	35000

<table>
<tr><td>3628
1714 'Prince Elector' Guinea</td><td>3630
Third bust</td><td>3631
Fourth bust</td></tr>
</table>

3628 Guinea. First laur. head r. R. Legend ends ET PR . EL (Prince Elector), die axis ↑↓

| 1714 | ....2500 | 6500 | 20000 |

3629 Guinea. Second laur. head, r. tie with two ends, R. Crowned cruciform shields,
   sceptres in angles normal legend ↑↓

| 1715 | ....1100 | 2500 | 9500 |

3630 Guinea. Third laur. head, r. no hair below truncation R. Similar die axis ↑↓

| 1715 | ....1050 | 2400 | 9500 |
| 1716 | ....1250 | 2750 | 10000 |

	F £	VF £	EF £
3631 Guinea. Fourth laur. head, r. tie with loop at one end R. Similar die axis ↑↓			
1716 1100		2500	9500
1716 Arms of Hanover at date	4500	–	–
1717 1250		2750	10000
1718 4250		–	–
1718/7 4000		–	–
1719 1100		2500	9500
1719/6 1250		2750	10000
1720 large or small 20 in date 1100		2500	9500
1721 1250		2750	10000
1722 1100		2500	9500
1722/0 1250		2750	10000
1723 1350		3000	10500
3632 Guinea. Fourth Laur. head, elephant and castle below R. Similar die axis ↑↓			
1721 .... *Extremely rare*			
1722 .... *Extremely rare*			

3633
Guinea, fifth bust

	F £	VF £	EF £
3633 Guinea. Fifth (older) laur. head, r. tie with two ends R. Similar die axis ↑↓			
1723 1100		2500	8500
1723 II for H in TH............. 1250		2750	9500
1724 1100		2500	8500
1724 R/I in GEORGIVS............. 1250		2750	9500
1725 1100		2500	8500
1725 large 5 in date 1100		2500	8500
1726 1000		2250	7500
1727 1350		3250	10000
3634 Guinea. Fifth laur. head, elephant and castle below, die axis ↑↓			
1726 5000		13500	35000

3635 Half-Guinea. First laur. head r. R. Crowned cruciform shields, sceptres in angles die axis ↑↓

1715	900	2250	8500
1717	600	1600	5500
1718	575	1500	5250
1718/7	650	1650	5750
1719	575	1500	5250
1720	650	1650	5750
1721	....*Extremely rare*		
1722	600	1600	5500
1722/0	625	1650	5750
1723	625	1650	5750
1724	750	2000	6750

3636 Half-Guinea. First laur. head elephant and castle below, die axis ↑↓

1721	....*Extremely rare*

3637	3638
Half-Guinea, second bust	Quarter Guinea

3637 Half-Guinea. Second (older) laur. head r. R. Crowned cruciform shields, sceptres in angles die axis ↑↓

1725	550	1450	5000
1726	575	1500	5250
1727	575	1500	5250

3638 Quarter-Guinea. Laur. head R. Similar die axis ↑↓

1718	275	525	1250

SILVER

3639A
1726 Crown - small roses and plumes

	F £	VF £	EF £

3639 Crown. Laur and dr. bust r. R. Roses and plumes in angles, regnal year on edge in words
(e.g. 1716 = SECVNDO) die axis ↑↓

1716 SECVNDO	600	1500	6750
1718/6 QUINTO	800	1850	8000
1720/18 SEXTO	750	1750	7500

3639A Crown. Similar R. small roses and plumes in angles

1720 SEXTO	950	2500	9500
1726 D. TERTIO	750	1750	7500

3640   Crown. Similar R. SSC (South Sea Company) in angles, die axis ↑↓

1723 DECIMO	625	1600	6750

3641
1715 Pattern Halfcrown

3641 Halfcrown. Laur and dr. bust r. R. Angles plain (pattern only), die axis ↑↓
1715 *FDC* £17500

3642
Halfcrown, roses and plumes

	F	VF	EF
	£	£	£

3642 Halfcrown. — R. Roses and plumes in angles, regnal year on edge in words (e.g. 1717 = TIRTIO)

1715 SECVNDO 400	950	4750
1715 Edge wording out of order.........................575	1350	6000
1715 Plain edge 750	2250	—
1717 TIRTIO 400	950	4750
1720/17 SEXTO 400	950	4750
1720 SEXTO 450	1100	5000

3643
1723 SSC Halfcrown

3643 Halfcrown. Similar R. SSC in angles, die axis ↑↓

1723 DECIMO 400	950	4750

3644
1726 Halfcrown small roses and plumes

3644 Halfcrown. — R. Small roses and plumes, die axis ↑↓

1726 D. TERTIO 4750	13500	30000

3645
Shilling, roses and plumes

3646
1721 Shilling, plain reverse

	F	VF	EF
	£	£	£

3645 Shilling. First laur. and dr. bust. r. R. Roses and plumes in angles, die axis ↑↓

1715	85	300	1100
1716	175	475	1650
1717	110	350	1350
1718	80	275	1000
1719	175	475	1650
1720	110	350	1350
1720/18	150	525	1750
1721	135	450	1500
1721/0	110	350	1350
1721/19	135	450	1500
1721/18 plumes and roses error	375	1500	—
1722	110	350	1350
1723	125	375	1350

3646 Shilling. First laur. and dr. bust r. R. angles plain (i.e. no marks either side) die axis ↑↓

1720	60	175	750
1720 large O	60	175	750
1721	200	675	2000
1721 O of GEORGIVS over zero			

3647
1723 SSC Shilling, first bust

3647 Shilling. First laur. and dr. bust r. R. SSC in angles, die axis ↑↓

1723	35	100	525
1723 French Arms at date	135	525	1350
1723 C/SS in 3rd quarter	45	120	575

LETTERING VARIETIES:
B·RVN on Rev., Large N in BRVN and stop between E.T. after BRVN.

3649	3650
1727 Shilling, second bust	1726 WCC Shilling

	F	*VF*	*EF*
	£	£	£

3648 Shilling. Second dr. bust, r. bow to tie. R. Similar, die axis ↑↓

1723 60   175   750

3649 Shilling. Similar R. Roses and plumes in angles die axis ↑↓

1723 110   350   1350
1724 120   375   1500
1725 110   350   1350
1725 no stops on obv 120   375   1500
1725 no stops on rev 150   450   1750
1726 no stops on obv 750   2500   —
1727 575   1850   —
1727 no stops on obv 500   1750   5250
1727 no stops on rev 675   2250   —

3650 Shilling. Second laur. and dr. bust r. W.C.C. (Welsh Copper Company) below bust die axis ↑↓

1723 850   3000   9000
1724 850   3000   9000
1725 900   3250   9500
1726 900   3250   9500

3651 Sixpence. Laur. and dr. bust r. R. Roses and plumes in angles, die axis ↑↓

1717 110   350   1000
1717   Plain edge ....*Extremely rare*
1720/17 100   300   850

3652	3653
1723 SSC Sixpence	1726 Sixpence, small roses and plumes

3652 Sixpence. Laur. and dr. bust r. R. SSC in angles, die axis ↑↓

1723 25   95   400
1723 larger lettering 30   110   425

3653 Sixpence. Similar R. Small roses and plumes, die axis ↑↓

1726 85   275   800

	F £	VF £	EF £
3654 Fourpence. Laur. and dr. bust r. ℞. Crowned 4, die axis ↑↓			
1717 15		40	100
1721 15		40	100
1723 20		50	160
1727 22		55	160
3655 Threepence. Laur. and dr. bust r. ℞. Crowned 3, die axis ↑↓			
1717 20		45	95
1721 25		48	95
1723 20		55	160
1727 small lettering 20		50	150
3656 Twopence. Laur. and dr. bust r. ℞. Crowned 2, die axis ↑↓			
1717 12		32	65
1721 12		25	60
1723 15		40	110
1726 12		25	60
1727 small lettering 15		32	85
3657 Penny. Laur. and dr. bust r. ℞. Crowned 1, die axis ↑↓			
1716 12		32	65
1718 12		32	65
1720 12		32	65
1720 HIPEX error...20		85	150
1723 15		30	80
1725 12		32	65
1726 15		40	70
1727 BRI·FR 20		50	110

3658

3658 Maundy Set. As last four. Uniform dates	F £	VF £	EF £
1723 150		275	800
1727 125		250	700

COPPER

3659

	F £	VF £	EF £
3659 Halfpenny. 'Dump' issue obv. legend continuous over bust, plain edge, die axis ↑↓			
1717 40		250	800
1717 no stops on obv. 100		525	—
1718 30		225	725
1718 R/B on rev....................50		250	900
1718 no stops on obv. 150		500	—
1719 1000		—	—
1719 grained edge................1000		—	—

(1719 is an extremely rare date, perhaps only 2 or 3 known to exist of each type)

3660

	F £	VF £	EF £
3660 Halfpenny. Second issue, second obverse, plain left shoulder strap, less hair to the right of tie knot, R. Britannia plain edge, die axis ↑↓			
1719 40		210	900
1719 grained edge................1000		—	—
1720 30		175	825
1721 30		165	725
1721 stop after date 40		200	800
1721/0 40		200	8000
1722 30		155	700
1722 Ⅴ for V on obv. 100		500	—
1723 30		155	750
1723 Thin Flan............................*Extremely rar*			
1723 no stop on rev............100		525	—
1724 30		155	70
3660A Halfpenny. Second issue, second obverse, ornate shoulder straps, die axis ↑↓			
1719 40		195	900

3661

	F £	*VF* £	*EF* £
3661 Farthing. 'Dump' issue, Similar die axis ↑↓			
1717 200		675	1250
1718			*Unique*

3662

3662 Farthing. Second issue laur. and cuir. bust r. R. Britannia, date in ex. die axis ↑↓

1719 small letters..60		330	775
1719 no stop on rev...70		380	—
1719 large lettering on obv. 30		165	650
1719 — no stops on obv. 70		410	—
1719 — no stops on rev 90		450	—
1719 last A/I on rev...80		350	—
1720 30		165	600
1720 milled edge 150		500	1150
1720 obv. large letters..80		350	—
1721 25		135	650
1721/0 40		165	675
1721 stop after date 35		165	625
1722 30		155	625
1722 obv. large letters..40		210	725
1723 R/⋈ in REX...100		330	900
1723 30		165	600
1724 30		165	625

George II was born on 30th October 1683 and was raised in Hanover, but upon his succession to the throne as George I's only son, he adapted himself to English society. His passions were the military, music and his wife – Caroline of Anspach, though he despised his eldest son Frederick as his own father despised him. George declared war on Spain in 1739 and he was the last King to have personally led his troops at the battle of Dettingen on 17th June 1743. Upon his death on 25th October 1760 the throne passed to his grandson George as Frederick had already died.

Silver was coined only spasmodically by the Mint during this reign; and no copper was struck after 1754. Gold coins made from bullion supplied by the East India Company bear the Company's E.I.C. initials. Some of the treasure seized by Admiral Anson during his circumnavigation of the globe, 1740-4, and by other privateers, was made into coin, which had the word LIMA below the king's bust to celebrate the expedition's successful harassment of the Spanish Colonies in the New World. Hammered gold was finally demonetized in 1733.

Engravers and designers: John Croker (1670-1741), John Rudolf Ochs Snr (1673-1748) and jnr (1704-88), Johann Sigismund Tanner (c.1706-75)

Prime Ministers: Sir Robert Walpole (1676-1745) Whig, 1721-43; Spencer Compton (1673-1743) Whig 1742-3; Henry Pelham (c.1695-1754) Whig 1743-54; William Cavendish (1720-1764) Whig 1756-7; Thomas Pelham-Holles (1693-1768) Whig 1754-6; 1757-62

GOLD

3663A
1741 Five Guineas - revised shield

	F £	VF £	EF £
3663 Five Guineas. Young laur. head l. R. Crowned shield of arms, die axis ↑↓ regnal year on edge in words (e.g. 1729 = TERTIO)			
1729 TERTIO	9500	24000	110000
1729 Plain edge proof *FDC* £250000			
3663A Five Guineas. Similar R. Revised shield garnish die axis ↑↓			
1731 QVARTO	12000	27500	125000
1731 QVARTO proof *FDC* £300000			
1735 NONO	12000	27500	125000
1738 DVODECIMO	10000	25000	115000
1741/38 D. QVARTO	9000	24000	110000
1741 D. QVARTO	8500	22500	100000
3664 Five Guineas. Young laur. head, E.I.C. (East India Company) below, die axis ↑↓			
1729 TERTIO	8000	20000	95000

3665
1746 LIMA Five Guineas

	F	*VF*	*EF*
	£	£	£

3665 Five Guineas. Old laur. head, l. LIMA below, ↑↓
1746 D. NONO...8500   22500   100000
3666 Five Guineas. Old laur. head plain below, R. Crowned shield, edge inscribed die axis ↑↓
1748 V. SECVNDO 8500   22500   100000
1753 V. SEXTO 8500   22500   100000
3667 Two Guineas. Young laur. head l. R Crowned shield with rounded arches, die axis ↑↓
1733 Proof *FDC* £75000
1734/3 6500   17500   —

3667A
1735 Two Guineas - new reverse

3667A Two Guineas. – R. Crown with pointed arches, new type of shield garnishing die axis ↑↓
1735 2000   6500   22500
3667B Two Guineas. Repositioned legend on obverse R. Similar
1738* 1050   3000   9000
1739 1100   3250   9500

Beware recent forgeries.

3668
1740 Two Guineas - Intermediate head

	F	VF	EF
	£	£	£
3668 Two Guineas. Intermediate laur. head l. R. Crowned shield of arms die axis ↑↓			
1739* 1050		3000	9000
1740/39 1250		3750	11000
1740 1100		3250	9500
3669 Two Guineas. Old laur. head l. R. Crowned shield of arms die axis ↑↓			
1748 1750		5250	20000
1753 2500		7500	25000
3670 Guinea. First young laur. head, l. small lettering, die axis ↑↓			
1727 2250		6500	22500

3671
1727 Guinea - small reverse shield

3671 Guinea. Similar larger lettering, smaller shield, die axis ↑↓			
1727 2500		7000	24000
1728 2500		7000	24000
3672 Guinea. Second (narrower) young laur. head l. die axis ↑↓			
1729 Proof *FDC* £40000			
1730 1100		3250	10000
1731 950		3000	9000
1732 1100		3250	10000
3673 Guinea. Second young laur. head, E.I.C. below R. Crowned shield of arms die axis ↑↓			
1729 3750		10000	30000
1731 3250		9500	27500
1732 2500		8500	25000

Beware recent forgeries.

	F	VF	EF
	£	£	£

3674 Guinea. Second young laur. head l. larger lettering R. Crowned shield of arms die axis ↑↓

1732	1100	3250	10000
1733	950	2850	8500
1734	950	2850	8500
1735	1000	3000	9000
1736	1000	3000	9000
1737	1050	3250	9500
1738	1050	3250	9500

3675 Guinea. — — E.I.C. below, die axis ↑↓

| 1732 | ....2000 | 7500 | 20000 |

3676

Note: All 1739-45 Guineas read GEORGIUS

3676 Guinea. Intermediate laur. head l. r. Crowned shield of arms die axis ↑↓

1739	1000	3000	9000
1740	1050	3250	9500
1741/39	2000	7500	20000
1743	2000	7500	20000

3677 Guinea. Similar E.I.C. below, R. Similar die axis ↑↓

| 1739 | ....2250 | 8000 | 22500 |

3678 Guinea. Similar larger lettering on *obv.*, GEORGIUS die axis ↑↓

| 1745 (also exists with small S in date) ....1000 | 3000 | 9000 |

3678A
1746 Guinea - GEORGIVS legend

3679
LIMA below bust Guinea

3678AGuinea. Similar as last but reads GEORGIVS die axis ↑↓

| 1746 | ....1050 | 3250 | 9500 |

3679 Guinea. Intermediate laur. head LIMA below, GEORGIUS die .axis ↑↓

| 1745 | ....3500 | 9000 | 32500 |

3680
Old head Guinea

	F £	VF £	EF £
3680 Guinea. Old laur. head l. R. Crowned shield of arms die axis ↑↓			
1747	750	2000	7000
1748	750	2000	7000
1749	750	2000	7000
1750	750	2000	7000
1751	750	2000	7000
1752	750	2000	7000
1753	850	2250	7500
1755	850	2250	7500
1756	800	2100	7000
1758	750	2000	6750
1759	725	1850	6500
1760	725	1850	6500
3681 Half-Guinea. Young laur. head. l. R First shield of arms, die axis ↑↓			
1728	850	2100	8000
1728 Proof *FDC* £22500			
1729	950	2250	8500

3681A
1731 Half-Guinea - modified shield

3681A Half-Guinea. Young laur. head l. R. Modified garnished shield die axis ↑↓			
1730	850	2100	7500
1731	750	1650	6250
1732	750	1750	6500
1734	750	1650	6250
1736	800	1750	6500
1737	850	2000	7500
1738	750	1650	6250
1739	750	1650	6250
3682 Half-Guinea. Young laur. head l. E.I.C. below R. Similar die axis ↑↓			
1729	1200	3250	11000
1730	1350	3500	12500
1731			*Extremely rare*
1732			*Extremely rare*
1739			*Extremely rare*

3683A
Half-guinea - GEORGIVS legend

	F £	VF £	EF £
3683 Half-Guinea. Intermediate laur. head l. R. Similar die axis ↑↓			
1740	750	1750	7500
1743		*Extremely rare*	
1745	850	2000	7500
3683A Half-Guinea. Similar, but reads GEORGIVS, die axis ↑↓			
1746	600	1500	5500

3684	3685
LIMA Half-Guinea	Half-Guinea, old head

	F	VF	EF
3684 Half-Guinea. Intermediate laur. head LIMA below, die axis ↑↓			
1745	1350	3500	12500
3685 Half-Guinea. Old laur. head l. R. Similar die axis ↑↓			
1747	800	1850	7000
1748	675	1650	6000
1749	1250	2750	—
1750	750	1750	6500
1751	675	1650	6000
1751/0	800	1750	—
1752	575	1200	4750
1753	575	1200	4750
1755	525	1100	4500
1756	500	1000	4000
1758	575	1200	4750
1759	475	900	3750
1759/8	525	1000	4000
1760	500	1000	4000

SILVER

3686
Crown, young head

	F	*VF*	*EF*
	£	£	£

3686 Crown. Young laur. and dr. bust. l. R. Crowned cruciform shields Roses and plumes in angles, regnal year on edge in words (e.g. 1736 = NONO), die axis ↑↓

1732 SEXTO 450	1350	6000
1732 Proof, plain edge *FDC* £30000		
1734 SEPTIMO..475	1350	6000
1735 OCTAVO 425	1250	5750
1736 NONO..425	1250	5750

3687

3687 Crown. Similar R. Roses in angles die axis ↑↓

1739 DVODECIMO 400	1100	5250
1741 D. QVARTO 400	1100	5250

3688
Crown, old head

	F £	VF £	EF £
3688 **Crown.** Old laur. and dr. bust l. R. Crowned cruciform shields Roses in angles, die axis ↑↓			
1743 D. SEPTIMO	400	1200	5500
3689 **Crown.** — LIMA below, die axis ↑↓			
1746 D. NONO	425	1250	5750

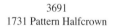

3690
Plain reverse

3691
1731 Pattern Halfcrown

3690 **Crown.** Old laur. and dr. bust l. R. angles Plain (i.e. no marks either side) die axis ↑↓

1746 Proof only, VICESIMO *FDC* £15000			
1750 V. QVARTO	475	1350	6250
1751 V. QVARTO	500	1450	6500

3691 **Halfcrown.** Young dr. bust l. R. angles plain (pattern only)

1731 *FDC* £12500

3692
1736 Halfcrown, roses and plumes

3693
1741 Halfcrown, roses on reverse

	F £	VF £	EF £
3692 Halfcrown. Young laur. and dr. bust l. ℞. Roses and plumes, regnal year on edge in words (e.g. 1732 = SEXTO), die axis ↑↓			
1731 QVINTO	175	475	2750
1732 SEXTO	175	475	2750
1734 SEPTIMO	225	525	3250
1735 OCTAVO	200	500	3000
1736 NONO	200	500	3000
3693 Halfcrown. Young laur. and dr. bust l. ℞. Roses in angles die axis ↑↓			
1739 DVODECIMO	165	425	2500
1741 D. QVARTO	165	425	2500
1741 Large *obv.* letters	200	500	3000
1741/39 D. QVARTO	175	475	2750
3694 Halfcrown. Old dr. bust. l. GEORGIUS ℞. Roses in angles die axis ↑↓			
1743 D. SEPTIMO	160	425	2400
1745 D. NONO	150	400	2250
1745/3 D. NONO	175	475	2750
3695 Halfcrown. Old laur. and dr. bust LIMA below die axis ↑↓			
1745 D. NONO	100	250	950
1745/3	135	400	1750
3695A Halfcrown. Old laur. and dr. bust as last LIMA below but reads GEORGIVS die axis ↑↓			
1746 D. NONO	90	225	900
1746/5 D. NONO	110	275	1250

3696
1751 Halfcrown

3696 Halfcrown. Old laur. and dr. bust l. ℞. Plain angles die axis ↑↓			
1746 proof only VICESIMO *FDC* £5250			
1750 V. QVARTO	225	575	3500
1751 V. QVARTO	250	625	3750

3697	3698	3699
1727 Plumes reverse	Shilling, young bust, small letters	Plain reverse

	F £	VF £	EF £
3697 Shilling. Young laur. dr. bust. l. R. Plumes in angles, die axis ↑↓			
1727	225	650	3500
1731	275	850	4250
3698 Shilling. Young laur. and dr. bust l. R. Roses and plumes in angles, die axis ↑↓			
1727	120	325	1750
1728	150	425	2500
1729	150	425	2500
1731	135	350	2250
1732	150	425	2500
3699 Shilling. Young laur. and dr. bust l. R. Plain, die axis ↑↓			
1728	135	350	2000

3700 - Shilling, larger lettering	3701 - Shilling, roses reverse

3700 Shilling. Similar larger lettering. R. Roses and plumes in angles die axis ↑↓			
1734	80	250	1350
1735	95	275	1500
1736	80	250	1350
1736/5	110	325	1750
1737	80	250	1350
1737 known with GR ΛTIΛ error			
1737 with 3/5 exists			
3701 Shilling. Young laur. and dr. bust l. R. Roses in angles die axis ↑↓			
1739 normal garter star	60	200	900
1739/7	100	275	1500
1739 smaller garter star	80	225	1250
1741	60	200	900
1741/39	100	275	1500

3702   3703
Shilling, old bust, roses   LIMA Shilling

	F	VF	EF
	£	£	£
3702 Shilling. Old laur. and dr. bust, l. R. Roses in angles die axis ↑↓			
1743 50	150	750
1743/1 90	225	1000
1745 75	200	950
1745/3 90	225	1000
1747 only known with GEORGIVS on obv 75	200	950
3703 Shilling. Old laur. and dr. bust LIMA below die axis ↑↓			
1745 40	135	675
1746 90	225	1000
1746/5 90	225	1000

N.B. In and after 1746 the 'U' was changed to 'V' on old Head Shillings.

3704
1758 Shilling

3704 Shilling. Old laur. and dr. bust R. plain angles die axis ↑↓
1746 Proof only *FDC* £2500

1750 60	150	800
1750/46 65	165	850
1750 Wide O..65	165	850
1751 135	375	2000
1758 also known with small 58 in date 20	60	275

3705
1728 Sixpence, young bust

3706
1728 Sixpence, plumeson reverse

| | F | VF | EF |
	£	£	£
3705 **Sixpence.** Young laur. and dr. bust. l. R. Angles plain, die axis ↑↓			
1728 50	150	575
1728 Proof *FDC* £3500			
3706 **Sixpence.** Similar R. Plumes in angles die axis ↑↓			
1728 45	145	550

3707
1728 Sixpence, roses and plumes

3707 **Sixpence.** Young laur. and dr. bust l. R. Roses and plumes in angles die axis ↑↓			
1728 35	125	425
1731 40	135	475
1732 40	135	475
1734 45	140	525
1735 45	140	525
1735/4 50	150	575
1736 50	175	600

3708
Sixpence, roses

3709
Sixpence, old bust, roses

3708 **Sixpence.** Young laur. and dr. bust l., R. Roses in angles, die axis ↑↓			
1739 35	130	475
1739 O/R in legend..40	135	500
1741 35	130	475
3709 **Sixpence.** Old laur. and dr. bust. l. R. Roses in angles die axis ↑↓			
1743 25	75	325
1745 25	75	325
1745/3 30	80	350

		F	VF	EF
		£	£	£

3710 Sixpence. Old laur. and dr. bust LIMA below bust R. angle plain die axis ↑↓

1745	45	140	525

3710A Sixpence. Similar as last but reads GEORGIVS die axis ↑↓

1746	25	80	350
1746/5	40	130	475

3711
Proof Sixpence

3711 Sixpence. Old laur. and dr. bust l. R. angles plain die axis ↑↓
1746 *proof only FDC* £1500

1750	30	80	375
1751	35	90	425
1757	15	30	140
1758	15	30	140
1758 ÐEI error	25	50	225
1758/7	20	40	175

3712 Fourpence. Young laur. and dr. bust l. R. Small dome-shaped crown
without pearls on arch, figure 4

1729	22	48	120
1731	20	45	110

3712A Fourpence. Similar R.Double arched crown with pearls, large figure 4, die axis ↑↓

1732	22	48	120
1735	22	48	125
1737	22	48	125
1739	20	45	110
1740	18	35	100
1743	35	80	250
1743/0	35	80	250
1746	15	30	85
1760	22	45	130

3713 Threepence. Young laur. and dr. bust l. R. Crowned 3, pearls on arch, die axis ↑↓

1729	18	38	90

3713A Threepence. Similar R. Ornate arch die axis ↑↓

1731 Smaller lettering	18	38	90
1731	18	38	90

3713B Threepence. Similar R. Double arched crown with pearls, die axis ↑↓

1732	18	38	85
1732 with stop over head	18	38	85
1735	18	38	90
1737	15	35	80
1739	15	30	80
1740	15	30	80
1743 Large lettering	15	30	80
1743 Small lettering	15	30	80

	F	VF	EF
	£	£	£
1743 — stop over head 18		35	85
1746 12		25	75
1746/3 14		30	75
1760 18		38	85

3714 Twopence. Young laur. and dr. bust l. R. Small crown and figure 2, die axis ↑↓

1729 15		25	70
1731 15		25	65

3714A Twopence. Young laur. and dr. bust l. R. Large crown and figure 2 die axis ↑↓

1732 15		25	70
1735 15		25	65
1737 15		25	70
1739 15		25	70
1740 22		35	90
1743 15		28	70
1743/0 15		28	70
1746 12		22	60
1756 12		25	50
1759 12		25	45
1760 18		30	75

3715 Penny. Young laur. and dr. bust l. head. R. Date over small crown and figure 1, die axis ↑↓

1729 12		25	70
1731 12		25	70

3715A Penny. Young laur. and dr. bust l. R. Large crown dividing date die axis ↑↓

1732 12		25	65
1735 15		30	60
1737 15		30	65
1739 12		25	60
1740 12		25	60
1743 10		22	60
1746 10		20	60
1746/3 12		32	65
1750 10		20	40
1752 10		20	40
1752/0 10		30	60
1753/2 10		25	45
1753 10		20	40
1754 10		25	45
1755 10		20	45
1756 10		20	45
1757 10		20	50
1757 GRATIA: 12		35	70
1758 10		20	45
1759 10		20	50
1760 18		30	75

3716

	F £	VF £	EF £
3716 Maundy Set. The four denominations. Uniform dates			
1729	80	225	500
1731	80	225	500
1732	80	200	450
1735	80	200	450
1737	80	200	450
1739	75	165	425
1740	75	165	425
1743	100	250	550
1746	70	150	400
1760	85	225	500

COPPER

3717

3717 Halfpenny. Young laur. and cuir. bust l. R. Britannia, date in ex. die axis ↑↓

1729	15	100	380
1729 rev. no stop	20	110	410
1730	10	100	360
1730 GEOGIVS error	20	150	470
1730 stop after date	20	110	380
1730 no stop after REX on obv.	25	160	470
1731	10	90	360
1731 rev. no stop	20	150	440
1732	10	100	360
1732 rev. no stop	20	150	440
1733	10	90	370
1734	10	90	370
1734 R/O on obv	20	145	450
1734/3	30	210	—
1734 no stops on obv.	30	210	—
1735	10	90	370
1736	15	110	400

	F	VF	EF
	£	£	£
1736/0	20	130	450
1737	15	100	400
1738	10	75	370
1738 V/S on obv.	20	145	450
1739	10	75	370

3718 Halfpenny. Old laur. and cuir. bust l., GEORGIUS R. Britannia, date in ex. die axis ↑↓

1740	10	70	300
1742	10	70	300
1742/0	20	130	425
1743	10	70	300
1744	10	70	300
1745	10	70	300

3719
1746 Halfpenny

3719 Halfpenny. Old laur. and cuir. bust l. GEORGIVS, R. Britannia, date in ex. die axis ↑↓

1746	10	65	300
1747	10	70	320
1748	10	70	320
1749	10	70	300
1750	10	70	320
1751	10	65	300
1752	10	65	300
1753	10	65	300
1754	10	70	320

3720

3720 Farthing. Young laur. and cuir. bust l. R. Britannia, date in ex. die axis ↑↓

1730	10	70	330
1731	10	70	330
1732	15	75	365
1732/1	20	110	385
1733	10	70	330
1734	15	75	365
1734 no stop on obv.	30	120	385
1735	10	65	300
1735 3 over 5	20	130	425
1736	10	70	330
1736 triple tie ribands	30	130	425
1737 small date	10	65	300
1737 large date	15	80	375
1739	10	65	300
1739/5	25	100	300

3721 Farthing. Old laur. and cuir. bust. GEORGIUS R. Britannia, date in ex. die axis ↑↓

1741	15	80	300
1744	10	65	275

3722 Farthing. Similar R. Britannia, date in ex. die axis ↑↓

1746	8	65	240
1746 V over U	90	250	—
1749	15	75	275
1750	15	75	275
1754	5	45	135
1754/0	25	130	300

George III, grandson of George II, was born on 4th June 1738. He married Charlotte of Mecklenburg and they had nine sons and six daughters. The French Revolution and the American War of Independence both happened in his long reign, the longest yet of any King. The naval battle of Trafalgar and the Battle of Waterloo also took place during his reign. Later in his reign, he was affected by what seems to be the mental disease porphyria, and the future George IV was appointed as regent. George III died at Windsor Castle on 29th January 1820.

During the second half of the 18th century very little silver or copper was minted. In 1797 Matthew Boulton's 'cartwheels', the first copper Pennies and Twopences, demonstrated the improvement gleaned from the application of steam power to the coining press.

During the Napoleonic Wars bank notes came into general use when the issue of Guineas was stopped between 1799 and 1813, but gold 7s. pieces, Third-Guineas; were minted to relieve the shortage of smaller money. As an emergency measure Spanish 'Dollars' were put into circulation for a short period after being countermarked, and in 1804 Spanish Eight Reales were overstruck and issued as Bank of England Dollars.

The transition to a 'token' silver coinage began in 1811 when the Bank of England had 3s and 1s. 6d. tokens made for general circulation. Private issues of token money in the years 1788-95 and 1811-15 helped to alleviate the shortage of regal coinage. A change over to a gold standard and a regular 'token' silver coinage came in 1816 when the Mint, which was moved from its old quarters in the Tower of London to a new site on Tower Hill, began a complete re-coinage. The Guinea was replaced by a 20s. Sovereign, and silver coins were made which had an intrinsic value lower than their face value. The St. George design used on the Sovereign and Crown was the work of Benedetto Pistrucci.

Engravers and Designers:– Conrad Heinrich Kuchler (c.1740-1810), Nathaniel Marchant (1739-1816), John Rudulf Ochs Jnr. (1704-88), Lewis Pingo (1743-1830), Thomas Pingo (d.1776) Benedetto Pistrucci (1783-1855), Johann Sigismond Tanner (c.1706-75), Thomas Wyon (1792-1817), William Wyon (1795-1851), Richard Yeo (d.1779)

GOLD

EARLY COINAGES

3723
1770 Pattern Five Guineas

3723 Five Guineas. Pattern only, young long haired bust r. R. crowned shield of arms, die axis ↑↑ (en medaille)

1770 *EF* £247500   *FDC* £495000
1773 *EF* £247500   *FDC* £495000

3723A Five Guineas. Pattern only, young bust right, hair extends under bust similar
1777 *EF* £247500   *FDC* £478500

3724
1768 Pattern Two Guineas

3724A
1777 Pattern Two Guineas

	F	VF	EF
	£	£	£

3724 Two Guineas. Pattern only, young long haired bust r. R. crowned shield of arms, die axis ↑↑ (en medaille)

1768   *EF* £93500   *FDC* £154000
1773   *EF* £93500   *FDC* £154000

3724A Two Guineas. Pattern only, thinner young bust right, hair extends under bust similar

1777   *EF* £93500   *FDC* £143000

There are six different bust varieties for 3723 and 3724, for further details see Wilson & Rasmussen

3725   3726
1761 Guinea first head, two leaf wreath   1763 Guinea second head

3725 Guinea. First laur. head r., 1761 (varieties with two or three leaves at top of wreath).

R. Crowned shield of arms die axis ↑↓ 2250	6500	15000

3726 Guinea. Second laur. head r. R. Crowned shield of arms die axis ↑↓

	F	VF	EF
1763 1300	4500	11500
1764 1300	4000	11000
1764 no stop over head..2250	5250	11500

Plain edge patterns exist of 1761 Guinea by John Tanner and 1763 by Richard Yeo. Both are extremely rare and trade too infrequently to price.

3727	3728	3729
Guinea, third head	Guinea, fourth head	Guinea, fifth head, 'spade' type

	F £	VF £	EF £
3727 Guinea. Third laur. head r. R. Crowned shield of arms die axis ↑↓			
1765 ...650		950	2500
1766 ...650		975	2650
1767 ...650		1200	3200
1768 ...525		950	2350
1769 ...650		950	2750
1770 ...1400		2850	8000
1771 ...650		950	2250
1772 ...650		950	2350
1773 ...650		950	2250
1773 first 7 over 1...650		1250	3000
3728 Guinea. Fourth laur. head r. Crowned shield of arms die axis ↑↓			
1774 ...600		850	1500
1774 Proof *FDC* £15000			
1775 ...600		850	1600
1776 ...600		875	2250
1777 ...600		850	1750
1778 ...600		1100	2750
1778 E over C in REX *exists*			
1779 ...600		850	1850
1779 9/7 error *exists*			
1781 ...600		850	1600
1782 ...600		850	1600
1783 ...600		850	1600
1784 ...600		850	1500
1785 ...600		850	1500
1786 ...600		850	1500
3729 Guinea. Fifth laur. head r. R. 'Spade'-shaped shield, die axis ↑↑			
1787 ...500		750	1300
1787 Proof *FDC* £14000			
1788 ...500		750	1300
1788 second 8/7 *exists*			
1789 ...500		750	1300
1790 ...500		750	1300
1791 ...500		750	1300
1792 ...500		750	1300
1793 ...500		750	1300
1794 ...500		750	1300
1795 ...500		750	1300
1796 ...500		750	1500
1797 ...500		750	1350

	F	VF	EF
	£	£	£
1798* 500		750	1100
1798/2 error *exists*			
1798/7 500		750	1700
1799 500		850	2500

3730	3731
1813 Guinea "Military type"	Half-Guinea, first head

3730 **Guinea.** Sixth laur. head. r. R. Shield in Garter, known as the Military guinea, die axis ↑↑

1813 1500	3200	6000

3731 Half-Guinea. First laur. head r. R. Crowned shield of arms die axis ↑↓

1762 750	2000	5500
1763 850	2650	6500

3732	3733
1764 Half-Guinea, second head	Half-Guinea, third head

3732 Half-Guinea. Second laur. head r. R. Crowned shield of arms die axis ↑↓

1764 400	700	1800
1765 600	1600	4000
1766 475	800	2000
1768 475	800	2000
1769 425	850	2100
1772 ....*Extremely rare*		
1773 450	850	2250
1774 500	900	2500
1775 500	1100	3500

3733 Half-Guinea Third laur. head (less fine style) r. R. Crowned shield of arms die axis ↑↓

1774 1950	4000	11000
1775 1375	3000	8500

* Beware counterfeits
Note: All figure 1's are Roman style I's for Guineas from 1781-1799.

| | 3734 | | 3735 | |
| | Half-Guinea, fourth head | | Half-Guinea, fifth head | |

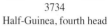

	F	VF	EF
	£	£	£

3734 Half-Guinea Fourth laur. head r. R. Crowned shield of arms die axis ↑↓

1775	350	600	1400
1775 Proof *FDC* £12500			
1776	400	650	1800
1777	350	600	1450
1778	350	600	1450
1779	350	600	1450
1781	350	600	1450
1783	600	1750	3950
1784	350	600	1450
1785	350	600	1450
1786	350	600	1450

3735 Half-Guinea Fifth laur. head. r. R. 'Spade' shaped shield, date below, die axis ↑↑

1787	350	500	950
1787 Proof *FDC* £8500			
1788	350	500	1050
1789	350	500	1100
1790	350	500	1050
1791	350	500	1050
1792	1500	4000	—
1793	350	500	1000
1794	350	500	1100
1795	350	525	1150
1796	350	500	1050
1797	350	500	1050
1798	350	500	950
1798/7	350	550	1250
1800	400	1000	2500

3736
Half-Guinea, sixth head

3736 Half-Guinea Sixth laur. head. r. R. Shield in Garter, date below die axis ↑↑

1801	350	500	900
1802	350	500	925
1803	350	500	975

3737

1813 Half-Guinea, seventh head

	F £	VF £	EF £

3737 Half-Guinea Seventh laur. head. r. with short hair. Ṟ. Shield in garter, date below die axis ↑↑

1804	300	450	875
1805			*Extremely rare*
1806	350	500	925
1808	350	500	875
1809	350	500	875
1810	350	500	875
1811	400	650	1600
1813	350	575	1250

1813 Proof *FDC* £5500

3738   3739

Third-Guinea, first reverse   Third-Guinea, second reverse

3738 Third-Guinea. First laur. head r. Ṟ. Crown, date in legend, die axis ↑↑

1797	220	350	725
1798	220	350	700
1799	475	1000	2000
1800	220	350	800

3739 Third-Guinea. First laur. head r. Ṟ. Similar but date below crown, die axis ↑↑

1801	220	400	900
1802	220	350	775
1803	220	350	775

3740
1804 Third Guinea, second head

3741
1762 Quarter Guinea

	F	VF	EF
	£	£	£

3740 Third-Guinea. Second laur. head r. with short hair, Ŗ. Similar, die axis ↑↑

1804	200	300	650
1806	200	325	725
1808	200	325	725
1809	200	325	725
1810	200	300	650
1811	550	1350	3000
1813	300	625	1350

3741 Quarter-Guinea. Laur. head r. R. Crowned shield die axis ↑↓

1762	250	525	900

For gold of the 'new coinage', 1816-20, see page 421.

SILVER

EARLY COINAGES

3742
1763 'Northumberland shilling'

3742 Shilling. Young laur. and dr. bust, r. known as the 'Northumberland' shilling, die axis ↑↓

1763*	300	600	1500

Plain edge patterns exist for 1764 and 1778. Both are extremely rare.

3743 Shilling. Older laur. and dr. bust, Ŗ. No semée of hearts in Hanoverian shield, die axis ↑↑

1787	 30	60	150
1787 Proof *FDC*			*Extremely rare*
1787 plain edge proof *FDC* £2750			
1787 plain edge pattern by Pingo, border of dots at perimeter *FDC* £1250			

3744 Shilling. — No stop over head, die axis ↑↑ 1787 ....40 | 85 | 300

*Beware, low grade counterfeits exist

3745
1781 No stops at date Shilling

	F	VF	EF
	£	£	£

3745 Shilling. — No stops at date, die axis ↑↑
1787 ....65 125 475
3745AShilling. — No stops on *obv.*, die axis ↑↑
1787 ....450 1000 2750
3746 Shilling. — R. With semée of hearts, die axis ↑↑
1787 ....30 60 150
1787 1/1 retrograde..55 185 425
1787 plain edge proof *FDC (Also known on large 27mm flan.)* £2500

Hanoverian Arms

No semée of hearts   With semée of hearts   3747 - 1798 Shilling

3747 Shilling. No stop over head, 1798: known as the 'Dorrien and Magens' shilling   *EF* £22000
3748 Sixpence. Laur. and dr. bust r. R. Without semée of hearts, die axis ↑↑
1787 ....25 50 115
1787 Proof *FDC* ....*Extremely rare*

3749
1787 Sixpence, with hearts

3749 Sixpence. Similar R. With semée of hearts, die axis ↑↑
1787 ....25 50 115

3750
1772 Fourpence

	F £	VF £	EF £
3750 Fourpence. Young laur. and dr. bust r. ℞. Crowned 4, die axis ↑↓			
1763	25	40	75
1763 Proof *FDC of highest rarity*			
1765	350	600	1250
1766	30	50	100
1770	30	50	100
1772	30	50	100
1772/0	30	50	100
1776	30	50	100
1780	30	50	100
1784	30	50	100
1786	30	50	100

3751	3753	3755
'Wire Money' Fourpence	Young bust Threepence	Older bust Threepence

	F	VF	EF
3751 Fourpence. Older laur. and dr. bust. ℞. Thin 4 ('Wire Money'), die axis ↑↑			
1792	40	80	160
3752 Fourpence. Older laur. and dr. bust r. ℞. Normal Crowned 4, die axis ↑↑			
1795	30	50	100
1800	25	40	80
3753 Threepence. Young laur. dr. bust r. ℞. Crowned 3, die axis ↑↓			
1762	20	35	60
1763	20	35	60
1763 Proof *FDC of highest rarity*			
1765	300	550	1250
1766	30	50	100
1770	30	50	100
1772 small III	30	50	100
1772 very large III	30	50	100
1780	30	50	100
1784	30	50	100
1786	30	50	100
3754 Threepence. Older laur. dr. bust. r. ℞. Thin 3 ('Wire Money'), die axis ↑↑			
1792	40	80	160
3755 Threepence. Older laur. and dr. bust r. ℞. Normal Crowned 3, die axis ↑↑			
1795	30	50	100
1800	25	40	80

3756
Young bust Twopence

	F	VF	EF
	£	£	£
3756 Twopence. Young laur. and dr. bust r. R. Crowned 2, die axis ↑↓			
1763 25		40	80
1763 Proof *FDC of highest rarity*			
1765 200		400	700
1766 25		40	80
1772 25		40	80
1772 second 7/6...25		40	80
1776 25		40	80
1780 25		40	80
1784 25		40	80
1786 25		40	80
1786 large obv. lettering..............................25		40	80
3757 Twopence. Older laur. and dr. bust. r. R. Thin 2 ('Wire Money'), die axis ↑↑			
1792 30		60	125
3758 Twopence. Older laur. and dr. bust r. R. Normal Crowned 2, die axis ↑↑			
1795 20		35	60
1800 20		30	50
3759 Penny. Young laur. and dr. bust r. R. Crowned 1, die axis ↑↓			
1763 25		40	80
1763 Proof *FDC* ....*Extremely rare*			
1766 20		40	80
1770 20		40	80
1772 20		40	80
1776 20		40	80
1779 20		40	80
1780 20		60	120
1781 20		40	80
1784 20		40	75
1786 20		30	70
3760 Penny. Older laur. and dr. bust. r. R. Thin 1 ('Wire Money'), die axis ↑↑			
1792 20		40	120
3761 Penny. Older laur. and dr. bust r. R. Normal Crowned 1, die axis ↑↑			
1795 20		30	60
1800 20		30	60
3762 Maundy Set. Young laur. and dr. bust. r. R. Crowned numerals.			
1763 115		200	425
1763 Proof set *FDC* £11500			
1766 125		240	425
1772 125		240	425
1780 125		240	425
1784 125		240	425
1786 125		240	425

	F	VF	EF
	£	£	£

3763 Maundy Set. — Older laur. and dr. bust. r. ℞. Thin numerals ('Wire Money'),
1792 ....175 350 1000
3764 Maundy Set. Older laur. and dr. bust r. ℞. Normal numerals.
1795 ....125 240 400
1800 ....125 240 375

N.B. Set prices are for matched sets, condition, toning etc.

EMERGENCY ISSUES, die axis ↑↑

3765 Dollar. Pillar type (current for 4s 9d). Spanish American 8 Reales, oval countermark with
head of George III.

Mexico City Mint — m mint mark in reverse legend........1350	3500	—
Bolivia, Potosi Mint – PTS monogram in reverse legend 1650	4250	—
Peru, Lima Mint – LIMÆ monogram in reverse legend 1750	4500	—

two initials of mint master

denomination

mint mark

3765A
Peru Mint Portrait type Dollar with oval countermark

3765A Dollar. Portrait type, oval countermark.

Mexico City Mint — m mint mark in reverse legend.........150	375	900
Bolivia, Potosi Mint — PTS monogram in reverse legend 175	650	1400
Chile, Santiago Mint — s mint mark in reverse legend 725	1950	—
Guatemala Mint — NG mint mark in reverse legend 900	2500	—
Spain, Madrid Mint mint mark in reverse left field..............400	1600	3500
Spain, Seville Mint mint mark in reverse left field 400	1500	3000
Peru, Lima Mint — LIMÆ monogram in reverse legend 250	800	1650

3765B Dollar. — Oval countermark on silver French Ecu of
crown size ....*Extremely rare*
3765C Dollar. — Oval countermark on USA Dollar..*Of highest rarity*
3765D Dollar. — Oval countermark on silver Italian crown size coins ....*Of highest rarity*

mint mark S   Mint Master
                                     Initials

3766   3766B
Seville Mint Portrait Dollar
with octagonal countermark

	F	VF	EF
	£	£	£
3766 Dollar octagonal countermarks with head of George III			
Mexico City Mint — m̊...425	975	2500	
Bolivia, Potosi Mint — PTS monogram 850	2150	4500	
Guatamala Mint — NG 1250	3500	—	
Peru, Lima Mint — LIME monogram 575	1650	4000	
Spain, Madrid Mint M to left of reverse shield.................1100	2750	—	
Spain, Seville Mint S to left of reverse shield...................1250	3250	—	
3766A Dollar. — Octagonal countermark on French Ecu			
or Italian Scudi ....*Of highest rarity*			
3766B Dollar. — Octagonal countermark on USA Dollar ....*Of highest rarity*			

3767
Half-Dollar with oval countermark, Madrid Mint

3767 Half-Dollar. With similar oval countermark of George III,			
Bolivia, Potosi Mint — PTS monogram 325	650	1500	
Chile, Santiago Mint — s° mint mark 475	1250	—	
Spain, Madrid Mint — Crowned M to left of shield............250	450	1100	
Spain, Seville Mint — Crowned S to left of shield..............250	450	1100	
3767A Half Dollar. With Octagonal countermark.			
Similar *from* ...850	1750	—	

BANK OF ENGLAND ISSUE, 1804-16

3768

	F £	VF £	EF £
3768 Dollar. (current for 5s. until 1811, revalued at 5s. 6d. until withdrawn from circulation in 1817). laur. and dr. bust of king. r. R̩. Britannia seated l., several varieties occur, die axis ↑↑			
1804 O. Top leaf to left side of E, R. Upright K to left of shield 125	300	690	
1804 — —no stops in CHK on truncation 175	400	1050	
1804 O. Top leaf to centre of E R. Similar 150	350	935	
1804 — —no stop after REX 125	300	880	
1804 —R. K inverted and incuse 175	475	1200	
1804 O. Top leaf to right side of E, R. normal K ....*Extremely rare*			
1804 —R. K inverted to left of shield 175	450	1100	

Various 1804 Proof strikings of varieties above *FDC from* £1950 to £4750

These dollars were re-struck from Spanish-American 8-Reales until at least 1811. Dollars that still show dates and Mint marks of original coin beneath are worth up to 25% more.

3769
1811 Three Shillings, first bust

	F	VF	EF
3769 Three Shillings. Dr and laur. bust in armour r. R. BANK / TOKEN / 3 SHILL. / date (in oak wreath), die axis ↑↑			
1811 30	75	275	
1811 Proof *FDC* £2000			
1812 30	75	300	

3770   3771
Three Shillings, second head   Eighteenpence, first bust

	F	VF	EF
	£	£	£

3770 Three Shillings. — Laureate head r. Top leaf between I/G ℞. As before
but wreath of oak and olive, die axis ↑↑

1812	30	75	275
1812 Proof *FDC* £2000			
1812 Proof in gold *FDC*	....*Extremely rare*		
1812 Proof in platinum *FDC*	....*Of the highest rarity*		
1813	30	75	325
1814	30	75	325
1815	30	75	325
1816*	375	800	2750

3771 Eighteenpence. Dr. and laur. bust r. in armour ℞ BANK/TOKEN/Is. 6D./date
(in oak wreath) ↑↑

1811	20	50	165
1811 Proof *FDC* £1500			
1812	20	50	165

3772   3773
Eighteenpence, second head   1812 Pattern Ninepence, 9D type

3772 Eighteenpence. Laureate head r. die axis ↑↑

1812	20	50	145
1812 Proof *FDC* £1500			
1812 Platinum proof	....*Of the highest rarity*		
1812 Proof ℞. Small letters *FDC* £3750			
1813	20	50	175
1813 Platinum proof *FDC*	....*Of the highest rarity*		
1814	20	50	185
1815	20	50	185
1816	20	50	185

3773 Ninepence. Similar, Laur. head 1812, ℞. 9D type (pattern only) die axis ↑↑ *FDC* £3000

3773A Ninepence. — — 1812, ℞. 9 pence type (pattern only) die axis ↑↑ FDC £5000

*Beware of counterfeits

COPPER

First Issue — Tower Mint, London

3774

3774 Halfpenny. Laur. and Cuir. bust r. R. Britannia l. date in ex., die axis ↑↓

1770	20	60	330
1770 Proof die axis ↑↑ *FDC* £2500			
1770 Proof in silver *FDC*	....*Extremely rare*		
1770 no stop on rev.	20	65	275
1771	20	50	220
1771 no stop on rev.	20	65	275
1771 ball below spear blade	20	50	220
1772 incuse hair coil on rev.	20	55	220
1772 GEORIVS error	50	150	440
1772 ball below spear blade	20	50	220
1772 no incuse hair coil	20	55	220
1772 — no stop on rev.	20	65	250
1773	20	55	220
1773 no stop after REX	20	65	275
1773 no stop on rev.	20	65	275
1774 different obv. profile	20	80	330
1775 —	20	75	330

3775
Rev. C, leaves point between A and N

	F	VF	EF
	£	£	£

3775 Farthing. Laur. and cuir. bust r. Ɍ. Britannia l. date in ex., die axis ↑↓
1771 Proof *FDC* £1750

1771 Rev A. leaf to r.of N..15	55	225
1771 Rev B. leaf to N..15	50	225
1771 Rev C..15	50	220
1771 1st 7/1 30	165	400
1773 15	40	175
1773 no stop on rev..15	55	250
1773 no stop after REX 15	65	275
1774 15	40	225
1775 15	40	225
1775 struck en medaille ↑↑ 15	65	255
1775 GEORGI Ɐ S..30	225	575

Note: 1771 varieties refer to the direction the top leaf of olive branch points in Britannia's hand

Second Issue—Soho Mint. Birmingham 'Cartwheel' coinage, die axis ↑↓

3776

3776 Twopence. Legends incuse on raised rim
1797 Copper proof *FDC* £2750
1797 Bronzed proof *FDC* £2500
1797 Silver proof *FDC* ....*Extremely rare*
1797 40   100   375
1797 Gold proof *FDC* ....*Extremely rare*
1797 Gilt copper *FDC* £3750

Prices for UNCIRCULATED copper coins are no longer quoted. Truly uncirculated copper coins of this period are too seldom traded on the market to fix a meaningful price. As a guide a truly uncirculated coin with full lustre or bloom should fetch 3-4 times the EF price.

3777

	F £	VF £	EF £
3777 Penny.			
1797 Similar, 10 leaves in wreath on obv. 25		60	175
1797 11 leaves in wreath on obv. 25		75	225
1797 Gilt copper proof *FDC* £2250			
1797 Copper proof *FDC* £1500			
1797 Bronzed proof *FDC* £1250			
1797 Silver proof *FDC* ....*Extremely rare*			
1797 Gold proof *FDC* ....*Extremely rare*			

Halfpence and Farthings of this issue are patterns.

Third Issue—Soho Mint, Birmingham, die axis ↑↓

3778

3778 Halfpenny. Laur. and dr. bust r., ℞. Britannia l. date below			
1799 Ship on rev. with 5 incuse gunports 12		20	80
1799 Ship with 6 relief gunports 12		20	100
1799 Ship with 9 relief gunports 12		20	100
1799 Ship with plain hull 12		20	100
1799 — raised line on hull 12		20	110
1799 Copper proof *FDC* £750			
1799 Bronzed proof *FDC* £700			
1799 Gilt copper proof *FDC* £1250			

3779

	F	VF	EF
	£	£	£
3779 Farthing. Laur. and dr. bust r. date below ℞. Britannia l.			
1799 Obv. with 3 berries in wreath 10	20	60
1799 Copper *FDC* £550			
1799 Bronzed proof *FDC* £500			
1799 Copper gilt proof *FDC* £975			
1799 Obv. with 4 berries in wreath.....................................10	20	80
1799 Gold proof *FDC* .... *Of the highest rarity*
1799 Silver proof *FDC* ....*Extremely rare*

Fourth Issue—Soho Mint, Birmingham, die axis ↑↓

3780

3780 Penny. Shorter haired, laur. and dr. bust r. date below. ℞. Britannia l. date below

| 1806 incuse hair curl by tie knot ....15 | 30 | 165 |
| 1806 no incuse hair curl ....15 | 30 | 185 |
| 1806 Copper proof *FDC* £800 |
| 1806 Bronzed proof *FDC* £800 |
| 1806 Gilt copper proof *FDC* £1450 |
| 1806 Silver proof *FDC* £6500 |
| 1807   ....15 | 30 | 165 |
| 1807 Copper proof *FDC* £800 |
| 1807 Bronzed proof *FDC* £750 |
| 1807 Gilt copper proof *FDC* £2000 |
| 1807 Silver proof *FDC* ....*Extremely rare* |
| 1807 Gold proof *FDC* ....*Extremely rare* |
| 1807 Platinum proof *FDC* ....*Extremely rare* |
| 1808 Proof *FDC* ....*Unique* |

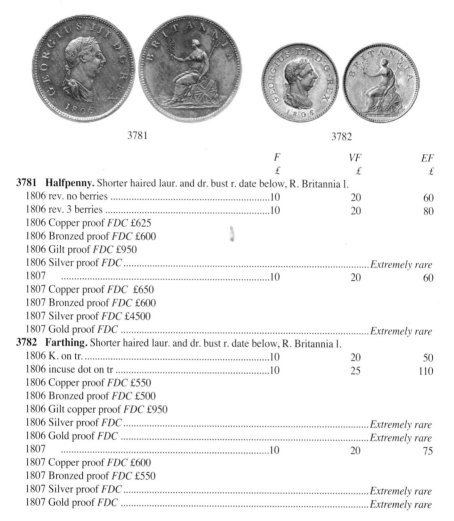

3781

3782

	F £	VF £	EF £
3781 Halfpenny. Shorter haired laur. and dr. bust r. date below, R. Britannia l.			
1806 rev. no berries	10	20	60
1806 rev. 3 berries	10	20	80
1806 Copper proof *FDC* £625			
1806 Bronzed proof *FDC* £600			
1806 Gilt proof *FDC* £950			
1806 Silver proof *FDC*			*Extremely rare*
1807	10	20	60
1807 Copper proof *FDC* £650			
1807 Bronzed proof *FDC* £600			
1807 Silver proof *FDC* £4500			
1807 Gold proof *FDC*			*Extremely rare*
3782 Farthing. Shorter haired laur. and dr. bust r. date below, R. Britannia l.			
1806 K. on tr.	10	20	50
1806 incuse dot on tr	10	25	110
1806 Copper proof *FDC* £550			
1806 Bronzed proof *FDC* £500			
1806 Gilt copper proof *FDC* £950			
1806 Silver proof *FDC*			*Extremely rare*
1806 Gold proof *FDC*			*Extremely rare*
1807	10	20	75
1807 Copper proof *FDC* £600			
1807 Bronzed proof *FDC* £550			
1807 Silver proof *FDC*			*Extremely rare*
1807 Gold proof *FDC*			*Extremely rare*

Prices for UNCIRCULATED copper coins are no longer quoted. Truly uncirculated copper coins of this period are too seldom traded on the market to fix a meaningful price. As a guide a truly uncirculated coin with full lustre or bloom should fetch 3-4 times the EF price.

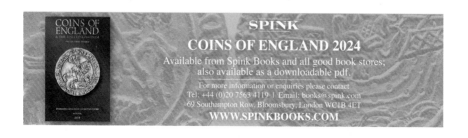

LAST OR NEW COINAGE, 1816-20

The year 1816 is a landmark in the history of our coinage. For some years at the beginning of the 19th century Mint production was virtually confined to small gold denominations, regular full production being resumed only after the Mint had been moved from the Tower of London to a new site on Tower Hill. Steam powered minting machinery made by Boulton and Watt replaced the old hand-operated presses and these produced coins which were technically much superior to the older milled coins.

In 1816 for the first time British silver coins were produced with an intrinsic value somewhat below their face value, the first official token coinage. The old Guinea was replaced by a Sovereign of twenty shillings in 1817, the standard of 22 carat (0.916) fineness still being retained.

Mint Master or Engraver's and/or designer's initials:

B.P. (Benedetto Pistrucci 1783-1855)   WWP (William Wellesley Pole)

GOLD

3783

3783   Five Pounds. 1820 LX (Pattern only) laur. head r. date below R. St George and dragon, edge inscribed die axis ↑↓   *EF* £275000   *FDC* £475000
   1820 Similar plain edge proof *FDC* (only two struck) .... *Of highest rarity*

3784

3784   Two Pounds. 1820 LX (Pattern only) laur. head r. date below R. St George and dragon, edge inscribed die axis ↑↓   *EF* £45000   *FDC* £95000
   1820 Similar plain edge proof *FDC* .... *Extremely rare*

3785   3785A

	F £	VF £	EF £	UNC £

3785 Sovereign. laur. head r. coarse hair, legend type A (Descending colon after BRITANNIAR, no space between REX and F:D:). R. St. George and dragon, die axis ↑↓

1817	600	1200	1950	5000
1817 Proof *FDC* £27500				
1817 ↑↑ die axis	1250	—	—	—
1818	850	1850	4850	12500
1819	45000	75000	250000	—

3785A Sovereign. Similar legend type B (Ascending colon after BRITANNIAR, space between REX and F:D:) ↑↓

1818	750	1500	5000	8500
1818 Proof *FDC* £37500				

3785B Sovereign. laur head r. hair with tighter curls, legend type A. R. Similar die axis ↑↓

1818	....*Extremely rare*

3785C   3786
Large date, open 2 variety   1817 Half-Sovereign

3785C Sovereign. Similar legend type B. (as above) die axis ↑↓

1818	....*Extremely rare*
1820 Roman I in date	....*Extremely rare*
1820 open 2, alignment of date varies	600	900	1300	4750
1820 thin date, smaller 0 Proof *FDC* £21500				
1820 short date height, alignment varies	600	950	2000	4750
1820 closed 2 alignment of date varies	600	900	1600	4500

The above 1820 entries are the main variations, there do exist other subtle differences which are merely sub-varieties and therefore are not included.

3786 Half-Sovereign. laur head r. date below R. Crowned shield, edge milled die axis ↑↓

1817	250	400	750	2250
1817 Proof *FDC* £12500				
1818/7*	450	1250	—	—
1818 Proof *FDC* £15000				
1818	275	400	950	2750
1820	265	375	800	2650
1820 Letter O for zero	350	500	950	2850

Note: 7 under 8 clearly visible at top right of 8, not to be confused with a defective last 8 punch.

SILVER

3787 - 1818 George III Crown

	F	VF	EF	UNC
	£	£	£	£

3787 Crown. Laur. head r. ℞. Pistrucci's St. George and dragon within Garter edge inscribed, die axis ↑↓

1818 LVIII, edge	45	120	650	2000
1818 LVIII error edge inscription				*Extremely rare*
1818 LVIII Proof *FDC*				*Extremely rare*
1818 LIX	45	120	675	2250
1818 LIX TUTΛMEN error	80	350	—	—
1819 LIX	40	120	600	2000
1819 LIX no stops on edge	65	200	800	2500
1819 LIX R. Thicker ruled garter	60	135	875	—
1819/8 LIX	70	250	900	—
1819 LX	50	120	600	2250
1819 LX no stop after TUTAMEN	60	150	750	—
1820 LX	45	120	625	2500
1820 LX R. S/T in SOIT	65	225	850	—
1820/19 LX	80	275	975	—

3788 - 1817 Halfcrown, large bust

3788 Halfcrown. Large laur. bust or 'bull' head r. date below R. Crowned garter and shield die axis ↑↑

1816	30	75	350	700
1816 Proof *FDC* £5750				
1816 Plain edge proof *FDC* £6750				
1817	30	75	325	675
1817 D/T in DEI	75	300	800	—
1817 E/R in DEI				*Extremely rare*
1817 S/I in PENSE	55	225	725	—
1817 Proof *FDC* £5750				
1817 Plain edge proof *FDC* £6250				

3789 - 1817 Halfcrown, small head

	F	VF	EF	UNC
	£	£	£	£

3789 Halfcrown. Small laur. head r. date below, R. Crowned garter and shield die axis ↑↑

1817* 30	75	300	675
1817 Proof *FDC* £5500			
1817 Plain edge proof *FDC* £6000			
1817 Reversed s's in garter..*Extremely rare*
1818 Reversed s's in garter..*Extremely rare*
1818** 40	100	400	800
1818 Proof *FDC* £6000			
1819 Proof *FDC* £5750			
1819 30	75	350	725
1819/8 ....*Extremely rare*
1820 40	100	425	725
1820 Proof *FDC* £5750			
1820 Plain edge proof *FDC* £6000			

3790
1819 Shilling

	F £	VF £	EF £	UNC £
3790 Shilling. laur head r. date below R. Crowned Shield in Garter edge milled, die axis ↑↑				
1816	15	30	75	200
1816 Proof *FDC* £1650				
1816 Plain edge proof *FDC* £1650				
1816 Proof in gold *FDC*				*Extremely rare*
1817	15	30	75	250
1817 RRITT flaw	25	50	175	400
1817 Plain edge proof *FDC* £2000				
1817 GEOE error	65	225	550	1000
1817 E over R in GEOR	85	125	475	650
1818	25	50	190	500
1818 High 8	30	65	250	475
1819/8	15	30	165	450
1819	15	30	100	275
1819 9/6 *exists*				
1820	15	30	100	250
1820 I/S in HONI	35	65	250	525
1820 Proof *FDC* £2250				

* Beware recent low grade forgeries
** Beware of silvered base metal contemporary forgeries

3791
1817 Sixpence

3791 Sixpence. laur head r. date below R. Crowned Shield in Garter edge milled, die axis ↑↑

1816	10	25	65	175
1816 Proof plain edge *FDC* £1500				
1816 Proof in gold *FDC*	....*Extremely rare*			
1817	10	25	75	175
1817 Proof plain edge *FDC* £1500				
1817 Proof milled edge *FDC* £1850				
1818	11	30	80	195
1818 Proof milled edge *FDC* £1900				
1819/8	14	30	90	220
1819	11	25	85	185
1819 small 8	11	25	80	195
1820	11	25	80	175
1820 inverted 1	70	300	575	—
1820 I/S in HONI	70	275	525	—
1820 obv. no colons	115	350	675	—
1820 milled edge Proof *FDC* £1650				

3792

3792 Maundy Set. (4d., 3d., 2d. and 1d.) laur. head, date below die axis ↑↑

1817	125	240	400	
1818	125	240	375	
1820	125	240	375	
3793 — Fourpence. 1817, 1818, 1820	...................*from* 20	35	65	100
3794 — Threepence. 1817, 1818, 1820	..................*from* 20	35	55	80
3795 — Twopence. 1817, 1818, 1820	......................*from* 20	35	50	80
3796 — Penny. 1817, 1818, 1820	...........................*from* 18	28	50	80

Maundy pennies are always the most requested oddment, it is the smallest coin in the set and is therefore the easiest to lose. Penny collectors also dictate supply and demand for this coin.

George IV, eldest son of George III, was born on 12th August 1762 and was almost the complete opposite to his father. He was very extravagant and lived in the height of luxury. He especially influenced fashion of the time which became known as the 'Regency' style. He had numerous mistresses, and had an arranged marriage with Caroline of Brunswick. She later left England and travelled Southern Europe, North Africa and the Holy Land, basing herself in Naples, but returned to claim her place as Queen upon George's accession. George banned her from ever being crowned, and he died without ever conceiving a son on 26th June 1830, when his younger brother William ascended the throne.

The Mint resumed the coinage of copper farthings in 1821, and pennies and halfpennies in 1825. A gold Two Pound piece was first issued for general circulation in 1823. A full cased proof set of the new bare head coinage was issued in limited quantities in 1826.

Engraver's and/or designer's initials on the coins:

B. P. (Benedetto Pistrucci)   W.W. P. (William Wellesley Pole) – Master of the Mint
J. B. M. (Jean Baptiste Merlen)

Engravers and Designers:– Francis Legett Chantrey (1781-1842) Jean Baptiste Merlen (1769-c.1850) Benedetto Pistrucci (1783-1855) William Wyon (1795-1851)

GOLD

3797

3797 Five Pounds. 1826 Bare head l. date below R. Crowned shield and mantle, inscribed edge, die axis ↑↓ Proof *EF* £55000   *FDC* £110000
1826 Piedfort proof *FDC* ....*Extremely rare*

3798   3799

	F £	VF £	EF £	UNC £

3798 Two Pounds.

1823 Proof *EF* £10000 *FDC* £20000

1823 Proof no JBM below truncation *FDC* ....*Extremely rare*

1823 Large bare head. l. R. St. George, inscribed

edge ↑↓ 1000   1500   2800   4500

3799 Two Pounds. Bare head l. date below R. Crowned shield and mantle

inscribed edge die axis ↑↓

1824 Proof *FDC* ....*Extremely rare*

1825 Proof plain edge *EF* £12500   *FDC* £21500

1826 Piedfort proof *FDC*..*Extremely rare*

1826 Proof *EF* £9250   *FDC* £15000

3800   3801
                                 Sovereign, second type

3800   Sovereign. Laur. head. l. R. St. George and dragon date in ex., die axis ↑↓

1821 500   1000   1850   3750

1821 Proof *EF* £7000   *FDC* £11500

1822* 500   1000   1850   4250

1823 1100   2750   8000   —

1824 500   1000   2250   4250

1825 750   2000   5750   9250

3801   Sovereign. Bare head. date below l. R. Crowned shield, die axis ↑↓

1825 500   1000   1650   3500

1825 Proof 8 heart semée *EF* £7000   *FDC* £13500

1825 Plain edge proof 7 heart semée *EF* £7500   *FDC* £14500

1826 500   1000   1575   4000

1826 Proof *EF* £6000   *FDC* £10500

1827* 500   1000   1750   4000

1828 6000   15000   29500   —

1829 500   1000   2000   4250

1830 500   1000   2000   4250

1830 die axis ↑↑ ....*Extremely rare*

1830 Milled edge proof ....*Extremely rare*

3802 Half-Sovereign. Laur. head. l. R. Ornately garnished Crowned shield. die axis ↑↓

1821 800   1650   2950   4750

1821 Proof *EF* £5850   *FDC* £8750

*Beware counterfeits

3803
Half-Sovereign, second reverse

3804
1825 Half Sovereign, bare head

	F	VF	EF	UNC
	£	£	£	£

3803 Half-Sovereign. Laur. head l. R. Plain Crowned shield die axis ↑↓

1823	400	700	1100	2350
1824	400	700	1000	2000
1825	400	700	1000	1800

3804 Half-Sovereign. Bare head. date below l. R. Crowned garnished shield die axis ↑↓

1826	400	700	1000	1850
1826 Proof *EF* £4250 *FDC* £6750				
1827	400	700	1000	2100
1828	400	700	1000	2000

3804A Half-Sovereign. Similar with extra tuft of hair to l. ear, much heavier border, die axis ↑↓

1826	400	700	1000	1850
1826 Proof *EF* £4250 *FDC* £6750				
1827	400	700	1000	2100
1828	400	700 ·	1000	2000

SILVER

WWP   B.P.

3805
1821 Laureate bust Crown

3805 Crown. Laur. head. l. R. St. George, date in exergue, B.P. to upper right,
tiny italic WWP under lance, die axis ↑↓

1821* edge SECUNDO	60	150	700	2250
1821 SECUNDO WWP inverted under lance	75	350	900	2500
1821 SECUNDO L - very clearly defined WWP Proof *FDC* £8000				
1821 SECUNDO Proof in copper	....*Extremely rare*			
1821 TERTIO Proof *FDC* £12000				
1822 SECUNDO	60	200	975	2850
1822 TERTIO	60	200	900	2350

* Beware of recent counterfeits in high grade

3806
1826 Proof Crown, bare head

	F £	VF £	EF £	UNC £

3806 Crown. Bare head. l. R̶. Shield with crest inscribed edge, die axis ↑↓
1825 Proof *FDC* £25000
1826 Proof *FDC* £18500

3807
Halfcrown, lightly garnished
shield, right thistle leaf
further from stem

3807
Heavy garnishing, right thistle leaf closer,
more parallel to its stem

3807 Halfcrown. Laur. head. l. R̶. Crowned Garnished shield, die axis ↑↓

	F	VF	EF	UNC
1820 35	100	300	750
1820 Proof *FDC* £4000			
1820 Plain edge proof *FDC* £5250			
1821 35	100	300	750
1821 Heavier shield garnishing 50	100	425	1000
1823 – 1250	4500	14850	—
1821 Proof *FDC* £3250			

3808
Halfcrown, second reverse

3809
1826 Halfcrown, bare head, third reverse

	F	VF	EF	UNC
	£	£	£	£

3808 Halfcrown. Laur. head l. R. Crowned Shield in garter and collar die axis ↑↓

1823	....	40	100	385	950
1823 Proof *FDC* £8000					
1824	....	50	140	425	1000
1824 Proof *FDC* £8000					

3809 Halfcrown. Bare head. date below l. R. Crowned Shield with crest die axis ↑↓

1824	....				*Extremely rare*
1824 Proof *FDC* £12500					
1825	....	40	100	350	750
1825 Proof *FDC* £3950					
1825 Plain edge proof *FDC* £3950					
1826	....	40	100	375	800
1826 Proof *FDC* £2500					
1828	....	110	300	1000	2750
1829	....	75	150	550	1100

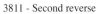

3810 - First reverse

3811 - Second reverse

3810 Shilling. Laur. head. l. R. Crowned garnished shield, die axis ↑↓

1821	....	25	60	200	450
1821 Milled edge Proof *FDC* £2000					

3811 Shilling. Laur. head l. R. Crowned shield in Garter die axis ↑↓

1823	....	55	90	295	795
1823 Proof *FDC* £3750					
1824	....	25	60	225	575
1824 Milled edge Proof *FDC* £3750					
1825	....	25	60	250	575
1825 Milled edge Proof *FDC* £3500					
1825/3	....				*Extremely rare*

3812
Third reverse

	F £	VF £	EF £	UNC £
3812 Shilling. Bare head l. date below R. Lion on crown die axis ↑↓				
1825	12	45	165	425
1825 Roman I	125	375	1100	2750
1825 Milled edge Proof *FDC* £1500				
1826	12	35	110	400
1826 Proof *FDC* £1100				
1826/2	—	—	—	2000
1827	45	110	395	875
1829	25	65	250	700
1829 Milled edge Proof *FDC* £4750				

3813	3814	3815
First reverse	Second reverse	Third reverse

	F £	VF £	EF £	UNC £
3813 Sixpence. Laur. head. l. R. Crowned Garnished shield, die axis ↑↓				
1821	20	50	150	450
1821 Proof *FDC* £1150				
1821 BBITANNIAR	100	325	900	—
3814 Sixpence. Laur. head l. R. Crowned Shield in Garter die axis ↑↓				
1824	20	50	175	450
1824 Proof *FDC* £2000				
1825	20	50	175	425
1825 Proof *FDC* £2000				
1826	30	85	300	650
1826 Proof *FDC* £2650				
3815 Sixpence. Bare head. l. with or without tuft of hair to l. of ear date below R. Lion on crown die axis ↑↓				
1826	20	50	150	385
1826 Proof *FDC* £1250				
1827	40	125	325	695
1828	20	60	250	550
1829	20	50	160	450
1829 Proof *FDC* £2250				

3816
1822 Maundy Set

	VF £	EF £	FDC £
3816 Maundy Set. (4d., 3d., 2d. and 1d.) laur head l. die axis ↑↓			
1822	250		450
1822 Proof set *FDC*		*Extremely rare*	
1823	175		400
1824	200		450
1825	175		400
1826	175		400
1827	175		400
1828	175		400
1828 Proof set *FDC*		*Extremely rare*	
1829	175		400
1830	165		400
3817 Maundy Fourpence. 1822-30	*from* 28	45	60
3818 — Threepence. small head, 1822	35	45	85
3819 — Threepence. normal head, 1823-30	*from* 28	45	60
3820 — Twopence. 1822-30	*from* 25	45	60
3821 — Penny. 1822-30	*from* 25	45	60

See note under 3796.

COPPER

3822
First Issue Farthing

	F £	VF £	EF £	BU £
First Issue, 1821-6. Obv. reads GEORGIUS IIII				
3822 Farthing. Laur. and dr. bust l. R. Britannia r. date in ex. die axis ↑↓				
1821 Proof *FDC* £1500				
1821	8	15	55	175
1822 leaf ribs incuse	8	15	45	150
1822—inv. A's legend	30	95	340	—
1822 leaf ribs raised	8	15	45	150
1822 Proof *FDC* £1500				
1822 Proof die axis ↑↑ *FDC* £1750				
1823 —	8	15	55	175
1823 — I for 1 in date	25	85	270	—

	F	VF	EF	BU
	£	£	£	£
1825 — 8	15	55	175
1825 — D/U in DEI 20	85	295	—
1825 leaf ribs raised.....................8	15	60	200
1825 gold proof *FDC* ....*Extremely rare*
1826 — 8	18	70	225
1826 R/E in GRATIA 20	80	270	—

See 3825 for Second Issue farthings of 1826 which have die axis ↑↑

3823
1826 Penny - plain saltire

Second issue, 1825-30. Obv. reads GEORGIUS IV

3823   Penny. Laur. head. l. R. Britannia, with shield bearing saltire of arms die axis ↑↑

1825 20	60	375	850
1825 Proof *FDC* £1750			
1826 plain saltire on rev. 20	60	225	775
1826 Proof *FDC* £1200			
1826 thin line on saltire 20	60	375	850
1826-Proof *FDC* £1000			
1826 thick line on saltire 20	60	300	925
1826-Proof *FDC* £1100			
1827 plain saltire 225	1250	7750	—

3824
1827 Halfpenny

3824   Halfpenny. die axis ↑↑ Laur. head. l. R. Britannia, with shield bearing saltire of arms

1825 10	40	160	450
1826 rev. two incuse lines on saltire 10	25	100	400
1826 Proof *FDC* £825			
1826 rev. raised line on saltire 10	30	175	350
1827 rev. two incuse lines on saltire 10	25	150	400

3825
1830 Farthing

	F	VF	EF	BU
	£	£	£	£

3825 Farthing. die axis ↑↑ Laur. head. l. R. Britannia, with shield bearing saltire of arms

1826 8	15	60	175
1826 Proof *FDC* £750				
1826 Roman I 15	55	350	675
1827 8	15	70	200
1828 8	15	75	185
1829 8	15	80	250
1830 8	15	75	185

3826	3827
1828 Half-Farthing	1827 Third-Farthing

3826 Half-Farthing. (for use in Ceylon). Laur. head. l. date below R.Britannia die axis ↑↑

1828 rev. helmet intrudes legend 30	50	125	350
1828 rev. helmet to base of legend 30	50	160	450
1830 rev. helmet to base of legend 22 70	300	—	
1830 rev. helmet intrudes legend 30	50	150	425

3827 Third-Farthing. (for use in Malta). Laur. head. l. date below R.Britannia die axis ↑↑

1827 20	40	80	225
1827 Proof *FDC* £900				

Copper coins graded in this catalogue as BU have full mint lustre.

PROOF SET
PS1 new issue, 1826. Five pounds to Farthing (11 coins) *FDC* £145000

William IV was born on 21st August 1765, and ascended the throne on his elder brother's death. From c.1791-1811 while Duke of Clarence, he was cohabiting with the actress Dorothea Jordan (1762-1816) who bore him ten illegitimate children. After the death of George IV's daughter, William was coerced into a legitimate marriage with Adelaide of Saxe-Coburg and Saxe-Meinigen. She bore him two daughters who both died in childhood. His reign was most notable for the introduction of the Reform bill and abolition of slavery. William was the last Hanoverian King of Britain. On his death on 20th June 1837 the throne passed to his niece Victoria.

In order to prevent confusion between the Sixpence and Half-Sovereign the size of the latter was reduced in 1834, although the weight remained the same. The smaller gold piece was not acceptable to the public and in the following year it was made to the normal size. In 1836 the silver Groat was again issued for general circulation: it is the only British silver coin which has a seated Britannia as the type and was revised upon the suggestion of Mr Joseph Hume thus rendering the nickname "Joey". Crowns were not struck during this reign for general circulation; but proofs or patterns of this denomination were made and are greatly sought after. Silver Threepences and Three-Halfpence were minted for use in the Colonies.

Engraver's and/or designer's initials on the coins:
W. W. (William Wyon)
Engravers and Designers:– Francis Legett Chantrey (1781-1842) Jean Baptiste Merlen (1769-c.1850) William Wyon (1795-1851).

GOLD

3828
1831 Proof Two Pounds

	F	VF	EF	BU
	£	£	£	£
3828 Two Pounds. bare head r. R. crowned shield and mantle, date below, edge plain. die axis ↑↓				
1831 (proof only) *EF* £13500 *FDC* £30000				
3829 Sovereign. First bust. r. top of ear narrow and rounded, nose to 2nd N of BRITANNIAR, fine obv. beading. R. Crowned shield. Die axis ↑↓				
1830 Proof plain edge *FDC* £26500				
1831 750	1600	2750	5500	
1832 800	1600	3750	7500	
1832 Proof *FDC* £27500				
3829A Sovereign. Similar, WW without stops die axis ↑↓				
1831 800	1750	3750	8000	

3829B
Second bust with broad ear top

	F	VF	EF	BU
	£	£	£	£

3829B Sovereign. Second bust. r. top of ear broad and flat, nose to 2nd I in BRITANNIAR,
coarser obv. beading.↑↓

1830 plain edge proof *FDC* 25000				
1831 6000	12500	—	—
1831 Proof plain edge *FDC* £12500				
1832* 750	1500	2400	4000
1833 750	1500	2400	4500
1835 750	1500	2400	5000
1836 750	1500	2400	4250
1836 N of ANNO struck in shield 6000	9000	17500	—
1837 750	1500	2650	4650
1837 Tailed 8 750	1500	3000	—

3830	3831
1834 Half-sovereign	Large size Half-Sovereign

3830 Half-Sovereign. Small size (17.9mm), bare head r.R. Crowned shield and mantle.
Die axis ↑↓

1831 Proof plain edge *FDC* £6000				
1831 Proof milled edge *EF* £9250 *FDC* £13500				
1834 450	900	1750	3250

3831 Half-Sovereign. Large size (19.4mm), bare head r.R. Crowned shield and mantle.
Die axis ↑↓

1835 450	900	1500	2750
1836 500	1200	—	—
1837 450	900	1700	3000

3832 Half-Sovereign. *Obv.* struck from Sixpence die (19.4mm) in error,

1836 3000	6000	12000	—

* Beware of counterfeits

SILVER

3833
1831 Crown. W.W. on truncation

	F £	VF £	EF £	BU £

3833 Crown. ℞. Shield on mantle
  1831 Proof only incuse W.W. on trun. struck ↑↓ *FDC* £35000
  1831 Proof struck in gold of five pounds weight *FDC* ....*Extremely rare*
  1831 Bare head r. raised W. WYON on trun. struck ↑↑ en medaille
    (medal die axis) *FDC* £45000
  1831 Bare head r. similar die axis ↑↓ *FDC* £40000
  1831 Bare head r. incuse WW over W. WYON on trun. *FDC* ....*Extremely rare*
  1834 Bare head r. W.W. on trun. struck die axis ↑↓ *FDC* £60000

WW script

3834

3834 Halfcrown. Bare head. WW in script on trun. ℞. Shield on mantle, die axis ↑↓
  1831 Plain edge proof *FDC* £3950
  1831 Milled edge proof *FDC* £4500

	F	VF	EF	BU
1834 40	120	475	1100
1834 Plain edge proof *FDC* £4950				
1834 Milled edge proof *FDC* £4250				
1835 40	125	575	1400
1836/5 45	125	775	1500
1836 40	120	450	1300
1836 Proof *FDC* £4750				
1837 60	240	550	1600

WW block

3834A

	F £	VF £	EF £	BU £

3834A Halfcrown. Bare head r. block WW on trun. R. Similar. die axis ↑↓

1831 Proof *FDC* £3750

1834 60   240   675   1500

3835   3836

1831 Shilling   1834 Sixpence

3835 Shilling. Bare head r. R. Value in wreath, date below. die axis ↑↓

1831 Plain edge Proof *FDC* £1500

1831 Milled edge proof *FDC* £3500

1834 18   60   250   600

1834 Milled edge Proof *FDC* £3500

1835 18   60   250   550

1835 Proof *FDC* £4000

1836 18   60   250   550

1836 Proof *FDC* £4000

1837 25   75   325   725

1837 Proof *FDC* £3500

3836 Sixpence. Bare head r. R. Value in wreath, date below. die axis ↑↓

1831 18   35   135   325

— Proof *FDC* die axis ↑↓ or ↑↑ £1000

1831 Proof milled edge *FDC* £1250

1834 18   35   145   350

1834 large date...18   35   200   450

1834 Proof *FDC* £1500

1835 18   35   135   375

1835 Proof *FDC* ....*Extremely rare*

1836 28   60   275   500

1836 Proof *FDC* ....*Extremely rare*

1837 30   75   275   500

1837 Proof *FDC* ....*Extremely rare*

1837 B/RRITANNIAR ....*Extremely rare*

3837 - 1836 Groat   3839 - 1835 Three-Halfpence

	F £	VF £	EF £	BU £
3837 Groat. Bare head r. R. Britannia seated, date in ex. die axis ↑↑				
1836 10		28	70	150
1836 Proof *FDC* £1350				
1836 Plain edge proof *FDC* £1250				
1836 Proof in gold *FDC* £17500				
1837 10		30	90	200
1837 Type 2 obv. 'more wiry hair' *values as above*				
1837 Proof *FDC* £1500				
1837 Plain edge proof *FDC* £1850				
3838 Threepence. Obverse 1, small head, low hair (for use in the West Indies). As Maundy threepence but with a dull surface, ↑↓				
1834 15		30	110	250
1835 15		30	100	225
1836 15		30	100	250
1837 15		30	115	265
3838A — Obverse 2, large head, high hair				
1834 15		30	100	225
1835 15		30	100	200
1836 15		30	100	200
1837 75		150	250	575
3839 Three-Halfpence (for Colonial use). Bare head r. R. Value, Crowned in wreath, die axis ↑↓				
1834 15		25	50	110
1835/4 15		25	55	130
1835 unconfirmed without 5/4				
1836 15		25	55	130
1837 15		50	150	375
1837 Proof *FDC* £1650				

3840 - 1831 Maundy Set

	EF £	FDC £
3840 Maundy Set (4d., 3d., 2d. and 1d.). Bare head r. Die axis ↑↓		
1831 220		475
— Proof *FDC* £1250		
1831 Proof struck in gold *FDC* £35000		
1832 200		450
1833 200		425
1834 200		425
1835 200		425
1836 200		450
1837 200		450

	VF	EF	FDC
	£	£	£
3841 — **Fourpence,** 1831-7 .... *from* 25	50	80
3842 — **Threepence,** 1831-7 .... *from* 25	50	80
3843 — **Twopence,** 1831-7 .... *from* 25	50	80
3844 — **Penny,** 1831-7 .... *from* 25	50	80

See note on under 3796.

COPPER

3845

	F	VF	EF	BU
	£	£	£	£

3845 Penny. Bare head r. No initials on trun. date below. R. Britannia r. die axis ↑↑

1831	25	65	300	1250
1831 Proof *FDC* ↑↓ £1250				
1831 Proof *FDC* ↑↑ £1400				
1834	25	80	425	1500
1837	55	175	825	2000

3846 Penny. Bare head r. date below. incuse initials on trun. R. Britannia r. die axis ↑↑

1831 W.W on trun 110	475	—	—
1831 .W.W on trun...30	115	475	1100

3847
1831 Halfpenny

3847 Halfpenny. Bare head r. date below. R. Britannia r. die axis ↑↑

1831	10	30	150	325
1831 Proof *FDC* ↑↓ £825				
1831 Proof *FDC* ↑↑ £925				
1834	12	35	165	375
1837	12	35	135	325

3848
1831 Farthing

	F	VF	EF	BU
	£	£	£	£
3848 Farthing. Bare head r. date below. R. Britannia r. die axis ↑↑				
1831 rev. incuse line on saltire 5	12	65	150
1831 Proof *FDC* ↑↓ £800				
1831 Proof *FDC* ↑↑ £850				
1834 incuse saltire 5	12	70	165
1834 rev. raised line on saltire 5	15	85	200
1835 die axis ↑↓ 5	25	135	325
1835 die axis ↑↑ 5	12	90	250
1835 rev. incuse line on saltire 5	15	85	200
1836 rev. raised line on saltire 5	12	85	200
1837 — 5	15	85	200

3849   3850
1837 Half-Farthing   1835 Third-Farthing

3849 Half-Farthing (for use in Ceylon). Bare head r. date below. R. Britannia r. die axis ↑↑
1837 80   280   495   —
3850 Third-Farthing (for use in Malta). Bare head r. date below. R. Britannia r. die axis ↑↑
1835 12   30   120   175
1835 Proof *FDC* £1100

Copper coins graded in this catalogue as UNC have full mint lustre

PROOF SET.
PS2 Coronation, 1831. Two pounds to farthing (14 coins). *FDC* £100000

Victoria was born on 24th May 1819, the only child of Prince Edward, Duke of Kent and Princess Victoria of Saxe-Coburg-Saalfeld, and ascended to the throne in 1837. In 1840 she married her cousin Prince Albert of Saxe-Coburg and Gotha, with whom she enjoyed 21 years of marriage producing nine children. Upon Albert's untimely death in 1861 she descended into a lengthy period of mourning, her excessive melancholy leading her to be nick-named 'the widow of Windsor'. She skilfully avoided conflict with other European powers, and produced connections with many Royal houses all over Europe. Victoria died on 22nd January 1901 at the age of 81, and was the last British monarch of the House of Hanover.

In 1849, as a first step towards decimalisation, a silver Florin (¹/10th pound) was introduced, but the coins of 1849 omitted the usual *Dei Gratia* and these so-called 'Godless' Florins were replaced in 1851 by the 'Gothic' issue. The Halfcrown was temporarily discontinued but was minted again from 1874 onwards. Between 1863 and 1880 reverse dies of the gold and silver coins were numbered in the course of Mint experiments into the wear of dies. The exception was the Florin where the die number is on the obverse below the bust.

The gold and silver coins were redesigned for the Queen's Golden Jubilee in 1887. The Double-Florin which was then issued was abandoned after only four years; the Jubilee Sixpence of 1887, known as the 'withdrawn' type, was changed to avoid confusion with the Half-Sovereign. Gold and silver were again redesigned in 1893 with an older portrait of the Queen, but the 'old head' was not used on the bronze coinage until 1895. The heavy copper Penny had been replaced by the lighter bronze 'bun' Penny in 1860. In 1874-6 and 1881-2 some of the bronze was made by Heaton in Birmingham, and these have a letter H below the date. From 1897 Farthings were issued with a dark surface.

Early Sovereigns had a shield-type reverse, but Pistrucci's St. George design was used again from 1871. In order to increase the output of gold coinage, branches of the Royal Mint were set up in Australia at Sydney and Melbourne and, later, at Perth for coining gold of imperial type.

Engraver's and/or designer's initials on the coins:
W. W. (William Wyon 1795-1851)   T. B. (Thomas Brock 1847-1922)
L. C. W. (Leonard Charles Wyon 1826-91)   B. P. (Benedetto Pistrucci, 1784-1855)
J. E. B. (Joseph Edgar Boehm 1834-90)
Engravers and Designers: George William De Saulle, (1862-1903) William Dyce (1806-64), Jean Baptiste Merlen (1769-c.1850) Edward Poynter (1836-1919)

GOLD

YOUNG HEAD COINAGE, 1838-87

3851
1839 Five Pounds - DIRIGIT reverse

3851 Five Pounds. 1839. Young filleted bust l. plain rear fillet R. 'Una and the lion' (proof only)
DIRIGIT legend, inscribed edge, die axis ↑↑ *FDC* ....*Extremely rare*
– 1839 Similar – DIRIGIT legend, struck on thick flan ....*Extremely rare*
– 1839 Similar – DIRIGIT legend, plain edge die axis ↑↑ ....*Extremely rare*
– 1839 –13 leaves to rear fillet, R. DIRIGE legend–proof   *EF* £175000   *FDC* £350000
– 1839 Similar – DIRIGE legend edge plain proof ....*Extremely rare*
– 1839 –9 leaves to rear fillet, DIRIGE legend   *EF* £175000   *FDC* £350000
– 1839 Similar – DIRIGE legend edge plain ....*Extremely rare*
– 1839 Similar – DIRIGIT legend edge plain proof ....*Extremely rare*
Truly FDC 1839 Five Pound coins are hardly ever encountered.

3852
Sovereign - first smaller young head

	F	VF	EF	BU
	£	£	£	£

3852 Sovereign. First (small) young head. l. date below. R. First shield. London mint, die axis ↑↓

	F	VF	EF	BU
1838 875	1500	3500	7250
1838 Proof *FDC* .... *Extremely rare*			
1838 Plain edge proof *FDC* £27500			
1839 1250	2500	4250	10000
1839 die axis ↑↓ Proof *FDC* £13500			
1839 die axis ↑↑ Proof *FDC* £13500			
1839 Milled edge proof *FDC* £25000			
1841 5000	10000	23000	—
1841 GRΛTIΛ 4500	9500	23500	—
1842 375	550	975	2250
1842 Open 2 600	1000	—	
1842 GRΛTIΛ 550	950	—	—
1843 ....BV	450	925	2000
1843 Roman I 675	1250	—	—
1843/2 or ⅔ 475	825	1500	2900
1844 wider date ....BV	450	900	2250
1844 closer date ....BV	450	950	2250
1844 first 4/Ϸ 750	1500	2500	—
1845 wider date ....BV	450	900	2250
1845 closer date ....BV	475	925	2250
1845 4/Ϸ 750	1500	2500	—
1845 Roman I 750	1400	—	—
1846 ....BV	500	950	2250
1846 4/Ϸ 750	1500	—	—
1846 Roman I 675	1250	—	—
1847 ....BV	500	950	2250
1847 Roman I 700	1450	—	—
1848 1250	2500	7500	—

3852A Sovereign. Similar R similar but leaves of the wreath arranged differently with tops of leaves closer to crown.

	F	VF	EF	BU
1838 5000	9500	23000	—

	F £	VF £	EF £	BU £

3852B Sovereign. Similar narrower shield. Considerably modified floral emblems, different leaf arrangement ↑↓

| 1843 | ....5500 | 11000 | 21000 | — |

3852C
Second large head

3852C Sovereign. Second (large) head. l. W W still in relief. date below R. Shield with repositioned legend die axis ↑↓

1848	....BV	425	900	2500
1849	....BV	425	900	2600
1849 Roman I	675	1250	—	—
1850	....BV	500	950	2400
1850 Roman I	675	1250	—	—
1850 ∀ICTORIA	1250	—	—	—
1850 8/5	....Extremely rare
1851	....BV	395	675	2000
1852 Roman I	675	1250	—	—
1852	....BV	395	775	2250
1853	....BV	395	700	2000
1853 F over E in DEF	750	1650	—	—
1853 ∀ICTORIA	1250	—	—	—
1854	....BV	475	1350	3100
1855	....BV	395	1000	—

3852D
WW Incuse on truncation

3852E
Extra line in ribbon - 'Ansell' named
after Royal Mint Chemist G.F. Ansell

3852D Sovereign. Similar — WW incuse on trun. die axis ↑↓

1853	....BV	575	1200	3000
1853 Roman I	675	1250	—	—
1853 Proof *FDC* £22500				
1854	....BV	395	750	2250
1854 C over rotated C	750	1650	—	—
1855 Roman I	650	1450	—	—
1855	....BV	395	750	2250
1856	....BV	395	750	2250

BV= Bullion value only (if gold price over £1600 an ounce)
NB Truly BU Victorian sovereigns without any surface marks or hairlines are very rarely encountered.

	F £	VF £	EF £	BU £
1857 ...... BV		395	750	2250
1857 ⱴ ICTORIA......1250		—	—	—
1857/5 ......Variety exists				
1858 small date......BV		395	750	1950
1858 large date ......BV		400	775	2250
1858 8/7......750		—	—	—
1859 ......BV		395	725	1650
1860 O over C in obv. leg......450		1100	—	—
1860 Roman I......650		1450	—	—
1860 ⱴ ICTORIA......1250		2750	—	—
1860 DEI GRⱯ 650		1500	—	—
1860 ......BV		395	500	1400
1860 large 0 ......BV		395	625	1500
1861 ......BV		395	575	1300
1861 Roman I......500		750	1750	3250
1861 C over rotated C in obv. leg......750		1650	—	—
1861 T over V in VICTORIA......400		750	—	—
1861 F/V in DEF narrow date 500		1250	—	—
1861 E over rotated E......750		1650	—	—
1862 R/E in BRIT......750		1650	—	—
1862 Roman I......500		975	—	—
1862 wide date ......BV		395	550	1300
1862 R/ Я in VICTORIA......1000		2500	—	—
1862 F/ⱴ in DEF 500		1250	—	—
1862 narrow date ......BV		395	550	1300
1863 ......BV		395	550	1300
1863 Roman I 500		975	—	—

3852E Sovereign. Similar — As 3852D 'Ansell' ribbon. Additional raised line on the lower part of the ribbon ↑↓

1859 750		1850	10000	18500

3852F Sovereign. Similar — As 3852D with die number 827 on trun. die axis ↑↓

1863 4750		10000	18500	—

3853
Die number location

3853 Sovereign. Similar As 3852D R. die number in space below wreath, above floral emblem, die axis ↑↓

1863 ......BV		BV	495	1100
1864 ......BV		BV	495	1100
1865 ......BV		BV	500	1200
1866 ......BV		BV	495	1100
1866/5 DIE 17 only 395		485	675	1350
1868 ......BV		BV	495	1100
1869 ......BV		BV	495	1100
1870 ......BV		BV	495	1100

BV= Bullion value only (if gold price over £1600 an ounce)

	F £	VF £	EF £	BU £

3853A Sovereign. Similar — As 3853 with die number 827 on trun. R. die number is always no. 22 die axis ↑↓

| 1863 | 4500 | 9000 | 15000 | — |

3853B Sovereign. Similar — WW in relief on trun. R. die number below wreath, above floral emblem die axis ↑↓

1870	BV	BV	450	1000
1871	BV	BV	425	900
1872	BV	BV	495	1100
1872 no die number	BV	BV	450	950
1873	BV	395	525	1000
1874	1925	1250	9000	—

3854
'M' Melbourne Mint mark

3855
'S' Sydney Mint mark

3854 Sovereign. Second (large) head. l. WW in relief date below R. M below wreath for Melbourne Mint, Australia ↑↓

1872 M	BV	BV	400	875
1872/1 M	BV	395	750	2250
1874 M	BV	BV	400	975
1880 M	450	1250	3000	7250

3854A Sovereign. Third young head. Similar but different hair arrangement.

1881 M	BV	BV	500	1500
1882 M	BV	BV	400	850
1883 M	BV	395	500	3250
1884 M	BV	BV	400	850
1885 M	BV	BV	400	950
1886 M	1500	4000	6000	13500
1887 M	775	2250	4250	9000

3855 Sovereign. Similar — As 3854. R. with S below wreath for Sydney Mint, Australia die axis ↑↓

1871 S	BV	BV	500	775
1872 S	BV	BV	500	975
1873 S	BV	BV	500	975
1875 S	BV	BV	500	975
1877 S	BV	BV	500	775
1878 S	BV	BV	500	775
1879 S	BV	BV	500	775
1880 S	BV	BV	500	975
1880 S VICTORIA	450	1500	2700	7500

3855A Sovereign. Second (large) head WW incuse on trun. date below R. with S below wreath for Sydney Mint die axis ↑↓

| 1871 S | BV | BV | 400 | 1400 |

BV= Bullion value only. At the time of going to press the spot price for gold was £1600 per oz.

	F £	VF £	EF £	BU £

3855B (Previously listed under 3855) as 3854A. Third head with different hair arrangements

1881 S	....BV	BV	500	900
1882 S	....BV	BV	500	900
1883 S	....BV	BV	500	900
1884 S	....BV	BV	500	900
1885 S	....BV	BV	500	900
1886 S	....BV	BV	500	900
1887 S	....BV	BV	500	1250

: The prices for Australian mint sovereigns are led by current trends in the Australian numismatic market place (which moved sharply downwards in 2014) and this trend has continued, although stabilising in 2017-2018. Being very condition conscious, it is truly UNC coins which command the highest price, any detraction from a true UNC coin should be taken at the EF guide price. The exchange rate of the Pound Sterling versus Australian Dollar also has an influence on price.

3856A	3857
Horse with long tail, small BP in exergue	Melbourne Mint, WW buried in truncation

3856 Sovereign. First young head. l. WW buried in narrow trun. R. St. George. London mint. Horse with short tail. Large BP and date in ex. die axis ↑↓

1871	....–	BV	500	850
1871 Proof milled edge*FDC* £18500				
1871 Plain edge proof *FDC* £12500				

3856A Sovereign. — — As 3856 R. Horse with long tail. Small BP and date in ex.die axis ↑↓

1871	....–	BV	465	850
1871 Proof *FDC* plain edge £11000				
1872	....–	BV	465	850
1873	....–	BV	465	850
1874	....–	BV	465	850
1876	....–	BV	465	850
1878	....–	BV	465	850
1879	600	1350	5000	–
1880	....–	BV	465	850

Horse tails - three variations in tail length exist across Melbourne and Sydney, all are defined more accurately by the number of spurs of extra hair, or not, at tail indent on left side.
Short tail - two spurs of hair in left indent.
Medium tail - no spurs of hair in left indent.
Long tail - one spur of hair in left indent.

3856B Sovereign. — — As 3856 R. Horse with short tail, small BP and date in ex.die axis ↑↓

1880	....–	BV	400	850
1880 Second 8/7	....BV	BV	485	1100
1884	....–	BV	465	850
1885	....–	BV	465	850

3856C Sovereign. — — As 3856 R. Horse with short tail, date but no BP in ex.die axis ↑↓

1880	....BV	BV	465	775
1880 Second 8/7	....BV	BV	500	850

BV= Bullion value only. At the time of going to press the spot price for gold was £1600 per oz.

	F £	VF £	EF £	BU £

3856D Sovereign. Second head. l. WW complete, on broad trun. R. Horse with long tail, small BP and date in ex.die axis ↑↓

1880 Second 8/7	BV	BV	465	950
1880	BV	BV	395	775

3856E Sovereign. — — As 3856D R. Horse with short tail. Date but no BP in ex. die axis ↑↓

1880	BV	BV	BV	775	

3856F Sovereign. — — As 3856E R. Horse with short tail, small BP and date in ex. die axis ↑↓

1880	BV	BV	BV	850
1884	BV	BV	BV	850
1885	BV	BV	BV	850

1887 Proof *FDC* £29500

3857 Sovereign. — — First head. l. WW buried in trun. M below head for Melbourne Mint, Australia. R. Horse with long tail, small BP and date in ex. die axis ↑↓

1872 M	BV	BV	475	2250
1873 M	BV	BV	425	800
1874 M	BV	BV	425	800
1875 M	BV	BV	425	800
1876 M	BV	BV	425	800
1877 M	BV	BV	425	675
1878 M	BV	BV	425	675
1879 M	BV	BV	425	755
1880 M	BV	BV	425	600
1881 M	BV	BV	425	600

3857A Sovereign. — — As 3857 R. horse with short tail, date but no BP in ex die axis ↑↓

1881 M	BV	BV	425	600
1882 M	BV	BV	425	575
1883 M	BV	BV	425	1100
1885 M	BV	BV	425	750

3857B Sovereign. First head l. WW buried in trun. M below head for Melbourne Mint, Australia R. Horse with short tail, small BP and date in ex. die axis ↑↓

1882 M	BV	BV	425	500
1883 M	BV	BV	425	500
1884 M	BV	BV	425	500
1885 M	BV	BV	425	595

3857C Sovereign. — — Second head. l. WW complete on broad truncation. R. Horse with short tail, small BP in ex.

1882 M	BV	BV	425	675
1883 M	BV	BV	425	450
1884 M	BV	200	425	400
1885 M	BV	BV	425	500
1886 M	BV	BV	425	500
1887 M	BV	BV	425	725

3857D Sovereign. First head. l. WW buried in trun. M below R. Horse with medium tail, small BP

1879 M	BV	BV	425	725
1880 M	BV	BV	425	725
1881 M	BV	BV	425	900
1882 M	BV	BV	425	900

3857E Sovereign. Second head. l. WW complete on trun. M below R. Horse with short tail, no BP in ex.

1884 M				*Extremely rare*
1885 M	BV	BV	425	600

BV= Bullion value only. At the time of going to press the spot price for gold was £1600 per oz.

	F £	VF £	EF £	BU £

3858 Sovereign First head. l. WW buried in narrow trun. S below head for Sydney Mint, Australia,
R. Horse with short tail, large BP and date in ex. die axis ↑↓

1871 S	...........BV	BV	585	1800

3858A Sovereign. — — As 3858 R. Horse with long tail, small BP and date in ex. die axis ↑↓

1871 S	...........BV	BV	425	2250
1872 S	...........BV	BV	425	900
1873 S	...........BV	BV	425	1550
1874 S	...........BV	BV	425	1100
1875 S	...........BV	BV	425	500
1876 S	...........BV	BV	425	500
1879 S	...........BV	BV	850	2250
1880 S	...........BV	BV	425	725

3858B Sovereign. First head. As 3858 R. Horse with short tail, date but no BP in ex. die axis ↑↓

1880 S	...........BV	BV	425	975
1881 S	...........BV	BV	425	675

3858C Sovereign. Second head. l. WW complete on broad trun. R. Horse with long tail,
small BP and date in ex. die axis ↑↓

1880 S	...........BV	BV	425	725

3858D Sovereign. — — As 3858C R. Horse with short tail, date but no BP in ex. die axis ↑↓

1881 S	...........BV	BV	425	585
1882 S	...........BV	BV	425	500

3858E Sovereign. — — As 3858D R. Horse with short tail small BP and date in ex. die axis ↑↓

1882 S	...........BV	BV	425	500
1883 S	...........BV	BV	425	1100
1884 S	...........BV	BV	425	500
1885 S	...........BV	BV	425	500
1886 S	...........BV	BV	425	500
1887 S	...........BV	BV	425	500

3858F Sovereign. Second head. Horse with long tail, no BP in ex.

1880 S	...........BV	365	500	775

3859
Type A1

3859A
Type A2

3859 Half-Sovereign. Type A1. First (smallest) young head. date below l. R. First shield,
die axis ↑↓

1838	225	325	1100	2000

1839 die axis ↑↓ or ↑↑ Proof only *FDC* £6500

1839 Milled edge proof *FDC* ....*Extremely rare*

1841	250	350	1350	3250
1842	225	300	800	1750
1843	225	325	850	2000
1844	225	325	800	1900
1845	300	800	3000	—
1846	225	325	800	1900
1847	225	325	800	1900

BV= Bullion value only. At the time of going to press the spot price for gold was £1600 per oz.

	F £	VF £	EF £	BU £
1848 Close date	225	325	850	2000
1848/7	300	500	1100	2350
1848 Wide date	225	325	1000	2000
1849	225	300	850	1900
1850	300	600	2250	—
1851	225	300	700	1600
1852	225	300	800	1750
1853	225	300	750	1600

1853 Proof small date *FDC* £12000
1853 Proof large date *FDC* £15000

	F	VF	EF	BU
1855	185	300	750	1700
1856	225	300	725	1750
1856/5	250	350	850	1850
1857	225	300	750	1600
1858	225	300	750	1600

3859A Half-Sovereign. Type A2, Second (larger) young head. date below. R̥. First shield die axis ↑↓

	F	VF	EF	BU
1858	225	300	625	1400
1859	225	300	625	1400
1860	225	300	600	1350
1861	225	300	700	1350
1862	850	2500	9000	—
1863	225	300	575	1350

3860	3860D	3860E	3860F
Die number location	Type A3	Type A4	Type A5

3860 Half-Sovereign. Type A2, second head, date below R̥. die number below shield, die axis ↑↓

	F	VF	EF	BU
1863	185	275	700	1500
1864	BV	225	600	1250
1865	BV	225	600	1250
1866	BV	225	600	1250
1867	BV	225	600	1250
1869	BV	225	600	1250
1870	BV	210	575	1100
1871	BV	210	575	1150

3860A Half-Sovereign. Second head, date below R̥. Re-engraved shield legend and rosettes closer to border, coarse boarder teeth both sides, with die number below shield die axis ↑↓

	F	VF	EF	BU
1870	325	675	1500	—
1871	265	575	1350	—

3860B Half-Sovereign. Second head, date below R̥. As last but with normal border teeth and no die number below shield die axis ↑↓

	F	VF	EF	BU
1871	300	750	1900	—

3860C Half-Sovereign. Second head, date below obv. with repositioned legend, nose now points to T in VICTORIA. R̥ Similar to last but with die number below shield die axis ↑↓

	F	VF	EF	BU
1871	300	875	1800	—
1872	265	575	1350	—

BV= Bullion value only. At the time of going to press the spot price for gold was £1600 per oz.

	F £	VF £	EF £	BU £
3860D Half-Sovereign. Type A3, Third (larger still) young head l, date below. R. As 3860A, with die number below shield die axis ↑↓				
1872 ....BV		210	500	1200
1873 ....BV		210	500	1200
1874 ....BV		200	525	1200
1875 ....BV		200	475	1100
1876 ....BV		200	475	1100
1877 ....BV		200	475	1100

3860E   3861
Half Sovereign   Type A5

3860E Half-Sovereign. Type A4. Fourth young head l. hair ribbon now narrow, date below. R.
As last with die number below shield die axis ↑↓

1876 ....BV		200	475	1100
1877 ....BV		200	475	1100
1878 ....BV		200	475	1100
1879 500		895	−	−

3860F Half-Sovereign. Type A5. Fifth young head l. in very low relief, date below. R.
As last with die number below shield die axis ↑↓

1880 185		235	675	1475

3860G Half-Sovereign. Type A4. Fourth young head, without die number below shield.

1876 ....*Extremely rare*

3861 Half-Sovereign. Fifth head, date below. R. Cross on crown buried in border. Legend and
rosettes very close to heavy border, no die number below shield die axis ↑↓

1880 ....BV		200	500	1200
1883 ....BV		200	450	1000
1884 ....BV		200	450	1000
1885 ....BV		200	450	900
1885/3 200		300	850	1650

3862 Half-Sovereign. Type A2, Second (larger) young head l. nose points between T and O.
Date below R. First crowned shield cross clear of border with S below shield for
Sydney Mint, Australia, die axis ↑↓

1871 S ....BV		225	800	8000
1871 S Proof..*Extremely rare*				

3862A Half-Sovereign. Similar obv. with repositioned legend, nose now points to T in VICTORIA.
Date below R Re-engraved shield cross touches border, S below shield die axis ↑↓

1872 S ....BV		225	800	8000

3862B Half-Sovereign. Type A3. Third (larger still) young head l. I of DEI points to rear fillet.
Date below R. As last die axis ↑↓

1875 S ....BV		225	800	8000

3862C Half-Sovereign. Type A4. Fourth young head l. front hair fillet now narrow. R. As last,
die axis ↑↓

1879 S ....BV		225	850	7500

* Beware recent forgeries
BV= Bullion value only. At the time of going to press the spot price for gold was £1600 per oz.

	F £	VF £	EF £	BU £

3862E Half-Sovereign. Fifth head, date below Ɍ. Cross on crown buried in border. Legend
and rosettes very close to heavy border, S below shield die axis ↑↓

1880 S	.... BV	225	500	11500
1881 S	.... BV	250	900	10000
1882 S	.... BV	600	2250	14000
1883 S	.... BV	200	650	4500
1883 S Proof	.... *Extremely rare*			
1886 S	.... BV	225	650	4750
1887 S	.... BV	225	550	3750

3863 Half-Sovereign. Type A3. Third (larger still) young head l. Date below Ɍ. Re-engraved
shield with M below shield for Melbourne Mint, Australia die axis ↑↓

1873 M	.... BV	225	1100	8000
1877 M	.... BV	275	2750	9500

3863A Half-Sovereign. Type A4, fourth young head l. hair ribbon now narrow. Ɍ.
As last die axis ↑↓

1877 M	.... BV	225	850	8000
1882 M	.... BV	225	2250	9500

3863B Half-Sovereign. Type A5. Fifth young head l. in low relief. Date below Ɍ.
As last die axis ↑↓

1881 M	.... BV	600	4000	12000
1882 M	.... BV	225	750	4500
1884 M	.... BV	275	2750	10000
1884 M Proof	.... *Extremely rare*			
1885 M	175	550	5000	11000
1886 M	.... BV	400	7000	12000
1886 M Proof	.... *Extremely rare*			
1887 M	.... BV	1250	10000	16500

JUBILEE COINAGE, 1887-93, die axis ↑↑

3864
1887 Five Pounds

3864* Five Pounds. Jubilee bust 1. Ɍ. St. George date in ex.

1887	1700	2250	2850	3850

— Proof *EF* £7500 *FDC* £20000
— Proof no B.P. in exergue £35000

3864A* Five Pounds. Jubilee bust 1. Ɍ. St George, S on ground for Sydney Mint, Australia

1887 S	.... *Extremely rare*

* Beware recent forgeries
BV= Bullion value only. At the time of going to press the spot price for gold was £1600 per oz.
For a detailed variety synopsis of Jubilee Head Sovereigns and their rarity see publication 'The Jubilee
Head Gold Sovereign' by David Iverson. (DISH)

	F	VF	EF	BU
	£	£	£	£

3865* Two Pounds. Jubilee bust 1. R. St George die axis ↑↑

1887 685	875	1150	1800

1887 Proof *EF* £2850 *FDC* £5500
1887 Proof no BP in exergue FDC *Extremely rare*

3865A* Two Pounds. R. St George, S on ground for Sydney Mint, Australia ↑↑

1887 S ....*Extremely rare*

3866
1887 Sovereign

3866* Sovereign. Normal JEB (angled J) designer's initials fully on trun. R. St. George.
die axis ↑↑ *(DISH L7, L8)*

1887	—	BV	365	425
1888 365	750	1250	2000
1889				*Exists?*
1890				*Exists?*

3866A Sovereign. Similar with tiny JEB (hooked J) closer designer's initials at base of truncation;
stops in an arc, die axis ↑↑ *(DISH L1, L4)*

1887 365	750	1250	2000

3866B Sovereign. Similar repositioned legend. G: of D:G: now closer to crown. Normal JEB
(angled J) designer's initials at base of trun. ↑↑ *(DISH L9, L11, L13, L14))*
1887 Proof *FDC* £4000

1888	—	BV	365	500
1889	—	BV	365	450
1890	—	BV	365	450
1891 600	1200	2000	—

3866C Sovereign. Similar obv. as last. R. Horse with longer tail, two variations of hair strands
die axis ↑↑ *(DISH L15, L16)*

1891	—	BV	365	450

1891 Proof *FDC* £22500

1892	—	BV	365	450

3866D Sovereign. First legend with tiny JEB (hooked J) with initials more spread across truncation;
stops all in line ↑↑ *(DISH L2, L3)*

1887 350	750	1250	2000

3867
"M' Melbourne Mint on groundline above 8's in date

3867 Sovereign. Similar with small spread JEB (hooked J) designer's initials fully on trun. R.
M on ground for Melbourne Mint, Australia, die axis ↑↑ *(DISH M1-M4)*

1887 M ....BV	650	1000	1850

* Beware recent forgeries
BV= Bullion value only. At the time of going to press the spot price for gold was £1600 per oz.

	F	VF	EF	BU
	£	£	£	£

3867A Sovereign. Similar with normal JEB designer's initials on trun. (angled J) die axis ↑↑ *(DISH M7, M9, M11)*

1887 M	—	BV	350	500
1888 M	BV	600	1100	2000
1889 M	—	BV	600	1850
1890 M				*Exists?*

3867B Sovereign. Similar repositioned legend. G: of D: G: now closer to crown. Normal JEB (angled J) initials at base of trun. die axis ↑↑ *(DISH M8, M10, M12, M14, M15)*

1887 M	—	BV	450	725
1888 M	—	BV	350	500
1888 Proof *FDC*				*Extremely rare*
1889 M	—	BV	350	500
1890 M	—	BV	350	500
1891 M	BV	600	1100	2000

3867C Sovereign. Similar obv. as last. ℞. Horse with longer tail, two variations of hair strands die axis ↑↑ *(DISH M16-M18)*

1891 M	—	BV	375	575
1892 M	—	BV	365	450
1893 M	—	BV	365	550

3868 Sovereign. First legend with closer JEB (angled J) stops in arc on trun. ℞. S on ground for Sydney Mint, Australia die axis ↑↑ *(DISH S9, S11, S13)*

1888 S	—	BV	375	600
1889S	—	BV	375	625
1890S	—	BV	600	1350

3868A Sovereign. Similar with spread JEB designer's initials stop level on left side of trun. (hooked J) die axis ↑↑ *(DISH S1-S8)*

1887 S	400	750	1500	3000
1887 S Proof	—	—	—	65000
1888 S	BV	600	1100	2000

3868B Sovereign. Similar repositioned legend. G: of D:G: now closer to crown. Normal JEB (angled J) initials on trun. die axis ↑↑ *(DISH S10, S12, S14)*

1888 S	—	BV	365	500
1889 S	—	BV	365	550
1890 S	—	BV	365	550

BV= Bullion value only. At the time of going to press the spot price for gold was £1600 per oz.

	F £	VF £	EF £	BU £

3868C Sovereign. Similar obv. as last. ℞. Horse with longer tail die axis ↑↑ (*DISH S15-S17*)

1891 S	....	—	BV	365	465
1892 S	....	—	BV	365	550
1893 S	....	—	BV	375	575

3868D Sovereign. First legend with spread JEB initials ending at right side of trun. (hooked J) ↑↑
(*DISH S2*)

1887 S	....	400	800	1500	3000

3869   3869D
higher shield, cross blends into border   Plain trun., lower shield, cross clear of border

3869 Half-Sovereign. Similar obv. normal JEB designer's initials. on trun. ℞. High shield
die axis ↑↑

1887	....	BV	BV	225	350
— Proof *FDC* £2250					
1890	....	BV	185	500	—

3869A Half-Sovereign. Similar small close JEB intitials. on trun. ℞. High shield die axis ↑↑

1887	....	BV	175	450	—

3869B Half-Sovereign. Similar normal JEB initials. on trun. ℞. Lower shield, date therefore
spread apart, complete cross at top, die axis ↑↑

1890	....	BV	175	475	—
1892	....	BV	175	475	—

3869C Half-Sovereign. Similar no JEB initials on trun. ℞. High Shield die axis ↑↑

1887	....	BV	175	450	—
1890	....	BV	175	240	400
1891	....	BV	175	450	—
1892	....	BV	175	450	—

3869D Half-Sovereign. Jubilee bust 1. ℞. Lower shield, date therefore spread apart die axis ↑↑

1890	....	—	175	225	350
1891	....	—	175	250	375
1892	....	—	175	225	350
1893	....	—	175	250	375

3870

3870 Half-Sovereign. Similar small very spread JEB initials on trun. ℞. High shield, M below for
Melbourne Mint, Australia, die axis ↑↑

1887 M	....	BV	225	400	1600
1887 M Proof	....*Extremely rare*				

BV= Bullion value only. At the time of going to press the spot price for gold was £1600 per oz.

	F	VF	EF	BU
	£	£	£	£

3870A Half-Sovereign. Similar small close JEB initials on trun. R̸. As last die axis ↑↑
1887 M .... BV   225   350   1400
1887 M Proof...*Extremely rare*

3870B Half-Sovereign. Similar normal JEB initials on trun. R̸. Lower shield, date therefore
    spread part die axis ↑↑
1893 M .... BV   250   500   2250

3871 Half-Sovereign. Similar small very spread JEB initials on trun. (hooked J) R̸. High shield S
    below for Sydney Mint, Australia ↑↑
1887 S .... BV   225   400   1200

3871A Half-Sovereign. Similar small close JEB initials on trun. R̸ As last. die axis ↑↑
1887 S .... BV   225   325   1100
1887 S Proof...*Extremely rare*

3871B Half-Sovereign. Jubilee bust 1. Normal JEB initials on trun. R̸. Lower shield,
    date therefore spread apart, S below for Sydney Mint, Australia die axis ↑↑
1889 S .... BV   250   1400   4500

3871C Half-Sovereign. Jubilee bust 1. Normal JEB initials on trun. R̸. High shield,
    S below for Sydney Mint, Australia die axis ↑↑
1891 S .... BV   300   1100   3750

3871D Half-Sovereign. Jubilee bust 1. No JEB initials on trun. R̸. As last die axis ↑↑
1891 S .... BV   250   700   3000

OLD HEAD COINAGE, 1893-1901, die axis ↑↑

3872
1893 Five Pounds

3872* Five Pounds. Old veiled bust 1. R̸. St. George and dragon, date and BP in ex.
1893 1750   2500   4000   6500
1893 Proof *EF* £8500   *FDC* £18500

3873
1893 Two Pounds

3873* Two Pounds. Old veiled bust 1. R̸. St. George and dragon, date and BP in ex. die axis ↑↑
1893 750   1000   1950   2750
1893 Proof *EF* £3850   *FDC* £7500

* Beware recent forgeries
BV= Bullion value only. At the time of going to press the spot price for gold was £1600 per oz.

3874 - 1893 Sovereign

	F	VF	EF	BU
	£	£	£	£

3874 Sovereign. Old veiled bust 1. R. St. George, London Mint die axis ↑↑

1893	—	—	BV	425
1893 Proof *FDC* £4000				
1894	—	—	BV	425
1895	—	—	BV	425
1896	—	—	BV	425
1898	—	—	BV	425
1899	—	—	BV	425
1900	—	—	BV	425
1901	—	—	BV	425

3875 Sovereign. Similar R. St. George. M on ground for Melbourne Mint, Australia die axis ↑↑

1893 M	—	—	BV	475
1894 M	—	—	BV	425
1895 M	—	—	BV	425
1896 M	—	—	BV	425
1897 M	—	—	BV	425
1898 M	—	—	BV	425
1899 M	—	—	BV	425
1900 M	—	—	BV	425
1901 M	—	—	BV	425

3876 - Perth Mint mark   3878 - 1893 Half -Sovereign

3876 Sovereign. Similar — P on ground for Perth Mint, Australia die axis ↑↑

1899 P	BV	BV	475	2250
1900 P	—	BV	BV	475
1901 P	—	BV	BV	475

3877 Sovereign. Similar — S on ground for Sydney Mint, Australia die axis ↑↑

1893 S	—	—	BV	425
1894 S	—	—	BV	425
1895 S	—	—	BV	425
1896 S	—	BV	BV	475
1897 S	—	BV	BV	475
1898 S	—	BV	BV	475
1899 S	—	—	BV	425
1900 S	—	—	BV	425
1901 S	—	—	BV	425

BV= Bullion value only. At the time of going to press the spot price for gold was £1600 per oz.
NB Truly BU old bust sovereigns are very scarce. Any surface defects will cause the value to drop significantly.

	F £	VF £	EF £	BU £
3878 Half-Sovereign. Old veiled bust 1.R. St. George. Date in ex. (no B.P. on this issue in exergue) London Mint die axis ↑↑				
1893	—	BV	195	325
— Proof *FDC* £2850				
1894	—	BV	195	325
1895	—	BV	195	325
1896	—	BV	195	325
1897	—	BV	195	325
1898	—	BV	195	325
1899	—	BV	195	325
1900	—	BV	195	325
1901	—	BV	195	325
3879 Half-Sovereign. Similar — M on ground for Melbourne Mint, Australia die axis ↑↑				
1893 M			*Extremely rare*	
1896 M	BV	250	400	2250
1899 M	BV	250	600	2500
1899 M Proof			*Extremely rare*	
1900 M	BV	250	650	2000
1900 M Proof			*Extremely rare*	
1896 M Proof			*Extremely rare*	
3880 Half-Sovereign. Similar — P on ground for Perth Mint, Australia die axis ↑↑				
1899 P Proof only			*unique*	
1900 P	185	300	750	4000
3881 Half-Sovereign. Similar — S on ground for Sydney Mint, Australia die axis ↑↑				
1893 S	BV	250	500	1650
1893 S Proof			*Extremely rare*	
1897 S	BV	250	425	2000
1900 S	BV	300	375	1200

BV= Bullion value only. At the time of going to press the spot price for gold was £1600 per oz.
NB Truly BU old bust sovereigns are very scarce. Any surface defects will cause the value to drop
significantly.

SILVER

YOUNG HEAD COINAGE, 1838-87, die axis ↑↓

3882
1844 Crown

Cinquefoil

Star

	F	VF	EF	BU
	£	£	£	£

†**3882 Crown.** Young head. l. R. Crowned shield, regnal year on edge in Roman figures
(eg 1847 = XI)

1839 Proof only *FDC* £27500

	F	VF	EF	BU
1844 Star stops, extra square of metal at tip of ponytail	150	350	1500	4500
1844 Star stops	60	200	1450	4000
1844 Cinquefoil stops	125	400	1750	4250
1844 Mistruck edge lettering	145	475	3500	–
1845 Cinquefoil stops	65	250	1500	4000
1847 XI Cinquefoil stops	125	375	2000	5000

3883 - 1847 Gothic Crown

3883*Crown. 'Gothic' type, bust l. R. Crowned cruciform Shields, emblems in angles.
inscribed edge, mdcccxlvii=

1847 Undecimo on edge die axis ↑↓	875	1350	3850	15000

1847 Septimo on edge of highest rarity.

1847 Proof in gold plain edge *FDC* .... *Of highest rarity*

1847 Proof, Plain edge die axis ↑↑ *FDC* £16500

1847 Proof in white metal plain edge *FDC*

3884 Crown. Similar mdcccliii=

1853. Septimo on edge die axis ↑↑ Proof *FDC* £32000

1853 plain edge proof *FDC* £42000

†*The Victorian young head Crowns are notoriously hard to grade. A truly BU coin must show all design elements clearly expecially on hair fillets and the reverse shield. All facial features and hair must also be present.*

**Beware of recent forgeries.*

	F £	VF £	EF £	BU £

3885 Halfcrown. Type A¹. Young head l. with one ornate and one plain fillet binding hair. WW in relief on trun. R. Crowned shield of arms, edge milled. Die axis ↑↓
1839 Milled edge Proof *FDC Extremely rare*
1839 Proof plain edge *FDC* £5000
3886 Halfcrown. Type A² Similar, but two ornate fillets binding hair.die axis ↑↓
1839 Proof only *FDC* £6750
3886A Halfcrown. Type A²ᐟ³ Similar, Two plain fillets, WW relief, die axis ↑↓ plain edge
1839 Proof *FDC* £7750
3887 Halfcrown. Type A³. Similar two plain fillets. WW incuse on trun. die axis ↑↓

	F	VF	EF	BU
1839 1250		3850	10750	—
1839 Milled edge Proof *FDC* £6750				
1839 Plain edge Proof *FDC* £6750				
1840 60		200	1100	2750

3888 Halfcrown. Type A⁴. Similar but no initials on trun. die axis ↑↓

	F	VF	EF	BU
1841 1200		2250	4850	8000
1842 60		200	700	1500
1843 125		450	1850	4250
1844 40		150	585	1500
1844 not in edge collar ....*Extremely rare*				
1845 40		150	585	1575
1845 5/3 ....*Extremely rare*				
1846 60		200	585	1575
1848/6 185		525	1500	3500
1848/7 ....*Extremely rare*				
1848 200		575	2000	4250
1849 large date....................65		200	975	2250
1849/7 ....*Extremely rare*				
1849 small date....................100		350	1100	2650
1850 65		275	900	2450

1850 Proof *FDC* £15750
1853 Proof *FDC* £7500
1862 Proof *FDC* £13500
1862 Plain edge Proof *FDC* £12500
1864 Proof *FDC* £13500
1864 Plain edge Proof *FDC* £12500

3889	3890
Type A5 Halfcrown	1849 'Godless' Florin

3889 Halfcrown. Similar Type A⁵. As last but design of inferior workmanship R. Crowned shield die axis ↑↓

	F	VF	EF	BU
1874 25		80	265	700

1874 Proof *FDC* £9500

	F	VF	EF	BU
	£	£	£	£
1875 25		80	225	685
1875 Proof *FDC* £9500				
1876 25		80	265	700
1876/5 30		80	355	900
1877 25		80	265	650
1878 25		80	265	675
1878 Proof *FDC* £8500				
1879 25		80	325	700
1879 Proof *FDC* £8500				
1880 25		80	200	600
1880 Proof *FDC* £8500				
1881 25		80	200	600
1881 Proof *FDC* £8500				
1881 Plain edge proof *FDC* £9750				
1882 25		80	325	600
1883 25		80	225	600
1883 Plain edge proof *FDC* £9750				
1884 25		80	225	600
1885 25		80	225	600
1885 Proof *FDC* £8500				
1886 25		80	225	600
1886 Plain edge proof *FDC* £9000				
1887 30		90	250	600
1887 Proof *FDC* £9000				

3890 Florin. 'Godless' type A (i.e. without D.G.), WW behind bust within linear circle, die axis ↑↓

	F	VF	EF	BU
1848 Plain edge (Pattern) *FDC* £3750				
1848 Milled edge ↑↑ or ↑↓ Proof *FDC* £5500				
1849 WW obliterated........50		100	400	800
1849 30		75	275	575

3891 Florin. 'Gothic' type B[1]. Reads brit:, WW below bust, date at end of obverse legend in gothic numerals (1851 to 1863) Crowned cruciform Shields, emblems in angles, edge milled. die axis ↑↓

	F	VF	EF	BU
1851 mdcccli Proof only *FDC* £32500				
1852 mdccclii 25		75	250	600
1852 mdccclii Proof *FDC* £5750				
1852/1 mdccclii, ii/i........25		75	375	760
1853 mdcccliii 25		75	300	675
1853 mdcccliii Proof *FDC* £6750				
1854 mdcccliv 850		1950	7000	—
1855 mdccclv........25		75	325	760
1856 mdccclvi 25		75	325	760
1857 mdccclvii 25		75	325	750
1857 mdccclvii Proof *FDC* £6500				
1858 mdccclviii 25		75	325	775
1858 mdccclviii Proof *FDC* £6500				
1859 mdccclix 25		75	325	775
1860 mdccclx 25		75	400	925
1862 mdccclxii 250		685	1850	5500
1862 mdccclxii Plain edge Proof *FDC* £8000				
1863 mdccclxiii 900		2250	7000	15000
1863 mdccclxiii Plain edge Proof *FDC* £12500				

3891
1853 Florin Type B¹

3893

	F	VF	EF	BU
	£	£	£	£

3892 Florin. Type B². Similar as last but die number below bust (1864 to 1867) die axis ↑↓

1864 mdccclxiv	.25	75	325	850
1864 mdccclxiv heavy flan	.350	800	2500	5775
1864 mdccclxiv heavy flan Proof *FDC* £9500				
1865 mdccclxv	.40	100	485	880
1866 mdccclxvi	.35	80	400	850
1867 mdccclxvii	.35	85	450	1015
1867 mdccclxvii Proof *FDC* £6500				

3893 Florin. Type B³. Similar reads britt:, die number below bust (1868 to 1879) die axis

1868 mdccclxviii	.30	90	485	900
1869 mdccclxix	.30	90	500	1050
1869 mdccclxix Proof *FDC* £6750				
1870 mdccclxx	.25	75	350	880
1870 mdccclxx Proof *FDC* £6750				
1871 mdccclxxi	.25	55	325	715
1871 mdccclxxi Proof *FDC* £6000				
1872 mdccclxxii	.20	55	250	715
1873 mdccclxxiii	.20	55	250	715
1873 mdccclxxiii Proof *FDC* £5750				
1874 mdccclxxiv	.25	75	300	715
1874/3 mdccclxxiv iv/iii	.35	80	325	935
1875 mdccclxxv	.25	75	300	755
1876 mdccclxxvi	.25	75	285	960
1877 mdccclxxvii	.25	50	300	715
1879 mdccclxxix				*Extremely rare*

3894 Florin. Type B⁴. Similar as last but with border of 48 arcs and no WW below bust
die axis ↑↓

1877 mdccclxxvii				*Extremely rare*

3895 Florin. Type B⁵. Similar but border of 42 arcs (1867, 1877 and 1878) die axis ↑↓

1867 mdccclxvii	.2850	—	—	—
1877 mdccclxxvii	.25	75	350	850
1878 mdccclxxviii	.25	75	300	800
1878 mdccclxxviii Proof *FDC*				*Extremely rare*

3896 Florin. Type B⁵/⁶. Similar as last but no die number below bust (1877, 1879) die axis ↑↓

1877 mdccclxxvii	.125	275	600	1540
1879 mdccclxxix	.110	275	725	1790

3897
1878 - Florin Type B[6]

	F	VF	EF	BU
	£	£	£	£

3897 Florin. Type B[6]. Similar reads britt:, WW; Border of 48 arcs (1879) die axis ↑↓

1878 mdccclxxviii ....*Extremely rare*

1879 mdccclxxix 25 75 295 770

3898 Florin. Type B[7]. Similar as last but no WW, Border of 38 arcs (1879) die axis ↑↓

1879 mdccclxxix 25 75 295 770

1879 mdccclxxix Proof *FDC* £6000

3899 Florin. Type B[3/8]. Similar as next but younger portrait (1880) die axis ↑↓

1880 mdccclxxx...*Extremely rare*

3900 Florin. Type B[8]. Similar but border of 34 arcs (1880 to 1887) die axis ↑↓

1880 mdccclxxx...25 60 350 635

1880 mdccclxxx Proof *FDC* £6000

1881 mdccclxxxi 25 60 275 690

1881 mdccclxxxi Proof *FDC* £5750

1881 mdccclxxxi/xxri 30 80 385 875

1883 mdccclxxxiii 20 60 285 690

1883 mdccclxxxiii Proof *FDC* £5000

1884 mdccclxxxiv 20 60 285 690

1885 mdccclxxxv...20 60 285 690

1885 mdccclxxxv Proof *FDC* £6000

1886 mdccclxxxvi 20 60 285 690

1886 mdccclxxxvi Proof *FDC* £6250

3901 Florin. Type B[9]. Similar but border of 46 arcs die axis ↑↓

1887 mdccclxxxvii 30 75 365 900

1887 mdccclxxxvii Proof *FDC* ....*Extremely rare*

3902 Shilling. Type A[1]. First head l., WW on trun. ℞. crowned mark of value within wreath, date below, die axis ↑↓

1838 ....25 60 195 495

1838 Proof *FDC* £4500

1839 ....35 90 275 880

1839 Proof *FDC* £3650

3903 Shilling Type A[2]. Second head, l. WW on trun. (proof only), 1839 die axis ↑↑ *FDC* £2000

3904 - Type A³ Shilling

	F £	VF £	EF £	BU £
3904 Shilling Type A³. Second head, l. no initials on trun. ℞. Similar die axis ↑↓				
1839 25	60	185	495
1839 Proof plain edge *FDC* £1750				
1839 Proof plain edge en medaille ↑↑ *FDC* £3000				
1839 Proof milled edge *FDC* £4000				
1840 25	60	225	580
1840 Proof *FDC* £4500				
1841 40	100	250	580
1842 25	60	225	550
1842 Proof *FDC* £4500				
1843 75	150	350	825
1844 25	50	225	535
1845 25	60	225	580
1846 25	60	200	495
1848 over 6 65	225	825	1925
1849 25	60	250	660
1850 800	2250	6250	—
1850/49 875	2000	6000	—
1851 80	200	650	1485
1851 Proof *FDC* £5500				
1852 25	60	180	470
1853 25	50	180	470
1853 Milled edge Proof *FDC* £3000				
1854 250	600	2500	5500
1854/1 300	875	3750	—
1855 20	45	165	470
1856 20	45	165	470
1857 20	45	165	470
1857 REG F: Ɔ:error 250	600	1950	—
1858 20	45	165	470
1859 20	45	165	470
1859 9/8 25	65	375	880
1859 Proof *FDC* £4500				
1860 20	45	225	580
1861 20	45	225	550
1861 D/B in FD 150	400	1000	—
1862 50	120	325	745
1863 100	250	650	1980
1863/1 120	350	900	—

	F	VF	EF	BU
	£	£	£	£

3905 Shilling Type A^4. Similar as last, R. Die number above date die axis ↑↓

1864	15	45	145	470
1865	15	45	145	470
1866	15	45	145	470
1866 BBITANNIAR	60	300	1100	2035
1867	15	45	145	470

3906 Shilling Type A^5. Third head, l. R. Similar no die number above date die axis ↑↓

1867 Proof £4500
1867 Proof plain edge £4750

1879	225	500	1250	2420

1879 Proof, milled edge, *FDC* £4500

3906A - Type A^6 Shilling   Die number location above date

3906A Shilling Type A^6. Third head, l. R. Similar die number above date die axis ↑↓

1867	200	500	1500	3025
1868	15	45	145	470
1869	20	50	190	470
1870	15	50	195	470
1871	15	45	135	470

1871 Plain edge proof *FDC* £4250
1871 Milled edge proof *FDC* £4000

1872	12	45	145	470
1873	12	45	145	470
1874	12	45	145	470
1875	12	45	145	435
1876	20	50	150	470
1877	12	45	145	460
1878	20	50	200	530

1878 Milled edge Proof *FDC* £4250
1879 uncertain to exist as normal coin or proof?

3907 Shilling Type A^7. Fourth head, l. R. Similar no die number above date die axis ↑↓

1879	12	40	130	435
1879 B over R in GBATIA	350	—	—	—

1879 Proof *FDC* £4500

1880	12	40	125	325

1880 Proof plain edge £4500
1880 Proof milled edge £3850

1881	12	40	100	250

1881 Proof plain edge £4500
1881 Proof milled edge £3750

1882	20	50	165	425
1883	12	40	135	360

1883 plain edge Proof *FDC* £4750

1884	12	40	110	330

1884 Proof *FDC* £3750

1885	12	40	100	325

	F	VF	EF	BU
	£	£	£	£
1885 Proof *FDC* £4250				
1886	12	40	110	285
1886 Proof *FDC* £4250				
1887	12	40	125	360
1887 Proof *FDC* £4000				

3907A Shilling. Type A⁷. Fourth head, R. Similar die number above date die axis ↑↓

1878	25	60	140	300
1878 Milled edge Proof *FDC* £4250				
1879	20	45	145	400

3908
Type A¹ Sixpence

3908 Sixpence. Type A¹. First head l. R. Crowned mark of value within wreath, date below
die axis ↑↓

1838	25	50	130	360
1838 Proof *FDC* £2750				
1839	25	50	130	385
1839 Proof *FDC* £1200				
1840	25	50	130	415
1841	25	50	150	440
1842	25	50	140	360
1843	25	50	140	360
1844 Small 44	18	40	140	415
1844 Large 44	18	40	150	440
1845	20	50	140	385
1846	20	50	140	440
1847 An example in fair condition sold at DNW, 29/9/10, lot 1773 for £850 + premium				
1848	90	275	950	3575
1848/6 or 7	90	275	950	3575
1850	25	50	140	330
1850/3	25	50	150	385
1851	25	50	150	385
1852	25	50	140	385
1853	20	40	120	435
1853 Proof *FDC* £1750				
1854	300	650	1500	3575
1855	20	50	140	385
1855/3	20	50	150	440
1855 Proof *FDC* ....*Extremely rare*				
1856	20	50	130	415
1857	20	50	130	415
1858	20	50	130	415
1858 Proof *FDC* ....*Extremely rare*				
1859	20	50	130	415
1859/8	20	50	130	415
1860	20	50	130	415
1862	110	285	750	1650
1863	75	175	525	1210
1866	....*Extremely rare*			

| 3909 | 3912 |
| Die number location above date | Type A⁵ Sixpence |

| | F | VF | EF | BU |
| | £ | £ | £ | £ |

3909 Sixpence. Type A². First head, ℞. Similar die number above date die axis ↑↓

1864	20	45	130	425
1865	20	45	150	400
1866	20	45	130	425
1867	20	45	150	435

| 3910 | 3911 |

3910 Sixpence. Type A³. Second head, l. ℞. Similar die number above date, die axis ↑↓

1867	20	50	120	330
1867 Proof *FDC* £3500				
1868	20	50	120	330
1869	20	50	150	470
1869 Proof *FDC* £3500				
1870	40	90	200	525
1870 plain edge Proof *FDC* £3500				
1871	20	50	110	360
1871 plain edge Proof *FDC* £3500				
1872	20	50	110	360
1873	20	50	125	360
1874	20	50	110	275
1875	20	50	110	330
1876	30	75	160	470
1877	20	50	110	330
1878	20	50	110	330
1878 DRITANNIAR	150	420	1250	—
1878 Proof *FDC* £3500				
1878/7	50	175	800	—
1879	20	50	125	360

3911 Sixpence. Type A⁴. Second head, l. ℞. Similar No die number, die axis ↑↓

1871	20	50	125	360
1871 Proof *FDC* £3000				
1877	20	50	125	360
1879	20	50	125	360
1879 milled edge Proof *FDC* £3000				
1879 plain edge Proof *FDC* £3250				
1880	20	50	110	305

3912 3913

	F £	VF £	EF £	BU £
3912 Sixpence. Type A⁵. Third head l. R. Similar, die axis ↑↓				
1880	15	40	90	200
1880 Proof *FDC* £2750				
1881	15	40	90	200
1881 plain edge Proof *FDC* ....*Extremely rare*				
1881 milled edge Proof *FDC* ....*Extremely rare*				
1882	25	50	110	350
1883	15	40	90	200
1883 Small R legend	25	50	150	400
1883 plain edge Proof *FDC Extremely rare*				
1884	15	40	90	200
1885	15	40	90	200
1885 Proof *FDC* £2750				
1886	15	40	90	200
1886 Proof *FDC* £2750				
1887	15	40	90	200
1887 Proof *FDC* £2850				
3913 Groat (4d.). Young head 1.R. Britannia seated r. date in ex, edge milled, die axis ↑↑				
1837 Plain edge Proof £13500				
1837 Milled edge Proof £12500				
1838	12	40	75	135
1838 plain edge Proof *FDC* £1500				
1838 Milled edge Proof £1350				
1838/∞ 8	30	100	175	300
1839	12	40	75	175
1839 die axis ↑↑ Proof plain edge *FDC* £750				
1839 die axis ↑↓ Proof plain edge *FDC* £800				
1840	12	40	75	150
1840 small round o	12	40	75	175
1841	12	40	100	250
1842	12	40	75	175
1842 Proof *FDC* £1500				
1842/1	12	40	75	225
1843	12	40	75	150
1843 4 over 5 *Exists*?	12	40	90	250
1844	12	40	75	150
1845	12	40	75	150
1846	12	40	75	150
1847/6 (or 8)	30	125	360	700
1848/6	15	50	90	200
1848	12	40	75	150
1848/7/6	12	40	110	325
1849	12	40	75	150
1849/8	12	40	75	150
1851	40	125	350	725
1852	100	250	600	1000

	F	VF	EF	BU
	£	£	£	£
1853 250	600	1200	–
1853 Proof *FDC* milled edge £1750			
1853 Proof *FDC* plain edge £1950			
1854 10	30	60	150
1855 10	30	60	150
1855/3 15	40	75	175
1857 Milled or plain edge proof *FDC* £2500			
1857 Plain edge pattern £3000			
1862 Plain or milled edge Proof *FDC* £3000			
1862 Plain edge pattern *FDC* £3750			

3914 Threepence. Type A[1]. First bust, young head, high relief, ear fully visible, die axis ↑↓
R̵ Crowned 3; as Maundy threepence but with a less prooflike surface.

	F	VF	EF	BU
1838* 25	50	100	200
1838 BRITANNIAB ....*Extremely rare*			
1839* 50	100	200	350
1839 Proof (see Maundy)			
1840* 25	50	100	250
1841* 60	100	150	250
1842* 60	100	150	275
1843* 10	30	75	200
1844* 25	50	100	200
1845 10	30	70	175
1846 100	200	400	800
1847* 100	200	400	800
1848* 100	200	650	–
1849 60	100	200	400
1850 20	40	90	350
1851 50	100	200	400
1851 reads 1551 650	–	–	–
1851 5 over 8 100	200	400	800
1852* 100	225	650	1100
1853 100	200	400	800
1854 20	50	100	225
1855 30	60	120	250
1856 15	40	90	200
1857 20	50	100	250
1858 20	50	75	200
1858 BRITANNIAB ....*Extremely rare*			
1858/6 30	60	200	–
1858/5 30	60	150	–
1859 15	40	75	200
1860 15	40	100	250
1861 15	40	75	20

*Issued for Colonial use only.

3914A - Type A²   3914C - Type A⁴   3914D - Type A⁵

	F £	VF £	EF £	BU £
3914A Threepence. Type A². First bust variety, slightly older portrait with aquiline nose ↑↓				
1859	15	30	75	175
1860	15	30	75	175
1861	15	30	75	175
1862	15	30	75	175
1863	30	50	100	200
1864	15	30	75	175
1865	15	30	100	200
1866	15	30	75	175
1867	15	30	75	175
1868	15	30	75	175
1868 RRITANNIAR			*Extremely rare*	
3914B Threepence. Type A³. Second Bust, slightly larger, lower relief, mouth fuller, nose more pronounced, rounded truncation, die axis ↑↓				
1867	15	30	100	225
3914C Threepence. Type A⁴. Obv. as last. ℞. Tie ribbon further from tooth border, cross on crown nearer to tooth border die axis ↑↓				
1866			*Extremely rare*	
1867	15	30	80	200
1868	15	30	80	200
1869	30	60	120	275
1870	12	25	70	150
1871	12	25	75	175
1872	10	20	75	175
1873	8	20	55	125
1874	8	20	55	100
1875	8	20	55	100
1876	10	20	55	100
1877	8	20	65	125
1878	8	20	65	125
1879	8	20	65	125
1879 Proof *FDC*			*Extremely rare*	
1884	8	10	55	100
3914D Threepence. Type A⁵. Third bust, older features, mouth closed, hair strands leading from 'bun' vary, die axis ↑↓				
1880	8	15	60	115
1881	8	15	45	100
1882	15	28	65	175
1883	8	15	45	100
1885	8	15	45	100
1885 Proof *FDC*			*Extremely rare*	
1886	8	15	45	100
1887	8	15	60	115
3914E Twopence. Young head 1. ℞ Date divided by a crowned 2 within a wreath, die axis ↑↓				
1838	12	25	40	75
1848	12	25	40	80

3915 - Three-Halfpence

	F £	VF £	EF £	BU £
3915 Three-Halfpence. (for Colonial use).Young head 1. R̥. Crowned value and date, die axis ↑↓				
1838 15		25	50	125
1838 Proof *FDC* £1000				
1839 15		25	50	125
1840 15		25	85	200
1841 15		25	50	125
1842 15		25	50	125
1843 15		25	50	125
1843 Proof *FDC* £1200				
1843/34 15		25	75	150
1843/34 Proof *FDC* £1000				
1860 15		25	70	175
1862 15		25	70	175
1862 Proof *FDC* £1500				
1870 Proof only £1750				

3916 - 1880 Maundy Set

	F	VF	EF	BU
3916 Maundy Set. (4d., 3d., 2d. and 1.) Young head 1., die axis ↑↓				
1838 ....—		—	400	800
1838 Proof *FDC* £2500				
1838 Proof in gold *FDC* £35000				
1839 ....—		—	300	500
1839 Proof die axis ↑↑ *FDC* £1650				
1840 ....—		—	600	1000
1841 ....—		—	400	800
1842* ....—		—	300	500
1843 ....—		—	250	450
1844 ....—		—	250	450
1845 ....—		—	250	450
1846* ....—		—	350	750
1847* ....—		—	350	750
1848* ....—		—	350	750
1849 ....—		—	250	500
1850 ....—		—	250	500
1851 ....—		—	250	500
1852* ....—		—	500	800
1853* ....—		—	350	750
1853 Proof *FDC* £2250				
1854 ....—		—	200	450
1855 ....—		—	200	450
1856 ....—		—	200	450
1857 ....*—		—	200	450

Issued for Colonial use only.

		F	VF	EF	BU
		£	£	£	£
1858		—	—	150	365
1859		—	—	150	365
1860		—	—	150	365
1861		—	—	150	365
1862		—	—	175	400
1863		—	—	175	400
1864		—	—	150	375
1865		—	—	150	375
1866		—	—	150	365
1867		—	—	150	365

1867 Proof set *FDC* £2500

		F	VF	EF	BU
1868		—	—	150	375
1869		—	—	150	400
1870		—	—	150	375
1871		—	—	125	365

1871 Proof set *FDC* £2500

		F	VF	EF	BU
1872		—	—	125	365
1873		—	—	125	365
1874		—	—	125	365
1875		—	—	125	365
1876		—	—	125	365
1877		—	—	125	365
1878		—	—	125	375

1878 Proof set *FDC* £2500

		F	VF	EF	BU
1879		—	—	125	365
1880		—	—	120	365
1881		—	—	120	365

1881 Proof set *FDC* £2500

		F	VF	EF	BU
1882		—	—	120	365

1882 Proof set *FDC* £2500

		F	VF	EF	BU
1883		—	—	120	365
1884		—	—	120	365
1885		—	—	120	365
1886		—	—	120	365
1887		—	—	150	375

3917 — Fourpence, 1838-87	*from* 20	40
3918 — Threepence, 1838-87	*from* 25	55
3919 — Twopence, 1838-87	*from* 20	40
3920 — Penny, 1838-87	*from* 20	50

Maundy Sets in good quality original cases are worth approximately £40 more than the prices quoted.
Refer to footnote after 3796.

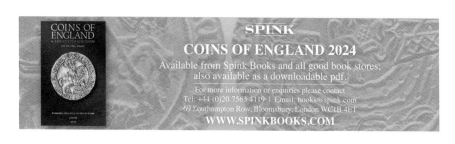

JUBILEE COINAGE 1887-93, die axis ↑↑

3921
1887 Crown

	F £	VF £	EF £	BU £
3921 Crown. Jubilee bust l. R. St. George and dragon,date in ex, edge milled, die axis ↑↑				
1887 40		60	120	250
1887 Proof *FDC* £3250				
1888 narrow date 40		60	185	425
1888 wide date..60		180	575	1100
1889 30		50	135	350
1890 40		60	165	425
1891 40		60	200	475
1892 40		65	250	600

3922 Double-Florin (4s.).Jubilee bust l. R. (As Florin) Crowned cruciform shields. Sceptre
in angles. Roman I in date, die axis ↑↑

1887 25		50	95	200
1887 Proof *FDC* £1250				

3923
1887 Double-Florin, Arabic 1 in date

3923 Double-Florin Jubilee bust l. R. Similar but Arabic 1 in date, die axis ↑↑

1887 25		50	75	175
1887 Proof *FDC* £1200				
1888 25		50	100	250
1888 inverted 1 for I in VICTORIA 40		90	200	550
1889 25		50	100	250
1889 inverted 1 for I in VICTORIA 45		85	275	575
1890 25		50	125	300

3924
1887 Halfcrown

3925
1890 Florin reverse

	F £	VF £	EF £	BU £
3924 Halfcrown. Jubilee bust 1. R. Crowned shield in garter and collar, die axis ↑↑				
1887 20		40	60	120
1887 Proof *FDC* £675				
1888 20		40	80	225
1889 20		40	80	250
1890 20		40	110	250
1891 20		40	120	350
1892 20		40	135	300
3925 Florin. Jubilee bust 1. R. Crowned cruciform shields, sceptres in angles, die axis ↑↑				
1887 15		25	50	90
1887 Proof *FDC* £500				
1888 obverse die of 1887 20		45	110	225
1888 20		35	70	185
1889 20		35	95	215
1890 15		45	185	450
1891 25		70	300	600
1892 35		110	350	700
1892 Proof *FDC* £10000				

3926
small head Shilling

	F	VF	EF	BU
3926 Shilling. Small Jubilee head. R. Crowned shield in Garter, die axis ↑↑				
1887 8		15	25	50
1887 Proof *FDC* £425				
1888 35		80	175	325
1888/7 8		15	55	125
1889 25		60	300	875
3927 Shilling. Large Jubilee head. R. Similar as before, die axis ↑↑				
1889 8		15	55	125
1889 Proof *FDC* £2850				
1890 8		16	65	150
1891 8		16	75	175
1891 Proof *FDC* £2850				
1892 8		16	75	175

3928
1887 'withdrawn type' Sixpence

	F £	VF £	EF £	BU £
3928 Sixpence. JEB designer's initials below trun. R. Shield in Garter (withdrawn type), die axis ↑↑				
1887 8	15	28	40	
1887 Proof *FDC* £425				
1887 JEB on trun. 30	75	130	350	
1887 R/V in VICTORIA..15	40	110	250	

3929	3930
Crowned value Sixpence	1888 Groat

3929 Sixpence. R. Jubilee bust 1. Crowned, value in wreath, die axis ↑↑

	F	VF	EF	BU
1887 8	10	20	35	
1887 Proof *FDC* £1500				
1888 8	12	30	85	
1888 Proof *FDC* £2000				
1889 8	12	30	85	
1890 8	12	40	100	
1890 Proof *FDC* ....*Extremely rare*				
1891 12	25	50	125	
1892 12	25	50	120	
1893 550	1100	3250	6500	

3930 Groat (for use in British Guiana). Jubilee Bust 1. R. Britannia seated r. date in axis, die axis ↑↑

	F	VF	EF	BU
1888 Milled edge Proof *FDC* £1250				
1888 20	40	75	150	

3931 Threepence. As Maundy but less prooflike surface, die axis ↑↑

	F	VF	EF	BU
1887 4	8	15	30	
1887 Proof *FDC* £225				
1888 4	8	18	55	
1889 4	8	13	45	
1890 4	8	13	45	
1891 4	8	16	50	
1892 4	8	18	55	
1893 18	60	185	450	

3932
1889 Maundy Set

		EF £	FDC £
3932 Maundy Set. (4d., 3d., 2d. and 1d.) Jubilee bust 1.die axis ↑↑			
1888		125	225
1888 Proof set *FDC*		*Extremely rare*	
1889		125	225
1890		125	225
1891		125	225
1892		125	225
3933 — Fourpence, 1888-92	*from*	25	40
3934 — Threepence, 1888-92	*from*	25	40
3935 — Twopence, 1888-92	*from*	25	40
3936 — Penny, 1888-92	*from*	25	40

Maundy Sets in the original undamaged cases are worth approximately £25 more than the prices quoted. Also see footnote after 3796.

OLD HEAD COINAGE 1893-1901, die axis ↑↑

3937
1893 Old Head Crown

	F £	VF £	EF £	BU £
3937 Crown. Old veiled bust l. R. St. George. date in ex. Regnal date on edge, die axis ↑↑				
1893 edge LVI	35	50	175	495
1893 Proof *FDC* £3250				
1893 LVII	35	75	325	800
1894 LVII	35	50	265	660
1894 LVIII	35	50	265	660
1895 LVIII	35	50	225	635
1895 LIX	35	50	200	605
1896 LIX	35	60	375	755
1896 LX	35	50	225	645
1897 LX	35	50	200	580
1897 LXI	35	50	200	580
1898 LXI	35	75	400	880
1898 LXII	35	50	275	645

	F	VF	EF	BU
	£	£	£	£
1899 LXII	35	50	200	715
1899 LXIII	35	50	225	770
1900 LXIII	35	50	200	635
1900 LXIV	35	50	200	605

3938
Halfcrown

3938 Halfcrown. Old veiled bust l. R. Shield in collar, edge milled, die axis ↑↑

1893	15	35	75	195
1893 Proof *FDC* £950				
1894	15	40	135	415
1895	15	35	100	305
1896	15	35	100	305
1897	15	35	75	250
1898	15	40	100	330
1899	15	35	75	275
1900	15	35	75	250
1901	15	35	75	260

3938A Small reverse design with long border teeth

1896	15	35	150	330

3939
Old Head Florin

3939 Florin. Old veiled bust l. R. Three shields within garter, die axis ↑↑

1893	12	30	75	180
1893 Proof *FDC* £650				
1894	12	30	110	315
1895	12	30	100	260
1896	12	30	100	260
1897	12	30	80	220
1898	12	30	95	275
1899	12	30	90	250
1900	12	30	80	195
1901	12	30	85	215

3940A
1901 Shilling

3941
1897 Sixpence

	F £	VF £	EF £	BU £
3940 Shilling. Old veiled bust l. R. Three shields within Garter, small rose, die axis ↑↑				
1893	8	15	55	120
1893 small lettering	8	15	50	110
1893 Proof *FDC* £450				
1894	8	15	60	160
1895	10	20	65	175
1896	8	15	60	165
3940A Shilling. Old veiled bust l. R. Second reverse, larger rose, die axis ↑↑				
1895	8	15	60	155
1896	8	15	55	155
1897	8	15	48	130
1898	8	15	55	155
1899	8	15	60	155
1900	8	15	50	130
1901	8	15	50	130
3941 Sixpence. Old veiled bust l. R. Value in wreath, die axis ↑↑				
1893	8	15	40	105
1893 Proof *FDC* £375				
1894	8	15	55	135
1895	8	15	50	130
1896	8	15	45	105
1897	8	15	40	105
1898	8	15	45	95
1899	8	15	45	105
1900	8	15	45	105
1901	8	15	40	95
3942 Threepence. Old veiled bust l. R. Crowned 3. As Maundy but less prooflike surface, die axis ↑↑				
1893	2	5	15	60
1893 Proof *FDC* £225				
1894	2	6	22	70
1895	2	6	20	60
1896	2	6	20	60
1897	2	5	15	45
1898	2	5	15	50
1899	2	5	15	50
1900	2	5	12	45
1901	2	5	15	45

3943
1901 Maundy Set

		EF £	FDC £
3943 Maundy Set. (4d., 3d., 2d. and 1d.) Old veiled bust l., die axis ↑↑			
1893	....	110	200
1894	....	110	200
1895	....	110	200
1896	....	110	200
1897	....	110	200
1898	....	110	200
1899	....	110	200
1900	....	110	200
1901	....	110	200
3944 — Fourpence. 1893-1901	*from*	20	40
3945 — Threepence. 1893-1901	*from*	25	40
3946 — Twopence. 1893-1901	*from*	20	40
3947 — Penny. 1893-1901	*from*	20	40

*Maundy Sets in the original undamaged cases are worth approximately £25 more than the prices quoted.
See footnote after 3796.*

COPPER AND BRONZE

YOUNG HEAD COPPER COINAGE, 1838-60, die axis ↑↑

3948
Penny
Rev. with ornamental trident prongs (OT)

	F £	VF £	EF £	BU £
3948 Penny. Young head l. date below R. Britannia seated r.				
1839 Bronzed proof *FDC* £2250				
1841 Rev. OT	90	150	350	1000
1841 Proof *FDC* £3500				
1841 Silver Proof *FDC* £9000				
1841 OT. no colon after REG	20	40	120	425
1843 OT. —	70	275	1650	4000

	F	VF	EF	BU
	£	£	£	£
1843 OT REG: 80	400	1850	4250
1844 OT 20	40	200	625
1844 Proof *FDC*			*Extremely rare*
1845 OT 20	40	300	825
1846 OT 20	40	275	600
1846 OT colon close to DEF 20	40	300	775
1847 – – 20	40	165	500
1847 OT DEF—: 20	40	190	500
1847 OT REG, raised lines to edge of crosses on shield, "Medusa" medallion ....*Extremely rare*
1848/7 OT 20	40	160	575
1848 OT 20	40	190	575
1848/6 OT 30	125	600	–
1849 OT 225	600	2250	4250
1851 OT 30	50	250	700
1851 OT DEF: 30	50	190	625
1853 OT DEF—: 12	30	110	475
1853 Proof *FDC* £3500
1853 Plain trident, (PT) DEF: 15	30	170	585
1854 PT 12	30	135	475
1854/3 PT 10	65	250	725
1854 OT DEF—: 12	30	120	500
1855 OT – 12	30	120	425
1855 PT DEF: 12	30	130	425
1856 PT DEF: 90	250	575	2450
1856 Proof *FDC* £4500
1856 OT DEF—: 100	350	900	3250
1857 OT DEF—: 12	30	100	400
1857 PT DEF: 12	30	95	395
1858 OT DEF—: 12	30	95	375
1858 – – with large rose on reverse ....*Extremely rare*
1858/7 – – 12	30	95	400
1858 OT DEF—: large rose 40	200	500	3000
1858/3 12	30	135	575
1858 no ww on trun 12	30	95	400
1859 20	40	110	475
1859 Proof *FDC* £4500
1860/59 800	1750	3250	8000

Copper coins graded in this catalogue as BU have full mint lustre.

3949 - 1845 Halfpenny

3949 Halfpenny. Young head l. date below R. Britannia seated r., die axis ↑↑ 1853 Rev. incuse dots

1838	15	25	75	250
1839 Bronzed proof FDC £1100
1841	15	25	75	300
1841 – Proof FDC £1750

	F	VF	EF	BU
	£	£	£	£
1841 Silver proof FDC ....*Extremely rare*				
1843 25		50	250	800
1844 20		50	165	375
1845 250		500	2000	–
1846 25		50	175	400
1847 25		50	160	360
1848 40		80	200	600
1848/7 25		50	190	400
1851 25		50	100	325
1851 Rev. incuse dots on shield 25		50	100	350
1852 Similar 25		50	100	325
1852 Rev. normal shield 25		50	110	350
1853 dots on shield 8		15	55	175
1853 — Proof FDC £900				
1853/2 — 25		50	165	400
1854 — 8		15	45	175
1855 — 8		15	45	185
1856 — 20		40	100	275
1857 — 8		15	60	215
1857 Rev. normal shield 8		15	55	200
1858 — 8		15	55	225
1858/7 — 8		15	55	225
1858/6 — 8		20	70	225
1859 — 8		20	70	225
1859/8 — 20		40	100	300
1860* — 1850		3500	7000	12500

Overstruck dates are listed only if commoner than normal date, or if no normal date is known.

*These 1860 large copper pieces are not to be confused with the smaller and commoner bronze issue with date on reverse (nos. 3954, 3956 and 3958).

Copper coins graded in this catalogue as UNC have full mint lustre.

3950	3950
1849 Farthing	1864 Proof

3950 Farthing. Young head l. date below R. Britannia seated r. die axis ↑↑

1838 WW raised on trun. 10	20	60	200
1839 10	20	55	150
1839 Bronzed Proof *FDC* £825			
1839 Silver Proof *FDC* ....*Extremely rare*			
1839 Copper Proof *FDC* £1250			
1840 10	20	60	170
1841 10	20	60	170
1841 Proof *FDC* ....*Extremely rare*			
1842 15	40	150	395

	F £	VF £	EF £	BU £
1843/2 10		25	110	350
1843 10		20	50	125
1843 I for 1 in date 75		325	700	1850
1844 65		220	750	1950
1845 10		20	58	165
1846 10		20	75	200
1847 10		20	58	165
1848 10		20	58	165
1849 35		95	375	775
1850 10		8	58	165
1850 5/4 15		40	100	325
1851 20		40	80	250
1851 D/ ɔ in DEI 80		275	650	1100
1852 20		40	80	250
1853 6		10	40	165
1853 WW incuse on trun 6		25	140	395
1853 Proof *FDC* £1100				
1854 6		10	45	150
1855 6		10	75	185
1855 WW raised 6		10	75	185
1856 WW incuse 6		18	80	250
1856 R/E in VICTORIA 15		60	325	600
1857 6		10	50	165
1858 6		10	50	165
1859 20		40	80	295
1860* 1600		3500	6500	13500
1864 IWW on truncation proof *FDC* £25000				

3951
Half-Farthing

3951 Half-Farthing. Young head l. R. Crowned Value and date, die axis ↑↑

	F £	VF £	EF £	BU £
1839 15		28	50	175
1839 Bronzed proof *FDC* £750				
1842 8		20	50	165
1843 5		10	28	100
1844 5		10	25	90
1844 E/N in REGINA 12		25	85	295
1847 15		28	50	160
1851 5/0 20		40	100	275
1851 20		40	80	175
1852 20		40	80	175
1853 20		40	80	190
1853 Proof *FDC* £750				
1854 25		50	100	325
1856 25		50	100	325
1856 Large date 45		135	350	825
1868 Proof *FDC* £950				
1868 Cupro nickel Proof *FDC* £1500				

3952
Third-Farthing

	F	VF	EF	BU
	£	£	£	£

3952 Third-Farthing (for use in Malta). Young head l. date below R. Britannia seated r.
   die axis ↑↑

	F	VF	EF	BU
1844	20	35	110	350
1844 RE for REG	30	65	375	800

3953
Quarter-Farthing

3953 Quarter-Farthing (for use in Ceylon). Young head l. R. Crowned Value and date,
   die axis ↑↑

	F	VF	EF	BU
1839	30	60	100	250
1851	30	60	100	275
1852	30	60	100	225
1852 Proof *FDC* £1500				
1853	30	60	125	375
1853 Proof *FDC* £1100				
1868 Proof *FDC* £900				
1868 Cupro-nickel Proof *FDC* £1450				

Copper coins graded in this catalogue as BU have full mint lustre.

*These 1860 large copper pieces are not to be confused with the smaller and commoner bronze issue with date on reverse (nos. 3954, 3956 and 3958).

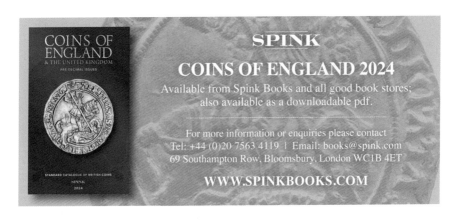

BRONZE COINAGE, "BUN HEAD" ISSUE, 1860-95, die axis ↑↑
When studying an example of the bronze coinage, if the minutiae of the variety is not evident due to
wear from circulation, then the coin will not be of any individual significance. Proofs exist of most
years and are generally extremely rare for all denominations.
3954 The Bronze Penny. The bronze coinage is the most complicated of the milled series from the point
of view of the large number of different varieties of obverse and reverse and their combinations. Below
are set out illustrations with explanations of all the varieties. The obverse and reverse types listed below
reflect those as listed originally by C W Peck in his British Museum Catalogue of Copper, Tin and
Bronze Coinage 1558-1958, and later in "The Bronze Coinage of Great Britain" by Michael J Freeman
which gives much fuller and detailed explanations of the types. Reference can also be compared to "The
British Bronze Penny" by Michael Gouby.

OBVERSES

Obverse 1 (1860) - laureate and draped bust
facing left, hair tied in bun, wreath of 15 leaves
and 4 berries, L C WYON raised on base of
bust, **beaded border** and thin linear circle.

Obverse 1* (1860) - laureate and draped bust
facing left, hair tied in bun, **more bulging
lowered eye with more rounded forehead**,
wreath of **15 leaves and 4 berries**, which are
weaker in part, L C WYON raised on base of
bust, **beaded border** and thin linear circle.

Obverse 3 (1860-61) - laureate and draped
bust facing left, hair tied in bun, **complete
rose to drapery**, wreath of 15 leaves and 4
berries, **two leaves have incuse outlines,**
L C WYON raised on base of bust **nearly
touches border**, toothed border and thin
linear circle both sides.

Obverse 2 (1860-62) - laureate and draped
bust facing left, hair tied in bun, wreath of 15
leaves and 4 berries, **L C WYON** raised **lower
on base of bust** and clear of border, **toothed
border** and thin linear circle both sides.

Obverse 4 (1860-61) - laureate and draped bust
facing left, hair tied in bun, **finer hair strands
at nape of neck**, wreath of 15 leaves and 4
berries, two leaves have incuse outlines, **L C
WYON below bust, nearly touches border,
toothed border of shorter teeth**, and thin linear
circle both sides.

OBVERSES *(continued)*

Obverse 7 (1874) - laureate and draped bust facing left, hair tied in bun, finer hair strands at nape of neck, **wreath of 17 leaves, leaf veins raised, 6 berries**, no signature, toothed border and thin linear circle both sides.

Obverse 5 (1860-61) - laureate and draped bust facing left, hair tied in bun, **finer hair strands at nape of neck**, wreath of 15 leaves and 4 berries, **leaf veins incuse**, two leaves have incuse outlines, **no signature below bust**, toothed border and thin linear circle both sides.

Obverse 8 (1874-79) - laureate and draped bust facing left, hair tied in bun, with **close thicker ties to ribbons**, wreath of 17 leaves, leaf veins raised, 6 berries, no signature, toothed border and thin linear circle both sides.

Obverse 6 (1860-74) - laureate and draped bust facing left, hair tied in bun, finer hair strands at nape of neck, **wreath of 16 leaves, leaf veins raised, no signature**, toothed border and thin linear circle both sides. There is a **prominent flaw** on the **top stop of the colon after D at the end of the legend**.

Obverse 9 (1879-81) - laureate and draped bust facing left, hair tied in bun, with close thicker ties, wreath of 17 leaves, **double leaf veins incuse**, 6 berries, no signature, toothed border and thin linear circle both sides.

OBVERSES *(continued)*

Obverse 10 (1880-81) - laureate and draped bust facing left, hair tied in bun, with close thicker ties, **wreath of 15 leaves, leaf veins raised and recessed, 4 berries**, no signature, toothed border and thin linear circle both sides.

Obverse 12 (1881-94) - laureate and draped bust facing left, hair tied in bun, with close thicker ties, **no curls at nape of neck**, nose more hooked, wreath of 15 leaves, leaf veins raised, 4 berries, no signature, **toothed border, more numerous teeth**, and thin linear circle both sides, weak on obverse, **larger lettering**.

Obverse 11 (1881-83) - laureate and draped bust facing left, more **hooked nose**, hair tied in bun, with close thicker ties, nose more hooked, wreath of 15 leaves, **leaf veins raised**, 4 berries, no signature, toothed border and thin linear circle both sides, **weak circle on obverse**.

Obverse 13 (1889) - laureate and draped bust facing left, hair tied in bun, with close thicker ties, no curls at nape of neck, nose more hooked, **wreath of 14 leaves, leaf veins raised**, no signature, toothed border and thin linear circle both sides, larger lettering.

REVERSES

Reverse A (1860) - Britannia seated right on rocks with shield and trident, **crosses on shield outlined with double raised lines**, L.C.W. incuse below shield, date below in exergue, lighthouse with 4 windows to left, ship sailing to right, **beaded border** and linear circle.

Reverse C (1860) - Britannia seated right on rocks with shield and trident, **crosses on shield outlined with wider spaced thinner double raised lines, thumb touches St. George Cross**, L.C.W. incuse below shield, date below in exergue, lighthouse with 4 windows to left, rocks touch linear circle, ship sailing to right, **beaded border** and linear circle.

Reverse B (1860) - Britannia with **one incuse hemline**, seated right on rocks with shield and trident, **crosses on shield outlined with treble incuse lines**, L.C.W. incuse below shield, date below in exergue, lighthouse with 4 windows to left, ship sailing to right, **beaded border** and linear circle.

Reverse D (1860-61) - Britannia seated right on rocks with shield and trident, crosses on shield outlined with wider spaced thinner double raised lines, thumb touches St. George Cross, L.C.W. incuse below shield, date below in exergue, lighthouse with 4 windows to left, rocks touch linear circle, ship sailing to right, **toothed border**.

REVERSES (*continued*)

Reverse E (1860) - Britannia seated right on rocks with **thick rimmed shield and trident**, crosses on shield outlined with wider spaced thinner double raised lines, thumb touches St. George Cross, **L.C.W. incuse below foot**, date below in exergue, lighthouse with **sharper masonry** to left, **rocks touch linear circle**, ship sailing to right, toothed border.

Reverse G (1861-75) - Britannia seated right on rocks with **convex shield and trident**, no signature, date below in exergue, bell-topped lighthouse to left, **lamp area depicted with five vertical lines, no rocks to left, sea crosses linear circle**, ship sailing to right, toothed border.

Reverse F (1861) - Britannia seated right on rocks with thick rimmed shield and trident, **incuse lines on breastplate**, crosses on shield outlined with wider spaced thinner double raised lines, thumb touches St. George Cross, **no L.C.W. extra rocks**, date below in exergue, **lighthouse with rounded top** and sharp masonry, **three horizontal lines** between masonry and top, rocks touch linear circle, ship sailing to right, toothed border.

Reverse H (1874-75, 1877) - Britannia seated right on rocks, **smaller head, thinner neck**, with convex shield and trident, no signature, **narrow date** below in exergue, **tall thin lighthouse** to left with **6 windows, lamp area of four vertical lines**, close date numerals, **tiny rock to left, sea touches linear circle**, ship sailing to right, toothed border.

REVERSES (*continued*)

Reverse I (1874) - Britannia seated right on rocks with convex shield and trident, **thick trident shaft**, no signature, **narrow date** below in exergue, **thicker lighthouse** to left with **4 windows**, lamp area of four vertical lines, close date numerals, tiny rock to left, sea touches linear circle, ship sailing to right, toothed border.

Reverse L (1880) - Britannia seated right on rocks with shield and trident, **extra feather to helmet plume, trident with three rings above hand**, date below in exergue, lighthouse with **cluster of rocks to left**, ship sailing to right, toothed border.

Reverse J (1875-81) - **larger Britannia** seated right on rocks with shield and trident, **left leg more visible, wider date** below in deeper exergue, lighthouse to left, ship sailing to right, **sea does not meet linear circle either side**, toothed border.

Reverse M (1881-82) - larger Britannia seated right on rocks with shield and trident, **flatter shield heraldically coloured**, date and **H** below in exergue, lighthouse to left with faint masonry, ship sailing to right, **sea does not meet linear circle**, toothed border.

Reverse K (1876, 1879) - Britannia with **larger head** seated right on rocks with convex shield and trident, **thicker helmet**, no signature, **narrow date** and in exergue, **tall thin lighthouse** to left, tiny rock to left, **sea touches linear circle**, ship sailing to right, toothed border.

REVERSES (*continued*)

Reverse O (1882 - proof only) – larger Britannia seated right on rocks with shield and trident, flatter shield heraldically coloured, date and **H in exergue**, lighthouse to left with faint masonry, ship sailing to right, **sea meets linear circle**, toothed border with more teeth.

Reverse N (1881-94) - thinner Britannia seated right on rocks with shield and thinner trident, **helmet plume ends in a single strand**, shield heraldically coloured with different thickness crosses, date in exergue, thinner lighthouse to left, ship sailing to right, sea meets linear circle, toothed border with more teeth.

Beaded border

Toothed border

Shield outlined with double raised lines

Shield outlined with treble incuse lines

Normal nose

More hooked nose

3954

	F	VF	EF	BU
	£	£	£	£

3954 Penny. Laur. bust l. R. Britannia seated r. date in ex. lighthouse l. ship to r., die axis ↑↑

1860 obv 1, rev A.....................60	125	625	1750
1860 obv 1, rev B 12	50	300	900
1860 obv 1*, rev A..................350	1200	2000	—
1860 obv 1, rev C 60	165	700	2650
1860 obv 1*, rev C 200	700	2000	—
1860 obv 1, rev D 600	950	2700	5500
1860 obv 2, rev B 525	975	3000	5750
1860 obv 2, rev D 5	20	75	325
1860 — heavy flan 2750	—	—	—
1860 N/Z in ONE, 2+D 80	275	575	1250
1860 obv 3, rev D 5	20	90	385
1860 obv 3, rev E...............110	325	875	2500
1860 obv 4, rev D 5	20	90	400
1860 obv 5, rev D 7	40	225	750
1860 obv 6, rev D 30	125	400	900
1861 obv 2, rev D 65	165	500	1350
1861 obv 2, rev F...*Extremely rare*
1861 obv 2, rev G 25	100	425	1200
1861 obv 3, rev D 225	550	1500	2850
1861 obv 4, rev D 5	20	95	385
1861 — — heavy flan 2750	—	—	—
1861 obv 4, rev F...............200	425	1750	—
1861 obv 4, rev G 50	200	750	2250
1861 obv 5, rev D 5	20	95	400
1861 obv 5, rev F...............950	—	—	—
1861 obv 5, rev G 100	375	1250	2500
1861 obv 6, rev D 5	20	85	300
1861 — — — 6 over 8 450	2150	—	—
1861 obv 6, rev F 150	550	1500	—
1861 obv 6, rev G 5	20	90	350
1861 — 8 over 6 450	2150	—	—
1862 obv 2, rev G 475	1250	2950	4000
1862 obv 6, rev G 5	20	70	265
1862 obv 6, rev G, reads VIGTORIA...............2500	—	—	—
1862 — 8 over 6 300	500	800	—
1862 — 2 over 1 ....*Extremely rare*
1862 — Halfpenny numerals...............900	2750	4250	—
1862 — VIGTORIA on obverse...*Extremely rare*
1863 obv 6, rev G 5	20	70	245
1863 Die number 2 ....*from* 1500	—	—	—
1863 Die number 3 ....*from* 1500	—	—	—
1863 Die number 4 ....*from* 1500	—	—	—
1863 Die number 5 ....*Extremely rare*

	F £	VF £	EF £	BU £
1863 slender 3	...........Extremely rare			
1863 Open 3	250	1500	–	–
1863/1 obv 6, rev G	...........Extremely rare			
1864 Upper serif	10	110	1200	3750
1864 Crosslet 4	15	150	1350	4250
1865 obv 6, rev G	6	18	200	695
1865/3 obv 6, rev G	45	125	450	1750
1866 obv 6, rev G	5	20	100	400
1867 obv 6, rev G	6	30	250	1000
1868 obv 6, rev G	8	40	300	1000
1869 obv 6, rev G	95	450	1650	4500
1870 obv 6, rev G	8	20	200	550
1871 obv 6, rev G	35	120	650	1950
1872 obv 6, rev G	5	20	95	300
1873 obv 6, rev G	5	20	95	350
1874 obv 6, rev G	5	20	135	650
1874 obv 7, rev G	5	30	125	400
1874 obv 8, rev G	18	45	250	900
1874 obv 8 rev H	12	40	185	750
1874 obv 6, rev H	30	85	385	850
1874 obv 7, rev H	5	30	150	425
1875 obv 8, rev G	12	50	275	675
1875 obv 8, rev H	5	20	80	300
1875 obv 8, rev J	5	20	85	325
1877 obv 8, rev J	5	20	90	325
1877 obv 8, rev H	3250	–	–	–
1878 obv 8, rev J	5	20	120	500
1879 obv 8, rev J	7	20	185	825
1879 obv 9, rev J	5	20	85	275
1879 obv 9, rev K	20	80	325	1250
1880 obv 9, rev J	5	12	135	500
1880 obv 9, rev L	5	10	120	475
1881 obv 9, rev J	5	12	125	600
1881 obv 10, rev J	20	80	295	875
1881 obv 11, rev J	50	135	500	1100
1882† obv 11, rev N	1500	4750	–	–
1883 obv 12, rev N	2	10	75	325
1883 obv11, rev N	2	10	75	375
1884 obv 12, rev N	2	10	70	235
1885 obv 12, rev N	2	10	70	235
1886 obv 12, rev N	2	10	75	265
1887 obv 12, rev N	2	10	70	225
1888 obv 12, rev N	2	10	60	200
1889 obv 12, rev N	3	12	85	395
1889 obv 13, rev N	2	10	55	225
1890 obv 12, rev N	2	10	55	225
1891 obv 12, rev N	2	10	55	225
1892 obv 12, rev N	2	10	55	225
1893 obv 12, rev N	2	10	55	225
1893 obv 12, rev N 3 over 2	100	325	400	700
1894 obv 12, rev N	2	12	80	285

†† *not to be confused with Heaton Mint - H - the mint letter is the first device to disappear on worn specimens*
Bronze coins graded in this catalogue as BU have full mint lustre

3955
H Mint mark location

3956
1860 Halfpenny Beaded border

	F	VF	EF	BU
	£	£	£	£

3955 Penny. Similar R. Britannia, H Mint mark below date – (struck by Ralph Heaton
& Sons, Birmingham)

	F	VF	EF	BU
1874 H obv 6, rev G 5	20	100	325
1874 H obv 6, rev H 10	25	145	575
1874 H obv 6, rev I 250	500	750	—
1874 H obv 7, rev G 10	25	120	385
1874 H obv 7, rev H 5	20	100	325
1874 H obv 7, rev I 550	—	—	—
1875 H obv 8, rev J 35	100	975	2250
1876 H obv 8, rev K 5	20	90	360
1876 H obv 8, rev J 8	25	165	500
1881 H obv 11, rev M 5	20	90	375
1881 H obv 9, rev M 475	1250	2750	—
1882 H obv12, rev M 10	20	150	525
1882 H obv 12, rev N 5	20	70	275
1882/1 H obv 11, rev M 8	20	150	825

3956 Halfpenny. Laur. bust l. R. Britannia seated r. date in ex. lighthouse l. ship to r.,
die axis ↑↑

	F	VF	EF	BU
1860 Beaded border 3	10	35	145
1860 no tie to wreath 5	12	100	300
1860 Toothed border 3	10	90	225
1860 Toothed border/Beaded border, mule 700	1400	2750	—
1860 round top light house 15	110	400	—
1860 5 berries in wreath 3	10	90	350
1860 — 15 leaves, berries 3	10	80	225
1860 — rounded lighthouse 3	10	100	250
1860 — Double incuse leaf veins 3	10	95	225
1860 — 16 leaves wreath 8	25	135	425
1861 5 berries in wreath 8	25	120	375
1861 15 leaves in wreath 5	18	95	325
1861 — R. no hemline to drapery 10	25	120	325
1861 — R. Door on lighthouse 3	10	95	325
1861 4 leaves double incuse veins 3	10	80	225
1861 16 leaves wreath 3	10	90	325
1861 — R. LCW incuse on rock 10	25	120	375
1861 — R. no hemline to drapery 3	10	90	285
1861 — R. door on lighthouse ....—	10	75	225
1861 HALP error 300	850	—	—
1861 6 over 8 275	800	—	—
1862 ....—	10	45	165

	F £	VF £	EF £	BU £
1862 Die letter to left of lighthouse				
A ...300	1250	2650	4000	
B ...600	2250	–	–	
C ...1000	2750	–	–	
1863 small 3 ...3	10	65	235	
1863 large 3 ...3	10	65	200	
1864 ...3	10	85	250	
1865 ...3	12	100	400	
1865/3 ...45	90	300	1000	
1866 ...3	10	100	375	
1867 ...3	10	100	325	
1868 ...3	10	100	375	
1869 ...20	85	400	1000	
1870 ...5	10	80	300	
1871 ...20	90	425	900	
1872 ...3	10	85	250	
1873 ...3	10	90	295	
1873 R. hemline to drapery ...3	10	90	300	
1874 ...10	25	125	400	
1874 narrow date ...15	50	300	700	
1874 older features ...5	20	135	400	
1875 ...3	6	80	250	
1877 ...3	6	80	250	
1878 ...4	20	125	450	
1878 wide date ...65	150	400	900	
1879 ...3	6	65	200	
1880 ...5	10	75	200	
1881 ...3	7	75	250	
1883 ...3	7	75	250	
1883 rose for brooch obv. ...20	50	150	295	
1884 ...2	6	55	185	
1885 ...2	6	55	185	
1886 ...2	6	55	185	
1887 ...2	6	50	175	
1888 ...2	6	75	200	
1889 ...2	6	75	200	
1889/8 ...15	45	165	400	
1890 ...2	6	50	150	
1891 ...2	6	50	150	
1892 ...3	6	75	200	
1893 ...2	6	70	175	
1894 ...3	6	75	200	

3957 Halfpenny. Similar R. Britannia, H Mint mark below date (struck by Ralph Heaton & Sons, Birmingham)

	F £	VF £	EF £	BU £
1874 H ...2	6	75	250	
1875 H ...2	6	80	275	
1876 H ...2	6	75	250	
1881 H ...2	6	75	250	
1882 H ...2	6	75	250	

Bronze coins graded in this catalogue as BU have full mint lustre

3958
1860 Farthing

	F £	VF £	EF £	BU £
3958 Farthing. Laur bust l. R. Britannia seated r. date in ex. lighthouse l. ship to r. die axis ↑↑				
1860 Beaded border	2	8	25	85
1860 Toothed border	2	8	20	95
1860 — 5 berries	2	8	30	95
1860 TB/BB mule	175	575	1100	—
1861 5 berries	2	8	40	110
1861 4 berries	2	8	30	100
1862	3	20	90	225
1862 large 8	55	200	425	—
1863	20	50	300	650
1864 4 no serif	2	8	50	165
1864 4 with serif	2	8	55	175
1865	2	8	45	125
1865/2	2	10	50	175
1866	2	8	40	125
1867	2	8	45	135
1868	2	8	45	135
1869	2	10	55	175
1872	2	8	45	125
1873	2	8	30	95
1875 large date	10	20	75	200
1875 small date	20	40	150	450
1875 —older features	20	40	100	325
1877 Proof only £11000				
1878	2	8	25	100
1879 large 9	2	8	40	125
1879 normal 9	2	8	35	110
1880	2	8	45	135
1881	2	8	35	120
1883	2	10	55	150
1884	2	6	20	75
1885	2	6	20	75
1886	2	6	20	75
1887	2	6	30	110
1888	2	6	30	100
1890	2	6	25	90
1891	2	6	20	90
1892	3	12	55	165
1893	2	6	20	90
1894	2	6	30	100
1895	15	40	95	225

Bronze coins graded in this catalogue as BU have full mint lustre

	F	VF	EF	BU
	£	£	£	£

3959 Farthing. Similar ℞. Britannia. H Mint mark below date (struck by Ralph Heaton & Sons, Birmingham)

	F	VF	EF	BU
1874 H older features 3	10	55	150
1874 H, both Gs over sideways G on obv. 125	350	900	–
1875 H younger features 80	250	400	850
1875 H older features 2	5	18	95
1876 H large 6 12	30	100	210
1876 H normal 6 10	20	65	150
1881 H 2	5	25	95
1882 H 2	5	25	90

3960
1868 Third-Farthing

3960 Third-Farthing (for use in Malta). Laur. head l. ℞. Crowned date and Value die axis ↑↑

1866	10	20	40	100
1868	10	20	40	100
1876	10	20	40	110
1878	10	20	40	110
1881	10	20	40	110
1884	10	20	40	100
1885	10	20	40	100

Old Head Issue, 1895-1901, die axis ↑↑

Proofs exist of most years and are generally extremely rare for all denominations

3961
1897 Penny

3961 Penny. Old veiled bust l. ℞. Britannia seated r. date in ex., die axis ↑↑

1895	2	6	30	125
1896	1	3	20	100
1897	1	3	20	100
1897 O'NE flawed 20	100	395	1300
1898	1	3	30	135
1899	1	3	20	100
1900	1	5	20	85
1901	1	3	12	70

3961 'Normal Tide'
Horizon is level with folds in robe

3961A 'Low Tide'
Horizon is level with hem line of robe

	F £	VF £	EF £	BU £
3961A Penny. Similar As last but 'Low tide' and 'P' 2mm from trident				
1895 25		100	380	950
3961B Penny. Similar, higher tide level above two folds of robe				
1897 25		100	400	1500

3962
Old Head Halfpenny

3964
Old Head Farthing

3962 Halfpenny. Old veiled bust l. ℞. Britannia seated r. date in ex., die axis ↑↑

1895	2	4	12	110
1896	2	4	10	105
1897	2	4	10	105
1897 Higher tide level	2	5	15	110
1898	2	4	12	110
1899	2	4	10	105
1900	2	4	10	100
1901	2	4	10	80

3963 Farthing. Old veiled bust l. ℞. Britannia seated r. date in ex. Bright finish, die axis ↑↑

1895	2	4	10	50
1896	2	4	10	55
1897	2	4	10	55

3964 Farthing. Similar Dark finish, die axis ↑↑

1897	2	4	10	35
1897 Higher tide level	2	4	12	55
1898	2	4	10	45
1899	2	4	10	35
1900	2	4	10	30
1901	2	4	10	25

PROOF SETS

PS3 Young head, **1839.** 'Una and the Lion' Five Pounds, and Sovereign to Farthing (15 coins) *FDC* £365000

PS4 — **1853.** Sovereign to Half-Farthing, including Gothic type Crown (16 coins) *FDC* £125000

PS5 Jubilee head. Golden Jubilee, **1887.** Five pounds to Threepence (11 coins)*FDC* £42500

PS6 — — **1887.** Crown to Threepence (7 coins) *FDC* £6000

PS7 Old head, **1893.** Five Pounds to Threepence (10 coins) *FDC* £48000

PS8 — — **1893.** Crown to Threepence (6 coins) *FDC* £7500

† *NB Truly 'FDC' proof sets are hardly ever encountered. Component coins showing any surface marks, hairlines or nicks will be worth less than the prices quoted above.*

THE HOUSE OF SAXE-COBURG-GOTHA, 1901-1917
EDWARD VII, 1901-10

'Edward the Peacemaker' was born on 9th November 1841, and married Princess Alexandra of Denmark. He indulged himself in every decadent luxury, while his wife tried to ignore his extra-marital activities. Edward travelled extensively and was crucial in negotiating alliances with Russia and France. Edward VII died on 6th May 1910.

Five Pound pieces, Two Pound pieces and Crowns were only issued in 1902. A branch of the Royal Mint was opened in Canada at Ottawa and coined Sovereigns of imperial type from 1908.

Unlike the coins in most other proof sets, the proofs issued for the Coronation in 1902 have a matt surface in place of the more usual brilliant finish.

Designer's initials: De S. (G. W. De Saulles 1862-1903)

B. P. (Benedetto Pistrucci, d. 1855)

Engravers and Designers: WHJ Blakemore, George William De Saulles (1862-1903), Benedetto Pistrucci (1784-1855)

GOLD

Die axis: ↑↑

3966
Matt Proof Five Pounds 1902

	F	VF	EF	BU
	£	£	£	£

3965 Five Pounds. Bare head r. Ṝ. St. George and dragon, date in ex.

1902 ....2000 | 2500 | 3000 | 4000

3966 Five Pounds. Similar Proof. 1902. *Matt surface FDC £4000*

3966A Five Pounds. Similar Proof 1902S. S on ground for Sydney Mint, Australia..*Extremely rare*

3967
1902 Two Pounds

3967 Two Pounds. Bare head r. R. St George and dragon, date in ex.

1902 ....900 | 1200 | 1400 | 1800

3968 Two Pounds. Similar Proof. 1902. *Matt surface FDC £2000*

3968A Two Pounds. Similar Proof 1902S. S on ground for Sydney Mint, Australia..*Extremely rare*

BV= Bullion value only. At the time of going to press the spot price for gold was £1600 per oz.

3969
1902 Sovereign

	F £	VF £	EF £	BU £
3969 Sovereign. Bare head r. R. St. George and dragon, date in ex. London mint, die axis ↑↑				
1902 Matt proof *FDC* £775				
1902	—	—	BV	395
1903	—	—	BV	425
1904	—	—	BV	425
1905	—	—	BV	425
1906	—	—	BV	425
1907	—	—	BV	425
1908	—	—	BV	425
1909	—	—	BV	425
1910	—	—	BV	425
3970 Sovereign. Similar R. C on ground for Ottawa Mint, Canada				
1908 C (Satin proof only) *FDC* £12500				
1909 C	—	350	475	1500
1909 C Satin finish specimen *FDC*			*Extremely rare*	
1910 C	—	350	450	1100
3971 Sovereign. Similar R. St. George M on ground for Melbourne Mint, Australia, die axis ↑↑				
1902 M	—	—	BV	425
1902 M Proof			*Extremely rare*	
1903 M	—	—	BV	425
1904 M	—	—	BV	425
1904 M Proof			*Extremely rare*	
1905 M	—	—	BV	425
1906 M	—	—	BV	425
1907 M	—	—	BV	425
1908 M	—	—	BV	425
1909 M	—	—	BV	425
1910 M	—	—	BV	425
1910 M Proof			*Extremely rare*	
3972 Sovereign. Similar R. P on ground for Perth Mint, Australia die axis ↑↑				
1902 P	—	—	BV	425
1903 P	—	—	BV	450
1904 P	—	—	BV	450
1905 P	—	—	BV	450
1906 P	—	—	BV	450
1907 P	—	—	BV	450
1908 P	—	—	BV	450
1909 P	—	—	BV	450
1910 P	—	—	BV	425
3973 Sovereign. Similar R. S on ground for Sydney Mint, Australia die axis ↑↑				
1902 S	—	—	BV	400
1902 S Proof			*Extremely rare*	

BV= Bullion value only. At the time of going to press the spot price for gold was £1600 per oz.

	F £	VF £	EF £	BU £
1903 S	—	—	BV	425
1904 S	—	—	BV	425
1905 S	—	—	BV	425
1906 S	—	—	—	425
1907 S	—	—	—	425
1908 S	—	—	—	425
1909 S	—	—	—	425
1910 S	—	—	—	425

3974A
1902 Half-Sovereign, no BP in exergue

3974A Half-Sovereign. Bare head r. R. St. George. London Mint no BP in exergue, die axis ↑↑
1902 Matt proof *FDC* £400

1902	—	BV	185	325
1903	—	BV	185	325
1904	—	BV	185	325

3974B Half-Sovereign. R. Similar with BP in exergue

1904	—	BV	185	325
1905	—	BV	185	325
1906	—	BV	185	325
1907	—	BV	185	325
1908	—	BV	185	325
1909	—	BV	185	325
1910	—	BV	185	325

3975 Half-Sovereign. Similar R. M on ground for Melbourne Mint, Australia, die axis ↑↑

1906 M	BV	325	850	—
1907 M	BV	185	250	750
1908 M	BV	185	265	500
1909 M	BV	185	275	700

3976A Half-Sovereign. — P on ground for Perth Mint, Australia R. no BP in exergue, die axis ↑↑

1904 P	BV	275	1250	5500

3976B Half-Sovereign. Similar R. P on ground for Perth Mint, Australia R. with BP in exergue, die axis ↑↑

1904 P				*Extremely rare*
1908 P	BV	250	1350	4500
1909 P	BV	250	750	2000

3977A Half-Sovereign. Similar R. S on ground for Sydney Mint, Australia R. No BP in exergue, die axis ↑↑

1902 S	BV	185	250	425
1902 S Proof				*Extremely rare*
1903 S	BV	185	250	600

3977B Half-Sovereign. — S on ground for Sydney Mint, Australia R. with BP in exergue, die axis ↑↑

1906 S	—	BV	185	500
1908 S	—	BV	185	350
1910 S	—	BV	185	325

BV= Bullion value only. At the time of going to press the spot price for gold was £1600 per oz.

SILVER

3978 - 1902 Crown

	F	VF	EF	BU
	£	£	£	£

3978 Crown. Bare head r. ℞. St. George and dragon date in ex. die axis ↑↑

1902	100	150	250	385
1902 error edge inscription				*Extremely rare*

3979 Crown. Similar Matt proof *FDC* £425

3980 - 1904 Halfcrown   3981 - Florin

3980 Halfcrown. Bare head r. ℞. Crowned Shield in Garter, die axis ↑↑

1902	20	40	100	225
1902 Matt proof *FDC* £225				
1903	150	485	2000	4850
1904	60	300	950	2650
1905*	550	1750	5250	10500
1906	20	60	250	725
1907	20	55	245	625
1908	20	55	475	1100
1909	20	50	275	750
1910	20	40	225	600

3981 Florin. Bare head r. ℞. Britannia standing on ship's bow die axis ↑↑

1902	20	40	75	140
1902 Matt proof *FDC* £200				
1903	20	40	175	500
1904	20	55	245	550
1905	65	260	950	2250
1906	20	40	150	475
1907	20	50	215	525
1908	20	60	300	650
1909	20	60	275	525
1910	20	50	145	300

Beware of 1970's forgeries.

3982
1902 Shilling

	F	VF	EF	BU
	£	£	£	£
3982 Shilling. Bare head r. R. Lion passant on crown die axis ↑↑				
1902 6	15	65	110	
1902 Matt proof *FDC* £175				
1903 15	40	175	425	
1904 15	40	150	425	
1905 110	350	1500	3250	
1906 6	15	80	225	
1907 6	15	85	250	
1908 6	25	200	500	
1909 6	25	225	600	
1910 6	15	80	175	

3983
1902 Sixpence

	F	VF	EF	BU
3983 Sixpence. Bare head r. R. Value in wreath die axis ↑↑				
1902 8	15	80	90	
1902 Matt proof *FDC* £135				
1903 10	25	60	150	
1904 10	25	125	265	
1905 10	25	90	200	
1906 8	15	45	100	
1907 8	15	45	110	
1908 8	15	60	135	
1909 8	15	60	135	
1910 8	15	50	100	
3984 Threepence. As Maundy but dull finish die axis ↑↑				
1902 3	15	25	40	
1902 Matt proof *FDC* £55				
1903 6	15	30	65	
1904 6	15	40	115	
1905 6	15	30	90	
1906 6	15	50	140	
1907 3	15	30	65	
1908 3	15	25	55	
1909 3	15	30	65	
1910 3	15	25	55	

3985
1903 Maundy Set

	F £	VF £	EF £	BU £
3985 Maundy Set (4d., 3d., 2d. and 1d.) Bare head r. die axis ↑↑				
1902	—	—	95	165
1902 Matt proof *FDC* £250				
1903	—	—	95	165
1904	—	—	95	165
1905	—	—	95	165
1906	—	—	95	165
1907	—	—	95	165
1908	—	—	95	165
1909	—	—	150	275
1910	—	—	150	275
3986 — **Fourpence**. 1902-10		*from*	20	30
3987 — **Threepence**. 1902-10		*from*	20	40
3988 — **Twopence**. 1902-10		*from*	20	30
3989 — **Penny**. 1902-10		*from*	20	35

Maundy sets in the original undamaged cases are worth approximately £25 more than the prices quoted. Also see footnote after 3796.

BRONZE

3990 - 1902 Penny

3990 Normal Tide　　　　　　　　　　'3990A 'Low Tide'

	F	VF	EF	BU
	£	£	£	£

3990 Penny. Bare head r. ℞. Britannia seated r. date in ex. die axis ↑↑

	F	VF	EF	BU
1902	1	4	12	40
1903 Normal 3	1	4	25	120
1903 Open 3	150	575	—	—
1904	1	4	35	140
1905	1	4	30	130
1906	1	4	20	110
1907	1	4	25	115
1908	1	4	20	120
1909	1	4	25	130
1910	1	4	15	100

3990A Penny. Similar ℞. As last but 'Low tide'

	F	VF	EF	BU
1902,'2' has wavy base line	—	5	40	100	300

3991 - Halfpenny

3991 Halfpenny. Bare head r. ℞. Britannia seated r. date in ex. die axis ↑↑

	F	VF	EF	BU
1902	2	6	12	45
1903	2	6	15	100
1904	2	6	20	125
1905	2	6	18	110
1906	2	6	18	100
1907	2	6	15	100
1908	2	6	15	100
1909	2	6	18	100
1910	2	6	15	90

	F £	VF £	EF £	BU £

3991A Halfpenny. Similar R. As last but 'Low tide'

| 1902 | 20 | 85 | 165 | 425 |

3992
Farthing

3992 Farthing. Bare head r. R. Britannia seated r. date in ex. Dark finish die axis ↑↑

1902	2	4	10	25
1903	2	4	10	25
1904	4	8	20	40
1905	2	4	10	25
1906	2	4	10	25
1907	2	4	10	25
1908	2	4	10	25
1909	2	4	10	25
1910	4	8	20	40

3993
1902 Third-Farthing

3993 Third-Farthing (for use in Malta) Bare head r. R. Crowned date and value
die axis ↑↑.

| 1902 | 8 | 12 | 20 | 40 |

No proofs of the bronze coins were issued in 1902

PROOF SETS
PS9 Coronation, **1902.** Five Pounds to Maundy Penny, matt surface, (13 coins) *FDC* £7250
PS10 — 1902. Sovereign to Maundy Penny, matt surface, (11 coins) *FDC* £2450

† *NB Truly 'FDC' proof sets are hardly ever encountered. Component coins showing any surface
marks, hairlines or nicks will be worth less than the prices quoted above.*

THE HOUSE OF WINDSOR, 1917-
GEORGE V, 1910-36

George V, the second son of Edward VII, was born on 3rd June 1865 and married Mary of Teck who bore him five sons and a daughter. He was King through World War I and visited the front on several occassions. He suffered a fall breaking his pelvis on one of these visits, an injury that would pain him for the rest of his life. He watched the Empire divide; Ireland, Canada, Australia, New Zealand and India all went through changes. He died on 20th January 1936 only months after his Silver Jubilee.

Paper money issued by the Treasury during the First World War replaced gold for internal use after 1915 but the branch mints in Australia and South Africa (the main Commonwealth gold producing countries) continued striking Sovereigns until 1930-2. Owing to the steep rise in the price of silver in 1919/20 the issue of standard (.925) silver was discontinued and coins of .500 silver were minted.

In 1912, 1918 and 1919 some Pennies were made under contract by private mints in Birmingham. In 1918, as Half-Sovereigns were no longer being minted, Farthings were again issued with the ordinary bright bronze finish. Crown pieces had not been issued for general circulation but they were struck in small numbers about Christmas time for people to give as presents in the years 1927-36, and in 1935 a special commemorative Crown was issued in celebration of the Silver Jubilee.

As George V died on 20th January, it is likely that all coins dated 1936 were struck during the reign of Edward VIII.

Engravers and Designers:– George Kuger Gray (1880-1943), Bertram MacKennal (1863-1931), Benedetto Pistrucci (1783-1855) Percy Metcalfe (1895-1970)

Designer's initials:
B. M. (Bertram Mackennal)   P. M. (Percy Metcalfe)
K. G. (G. Kruger Gray)   B. P. (Benedetto Pistrucci; d. 1855)

Die axis: ↑↑

GOLD

3994 Five Pounds.* Bare head l. R. St. George and dragon, date in ex., 1911 (Proof only) £10500
3995 Two Pounds.* Bare head l. R. St. George and dragon, date in ex., 1911 (Proof only) £3250

3996

	F £	VF £	EF £	BU £
3996 Sovereign. Bare head l. R. St. George and dragon. London Mint die axis: ↑↑				
1911	—	BV	BV	400
1911 Proof *FDC* £1750				
1911 Matt Proof *FDC of highest rarity*				
1912	—	BV	BV	375
1913	—	BV	BV	375
1914	—	BV	BV	375
1915		BV	BV	375
1916	—	BV	400	650
1917*	—	5500	15000	—
1925	—	BV	BV	350

*Forgeries exist of these and of most other dates and mints.
BV= Bullion value only. At the time of going to press the spot price for gold was £1600 per oz.

3997 - Canada 'c' Mint mark

	F £	VF £	EF £	BU £
3997 Sovereign. Bare head l. R. St George, C on ground for the Ottawa Mint, Canada die axis: ↑↑				
1911 C	—	BV	365	550
1913 C	—	450	1200	—
1914 C	—	400	850	—
1916 C*	—	7500	17500	—
1917 C	—	BV	BV	500
1918 C	—	BV	BV	500
1919 C	—	BV	BV	500
3998 Sovereign. Similar R. I on ground for Bombay Mint, India				
1918	—	BV	375	550
3999 Sovereign. Similar R. M on ground for Melbourne Mint, Australia die axis: ↑↑				
1911 M	—	—	BV	400
1912 M	—	—	BV	400
1913 M	—	—	BV	400
1914 M	—	—	BV	400
1915 M	—	—	BV	400
1916 M	—	—	BV	400
1917 M	—	—	BV	400
1918 M	—	—	BV	400
1919 M	—	—	BV	400
1920 M	700	1400	2300	4500
1921 M	2750	5000	7500	17000
1922 M	1750	4000	7500	13500
1923 M	—	BV	BV	400
1924 M	—	BV	BV	400
1925 M	—	—	BV	395
1926 M	—	BV	BV	400
1928 M	450	900	1350	2350

4000 - 1930 M Sovereign, small head

4000 Sovereign. Similar small bare head l. die axis: ↑↑				
1929 M	375	750	1350	2500
1929 M Proof *FDC*				*Extremely rare*
1930 M	—	BV	385	475
1931 M	BV	BV	475	600

* Beware of recent forgeries

<table>
<tr><td>4001</td><td>4003</td></tr>
<tr><td>Perth Mint Sovereign</td><td>1921 Sydney 's' Sovereign</td></tr>
</table>

	F £	VF £	EF £	BU £

4001 Sovereign. Similar R. P on ground for Perth Mint, Australia die axis: ↑↑

	F	VF	EF	BU
1911 P	—	—	BV	385
1912 P	—	—	BV	385
1913 P	—	—	BV	385
1914 P	—	—	BV	385
1915 P	—	—	BV	385
1916 P	—	—	BV	385
1917 P	—	—	BV	385
1918 P	—	—	BV	385
1919 P	—	—	BV	385
1920 P	—	—	BV	385
1921 P	—	—	BV	385
1922 P	—	—	BV	385
1923 P	—	—	BV	385
1924 P	—	BV	BV	425
1925 P	BV	BV	325	600
1926 P	400	675	1100	2500
1927 P	BV	BV	375	500
1928 P	—	BV	BV	425

4002 Sovereign. Similar — small bare head l. die axis: ↑↑

	F	VF	EF	BU
1929 P	—	BV	BV	450
1930 P	—	BV	BV	450
1931 P	—	—	BV	375

4003 Sovereign. Similar R. S on ground for Sydney Mint, Australia die axis: ↑↑

	F	VF	EF	BU
1911 S	—	—	BV	385
1912 S	—	—	BV	385
1913 S	—	—	BV	385
1914 S	—	—	BV	385
1915 S	—	—	BV	385
1916 S	—	—	BV	385
1917 S	—	—	BV	385
1918 S	—	—	BV	385
1919 S	—	—	BV	425
†1920 S				*Of highest rarity*
1921 S	500	800	1600	2500
1922 S	5000	9500	14000	27500
1923 S	3500	6500	12000	25000
1924 S	400	800	1450	2500
1925 S	—	—	BV	400
1926 S	6000	12500	20000	31500

† *An example of the proof 1920 S sold at a UK auction in May 2012 for £780,000*
BV= Bullion value only. At the time of going to press the spot price for gold was £1600 per oz.

	F £	VF £	EF £	BU £
4004 Sovereign. Similar R. SA on ground for Pretoria Mint, South Africa die axis: ↑↑				
1923 SA	—	3000	10000	—
1923 SA Proof *FDC* £2750				
1924 SA	—	2500	6500	9000
1925 SA	—	—	BV	385
1926 SA	—	—	BV	385
1927 SA	—	—	BV	385
1928 SA	—	—	BV	385
4005 Sovereign. Similar — small head die axis: ↑↑				
1929 SA	—	—	BV	385
1930 SA	—	—	BV	385
1931 SA	—	—	BV	385
1932 SA	—	—	BV	385

4006
1914 Half-sovereign

4006 Half-Sovereign. Bare head l. R. St. George and dragon date in ex. London Mint die axis: ↑↑				
1911	—	BV	BV	250
1911 Proof *FDC* £1100				
1911 Matt Proof *FDC* .... *Of highest rarity*				
1912	—	BV	BV	250
1913	—	BV	BV	250
1914	—	BV	BV	250
1915	—	BV	BV	250
4007 Half-Sovereign. Similar R. M on ground for Melbourne Mint, Australia die axis: ↑↑				
1915 M	—	BV	BV	250
4008 Half-Sovereign. Similar R. P on ground for Perth Mint, Australia die axis: ↑↑				
1911 P	—	BV	175	350
1915 P	—	BV	175	325
1918 P	200	600	2000	3750
4009 Half-Sovereign. Similar R. S on ground for Sydney Mint, Australia die axis: ↑↑				
1911 S	—	BV	BV	215
1912 S	—	BV	BV	215
1914 S	—	BV	BV	215
1915 S	—	BV	BV	215
1916 S	—	BV	BV	215
4010 Half-Sovereign. Similar R. SA on ground for Pretoria Mint, South Africa die axis: ↑↑				
1923 SA Proof *FDC* £1500				
1925 SA	—	BV	BV	215
1926 SA	—	BV	BV	215

BV= Bullion value only. At the time of going to press the spot price for gold was £1600 per oz.

SILVER

FIRST COINAGE, 1911-19 Sterling silver (.925 fine)

4011
1911 Halfcrown

	F £	VF £	EF £	BU £
4011 Halfcrown. Bare head l. R. Crowned shield in Garter die axis: ↑↑				
1911 15	25	85	275	
1911 Proof *FDC* £325				
1912 15	25	75	350	
1913 15	30	85	375	
1914 12	18	45	175	
1915 12	18	40	120	
1916 12	18	40	120	
1917 12	20	60	150	
1918 12	18	45	125	
1919 12	20	55	150	

4012
1912 Florin

4012 Florin. Bare head l. R. Crowned Cruciform shields sceptres in angles die axis: ↑↑				
1911 10	18	60	195	
1911 Proof *FDC* £225				
1912 10	18	70	275	
1913 10	25	85	300	
1914 10	18	50	125	
1915 10	20	65	200	
1916 10	18	50	125	
1917 10	18	55	150	
1918 10	18	45	110	
1919 10	18	55	150	

	4013	4014
	1911 Proof	1911 Sixpence

	F	VF	EF	BU
	£	£	£	£

4013 Shilling. Bare head l. R. Lion passant on crown, within circle die axis: ↑↑

	F	VF	EF	BU
1911	6	15	40	90
1911 Proof *FDC* £150				
1912	6	15	45	135
1913	6	15	75	250
1914	6	10	40	90
1915	6	10	30	75
1916	6	10	30	75
1917	6	15	40	135
1918	6	10	35	85
1919	6	15	45	100

4014 Sixpence. Bare head l. R. Lion passant on crown, within circle die axis: ↑↑

	F	VF	EF	BU
1911	5	10	30	60
1911 Proof *FDC* £115				
1912	5	10	40	80
1913	5	10	45	85
1914	5	10	30	65
1915	5	10	30	75
1916	5	10	30	60
1917	5	10	55	160
1918	5	10	30	65
1919	5	10	35	75
1920	5	10	45	90

4015 Threepence. As Maundy but dull finish die axis: ↑↑

	F	VF	EF	BU
1911	—	2	10	30
1911 Proof *FDC* £55				
1912	—	2	10	30
1913	—	2	10	30
1914	—	2	5	30
1915	—	2	5	35
1916	—	2	5	25
1917	—	2	5	25
1918	—	2	5	25
1919	—	2	5	25
1920	—	2	10	35

4016 - 1915 Maundy Set

		EF £	FDC £
4016 Maundy Set (4d., 3d., 2d. and 1d.) die axis: ↑↑			
1911		110	200
1911 Proof *FDC* £300			
1912		110	200
1913		110	200
1914		110	200
1915		110	200
1916		110	200
1917		110	200
1918		110	200
1919		110	200
1920		135	200
4017 — **Fourpence.** 1911-20	from	20	30
4018 — **Threepence.** 1911-20	from	20	32
4019 — **Twopence.** 1911-20	from	20	30
4020 — **Penny.** 1911-20	from	20	35

See footnote after 3796

SECOND COINAGE, 1920-27 Debased silver (.500 fine). Types as before.

	F £	VF £	EF £	BU £
4021 Halfcrown. Deeply engraved. Bare head l. R. Crowned shield in garter die axis: ↑↑				
1920	5	12	60	225
4021A — recut shallow portrait				
1920	5	15	75	250
1921	5	12	60	185
1922	5	10	60	195
1923	5	10	40	95
1924	5	10	60	160
1924 Specimen Finish £4250				
1925	12	75	375	875
1926	5	18	85	200
1926 No colon after OMN	15	45	175	395
4022 Florin. Deeply engraved. Bare head l. R. Crowned cruciform shields, sceptres in angles die axis: ↑↑				
1920	3	12	60	175
4022A — recut shallow portrait				
1920	5	18	75	175
1921	5	10	55	120
1922	5	10	50	120
1922 Proof in gold *FDC*				*Of highest rarity*
1923	5	10	40	85
1924	5	12	65	150
1924 Specimen Finish £3500				
1925	10	55	200	500
1926	5	12	65	165

	F	VF	EF	BU
	£	£	£	£

4023 Shilling. Deeply engraved. Bare head l. R. Lion passant on crown within circle
die axis: ↑↑

1920	3	12	45	110
1921 nose to S	12	30	90	225

4023A — recut shallow portrait

1920	4	15	65	160
1921 nose to SV	3	15	65	160
1922	3	10	45	95
1923	3	10	35	90
1924	3	10	35	95
1924 Specimen Finish £3500				
1925	3	10	65	160
1926	3	10	35	100

Note: 1923 and 1924 Shillings exist struck in nickel and are valued at £2850 each FDC.

4024 Sixpence. Bare head l. R. Lion passant on crown within circle die axis: ↑↑

1920	2	8	30	85
1921	2	8	25	80
1922	2	8	25	80
1923	10	25	40	110
1924	2	8	20	65
1924 Specimen Finish *FDC* £3000				
1924 Proof in gold	....*Extremely rare*			
1925	5	12	70	

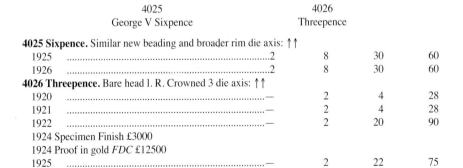

4025
George V Sixpence

4026
Threepence

4025 Sixpence. Similar new beading and broader rim die axis: ↑↑

1925	2	8	30	60
1926	2	8	30	60

4026 Threepence. Bare head l. R. Crowned 3 die axis: ↑↑

1920	....—	2	4	28
1921	....—	2	4	28
1922	....—	2	20	90
1924 Specimen Finish £3000				
1924 Proof in gold *FDC* £12500				
1925	....—	2	22	75
1926	2	8	45	150

	EF £	FDC £
4027 Maundy Set. (4d., 3d., 2d. and 1d.) die axis: ↑↑		
1921	120	200
1922	120	200
1923	120	200
1924	120	200
1925	120	200
1926	120	200
1927	120	200
4028 — **Fourpence.** 1921-7 ....*from*	20	35
4029 — **Threepence.** 1921-7 ....*from*	20	30
4030 — **Twopence.** 1921-7 ....*from*	20	30
4031 — **Penny.** 1921-7 ....*from*	20	40

2nd coinage   3rd coinage
BM more central on tr.   Modified Effigy, BM to right of tr

THIRD COINAGE, 1926-27. As before but modified effigy, with details of head more clearly defined. The BM on truncation is nearer to the back of the neck and without stops; beading is more pronounced.

	F £	VF £	EF £	BU £
4032 Halfcrown. Modified effigy l. R. Crowned Shield in Garter die axis: ↑↑				
1926	5	20	75	200
1927	5	10	45	110
1927 Proof in gold *FDC* ....*Of highest rarity*				
4033 Shilling. Modified effigy l. R. Lion passant on crown, within circle die axis: ↑↑				
1926	2	8	30	65
1927	2	8	40	75
4034 Sixpence. Modified effigy l. R. Lion passant on crown, within circle die axis: ↑↑				
1926	2	5	20	50
1927	2	5	25	55
4035 Threepence. Modified effigy l. R. Crowned 3 die axis: ↑↑				
1926	2	4	12	55

FOURTH COINAGE, 1927-36

VIP proofs are thought to exist for all denominations from 1928 through to 1936 and are all extremely rare.

4036
1927 'Wreath' Crown proof

	F £	VF £	EF £	BU £
4036 Crown. Modified Bare head l. R. Crown and date in wreath die axis: ↑↑				
† 1927 –15,030 struck Proof only *FDC* £325				
1927 Matt Proof *FDC Extremely rare*				
1928* –9034 struck 105	165	275	475
1929 –4994 struck 110	195	300	525
1930 –4847 struck 110	195	310	545
1931 –4056 struck 115	155	310	575
1932 –2395 struck 170	305	525	1000
1933* –7132 struck 115	200	325	535
1934 –932 struck... 1000	1920	2950	4750
1936 –2473 struck 175	320	525	985

4037
1931 Halfcrown

	F £	VF £	EF £	BU £
4037 Halfcrown. Modified bare head l. R. Shield die axis: ↑↑				
†1927 Proof only *FDC* £150				
1927 Matt Proof *FDC of highest rarity*				
1928 5	8	18	50
1929 5	8	20	55
1930 20	95	300	825
1931 5	8	25	75
1932 5	8	25	85
1933 5	8	15	75
1934 5	10	75	200
1935 5	8	15	50
1936 5	8	12	40

†*N.B. Proofs of other dates from 1927 also exist, but are extremely rare as they were for V.I.P. issue*
* *Beware recent counterfeits*

4038
Florin

	F	VF	EF	BU
	£	£	£	£

4038 Florin. Modified bare head l. R. Cruciform shields, sceptre in each angle die axis: ↑↑

†1927 Proof only *FDC* £150

1927 Matt Proof *FDC* ....*Extremely rare*

1928	4	8	14	40
1929	4	8	18	55
1930	4	8	40	95
1931	4	8	20	70
1932	15	70	400	900
1933	4	8	15	65
1935	4	8	12	50
1936	4	8	10	40

4039   4040
Shilling   Sixpence

4039 Shilling. Modified bare head l. R. Lion standing on crown, no inner circles die axis: ↑↑

1927	3	6	20	60

†1927 Proof *FDC* £75

1927 Matt Proof *FDC* ....*Extremely rare*

1928	3	6	15	50
1929	3	6	15	50
1930	3	12	50	130
1931	3	6	15	55
1932	3	6	15	55
1933	3	6	15	55
1934	3	6	20	65
1935	3	6	15	50
1936	3	6	10	40

4040 Sixpence. Modified bare head l. R. Three oak sprigs with six acorns die axis: ↑↑

†1927 Proof only *FDC* £85

1927 Matt Proof *FDC* ....*Extremely rare*

1928	2	5	12	40
1929	2	5	12	40
1930	2	5	12	45

†N.B. Proofs of other dates from 1927 also exist, but are extremely rare as they were for V.I.P. issue

	F	VF	EF	BU
	£	£	£	£

4041 Sixpence. Similar closer milling die axis: ↑↑

	F	VF	EF	BU
1931	2	5	12	45
1932	2	5	12	65
1933	2	5	12	45
1934	2	5	12	55
1935	2	5	12	35
1936	2	5	12	30

4042
Threepence

4042 Threepence. Modified Bare head l. ℞. Three oak sprigs with three acorns die axis: ↑↑

†1927 Proof only *FDC* £150

1927 Matt Proof *FDC*...*Extremely rare*

	F	VF	EF	BU
1928	5	10	30	80
1930	2	5	20	65
1931	—	1	2	20
1932	—	1	2	20
1933	—	1	2	20
1934	—	1	2	18
1935	—	1	2	20
1936	—	1	2	15

4043
George V Maundy Set

	EF	FDC
	£	£

4043 Maundy Set. As earlier sets die axis: ↑↑

	EF	FDC
1928	120	185
1929	120	185
1930	150	185
1931	120	185
1932	120	185
1933	135	185
1934	135	185
1935	135	185
1936	145	185

The 1936 Maundy was distributed by King Edward VIII

		EF	FDC
4044 — Fourpence. 1928-36	*from*	20	30
4045 — Threepence. 1928-36	*from*	20	30
4046 — Twopence. 1928-36	*from*	20	30
4047 — Penny. 1928-36	*from*	25	40

†N.B. Proofs of other dates from 1927 also exist, but are extremely rare as they were for V.I.P. issue

Silver Jubilee Commemorative issue, die axis: ↑↑

4048
1935 'Jubilee' Crown

	F £	VF £	EF £	BU £
4048 Crown.				
1935. ℞. St. George, incuse lettering on edge –				
714,769 struck	—	25	35	50
1935 — error edge ....*Extremely rare*				
4049 Crown. Similar Specimen striking issued in box .... —		—	—	75

4050 Crown. Similar raised lettering on edge 2,500 struck.
  Proof (.925 ℞) *FDC* £1000
  — error edge inscription Proof *FDC* £5000
  — Proof in gold –28 struck £87500

BRONZE

H Mint mark location – 4052

4052
1912 H Penny

KN Mint mark location
as above – 4053

4051 Penny. Bare head l. ℞. Britannia seated right die axis: ↑↑

1911	1	3	15	60
1912	1	3	20	70
1913	1	3	30	95
1914	1	3	22	75
1915	1	3	25	80
1916	1	3	22	75
1917	1	3	15	65
1918	1	3	15	65
1919	1	3	18	65
1920	1	3	18	70
1921	1	3	18	65
1922	1	3	35	135
1922 Rev. of 1927	3500	11500	—	—
1922 Specimen finish	....*Extremely rare*			
1926	1	4	40	140

	F	VF	EF	BU
	£	£	£	£

4052 Penny. Bare head l. R. Britannia, H (Heaton Mint, Birmingham, Ltd.) to l. of date die axis: ↑↑

1912 H	1	10	100	285
1918 H	2	25	325	800
1919 H	2	30	475	1150

4053 Penny. Bare head l. R. Britannia KN (King's Norton Metal Co.) to l. of date die axis: ↑↑

1918 KN	5	75	250	1450
1919 KN	7	90	450	2000
1919 KN Cupro-nickel				*Unique*

4054 Penny. Modified effigy l. R. as 4051

1926	15	50	650	3500

4054A Penny. Modified effigy. R. Britannia sl. smaller. Shorter right thumb, date in ex. die axis: ↑↑

1922				*Of the highest rarity*
1926				*Of the highest rarity*
1927		—	1	12	40

4055 Penny. Small bare head l. R. Britannia Seated r. date in ex. die axis: ↑↑

1928	—	1	12	45
1929	—	1	12	55
1930	—	1	20	75
1931	—	1	18	60
1932	—	1	35	140
1933				*Extremely rare*
1934*	—	1	45	250
1935	—	1	10	28
1936	—	1	7	24

4056 - Halfpenny

4056 Halfpenny. Bare head l. R. Britannia Seated r. date in ex. die axis: ↑↑

1911	1	3	8	45
1912	1	3	10	50
1913	1	3	10	50
1914	1	3	12	55
1915	1	3	18	60
1916	1	3	18	60
1917	1	3	10	50
1918	1	3	10	50
1919	1	3	10	50
1920	1	3	20	60
1921	1	3	10	50
1922	1	3	22	90
1923	1	3	10	50
1924	1	3	10	50
1924 Specimen finish				*Extremely rare*
1925	1	3	10	50

Matt proofs also exist of some dates for most denominations and are all extremely rare.
* Most 1934 pennies were mint darkened. Coins with original lustre are rare.

	VF	EF	BU
	£	£	£

4057 Halfpenny. Modified effigy l. R. Britannia Seated r. date in ex. die axis: ↑↑

1925	 3	20	75
1926	 2	12	55
1927	 2	8	45

4058
Small head

4058 Halfpenny. Small bare head l. R. Britannia Seated r. date in ex. die axis: ↑↑

1928	 1	7	35
1929	 1	7	35
1930	 1	7	45
1931	 1	7	40
1932	 1	7	40
1933	 1	7	40
1934	 1	7	35
1935	 1	7	30
1936	 1	5	20

4059
Farthing

4059 Farthing. Bare head l. R. Britannia Seated r. date in ex. Dark finish die axis: ↑↑

1911	 1	4	20
1912	 1	3	18
1913	 1	3	18
1914	 1	3	18
1915	 1	5	25
1916	 1	3	18
1917	 1	3	14
1918	 1	10	40

4060 Farthing. Similar Bright finish, die axis: ↑↑

1918	 1	3	18
1919	 1	3	18
1920	 1	4	20
1921	 1	4	20
1922	 1	4	25
1923	 1	5	20
1924	 1	5	20
1925	 1	4	20

	VF	EF	BU
	£	£	£

4061 Farthing. Modified effigy l. R. Britannia Seated r. date in ex. die axis: ↑↑

	VF	EF	BU
1926	1	3	18
1927	1	3	18
1928	1	3	14
1929	1	3	18
1930	1	3	20
1931	1	3	18
1932	1	3	14
1933	1	3	18
1934	2	5	18
1935	3	5	30
1936	1	3	14

4062
Third-Farthing

4062 Third-Farthing (for use in Malta). Bare head l. R. Crowned date and Value die axis: ↑↑

	VF	EF	BU
1913	12	20	40

PROOF SETS

PS11 Coronation, **1911.** Five pounds to Maundy Penny (12 coins) *FDC* £19500

PS12 — **1911.** Sovereign to Maundy Penny (10 coins) *FDC* £4750

PS13 — **1911.** Half crown to Maundy Penny (8 coins) *FDC* £1100

PS14 New type, **1927.** Wreath type Crown to Threepence (6 coins) *FDC* £750

† *NB Truly 'FDC' proof sets are hardly ever encountered. Component coins showing any surface marks, hairlines or nicks will be worth less than the prices quoted above.*

Edward VIII succeeded his father on 20th January 1936 and abdicated 10th December. He was born 23rd June 1894, and was very popular as Prince of Wales. He ruled only for a short time before announcing his intended marriage to the American divorcee Wallis Simpson; a potential religious and political scandal. Edward was not a traditionalist, as evidenced on the proposed coinage, where he insisted against all advice on having his effigy face the same way as his father's, instead of opposite. He abdicated in favour of his brother, and became Edward, Duke of Windsor, marrying Mrs Simpson in France, where they lived in exile. He governed the Bahamas from 1940-45 and died on 28th May 1972.

No coins of Edward VIII were issued for currency within the United Kingdom bearing his name and portrait. The Mint had commenced work on a new coinage prior to the Abdication, and various patterns were made. No Proof Sets were issued for sale and only a small number of sets were struck.

Coins bearing Edward's name, but not his portrait, were issued for the colonial territories of British East Africa, British West Africa, Fiji and New Guinea. The projected U.K. coins were to include a Shilling of essentially `Scottish' type with twelve sides which might supplement and possibly supersede the inconveniently small silver Threepence.

Engravers and Designers:– George Kruger Gray (1880-1943), Thomas Humphrey Paget (1893-1974), Benedicto Pistucci (1784-1855) Frances Madge Kitchener, Percy Metcalfe (1895-1970), H Wilson Parker (1896-1980)

Designer's initials: H. P. (T. Humphrey Paget)   B.P. (Benedetto Pistrucci, d. 1855)
                  K. G. (G. Kruger Gray)   M. K. (Madge Kitchener)
                  W. P. (H. Wilson Parker)

Die axis ↑↑

GOLD

4063
Edward VIII Proof Five Pounds

4063 Proof Set
Gold, Five Pounds, Two Pounds and Sovereign, Silver Crown, Halfcrown, Florin, Scottish Shilling, Sixpence and Threepence, Brass Threepence, Penny, Halfpenny and Farthing, 1937 *FDC*.
Only one complete set known in private hands..

FDC
£

Five Pounds, Bare head 1. R St George and dragon, date in ex 715000
Two Pounds, Bare head 1. R St George and dragon, date in ex 330000
Sovereign, Bare head l. R. St George and dragon date in ex 660000
Crown, Bare head l. R. Crowned Shield of arms and supporters.. 305000
Halfcrown, Bare head l. R. Quartered Standard of arms 150000
Florin, Bare head l. R. Crowned rose and emblems 110000
Shilling, Bare head l. R. Lion seated facing on crown 85850
Sixpence, Bare head l. R. Six interlinked rings.. 60500
Threepence, Bare head l. R. three interlinked rings 46750

4064A

4064A Nickel brass. **Threepence,** 1937 Bare head l. R. Thrift plant below 60500
    Bronze. **Penny,** 1937 110000
    Halfpenny, 1937 49500
    Farthing, 1937 44000

Note: Matt proofs exist of most denominations

Pattern

Edward VIII Brass Threepence

UNC
£

4064B Nickel brass dodecagonal **Threepence,** 1937. Bare head l. R. Thrift plant of more
    naturalistic style than the modified proof coin. A small number of these coins were
    produced of differing thickness for experimental purposes and a few did get into
    circulation 50000

George VI was born on 14th December 1895 and never expected to be King. He suffered ill-health through much of his life and had a stammer. He married Elizabeth Bowes Lyon and together they became very popular especially through the ravages of World War II, when Buckingham Palace was bombed. The war took its toll on George, and ever a heavy smoker he succumbed to lung cancer on 6th February 1952. Elizabeth, known after his death as 'Queen Elizabeth the Queen Mother', lived on to the age of 101 dying on 30th March 2002.

Though they were at first issued concurrently, the twelve-sided nickel-brass Threepence superseded the small silver Threepence in 1942. Those dated 1943-4 were not issued for circulation in the U.K. In addition to the usual English 'lion' Shilling, a Shilling of Scottish type was issued concurrently. This depicts the Scottish lion and crown flanked by the shield of St. Andrew and a thistle. In 1947, as silver was needed to repay the bullion lent by the U.S.A. during the war, silver coins were replaced by coins of the same type and weight made of cupro-nickel. In 1949, after India had attained independence, the title IND:IMP (Indiae Imperator) was dropped from the coinage. Commemorative Crown pieces were issued for the Coronation and the 1951 Festival of Britain.

Engravers and Designers:– Frances Madge Kitchener, George Kruger Gray (1880-1943), Percy Metcalfe (1895-1970) Thomas Humphrey Paget (1893-1974), H Wilson Parker (1896-1980), Benedetto Pistrucci (1784-1855)

Designer's initials: K. G. (G. Kruger Gray)   B. P. (Benedetto Pistrucci, d. 1855)
                          H. P. (T. Humphrey Paget)   W. P. (Wilson Parker)

Die axis ↑↑

GOLD

4074
1937 Proof Five Pounds

4076
1937 Proof Sovereign

	FDC
	£
4074 Five Pounds. Bare head l. R. St. George, 1937. Proof plain edge only (5001 struck)	7000
4074-4077 Proof Struck to Matt finish *FDC of highest rarity*	
4075 Two Pounds. Similar, 1937. Proof plain edge only (5001 struck)	2750
4076 Sovereign. Similar, 1937. Proof plain edge only (5001 struck)	3500
4077 Half-Sovereign. Similar, 1937. Proof plain edge only (5001 struck)	1000

SILVER

FIRST COINAGE, 1937-46 Silver, .500 fine, with title IND:IMP
VIP proofs are thought to exist for all denominations from 1938 through to 1952 and are all
extremely rare.

4078 - 1937 Crown

	VF £	EF £	BU £
4078 Crown. Coronation commemorative			
1937. ℞. Arms and supporters 25	25	35	50
4079 Crown. Similar 1937 Proof *FDC* £90			
Similar 1937 Frosted 'VIP' Proof £1500			

4080 - Halfcrown   4081 - 1937 Florin

4080 Halfcrown. Bare head l. ℞. Shield die axis: ↑↑

1937	5	5	10	25
1937 Proof *FDC* £40				
1938	5	5	10	55
1939	5	5	10	30
1940	5	5	10	35
1941	5	5	10	30
1942	5	5	10	25
1943	5	5	10	30
1944	5	5	10	25
1945	5	5	10	20
1946	5	5	10	20

4081 Florin. Bare head l. ℞. Crowned rose, etc. die axis: ↑↑

1937	4	4	8	25
1937 Proof *FDC* £35				
1938	4	4	8	50
1939	4	4	8	25
1940	4	4	8	30
1941	4	4	8	25
1942	4	4	8	20
1943	4	4	8	25
1944	4	4	8	25
1945	4	4	8	20
1946	4	4	8	20

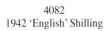

4082
1942 'English' Shilling

4083
1945 'Scottish' Shilling

	VF	EF	BU
	£	£	£

4082 Shilling. 'English' reverse. Bare head l. R. Lion standing on large crown die axis: ↑↑

1937	3	6	25
1937 Proof *FDC* £28			
1938	3	6	50
1939	3	6	25
1940	3	6	30
1941	3	6	25
1942	3	6	25
1943	3	6	25
1944	3	6	25
1945	3	6	18
1946	3	6	18

4083 Shilling. 'Scottish' reverse. Bare head l. R. Lion seated facing on crown die axis: ↑↑

1937	3	6	20
1937 Proof *FDC* £28			
1938	3	6	45
1939	3	6	25
1940	3	6	30
1941	3	6	30
1942	3	6	30
1943	3	6	25
1944	3	6	25
1945	3	6	18
1946	3	6	18

4084
1945 Sixpence

4084 Sixpence. Bare head l. R. GRI crowned die axis: ↑↑

1937	2	5	15
1937 Proof *FDC* £25			
1938	2	5	30
1939	2	5	25
1940	2	5	30
1941	2	5	25
1942	2	5	20
1943	2	5	20
1944	2	5	20
1945	2	5	15
1946	2	5	15

4085
1944 Threepence

	VF £	EF £	BU £
4085 Threepence. Bare head l. ℞. Shield on rose die axis: ↑↑			
1937 2		5	15
1937 Proof *FDC* £20			
1938 2		5	20
1939 2		6	35
1940 2		5	30
1941 2		5	30
1942* 6		20	45
1943* 8		25	55
1944* 15		40	110
1945* .... *Extremely rare*			

* issued for Colonial use only

4086
1937 Maundy Set

	EF £	FDC £
4086 Maundy Set. Silver, .500 fine. Die axis: ↑↑		
1937 90		175
1937 Proof *FDC* £200		
1938 110		175
1939 110		175
1940 125		175
1941 110		175
1942 110		175
1943 110		175
1944 110		175
1945 110		175
1946 110		175

	EF £	UNC £
4087 — Fourpence. 1937-46 .... *from*	20	40
4088 — Threepence. 1937-46 .... *from*	22	35
4089 — Twopence. 1937-46 .... *from*	20	30
4090 — Penny. 1937-46 .... *from*	30	40

	EF	FDC
	£	£

SECOND COINAGE, 1947-48, Silver, .925 fine, with title IND:IMP (Maundy only)
4091 Maundy Set (4d., 3d., 2d. and 1d.). Die axis: ↑↑

1947	110	175
1948	110	175

4092 — **Fourpence,** 1947-8	40
4093 — **Threepence,** 1947-8	35
4094 — **Twopence,** 1947-8	30
4095 — **Penny,** 1947-8	40

THIRD COINAGE, 1949-52, Silver, .925 fine, but omitting IND:IMP. (Maundy only)
4096 Maundy Set (4d., 3d., 2d. and 1d.). Die axis: ↑↑

1949	120	175
1950	135	175
1951	135	175
1952	160	220

1952 Proof in copper *FDC* £7500

The 1952 Maundy was distributed by Queen Elizabeth II.

4097 — **Fourpence,** 1949-52	*from*	40
4098 — **Threepence,** 1949-52	*from*	35
4099 — **Twopence,** 1949-52	*from*	30
4100 — **Penny,** 1949-52	*from*	40

See footnote re Maundy Pennies after 3796.

CUPRO-NICKEL

	VF	EF	BU
	£	£	£

SECOND COINAGE, 1947-48, Types as first (silver) coinage, IND:IMP.
4101 Halfcrown. Bare head l. R. Shield die axis: ↑↑

1947	1	2	15
1948	1	2	12

4102 Florin. Bare head l. R. Crowned rose die axis: ↑↑

1947	1	2	15
1948	1	2	15

4103 Shilling. 'English' reverse. Bare head l. die axis: ↑↑

1947	1	2	15
1948	1	2	15

4104 Shilling. 'Scottish' reverse. Bare head l. die axis: ↑↑

1947	1	2	15
1948	1	2	15

4105 Sixpence. Bare head l. R. GRI crowned die axis: ↑↑

1947	1	2	12
1948	1	2	12

THIRD COINAGE, 1949-52, Types as before but title IND:IMP. omitted

4106	4110
1949 Halfcrown	1952 Sixpence

	F £	VF £	EF £	BU £
4106 Halfcrown. Bare head l. R. Shield die axis: ↑↑				
1949		1	3	30
1950		— 1	8	45
1950 Proof *FDC* £45				
1951		1	8	45
1951 Proof *FDC* £45				
1952				*Unique*
1952 Proof *FDC* £90000				
4107 Florin. Bare head l. R. Crowned rose die axis: ↑↑				
1949		1	5	40
1950		1	8	40
1950 Proof *FDC* £45				
1951		1	8	45
1951 Proof *FDC* £45				
4108 Shilling. 'English' reverse. Bare head l. die axis: ↑↑				
1949		1	5	35
1950		1	8	35
1950 Proof *FDC* £40				
1951		1	6	35
1951 Proof *FDC* £35				
1952 Proof *FDC* £47500				
4109 Shilling. 'Scottish' reverse. Bare head l. die axis: ↑↑				
1949		1	5	35
1950		1	8	35
1950 Proof *FDC* £40				
1951		1	6	35
1951 Proof *FDC* £30				
4110 Sixpence. Bare head l. R. Crowned cypher die axis: ↑↑				
1949		1	1	15
1950		1	3	20
1950 Proof *FDC* £30				
1951		1	5	25
1951 Proof *FDC* £30				
1951 Matt Proof *FDC* £1500				
1952	8	15	45	135

Festival of Britain issue die axis: ↑↑

4111 - Festival of Britain Crown

	F	VF	EF	BU
	£	£	£	£

4111 Crown. Bare head l. R. St. George and dragon, date in ex, 1951. *Proof-like*.

Two reverse types exist .... —   4   12
Similar — 1951 Frosted 'VIP' Proof £2750, narrow edge lettering
Similar — 1951 Matt Proof *FDC* £4000
Similar — 1951 Plain edge Proof *FDC* £2500

NICKEL BRASS

FIRST ISSUE, 1937-48, with title IND:IMP.

4112 - 1941 Brass Threepence   4113 - Second issue obverse

4112 Threepence (dodecagonal). Bare head l. R. Thrift plant die axis: ↑↑

1937		—	2	15
1937 Proof *FDC* £22				
1938		—	6	30
1939		—	10	50
1940		—	6	30
1941		—	3	20
1942		—	2	15
1943		—	2	15
1944		—	2	20
1945		—	5	20
1946	6	15	150	950
1948		—	10	65

SECOND ISSUE, 1949-52, omitting IND:IMP.
4113 Threepence. Bare head l. R. Similar die axis: ↑↑

1949	8	30	200	750
1950			25	150
1950 Proof *FDC* £50				
1951	3		30	150
1951 Proof *FDC* £55				
1951 Matt Proof *FDC* £1250				
1952		—	5	25

BRONZE

FIRST ISSUE, 1937-48, with title IND:IMP.

4114 - 1938 Penny   4115 - 1937 Halfpenny

	VF £	EF £	BU £
4114 Penny. Bare head l. R. Britannia Seated r. date in ex die axis: ↑↑			
1937	—	1	10
1937 Proof *FDC* £28			
1938	—	3	12
1939	—	4	20
1940	—	10	60
1940 Double exergue line	—	4	25
1944* —	—	6	30
1945* —	—	5	25
1946* —	—	2	12
1947 —	—	1	10
1948 —	—	1	10
1946 ONE' die flaw	25	150	350

most pennies of these date were darkened at the mint.

4115 Halfpenny. Bare head l. R. Ship sailing l. date below die axis: ↑↑			
1937	—	1	10
1937 Proof *FDC* £22			
1938	—	2	15
1939	—	3	30
1940	—	3	30
1941	—	2	12
1942	—	1	10
1943	—	1	10
1944	—	1	10
1945	—	1	10
1946	—	3	25
1947	—	1	12
1948	—	1	12

4116 - 1943 Farthing

4116 Farthing. Bare head l. R. Wren l. date above die axis: ↑↑			
1937	—	1	7
1937 Proof *FDC* £16			
1938	—	2	15

	VF	EF	BU
	£	£	£
1939	—	1	8
1940	—	1	8
1941	—	1	8
1942	—	1	7
1943	—	1	7
1944	—	1	7
1945	—	1	7
1946	—	1	7
1947	—	1	7
1948	—	1	7

SECOND ISSUE, 1949-52

4117 Penny. Bare head l. R. Britannia Seated r. date in ex. die axis: ↑↑

1949	—	1	10
1950	10	20	75
1950 Proof *FDC* £40			
1951	30	40	75
1951 Proof *FDC* £55			
1952 Proof only *FDC*			*Unique*

4118   4119
Second issue Halfpenny   Second issue Farthing

4118 Halfpenny. Bare head l. R. Ship Sailing l. date below die axis: ↑↑

1949	—	4	20
1950	—	3	15
1950 Proof *FDC* £20			
1951	—	5	30
1951 Proof *FDC* £22			
1952	—	1	7

4119 Farthing. Bare head l. R. Wren l. date above die axis: ↑↑

1949	—	1	8
1950	—	1	7
1950 Proof *FDC* £20			
1951	—	2	9
1951 Proof *FDC* £22			
1952	—	1	7

The coins dated 1952 were issued during the reign of Elizabeth II.

PROOF SETS

PS15 Coronation, **1937.** Five pounds to Half-sovereign (4 coins) *FDC* £13000
PS16 — **1937.** Crown to Farthing, including Maundy Set (15 coins) *FDC* £400
PS17 Mid-Century, **1950.** Halfcrown to Farthing (9 coins) *FDC* £175
PS18 Festival of Britain, **1951.** Crown to Farthing (10 coins) *FDC* £235

Elizabeth II was born on 21st April 1926. Our current Monarch has lived a long and glorious reign celebrating her Golden Jubilee in 2002. She married Philip, a distant cousin, in 1947 and has four children, Charles, Anne, Andrew and Edward. Significantly she is the first Monarch to pay taxes and her coinage has been an interesting one with the change to decimal coinage and the numerous bust changes since 1953.

The earliest coins of this reign have the title BRITT:OMN, but in 1954 this was omitted from the Queen's titles owing to the changing status of so many Commonwealth territories. The minting of 'English' and 'Scottish' shillings was continued. A Coronation commemorative crown was issued in 1953, another crown was struck on the occasion of the 1960 British Exhibition in New York and a third was issued in honour of Sir Winston Churchill in 1965. A very small number of proof gold coins were struck in 1953 for the national museum collections, but between 1957 and 1968 gold sovereigns were minted again in quantity for sale in the international bullion market and to counteract the activities of counterfeiters.

Owing to inflation the farthing had now become practically valueless; production of these coins ceased after 1956 and the coins were demonetised at the end of 1960. In 1965 it was decided to change to a decimal system of coinage in the year 1971. As part of the transition to decimal coinage the halfpenny was demonetized in August 1969 and the halfcrown in January 1970. (See also introduction to Decimal Coinage.)

Designer's initials:

A. V. (Avril Vaughan, 1937-2006)
B. P. (Benedetto Pistrucci, 1783-1855)
B. R. (Bruce Rushin)
C.D. (Clive Duncan)
C. T. (Cecil Thomas, 1885-1976)
D. C. (David Cornell)
E. F. (Edgar Fuller)
G. L. (Gilbert Ledward, 1888-1960)
I. R. B. (Ian Rank-Broadley)
J. B. (James Butler)
J. C. (Jody Clark)
J. M. (Jeffrey Matthews)
J. M. M. (John Mills)
M. B. (Matthew Bonaccorsi)

M. G. (Mary Gillick, 1881-1965)
M. M. D. (Mary Milner Dickens)
M. N. (Michael Noakes)
M. R. (Michael Rizzello, 1926-2004)
N. S. (Norman Sillman, 1921-2013)
P. N. (Philip Nathan)
R. D. (Ron Dutton)
R. D. M. (Raphael David Maklouf)
R. E. (Robert Elderton)
r. e. (Robert Evans)
R. L. (Robert Lowe)
T. N. (Timothy Noad)
W. G. (William Gardner, 1914-2000)
W. P. (Wilson Parker 1896-1980)

Other designers whose initials do not appear on the coins:

Christopher Ironside (1913-1992)
Arnold Machin (1911-1999)
David Wynne (1926-2014)
Professor Richard Guyatt (1914-2007)
Eric Sewell
Oscar Nemon (1906-1985)

Leslie Durbin (1913-2005)
Derek Gorringe
Bernard Sindall (1925-1998)
Tom Phillips
Edwina Ellis
David Gentleman
Matthew Dent

PRE-DECIMAL ISSUES, 1952-71
Die axis ↑↑

GOLD

FIRST COINAGE, with title BRITT.OMN, 1953. *Proof only. Originally produced for institutional collecting.*

4120 Five Pounds. Young laur. head r. R. St. George 1953 .... *Of the highest rarity*
4121 Two Pounds. Young laur. head r. R. St. George 1953 .... *Of the highest rarity*
4122 Sovereign. Young laur. head r. R. St. George 1953 .... *£425000*
4123 Half-Sovereign. Young laur. head r. R. St. George 1953 .... *Of the highest rarity*

SECOND ISSUE, BRITT.OMN omitted

4125
1958 Sovereign

	EF £	BU £
4124 Sovereign. Young laur head r. Ŗ. St. George, fine graining on edge		
1957 ....BV		375
1957 Proof *FDC* £15000		
4125 Sovereign. Similar, but coarser graining on edge		
1958 ....BV		375
1958 Proof *FDC* £15000		
1959 ....BV		375
1959 Proof *FDC* £15000		
1962 ....BV		375
1963 ....BV		375
1963 Proof *FDC* £15000		
1964 ....BV		375
1965 ....BV		375
1966 ....BV		375
1967 ....BV		375
1968 ....BV		375

SILVER

The Queen's Maundy are now the only coins struck regularly in silver.
The location of the Maundy ceremony is given for each year.

FIRST ISSUE, with title BRITT:OMN:

4126
Maundy Set

	EF £	FDC £
4126 Maundy Set (4d., 3d., 2d. and 1d.), 1953. *St Paul's Cathedral* 350		1350
1953 Proof struck in gold *FDC* ....*Extremely rare*		
1953 Proof struck in nickel bronze *FDC* ....*Extremely rare*		
4127 — Fourpence. 1953 225		
4128 — Threepence. 1953..200		
4129 — Twopence. 1953..200		
4130 — Penny. 1953 325		

BV= Bullion value only. At the time of going to press the spot price for gold was £1600 per oz.

	EF £	FDC £

SECOND ISSUE, with BRITT:OMN: omitted

4131 Maundy Set (4d., 3d., 2d. and 1d.).

	EF £	FDC £
1954 *Westminster*	—	165
1955 *Southwark*	—	165
1956 *Westminster*	—	165
1957 *St. Albans*	—	165
1958 *Westminster*	—	165
1959 *Windsor*	—	165
1960 *Westminster*	—	165
1961 *Rochester*	—	165
1962 *Westminster*	—	165
1963 *Chelmsford*	—	165
1964 Westminster	—	165
1965 Canterbury	—	165
1966 Westminster	—	165
1967 Durham	—	165
1968 Westminster	—	165
1969 Selby	—	165
1970 Westminster	—	165

For a continuation of these issues see 'Coins of England, Decimal Issues'.

	EF £	UNC £
4132 — **Fourpence.** 1954-70	*from* 20	40
4133 — **Threepence.** 1954-70	*from* 25	35
4134 — **Twopence.** 1954-70	*from* 20	30
4135 — **Penny.** 1954-70	*from* 35	50

See footnote after 3796

CUPRO-NICKEL

FIRST ISSUE, 1953, with title BRITT.OMN.
VIP proofs are thought to exist for all denominations from 1954 through to 1964 and are all extremely rare.

4136
1953 Coronation Crown

	EF £	BU £	Proof FDC £

4136 Crown. Queen on horseback. R. Crown in centre of emblematical cross, shield of
Arms in each angle

	EF £	BU £	Proof FDC £
1953	3	8	35

Similar 1953 Frosted 'VIP' proof with more fine detail apparent £1450

4137A   4138
1953 Halfcrown - 2nd obverse die   1953 Florin

	BU	*Proof* FDC
	£	£

4137 Halfcrown. First obverse die, I of DEI points to a space between beads 5   1700
4137A Halfcrown. Second obverse die, I of DEI points to a bead, with title BRITT:OMN:
    Young laur. head r. R. Arms
1953   5   20
4138 Florin. Young laur. head r. R. Double rose
1953   4   12

4139   4140
1953 'English' Shilling - 1st obv. die   'Scottish' reverse

4139 Shilling. 'English' reverse. Young laur. head r. R. Three lions
1953   2   10
4140 Shilling. ' — 'Scottish' reverse. Young laur. head r. R. Lion rampant in shield
1953   2   10

4141
1953 Sixpence - 2nd obv. die

4141 Sixpence. Young laur. head r. R. Interlaced rose, thistle, shamrock and leek
1953   1   8
4142 Set of 9 uncirculated cu-ni, ni-br and Æ coins (2/6 to 1/4d.)
in Royal Mint plastic envelope 30   —

SECOND ISSUE, similar types but omitting BRITT.OMN.

4143	4144
1960 Crown	1965 Churchill Crown

	UNC	BU
	£	£

4143 Crown, 1960. Young laur. head r. Ṛ. As 4136 ....5 — 12
— — Similar, from polished dies (New York Exhibition issue) .... 10 — 35
— — 'VIP' *Proof*, frosted design *FDC* £1200
4144 Crown, Churchill commemorative, 1965. As illustration. Ṛ. Bust of
Sir Winston Churchill r. 2
— — Similar, "Satin-Finish". VIP *Specimen* 2500
— — —, with 'ON' designer's initials on reverse ....*Of the highest rarity*

	EF	BU
	£	£

4145 Halfcrown. Young laur. head r. Ṛ. As 4137

	EF	BU
1954	8	50
1955	1	12
1956	1	18
1957	1	8
1958	8	45
1959	8	55
1960	1	20
1961	1	6
1961 Polished die	1	25
1962	1	6
1963	1	6
1964	1	8
1965	1	5
1966	1	3
1967	1	3

1970 Proof *FDC* £8

4146
1957 Florin

	EF £	BU £
4146 Florin. Young laur. head r. R. As 4138		
1954	8	55
1955	1	12
1956	1	12
1957	8	50
1958	10	55
1959	10	65
1960	1	12
1961	1	12
1962	1	5
1963	1	4
1964	1	4
1965	1	4
1966	1	3
1967	1	3
1970 Proof *FDC* £6		
4147 Shilling. 'English' reverse. Young laur. head r. R. As 4139		
1954	1	6
1955	1	6
1956	1	12
1957	1	5
1958	8	65
1959	1	5
1960	1	8
1961	1	3
1962	1	2
1963	1	2
1964	1	2
1965	1	2
1966	1	2
1970 Proof *FDC* £5		
4148 Shilling. 'Scottish' reverse. Young laur. head r. R. As 4140		
1954	—	6
1955	—	8
1956	—	12
1957	5	35
1958	—	4
1959	10	110
1960	—	8
1961	—	20
1962	—	5

	EF	BU
	£	£
1963	—	2
1964	—	2
1965	—	2
1966	—	2

1970 Proof *FDC* £5

4149 Sixpence. Young laur. head r. ℞. As 4141

1954	—	8
1955	—	4
1956	—	5
1957	—	4
1958	—	10
1959	—	3
1960	—	7
1961	—	6
1962	—	2
1963	—	2
1964	—	2
1965	—	1
1966	—	1
1967	—	1

1970 Proof *FDC* £5

NICKEL BRASS

FIRST ISSUE, with title BRITT.OMN.

4152
1953 Brass Threepence - 2nd obv. die Proof

4153
Second issue

4152 Threepence (dodecagonal). Young laur. head r. ℞. Crowned portcullis

1953		4

— Proof *FDC* £12

SECOND ISSUE (omitting BRIT.OMN)

4153 Threepence Similar type

1954	—	8
1955	—	10
1956	—	10
1957	—	6
1958	—	15
1959	—	6
1960	—	7
1961	—	3
1962	—	2
1963	—	2
1964	—	2
1965	—	2
1966	—	1
1967	—	1

1970 Proof *FDC* £5

BRONZE

FIRST ISSUE, with title BRITT.OMN.

4154	4155	4156
1953 Penny - 1st obv. die	1953 Halfpenny 2nd obv. die	1953 Farthing

	VF	EF	BU	Proof FDC
	£	£	£	£

4154 Penny. Young laur. head r. ℞. Britannia (only issued with Royal Mint set in plastic envelope)

1953 Beaded border	1	3	10	25
1953 Toothed border *FDC* £3250				

4155 Halfpenny. Young laur. head r. ℞. Ship

1953	—	—	3	12

4156 Farthing. Young laur. head r. ℞. Wren

1953	—	—	2	10

	EF	BU
	£	£

SECOND ISSUE, omitting BRITT.OMN.

4157 Penny. Young laur. head r. ℞. Britannia (1954-60 *not issued*)

1954 *Unique*		100000
1961	—	3
1962	—	1
1963	—	1
1964	—	1
1965	—	1
1966	—	1
1967	—	1
1970 Proof *FDC* £6		

4158 Halfpenny. Young laur. head r. ℞. Ship (1961 *not issued*)

1954	—	8
1954 larger border teeth	—	10
1955	—	6
1956	—	8
1957	—	4
1957 calm sea	10	50
1958	—	3
1959	—	2
1960	—	2
1962	—	1
1963	—	1
1964	—	1
1965	—	1
1966	—	1
1967	—	1
1970 Proof *FDC* £5		

	EF £	BU £
4159 Farthing. Young laur. head r. ℞. Wren		
1954	—	6
1955	—	6
1956	3	10

PROOF SETS

PS19 Coronation, **1953.** Crown to Farthing (10 coins) ....*FDC* 150
PS20 'Last Sterling', **1970.** Halfcrown to Halfpenny plus medallion ....*FDC* 30

PRE-DECIMAL PROOF SETS

All prices quoted assume coins are in their original case. Issued by the Royal Mint in official case from 1887 onwards, but earlier sets were issued privately by the engraver. All pieces have a superior finish to that of the current coins.

		No. of coins	FDC £
PS1	**George IV, 1826.** New issue, Five Pounds to Farthing	(11)	145000
PS2	**William IV, 1831.** Coronation, Two Pounds to Farthing	(14)	100000
PS3	**Victoria, 1839.** Young head. "Una and the Lion" Five Pounds and Sovereign to Farthing	(15)	375000
PS4	— **1853.** Sovereign to Half-Farthing, including Gothic type Crown	(16)	125000
PS5	— **1887.** Jubilee bust for Golden Jubilee, Five Pounds to Threepence	(11)	42500
PS6	— **1887.** Silver Crown to Threepence	(7)	6000
PS7	— **1893.** Old bust, Five Pounds to Threepence	(10)	48000
PS8	— **1893.** Silver Crown to Threepence	(6)	7500
PS9	**Edward VII, 1902.** Coronation, Five Pounds to Maundy Penny. Matt finish to surfaces	(13)	6750
PS10	— **1902.** Sovereign to Maundy Penny. Matt finish	(11)	2250
PS11	**George V, 1911.** Coronation, Five Pounds to Maundy Penny	(12)	19500
PS12	— **1911.** Sovereign to Maundy Penny	(10)	4750
PS13	— **1911.** Silver Halfcrown to Maundy Penny	(8)	1350
PS14	— **1927.** New Coinage. Wreath type Crown to Threepence	(6)	675
PS15	**George VI, 1937.** Coronation. Five Pounds to Half-Sovereign	(4)	13000
PS16	— **1937.** Coronation. Crown to Farthing, including Maundy Set	(15)	450
PS17	— **1950.** Mid-Century, Halfcrown to Farthing	(9)	175
PS18	— **1951.** Festival of Britain, Crown to Farthing	(10)	235
PS19	**Elizabeth II, 1953.** Coronation. Crown to Farthing	(10)	150
PS20	— **1970.** "Last Sterling" set. Halfcrown to Halfpenny plus medallion	(8)	30

Truly flawless FDC sets of the earlier period are commanding prices in excess of catalogue values'

A SELECT NUMISMATIC BIBLIOGRAPHY

Listed below is a selection of general books on British numismatics and other works that the specialist collector will need to consult.

General Books:
BROOKE, G. C. *English Coins*. 3rd ed., 1966.
BULL, M., *English Silver Coinage since 1649* (Spink 2015)
CHALLIS, C. E. (ed.) *A New History of the Royal Mint*. 1992
GRUEBER, H. A. *Handbook of the Coins of Great Britain and Ireland*. Revised 1970
KENYON, R. Ll. *Gold Coins of England*. 1884
NORTH, J. J. *English Hammered Coinage*, Vol. I, c. 650-1272. 1994; Vol. II, 1272-1662. 1991
STEWARTBY, Lord. *English Coins 1180-1551*. 2009
SUTHERLAND, C. H. V. *English Coinage, 600-1900*. 1972

Specialist Works:
ABRAMSON, T. *Sceattas, An Illustrated Guide*. 2006
ALLEN, D. *The Origins of Coinage in Britain: A Reappraisal*. Reprint 1978
ALLEN, D. F. *The Coins of the Coritani*. (SCBI no. 3) 1963
ALLEN, D. F. *English Coins in the British Museum: The Cross-and-Crosslets* (*'Tealby'*) type of Henry II. 1951
ALLEN, M. *The Durham Mint*. 2003
ARCHIBALD, M. M. and BLUNT, C. E. *British Museum. Anglo-Saxon Coins. Athelstan to the reform of Edgar*. 924-c.973. 1986
ASKEW, G. *The Coinage of Roman Britain*. (1951) Reprinted 1980.
BESLY, E. M. *Coins and Medals of the English Civil War*. 1990
BIDDLE, M., with HARVEY, Y., *The Winchester Mint* (Oxford 2012)
BLACKBURN, M. A. S. *Anglo-Saxon Monetary History*. 1986
— — *Viking Coinage and Currency in the British Isles*. 2011
BLUNT, C. E. and WHITTON, C. A. *The Coinages of Edward IV and of Henry VI (Restored)*.
BLUNT, C. E., STEWART, B.H.I.H. and LYON, C.S.S. *Coinage in Tenth-Century England. From Edward the Elder to Edgar's Reform*. 1989
BOON, G. C. *Coins of the Anarchy. 1135-54*. 1988
BRAND, J. D. *The English Coinage 1180-1247: Money, Mints and Exchanges* 1994
BROOKE, G. C. *English Coins in the British Museum: The Norman Kings*. 1916
BROWN, I. D., COMBER, C. H. & WILKINSON, W. *The Hammered Silver coins produced at the Tower Mint during the reign of Elizabeth I*. 2006
BROWN, I. D. and DOLLEY, M. *Bibliography of Coin Hoards of Great Britain and Ireland 1500-1967*. 1971
BUCK, I. *Medieval English Groats*. 2000
CARSON, R. A. G. *Mints, Dies and Currency. Essays in Memory of Albert Baldwin*. 1971
CHICK, D. *The Coinage of Offa and his Contemporaries*. 2010
CHURCHILL, R. *Mints and Moneyers during the reign of Henry III*. 2012
CHURCHILL, R. and THOMAS B. *The Brussels Hoard of 1908. The Long Cross Coinage of Henry III*. 2012
CLOKE, H.J. and TOONE, L., *The London Mint of Constantius and Constantine* (Spink 2015)
DAVIES, P. J. *British Silver Coins Since 1816 with Engravers' Patterns and Proofs and Unofficial Pieces*. 1982
DE JERSEY, P. *Coinage in Iron Age Armorica*. 1994
DOLLEY, R. H. M. (ed.). *Anglo-Saxon Coins; studies presented to Sir Frank Stenton*. 1964

EAGLEN, R.J., *The Abbey and Mint of Bury St. Edmunds*, Vol I, to 1279, Vol II, from 1279 (Spink 2006, 2014)

EVERSON, T. *The Galata Guide to The Farthing Tokens of James I & Charles I.* 2007

FREEMAN, M. J. *The Bronze Coinage of Great Britain.* 2006

GRIERSON, P. and BLACKBURN, M. A. S. *Medieval European Coinage, vol. 1, The Early Middle Ages.* 1986

HOBBS, R. *British Iron Age Coins in the British Museum.* 1996

KEARY, C. and GREUBER, H. *English Coins in the British Museum: Anglo-Saxon Series.* 1887, reprinted, 1970, 2 volumes.

LAKER, A. J. *The portrait Groats of Henry VIII.* 1978

LAWRENCE, L. A. *The Coinage of Edward III from 1351.*

LINECAR, H. W. A. *The Crown Pieces of Great Britain and the British Commonwealth.* 1962
– – *English Proof and Pattern Crown-Size Pieces.* 1968

MACK, R. P. *The R. P. Mack Collection, Ancient British, Anglo-Saxon and Norman Coins.* (SCBI no. 20) 1973

MANVILLE, H. E. *Encyclopedia of British Numismatics. Numismatic Guide to British and Irish Periodicals 1731-1991.* 1993

MANVILLE, H. E. and ROBERTSON, T. J. *An Annotated Bibliography of British Numismatic Auction Catalogues from 1710 to the Present.* 1986

MARSH, M. A. *The Gold Half Sovereign.* 2nd Edition, revised 2004

MARSH, M. A. *The Gold Sovereign.* 2nd Edition 1999

MASS, J. P. *The J. P. Mass collection of English Short Cross Coins 1180-1247. (SCBI 56).* 2001

MOSSOP H.R., *The Lincoln Mint c.890-1279* (1970)

NAISMITH, R. *The Coinage of Southern England, 796-c.865.* 2011

NORTH, J. J. *Edwardian English Silver Coins 1279-1351. (SCBI 39)* 1989

NORTH J.J., *English Hammered Coinage*, Vol I, c.600-1272, and Vol II, 1272-1662, third edition (Spink 1994, 1991)

NORTH, J. J. and PRESTON-MORLEY, P. J. *The John G. Brooker Collection: Coins of Charles I. (SCBI 33)* 1984

PECK, C. W. *English Copper, Tin and Bronze Coins in the British Museum, 1558-1958.* 1970

RAYNER, P.A. *The English Silver Coinage from 1649.* 5th ed. 1992

REECE, R. *Coinage in Roman Britain,* 1987

ROBINSON, Dr. B. *The Royal Maundy.* 1992

RUDD, C. *Ancient British Coins (ABC).* 2009

RUDING, REV. R. *Annals of the Coinage of Great Britain.* 3rd Edition 1840

SEAR, D. R. *Roman Coins and their Values. 4th Edition* (1999) Reprinted 2000

SILLS, J. *Gaulish and Early British Gold Coinage.* 2003

THOMPSON, J. D. A. *Inventory of British Coin Hoards, A.D. 600-1500.* 1956

VAN ARSDELL, R. *Celtic Coinage of Britain.* 1989

VAN ARSDELL, R. D. *The Coinage of the Dobunni.* 1994

WHITTON, C. A. *The Heavy Coinage of Henry VI.*

WILSON, A. and RASMUSSEN, M. *English Patten, Trial and Proof Coin in Gold, 1547-1968.* 2000

WITHERS, P. & B. R. *The Galata Guide to the Pennies of Edward I and II and the Coins of the mint of Berwick-upon-Tweed.* 2006

WOODHEAD, P. *English Gold Coins 1257-1603. The Herbert Schneider Collection, vol. 1 (SCBI 47)* 1996

— — *English Gold Coins 1603-20th Century. The Herbert Schneider Collection, vol. 2 (SCBI 57)* 2002

WREN, C. R. *The Short-cross coinage 1180-1247. Henry II to Henry III. An illustrated Guide to Identification.* 1992

— — *The Voided Long-Cross Coinage 1247-1279. Henry III and Edward I.* 1993

— — *The English Long-Cross Pennies 1279-1489. Edward I-Henry VII.* 1995

For further references to British hammered coinage see *Sylloge of Coins of the British Isles,* a serial publication now comprising 68 volumes cataloguing collections in private hands and institutions. For a full list of the volumes published to date in this series, please contact Spink at the address below.

Other authoritative papers are published in the *Numismatic Chronicle and British Numismatic Journal.* A complete book list is available from Spink & Son Ltd., 69 Southampton Row, Bloomsbury, London WC1B 4ET, Tel: 020 7563 4119. Email: Books@spink.com or by visiting the Spink Books website, www.spinkbooks.com. We carry a wide range of numismatic titles both new and old, including some titles from other publishers. Please feel free to come and browse our showroom if you are in the area.

Further information regarding membership of the British Numismatic Society can be found at www.britnumsoc.org

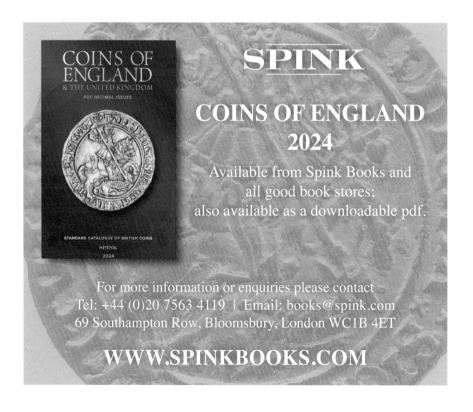

APPENDIX II

LATIN OR FOREIGN LEGENDS ON ENGLISH COINS

A DOMINO FACTUM EST ISTUD ET EST MIRABILE IN OCULIS NOSTRIS. (This is the Lord's doing and it is marvellous in our eyes: *Psalm 118.23*.) First used on 'fine' sovereign of Mary.

AMOR POPULI PRAESIDIUM REGIS. (The love of the people is the King's protection.) Reverse legend on angels of Charles I.

ANNO REGNI PRIMO, etc. (In the first year of the reign, etc.) Used around the edge of many of the larger milled denominations.

CHRISTO AUSPICE REGNO. (I reign under the auspice of Christ.) Used extensively in the reign of Charles I.

CIVIUM INDUSTRIA FLORET CIVITAS. (By the industry of its people the State flourishes.) On the 1951 Festival Crown of George VI.

CULTORES SUI DEUS PROTEGIT. (God protects His worshippers.) On gold double crowns and crowns of Charles I.

DECUS ET TUTAMEN. (An ornament and a safeguard: Virgil, *Aenid*, v.262.) This inscription on the edge of all early large milled silver was suggested by Evelyn, he having seen it on the vignette in Cardinal Richelieu's Greek Testament, and of course refers to the device as a means to prevent clipping. This legend also appears on the edge of U.K. and Northern Ireland one pound coins.

DIEU ET MON DROIT. (God and my right.) On halfcrowns of George IV and later monarchs

DIRIGE DEUS GRESSUS MEOS. (May God direct my steps: *Psalm 118.133*.) On the 'Una' Five pounds of Queen Victoria.

DOMINE NE IN FURORE TUO ARGUAS ME. (O Lord, rebuke me not in Thine anger: *Psalm 6, 1.*). First used on the half-florin of Edward III and then on all half-nobles. D*omiN*us *Deus Omnipotens* REX. (Lord God, Almighty King.) Viking coins.

DUM SPIRO SPERO. (Whilst I live, I hope.) On the coins struck at Pontefract Castle during the Civil War after Charles I had been imprisoned.

EXALTABITUR IN GLORIA. (He shall be exalted in glory: *Psalm 111.9*.) On all quarter-nobles.

EXURGAT DEUS ET DISSIPENTUR INIMICI EIUS. (Let God arise and let His enemies be scattered: *Psalm* 68, 1.) On the Scottish ducat and early English coins of James I (VI) and was chosen by the King himself. Also on Charles I, civil war, and Declaration coins,

FACIAM EOS IN GENTEM UNAM. (I will make them one nation: *Ezekiel, 37, 22.*) On unites and laurels of James I.

FLORENT CONCORDIA REGNA. (Through concord kingdoms flourish.) On gold unite of Charles I and broad of Charles II.

HANC DEUS DEDIT. (God has given this, i.e. the crown .) On siege-pieces of Pontefract struck in the name of Charles II.

HAS NISI PERITURUS MIHI ADIMAT NEMO. (Let no one remove these [letters] from me under penalty of death.) On the edge of crowns and half-crowns of Cromwell.

HENRICUS ROSAS REGNA JACOBUS. (Henry united the roses, James the kingdoms.) On English and Scottish gold coins of James I (VI).

HONI SOIT QUI MAL Y PENSE. (Evil to him who evil thinks.) The Motto of the Order of the Garter, first used on the Hereford (?) halfcrowns of Charles I. It also occurs on the Garter Star in the centre of the reverse of the silver coins of Charles II, but being so small it is usually illegible; it is more prominent on the coinage of George III.

ICH DIEN. (I serve.) Aberystwyth Furnace 2d, and Decimal 2p. The motto of The Prince of Wales.

INIMICOS EJUS INDUAM CONFUSIONE. (As for his enemies I shall clothe them with shame: *Psalm* 132, 18.) On shillings of Edward VI struck at Durham House, Strand.

JESUS AUTEM TRANSIENS PER MEDIUM ILLORUM IBAT. (But Jesus, passing through the midst of them, went His way: *Luke iv. 30.*) The usual reverse legend on English nobles, ryals and hammered sovereigns before James I; also on the very rare Scottish noble of David II of Scotland and the unique Anglo-Gallic noble of Edward the Black Prince.

JUSTITIA THRONUM FIRMAT. (Justice strengthens the throne.) On Charles I half-groats and pennies and Scottish twenty-penny pieces.

LUCERNA PEDIBUS MEIS VERBUM EST. (Thy word is a lamp unto my feet: *Psalm 119, 105.*) Obverse legend on a rare half-sovereign of Edward VI struck at Durham House, Strand.

MIRABILIA FECIT. (He made marvellously: *Psalm 97.1.*) On the Viking coins of (?) York.

NEMO ME IMPUNE LACESSIT. (No-one provokes me with impunity.) On the 1984 Scottish one pound. Motto of The Order of the Thistle.

NUMMORUM FAMULUS. (The servant of the coinage.) The legend on the edge of the English tin coinage at the end of the seventeenth century.

O CRUX AVE SPES UNICA. (Hail! O Cross, our only hope.) On the reverse of all half-angels.

PAX MISSA PER ORBEM. (Peace sent throughout the world.) The reverse legend of a pattern farthing of Anne.

PAX QUÆRITUR BELLO. (Peace is sought by war.) The reverse legend of the Cromwell broad.

PER CRUCEM TUAM SALVA NOS CHRISTE REDEMPTOR. (By Thy cross, save us, O Christ, our Redeemer.) The normal reverse of English angels.

PLEIDIOL WYF I'M GWLAD. (True am I to my country.) Used on the 1985 Welsh one pound. Taken from the Welsh National Anthem.

POST MORTEM PATRIS PRO FILIO. (After the death of the father for the son.) On siege-pieces struck at Pontefract in 1648 (old style) after the execution of Charles I.

POSUI DEUM ADJUTOREM MEUM. (I have made God my Helper: *comp. Psalm* 54, 4.) Used on many English and Irish silver coins from Edward III until 1603. Altered to POSUIMUS and NOSTRUM on the coins of Philip and Mary.

PROTECTOR LITERIS LITERÆ NUMMIS CORONA ET SALUS. (A protection to the letters [on the face of the coin], the letters [on the edge] are a garland and a safeguard to the coinage.) On the edge of the rare fifty-shilling piece of Cromwell.

QUÆ DEUS CONJUNXIT NEMO SEPARET. (What God hath joined together let no man put asunder: *Matthew 19, 6.*) On the larger silver English and Scottish coins of James I after he succeeded to the English throne.

REDDE CUIQUE QUOD SUUM EST. (Render to each that which is his own.) On a Henry VIII type groat of Edward VI struck by Sir Martin Bowes at Durham House, Strand.

RELIGIO PROTESTANTIVM LEGES ANGLIÆ LIBERTAS PARLIAMENTI. (The religion of the Protestants, the laws of England, the liberty of the Parliament.) This is known as the 'Declaration' and refers to Charles I's declaration to the Privy Council at Wellington, 19 September, 1642; it is found on many of his coins struck at the provincial mints during the Civil War. Usually abbreviated to REL:PROT:LEG: ANG:LIB:PAR:

ROSA SINE SPINA. (A rose without a thorn.) Found on some gold and small coins of Henry VIII and later reigns.

RUTILANS ROSA SINE SPINA. (A dazzling rose without a thorn.) As last but on small gold only.

SCUTUM FIDEI PROTEGET EUM or EAM. (The shield of faith shall protect him, or her.) On much of the gold of Edward VI and Elizabeth.

SIC VOS NON VOBIS (Thus we labour but not for ourselves). 1994 £2 Bank of England.

TALI DICATA SIGNO MENS FLUCTUARI NEQUIT. (Consecrated by such a sign the mind cannot waver: from a hymn by Prudentius written in the fourth century, entitled 'Hymnus ante Somnum'.) Only on the gold 'George noble' of Henry VIII.

TIMOR DOMINI FONS VITÆ. (The fear of the Lord is a fountain of life: *Proverbs, 14, 27.)* On many shillings of Edward VI.

TVAETVR VNITA DEVS. (May God guard these united, i.e. kingdoms.) On many English Scottish and Irish coins of James I.

VERITAS TEMPORIS FILIA. (Truth, the daughter of Time.) On English and Irish coins of Mary Tudor.

Some Royal Titles:

REX ANGL*orum*—King of the English.

REX SAXONIORVM OCCIDENTALIVM —King of the West Saxons.

DEI GRA*tia* REX *ANGL*iae ET FRANC*iae DomiNus HYBerniae ET AQVITaniae*—By the Grace of God, King of England and France, Lord of Ireland and Aquitaine.

D*ei GRAtia Magnae Britanniae, FRanciae ET Hiberniae REX Fidei Defensor BRunsviciensis ET Luneburgen-sis Dux, Sacri Romani Imperii Archi-THesaurarius ET ELector=*By the Grace of God, King of Great Britain, France and Ireland, Defender of the Faith, Duke of Brunswick and Luneburg, High Treasurer and Elector of the Holy Roman Empire.

BRITANNIARUM REX —King of the Britains (i.e. Britain and British territories overseas).

BRITT:OMN:REX:FID:DEF:IND:IMP: —King of all the Britains, Defender of the Faith, Emperor of India.

VIVAT REGINA ELIZABETHA — Long live Queen Elizabeth. On the 1996 £5 Queen's 70th birthday £5 crown.

APPENDIX III

NUMISMATIC CLUBS AND SOCIETIES

Coin News, The Searcher and *Treasure Hunting*, are the major monthly magazines covering numismatics. Many local numismatic societies and clubs in the British Isles are affiliated to the British Association of Numismatic Societies (BANS) which holds an annual Congress and an annual Conference (weekend meetings) with a range of speakers in convivial surroundings. Details and contacts for a club or society near can be found online, www.coinclubs.org.uk or by contacting the Secretary, Bill Pugsley, at the following email address: bill@pugsley.co.uk.

The two principal learned societies are the Royal Numismatic Society (RNS), c/o Department of Coins and Medals, the British Museum, Great Russell Street, Bloomsbury, London WC1B 3DG, and the British Numismatic Society (BNS), c/o The Secretary, Peter Preston-Morley, c/o Dix, Noonan, Webb, 16 Bolton Street, London, W1J 8BQ, email: ppm@dnw.co.uk. Both these societies publish an annual journal. To find out more about membership, meetings and publications, for the RNS go to www.numismatics.org.uk and for the BNS, go to www.britnumsoc.org.uk

MINTMARKS AND OTHER SYMBOLS ON ENGLISH COINS

A Mintmark (*mm.*), is a term borrowed from Roman and Greek numismatics where it showed the place of mintage; it was generally used on English coins to show where the legend began (a religious age preferred a cross for the purpose). Later, this mark, since the dating of coins was not usual, had a periodic significance, changing from time to time. Hence it was of a secret or 'privy' nature; other privy marks on a coin might be the code-mark of a particular workshop or workman. Thus a privy mark (including the *mintmark*) might show when a coin was made, or who made it. In the use of precious metals this knowledge was necessary to guard against fraud and counterfeiting.

Mintmarks are sometimes termed 'initial marks' as they are normally placed at the commencement of the inscription. Some of the symbols chosen were personal badges of the ruling monarch, such as the rose and sun of York, or the boar's head of Richard III, the dragon of Henry Tudor or the thistle of James I; others are heraldic symbols or may allude to the mint master responsible for the coinage, e.g. the *mm.* bow used on the Durham House coins struck under John Bowes and the WS mark of William Sharrington of Bristol.

A table of mintmarks is given overleaf. Where mintmarks appear in the catalogue they are sometimes referred to only by the reference number, in order to save space, i.e. *mm. 28* (=mintmark Sun), *mm.28/74 (=mm.* Sun on obverse, *mm.* Coronet on reverse), *mm. 28/-* (=*mm.* Sun on obverse only).

1 Edward III, Cross 1 (Class B+C).
2 Edward III, broken Cross 1 (Class D).
3 Edward III, Cross 2 (Class E)
4 Edward III, Cross 3 (Class G)
5 Cross Potent (Edw. III Treaty)
6 Cross Pattée (Edw. III Post Treaty Rich. III).
7 (a) Plain of Greek Cross.
   (b) Cross Moline.
8 Cross Patonce.
9 Cross Fleuree.
10 Cross Calvary (Cross on steps).
11 Long Cross Fitchée.
12 Short Cross Fitchée.
13 Restoration Cross (Hen. VI).
14 Latin Cross.
15 Voided Cross (Henry VI).
16 Saltire Cross.
17 Cross and 4 pellets.
18 Pierced Cross.
19 Pierced Cross & pellet.
20 Pierced Cross & central pellet.
21 Cross Crosslet.
22 Curved Star (rayant).
23 Star.
24 Spur Rowel.
25 Mullet.
26 Pierced Mullet.
27 Eglantine.
28 Sun (Edw. IV).
29 Mullet (Henry V).
30 Pansy.
31 Heraldic Cinquefoil (Edw. IV).
32 Heraldic Cinquefoil (James I).
33 Rose (Edw. IV).
34 Rosette (Edw. IV).
35 Rose (Chas. I).
36 Catherine Wheel.
37 Cross in circle.
38 Halved Sun (6 rays) & Rose.
39 Halved Sun (4 rays) & Rose.
40 Lis-upon-Half-Rose.
41 Lis-upon-Sun & Rose.
42 Lis-Rose dimidiated.
43 Lis-issuant-from-Rose.
44 Trefoil.

45 Slipped Trefoil, James I (1).
46 Slipped Trefoil, James I (2).
47 Quatrefoil.
48 Saltire.
49 Pinecone.
50 Leaf (-mascle, Hen. VI).
51 Leaf (-trefoil, Hen. VI).
52 Arrow.
53 Pheon.
54 A.
55 Annulet.
56 Annulet-with-pellet.
57 Anchor.
58 Anchor & B.
59 Flower & B.
60 Bell.
61 Book.
62 Boar's Head (early Richard III).
63 Boar's Head (later Richard III).
64 Boar's Head, Charles I.
65 Acorn   (a) Hen. VIII
                     (b) Elizabeth.
66 Bow.
67 Br. (Bristol, Chas. I).
68 Cardinal's Hat.
69 Castle (Henry VIII).
70 Castle with H.
71 Castle (Chas. I).
72 Crescent   (a) Henry VIII
                     (b) Elizabeth.
73 Pomegranate. (Mary; Henry VIII's is broader).
74 Coronet.
75 Crown.
76 Crozier   (a) Edw. III
                     (b) Hen. VIII.
77 Ermine.
78 Escallop (Hen. VII).
79 Escallop (James I).
80 Eye (in legend Edw. IV).
81 Eye (Parliament).
82 Radiate Eye (Hen. VII).
83 Gerb.
84 Grapes.
85 Greyhound's Head.
86 Hand.
87 Harp.
88 Heart.
89 Helmet.
90 Key.
91 Leopard's Head.

91A Crowned Leopard's Head with collar (Edw. VI).
92 Lion.
93 Lion rampant.
94 Martlet.
95 Mascle.
96 African Head.
97 Ostrich's Head.
98 P in brackets.
99 Pall.
100 Pear.
101 Plume.
102 Plume. Aberystwyth and Bristol.
103 Plume. Oxford.
104 Plume. Shrewsbury.
105 Lis.
106 Lis.
107 Portcullis.
108 Portcullis, Crowned.
109 Sceptre.
110 Sunburst.
111 Swan.
112 R in brackets.
113 Sword.
114 T (Henry VIII).
115 TC monogram.
116 WS monogram.
117 y or Y.
118 Dragon (Henry VII).
119 (a) Triangle
      (b) Triangle in Circle.
120 Sun (Parliament).
121 Uncertain mark.
122 Grapple.
123 Tun.
124 Woolpack.
125 Thistle.
126 Figure 6 (Edw. VI).
127 Floriated cross.
128 Lozenge.
129 Billet.
130 Plume. Bridgnorth or late declaration
131 Two lions.
132 Clasped book.
133 Cross pommée.
134 Bugle.
135 Crowned T (Tournai, Hen VIII)
136 An incurved pierced cross

The reign listed after a mintmark indicates that from which the drawing is taken. A similar mm. may have been used in another reign and will be found in the chronological list at the beginning of each reign.

NOTES

Standard Catalogue of British Coins

COINS OF ENGLAND

& THE UNITED KINGDOM
Pre-Decimal Issues

59th Edition

LONDON

A Catalogue of the Coins of Great Britain
and Ireland
first published 1929

Standard Catalogue of British Coins
Coins of England and the United Kingdom
59th edition, 2024

© Spink & Son Ltd, 2023
69 Southampton Row, Bloomsbury
London WC1B 4ET
www.spinkbooks.com

www.spink.com

Typeset by Design to Print UK Ltd,
9 & 10 Riverview Business Park, Forest Row, East Sussex RH18 5DW
www.designtoprintuk.com
Printed and bound in Malta
by Gutenberg Press Ltd.

Cover design: Russell Whittle
Email: uk47@icloud.com

ISBN 978-1-912667-95-6

CONTENTS

ACKNOWLEDGEMENTS

We wish to acknowledge the valuable contributions of the following.

Richard Abdy *(The British Museum)*
Tony Abramson
Dr Martin Allen
Keith Bayford
Joe Bispham
Jon Blyth
James Booth
Ron Churchill
Nigel Clark
Chris Comber
Barrie Cook *(The British Museum)*
Simon Cope
Jonathan Cope
Dave Craddock
Joe Cribb *(The British Museum)*
Mike Cuddeford
Paul Davies
Charles Davis
Alan Dawson
Tim Everson
David Fletcher
Glen Gittoes
Eric Green
Dave Greenhalgh
David Guest
Peter Hendra

Heritage Auctions UK
Steve Hill
Peter Jackson
Richard Kelleher *(The Fizwilliam Museum)*
Geoff Kitchen
Stewart Lyon
William MacKay
Nigel Mills
Graeme Monk
Neil Paisley
Rob Pearce
Gary Poole
Nigel Prevost
Mark Rasmussen
Mark T Ray
Martin Roberts
The Schneider Family
Dr Irving Schneider
Peter D Spencer
Bob Thomas
Andrew Wayne
Graham Warboys
Tim Webb Ware
Walter Wilkinson
Gareth Williams *(The British Museum)*
Paul & Bente R Withers

Museums/Institutions
The Trustees of the British Museum, London
The Fitzwilliam Museum, Cambridge

Photography
Richard Hodges
Paul & Bente R. Withers
Wioletta Madaj

ABBREVIATIONS

Archb.	Archbishop	laur.	laureate
Æ	bronze	mm.	mintmark
Ↄ	silver	mon.	monogram
Ⱥ	gold	O., obv.	obverse
Bp.	Bishop	p.	new penny, pence
BV	bullion value	pl	plume
cuir.	cuirassed	quat.	quatrefoil
d.	penny, pence	qtr.	quarter
diad.	diademed	rad.	radiate
dr.	draped	R., rev.	reverse
ex.	exergue	r.	right
grs.	grains	s.	shillings
hd.	headstg.	stg.	standing
i.c.	inner circle	trun.	truncation
illus.	illustration	var.	variety
l.	left	wt.	weight

FOREWORD

Welcome to Coins of England 2024! Another year has whirled around already! Only yesterday we mourned the loss of Queen Elizabeth II and simultaneously heralded the new Carolean age. Sadly the peace and tranquility that marked her lengthy reign has given way to bloodshed once more in Europe and the Middle East. This geopolitical uncertainty firmly feeds into the market dynamics at play in our now not-so-small world of numismatics.

It also affords us an apt introduction to our chosen cover coin - the iconic 'George Noble' of King Henry VIII. This dramatic Tudor emblem was conceived at a time of similar ideological and religious conflict, and dare I condemn it so simply as 'map redrawing'. The propaganda was simple - a youthful King of England backed by his Patron Saint George - and supported by his consort Katharine of Aragon. This Queen had already proven herself a worthy tactician on the blood-soaked fields of Flodden. Surviving personal letters from Henry to Katharine almost whimsically recall an exchange of the French banner for a piece of the fallen Scottish King's coat in celebration of their military victories on the Continent and north of the border.

However much like the fluid political vista of our age, these best laid plans were not to stand up to rigorous scrutiny; for Henry was to grow impatient for a male heir. He determined the fate of the Kingdom, but more crucially his own virility upon the matter. His first years as head of state had witnessed the agony of loss of a neo-natal son, and not even the extravagance of the 'Field of Cloth of Gold' could distract his increasing ire towards poor Katharine. Indeed even Cardinal Wolsey, the man who had masterminded the recoinage of 1526, and oversaw the introduction of this unique numismatic evolution, would barely outlast the three years in which it would be produced. The Prudential invocation: TALI DICATA SIGNO MENS FLVCTVARE NESCIT - "the sign of the cross seals thy brow and the place where lies thy heart" began to ring increasingly hollow for Henry and Katharine's communion. And thus, rather poetically, this emphatically personal and utterly naked symbol of Tudor authority records both the apogee and perigee of Henry's reign. No wonder that his George Noble was almost instantaneously recognised as a collector's coin - arguably Britain's first! Records survive from as early as February 1538 confirming not only their inherent rarity to even Royal courtiers, but their enhanced secondary market value. Thomas Howard, 3rd Duke of Norfolk happily paid three pounds for one! When our cover coin surfaced in the Spink auction room back in September 2021, it was speculated that Howard's very coin was that actually being offered. In the event, its lineage could be traced confidently back only to the 18th Century, but still it would achieve an as yet unbeaten sum.

Imagine our delight therefore when a very fortunate metal detectorist contacted us with a new example, fresh from the unforgiving Chiltern soil in January! As many of our regular readers will have noted, Spink has been on a concerted drive to re-embrace the community that provides us with the most new discoveries and additions every year. A community who seek to add, compare and contrast their latest discoveries with the types and denominations in the pages that follow, and who so eagerly purchase this book every year. With our support of the Rodney Cook Memorial Rally since 2022, we have been privileged to handle many outstanding finds of regional and national significance including the Ashley Green hoard of 2nd Century BC gold Staters; a plethora of Saxo-Norman Pennies of the Heptarchic Kingdoms; and not one, but two excessively rare round Halfpennies of King Eadgar. This year also marks the amendment to the Treasure Act of 1996 to now include single coin finds of significance, largely I hasten to add, in light of the Spink sale of the Henry III Gold Penny! Time will tell how many new discoveries will be permitted to enter the private collector domain and how this will impact market prices.

Across the board, 2023 has translated into a year of consolidation rather than growth. Fresh-to-market material continues to perform exceedingly well on the rostrum, but the Covid-era approach of buying to re-offer in short time frames has begun to test auction patience. The full return of in-person coin shows has furthered this slide in selling rates, as the natural appeal for human interaction and discussion at the point of purchase has returned to the top of collector pursuit, even if many in the trade continue to struggle to compete for material to restock.

In January, Spink hosted its annual Collectors Series Sale at the New York International Numismatic Congress with our usual fanfare. The highlights of the English portion were the sensational run of King George IV Gold Pattern Proof Five-Pounds to Half-Sovereign. Despite the appeal of third-party grading continuing unabated, this 'raw' offering blasted past expectations to attain over $150,000 for the four 1826-issued coins. It would take a full Proof Set appearing in September to top this impressive feat!

With the dust barely settled, Spink breathlessly shifted to auctioning the first portion of the "St. Helier Collection" of English Gold Proofs and Patterns alongside the remarkable numismatic selection of the 'White Rose' Cabinet unseen to commerce, or indeed Spink's rooms, since it had been purchased from us in the 1940s! To feature an 1820 Pattern Five-Pounds is special, to offer it in tandem with a legendary 'Una and the Lion' 1839 Pattern Five-Pounds and a Queen Anne 1713 Farthing in gold truly humbling. Records would continue to tumble in this extravaganza, as Spink would break its own house record for an ancient coin not once, but twice in the same day with the dispersal of a Nektanebo II 'hieroglyph' Gold Stater and an extraordinary 'Death Mask' Portrait of Julius Caesar and Gaius Octavianus gold Aureus struck mere months after the 'Perpetual Dictator's brutal assassination. With over £4.88 million pounds in numismatic auctions posted by April 2023, it is unsurprising to note this as one our strongest ever Spring performances! Much like buses though, no sooner had one Queen Anne Gold Farthing appeared, than a second surfaced across London and reportedly posted a similar six-figure result. How considerate of King Charles III to hold his Coronation in May to give us all the double-bank holiday to recuperate!

With the summer recess came the announcement of Spink's appointment as the British Numismatic Trade Association's Official Coinex Auctioneer for 2023. This appointment was all the more prestigious as 2023 also marked 50 Years of Service for the trade body of which Spink had been a founding member. In celebration of this feat, Spink elected to reveal here the discovery of a new Iron Age ruler - Esunertos. The story of buried treasure always captures the attention of the national media, but not even we could appreciate how much it did actual Celtic collectors. On 28 September it eclipsed our previous world record for a British-made Quarter-Stater by posting an emphatic £20,400. Cue press call! Coinex also saw Spink re-enter another numismatic arena with its first ancient-only room auction for over two decades headlined by the 'Kyrios' Collection which helped to realise over £500,000. Therefore, as I sit to write this final chapter of an eventual year that was, I am delighted to confirm a second instalment to the "St. Helier Collection" to be auctioned in December. With it, Spink will offer a previous world-record-holding William IV Pattern 'Crown' in gold, thereby completing its envious calendar year of early 'Five Pound Pieces' of 1820; 1826; 1831 and 1839 - the last time this occurred under one London auctioneer was Spink in 1993!

As we look forward to 2024, in anticipation of the next twist and turn in our beloved collectors market, we also reminisce about the radical change already undertaken in the numismatic world. From the now unassailable dominance of the online auction model, to the booming participation on online social media fora driving interest in new and old coins alike. Will the decline in physical cash use spell another evolution, or will the Royal Mint's initiative to encourage 'early learning' with the King's new 'definitives' breed a whole new generation of collector? Or like NFTs, will that become simply yesterday's chip paper? Only time will tell, but you can be sure that Spink will continue to keep its finger on the numismatic pulse to share as it looks ahead further still to the 2025 Centenary of its first English numismatic publication: *The Milled Silver Coinage of England from Charles II to the Present Day*, the forerunner of the book you know and love today.

This leaves me only to wish you a very successful collecting year ahead and repeat the ode of King Henry VIII himself: *Pastime with good company!*

Gregory Edmund
Head of Numismatics

A note from Emma Howard, Editor, Coins of England: our thanks to everyone who has submitted suggestions for new inclusions or corrections to existing entries. As ever, all submissions are subject to the scrutiny and approval of our editorial committee, who have approved any corrections and provided a complete overhaul of price changes to reflect the activity in the market over the past year.

A note on bullion value in this edition: we have listed the 2024 spot price for gold quoted on page 495 onwards at £1,600 an ounce, but obviously this is subject to fluctuation because the price of gold has been and continues to be so volatile.

Arrangement

The arrangement of this catalogue is not completely uniform, but generally it is divided into metals (gold, silver, copper, etc) under each reign, then into coinages, denominations and varieties. In the Celtic section the uninscribed coins are listed before the dynastic coins; under Charles II all the hammered coins precede the milled coinage; the reign of George III is divided into coins issued up to 1816 and the new coinage from 1816 to the end of the reign; and under Elizabeth II the decimal issues are separated from the pre-decimal *(£.s.d.)* coinages and listed in a separate volume of the SCBC since 2015. For the first time in 2020 the two volumes have been made available for purchase independently of one another.

Every major coin type is listed though not every variety. We have endeavoured to give rather more coverage to the varieties of relatively common coins, such as the pennies of Edward I, II and III, than to the very much rarer coins of, for instance, King Offa of Mercia.

Values

The values given represent the range of retail prices at which coins are being offered for sale at the time of going to press and **not** the price which a dealer will pay for those coins. These prices are based on our knowledge of the numismatic market, the current demand for particular coins, recent auction sale prices and, in those cases where certain coins have not appeared for sale for some years, our estimation of what they would be likely to sell at today, bearing in mind their rarity and appeal in relation to somewhat similar coins where a current value is known. Values are given for two grades of preservation from the Celtic period onwards and three to four grades of preservation for coins of the 17th to the 20th century.

Collectors normally require coins in the best condition they can afford and, except in the case of a really rare coin, a piece that is considerably worn is not wanted and has little value. The values given in the catalogue are for the exact state of preservation stated at the head of each column and bearing in mind that a score of identical coins in varying states of wear could be lined up in descending order from mint condition (FDC, *fleur de coin*), through very fine (VF) to *poor* state. It will be realized that only in certain instances will the values given apply to particular coins. A 'fine' (F) coin may be worth anything between one quarter and a half of the price quoted for a 'very fine' (VF); on the other hand, a piece in really mint condition will be valued substantially higher than the price quoted for 'extremely fine' (EF). The designation BV has been adopted for coins whose value on the market has yet to exceed its bullion value. Purchasing sovereigns, catalogued as BV, will attract a dealers' premium.

We emphasise again that the purpose of this catalogue is to give a general value for a particular class of coin in a specified state of preservation, and also to give the collector an idea of the range and value of coins in the English series. The value of any particular piece depends on three things:

Its exact design, legend, mintmark or date.

Its exact state of preservation; this is of prime importance.

The demand for it in the market at any given time.

Some minor varieties are much scarcer than others and, as the number of coins issued varies considerably from year to year, coins of certain dates and mintmarks are rarer and of more value than other pieces of similar type. The prices given for any type are for the commonest variety, mintmark or date of that type.

The Scope

Coin collecting, numismatics, is a fascinating hobby. It requires very little physical exertion and only as much mental effort as one wishes or is able to put into it at any time. There is vast scope and boundless ramifications and byways encompassing not only things historical and geographical, but also touching on economics, metallurgy, heraldry, literature, the fine arts, politics, military history and many other disciplines. This catalogue is solely concerned with British coinage from its earliest times right up to date. From the start the beginner should appreciate that the coinage of our own nation may be seen as a small but very important part of the whole story of world currency.

The first coins, made of electrum, a natural alloy of gold and silver, were issued in western Asia Minor (Lydia) in the later seventh century BC. Over the next century or so coinage of gold and silver spread across the Aegean to mainland Greece, southwards to the eastern Mediterranean lands and eventually westward to the Greek colonies in southern Italy, Sicily (Magna Graecia) and beyond. The coins of the Greeks are noted for their beautiful, sometimes exquisite craftsmanship, with many of the coin types depicting the patron deities of their cities. Coins of Philip II of Macedon (359-336 BC), father of Alexander the Great, circulated amongst the Celtic peoples of the Danubian Basin and were widely copied through central Europe and by the Gauls in France. Gold Gaulish staters were reaching Britain around the beginning of the first century BC and the earliest gold to be struck in the island must have been produced shortly afterwards. Although their types and designs copy the Apollo head and racing charioteer of Philip II's gold coins, they are stylistically much removed from the original representation and very individually Celtic in concept.

The coins of the Romans cover some seven centuries and include an enormous number of different types that were current throughout a major part of the civilised world from Spain to Syria and from the Rhine in the north to the Sudan in the south. The Roman province of Britain was part of this vast empire for four hundred years from AD 43 until the early fifth century. Innumerable Roman coins have been recovered from sites in this country, most being made of brass or bronze. Many of these are quite inexpensive and very collectable. In recent years many hoards of gold and silver coins have been found, usually by use of metal detectors.

Following the revival of commerce after the Dark Ages, coinage in Western Europe was virtually restricted to silver until the thirteenth century, though gold was still being minted in Byzantium and in the Islamic world. In the Middle Ages many European cities had their own distinctive coinage and money was issued not only by the kings but also by nobles, bishops and abbots. From the time of the later Crusades gold returned to the West, and the artistic developments of the Renaissance in the fifteenth century brought improved portraiture and new minting techniques.

Large silver crown-size thalers were first minted at Joachimsthal in Bohemia early in the sixteenth century. The substantial shipments of silver coming to Europe from the mines of Spanish America over the next couple of centuries led to a fine series of larger coins being issued by the European states and cities. The larger size allowed greater artistic freedom in the designs and the portraits on the coins.

Both Germany and Italy became unified nation states during the later nineteenth century, thereby substantially reducing the number of mints and coin types. Balancing the reduction in European minting authorities were the new coins that were issued by the independent states of South and Central America. Since the 1950s many new nations have established their independence and their coinage provides a large field for the collector of modern coins.

It can be seen that the scope for the collector is truly vast, but besides the general run of official coinage there is also the large series of token coins—small change unofficially produced to supplement the inadequate supply of authorised currency. These tokens were issued by merchants, innkeepers and manufacturers in many towns and villages in the seventeenth, eighteenth and nineteenth centuries and many collectors specialise in their local issues.

Some coins have designs of a commemorative nature; an example being the Royal Wedding crown of 1981, but there are also large numbers of commemorative medals which, though never intended for use as coinage, are sometimes confused with coins because they are metal objects of a similar shape and sometimes a similar size to coins. This is another interesting field for collectors as these medals often have excellent portraits of famous men or women, or they may commemorate important events or scientific discoveries. Other metallic objects of coin-like appearance that can be confusing for the beginner are reckoning counters, advertising tickets, various other tickets and passes, and items such as brass coin weights.

Minting processes

From the time of the earliest Greek coins in the late seventh century BC to about the middle of the sixteenth century AD, coins were made by hand. The method of manufacture was simple. The obverse and reverse designs were engraved or punched into the prepared ends of two bars of bronze or iron, shaped or tapered to the diameter of the required coin. The obverse die, known as the *pile*, was usually spiked so that it could be anchored firmly into a block of wood or metal. The reverse die, the *trussel*, was held by hand or grasped by tongs.

The coin was struck by placing a metal blank between the two dies and striking the trussel with a hammer. Thus, all coinage struck by this method is known as 'hammered'. Some dies are known to have been hinged so there would be an exact register between the upper and lower die. Usually a 'pair of dies' consisted of one obverse die (normally the more difficult to make because it had the finer detail, such as the ruler's portrait) and two reverse dies. This was because the shaft of iron bearing the reverse design eventually split under the constant hammering; two reverse dies were usually needed to last out the life of the obverse die.

Some time toward the middle of the sixteenth century, experiments, first in Germany and later in France, resulted in the manufacture of coins by machinery.

The term 'milled', which is applied to all machine-made coins, comes from the type of machinery used – the mill and screw press. With this machinery the obverse die was fixed as the lower die and the reverse die brought down into contact with the blank by heavy vertical pressure applied by a screw or worm-drive connected to a cross bar with heavy weights at each end. These weights usually had long leather thongs attached which allowed a more powerful force to be applied by the operators who revolved the arms of the press. New blanks were placed on the lower die and the struck coins were removed by hand. The screw press brought more pressure to bear on the blanks and this pressure was evenly applied, producing a far better and sharper coin.

Various attempts were made during the reigns of Elizabeth I and Charles I to introduce this type of machinery with its vastly superior products. Unfortunately problems associated with the manufacture of blanks to a uniform weight greatly reduced the rate of striking and the hand manufacture of coins continued until the Restoration in 1660, when Charles II brought to London from Holland the Roettiers brothers and their improved screw press.

The first English coins made for circulation by this new method were the silver crowns of 1662, which bore an inscription on the edge, DECVS ET TVTAMEN, 'an ornament and a safeguard', a reference to the fact that the new coins could not be clipped, a crime made easy by the thin and often badly struck hammered coins.

The mill and screw press was used until new steam-powered machinery made by Boulton and Watt was installed in the new mint on Tower Hill in London. This machinery had been used most successfully by Boulton to strike the large 'cartwheel' two- and one- penny pieces of 1797 and other coins, including 'overstriking' Spanish *eight-reale* pieces into Bank of England 'dollars' since the old Mint presses were not able to exert sufficient power to do this. This new machinery was first used at the Mint to strike the 'new coinage' halfcrowns of 1816, and it operated at a far greater speed than the old type of mill and screw presses and achieved a greater sharpness of design.

The very latest coining presses now operating at the Royal Mint at Llantrisant in South Wales, are capable of striking at a rate of up to 800 coins a minute.

Condition

One of the more difficult problems for the beginner is to assess accurately the condition of a coin. A common fault among collectors is to overgrade and, consequently, to overvalue their coins.

Most dealers will gladly spare a few minutes to help new collectors. Many dealers issue price lists with illustrations, enabling collectors to see exactly what the coins look like and how they have been graded.

Coins cannot always be graded according to precise rules. Hammered coins often look weak or worn on the high parts of the portrait and the tops of the letters; this can be due to weak striking or worn dies and is not always attributable to wear through long use in circulation. Milled coins usually leave the Mint sharply struck so that genuine wear is easier to detect. However a x5 or x10 magnifying glass is essential, especially when grading coins of Edward VII and George V where the relief is very low on the portraits and some skill is required to distinguish between an uncirculated coin and one in EF condition.

The condition or grade of preservation of a coin is usually of greater importance than its rarity. By this we mean that a common coin in superb condition is often more desirable and more highly priced than a rarity in poor condition. Coins that have been pierced or mounted as a piece of jewellery generally have little interest to collectors.

One must also be on the lookout for coins that have been 'plugged', i.e. that have been pierced at some time and have had the hole filled in, sometimes with the missing design or letters re-engraved.

Badly cleaned coins will often display a complexity of fine interlaced lines and such coins have a greatly reduced value. It is also known for coins to be tooled or re-engraved on the high parts of the hair, in order to 'increase' the grade of coin and its value. In general it is better to have a slightly more worn coin than a better example with such damage.

Professional grading services have come to exert considerable influence over the grading of coins and the subsequent prices they can command. Whilst such services can provide an accurate way to grade coins, and are well-suited to milled and machine made issues, the resulting grading remains an opinion with grading of hammered and ancient requiring different considerations to milled and machine-made coins. Associated with professional grading is the practise of sealing the coin within a clear plastic container, colloquially referred to as slabbing. Whilst now a well-established practice in the US market it has had less impact in the UK where collectors prefer to handle a coin which allows for closer examination of the surfaces and the edges, a necessity for a milled coin with an inscribed edge which once enscapulated cannot be examined.

Cleaning coins

Speaking generally, *do not* clean coins. More coins are ruined by injudicious cleaning than through any other cause, and a badly cleaned coin loses much of its value. A nicely toned piece is usually considered desirable. Really dirty gold and silver can, however, be carefully washed in soap and water. Copper coins should never be cleaned or washed, they may be lightly brushed with a brush that is not too harsh.

Buying and selling coins

Exchanging coins with other collectors, searching around the antique shops, telling your relatives and friends that you are interested in coins, or even trying to find your own with a metal detector, are all ways of adding to your collection. However, the time will come when the serious collector needs to acquire specific coins or requires advice on the authenticity or value of a coin.

At this point an expert is needed, and the services of a reputable coin dealer or independent numismatic consultant are necessary. There are now a large number of coin dealers in the UK, many of whom belong to the B.N.T.A. (The British Numismatic Trade Association). Many dealers publish their own lists of coins. Studying these lists is a good way for a collector to learn about coins and to classify and catalogue their own collections.

The internet has made it very much easier to locate, view and acquire coins online not just in the United Kingdom but worldwide. Many dealers now offer lists of stock online. It has also revolutionised the availability of coins at auction with printed catalogues supplemented by online catalogues and the increasing use of online bidding making the need to attend an auction on the day less critical than it once was. As a result buying and selling at auction has grown as a way to add to and dispose of collections. In buying at auction it is always advisable to examine the coin before deciding to bid and it should be borne in mind that the description given will only be as good as the expertise of the person describing the coin. It is still possible to find and acquire bargains at auction, but the chance of doing so is perhaps less these days than it once was. It should also be pointed out that auction houses charge the buyer a premium on the hammer price, generally at 20%, on which, in the United Kingdom , VAT is applicable with the total price paid generally hammer price plus 24%. Coins disposed of at auction will be subject to a vendor's commission charge made by the auction house which can be up to 15% of the price realised. An active market for buying and selling coins exists also on e-bay, however in general items offered here should be treated with caution with the onus on checking the veracity of the coin very much with the bidder.

The Standard Catalogue of British Coins has been published since 1929. It serves as a price guide for all coin collectors. Spink also publish books on many aspects of English, Greek, Roman and Byzantine coins and on British tokens which serve as a valuable source of information for coin collectors. Our books are available directly from Spink at www.spinkbooks.com selected high street booksellers and online outlets such as Amazon.

Numismatic Clubs and Societies

There are over thirty numismatic societies and clubs in the British Isles. Joining one is the best way to meet fellow enthusiasts, learn about your coins and other series in a friendly and informative way. For details and contacts for a club or society near you see Appendix III, page 596 or online, www.coinclubs.org.uk. The British Association of Numismatic Societies (BANS), which acts as the national body for all Societies, holds two weekend meetings each year with a range of speakers in convivial surroundings.

Useful suggestions

Security and insurance. The careful collector should not keep valuable coins at home unless they are insured and have adequate protection. Local police and insurance companies will give advice on what precautions may be necessary.

Most insurance companies will accept a valuation based on *The Standard Catalogue*. It is usually possible to have the amount added to a householder's contents policy but particularly valuable individual coins may have to be separately listed. A 'Fire, Burglary and Theft' policy will cover loss only from the insured's address, but an 'All Risks' policy will usually cover accidental damage and loss anywhere within the U.K.

Until fairly recently most high street banks offered safe-deposit boxes which formed a useful way for holding a collection in a secure environment. However in recent years many high street banks have stopped providing such services. The alternative is to acquire and install a safe at your home where coins can be stored. There are many options available here and most insurance companies will offer reduced premiums for coins securely stored at the home.

Keeping a record. All collectors are advised to have an up-to-date record of their collection and, if possible, photographs of the more important and more easily identifiable coins. This should be kept in a separate place from the collection so that a list and photographs can be given to the police should loss occur. Note the price paid, from whom purchased, the date of acquisition and the condition of the coin.

Storage and handling. New collectors should get into the habit of handling coins by the edge. This is especially important as far as highly polished proof coins are concerned.

Collectors may initially keep their coins in paper or plastic envelopes housed in boxes, albums or special containers. Many collectors will eventually wish to own a hardwood coin cabinet in which the collection can be properly arranged and displayed. If a home-made cabinet is being constructed avoid using oak and cedar wood; mahogany, walnut and rosewood are ideal. It is important that coins are not kept in a humid atmosphere; especial care must be taken with copper and bronze coins which are very susceptible to damp or condensation which may result in a green verdigris forming on them.